The Art of
COMPUTER
GRAPHICS
Programming

A STRUCTURED INTRODUCTION
for ARCHITECTS and DESIGNERS

William J. Mitchell

Robin S. Liggett

Thomas Kvan

The Art of
COMPUTER
GRAPHICS
Programming

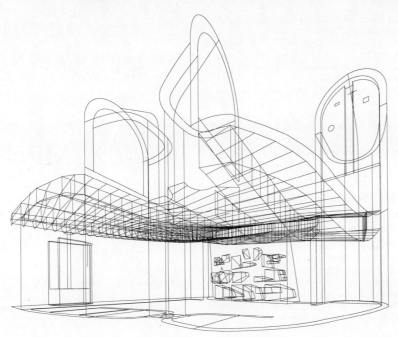

VNR VAN NOSTRAND REINHOLD COMPANY
—————————————————————— NEW YORK

Printed in the United States of America

Designed by Ernie Haim

Van Nostrand Reinhold Company, Inc.
115 Fifth Avenue
New York, New York 10003

Van Nostrand Reinhold Company Limited
Molly Millars Lane
Wokingham, Berkshire RG11 2PY, England

Van Nostrand Reinhold
480 La Trobe Street
Melbourne, Victoria 3000, Australia

Macmillan of Canada
Division of Canada Publishing Corporation
164 Commander Boulevard
Agincourt, Ontario M1S 3C7, Canada

16 15 14 13 12 11 10 9 8 7 6 5 4 3 2 1

Library of Congress Cataloging-in-Publication Data

Mitchell, William J. (William John), 1944–
  The art of computer graphics programming.

  Bibliography: p.
  Includes index.
  1. Computer graphics. 2. PASCAL (Computer program
language) 3. Structured programming. I. Liggett,
Robin. II. Kvan, Thomas. III. Title.
T385.M58 1986   006.6   86-4017
ISBN 0-442-25991-3 (pbk.)

Contents

Preface   *VII*

Part One: Introduction to the Medium
1. Line Drawings   *3*
2. Continuous Tone and Color   *31*
3. The Computer as a Graphics Machine   *63*
4. Writing, Compiling, and Executing a Graphics
   Program   *89*

Part Two: Elementary Graphics Programs
5. The Pascal Programming Language   *109*
6. Programs to Generate Simple Line Drawings   *135*
7. Coordinate Calculations   *145*
8. Graphic Vocabularies   *161*
9. Repetition   *201*
10. Curves   *251*
11. Conditionals   *273*
12. Hierarchical Structure   *323*

Part Three: Advanced Techniques
13. Storing Pictures: Data Structures   *357*
14. Transformations   *415*
15. Simple Drawing Editors   *477*
16. Going On from Here   *505*

Appendix: Implementation Details   *527*

Acknowledgments   *551*

Bibliography   *553*

Index   *557*

Preface

The Computer Graphics Revolution

The technology of computer graphics is on the threshold of transforming our culture. Cheap and powerful drawing processors will soon be as familiar to most of us as word processors. Drawing, like reading and writing, will cease to be a specialized skill practiced by a few favored individuals; rapid generation and editing of high-quality graphics will be within the grasp of all. Draftsmen will be as obsolete as scribes.

This emerging transformation is the result, in large part, of the advances made in silicon-chip technology since the 1950s, which have reduced the costs of computer processing of information almost to zero. We have learned how to manufacture abundant computer intelligence out of sand—something of much greater value than alchemists' project to transmute base metals into gold. The graphic arts and design represent only one aspect of our cultural life that will be changed profoundly by this—much as medieval culture was shaken to its foundations by the invention of printing and by the mass literacy that followed.

Objectives of This Text

This book provides a step-by-step, practical introduction to computer graphics for those who want to understand and use it. It is directed at graphics and design professionals: architects, urban designers, landscape architects, interior designers, product designers, graphic artists, animators, and others. But we hope that it will also serve the needs of those who have never learned to draw well in the conventional way. Lack of highly developed hand-eye skills and of facility with conventional graphic media is no handicap in computer graphics. Once you become familiar with the technology and thoroughly grasp some basic principles, it is your level of understanding of line, tone, color, and composition, not your manual dexterity, that determines what you can do with a computer graphics system. We are at least as concerned here with issues of design theory and visual aesthetics as we are with computer technology.

We do not assume any previous background in computing, nor do we expect any mathematics beyond elementary algebra and trigonometry. Where you must understand some specialized technical material, we introduce and explain it. And do not worry if you cannot type; two-finger typing will suffice for everything covered in this text.

Our central objective is to teach you how to write concise, elegant, well-structured computer *programs* to generate graphic displays. A program is simply a sequence of instructions that you give to the computer. These instructions may be interpreted and executed one by one, as they are typed in at a keyboard or selected from some kind of menu, or they may form a lengthy sequence that is first entered, then later executed. The *language* in which the instructions are expressed might be very simple and specialized—perhaps consisting of just a few one-word commands—or it might be rich, general, and extensive—with an elaborate syntax governing the construction of a wide range of expressions. Here we shall introduce and employ the popular Pascal programming language, since this language is simple enough to learn quickly, yet includes all the constructs that we will need to express sophisticated programs. However, we will not confine our attention merely to the capabilities and syntactic coventions of Pascal itself. We will, instead, use Pascal to introduce basic principles of graphic programming that can be applied, on the one hand, to programming in comparable languages such as Fortran, Basic, PL/1, C, Modula, and Ada, and on the other hand, to the instruction of specialized interactive computer graphics systems such as drafting and paint systems, which use command languages or menus.

We must recognize that Pascal is not the last word in programming languages. Its successor, before too long, is likely to be Modula-2. However, since Pascal is still very much more widely used than Modula-2, and since much of Modula-2 is almost identical to Pascal, it makes sense to use Pascal here. In any case, it is in the nature of programming languages to become obsolete eventually, so it is wise to begin with a convenient and popular language like Pascal and be prepared to learn new languages as the need arises. Once you have learned one language, fortunately, this is not difficult.

We treat computer programming for the production of graphics as an art form that (much like musical composition, playwriting, and choreography) involves a distinction between *specifying* and *performing* a work. Such a distinction has not been traditional in the graphic arts; drawings and paintings are usually executed directly. But in computer graphics, a program is like a score, the computer is like a pianist, and the production of a picture is like a very meticulous and faithful performance.

The only way to become skilled in any art form is by *doing*. You must become familiar with the characteristics of your medium, and you must develop your skills through practice—starting with simple exercises and gradually moving to more ambitious projects. This book therefore takes a hands-on approach; it introduces the principles of graphics programming in Pascal, illustrates these with numerous examples, and suggests a carefully graduated series of Pascal programming exercises.

Use As a Text

The material is organized into three parts, and structured for use either in private study or as an accompaniment to classroom exposition. The first, *Introduction to the Medium*, describes the devices that are used in computer graphics, discusses their characteristics, and compares computer graphics to more traditional graphic media. The next, *Elementary Graphics Programs*, introduces the basic constructs needed to write programs that will generate two-dimensional drawings, such as elevations of simple buildings. The final section, *Advanced Techniques*, considers some methods of producing more ambitious images.

This book is intended to be compatible with a wide variety of computing environments, ranging from low-cost home computers to major installations with powerful processors and sophisticated display devices. We have been careful not to assume that anything more than the Pascal language and a simple graphic display or plotting device will be available to the reader.

Code listings for the software that you will need to get started are provided in the appendix. If you are a student using this book in a course, you probably do not need to worry about this; your instructor will have taken care of implementing the software on the computer system that you will be using. But if you are an instructor preparing to teach a course, or if you intend to work on your own home computer, you will probably need to consult the appendix and follow the implementation instructions.

The material presented herein was originally developed for our introductory courses in computer graphics at the Graduate School of Architecture and Urban Planning at UCLA and at the Harvard Graduate School of Design. We have found that you can get through it all in a one-semester course that meets twice a week. A student typically needs about an hour of workstation time a day in order to complete an adequate number of exercises successfully.

PART ONE

Introduction to the Medium

a. "An active line on a walk, moving freely, without goal. A walk for a walk's sake. The mobility agent is a point, shifting its position forward."

b. "The same line, accompanied by complementary forms."

c. "The same line, circumscribing itself."

d. "Two secondary lines, moving around an imaginary main line."

e. "An active line, limited in its movement by fixed points."

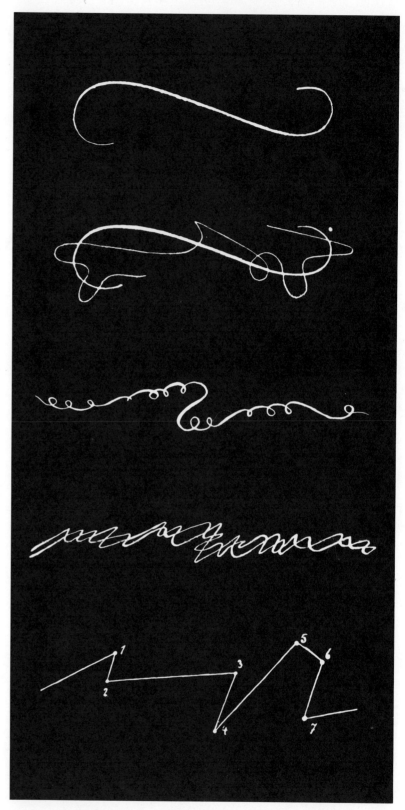

1-1. Lines as introduced by Paul Klee in his *Pedagogical Sketchbook*.

2

1.

Line Drawings

Drawings as Sets of Lines

How do you make a drawing? You begin a simple drawing by moving some kind of marker over a reasonably flat surface to form a line. By repeating this action to produce a set of lines, you can create a drawing of any complexity. There are many possible combinations of marker and surface. You can, for example, draw with a stick in the sand, chalk on a blackboard, pencil on paper, or drafting pen on acetate. Your choice of medium will depend on what is at hand, the accuracy and line quality that you must achieve, and the size, durability, and portability required for the final product.

If you want to develop a systematic understanding of the art of drawing, a logical way to begin is with careful consideration of the various lines that can be produced by different combinations of marker, surface, and hand movement. You can then look at ways of combining lines into more complex graphic structures and at possible transformations of such structures. This strategy has much in common with that of approaching musical composition first by the consideration of notes and scales, then by the combination of notes into sequences and chords, and finally the potential transformations of musical structures.

The idea is not new. In the 1920s, the great Swiss painter, Paul Klee, began his *Pedagogical Sketchbook* (Klee 1925) by speaking of a line as "a point, shifting its position forward," then demonstrating some of the many different ways to form a line (fig. 1-1). In *Point and Line to Plane*, Klee's Bauhaus colleague Wassily Kandinsky considered a line as the result of applying a "force" to a point to produce movement (Kandinsky 1926). A constant force produces a straight line; a sudden change in direction of the force produces an angle; and a smoothly varying force produces a curve (fig. 1-2).

1-2. Wassily Kandinsky's illustration, in *Point and Line to Plane*, of "forces" applied to a point to produce straight, zigzag, and curved lines.

The Cathode Ray Tube

In computer graphics we simply use a computer-controlled machine rather than the hand to apply the force that moves a point across a surface. The most common device for this purpose is the *cathode ray tube*. Its operation is illustrated schematically in figure 1-3.

The basic physical action involved in a cathode ray tube is the attraction

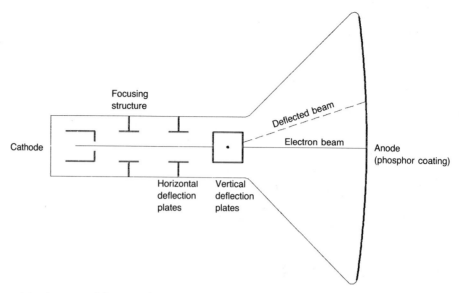

1-3. The essential features of a cathode ray tube.

of electrons from the negatively charged *anode* at the back of the tube to a positively charged *cathode* that covers the front of the tube. The electrons are focused into a narrow beam by application of a magnetic field. Where this beam strikes the cathode, it excites a *phosphor* coating, producing a small, glowing point. Before it strikes the cathode, though, the beam passes between *deflection plates,* which apply magnetic fields to deflect the beam horizontally and vertically. By adjustment of the deflection plates, then, the glowing point can be moved around the surface of the screen.

Several variants on the principle of the cathode ray tube (CRT) display can be produced by using different kinds of deflection apparatuses in conjunction with different kinds of phosphors. They are known, respectively, as the *storage tube* display, the *refreshed vector* display, and the *raster* display. We shall consider these in turn.

Storage Tube Displays

The phosphors used in CRT displays may be classed as either *low persistence* or *high persistence*. If the phosphor is low persistence, then the electron beam striking a point on the screen only excites it for a fraction of a second, so that the moving beam creates a glowing point that travels across the screen surface, dragging a "tail" behind it. No permanent image appears. If the phosphor is high persistence, however, the electron beam excites the phosphor more permanently, so that the moving beam traces out a line that remains on the screen until it very slowly fades away, or is erased in a flash of light by flooding the whole screen with electrons, or the display is turned off. Because a CRT with a high persistence phosphor *stores* an image on the surface of the screen, it is called a *storage tube* display. Such displays have been in use as computer graphics devices since the 1960s (fig. 1-4), but, as other technologies have developed, they have lost the great popularity they once enjoyed.

The display area of a standard no-frills storage tube is about the same as that of an 8½- by 11-inch pad of paper. Glowing lines appear on a dark background. The intensity is fairly low, so room lights must usually be dimmed.

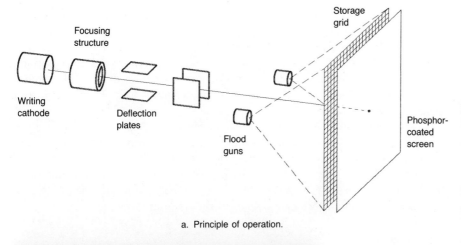

a. Principle of operation.

b. A typical model (Tektronix).

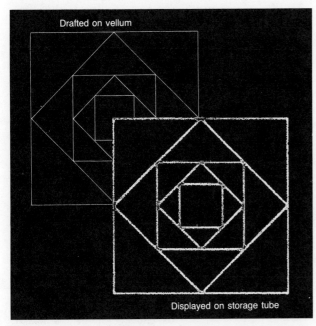

1-5. Comparison of lines drawn on vellum, using a fine drafting pen, with lines displayed on a storage-tube screen.

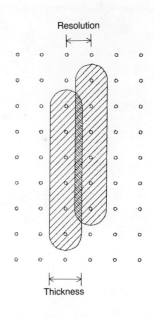

1-6. Enlarged diagram of lines displayed on a storage tube, illustrating resolution, line thickness, and the potential overlap of closely spaced lines.

Phosphors can be produced in many different colors, but green is by far the most common. Figure 1-5 shows some lines photographed from a storage tube and reproduced at actual size, compared with some lines made by technical pen. You can see that the storage tube lines are fairly thick, and there is perceptible fuzziness.

The display also has limited *resolution*. This is not to be confused with line thickness; the resolution is the minimum distance at which lines can be spaced. A typical storage tube screen has a resolution of 1,024 points across its widest dimension, amounting to about 150 points to the inch. Larger storage tubes, with 14- or 18-inch-wide screens, sometimes have resolutions of 4,096 points. Since line thickness on a storage tube is usually greater than the minimum possible spacing of lines, lines placed too close together will fuse into solid areas (fig. 1-6).

The 1,024 (or 4,096) points across a storage tube screen are called its *addressable points*. The deflection apparatus can be set to draw a straight line from any addressable point on the screen to any other. Thus a storage tube picture is composed of uniform straight lines connecting locations in the grid of addressable points (fig. 1-7a). Refer to the different kinds of lines illustrated by Paul Klee in figure 1-1. In his terms, a storage tube displays the kind of line that is "limited in its movement by fixed points" (fig. 1-7b); these fixed points are addressable points on the screen.

The distortion that is necessary to map regular shapes onto a square grid of addressable points of finite resolution can sometimes cause unexpected, unwanted effects. Consider figure 1-8, for example. It shows a nominal circle superimposed on a grid and the shape that appears when approximation is made to the nearest grid points. This sort of effect can sometimes degrade fine detail and small lettering displayed on a storage tube.

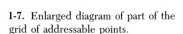

1-7. Enlarged diagram of part of the grid of addressable points.

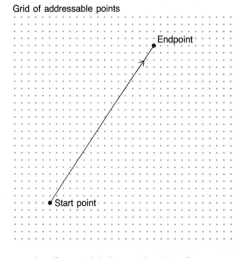

a. A uniform straight line can be drawn from any addressable point on the screen to any other.

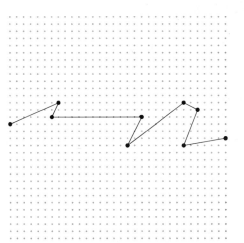

b. The "fixed points" of Klee's line that is "limited in its movement" (see fig. 1-1e) become the addressable points on the screen.

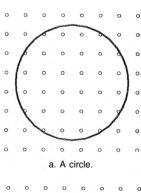

a. A circle.

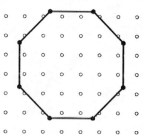

b. Approximation of the circle by equal straight segments.

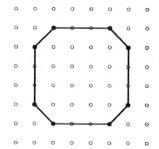

c. Distortion of lengths and angles when endpoints of line segments are moved to the nearest locations on a square grid.

1-8. Distortion results when a regular shape is approximated by straight line segments connecting addressable points.

In general, then, generating displays on a standard storage tube is rather like drawing with a thick, soft pencil on a small sketchpad. You can get better quality for a higher price. In the more expensive models, larger screens and finer lines provide the capability to display more intricate drawings (fig. 1-9).

Special electrostatic printing devices (fig. 1-10) can be connected to storage tubes, so screen images can be copied onto paper at the touch of a button. These reverse the tonality, yielding black lines on a white background (fig. 1-11). Unfortunately, the line quality is usually poor. Prints produced with these device are adequate for working purposes, but do not provide good final copies. Another way to record a storage tube image is to photograph the screen. You must avoid reflections on the screen and experiment with exposure, but it is possible to produce bright, crisp slides and publication-quality prints in this way.

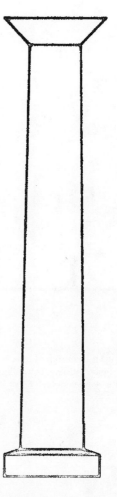

1-11. Electrostatic print of a drawing displayed on a storage tube.

1-9. A drawing displayed on a large, high-resolution storage tube.

1-10. An electrostatic printer connected to a storage tube.

The major disadvantages of standard storage tube displays are that they are static, do not allow selective erase operations, and are monochromatic. A *dynamic* display allows moving pictures to be displayed, but by their basic physical nature, standard storage tubes do not have this capacity. You therefore cannot use a storage tube to display an animated scene; you cannot see an object rotate on the screen; and you cannot drag graphic elements from one location to another across the screen.

Whereas all the marks on a screen can be erased by flooding it with electrons, there is no way to *selectively erase* lines—except by erasing the screen completely and redrawing the picture with the indicated lines removed. This can make alteration of a drawing a tedious and cumbersome process, and if the drawing is complex, the regeneration of the image can take a significant amount of time.

Also because of their physical nature, storage tubes display lines of just one color. If you want colored drawings, you must use another type of technology.

Some of these limitations have been partially overcome in recent advanced models of storage tubes. But a storage tube display should basically be thought of as a fairly low-cost device for displaying static, monochromatic line drawings at medium resolution on a rather small screen.

Refreshed Vector Displays

The basic difference between a refreshed vector display and a storage tube is that the refreshed vector display uses a very low-persistence phosphor. The deflection apparatus moves the electron beam around very rapidly to trace out a line drawing on the screen and constantly repeats this operation. When this *refresh cycle* is fast enough (at least thirty times per second, and preferably forty or fifty), the illusion of a constant image is created—much as individual frames in rapid succession create the illusion of a constant image on a movie screen.

In addition to the CRT, a refreshed vector display must incorporate a *display buffer* and a *display controller* (fig. 1-12). The display buffer is a memory device storing all the information needed to refresh the drawing. The display controller's function is to cycle through this information and translate it into appropriate movements of the electron beam.

Refreshed vector displays have been in use in computer graphics since the 1950s—even longer than storage tubes. Figure 1-13 illustrates a typical refreshed vector display device. These are inherently more expensive than storage tubes, because the electron beam deflection apparatus of a refreshed vector tube must be built to more exacting standards, and because computer resources must constantly be devoted to the task of refreshing the image.

There is an important performance disadvantage too. The amount of work that must be done to refresh a drawing is proportional to the number of lines

1-12. The relationships between the display buffer, display controller, and CRT in a refreshed vector display.

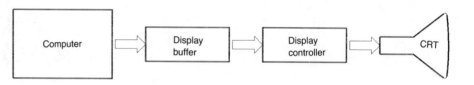

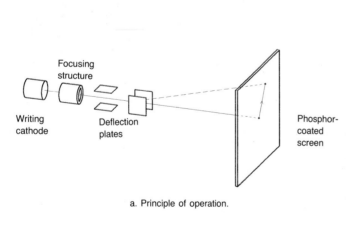

a. Principle of operation.

1-13. A refreshed vector display device.

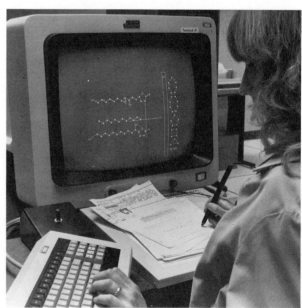

b. A typical model.

in the drawing, so that it takes longer to refresh a complex drawing than to refresh a simple one. If the refresh cycle becomes too long, the image begins to flicker. At best this is annoying, and looking at a flickering image can eventually make you ill. If the refresh cycle becomes longer still, the image will decay completely. In addition to this limitation—imposed by the limited speed of the display controller—there is a second limitation imposed by the capacity of the display buffer; it will only be able to store some finite number of lines. Thus a refreshed vector display not only has (like a storage tube) limitations on resolution, but also on the complexity of the drawings it can handle.

Refeshed vector technology does, however, have the important advantage of allowing the display of moving images. This is accomplished by generating and displaying successive drawings that differ slightly from each other to create the illusion of continuous motion. Thus you can rotate three-dimensional objects, simulate movement through a landscape, and display animated scenes. Selective erasing is also possible. If a line is indicated for erasure, the computer can delete it at the next refresh cycle, so that it seems to disappear instantly. Furthermore, it is possible to build multicolor refreshed vector displays. These are, however, considerably more expensive than models that produce mono-chromatic images.

Refreshed vector displays are available at a wide variety of cost and performance levels. Cheaper models tend to have smaller screens, lower resolution, and a more limited capacity for displaying complex drawings before flicker sets in. More expensive models typically display larger, more complex drawings at higher resolution, with better line quality; these sometimes have color capability as well.

Although some capabilities overlap, storage tube and refreshed vector displays are appropriate for different applications. Where low cost is important, complex drawings must be displayed, and color and dynamic display capabilities are not essential (in architectural drafting applications, for example), storage tubes are attractive. But where dynamics and color *are* important, drawing complexity is limited, and cost is less of a consideration (for example, in aircraft-landing simulators), refreshed vector displays meet the requirements.

Raster Displays of Line Drawings

An increasingly popular alternative to the storage tube or the refreshed vector display is the *raster* CRT display. In fact, raster displays have now become the standard, especially on low-cost personal computers; other types of displays are used only in specialized applications.

Raster displays are usually produced on video monitors. Some inexpensive home computers, in fact, use ordinary television sets as display devices, but special high-precision monitors are used in more sophisticated computer graphics systems.

Where the phosphor of a storage or refreshed vector CRT covers the screen surface continuously, the phosphor of a video monitor is disposed in a grid of small discrete dots. Each horizontal line of dots is called a *raster* (fig. 1-14). Another difference is that in a raster display, the electron beam does not trace out a drawing in a line-by-line (calligraphic) fashion. Instead, it sweeps out the entire surface of the screen, moving from left to right along each raster and from the top of the screen to the bottom (fig. 1-15). This process is repeated thirty times per second. A dot can be drawn on a raster display by intensifying the electron beam each time that it passes over the specified position. So lines can be constructed out of dots (fig. 1-16). Perfectly vertical and horizontal lines will appear smooth, but diagonal lines appear slightly jagged, since the resolution at which the dots can be displayed is limited.

In addition to the video monitor, a typical raster device incorporates a *frame buffer* and a *digital-to-analog converter* (DAC). Their arrangement is schematically depicted in figure 1-17. The frame buffer is a memory device,

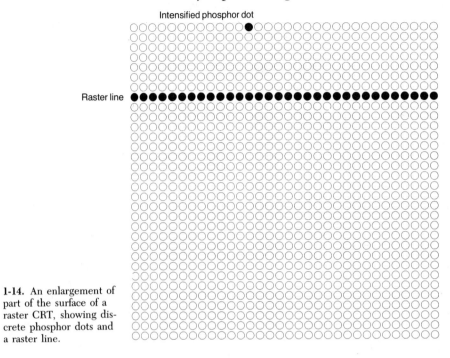

1-14. An enlargement of part of the surface of a raster CRT, showing discrete phosphor dots and a raster line.

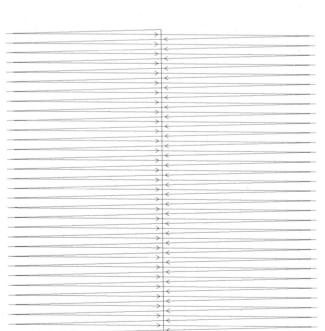

1-15. Scan pattern of the electron beam on a raster CRT.

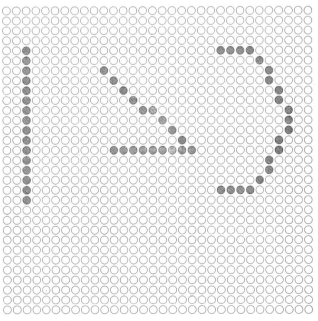

1-16. An enlargement of lines displayed on a raster CRT, showing how they are constructed out of dots.

which stores numbers specifying how each dot on the screen is to be intensified. The DAC converts these numbers to intensity levels for the electron beam as it sweeps out the screen.

Because a raster CRT display constructs pictures out of discrete dots rather than continuous straight lines, a line drawing may look quite different when it is displayed on a raster device and on a calligraphic device (fig. 1-18). The difference is most pronounced, of course, where resolution is low.

Raster displays can be used to produce not only line drawings, but also continuously toned and colored images. We shall say a great deal more about them in our discussion of tone and color in chapter 2.

Frame buffer

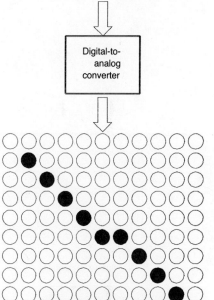

1-17. The relationships between the frame buffer, digital-to-analog converter (DAC), and CRT in a raster display.

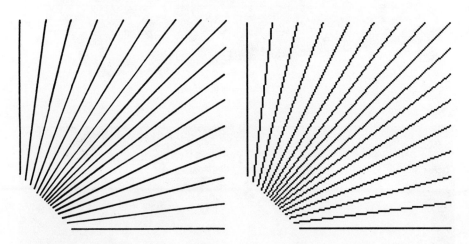

a. A drawing displayed on a calligraphic device.   b. The same drawing displayed on a raster device.

1-18. The effect of CRT display technology on the appearance of a line drawing.

Pen Plotters

CRT displays generate line drawings by the movement of an electron beam across a phosphor. A *pen plotter* generates line drawings in a much more conventional way—by moving a pen across paper. Electric motors are used to produce the movement; plotters, unlike CRT displays, are electro-mechanical rather than electronic devices. They have many complicated moving parts and, compared to CRT displays, are relatively slow, noisy, and unreliable. However, they can be used to produce good-quality computer-generated line drawings on paper.

Several different arrangements are used to produce, under computer control, the required movement. In a *flat-bed* plotter (fig. 1-19) the paper remains motionless, while computer-controlled electric motors drive a cross-arm (very much like a draftsman's parallel rule) back and forth in one direction and drive a plotting head back and forth along the cross-arm in the perpendicular direction. The plotting head's pen can also be raised and lowered under computer control. This arrangement imposes a definite limitation (determined by the size of the bed) on the size of drawings.

In a *drum* plotter (fig. 1-20) paper on a continous roll is scrolled back and forth in one direction, while a plotting head is moved back and forth, along a fixed cross-arm, in the perpendicular direction. Drum plotters tend

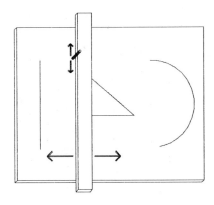

a. Principle of operation.

1-19. A flat-bed plotter.

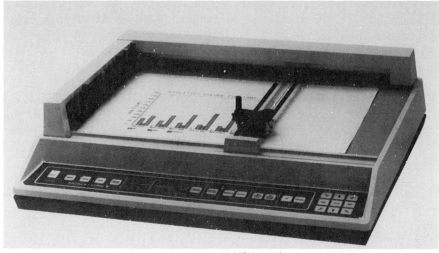

b. A typical model (Calcomp).

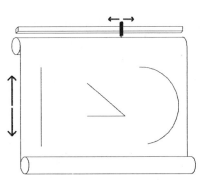

a. Principle of operation.

1-20. A drum plotter.

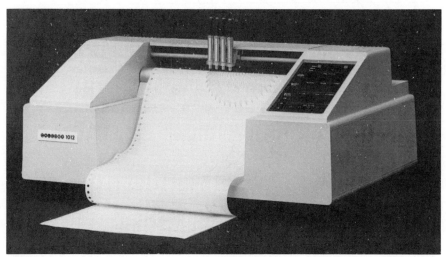

b. A typical model (Calcomp).

to be slower and less precise than flat-bed plotters, but they can produce drawings of unlimited length (though width is limited by the width of the drum).

Flat-bed and drum plotters are most common, but plotters that move the paper on a belt (fig. 1-21) or that roll the paper back and forth between wheels at either edge (fig. 1-22) are also available.

Virtually any kind of paper or drafting film can be used in a flat-bed plotter. Indeed, flat-bed plotters (equipped with suitable heads) can even be used to etch sheets of metal or cut sheets of cloth. Drum plotters are a bit more limited, since the plotting medium must be adequately flexible and not too fragile. But most familiar drafting media (such as tracing paper, vellum, and acetate) can be used without difficulty.

A wide variety of pens can be mounted on plotting heads as well. Ballpoint pens are very popular, since they fail infrequently and do not often need to

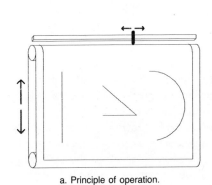

a. Principle of operation.

1-21. A belt plotter.

b. A typical model (Calcomp).

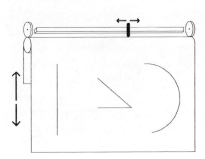

a. Principle of operation.

1-22. The movement of plotter paper between wheels.

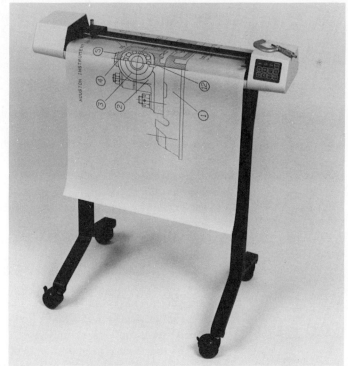

b. A typical model (Houston Instrument).

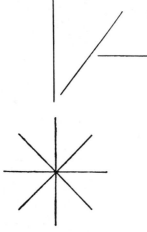

a. Three "basic types of straight lines," as illustrated by Kandinsky in *Point and Line to Plane*.

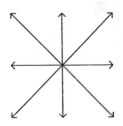

b. The eight possible directions of movement in incremental plotting.

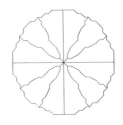

c. Incremental approximation of various lines.

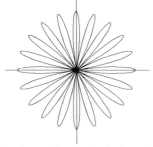

d. The effect on line quality of a large step size.

1-23. The principle of incremental plotting.

be refilled or replaced. But the line quality that results is no better than you would expect from a ballpoint, so they are best used for producing working plots rather than final copy.

Heavy-duty versions of the familiar tubular-nib drafting pen are normally used for producing high-quality plots. They usually produce results that would be the envy of even the most sure-handed draftsman. Even in the context of sophisticated computer technology, however, you cannot escape the fundamental and irksome physical limitations of liquid ink pens. Under unfavorable circumstances, plotter pens can dry up, blot, skip, and produce uneven lines.

Many drum plotters use the *incremental* plotting method, in which the pen can move one small, fixed increment at a time to the left or to the right, while the paper can move a similar increment up or down. This action produces a short line segment in any one of eight directions (fig. 1-23). The effect of such stepping is imperceptible when a drawing is composed entirely of horizontal, vertical, and 45-degree diagonal lines. But lines at other angles and curves must be approximated as illustrated in figure 1-23c. If the step size is too large, line quality can become unacceptable—particularly when a fine pen is being used (fig. 1-23d). Unfortunately, there is a trade-off to be made between line quality and plotting speed, since a larger step size allows faster operation.

Flat-bed plotters commonly use the *line-plotting* method. In this case, straight lines of any length, and at any angle, are produced between specified pairs of points. Curves, however, must still be approximated by short straight segments.

The plotter's *resolution, repeatability,* and *accuracy* also affect the graphic quality of a plotted drawing. In the kinds of design and graphic applications that will concern us here, the resolution of a plotter rarely presents a problem. Usually we find that a plotter can produce drawings at a higher resolution than the most skilled hand draftsman working with the finest pen on the smoothest surface.

Repeatability describes the capability of a pen plotter to return to a previously plotted point, whereas accuracy refers to the difference between the actual and the specified pen location. Poor repeatability and accuracy in a pen plotter produce the same undesirable results as sloppy hand drafting—polygons that do not close, corners that cross, uneven hatching, and so on. However, repeatability and accuracy to better than one-thousandth of an inch are achievable with many pen plotters.

Pen plotters seem impressively fast when you first see them in operation. When productivity is important, however, plotting time for drawings can become a significant issue, and it is not unusual for a large and intricate drawing to take many minutes, or even hours, to plot.

Pen plotters on the market today cover an enormous spectrum of cost and performance levels. The cheapest (intended for use with inexpensive personal computers) plot on 8½- by 11-inch paper, are extremely slow, and produce results of limited graphic quality. They are, however, adequate for many practical purposes. More expensive models can cost tens, or even hundreds, of thousands of dollars and offer large formats, very high precision, excellent quality (fig. 1-24), and high-speed operation.

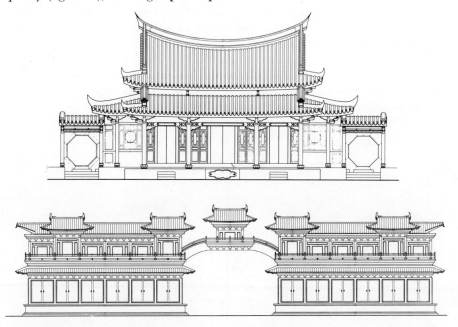

1-24. Examples of line drawings produced on a good-quality pen plotter. (Images by John Chu, Yi-Mei Fan, and Ranjit Makkuni.)

Device Coordinate Systems

The rectangle of a CRT display screen, or of a plotting surface, constitutes a *picture plane* (defined by Kandinsky in *Point and Line to Plane* as "that material plane which is called upon to accommodate the content of the work of art"), on which we can dispose lines to create a drawing (fig. 1-25). How can we, then, create a specific *kind* of line in a specific *place* on the drawing surface of a computer graphics display?

We first must choose some method for specifying *position* on the picture plane analogous to the use of latitude and longitude to specify the position of a ship or aircraft on the surface of the earth, or to the use of a street address to specify the location of a house in a city. The standard approach is to establish a *device coordinate system,* which allows any position on the screen or plotting surface to be specified by giving an X and a Y coordinate. Usually the origin of this coordinate system is set at a corner of the drawing surface, so all coordinates are positive (fig. 1-26).

In CRT displays, device coordinates are typically specified in *raster units*, with the origin at the bottom-left corner of the screen (fig. 1-27). The size of a raster unit is determined by the resolution of the display; it is the smallest possible distance between two distinct points. Storage tube and refreshed vector displays, for example, typically have systems of 1,024 by 1,024 raster units, and raster displays typically have 256 by 256, 512 by 512, or 1,024 by

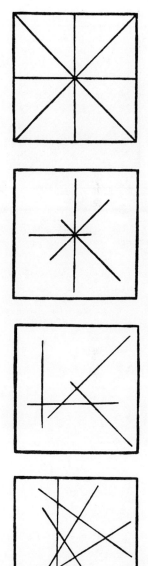

1-25. Lines disposed on a picture plane, as illustrated by Kandinsky in *Point and Line to Plane*.

1,024 systems. Note that in this type of system, coordinates will always have integer values; fractions would be meaningless.

Flat-bed plotters are very often used to produce drawings at some definite scale, so it is convenient to specify device coordinates in inches (or millimeters, where the metric system is used). The limits of the coordinate system, then, are determined by the size of the available plotting surface (fig. 1-28). Since resolution is very much better than one inch (or even one millimeter), coordinates have real number rather than integer values.

Drum plotters are slightly trickier, since the plotting surface is limited in one direction (by the width of the drum), but not in the other, and because there is no fixed point on the paper to take as the origin. Usually, then, the device coordinate system is set up as shown in figure 1-29.

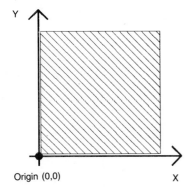

Origin (0,0)   X

1-26. A device coordinate system with its origin at the bottom-left corner.

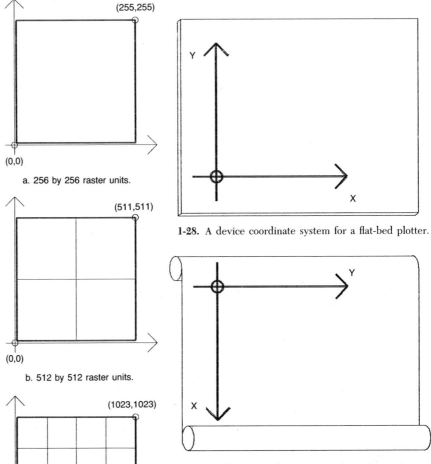

a. 256 by 256 raster units.

b. 512 by 512 raster units.

c. 1,024 by 1,024 raster units.

1-27. Typical device coordinate systems for CRT displays.

1-28. A device coordinate system for a flat-bed plotter.

1-29. A device coordinate system for a drum plotter.

Vectors as Graphic Primitives

Once a device coordinate system has been established, we can specify a line that we want to draw within the coordinate system by giving the coordinates of its endpoints (fig. 1-30a). Thus a straight line segment (usually referred to in computer graphics as a *vector*) is encoded as four numbers:

BEGINNING	X1	Y1
END	X2	Y2

Another approach, illustrated in figure 1-30b, is to specify the beginning coordinates, followed by a direction and a length:

BEGINNING	X1	Y1
DIRECTION	THETA	
LENGTH	L	

These approaches are mathematically equivalent; you need four numbers, in either case, to specify a vector.

A dot or point may be treated as a degenerate case of a vector with the same beginning and end points (fig. 1-31). The precise size and shape of the mark that results will depend on the physical characteristics of the display device.

What if we want to specify a curved line? The standard approach in computer graphics is to approximate the curve by a sequence of vectors. This can be done more or less closely as illustrated in figure 1-32. A limit to this is ultimately set, of course, by the resolution of the device.

a. Endpoint coordinates (X1, Y1) and (X2, Y2).

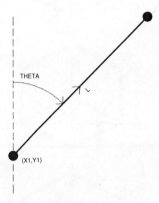

b. Endpoint (X1,Y1), direction Theta, and length L.

1-30. Encoding a vector as four numbers.

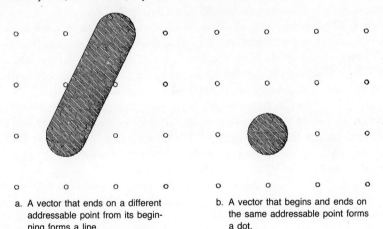

a. A vector that ends on a different addressable point from its beginning forms a line.

b. A vector that begins and ends on the same addressable point forms a dot.

1-31. Degeneration of a vector to a point.

We now have a way to write instructions for the generation of a line drawing. We take vectors as our graphic *primitives*. The complete drawing is thus a set of vectors, and any part of the drawing is a subset. Each vector to be drawn is specified in the device coordinate system by four numbers at some finite level of resolution. The drawing instructions can be executed by a human draftsman who knows how to interpret them, or (when suitably encoded as electrical impulses) by numerically controlled machines such as CRT displays and pen plotters.

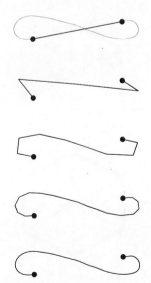

1-32. A curved line and increasingly accurate approximations with sequences of vectors.

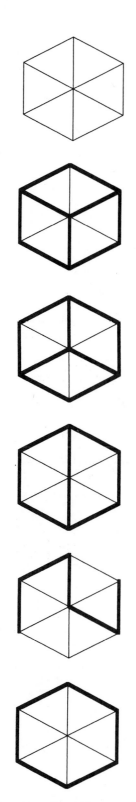

Line Thickness and Quality

When we take this simple approach to line graphics, the positions and lengths of vectors are the only graphic variables that we have to work with when composing a drawing. These vectors are of the same weight, color, and style. Although working within these constraints can yield very elegant results, we often want more graphic variables at our command.

It is very common, for example, to vary the thickness of lines in a drawing. This might, for example, be done to give special emphasis to part of a drawing, or to provide depth cues (fig. 1-33). Furthermore, an artist might employ variation in the line weight for the purely formal purpose of creating contrasts, tensions, and rhythms, as in the composition by Josef Albers shown in figure 1-34.

In hand drafting, line thickness can be varied by selecting different tubular-tipped pens. This can be done with a plotter too; most plotters have several pens, which can be selected under computer control. Either the pens are mounted side by side on the plotting head (fig. 1-35a), or there is a rack at the side of the plotting surface from which pens can be selected and mounted on the head (fig. 1-35b).

If we want to make use of this capability, we must have some way to specify the pen with which a vector is to be drawn. An obvious approach is to number the pens, then to specify the pen number for each vector as follows:

BEGINNING	X1	Y1
END	X2	Y2
THICKNESS	PEN_NUMBER	

Since we have introduced an additional graphic variable, it now takes five numbers rather than four to specify a graphic primitive.

In CRT displays, the electron beam traversing the phosphor normally generates a line of constant thickness. However, lines of greater thickness can be produced by drawing closely spaced parallel lines, which fuse into a single line, whose thickness is controlled by specifying the number of parallel lines to be drawn—a technique often used in hand drawing (fig. 1-36).

Some hand media, for example, flexible-nib pens or brushes, allow variation of thickness not only from line to line, but also continuously within a line, as illustrated by Kandinsky in figure 1-37. Usually this is controlled by varying the pressure or speed as the line is drawn. In pen or brush calligraphy, control of such variation is critically important (fig. 1-38).

The line-drawing devices used in computer graphics do not provide for this kind of variation. Its effect can be approximated where necessary, however, by building up a line out of short vectors. One approach is to break the line into short, straight segments and draw approximately parallel vectors to build up the required width for each segment (fig. 1-39a). Another possibility is to draw short, closely spaced vectors perpendicular to the direction of the line (fig. 1-39b). Alternatively, the thickness of the line may be filled by parallel hatching in an arbitrary direction (fig. 1-39c).

Where a drawing includes lines of substantial thickness, the styles of ending a line and of forming corners become significant graphic issues. A tubular-tipped pen, for example, characteristically produces rounded ends and corners (fig. 1-40a); a chisel-tipped pen produces square ends (fig. 1-40b); and tape can be cut to produce chamfered corners (fig. 1-40c). In calligraphy, a

1-33. Variation in line thickness used to emphasize different parts of a figure and to provide depth cues.

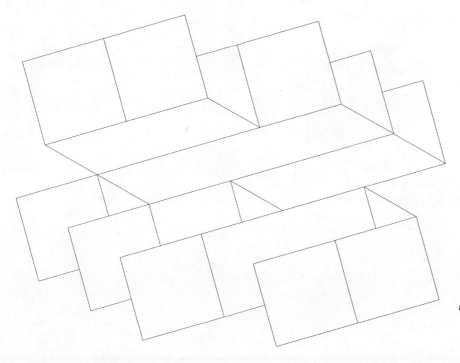

a. An arrangement of parallels, perpendiculars, and diagonals, with no variations in line thickness.

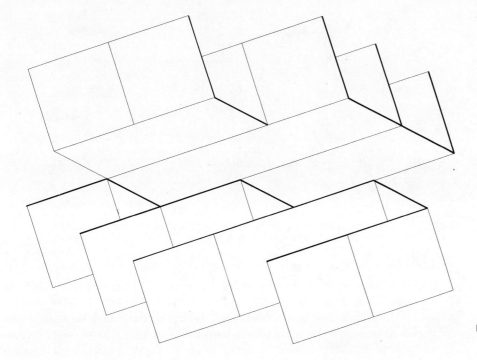

b. Variations in line thickness are introduced.

1-34. Variations in line thickness can be used to create contrasts, tensions, and rhythms. (After a composition by Josef Albers in *Despite Straight Lines.*)

a. Several different pens mounted on the plotting head.

b. Pens are selected from a rack at the side of the plotter.

1-35. Pen plotters that allow variation in line thickness.

1-36. Closely spaced parallel lines read as a single thick line; Paul Klee, *Architecture of Variations*, 1927. (Paul Klee Foundation, Museum of Fine Arts Berne. Copyright © 1986 by Cosmopress, Geneva.)

1-37. Variation of thickness within a line; illustration of some possibilities by Kandinsky in *Point and Line to Plane*.

thick line may be made to end with a sharp point by lifting the brush from the paper as it approaches the end. Lines can meet exactly to form corners (fig. 1-41a); there may be overshoot (fig. 1-41b), or there may be a slight gap at the corners (fig. 1-41c). Skilled draftsmen carefully choose one of these methods of handling corners in order to give a particular feel to a drawing and to make it read more clearly. In computer graphics this subtlety is usually ignored, and all corners are formed exactly, although systems can be set up to treat corners in different ways.

Many of these effects of different types of pens, brushes, and styles of handling can be simulated on line-drawing devices by constructing lines out of parallel strokes and calculating thicknesses and end conditions as if the constructed line were formed by a tool of specified shape. On raster devices, similar effects can be produced by building up lines from dots. Figure 1-42, for example, illustrates the use of simulated circular, square, horizontal, vertical, and diagonal "pens."

When we choose among different graphic tools (whether real or simulated), we introduce yet another graphic variable. Thus we might, for example, number each tool, then specify each vector in a picture as follows:

BEGINNING	X1	Y1
END	X2	Y2
THICKNESS	T	
TOOL TYPE	N	

Line Intensity

Intensity is another property of lines that can vary within a drawing. In hand drafting this might be done, for example, by diluting ink to different levels or by varying pressure on a pencil to emphasize parts of a drawing (fig. 1-43).

In plotting we can imitate hand methods by using pens with inks in different dilutions. Many lower-cost CRT displays do not provide any differential intensity control. However, some more sophisticated models provide not only for intensity variation from vector to vector, but also for continuous intensity variation along a vector. Intensity control is particularly useful for providing depth cues in three-dimensional scenes (fig. 1-44).

The usual way to specify intensity (where this is to be controlled in a CRT display) is to give a number between zero (minimum intensity) and one (maximum intensity). Thus, where thickness, tool type, and intensity are all controlled, we have seven graphic variables with which to work.

BEGINNING	X1	Y1
END	X2	Y2
THICKNESS	T	
TOOL TYPE	N	
INTENSITY	I	

Line Color

Yet another potential graphic variable is the color of lines. Color variation is traditionally made possible by using sets of colored pens, pencils, or crayons. Color is often used, like line thickness and intensity, to direct the viewer's attention, to emphasize, and to provide depth cues. It might also be used to imply the color of an enclosed shape (without actually coloring in the shape).

In technical drafting, line color can be used very effectively to separate different layers of information. The floor plan of a building, for example, might be drawn with the structural system in one color, the mechanical system in a second, and the furniture and partitions in a third. This separation allows much greater density of information on a drawing without confusion and brings

1-38. An example of Chinese calligraphy; pressure and speed are varied to control the thickness of strokes.

a. Vectors parallel to the direction of movement.

b. Vectors perpendicular to the direction of movement.

c. Vectors independent of the direction of movement.

1-39. The use of short vectors to create a line of continuously varying thickness.

a. Rounded ends and corners, as produced by tubular-tipped pens.

b. Square ends and corners, as produced by chisel-tipped pens.

c. Angled ends and chamfered corners, as produced by cutting tape.

1-40. Enlargements of ends of lines.

a. Exact.

b. Overshoot.

c. Gap.

1-41. Styles of corner formation.

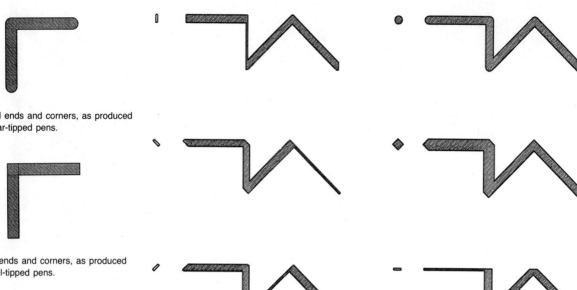

1-42. Pen tip shapes and corresponding types of lines; these can be simulated using short vectors.

out the relationships between systems. You can immediately tell, for example, where the different systems have spatial conflicts.

Pen plotters allow color variation through use of pens with different colored inks. Refreshed vector displays with color capability usually have a very limited palette. In either case, each option is numbered, and you control the color of a vector by specifying the identification number of the desired color. Raster displays may provide extensive palettes of colors and allow sophisticated color control; this is discussed in chapter 2.

Constructed Line Styles

We began our disussion of graphic variables by pointing out that the basic ones are the length and position of a vector. We have now seen that the thickness, style, intensity, and color of lines can also be controlled. Yet another possibility is to construct lines out of repeating motifs. For the moment we shall limit outselves to a brief survey of the graphic possibilities and defer until Section 2 discussion of techniques of construction.

The most common constructed line styles are dotted and dashed lines (fig. 1-45). Different characters can be given by controlling the length and spacing of the strokes. Or, more elaborately, a line might be constructed out of discrete symbols, each composed of several vectors (fig. 1-46).

Tone and Texture

Areas of different tone and texture in a drawing can be built up out of vectors. *Hatching*, for example, is a traditional device in both freehand drawing and technical drafting (fig. 1-47) and can also be incorporated into drawings generated by line-drawing devices. Another possibility is to use *dot screens* of varying density (fig. 1-48). In hand drafting such screens are usually preprinted and applied on sticky-backed transparent paper. Using a computer graphics

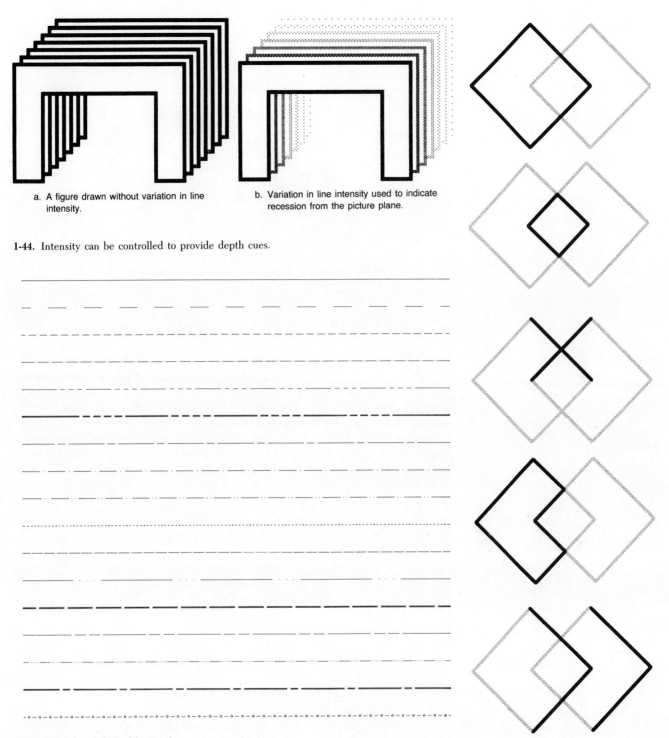

a. A figure drawn without variation in line intensity.

b. Variation in line intensity used to indicate recession from the picture plane.

1-44. Intensity can be controlled to provide depth cues.

1-45. Dotted and dashed line styles.

line-drawing device, each dot is a zero-length vector. Finally, regular textures of any complexity can be constructed from lines, dots, and symbols of various kinds (fig. 1-49).

Every draftsman knows that hatched and textured line drawings are very laborious to produce, since they require a great many individual pen strokes.

1-43. Variations of a figure produced by changing line intensity.

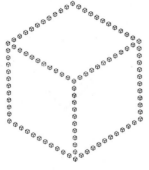

1-46. Lines constructed out of repeating symbols.

a. Mechanical hatching. (Perspective rendering of the Yale Mathematics Building by Venturi, Rauch and Scott-Brown.)

1-47. Hatching is used to render tone and texture (above and right).

Similarly, a line-drawing device must generate a great many vectors. Even though a pen plotter is much faster than the hand, and a CRT display is faster still, it does take a finite amount of time to generate a vector, and it can easily take an unacceptably long time for a line-drawing device to produce a large amount of hatching or texturing. There can be other problems, too. Limited resolution (especially on storage tubes) can result in the clotting of fine detail and fusion of close hatching. And the large number of vectors involved is very likely to cause flicker in a refreshed vector CRT. So hatching, screens, and texturing generated from vectors should be used very sparingly where line-drawing devices are employed.

Lettering

Lettering on drawings produced using line-drawing devices is also generated from short vectors. Although (as we have seen) it is technically feasible to vary line thickness, such variation greatly increases the time required to generate a character, so characters are typically formed out of strokes of even weight. It is also common practice to attempt to limit the number of vectors used to form a character. Thus the lettering that results tends to be similar to that produced using drafting pens and lettering stencils (fig. 1-50). Results improve by increasing the number of vectors used per character (and therefore computational effort) to produce smoother curves (fig. 1-51).

The most significant problem with simple vector lettering is that the strokes forming characters do not become thicker as the characters are drawn at larger scale. Thus, as shown in figure 1-52, small lettering appears relatively dense and bold compared with larger lettering.

There are various ways to achieve better character form and better control of density and boldness by using more vectors. One is to allow variation of thickness in conjunction with use of a simulated tool. Some examples of this technique are shown in figure 1-53.

b. Freehand hatching. (Kleinstadt-Rathaus, by Heinrich Tessenow.)

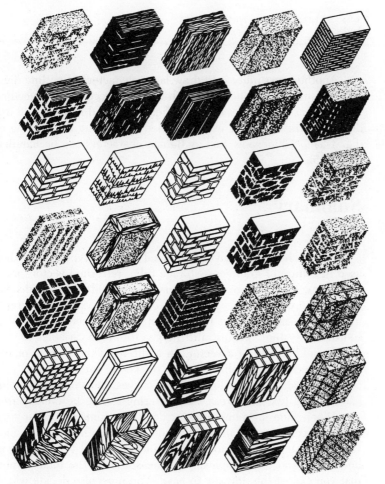

1-49. Some regular textures constructed from lines. (Chris Yessios, Ohio State University.)

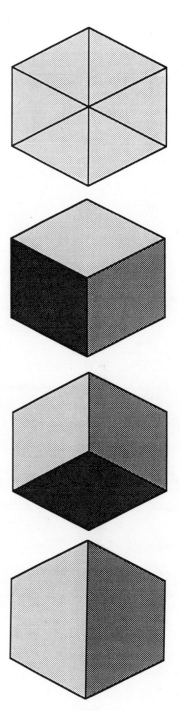

1-48. The use of dot screens to render tone and texture.

ABCDEF
GHIJKL
MNOPQR
STUVWX
YZ1234
567890

1-50. A font, with a minimum number of vectors per character, designed for use with a pen plotter.

ABCDEF GHI JKLMNOPQRSTUVWXYZ1234567890
ABCDEFGHI JKLMNOPQRSTUV
ABCDEFGHI JKLMNOPQR
ABCDEFGHI JKLMNOP
ABCDEFGHI JKLMN
ABCDEFGHI JKLM

1-52. Vector characters drawn with the same pen at different scales; the smaller lettering appears denser and bolder.

5 5 5

1-53. A character drawn with simulated horizontal, vertical, and diagonal pens.

ABCDEF
GHIJKL
MNOPQR
STUVWX
YZ1234
567890

1-51. A font with a larger number of vectors per character.

Another possibility is to draw large characters in outline (fig. 1-54a). Now imagine such an outline filled with closely spaced parallel vectors (fig. 1-54b). Each of these vectors can be specified by its endpoints in the usual way. The density of the character may be varied by altering the spacing of the vectors (fig. 1-54c). Chinese as well as Roman characters can be handled in this way (fig. 1-55).

Summary

In this chapter we have introduced the basic types of line-drawing devices used in computer graphics—storage tube, refreshed vector, and raster CRTs; and flat-bed and drum pen plotters. Associated with the display or plotting surface of any such device is a device coordinate system. The graphic primitive, from which any drawing is constructed, is a vector defined in the device coordinate system. Values must be given to four variables to specify fully the length and position of a vector. In addition, if the display or plotting device has the necessary capabilities, the thickness, intensity, and color of vectors can be varied. Complex line figures, curves, lines of varying width and style, hatched and textured areas, and lettering can all be created from vectors.

When choosing a line-drawing device for some particular graphic purpose, you must consider the image size and resolution needed, the kinds of graphic variables that you want to control (thickness, tool type, color, intensity, and line style), and the complexity (as measured by the total number of vectors) that you expect the drawing to have. You must also decide whether you want hard copy and whether the dynamic manipulation of displays is important.

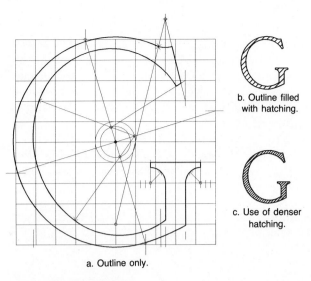

b. Outline filled
with hatching.

c. Use of denser
hatching.

a. Outline only.

1-54. Outlined characters.

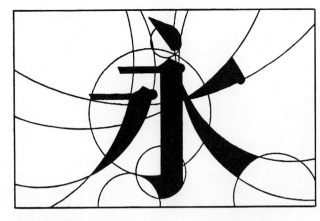

1-55. The construction of a Chinese character from vectors and arcs.

Exercises

1. Look at some books of drawings, or go to the drawing section of your local art museum, and examine closely examples of interesting line drawings or prints in some of the following media:

- hard pencil on fine paper
- chalk or charcoal on rough paper
- ruling pen
- flexible-nib pen
- brush (as in Chinese calligraphy)
- lithograph
- copper engraving
- steel engraving
- mechanical engraving (as on banknotes)
- wood cut
- felt-tip marker

Add a few that you will not usually find in books or museums, such as:

- stick in wet cement or beach sand
- finger on steamy window
- aerosol can graffiti
- skywriting
- neon tubing
- toothpaste on a mirror

In each case try to discover and characterize the type of elementary, primitive stroke that the artist has used. What graphic variables (length, weight, color, and so on) did the artist manipulate each time that he or she executed such a stroke? How was this accomplished physically (selection of instrument, pressure, wrist action, and so on)? What effects was the artist achieving by manipulating graphic variables in this way? Write a brief, illustrated critical analysis of each example, answering these questions.

2. Examine the graphic output device (display or plotter) that you intend to

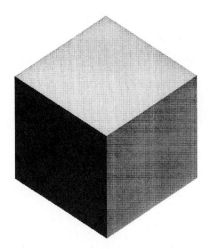

a. Cube.

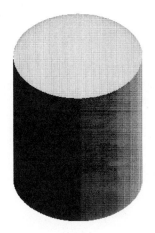

b. Cylinder.

c. Sphere.

1-56. Shaded objects rendered by hatching.

use to carry out the graphics programming exercises given in later chapters. If you can, obtain its technical specifications. Compare the graphic variables that it offers with those of some manual techniques for producing line drawings. Also, compare resolution and accuracy. What are the relative strengths and limitations of each technique? For what types of imagery are these characteristics suitable? Write a brief, illustrated evaluation.

3. The seventeenth-century Chinese *Mustard Seed Garden Manual of Painting* (Princeton, NJ: Princeton University Press, 1956) lists and illustrates many different types of brushstrokes:

- like spread-out hemp fibers
- like entangled hemp fibers
- like sesame seeds
- like big ax cuts
- like small ax cuts
- like cloud heads or thunderheads
- like raindrops
- like an eddy or whirlpool
- like the veins of a lotus leaf
- like lumps of alum
- like skull bones
- like the wrinkles on a devil's face
- like raveled rope
- like brushwood
- like hair of cattle
- like horses' teeth

It then describes how to construct line drawings of plants, animals, and landscape features by combining brushstrokes. Study the formation and use of some of these strokes. What graphic variables does the artist manipulate? What are the roles of these variables in composition? Compare these brushstrokes with the primitives available on line-drawing devices.

4. In this chapter we have introduced the idea of a device coordinate system suitable for describing positions of graphic elements on rectangular picture planes. But artists sometimes work on other types of surfaces. Design coordinate systems that would be suitable for use by artists working in the following ways:

- painting a mural on the inside surface of a barrel vault
- painting a mural on the inside surface of a hemispheric dome
- painting the outside of a vase
- painting a balloon (before it is inflated)

5. Imagine that you are standing on a very large picture plane. You can trace out a vector simply by moving in a specified direction for a specified distance; you do not need to know where you are relative to the origin of some fixed coordinate system in order to do this. Compare the advantages and disadvantages, for graphic purposes, of this method for specifying vectors and the method that we have introduced in this chapter.

6. Figure 1-56a illustrates a shaded cube against a uniform background. Similarly, figure 1-56b shows a cylinder, and figure 1-55c depicts a sphere. Render each of these objects in ink as accurately as you can, using a parallel rule and triangle and using each of the following hatching techniques:

- evenly spaced horizontal lines with line weight varying as required
- lines at a 45-degree angle from the base, of uniform weight but with varied spacing as required
- cross-hatching using lines that are vertical, horizontal, and at a 45-degree angle

7. What do you think is the smallest number of straight lines that you could use for each character to create a satisfactory uppercase Roman alphabet? Choose some number and design an alphabet according to this limitation. Try the same exercise for, say, Chinese, Japanese, Korean, Hebrew, and Arabic characters.

2.

Continuous Tone and Color

Continuous Tone and Color Media

In chapter 1 we considered how drawings can be built up out of lines. Not all drawings, however, are created this way. Sometimes we construct drawings out of continuous areas of tone and color. One way to do this is to cut out shapes and arrange them on the picture plane. Indonesian shadow puppets, for example, are made this way. Paint can be applied in flat polygonal areas to get a similar effect; Kasimir Malevich's famous *Black Square* (fig. 2-1) is a radical reduction of this kind of painting to its bare essentials. The technique can be elaborated, as in colored-paper collage or in quilts or analogous painting and printing methods, by using differently colored or shaded polygons (fig. 2-2).

With paint, pigments and substrate can be mixed in different proportions to produce color variation. Another traditional way to achieve variation, both with paint and with dry media, such as charcoal, is to control the thickness of application.

Various tools and techniques are used to control the mixture and application of pigments. In watercolor painting, for example, soft brushes are used to apply layers of wash. In oil painting, stiffer brushes can be used in an impasto technique. You might use your fingers to smear chalk or charcoal. Or you might use an airbrush to spray a surface.

One way to handle these sorts of media is to keep the edges of forms sharp and well defined, but to create smooth transitions of tone or color across forms (fig. 2-3). Watercolor can be applied in well-defined patches of wash within which gradations take place (fig. 2-4). And, of course, Renaissance and neoclassical painters used oils, tempera, and fresco in this fashion (fig. 2-5).

Another possibility is to allow the edges of forms to erode and fade into each other to produce a continuously varying surface, rather than a composition of well-defined distinct shapes. In J. M. W. Turner's watercolors, for instance, the washes of color flow smoothly into each other, and there are few sharp edges or clearly bounded shapes. His oil paintings, similarly, dissolve into continuously varying fields of light (fig. 2-6).

Construction from Discrete Points

One of the innovations of the French impressionists was to recognize that varying the mixtures of pigments and the thicknesses in which pigments are

2-1. A uniformly colored polygon on the picture plane. (*Black Square*, from Kasimir Malevich's *Suprematism: Thirty-Four Drawings.*

2-2. A composition of polygons in two colors. (*Three Black and Five Grey Elements*, from Kasimir Malevich's *Suprematism: Thirty-Four Drawings.*)

31

2-3. A composition with gradations across polygons. (*Composition with Four Grey Elements*, from Kasimir Malevich's *Suprematism: Thirty-Four Drawings.*)

2-4. Rendering of an Ionic capital from the Colisseum by the Beaux Arts architect Louis Duc. The shading of three-dimensional forms was rendered with layers of graded watercolor wash.

2-5. Raphael's *The Marriage of the Virgin* used blended oil paint to render smooth shading on buildings and human figures (Pinacoteca di Brera, Milan).

2-6. J. M. W. Turner's *Valley of Aosta, Snowstorm, Avalanche and Thunderstorm* shows continuous variation across the picture plane. (Courtesy of the Art Institute of Chicago.)

applied are not the only ways to achieve variation in tone and color across a painting surface. They found that if you apply paint in small discrete patches that blend together when viewed from a distance, you can construct nuances and transitions in point-by-point fashion. The postimpressionist Georges Seurat was to carry this approach to its limit (fig. 2-7).

There was some precedent for this in the technique of mosaic (fig. 2-8), which dates back to ancient times. Mosaic artists construct pictures from tiny fragments of colored stone, glass, or ceramic (tesserae). Their graphic variables are the size, shape, and placement of tesserae; color (selected from a limited range of available possibilities); and sometimes the alignment of the tesserae surfaces.

Seurat's dots of pigment were arranged in a random pattern across the picture plane, like grains of sand on a beach. Mosaic artists frequently arrange tesserae to follow and reinforce the contours of forms. A third possibility,

a. Georges Seurat, *Sunday Afternoon on the Island of La Grande Jatte*. (Courtesy of the Art Institute of Chicago.)

2-7. Pointillist technique.

b. A detail of the brushwork.

when constructing a composition from discrete points, is to locate the points within a checkerboard grid (fig. 2-9).

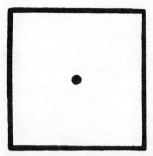

a. A point on the picture plane is taken as the graphic primitive. (Diagram by Kandinsky in *Point and Line to Plane*.)

2-8. Mosaic technique.

b. Designs formed by arranging uniform points. (Windows by Filippo Brunelleschi in the cupola of the Old Sacristy, San Lorenzo, Florence.)

c. Sizes, shapes, and colors of tesserae become additional graphic variables in a mosaic at Ravenna.

The Raster Grid

In computer graphics, a checkerboard grid covering a display surface is known as a *raster grid* (fig. 2-10). Each cell of such a grid is usually referred to as a *pixel* (for picture element) and each horizontal line of cells as a *raster*. Each pixel in a raster grid can be uniquely identified by *indexing* along the two axes (fig. 2-11). Indexing usually begins at the bottom-left corner, as with

2-9. The construction of designs within square grids. (Sketches from Paul Klee's *Notebooks*.)

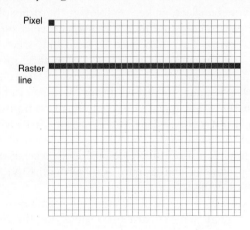

2-10. Pixels, raster line, and raster grid.

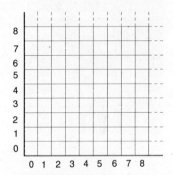

a. The standard convention—indexing from the bottom-left corner.

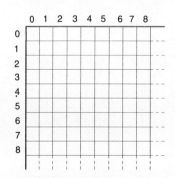

b. An alternative—indexing from the top-left corner.

2-11. Indexing the raster grid.

CONTINUOUS TONE AND COLOR **33**

2-12. A lacework pattern constructed by filling some square cells and leaving others open. The design was taken from Frederico Venciolo's *Les singuliers et nouveaux pourtraicts . . . pour toutes sortes d'ouvrages de Lingerie*, Paris, 1587.

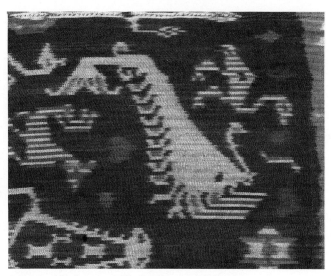

2-13. Detail of a woven blanket from Sumba (Indonesia), the structure of the weave defines a grid within which patterns are constructed by varying the color of the thread.

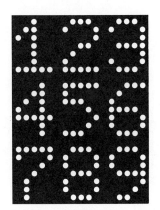

2-14. A grid of lights.

2-15. An enlarged detail of a halftone picture showing the regular grid of dots.

a coordinate system (fig. 2-11a). In some contexts, however, it is more convenient to index from the top-left corner (fig. 2-11b).

Traditional Raster Media

Venetian lace makers employed the principle of the raster grid; designs were constructed by filling some square cells and leaving others open (fig. 2-12). Weavers have also used it; here the structure of the weave defines the grid, and thread color is varied within this, pixel by pixel, to create motifs and patterns (fig. 2-13). The process of weaving is one of constructing the complete rectangular surface, raster by raster. In both lace making and weaving, instructions that specify the contents of each pixel can be written. Sequences of such instructions constitute programs (which might be followed either by human craftsmen or by suitable machines) for the creation of particular designs. The nineteenth-century Jacquard loom was an early machine built to follow such programs, and so may be regarded as the ancestor of today's computer graphics devices.

Mosaics, too, can be constructed within raster grids. Here the artist might write a sequence of instructions specifying the color of tile to be used at each location. Workmen could then execute this program to produce the design.

Another traditional raster medium is the grid of electric lights that is sometimes used for the large-scale display of messages or black-and-white pictures (fig. 2-14). In this case, each pixel is controlled by a switch, which can be either on or off. A program to generate a picture, then, consists of a sequence of switch settings. If the switch settings are rapidly changed, moving messages and animated pictures can be generated.

Halftone printing, as in newspapers and magazines, is also a raster technique. The resolution of the grid varies from about fifty dots per inch for low-quality newspaper illustrations to several hundred dots per inch for high-quality printing. Tonal variation across the picture surface is achieved by varying the size of the dot displayed at each grid location (fig. 2-15). Halftones can also be displayed on grids of lights if each light is controlled by a rheostat, or some similar device that allows continuous variation, rather than by an on/off switch.

Video Monitors

The most common and familiar type of raster display by far is an ordinary *video monitor*. In chapter 1 we briefly considered video monitors as devices for displaying line drawings. Here we shall examine them in more detail as devices for the display of continuous tone and color pictures.

A video monitor has a fairly coarse raster grid. Broadcast television in the United States operates at a standard of 525 scan lines, with a horizontal resolution of about 300 points, to yield a display of 157,500 distinct points. European broadcast television operates at slightly higher resolution, with 625 scan lines. High-performance video monitors used in computer graphics may have a resolution in the order of 1,000 by 1,000 points or even higher.

A standard video monitor has a horizontally oriented screen with an aspect ratio (width to height) of 4:3. The electron beam scans the surface of the screen in a left-to-right and top-to-bottom pattern. The input signal to the monitor specifies the tone or color to be displayed in each pixel at each scan. In U. S. broadcast television, thirty full pictures are scanned per second. To reduce the flicker of the image, a technique known as *interlacing* is used; each full picture actually consists of two successive 262-line pictures, with scan lines of the two offset from each other, so that there are sixty interlaced fields per second (fig. 2-16).

A monochrome video monitor has a single electron beam, and variations in intensity across the picture surface are produced by varying the intensity of this beam, so that it excites the phosphor to different levels. A color video monitor is a little more complicated. Here there are phosphor dots that glow red, green, and blue (the additive color primaries), arranged in a triangular pattern on the screen (fig. 2-17). The eye integrates the dots forming each triad, so that a single color is perceived. By varying the intensities of red, green, and blue, different colors can be displayed. This requires the use of three electron beams, one for each primary (fig. 2-18). A perforated metal grid called the *shadow mask* is placed between the electron guns and the face of the CRT, so that each beam is directed to the right type of phosphor.

In broadcast television, a signal from the receiver controls the electron beam and so produces images on the screen. But we can also use a computer to generate the signal so that the monitor functions as a computer graphics output device.

Other Electronic Raster Display Devices

A few other electronic raster display technologies have been developed and are used in specialized contexts. The *plasma panel* (fig. 2-19), for example, consists of a grid of gas-filled cells sandwiched between glass. When a current is passed through a cell, it glows. Each cell can be individually controlled so that a picture can be constructed by turning on appropriate cells.

An alternative is the *liquid crystal display* (LCD). This is most familiar from its use in the display of numerals in digital watches. It is also possible to fabricate LCD grids a few inches square. These are now commonly used in miniature televisions, portable computers, and electronic games (fig. 2-20).

Extremely large raster display screens can also be constructed from discrete cells. Sony's Jumbotron (fig. 2-21), which was erected near Tokyo for the Tsukuba Expo in 1985, has a display surface of 82 by 131 feet and is a raster grid of 378 by 400 light-emitting cells. Each cell is an assembly of a red, a green, and a blue phosphor rectangle.

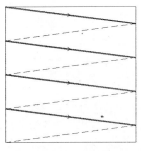

a. First field of scan lines.

b. Second field of scan lines.

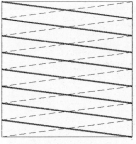

c. The two fields interlaced.

2-16. The principle of interlacing.

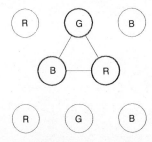

2-17. An enlargement of part of the display surface of a color video monitor, showing the pattern of red, green, and blue phosphor dots arranged in triads.

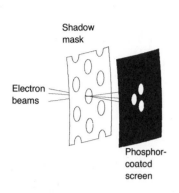

Shadow
mask

Electron
beams

Phosphor-
coated
screen

2-18. A shadow mask is used to direct the electron beams in a color video monitor.

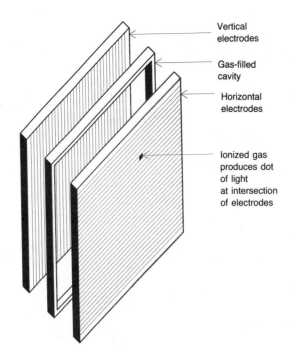

Vertical
electrodes

Gas-filled
cavity

Horizontal
electrodes

Ionized gas
produces dot
of light
at intersection
of electrodes

a. Principle of operation.

b. A typical model (SAI Technology).

2-19. A plasma-panel display screen.

2-20. A liquid-crystal display screen on a miniature television receiver (Seiko).

2-21. Sony's Jumbotron, a 40-by-25-meter video display screen, consisting of 151,200 light-emitting cells, built for the Tsukuba Expo, 1985.

Display Generators

In addition to a CRT or some other kind of monitor, a raster display device used in computer graphics has a *display generator*. As we saw in chapter 1, this contains a high-speed electronic *display memory* (often called a *bitmap* or a *frame buffer*) that stores information specifying the tone or color for each pixel in the raster grid (fig. 2-22). This information then controls the intensity of the electron beam as it sweeps the screen.

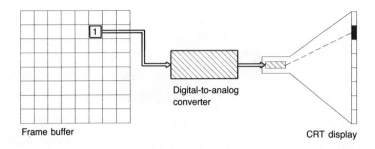

Frame buffer

Digital-to-analog
converter

CRT display

2-22. The bitmap or frame buffer stores information that specifies the tone or color for each pixel in the raster grid. (See Klee's design drawings in fig. 2-9).

Display generators in use today range from small inexpensive devices fabricated on single silicon chips (mostly used for video games and home computers) to bulkier and more sophisticated devices that cost thousands of dollars. In a raster graphic display device, the display generator may be hidden within the monitor, or it may be a separate component connected to the monitor (fig. 2-23). Some popular personal computers come with built-in display generators. Others allow display cards to be plugged in (fig. 2-24).

Describing a Pixel

Whereas a vector is the graphic primitive of a line-drawing device, a pixel is the graphic primitive of a raster display device. And just as we must numerically describe vectors to control a line-drawing device, so we must numerically encode pixel values to control a raster device.

Just as the raster grid divides the continuous surface of the picture plane into discrete cells (forcing us to think about the resolution needed for our particular graphic purposes), methods for numerically encoding pixel values divide the continuity of possible intensity or color variation into a finite number of distinct steps. We must, then, consider the number of intensity or color distinctions that we will want to be able to make in order to produce different types of pictures. (Kasimir Malevich pointedly raised this question when he painted his famous white square on a white ground: the ultimate reductionist gesture.)

2-23. A frame buffer packaged as a separate device (Raster Technologies).

2-24. A display card (Matrox).

Intensity

We need, at least, to be able to specify two different intensity levels. In an array of electric lights, as we saw earlier, we might do this by having a switch to control each light; you can think of the array of switches as a memory for storing a picture. A logical equivalent is to store a value of either zero or one at each location in a frame buffer, specifying whether or not the corresponding pixel is to be intensified. In either case, one *bit* (the minimum unit of information) is stored for each pixel. The grid of bits is known as a *bitplane*. A simple raster display, with a single bitplane, is shown schematically in figure 2-25.

A single bitplane allows us to specify bilevel pictures (fig. 2-26). Some

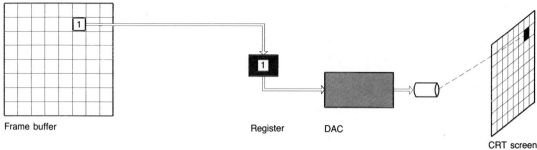

2-25. A raster display device with a single bitplane.

Frame buffer   Register   DAC   CRT screen

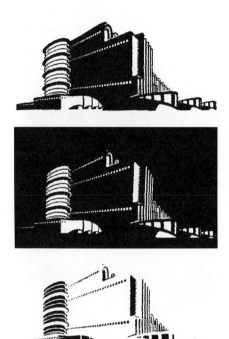

2-26. Bilevel raster displays of a sketch by Erich Mendelsohn.

display devices only have bilevel capability anyway, but others (such as ordinary black-and-white video monitors) can display many more levels. To take advantage of this capability, it is necessary to store more information per pixel.

If we allow ourselves two bits of information to describe a pixel, then we can select from a range of two to the second power, that is, four possibilities for each pixel. This allows us to work with four different intensity levels (black, dark gray, light gray, and white). This is analogous to making a montage using four different shades of paper, silk screening with four different stencils and inks, or weaving with threads of four different shades (fig. 2-27). A raster display with this capability has two bitplanes. Its construction is shown schematically in figure 2-28.

Three bits per pixel gives us a palette of eight different intensities, four bits per pixel yield sixteen choices, and five bits per pixel yield thirty-two. The relation between the number of bitplanes and the number of intensity levels is made clear in figure 2-29.

With only two or three bits per pixel at your disposal, it is impossible to create the illusion of smooth tonal graduation in a picture, no matter how fine the resolution of the display. At best you can hope to approximate it by sequences of distinct "layers" (fig. 2-30). But you can sometimes do it with four bits (64 levels) and almost always with five (128 levels). Thus you can begin to use a graphic technique analogous to that of smoothly graded charcoal or monochromatic watercolor wash (fig. 2-31).

The construction of a raster display with five bitplanes is shown in figure 2-32a. There is however, a more efficient arrangement (fig. 2-32b). A value

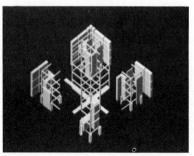

2-27. A four-level raster image. (Image by Michel Mossessian.)

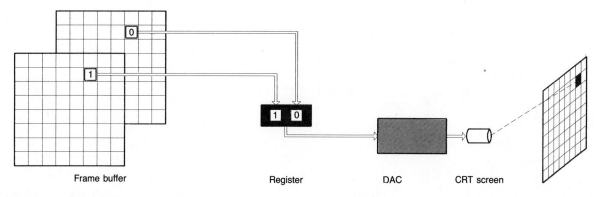

Frame buffer   Register   DAC   CRT screen

2-28. A raster display device with two bitplanes.

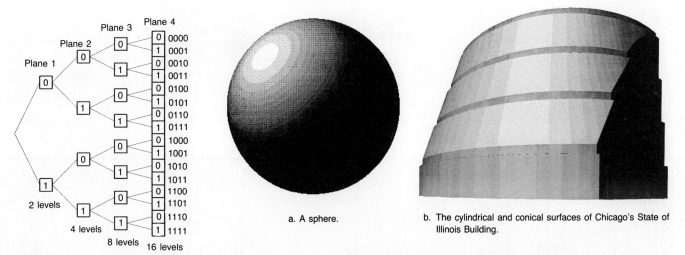

a. A sphere.

b. The cylindrical and conical surfaces of Chicago's State of Illinois Building.

2-29. A tree diagram illustrating the relation between the number of bitplanes and the number of intensity levels.

2-30. The shading of curved surfaces approximated by a sequence of distinct layers.

from the frame buffer is used as an index to a *look-up table* stored in memory. Where each entry in the frame buffer has m bits, each entry in the look-up table has n bits, where n is greater than m. Thus the look-up table defines a palette of 2^n different intensities, but only 2^m of these can be displayed at any one time. If M is 3 and N is 5, for example, there are $2^5 = 32$ different intensities from which to choose, but only $2^3 = 8$ of these may be displayed at any one time (fig. 2-33). This is a very common arrangement, since a picture is unlikely to have its intensity levels distributed evenly across the entire range; they are more likely to be bunched in some particular part, or parts, of the range, and entries in the look-up table can be chosen to fall within the relevant parts of the range. The entries in the look-up table will not be the same for a bright, high-key, image as they will be for a shadowy one, or the same for high-contrast and low-contrast images.

Color

Where a monitor is capable of generating color rather than monochromatic images, the numbers in a frame buffer can be used to specify different colors, rather than different intensities. Since there are three primary colors (red,

2-31. A smoothly shaded image on a high-resolution raster display. (Image by Carlos Dell Acqua.)

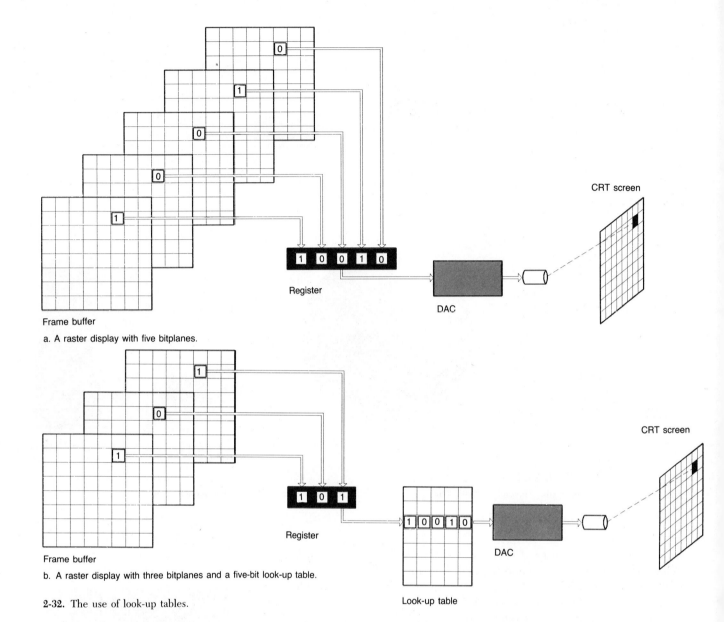

Frame buffer

a. A raster display with five bitplanes.

Frame buffer

b. A raster display with three bitplanes and a five-bit look-up table.

2-32. The use of look-up tables.

green, blue), we need a minimum of three bitplanes (fig. 2-34a). Each bitplane, then, specifies whether the corresponding electron gun is on or off for each pixel.

Eight different colors can be produced in this way:

Red	Green	Blue	Result
on	on	on	white
on	off	on	magenta
off	on	on	cyan
on	on	off	yellow
off	off	on	blue
off	on	off	green
on	off	off	red
off	off	off	black

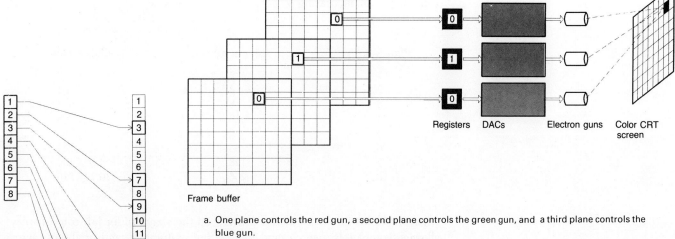

Frame buffer

a. One plane controls the red gun, a second plane controls the green gun, and a third plane controls the blue gun.

2-33. The effect of a look-up table; eight colors are selected from a palette of thirty-two.

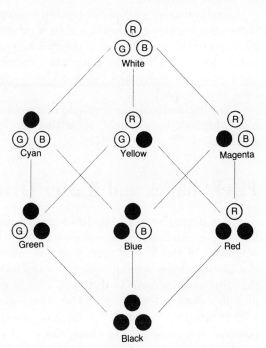

b. The lattice of available colors. Each point represents a subset of colored dots in a triad, and the links represent union and intersection operations.

2-34. A color display with three bitplanes.

This system may also be represented by a lattice (fig. 2-34b). Mathematically minded readers will recognize that it constitutes, in fact, a *Boolean algebra* of color. Incidentally, it has a long history in color theory; Johann Wolfgang Von Goethe, in particular, was fascinated by it.

By increasing the number of bitplanes controlling each electron gun, we can specify an increasing variety of colors as follows:

Planes/gun	Levels/gun	Available colors
1	2	8
2	4	64
3	8	512
4	16	4,096
5	32	32,768
6	64	262,144
7	128	2,097,152
8	256	16,777,216

Eight bitplanes for each gun are considered the standard for full-color display, allowing completely smooth gradations of hue, saturation, and brightness across the picture surface.

A color display with one or two bitplanes per gun allows the use of graphic techniques analogous to collage with a palette of different colored paper, or silk screen. More bitplanes allow you to use techniques similar to layered watercolor wash. With the full eight bitplanes per gun, you can use a full-color technique much like that used in renaissance and baroque painting, or color photography.

As with monochrome displays, it is common to introduce a look-up table. Many displays, for example, allow simultaneous use of $2^8 = 256$ colors from a pallette of $2^{24} = 16,777,216$.

Pixel Shapes and Raster Grid Formats

It is important to distinguish between the *logical* resolution of the frame buffer (the number of pixel values that it stores in memory) and the *physical* resolution of the display screen (the number of phosphor dots or triads on the surface of the screen). Often the resolution of the frame buffer is lower than that of the screen. In this case, a single pixel will be composed of several phosphor dots or triads (fig. 2-35a). These dots or triads may form a square, or they may form rectangles of different proportions (fig. 2-35b). As Kandinsky noted in *Point and Line to Plane*, the shaping of point elements of a picture can become an important graphic issue: "Thought of in the abstract, or in one's imagination, the ideal point is small and round. . . . In reality, a point can assume an infinite variety of shapes" (fig. 2-35c).

Most frame buffers use a square raster grid. When a square grid of square pixels is displayed on a standard video monitor (of aspect ratio 4:3), however, part of the screen area is wasted (fig. 2-36a). This problem can be solved by using a frame buffer with a rectangular grid and square pixels; the 640 by 480 format is quite common, for instance (fig. 2-36b). Another possibility is to use rectangular pixels of a proportion given by the dot matrix used to display characters (fig. 2-36c). This is quite common, particularly with low-cost personal computers, but it makes any kind of serious graphics work very difficult, since it results in distorted shapes. A circle, for example, becomes an ellipse (fig. 2-37).

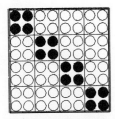

a. If the resolution of the frame buffer is lower than the screen resolution, each pixel will be composed of several phosphor dots or triads.

b. Rectangular pixels.

c. Examples of points of different shapes given by Kandinsky in *Point and Line to Plane*.

2-35. The relation between frame buffer and screen resolution.

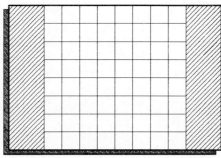

a. Part of the screen area is wasted with a square grid of square pixels.

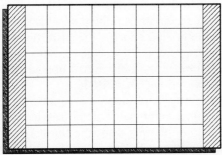

b. The use of a frame buffer with a rectangular grid of square pixels.

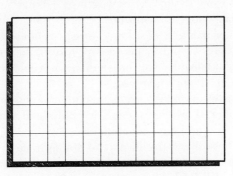

c. The use of rectangular pixels.

2-36. Mapping a frame buffer onto a rectangular video screen.

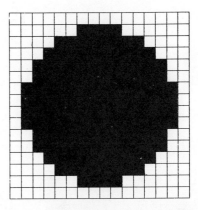

a. A circle represented in the frame buffer.

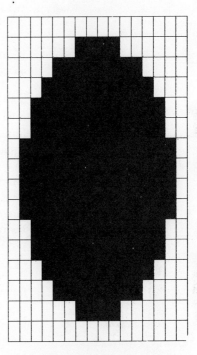

b. An ellipse results when the pixels become rectangular on the screen.

2-37. Distortion results from the use of rectangular pixels.

Resolution

Since a pixel displayed on a CRT screen is of finite size, individual pixels may sometimes be perceptible, just as the viewer of a mosaic may perceive the individual tesserae, the viewer of a painting may perceive brush strokes, and the viewer of a photograph may perceive grain. In all cases, the aesthetic issue is the same; the artist must design the picture to read satisfactorily close up as a pattern of primitives (tesserae, brush strokes, or pixels), and at a distance, where the eye integrates patterns of primitives so that larger objects are perceived.

Sometimes the representation of continuous objects such as lines, circles, and smoothly graded surfaces within a discrete pixel grid presents particular problems. Figure 2-38, for example, shows a circle displayed in successively finer raster grids. At low resolution, the edges of the shape become very ragged; the characteristic stair-step effect is known as the *jaggies* or as *aliasing*. A more subtle aliasing effect is the distortion of fine detail. A colonnade, for example, may appear as a few wide columns rather than as the correct number of smaller columns (fig. 2-39). Small objects may disappear entirely, or their shapes may be seriously distorted.

Since the effects of aliasing are mitigated by increasing the resolution and are eventually eliminated if the resolution can be made fine enough, it is obvious that we usually want the finest resolution possible. But there is a fundamental problem. The number of pixels in the image increases with the square of the resolution; whenever the resolution is doubled, there are four times as many pixels. This usually creates a lot more work: fine weaving is more laborious than coarse weaving; mosaics made out of small tiles take longer than mosaics made out of large tiles; and pointillistic painting takes longer than painting in a broad-brush technique. Thus, in construction of a raster image, we must often accept a resolution significantly lower than that physically attainable, and lower than we would ideally like, in order to limit the amount of work involved.

In raster graphics, image resolution is determined by the capacity of the frame buffer. Low-cost home computers and video games store only a few bits per pixel and have resolutions of 128 by 128, 256 by 256, or 512 by 512 pixels. These allow the display of simple images. Higher-cost models, used for professional applications, may store up to twenty-four bits per pixel, at resolutions of 512 by 512, 1,024 by 1,024, and occasionally even higher. The amounts of information (in bits) that must be stored to produce pictures at these levels of resolution are summarized in the following table.

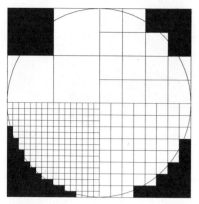

2-38. A circle displayed in successively finer raster grids; the lower the resolution the more jagged the edge.

a. A colonnade.

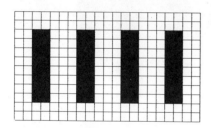

b. A colonnade mapped onto a fine raster grid.

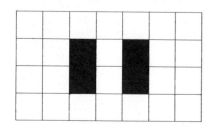

c. A colonnade mapped onto a coarse raster grid.

2-39. The distortion of fine detail.

Resolution	1 bit per pixel	3 bits per pixel	24 bits per pixel
128 × 128	16,384	49,152	393,216
256 × 256	65,536	196,608	1,572,864
512 × 512	262,144	786,432	6,291,456
1,024 × 1,024	1,048,576	3,145,728	25,165,824

The amount of information stored in the frame buffer for a 1,024 by 1,024 twenty-four-bit image is more than 1,500 times more than that required for a 128 by 128 black-and-white image. Furthermore, the display generator must handle more than 1,500 times as much information to refresh the image. It is hardly surprising, then, that the cost of raster displays varies by several orders of magnitude from that of low-resolution models to that of very high–precision color displays.

Antialiasing and the Aesthetics of Edges and Details

An apparent paradox in raster graphics is that broadcast television images, although of low resolution (525 × 300), do not manifest the jagged edge-lines that are frequently evident even in high-resolution computer-generated raster displays. How can this be so?

Figure 2-40 illustrates the answer. One way to approximate a continuous object to a discrete raster grid is to take an all-or-nothing approach; if the boundary of a colored object passes through a pixel, then the pixel becomes the color that covers the larger part of its area (fig. 2-40a). This results in pronounced jaggedness. Increasing the resolution mitigates but does not eliminate this effect (fig. 2-40b). An alternative approach, shown in figure 2-40c, is to *average* the contents of each pixel, which is what a video camera does. Some of the crispness of the image is lost, but jagged edges disappear.

It is possible to construct display generators that will perform this averaging operation to produce much smoother-looking computer-generated images. This is known as *antialiasing*. A display memory with a sufficient number of bits per pixel is needed to represent the averaged values, and the system must be built to handle the substantial amount of computation that is involved in performing the averaging operations. Generally then, antialiasing is featured only by the more sophisticated and expensive raster graphics displays.

There are several different approaches to antialiasing based, ultimately, on the mathematical theory of *sampling* (representing a large set of values by an appropriately chosen smaller set of values). We will not go into the details here, since those are given in any of the standard technical texts on computer graphics (see bibliography). They all render edges and small objects slightly differently and so produce slightly different images.

The handling of edges is, of course, of general concern in painting and graphic design. A watercolorist might, for example, work on damp paper to produce edges that bleed, or use dry brush techniques to produce crisp, ragged edges. Stencil and colored screen cutout techniques are often used when very smooth, crisp edges are desired. Mosaic artists and weavers sometimes use techniques that are very closely akin to antialiasing on a raster display (fig. 2-41). When you work with a raster graphic display, you should, then, think as carefully about the handling of edges as you would with more traditional graphic media and choose an antialiasing technique accordingly.

Artists have also been concerned with techniques for handling fine detail. A woodcut artist, for example, cannot make extremely fine lines, small dots, or sharp curves, and this limits the capability to render fine detail accurately. If fine detail must be shown, it is necessary either to use a higher-resolution medium (such as engraving on a metal plate), or to find some "averaging" technique analogous to those used in raster graphics.

Trading Off Graphic Qualities

A raster display device should ideally be of high resolution; it should allow the display of continuous tone and color; and it should perform antialiasing.

a. Low-resolution raster image of a shaded cylinder.

b. Less ragged edges result when the resolution is doubled.

c. Edges are smoothed by pixel-averaging.

2-40. The effect of averaging pixels.

2-41. A three-color twill weave pattern has an effect similar to antialiasing.

a. A motif consisting of black lines on a white ground.

b. The reverse-video version.

2-42. Enlargements of part of a bilevel raster display.

But, since any display generator has a limited memory (and these features all require memory) all but the most sophisticated and expensive raster display devices emphasize one feature or the other. Some are designed as crisp, high-resolution (1,024 × 1,024) black-and-white-only displays. Others provide twenty-four bits of color control at 512 by 512 resolution. Others provide eight bits of color control, 512 by 512 resolution, and antialiasing.

Personal computers often provide the choice of either higher-resolution black-and-white or lower-resolution color display. The IBM PC, for example, provides both a 640 by 200 mode for black-and-white, and a 320 by 200 four-color mode. The Apple Macintosh II provides 1,280 by 960 black-and-white or 640 by 480 color.

Classes of Displayed Images

A raster CRT is obviously very versatile and can display a wide variety of images. For our purposes here, it will be useful to divide these into the following broad classes:

- monochrome line drawings
- bilevel pictures with pattern and texture
- halftones
- colored line drawings
- pictures with solid-colored polygons
- pictures with colored patterns
- full-color pictures

We shall consider these in turn.

Monochrome Line Drawings

As noted in chapter 1, raster displays can be used, much like storage tube and vector displays, for the display of monochromatic line drawings. A bilevel (single bitplane) display is adequate. Resolution must be adequate to deal with the fineness and density of the line work required for the application.

For professional drafting work, displays with resolutions of at least 1,024 by 1,024 (or the equivalent in a rectangular format) are needed. Displays of this type can now be produced at prices that are highly competitive with storage tube and refreshed vector displays and have mostly displaced these older technologies in computer-aided design and drafting applications.

Unlike storage tube and refreshed vector displays, this type of raster device normally displays black lines on a white background (fig. 2-42a). However, they can also be operated in *reverse-video* mode—white lines on a black background (fig. 2-42b). The lines appear very fine and crisp, but some jaggedness is apparent on curves and diagonals.

As E. H. Gombrich has pointed out, artists have long been familiar with the effect of reversing figure and ground (Gombrich 1960). Greek vase painters did this, for example, when they switched from the black-figured to the red-figured technique (fig. 2-43).

Most popular personal computers have built-in or plug-in display generators that can be used to produce black-and-white line drawings at low to medium resolution. (The vendors often refer to their "high-resolution" display generators, but this is usually salesmen's hyperbole.) Here are some of the options available on some of the first inexpensive personal computers to provide useful graphics capabilities:

Apple II	280 × 192
Apple III	560 × 192
Apple Macintosh	512 × 342
Atari ST	640 × 400
Commodore Amiga	640 × 400
DEC Rainbow	384 × 240
IBM PC	640 × 200
TRS-80 Model II	640 × 240

At these resolutions, fine line work and dense detail are impossible, and jaggedness on curves and diagonals is very noticeable (fig. 2-44). These devices, then, are not entirely adequate for professional applications, such as architectural drafting. Their low cost, however, makes them attractive as devices on which to learn basic principles of computer graphics by carrying out simple exercises.

The choice of an appropriate way to map continuous straight lines onto a discrete raster grid is an important issue when using a bilevel display to produce line drawings. This presents no difficulty when lines are parallel to the coordinate axes (fig. 2-45a). It is straightforward, too, when lines are at a 45-degree angle from these axes (fig. 2-45b). But what is to be done with lines at other angles (fig. 2-45c)? Techniques for dealing with this problem are known as *scan conversion* methods. Scan conversion is typically built in to a raster display, so you do not have to choose a scan conversion method. But it is important to know what scan conversion methods are intended to accomplish visually, and what their limitations are, just as it is important to know the line-formation capabilities of different types of pens and pencils.

What are the visual objectives? First, lines should appear as straight as possible; that is, jaggedness of diagonals should be minimized. Figure 2-46 shows the effects of two of the available scan conversion methods. There are clear differences in line character and graphic effect. Second, lines should appear to be of even weight along their length. In other words, the pixels that form the line should be as evenly spaced as possible. Unfortunately, some scan conversion methods can produce "bunching" of pixels (fig. 2-47). This is read either as variation in width or in intensity. Line weight should also be independent of length and angle. Consider, for example, a line parallel to and a line at a 45-degree angle from the coordinate axes (fig. 2-48). If we simply represent each line by the pixels that it intersects, the diagonal line will be lighter than the horizontal. Finally, lines should terminate accurately. The approximations that are made in scan conversion should not, for example, result in a gap where two lines are meant to intersect (fig. 2-49).

The standard technical texts on computer graphics (see bibliography) describe available scan conversion methods in detail and compare their visual characteristics. Each method has its advantages and disadvantages, but none is perfect. Thus a drawing composed of straight lines (especially when there are many diagonals) and regular curves will never appear as clean, crisp, and precise when displayed on a bilevel raster device as when it is displayed on a true line-drawing device of comparable resolution. This effect shows up particularly clearly in architectural drafting.

Raster displays, however, inherently provide much greater capability to

a. Black figure side.

b. Red figure side.

2-43. Bilingual Amphora, with an effect similar to that of reverse video. (*Herakles and the Cretan Bull*, Lysippides Painter and the Andokides Painter, Greek, c. 525 B.C. Courtesy of Museum of Fine Arts, Boston).

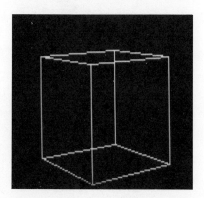

2-44. Jagged lines on a low-resolution raster display.

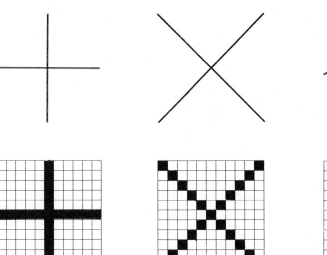

a. Lines parallel to the coordinate axes have unique mappings onto grid locations.

b. Lines at a 45-degree angle from the axes also have unique mappings.

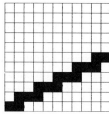

c. Lines at other angles may be mapped in alternative ways.

2-45. Mapping continuous straight lines onto the raster grid.

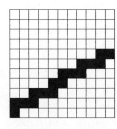

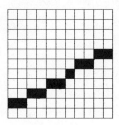

2-46. The effects of different scan conversion methods on jaggedness.

vary line styles than vector displays. Since lines are built up out of small pixels, it is possible to vary width and texture freely in order to simulate the effects of specific tools, such as pens, brushes, crayons, and even spray cans (fig. 2-50).

Where drawings are composed of lines of varying weight and style rather than uniform lines, used freehand rather than mechanically, aliasing effects become much less objectionable (fig. 2-51). Here they merely introduce some inconspicuous, random, visual noise into the picture (much like the effect of the grain of rough drawing paper) and do not work against the aesthetic intention.

Bilevel Pictures with Pattern and Texture

As Kandinsky noted in *Point and Line to Plane*, points distributed over a picture plane can be used to create *textures* (fig. 2-52). A bilevel raster display provides the capability to generate innumerable patterns and textures in this way and to thereby construct drawings.

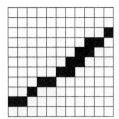

2-47. The bunching of pixels.

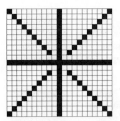

2-48. A diagonal composed of adjacent pixels appears lighter than a horizontal or a vertical line.

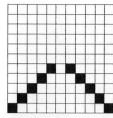

2-49. An approximation to the grid may result in a gap where two lines are meant to intersect.

2-50. A variety of line styles on a raster display.

A common and simple method of regular pattern construction is illustrated in figure 2-53. A motif is defined in a small, square array of pixels (8 × 8 is typical), then regularly repeated as shown. Figure 2-54 illustrates some of the many regular patterns that can be produced in this way.

Such patterns can be deployed by themselves on the picture plane to produce compositions (fig. 2-55), or they can be combined with line work (fig. 2-56). In either case, the graphic possibilities are analogous to those of fairly low-resolution mechanical screens, as used by comic-strip artists and newspaper illustrators. If you want to use a bilevel raster display in this way, it is useful to study the work of the best illustrators working with mechanical screens and learn their techniques of bold form, effective tonal contrast, and careful combinations of patterns.

2-51. A freehand line drawing on a raster display; aliasing effects merely introduce some inconspicuous, random visual noise and are much less objectionable.

Halftones

Given a square of four pixels, you can construct sixteen different pixel patterns within it, as shown in figure 2-57. One of these is all white, four read as light gray (that is, 25 percent black), six read as middle gray (50 percent black), another four read as dark gray (75 percent black), and one is

a. A motif defined in a small, square array of pixels.

b. Repetition of the motif to generate a pattern.

2-53. Regular pattern construction in the raster grid.

2-52. Textures as "accumulations of points," illustrated by Kandinsky in *Point and Line to Plane*.

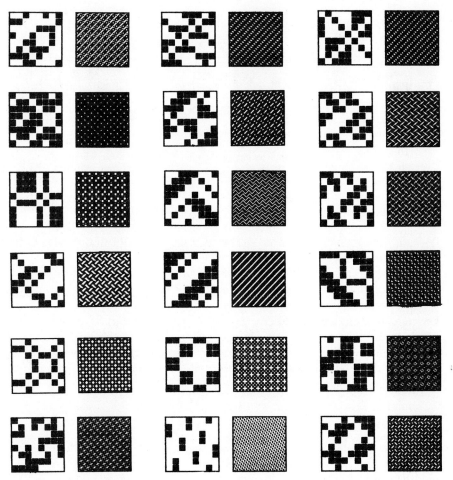

2-54. Examples of traditional twill weave patterns generated by repeating motifs defined in 8 by 8 square arrays of pixels.

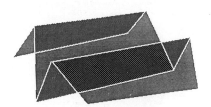

2-55. A composition of regular patterns on a bilevel raster display.

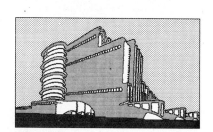

2-56. Regular patterns combined with line work.

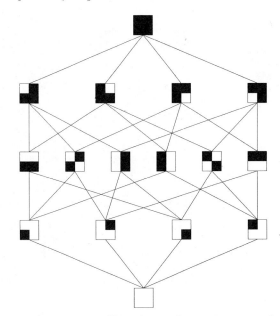

2-57. The $2^4 = 16$ pixel patterns possible within a 2 by 2 square array, shown on a lattice.

black. These patterns enable you, in effect, to produce a four-level picture on a two-level display at the cost of halving the resolution. Similarly, you can take a 3 by 3 square of pixels as the unit. This gives you 1,024 different patterns, with ten different gray levels, at a cost of dividing the resolution by three.

Pattern cells should not introduce irrelevant and distracting small-scale structure into a picture when they are combined. The 3 by 3 pattern cells shown in figure 2-58, for example, produce bold stripes when combined. These are an unwanted intrusion when, for example, you want to render smooth shading across a curved surface. However, pattern cells can be judiciously chosen to minimize those sorts of effects. Figure 2-59, for example, shows a widely used set of ten 3 by 3 pattern cells. These can be used to generate surprisingly good halftones, even on very low-resolution bilevel displays (fig. 2-60). There are many other methods for generating halftones on bilevel raster displays (see Jarvis, Judice, and Ninke 1976). All aim, however, to provide enough variation to render smooth tonal gradations while avoiding the introduction of unwanted patterning.

Another way to produce halftones is to use a multilevel rather than a bilevel display. If the resolution of the display is fine, techniques that produce results similar to gray watercolor wash, smoothly shaded charcoal or pastel, or black-and-white photography can be used. Figure 2-61 shows the same image on a bilevel display, with use of patterns for halftoning, and on an eight bitplane (256-level) display. Notice how the dot pattern produces an effect similar to that of the grain of rough paper with charcoal; this can be used to aesthetic advantage. The smoothly shaded multilevel image, on the other hand, is reminiscent of the way that neoclassical painters like Jacques-Louis David and Jean-Auguste-Dominique Ingres handled tonal nuances and transitions in their oil paintings.

Colored Line Drawings

A frame buffer with two bitplanes and a color video monitor can generate four-color (including background) line drawings. With three bits per pixel you get eight colors and with four bits you get sixteen. Many personal computers provide color capabilities of this type, usually at lower resolution than with their black-and-white options.

Today, many professional computer-aided design and drafting systems offer medium-resolution (512 × 512) or high-resolution (1,024 × 1,024) color raster displays. These usually offer a wider palette than personal computers—typically 256 colors.

The introduction of additional line colors can be used to pack more information into an image without producing confusion. Compare, for example, the two-color (black-and-white) woodcut by Baldung Grien, shown in figure 2-62a with the three-color (black, gray, and white) chiaroscuro woodcut version in figure 2-62b. An additional line color has allowed more information about surfaces to be included: curvature is shown more completely; highlights are depicted explicitly rather than merely implied, and textures (the rabbits' fur, the serpent's scales, the blades of grass) are shown more clearly. The result is a much richer but no less legible picture.

Colored line drawings are widely used in technical graphics, where different layers of information on a drawing need to be separated; for example, where graphs representing several different variables are to be represented on the

2-58. Examples of 3 by 3 pattern cells that produce bold stripes when combined.

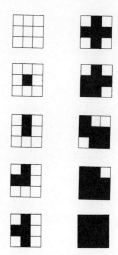

2-59. A set of 3 by 3 pattern cells that do not introduce unwanted stripes, or other objectionable effects.

2-60. A low-resolution halftone produced with pattern cells.

same coordinate axes, or where several different layers of architectural information must be shown on the same floor plan (fig. 2-63).

Pictures with Solid-colored Polygons

Another way to employ color capabilities is to use *solid polygons* (many-sided plane figures), rather than lines, as the graphic primitives. A solid polygon can be thought of as a set of contiguous pixels of the same color as shown in figure 2-64. A display composed of solid polygons is like a collage made from pieces of colored paper.

Where the frame buffer has only one bitplane, solid polygon pictures are simple black-on-white or white-on-black silhouettes. With the four, eight, or sixteen color palettes that the color display generators of many personal computers provide, you can display more complex maps, graphs, and so on. The IBM PC color display generator, for example, at a resolution of 320 by 200, allows you to work with either one of the following four-color palettes:

- background, cyan, magenta, white
- background, green, red, yellow

The background can be chosen from a palette of sixteen colors.

High-resolution raster displays, with up to twenty-four bits per pixel, can produce more sophisticated solid polygon images. These allow use of a poster technique (fig. 2-65).

Pictures with Colored Patterns

Just as pattern cells can be used, at the cost of spatial resolution, to render multiple gray levels on a bilevel display, so pattern cells with colored pixels can be used to extend the palette of a display with limited color capability.

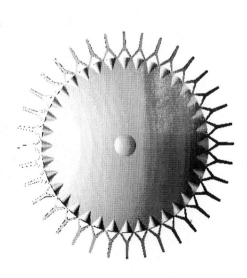

a. Produced on a bilevel display with the use of patterns for halftoning.

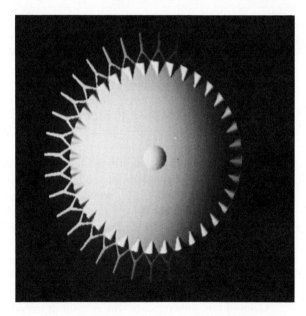

b. Produced on an eight bitplane (256 level) display.

2-61. Different versions of the same halftone. (Images by Ehud Rapoport.)

a. One line color.

b. Two line colors.

2-62. Two versions of Baldung Grien's woodcut, *The Fall of Man*, 1511. (Metropolitan Museum of Art, New York.)

Consider, for example, a 2 by 2 pattern cell in which each pixel can be either red or green or blue. This yields fifteen color mixes:

Red Pixels	Green Pixels	Blue Pixels	Result
0	0	4	blue
0	1	3	greenish blue
0	2	2	cyan
0	3	1	bluish green
0	4	0	green
1	0	3	purplish blue
1	1	2	pastel blue
1	2	1	pastel green
1	3	0	yellowish green
2	0	2	magenta
2	1	1	pink
2	2	0	yellow
3	0	1	red/magenta
3	1	0	orange
4	0	0	red

This technique can be useful with low-cost personal computers, which often allow display of only four or eight different colors. The injudicious selection of pattern cells, however, can result in extremely discordant effects.

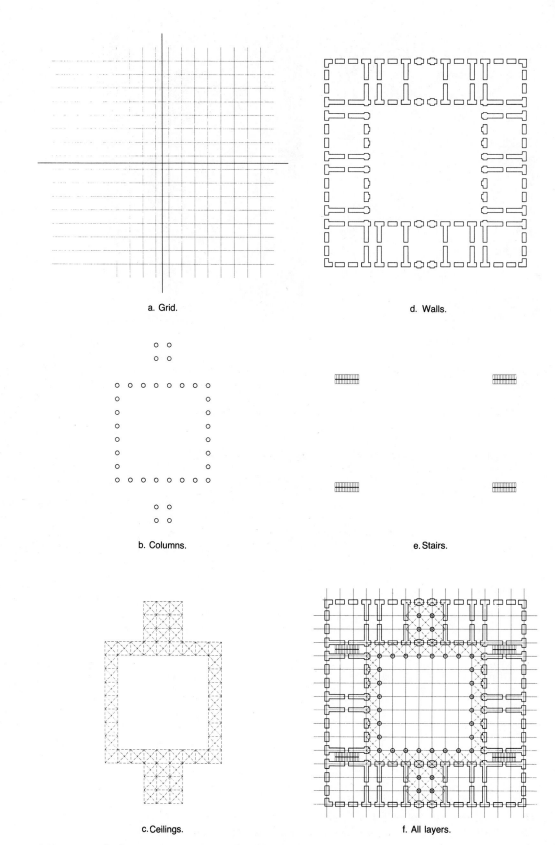

a. Grid.

d. Walls.

b. Columns.

e. Stairs.

c. Ceilings.

f. All layers.

2-63. Layers of information on a technical drawing.

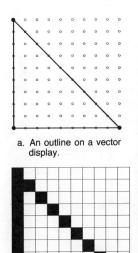

a. An outline on a vector
   display.

b. An outline on a raster display.

c. A solid.

d. A set of contiguous pixels
   of the same color.

2-64. The depiction of polygons.

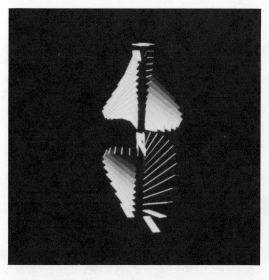

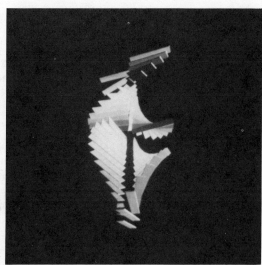

2-65. Pictures composed of colored polygons on an eight bitplane (256-level) high-resolution raster display. (Images by Felix Wettstein.)

Full-color Pictures

High-resolution raster displays with twenty-four bitplanes allow smooth gradations of hue, saturation, and brightness in a picture, as when a painter works with a full palette of pigments and can mix in black and white to produce shades and tints. Thus, effects similar to those achievable with oils, airbrush, or color photography can be produced. The cover of this book shows an example, and you can see many more in commercial and theatrical animated film that is produced using computer animation techniques.

Characters

Whereas characters on line-drawing devices are composed of short vectors, characters displayed on raster CRTs are patterns of pixels. A minimally adequate character cell size is 5 by 7 pixels, and this is commonly used on low-resolution devices. Figure 2-66 illustrates an uppercase font in 5 by 9 format. Where higher resolution is available, 7 by 10 cells are often used to produce more elegantly formed characters.

Sophisticated raster display and plotting devices permit characters to be presented at very high resolution. This allows the use of a wide variety of fonts and the introduction of numerous typographic subtleties (fig. 2-67). Where a multilevel display is available, characters can be antialiased (fig. 2-68), which results in a considerably improved appearance.

2-66. An uppercase font in cells of 5 by 9 pixels.

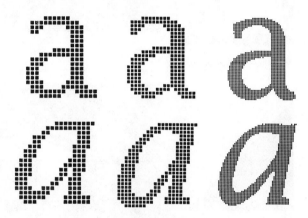

a. Outlines of characters.

b. Corresponding bitmaps.

**After the prime necessities of life
nothing is more precious to us than books.**
The art of typography, their creator,
renders a signal service to society and lends it invaluable support,
serving, as it does, to educate the citizen,
to widen the field for the progress of sciences and arts,
to nourish and cultivate the mind, to elevate the soul,
and, generally, taking upon itself to be the messenger
and interpreter of wisdom and truth.
It is, in fine, the portrayer of mind.
**Therefore we may call it essentially the art of all arts
and the science of all sciences.**

Pierre Simon Fournier
Manuel Typographique (1764–1766)

c. Text produced from bitmapped characters at normal size.

2-67. High-resolution raster characters. (*Lucida* type copyright © by Bigelow and Holmes).

2-68. The enlargement of a character with antialiasing.

Raster Printers and Plotters

Sometimes it is useful to produce a raster image not on a CRT screen, but as hard copy on paper or photographic film. Various types of raster printers and plotters can be used for this purpose.

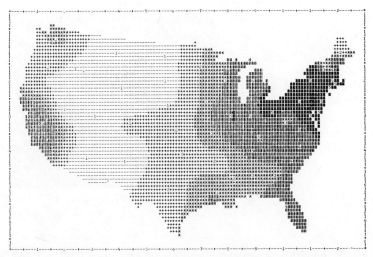

2-69. An image produced by overprinting combinations of characters on a line printer. (Harvard Laboratory for Computer Graphics and Spatial Analysis.)

a. A typical low-cost dot-matrix printer (Epson).

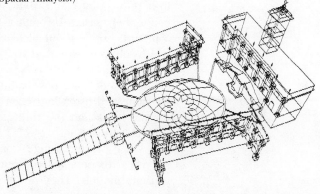

b. A low-resolution graphic image produced on a dot-matrix printer. (Image by Horacio Reggini.)

2-70. Impact dot-matrix printers.

Any kind of text printer that is used as a computer output device can, in fact, be used to plot raster images. Each line of characters on a page can be thought of as a raster line and each character position as a pixel. Thus gray scale pictures can be built up by selecting an appropriate character, or overprinted combinations of characters, for each position. In the early days of computing, before better alternatives were widely available, line printers were often used this way to produce crude graphic output (fig. 2-69).

Today raster images are most commonly output on printers that transfer small dots within a raster grid. *Impact dot matrix* printers (fig. 2-70) use electromechanically driven needles and an ink ribbon. The impact of a needle is used to transfer a dot onto the paper. Multicolor ribbons, or multiple ribbons of different colors, can be used to produce color. Generally impact matrix printers tend to be relatively cheap, but noisy, slow, and of fairly poor resolution. They are commonly used as low-cost hard copy devices for personal computers.

There are several different methods of *inkjet* printing (fig. 2-71), but they all use a nozzle that emits very fine droplets of ink to create dots on the surface of the paper. Resolution is good, ranging from about 80 dots per inch up to better than 400 dots, and color printing is possible with multiple nozzles.

2-71. An inkjet printer (Chromajet).

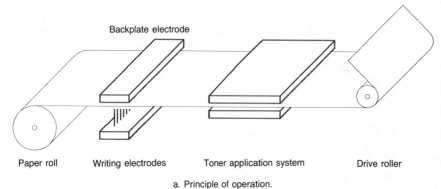

Backplate electrode

Paper roll   Writing electrodes   Toner application system   Drive roller

a. Principle of operation.

b. A typical model (Versatec).

2-72. Electrostatic plotters.

An *electrostatic plotter* (fig. 2-72) works by passing a continuous roll of paper under a comblike array of very fine metal teeth. These can be controlled to deposit point electrostatic charges in rows at closely spaced intervals. The paper then passes through a toner (as in an electrostatic copier) to produce a picture built up out of black dots. Electrostatic plotters are now made in widths of up to seventy-two inches. Early models had a resolution of 100 dots to the inch; 200 dots is a widely accepted current standard (fig. 2-73); and 400-dot models are now coming into use. Color electrostatic plotters are now available and use a four-layer system. The paper is successively printed with dots in black and the three additive primaries, much as in traditional color separation printing.

Laser printers range from small, inexpensive desktop models designed for use with personal computers (fig. 2-74) to large, expensive, very high–capacity models. They produce excellent quality, small format (typically 8½-by 11-inch) images.

Yet another possibility is *thermal transfer* printing, which makes use of ribbons with ink in a wax binder. A printhead melts the wax in order to transfer dots to the paper.

Raster plotting devices tend to be expensive where high resolution, color, and large formats are required. Electrostatic plotters typically cost tens, and sometimes hundreds, of thousands of dollars. At the other end of the cost scale are small-format, low-resolution, monochrome impact printers that cost only a few hundred dollars.

Photographic Output

An obvious way to produce a permanent record of an image displayed on a raster CRT screen is simply to photograph it using an ordinary 35 mm camera. Darken the room to avoid screen reflections and use a tripod so the image can be framed precisely. Screen images often have very high contrast, making it difficult to find the correct exposure, so expose for the dominant color in the picture, and bracket additional exposures around this. Exposure time should be much longer than the one-thirtieth of a second needed for scanning a full frame to avoid visible unevenness in the picture, resulting from a scan that is only partially completed during the exposure. One second

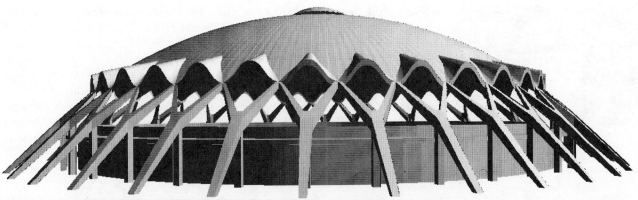

a. Computer-generated image of a stadium by Pier Luigi Nervi. (Image by Ehud Rapoport.)

b. A detail of the plot at actual size.

2-73. Output from an electrostatic plotter.

2-74. An inexpensive laser printer (Quality Micro Systems).

2-75. A recording camera (Dunn Instruments).

is about right. Use a long lens, if possible; the foreshortening effect eliminates distortions due to screen curvature. Different types of color film will distort screen colors in different ways, so experiment to find the one that is the most satisfactory. Excellent slides and prints can result.

Even better results can be obtained, much more conveniently, using special *recording cameras* (fig. 2-75). These either contain a camera focused on a small CRT screen, or have some arrangement for plotting pixels directly on photographic film. The most sophisticated have very high resolution. Some, used in theatrical film animation, have resolutions of 4,000 by 4,000, sufficient to produce synthesized color images that are impossible to distinguish from photographs of complex three-dimensional scenes (fig. 2-76).

2-76. A very-high-resolution image of a spaceship from the 1984 Lorimar film, *The Last Starfighter*. (Digital Scene Simulation by Omnibus Simulation, Inc. Copyright © 1984, 1985 by Omnibus Simulations, Inc. All rights reserved.)

Summary

The raster CRT display is an extraordinarily versatile device. At the low end of the cost range, raster displays provide low-to-medium resolution black-and-white and elementary color graphics capabilities on popular personal computers. More expensive models are designed for different professional graphics tasks. Some are designed for display of fine, detailed line work, whereas others are designed for display of realistic, smoothly shaded and colored images.

Depending on the capabilities of the display generator and monitor, you can use raster display technology to work in a wide variety of graphic styles. We have considered monochrome line drawings, monochrome pattern and texture, halftoning, colored lines, polygons and patterns, and full-color pictures.

Although the capabilities of vector and raster devices overlap, their fundamental differences must be understood and respected. A vector device places uniform, straight lines very precisely, one by one, on the picture plane.

It also suggests an economy of graphic means, since the time taken to plot a picture vector by vector is proportional to the number of vectors in it. Complex line styles, hatching, and texture must therefore be used very sparingly. A raster device, on the other hand, builds an image out of uniform pixels arranged in a grid that completely covers the picture plane. This makes it harder to produce uniform lines and clean, crisp edges, but results in greater versatility. Graphic techniques that use a wide variety of line styles, patterns, textures, and colors and that modulate the surface in complex ways are appropriate with raster devices.

Exercises

1. Examine a few good examples of graphic designs or paintings in some of the following continuous tone and color media:

- colored paper collage
- woodblock print
- stained glass
- batik
- gouache
- oils
- watercolor wash
- airbrush
- continuously applied pastel or chalk

What can you identify, in each case, as the artist's graphic primitives? What are the graphic variables that the artist manipulates each time that an operation is performed to generate a primitive? How is this manipulation accomplished physically? Would it be possible to design a machine to perform such manipulations, and if so, what might it be like? Write a brief, illustrated comparison of several examples, with answers to these questions.

2. See if you can find examples of mosaics constructed from the following primitives:

- smooth, irregular pebbles (look at the paving patterns in traditional Chinese gardens)
- small, irregular, straight-edged polygonal tesserae
- roughly regular, square tesserae, placed at varying angles (look at Roman and Byzantine examples)

What graphic variables does the artist work with? How are the following effects produced?

- continuous areas of tone or color
- gradations of tone or color across a surface
- straight and curved lines

Compare these mosaic techniques to each other and to the use of a raster grid in computer graphics.

3. Collect some examples of fabric designs executed in multicolored thread and using various techniques. Some suggestions:

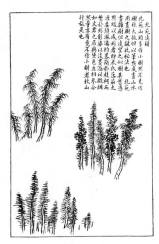

a. Close-up

b. Middle distance.

c. Far distance.

2-77. Illustrations of techniques for painting trees from *The Mustard Seed Manual of Painting*.

- needlepoint and tapestry
- Navajo rugs
- Sumba blankets (from Indonesia)
- Suzhou embroidery (from China)
- woven reed baskets
- modern woven fabrics

Make an illustrated comparison considering, for each case, the following questions:

- How many different kinds of thread are employed?
- What graphic variables are manipulated, and how is this accomplished physically?
- Was the design executed by a machine; if not, could it have been?

4. The traditional Japanese game of *go* is played on a square grid with circular black and white pieces. In effect, a board covered with pieces is a low-resolution, one-bit-per-pixel raster display device. Obtain a go board and a supply of pieces, and experiment to see what kinds of images can satisfactorily be constructed at this resolution. Experiment with creating recognizable images of various motifs using the smallest possible number of pieces.

5. Examine an available raster CRT display device and, if possible, its technical specifications. Compare its graphic variables and its spatial and color resolution and accuracy with those of some of the traditional media that you considered in earlier exercises. What are the relative strengths and limitations? Provide a concise evaluation.

6. A medium like watercolor wash allows continuous variation of tone and color across the picture plane; a raster display breaks the picture plane into distinct cells, within which intensity or color may vary only in discrete steps. Experiment with continuous and discrete renderings of the same motif. What are the representational and aesthetic advantages and disadvantages of each technique?

7. The picture plane could be broken into triangular or hexagonal cells, instead of a square raster grid. Experiment with mapping the same motif into square, triangular, and hexagonal grids. What are the advantages and disadvantages of each grid?

8. Figure 2-77 compares methods, described in *The Mustard Seed Manual of Painting*, for depicting trees close up, in the middle distance, and in the far distance. How is fine detail handled in each case? How would it be handled by mapping successively smaller images of trees onto a bilevel raster grid? What would be the effects of using pixel averaging for antialiasing? Make a critical comparison.

9. Nelson Goodman (1976) has distinguished between *dense* symbol systems, in which marks on a surface vary continuously and cannot be isolated from each other, and *differentiated* symbol systems that work with discrete, distinct elements. Painting, he claims, is dense, whereas printed text is differentiated. How do raster images fit into this scheme? Discuss.

3.

The Computer as a Graphics Machine

We have now seen how Kandinsky's graphic primitives—the *point*, the *line*, and the *plane*—become the *pixel*, the *vector*, and the *filled polygon* on display and plotting devices. Our next step is to consider the computer that controls the generation and disposition of these elements on a display screen or plotting surface.

You need not know all the technical details governing the operation of a computer in order to produce graphics successfully any more than you need to be an expert in automobile technology in order to drive a car. You must, however, know the basic terminology, understand the roles of the various fundamental components of a computer system, and know where limitations on capacity and performance are likely to appear.

In this chapter, then, we will introduce the organization and functions of a computer system and briefly describe some of the technology involved.

Input, Process, and Output

The functions of many machines can be described by specifying their *input*, *process*, and *output*. The process transforms something that we have into something that we want. Here are some familiar examples:

- **Toaster**
  Input: bread
  Process: application of radiant heat
  Output: toast

- **Coffee grinder**
  Input: beans
  Process: grinding
  Output: ground coffee

- **Pencil sharpener**
  Input: blunt pencil
  Process: rotary shaving
  Output: sharp pencil

The basic functions of a computer can be described in this fashion as well. The input consists of information in some form (for example, numbers typed in at a keyboard); the process consists of arithmetic and logical operations applied to that information (adding numbers, for instance); and the output consists of the new information that results from the operations performed upon the input (the total, for example). We are particularly concerned here with input information that specifies how a picture is to be made, output in the form of the displayed or plotted picture, and processes for converting one into the other. Figure 3-1 illustrates this basic organization.

The physical configuration of a simple computer system usually reflects this organization in a very direct way (fig. 3-2). There is an *input device*—in this case a keyboard, which is connected to a box containing the *central processing unit* (CPU). The *output device* (here a CRT screen) is also connected to the CPU. This basic scheme is frequently elaborated by connecting several different input and output devices to a CPU—much as a building might have several different entrances and exits (fig. 3-3). Further, a number of CPUs can be interconnected to form a *network* (fig. 3-4) within which information can be passed from computer to computer. It will be useful to survey the range of different types of input devices, CPUs, and output devices before going further.

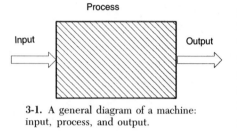

3-1. A general diagram of a machine: input, process, and output.

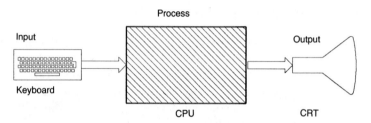

3-2. The physical configuration of a simple computer system: input device (keyboard); central processing unit; and output device (CRT).

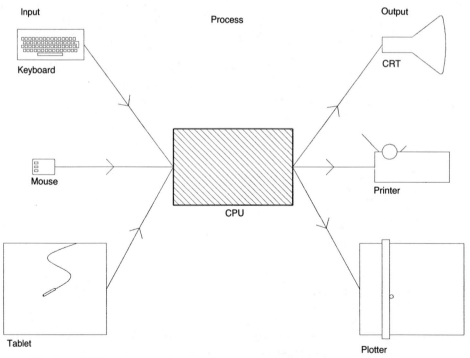

3-3. Several different input and output devices connected to a CPU.

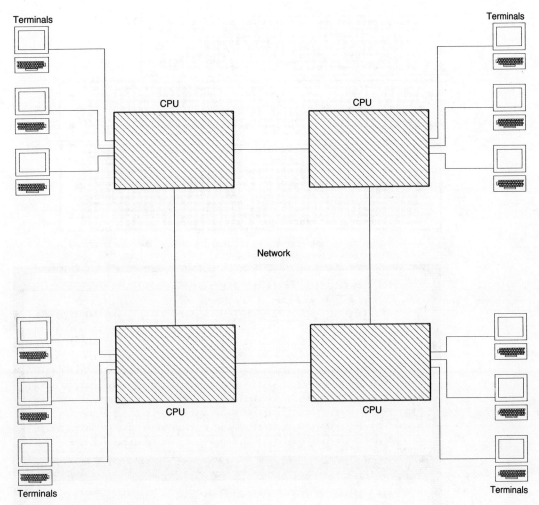

3-4. Several CPUs constituting a network.

Input Methods

Computer input methods are ways of capturing textual, graphic, audible, and other forms of information and converting these into an electronic form processable by the computer. The information may either be recorded on some input medium, which is then read, or it may be input directly.

Input Media

A variety of different media can be used for recording information: printed and punched paper, magnetic tape, photographic film, laser videodisc, and digital audio recordings to name just a few of the most familiar. Any device that reads recorded information and converts it into electrical impulses is potentially an input device for a computer. Many common input media, and the associated reading devices, actually predate the computer, or were originally developed for other purposes and have since been adapted for use in computing.

The technology for recording data on *punch cards* (fig. 3-5), for example, was developed in the nineteenth century. Card punches, readers, and sorters

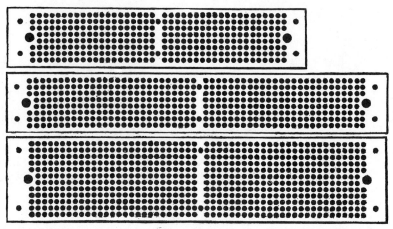

a. Cards for encoding patterns to be woven by Jacquard looms—the nineteenth century ancestors of today's computer graphics devices.

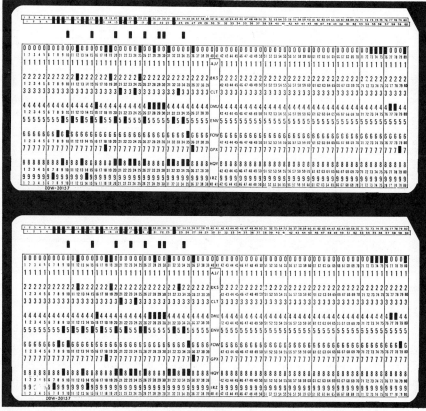

b. Punch cards with characters encoded as patterns of holes.

3-5. Punch cards.

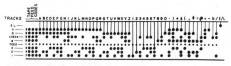

3-6. Punched paper tape, showing how characters are encoded as patterns of holes.

were used extensively in the 1890 U.S. Census, and the success of this led to the development of a large office data-processing industry based on punch card technology. So, when the first computers were developed in the 1940s and 1950s, they used punch card readers as input devices. Punched paper tape (fig. 3-6) readers were also commonly used. Punched paper remained the standard computer input medium until the 1970s, but is now obsolete.

Magnetic tape found its first commercial application in the recording and reproduction of sound; a well-developed technology already existed when computers first appeared. Not only sound but also digitally encoded numerals and characters can be recorded on magnetic tape. The method is to create tiny magnetized spots on the surface of the tape, much as holes are punched in paper tape. A similar coding scheme is used. Magnetic tape readers, however, operate at a much higher speed than paper tape readers. Today, both cassettes (fig. 3-7) and large reel-to-reel tapes (fig. 3-8) are commonly used as computer input media.

3-7. Cassette tape (Data Electronics).

In the audio and video recording fields, disk format is preferred over tape format for certain purposes. There are phonograph records, for example, and laser videodiscs. Similarly, the *floppy disk* (fig. 3-9), a coated plastic disk on which information is recorded magnetically, has now become a very popular input medium—particularly for home computers. Where a phonograph disk has one spiraling track, a floppy disk has concentric tracks for recording information on its surface. A *floppy disk drive* (fig. 3-10) is used to read and write information on the disks. The drive spins the disk at high speed and can position its head to read or write on any track. Software from a computer store is usually on floppy disks or tape cassettes. These have become publishing media.

3-8. Reel-to-reel magnetic tape (Memorex).

Bar codes (fig. 3-11) printed on products in the supermarket are yet another scheme for encoding digits and characters. These may be read by light-sensitive wands, or by the sophisticated laser-scanning devices that are installed at checkout counters to input the encoded information to a computer.

You can, with some effort, learn the codes that are used with punch cards, paper tape, and bar coding and read the information yourself. But these certainly are not convenient formats in which to present information to human beings. And human beings cannot read magnetic media at all. Another class of input devices known as *document readers* has therefore been developed.

3-9. Floppy disks (Memorex).

3-10. A floppy disk-drive mechanism (Tandon).

3-11. Bar code—characters are encoded as patterns of narrow and wide bars (Intermec).

3-12. Numerals used with magnetic ink character recognition (MICR) reading devices.

These read alphabetic characters and numbers directly from a printed page. Magnetic ink character recognition (MICR) devices read characters in a special font (fig. 3-12) printed in magnetic ink. There are also special optical character recognition (OCR) fonts. Some document readers can accept cleanly typed characters in standard styles.

Direct Input Devices

The alternative to an input medium and a reader is a device that allows an operator to communicate directly with the computer by performing certain input actions. The most common such device is the *keyboard* (fig. 3-13), adapted from its original use in the typewriter. Here the action is a *keystroke*, which results in input of a single character or digit. Most computer keyboards are more extensive than a standard typewriter keyboard; in addition to the standard layout of keys, they can have a *numeric pad* for convenient input of numerical data, plus *function keys* that have various specialized uses. Keyboards are also found on musical instruments. In this case, depression of a key generates a corresponding sound. Similarly constructed keyboards can be used to input information describing a musical composition to a computer (fig. 3-14).

The *microphone* can also be used as a direct input device (fig. 3-15). Here the action is that of speaking a single-word command that is drawn from some fairly limited vocabulary. Until quite recently the technology associated with this was expensive and unreliable. Today, though, personal computers that respond to spoken commands are becoming increasingly common. In computer graphics, voice input becomes particularly useful when you have both hands occupied by keyboards and other devices, and you need an additional communication channel. Continuous speech recognition by computer is more difficult, but the technology for this is developing rapidly.

Just as a microphone can equip a computer with ears, a *video camera* can equip it with eyes (fig. 3-16a). Other types of scanners, including X-ray, ultrasonic, and laser are also used (fig. 3-16b). These are all raster-scanning devices and input a picture encoded as an array of intensity levels. It is difficult to develop a computer system that can recognize vectors in pictures that are input in this way, and (so far, at least) this severely limits the usefulness of scanned input of line drawings. However, scanned pictures are of great importance in the fields of computer enhancement and interpretation of satellite and medical imagery and in robotic vision systems.

3-13. A typical computer keyboard with numeric pad and function keys (Key tronic).

3-14. A keyboard to input information describing a musical composition (Ensoniq).

3-15. A headset with microphone is used to input spoken commands (Key tronic).

a. A video camera (Datacopy).

b. A laser scanner (Datacopy).

3-16. Various types of scanners can be used to encode a picture as an array of intensity levels.

Pointing Devices

Many different *pointing devices* have been developed for direct input of coordinates on a surface, or even within a cube of three-dimensional space. Here the action is one of indicating a point in some way, with the result that a corresponding coordinate pair or triplet is input. These devices are of special interest in computer graphics, since they can be used to input vectors by indicating their endpoints and also to select graphic elements from menus and locate them in a picture.

A pointer must have a sufficiently fine tip, and there must be a precise way to record the coordinates of the tip. The most obvious and available pointer is, of course, your finger. When used in conjunction with a *pressure-sensitive touchpad* (fig. 3-17), it becomes a very convenient, direct input device. Touchpads are low-cost devices and have become fairly popular in educational and recreational computer graphics applications. However, they are not very accurate and tend to be unreliable so are not often used in professional contexts.

Touch screens (fig. 3-18) are most commonly used in conjunction with raster CRT displays. They are transparent and fit in front of the display screen. A variety of techniques are used to sense the position of the finger: some sense where light beams are broken; others sense a capacitance change; and others use two closely spaced, flexible, transparent plastic sheets that come into contact and close a switch at the point of pressure. These devices are very easy to use, but they do have some limitations: accuracy is very limited, your arm gets tired, and the screen gets covered with finger marks.

Light pens (fig. 3-19) can be employed for pointing at a display screen more accurately. These devices work with refreshed vector or raster CRT displays, but not with storage tubes. A light pen contains a receptor that detects the scanning beam. A timing circuit is then used to calculate the location at which the beam was detected. It follows from this principle of operation that a light pen cannot detect an arbitrary point on a refreshed vector display, but only illuminated points. The high degree of accuracy (usually to the resolution of the display) of a light pen is attractive, and inexpensive models for use with low-cost raster displays are now available. They are not very pleasant to use, however, as arm fatigue is a problem here too. Furthermore, the curvature of the CRT screen, and the distance between the phosphor and the protective screen in front results in parallax problems.

Most professional computer graphics work today is done with *graphic*

3-17. A touchpad (Tandy).

3-18. A touch screen is used with a raster CRT for input of coordinates (Hewlett-Packard).

tablets (fig. 3-20a). These look like ordinary drawing boards and range in size from about 8 by 10 to about 40 by 60 inches. A *stylus* or a *crosshair* device (fig. 3-20b) is used to detect points on the working surface. The resolution to which stylus or crosshair locations may be distinguished is very good: typically from 20 to 1,000 points to the inch. Small, low-resolution units are inexpensive, but higher performance costs more.

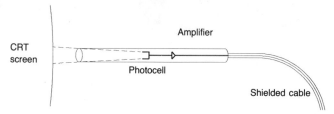

CRT screen · Amplifier · Photocell · Shielded cable

3-19. A light pen.

a. The digitizing surface.

b. Stylus and crosshair devices (Houston Instrument).

3-20. Graphic tablets.

Any one of several different detection systems may be used in a graphic tablet. Today most use *electromagnetic arrays*: a grid of fine wires is concealed beneath the tablet surface; electrical pulses are sent down the wires in sequence; and a coil in the stylus or crosshair device picks up an induced current as pulses pass underneath (fig. 3-21a). *Ultrasonic* tablets (fig. 3-21b) generate a sound pulse from the stylus tip and measure the time taken for the sound to arrive at two strip microphones along the tablet edge in order to establish the stylus position. *Mechanical* tablets (fig. 3-21c) work like pantographs.

Since an existing drawing can be taped to the surface of a tablet without impeding its operation, tablets are very commonly used to input existing drawings by means of point-by-point tracing. Large surface area and high resolution do, of course, make this easier. Since electromagnetic array and ultrasonic tablets detect stylus or crosshair locations hundreds of times a second, these can also be used for freehand sketching.

The principle of the tablet can be extended from two to three dimensions (fig. 3-22). When three perpendicular strip microphones are used in conjunction with an ultrasonic stylus, for example, coordinates of points within a cube can be detected. Advanced models work with cubes up to about ten feet on edge,

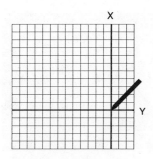

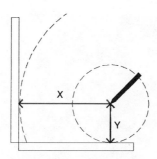

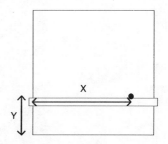

a. An electromagnetic array is made up of a grid of fine wires from which the stylus or crosshair device picks up an induced current as an electrical impulse passes underneath.

b. Strip microphones measure the time taken for an ultrasonic sound pulse to travel from the stylus tip.

c. Mechanical linkages measure X and Y displacements of the stylus.

3-21. Detection systems for graphic tablets.

with a resolution of more than 200 points per inch. This is not a cheap technology, however. Detection of point light sources, electromagnetic devices, and mechanical linkages have also been used for digitizing three-dimensional coordinates.

Positioning Devices

Several devices are commonly used for positioning a pulsing *cursor* on a CRT screen. Most common are cursor keys (fig. 3-23); when one of the four keys is depressed, the cursor moves in the direction of the arrow. Almost all home computers, professional personal computers, and word processors have these. A few have cursor disks (fig. 3-24), which sense the position and pressure of a finger or foot and use this information to control cursor movement.

A particularly simple and inexpensive positioning device is a pair of *thumbwheels* (fig. 3-25). Rotation of one sets an X coordinate, while rotation of the other sets a Y coordinate. Storage-tube terminals frequently come equipped with thumbwheels, which are used to control the position of nonstored crosshairs displayed on the screen.

Arcade video games (which are, in fact, sophisticated computer graphics systems) have made two more positioning devices popular—the *trackball* (fig. 3-26) and the *joystick* (fig. 3-27)—to control the positions of the objects displayed on screen.

Yet another popular positioning device is the *mouse*. The mechanical-ball mouse (fig. 3-28) works like an upside-down trackball and can be used on any reasonably flat surface. An optical mouse (fig. 3-29) works over a gridded surface and detects grid points passing underneath. Mice, unlike most other positioning devices, register *relative* motion from their last location, rather than absolute location; if you pick up a mouse and replace it at a new location on the surface, a new reference point is established. Mice are very easy to use and are becoming increasingly popular on personal computers.

For professional work in computer graphics, you usually need convenient, high-performance input devices. But they are not necessary if your main objective is to learn the basic principles of computer graphics. In this book, then, we shall not assume access to any expensive or unusual devices. A keyboard is all that is absolutely necessary. For advanced work, it is useful to have a mouse as well.

a. Electromagnetic digitizer (Polhemus Navigation Sciences).

b. Digitizer with mechanical linkages (Micro Control Systems).

3-22. Three-dimensional digitizers.

3-23. Cursor keys.

3-24. A foot-operated cursor disk (Versatron).

3-25. Thumbwheels controlling crosshairs on a storage tube.

The Processor

The reason for putting information into a computer is, of course, that you want to *process* it in some way. The part of the computer that actually does this work is therefore called the *processor*. The processor does not do anything that cannot, in principle, be done with pencil and paper. In fact, its basic operations are extremely simple. But it performs them at almost unimaginably high speed and with extraordinary reliability.

The processor has two basic parts: its *memory* and its *central processing unit* (CPU). The memory is used to store the information that is being worked with, much as a scratchpad is used in a hand calculation. The CPU performs operations on this information. In a typical operation, for example, it might retrieve two numbers from memory, add them, and put the result back in memory. The basic relationship of CPU and memory is illustrated in figure 3-30.

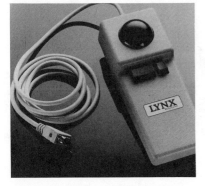

3-26. A trackball (Disc Instruments).

Memory

Memory can be thought of as an array of pigeonholes, each with a unique serial number (index), and each capable of storing a coded representation of

3-27. A joystick (Tandy).

3-28. A mechanical-ball mouse (Logitech).

3-29. An optical mouse (Mouse Systems Corp.).

a number or a character (fig. 3-31). Two kinds of information are stored in memory: information that is to be operated upon, the *data*; and information specifying the sequence of operations to be performed, the *program* (fig. 3-32). Both data and programs may be entered into memory from the computer's input devices. (When discussing certain kinds of computational processes, it is convenient to drop the distinction between program and data. For our purposes, however, it will be useful to maintain it.)

Memory physically consists of thousands of two-state electronic devices. Each one of these can represent a *binary digit* (a *bit* of information): zero when the device is in the charged state, one when it is uncharged. Most computers today have their memories organized into eight-bit chunks called *bytes*. Each byte can store an item of data (an integer, a real number, or a character) in digitally encoded format. This scheme has its limitations: you can store integers only within a limited range, or real numbers with limited precision. More powerful computers therefore group bytes into *words* of two bytes (sixteen bits), four bytes (thirty-two bits), or even eight bytes (sixty-four bits).

Computer memory has traditionally been a very expensive component of the hardware (though it is rapidly becoming less so). As a result, most computers have just enough memory; programmers should not waste it.

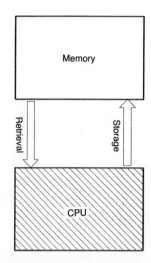

3-30. The relationship between the CPU and memory of a computer.

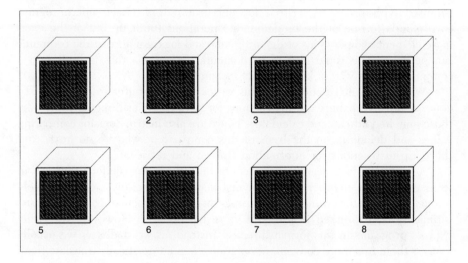

3-31. Memory can be thought of as an array of pigeonholes, each with a unique serial number (index), and each capable of storing a coded representation of a number or a string of characters.

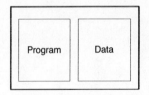

3-32. Two kinds of information are stored in memory: programs and data.

The CPU

The idea of a *logic circuit* underlies the construction and operation of the CPU. Where memory consists of two-state storage devices, logic circuits are composed of two-state (on and off) *switches*. Conceptually (although the physical distinction is not always clear) the CPU is broken down into the *execution registers*, the *arithmetic and logical unit*, and the *control unit*.

The execution registers are used to hold information that is needed right away, for example, numbers that are being added, the results of the addition, and currently active locations in memory. When information is to be operated upon by the CPU, it is first retrieved from memory and loaded into execution registers.

As the name implies, the arithmetic and logical unit actually performs fundamental arithmetic operations: addition, subtraction, multiplication, and division. In this respect, it is very much like the familiar four-function calculator. In addition, however, it can perform the logical operation of comparing numbers to determine which is greater. The arithmetic and logical unit actually consists of an array of logic circuits that performs the required operations. The logic circuits are organized into basic configurations called *and*, *or*, and *not gates*, which physically model the operations of Boolean algebra and binary arithmetic applied to the binary numbers stored in the registers. In the end, all digital computation comes down to this. (But do not be misled into taking too reductionist a view. It is just as true to say that all life, in the end, comes down to a few hydrocarbons.)

The essential function of the control unit is to guide the computer through execution of the sequence of instructions (that is, the program) that is stored in the memory. It retrieves instructions one by one from memory, interprets each one, activates the arithmetic and logical unit or an input or output device to execute the instruction, then repeats the cycle for the next instruction.

The Instruction Set

Within the control unit are circuits known as *microprograms* (not to be confused with programs written for microcomputers). Each microprogram corresponds to one of the fundamental operations (built up out of the even more elementary operations of the arithmetic and logical unit) that the computer can perform. The repertoire of fundamental operations that is built into a computer in this way is known as its *instruction set*.

What is the instruction set? This varies from computer to computer. In general, however, there are instructions for performing arithmetic, much like those punched into a hand calculator. There are also instructions for comparing values and deciding, on the basis of this comparison, what to do next. And there are instructions for information storage and retrieval.

A computer can accept and execute only those instructions that are in its instruction set; in other words, the instruction set precisely and exhaustively defines a computer's functions. A program for a particular computer must ultimately be expressed in terms of its instruction set. However, we rarely express programs in this format directly. Instead, as we shall see, we usually express them in a more convenient notation, then automatically translate them into sequences of instructions in the instruction set.

The range of different instructions contained in the instruction set is important, as the more instructions there are, the more versatile the CPU, and the easier it will be to program it to do something useful. We are also interested in the *speed* with which the instructions are performed, since this ultimately determines how fast programs (that is, sequences of instructions) can be executed.

The Data Bus and Clock

In addition to memory, an arithmetic and logical unit (with its registers and logic circuits), and a control unit microprogrammed with an appropriate instruction set, two more things are needed to complete a CPU. There must be a *data bus* connecting the various parts and a *clock* to time and coordinate the CPU's operation.

The Instruction Cycle

The relationships between the input unit, memory, arithmetic and logical unit, control unit, and output unit are summarized by the block diagram in figure 3-33. It depicts both flows of information and control links. We can see how information flows in and out of the memory and how the control unit (following the stored instructions comprising the program) controls the flow of information and its transformation. Figure 3-34 summarizes the way in which an *instruction cycle* is performed by a computer that is organized in this fashion. We can see how instructions are retrieved, interpreted, and executed one by one.

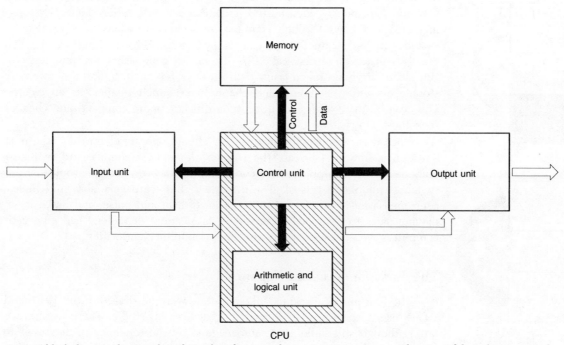

3-33. A block diagram showing the relationships between the input unit, memory, arithmetic and logical unit, control unit, and output unit of a computer.

Strictly speaking, this functional organization and this kind of instruction cycle characterize one particular type of computer known as the *von Neumann machine* (after the mathematician and computer pioneer John von Neumann). There are other types that are organized and perform in different ways. All of the commercially available computers that you are likely to encounter, however, are von Neumann machines, and the Pascal programming language, which we use in this text, is designed to run on these machines.

In summary, you should keep in mind three basic facts about processors:

- They store and perform elementary operations on data in binary form. More complex information can be encoded in binary form for processing, and more complex operations can be built up as sequences of the elementary operations in the instruction set.
- The operation of the processor is controlled by a stored program.
- Execution of the program is strictly sequential. Instructions are retrieved from memory and executed one by one.

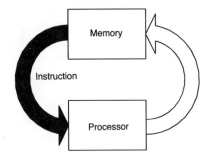

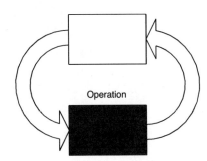

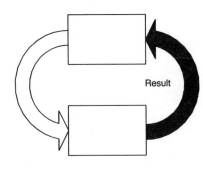

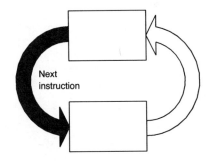

3-34. The instruction cycle.

The Development of CPU and Memory Technology

It is useful to know something of the historical development of CPU and memory technology as well as the associated cost and performance trends. This provides insight into the practical uses of computers—the applications that have become technically feasible and cost-effective. In particular, it makes clear why computer graphics has become such an exciting and explosively developing field.

CPUs are essentially electrical networks containing large numbers of interconnected storage and switching elements. A useful analogy is that of a vast and enormously complicated irrigation network, where water is stored in ponds and flows through channels and where the flow is controlled by switches in the channels. You can, in fact, construct a hydraulic CPU. You can also construct a mechanical CPU—like a very complicated toy train network. But electricity flows much faster than water or toy engines, and the necessary storage elements, switches, and channels are much smaller, so an electric CPU can be many orders of magnitude quicker, more compact, and cheaper than these alternatives.

Once it is established that the CPU should operate electrically, the next question is how to fabricate the storage elements, channels, and switches. Some very early computers were constructed with wires and electromechanical switches (telephone relays). These worked, but were very slow and bulky, consumed a lot of power, generated a lot of heat and noise, and had a lot of moving parts to wear out. If no better fabrication technology had emerged, computers would have merely remained laboratory curiosities.

The First Generation: Vacuum Tubes

The first practical and useful computers were fabricated in the 1940s and 1950s, using vacuum tubes as switching devices (fig. 3-35). These were much faster, though still bulky, hot, and plagued by the tendency of the tubes to burn out. The most famous and significant of the pioneering vacuum-tube machines were the ENIAC (an 18,000-tube, 200-kilowatt machine, completed at Harvard in 1946), the EDVAC (a much more powerful machine, completed in 1952), and the UNIVAC (a commercial machine, the first model of which was delivered to the U.S. Bureau of the Census in 1951). If the fabrication technology had stayed at this level, computing would have remained the preserve of big science, big government, and big business.

The development of computer graphics began with MIT's Whirlwind—a vacuum-tube machine that was put into operation in 1950. This was equipped with two refreshed vector CRTs for the display of graphics.

The Second Generation

The timely invention of the *transistor* in 1948 produced the next major step forward. The transistor served as a solid-state replacement for the vacuum tube. It was smaller, more robust, more reliable, less power hungry, cooler, and cheaper to fabricate. By the mid-1950s, cheap, portable transistor radios had appeared, and the vacuum-tube radio was soon consigned to oblivion as was the vacuum-tube computer. A *second generation* of computers emerged based on the new transistor technology. They were being delivered by the end of the 1950s. Machines such as the IBM 7090 and the CDC 6600 enjoyed considerable commercial success and were installed by universities, government departments, and large corporations. The associated data-processing industry began to develop rapidly. By the mid-1960s, second-generation computers were in widespread use, but were usually accessible only to trained specialists and at relatively few centralized locations.

It was second-generation computers that excited speculation then serious research into the possibilities of computer graphics. An article in *Fortune* magazine in 1956 described the idea of a "design machine" (fig. 3-36) that, as it turns out, anticipated many of the features of today's computer graphics systems. Then, at the 1963 Spring Joint Computer Conference, Ivan E. Sutherland presented a full-fledged, operational computer-aided design system (fig. 3-37). This ran on the second-generation TX-2 computer at MIT's Lincoln Laboratory and made use of a refreshed vector display and a light pen.

The Third Generation: Integrated Circuits

In electronic circuitry, the interconnections of discrete electronic components cause a lot of problems. They are costly, take up excessive space, are a major source of unreliability and noise problems, and increase power requirements. It therefore makes sense to fabricate integrated circuits (ICs) that contain a number of individual components (such as transistors and capacitors) in a monolithic unit whenever possible. Research into integrated electronic circuits began in the mid-1950s, and the first mass-produced commercial integrated circuits, fabricated on small silicon chips, emerged in the early 1960s. This new technology brought the reign of the second-generation computers to an abrupt end. By the mid-1960s, more powerful and cost-effective *third-generation* computers, which made extensive use of ICs, were coming onto the market. Among the best known of these were the IBM 360 series of large mainframes and the DEC PDP-11 series of minicomputers.

3-35. Eniac, an early vacuum-tube computer. (Courtesy of Smithsonian Institution, Washington.)

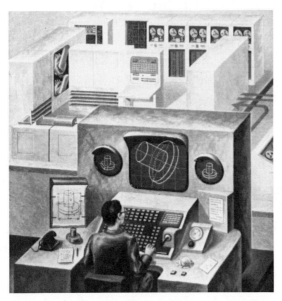

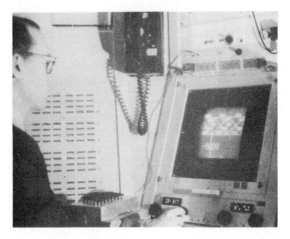

3-37. Ivan. E. Sutherland's pioneering *Sketchpad* computer-aided design system (1963).

3-36. An artist's conception of a computer graphics system for use in design. (*Fortune* magazine, November 1956.)

The Fourth Generation: VLSI

The next step in the development of processor technology was to go from ICs to *very large scale integrated circuit* (VLSI) chips. The trend over the last two decades has been toward the fabrication of integrated circuits of increasing complexity on single, thumbnail-sized silicon chips. This brings with it, in general, increasingly powerful and sophisticated functions performed by a single chip, decreasing cost of computation, and greater reliability. By the early 1970s, the first *microprocessors* (complete computer processors on a single chip) were being produced commercially. Intel Corporation produced its 4004 in 1971, its 8008 in 1972, and its famous 8080 in 1974. A very diverse *fourth generation*, based heavily on VLSI and ranging from inexpensive home computers to enormously powerful supercomputers, began to emerge.

Memory Chips

As the technology for fabrication of CPUs progressed from vacuum tubes, through discrete transistors and ICs, to microscopic VLSI circuits on tiny silicon chips, the development of memory fabrication technology was following a similar evolutionary path. Early computers used a variety of memory devices: magnetic delay lines, electrostatic storage devices, and magnetic drums. *Magnetic core* memory emerged in the early 1950s and soon became standard. This consisted of thousands of tiny doughnut-shaped magnets strung on a grid of fine wires. Memory chips, fabricated using VLSI techniques, began to appear around 1970. These rapidly made magnetic core obsolete, but the name has not died; computer memory is still commonly referred to as *core*. A more up-to-date term, gaining increasing favor, is *random access memory* (RAM).

VLSI technology is now also used to produce read only memory (ROM), another type of computer memory. Whereas information can be both written into and read out of RAM, ROM permanently stores information that the computer can read, but cannot replace with new information. Typically, ROM is used for permanent storage of frequently used programs within a computer.

Computation as a Free Commodity

A complete microcomputer (performing all processor functions) can now be put together out of CPU, memory, and other chips on a *circuit board* a few inches square. Further integration can be achieved by fabricating a microcomputer on a single chip. The Texas Instruments TM 1000, one of the earliest and most popular microcomputers, is about an eighth of an inch square and sells for around two dollars. Somewhere around a hundred million of them have been sold to date.

The astonishing growth of the computer industry in the 1970s and 1980s has been due primarily to the success of VLSI technology. Increasingly powerful processor, memory, and microcomputer chips are now produced in enormous quantities at a unit cost, typically of just a few dollars. As a result, computer intelligence has become virtually a free commodity; computers have become consumer items; and computing is now a mass medium.

Measures of Processor Performance

The performance of a processor is measured in several different ways, just as the performance of an automobile is measured in terms of horsepower, seating capacity, gasoline consumption, and so on. One of the most fundamental measures, which is often used to characterize classes of processors, is the number of bits of information that the CPU can accept and operate on in a single chunk. This is determined by the capacities of the CPU chip's registers and of its internal data pathways. Assuming the same fabrication technology, the more bits a CPU has, the faster it operates. The amount of memory that a CPU can control is also determined by the number of bits, since this limits the size of the integers that can be used for indexing memory locations.

There is obvious motivation, then, to produce CPU chips that can handle as many bits at once as possible. The catch is that the complexity of a circuit, and hence the difficulty of its design and fabrication, increases very rapidly with the number of bits that it can handle. The development of CPU technology over the last twenty years has essentially been a story of the miniaturization of increasingly complex circuits onto thumbnail-sized silicon chips. One way to grasp this trend is to compare the circuit on a CPU chip to the street network of a town. Chips created before 1960 had circuits equivalent to the street network of a small village, or a university campus. By around 1970, circuits equivalent to a street network of about fifty square kilometers represented the state of the art. The technology of the 1980s allows fabrication of circuits corresponding to five-thousand-square-kilometer street networks—larger than any existing city. We can expect, with reasonable confidence, that the technology of the 1990s will allow fabrication of networks that would cover the state of California (just a little while, perhaps, before a street network actually does cover all of California), and in the more distant future, we can anticipate networks that would cover continents.

Four- to Thirty-two-Bit Chips

The result of this development has been a progression from four-bit CPU chips to eight-bit, sixteen-bit, and most recently thirty-two-bit chips. The TM 1000, mentioned earlier, is a four-bit device. As such, its capabilities are very limited, and it is used as a controller in machines like copiers and microwave ovens rather than as a general purpose computer. Inexpensive, mass-produced eight-bit CPU chips (such as the Zilog Z80) first appeared in the early 1970s, and by 1975, the first eight-bit home microcomputer (the Altair, now all but forgotten) had appeared on the market. Since eight-bit chips cost only a few dollars, but are adequate for many common applications (such as word processing), the personal computer industry grew explosively. Apple, Radio Shack, and Commodore soon emerged as leaders. The popularity of eight-bit machines peaked in 1981 and 1982 and has since declined.

Sixteen-bit chips, such as the Intel 8088, became available in the early 1980s and made it possible to build much more powerful personal computers at only insignificantly greater inherent cost than the eight-bit machines, which were rapidly displaced. The 8088-based IBM PC quickly rose to dominate the personal computer industry; many other vendors brought out sixteen-bit machines as well. Whereas eight-bit personal computers can support only very crude and simple graphics, the IBM PC, the Apple II, the DEC Rainbow, and similar popular sixteen-bit machines began to provide an adequate environment for learning and doing elementary computer graphics.

Another sixteen-bit chip to gain great popularity in the 1980s was the Motorola 68000. This is considerably more powerful than the 8088 (indeed, it performs in many ways like a thirty-two-bit CPU), and it has been used in more expensive, high-performance personal computers such as the Apollo and Sun lines, and the Xerox Star. Many of these have excellent, high-resolution raster graphics capabilities. In 1984 the Apple Macintosh, a low-cost Motorola 68000 machine with much more sophisticated graphics capabilities than earlier low-cost personal computers, was introduced. These machines represented the beginning of moderately priced high-quality computer graphics.

The first of the mass-produced thirty-two-bit chips was from Hewlett-Packard. The earliest personal computers based on thirty-two-bit chips were very expensive—far out of the range for home, educational, or even most professional uses. But the trend is for costs to drop, and as they have done so, thirty-two-bit machines have become increasingly popular. These can support very fast, very high-quality graphics.

Speed

The speed of a CPU is given as the time it takes to execute a single instruction. Second-generation computers of the early 1970s typically took a few *microseconds*—millionths of a second. There are a thousand *nanoseconds* in a microsecond. Some fourth-generation computers, twenty years later, take only a few nanoseconds. In the future, we can look forward to instruction execution times measured in *picoseconds* (thousandths of nanoseconds). These numbers are inconceivably small, but even a relatively simple program may require execution of many billions of instructions, so the differences in speed are apparent at a practical level. Execution times for programs may be measured in seconds, minutes, or even hours.

Sometimes the speed of a computer is specified in *MIPS*—millions of instructions per second. A low-cost personal computer is likely to be in the 0.1 to 1.0 MIPS range; a large computer might operate at about 10 MIPS; and the most powerful computers exceed 50 MIPS. The throughput that can be achieved depends both on the number of instructions processed per second and the amount of computational work accomplished per instruction; larger computers typically achieve more per instruction than smaller computers.

Storage Capacity

The amount of information that can be stored by a computing device is often given by the largest integer that can be represented by n bits of information; this is 2^n. Thus the powers of two (2, 4, 8, 16, 32, 64, 128, 256, 512, 1,024 . . .) show up frequently in specifications of storage capacity. The integer $2^{10} = 1,024$ closely approximates $10^3 = 1,000$, so the prefix "kilo," which is frequently abbreviated K, is used to denote either 1,000 or 1,024. The prefix "mega" (M) denotes 10^6, and the prefix "giga" denotes 10^9.

Memory capacity is usually determined by two factors: the amount of memory that the associated CPU is capable of controlling and the cost of fabricating memory. The capacity of an individual memory chip is measured in units of 1,024 (1K) bits. In general, the more bits on a chip, the cheaper memory becomes. The evolution of processor chips has been paralleled by the evolution of memory chips from 16K to 64K, then (by 1984) to 256K and beyond. The complete memory of a computer is an assembly of memory chips. As we noted earlier, it is organized into eight-bit chunks called bytes, so it is usual to measure total memory capacity in units of 1,024 (1K) bytes, referred to as *kilobytes*. Computers with eight-bit CPUs usually have memories in the range from 4K bytes to 128K bytes. Computers with sixteen-bit CPUs may have up to 1,024K bytes. Machines with thirty-two-bit CPUs may have even more.

Trends

These advances are causing changes in computer terminology. In the 1970s, eight-bit chip-based machines were known as *microcomputers*; sixteen-bit machines with larger memories were referred to as *minicomputers*; and powerful thirty-two-bit macines were called *super-minicomputers* or *mainframes*. Even more powerful machines are known as *supercomputers*. With continuing advances in VLSI technology, though, these distinctions are being obliterated.

Figure 3-38 summarizes the dramatic trends in processor performance and cost from 1960 to 1990. Note in particular that processing cost has decreased by a factor of about thirty thousand. Boastful members of the computer industry enjoy pointing out that if the automobile industry had done as well, a car today would cost less than a dollar and would run indefinitely on a single tank of gasoline.

Auxiliary Memory

A basic problem with the computer described so far is that the memory is too limited and volatile for many purposes. In other words, you cannot store very much information, and whatever can be stored is lost when the power is turned off. Any serious computer therefore incorporates some *auxiliary*

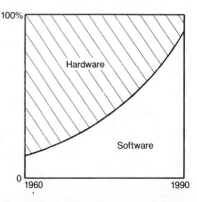

a. Hardware cost has been a decreasing percentage of the total cost of performing a computational task.

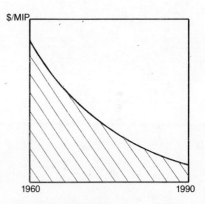

b. Cost/performance ratios (measured here in $/MIP) have been improving.

3-38. Trends in processor performance and costs from 1960 to 1990.

memory as well (fig. 3-39). This is much slower than RAM, but it is more capacious and nonvolatile, allowing semipermanent storage of large amounts of data within a computer.

There are two basic types of auxiliary memory: *sequential* and *random access*. The standard sequential auxiliary memory device is a magnetic tape drive. Since the process of winding and rewinding tape to access arbitrary locations is very slow, use of sequential auxiliary memory is satisfactory only when you can organize processes of reading and writing data on tape in strictly sequential fashion.

The standard random-access auxiliary memory device is a magnetic disk drive (fig. 3-40). Information is recorded on concentric tracks on a rapidly spinning disk. The read/write head can be moved radially to position it over any track. The time taken to access a location is that of moving the head to the appropriate track, plus that required for the given location on the track to spin to a position beneath the head.

Until the early 1970s, disks were invariably made of metal; the drives had retractable heads; and *disk packs* could be removed from the drives. *Floppy disks*, which were introduced in the 1970s, are made of Mylar plastic. *Winchester disks*, another 1970s innovation, differ both from traditional diskpack and floppy disk devices in that the head and disks are contained in a sealed assembly; the disks are not removable. All of these devices are considerably slower than RAM, but faster than magnetic tape.

The capacity of a disk unit is measured in *megabytes*—units of one million bytes (one thousand kilobytes). Floppy disks store less than a megabyte; Winchester disks typically store ten to forty megabytes; and disk packs may store hundreds of megabytes. Capacities of very large disk devices are now measured in *gigabytes*—units of one thousand megabytes. For comparison, a book typically contains a few megabytes of character information. A 1,024 by 1,024 bilevel raster picture requires 128 kilobytes (one-eighth of a megabyte) of memory. If each pixel is represented by one byte to achieve smooth shading,

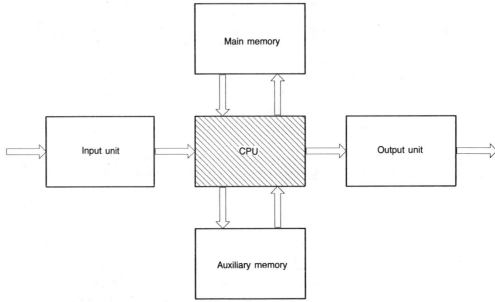

3-39. The relationship of main memory and auxiliary memory. Main memory is larger, and it is not volatile. Information can be transferred from auxiliary to main memory and back as required.

a 1,024 by 1,024 pixel picture requires a megabyte, and if three bytes per pixel are used, three megabytes are needed to produce full color. A 4,096 by 4,096 full-color picture requires about fifty megabytes.

It should now be evident that a computer system has a *storage hierarchy*. First there are the registers in the CPU itself; there are very few of these, but access to data in them is very fast. Then comes main memory, with many more locations, but slower access. Next comes disk memory, which is much more capacious, cheaper, and nonvolatile, but also much slower. Finally come very slow, inexpensive removable media, such as magnetic tape and floppy disk, which provide unlimited archival storage. This hierarchy is analogous to the organization that we give to information that we use ourselves; we keep some information in front of us as we work, we retrieve additional information from nearby files and bookshelves as needed, and we rely on more distant libraries for information that we need only occasionally.

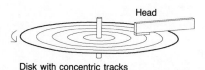

Disk with concentric tracks

3-40. A disk-drive mechanism—information is recorded magnetically on concentric tracks on a rapidly spinning disk, and the read/write head can be moved radially to be positioned over any track.

Output Devices

When you have finished a computation, you need to get the results out of the computer in a convenient form. Output devices convert data stored in computer memory into printed, graphic, audible, or other required forms. They are, then, the exact converse of input devices.

Text Output

We have already covered graphic output devices at length, since the production of graphics is our focus of interest here. But you will encounter other kinds as well, in even the most elementary computer applications. The most common output device today is the *alphanumeric display*, which shows characters on a screen. CRTs, light-emitting diodes (LEDs), and liquid crystal devices (LCDs) are most familiar in this role.

A *printer* of some kind is needed to get numbers and text on paper. There are numerous printing technologies in current use, but it is not necessary to go into the details here. One major difference among them is whether the ink-transfer mechanism is impact, thermal, or electrostatic. There are page printers, which print a page at a time, line printers, which print a line at a time, and character printers. The latter are further divided into those that print fully formed characters, and those that build up characters using dot matrices. Low-cost, dot-matrix printers are most commonly used with personal computers. Slower and more expensive daisy-wheel printers produce better results. Large computer installations may make use of high-speed impact line printers and (increasingly) high-capacity, high-quality laser printers.

Audio Output

A *speaker* can be used to produce simple beeps and buzzes, synthesized speech, and synthesized music. Computer games make extensive use of primitive (and often annoying to the nonparticipant) sound effects. Digitally synthesized speech is now common in games, too, and is also incorporated in machines such as automobiles and copiers. It can turn any telephone into a computer output device. A computer can even become a music processor—just as it can be a word or drawing processor.

Device Drivers

Not every output device can be connected to every computer. First, there must be hardware compatibility. Computer manufacturers normally produce a range of displays, printers, and so on, that are compatible with their machines. For popular computers, there are usually numerous "plug-compatible" output devices produced by third-party manufacturers. But hardware compatibility alone is not enough; the computer must have *device drivers* for its output devices. These are programs, or special circuitry, that generate the signals that control the output device. If you want to connect an unusual output device to a computer, you may find that the necessary driver is not available, and you must write it yourself, which requires considerable technical competence.

Networking and Data Communications

Early computers were stand-alone devices—not surprising, since there was not much else with which to connect them. Today's personal computers are often used in this mode as well. It is possible, however, to connect computing devices to form spatially dispersed *networks*. The network illustrated in figure 3-41a features remote input/output *terminals* (usually CRTs with keyboards) connected to a single CPU. This organization evolved in the days when CPUs were extremely expensive and found widespread use in applications such as the processing of airline reservations. Another kind of network, which has become increasingly popular as processor costs have dropped, is diagrammed in figure 3-41b. In this case, the intelligence is distributed; each node has its own CPU. Modern office automation networks, for example, typically have this structure.

Networking computers adds the data transmission function to those of input, storage, processing, and output. The French have coined a useful term, *télématique* (telematics) for this extraordinarily powerful combination of functions.

A distinction is made between long-distance computer networks and local-area networks (LANs). A long-distance network can be nationwide, or even worldwide, and can incorporate microwave and satellite links. A LAN is usually restricted to a single building or campus and uses electrical cable or fiber-optic links.

Most existing communication networks, such as the telephone network, have been designed for voice communication. For digital communication between computer equipment on such networks, the electronic signal must be specially encoded for voice frequency transmission, then decoded at the other end. A device known as a *modem* (modulator-demodulator) is used to perform this task; the arrangement is illustrated in figure 3-42. Modems are commonly used today to allow personal computers to communicate with each other, and with dial-up data-base services, via the telephone network. Modems are not needed where networks are specially designed to carry digital data.

The key performance issues in a network are the rate at which data can be transmitted (the *channel capacity*) and the reliability of the channels. Channel capacity is measured in *bits per second* (bps). A network operated over ordinary voice-grade telephone lines might typically transmit at 2,400 bps. Arpanet, one of the most extensive long-distance networks, transmits at

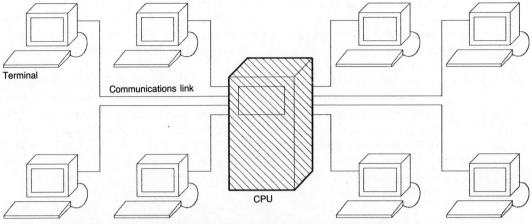

a. Time sharing—remote terminals are connected to a single, central CPU.

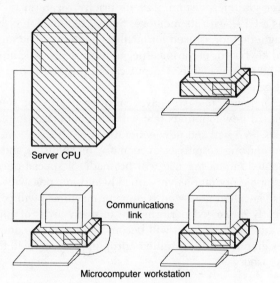

b. Distributed intelligence—CPUs communicate with each other, and a "server" CPU directs communications.

3-41. Structures of computer networks.

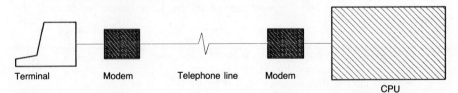

3-42. The use of modems to encode and decode digital signals for transmission over telephone lines.

about one-half million bps. Ethernet, a popular LAN system, transmits at about ten-million bps. A cable television network transmits at around 3,000 megabits per second.

The obvious importance of networking, for our purposes, is that it allows the transmission of digitally encoded pictures. Channel capacity can become a limiting factor, however. Consider, for example, a 1,024 by 1,024 color raster image, encoded with twenty-four bits per pixel. This amounts to about twenty-four million bits. It would take about three hours to transmit it over a 2,400 bps channel. It would take about a minute over Arpanet—still too long for high-performance graphics. Ethernet transmission reduces the time to less than three seconds—a tolerable delay for most practical purposes, but certainly a perceptible one.

If the channels of a network are not sufficiently reliable, *line noise* will be introduced into transmissions. This shows up as random characters in text, random lines in a vector drawing, and random pixels in a raster picture. It can become a significant problem when ordinary telephone lines are used for the transmission of data.

Summary

We have now introduced and discussed all of the basic, essential elements of a computer graphics system. Let us briefly recapitulate. At the heart of the system is a CPU with its memory. Some combination of hard disk, floppy disk, and magnetic tape is used for auxiliary memory. The input device might be a standard keyboard, or various special-purpose graphic input devices, such as tablets, might be available. Output can be displayed on a vector or raster screen, or it can be plotted.

The technologies that we have considered are not static, and we can expect continued developments that will have important implications for computer graphics. We will see new generations of CPU and memory chips that will make computing resources even more inexpensive and therefore more widely available. Increasing use will be made of special-purpose CPU chips to perform graphic operations very quickly and inexpensively. New computer architectures (so-called non–von Neumann machines) will come into use and will offer greatly enhanced performance in many areas of application. Large-scale networking of computers will become increasingly commonplace. High-quality raster graphics will continue to drop in price and will therefore become more widely used.

Exercises

1. Investigate the basic technical specifications of the computer that you will be using to carry out the exercises given in the later chapters. Answer the following questions:

- What kind of processor does it have? How many bits?
- How much memory does it have?
- What kind of disk memory does it have? What is its capacity?
- What input and output devices are available?
- Does your terminal or personal computer connect to a remote processor? If so, what is the line speed of the connection?

2. Assume that a computer takes a microsecond to transform a black pixel to white or white to black in a 1,024 by 1,024 raster picture. How long will it take to transform a black-on-white line drawing into a white-on-black drawing?

3. Assume that each coordinate defining a vector in a device coordinate system

is represented by one byte, so that a vector is fully represented by four bytes. Analyze some line drawings to find how much memory would be needed to store them, vector by vector, in this way. How long would it take to transmit them over a 2,400 bps channel?

4. Imagine a computer designed to produce three-dimensional sculptures, rather than two-dimensional images. What kinds of machines might be used as output devices? How might a sculptor input information specifying a piece?

5. Many technologies that preceded the computer contributed ideas and techniques that were instrumental in the development of computer graphics. Among the most important have been:

- weaving (particularly the Jacquard loom)
- automatic plotting of scientific data
- television
- telecommunications.

What are the lines of ancestry of computer graphics technology? Write a brief historical analysis.

6. It has been suggested that, in the near future, computers will be as ubiquitous as telephones, and that most graphic information will be generated, stored, processed, and transmitted in digital form. Is this plausible? If so, what will be the effect on the visual arts? Write a brief critical discussion.

7. It might be argued that the video game is to VLSI technology what the first popular novels were to the printing press. What new popular artforms do you expect to emerge from the VLSI revolution, and how do you expect them to develop?

8. A close analogy can be drawn between computer graphics and digitally synthesized music. Compare these two art forms in terms of the input and output devices that are used, the processing that is involved, and the historical development that has taken place.

4.

Writing, Compiling, and Executing a Graphics Program

To put a computer to work for you, you must be able to perform several tasks. First, you must be able to switch the computer on. You will want it to input, file, and retrieve data and programs. You will need to specify which of the programs that it has stored in memory is to be executed, and you might want to create new programs. You may want to specify how output is to be printed or displayed on the devices that are available. Finally, you will terminate your work session and sign off.

In this chapter we will describe these steps and discuss the software needed to accomplish them. In particular, we will focus on the process of writing, compiling, and executing graphics programs.

Starting Up

When you start an automobile, you go through a sequence of operations specified in the owner's manual. Perhaps, for example, you buckle the seat belt, pull out the choke, make sure that the transmission is in neutral, depress the clutch, turn the key while depressing the gas pedal, release the hand brake, put the gearshift into first, engage the clutch, and drive off. Similarly, you must go through a sequence of operations to start a computer. Depending on the type of computer, the sequence may be very simple or quite complex.

On many personal computers, the start-up procedure has been reduced to an absolute minimum; you just switch on the power and they are ready to be used. This is made possible by permanently storing the operating system (which we will discuss in a moment) in ROM or on a hard disk. On other personal computers you must load the operating system from floppy disks before you can proceed.

On a large computer system, the process of activating the various hardware components and loading in the operating system can be lengthy and complex. It is usually performed by a specialist operator, and users do not need to know about it. Once the system is "up," a user need only switch on a terminal and depress a key (or perform some equivalent action) to "get the system's attention."

If you are working at a remote terminal connected to a central processor, you need to establish communication between the terminal and the processor before you can begin. This is accomplished by activating the modem, then dialing the processor.

You will find the start-up procedure for the particular computer system that you will be using documented in a beginner's manual or in an instruction sheet. You should consult this before reading on.

The Operating System and Its Basic Functions

When you have started up the computer or connected your terminal to it, you can begin to enter *commands*, which are usually typed from the keyboard. Some systems allow commands to be entered in other ways—by using a mouse to select from a menu, by voice input, or by using special command keys.

What repertoire of basic commands should a computer be able to interpret and execute? Of course there are many possible answers depending on what you want to accomplish, but there are some basic commands that are almost always essential. First, you need commands that will enable you to create and manipulate *files*—collections of related information stored on disk. A file might contain data to be processed, or it might contain a program to perform some task. You must be able to open and name files, to enter and edit information in files, to find and access files that already exist, and to delete files that are no longer needed.

Second, you should be able to select and execute *applications programs*, which perform useful tasks, such as generating graphics, and are stored in files within the system. These may be programs that you have written yourself, or those written by others. When you execute an applications program, you may need to tell the computer where to get the input data and what to do with the output.

If you are going to write your own applications programs, you must be able to have the computer translate the instructions that you have written into a form that it can execute. (This process is called *compilation*, or *interpretation*, and we shall consider it in more detail later in this chapter.) You may also need to *link* parts written separately into a single program. And you will probably want the computer to help you find and eliminate errors in your programs (a process known as *debugging*).

If you are working on a terminal linked to a central processor, or on a personal computer that can communicate with other personal computers, you may want to send information to and receive information from other users. *File transfer* commands, which enable you to send files from your computer to others, and *electronic mail* commands, which enable you to send and receive messages, are needed for this.

When the computer executes a program, it calls into action its various resources (CPU, memory, disk space, input and output devices) as they are needed to perform specified operations. You may need *resource management* commands to specify what resources are available and how they are to be allocated to various possible uses.

The *operating system* of a computer is a program that accepts, interprets, and executes these essential commands (and often many more as well). It controls the overall operation of the computer on which it resides and provides the user with a basic set of tools for performing useful computational work.

Figure 4-1, for example, diagrammatically illustrates the structure of Unix, a popular operating system that runs on many different computers. It consists of three major parts. The *Shell* is the command interpreter—the part of Unix

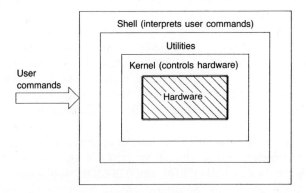

4-1. The structure of the Unix operating system.

that is visible to the user. It "listens" for commands from the keyboard or elsewhere and translates these into action. The *file system* consists of software for performing operations on files. The *kernel* is the part of the system that keeps track of disks, input devices, output devices, communications devices, and other hardware.

Types of Operating Systems

Operating systems have been developed for different classes of computers and to provide appropriate environments for users with a variety of needs. They also represent different stages in the evolution of operating system technology. We need not go into all the intricacies here, but it will be useful to articulate a few fundamental distinctions between batch and interactive operating systems; between single-task and multitasking systems; between single-user and multi-user systems; and between systems that operate a single machine and systems that operate a network.

In the past, it was standard to submit a program and data to a computer on punch cards, along with special *control cards* that told the computer what to do with them. The system would read the cards, execute the program, and output the results. A *batch* operating system controlled this sort of processing. Fortunately, such systems are mostly a thing of the past. The *interactive* operating systems common today allow you to type in commands at a terminal keyboard and read output at a display screen—a much more convenient and efficient arrangement.

As the name suggests, a *single-task* operating system allows only one task (for example, the execution of a user program) to be performed at a time. But a *multitasking* system can perform several tasks at once. This allows you to instruct the system to run some program in the "background" while you interact with another program in the "foreground."

A *single-user* operating system allows only one user to interact with it at a time, whereas a *multi-user* operating system allows many terminals to be connected to a computer and many users to interact with the operating system at the same time. This arrangement allows users to share the programs and data that reside on the computer and to communicate with each other via electronic mail.

Most operating systems reside on a single computer. Increasingly, though, computers can be connected to form *networks*. Some sophisticated modern operating systems, then, are designed to keep track of, and allocate as required, the resources of a network.

A low-cost personal computer, will almost certainly have a very simple, single-user, single-task operating system. Among the most widely used of these are CP/M and MS-DOS. More powerful personal computers typically have more sophisticated multitasking operating systems; the Unix system is particularly popular in this type of environment. Minicomputers, super-minis, and mainframes often have very elaborate, multi-user, multitasking operating systems.

Some computers run several different operating systems. The Rainbow personal computer, which was introduced by DEC in the mid-1980s, for example, was designed to run both CP/M and MS-DOS. When you switch it on, it asks you to choose one or the other.

You should obtain a copy of the user's manual for the operating system with which you expect to be working and have it on hand as you go through this chapter.

Windows, Menus, and Icons

Teletypes and electric typewriters were early devices for communicating with computers, and many older operating systems preserve a style of communication characteristic of these devices. Commands are typed from the keyboard, then entered by hitting the *return* key. Commands and responses appear on the screen as lines of text, one beneath the other. Raster CRTs, however, allow the use of windows, menus, and icons to facilitate communication, and modern operating systems often take advantage of this.

Windows on a display screen are like rectangular pieces of paper with text and drawings arranged on a desktop (fig. 4-2). They can be overlaid, and a mouse can be used to shift and resize them. Different windows are used

4-2. Windows on a raster CRT display (Xerox).

for different purposes. One, for example, might be used for communication with the operating system, whereas a second displays the text of an application program that is being run, and a third displays a picture that is generated by the program.

Menus are lists of commands available to the user. Menu headings are usually displayed along the top of the screen, and menus can be pulled down as required (like roller blinds) by pointing at the appropriate heading with the mouse (fig. 4-3). A command can then be selected by pointing.

Icons are small pictures that are used, instead of text, to represent objects and actions (fig. 4-4). A picture of a file folder might stand for a file, for example. Commands can be given by pointing at icons, or by moving them around on the screen. Responses are sometimes made by displaying icons rather than text.

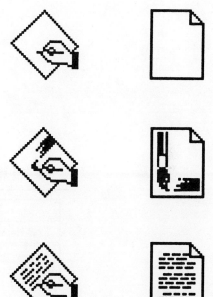

Edit	
Undo	⌘Z
Cut	⌘X
Copy	⌘C
Paste	⌘V
Clear	
Invert	
Fill	
Trace Edges	⌘E
Flip Horizontal	
Flip Vertical	
Rotate	

Style	
✓Plain	⌘P
Bold	⌘B
Italic	⌘I
Underline	⌘U
Outline	⌘O
Shadow	⌘S
Align Left	⌘L
✓Align Middle	⌘M
Align Right	⌘R

4-3. Examples of pull-down menus.

4-4. Examples of icons, representing different kinds of files.

These techniques were developed in the early 1970s at the Xerox Palo Alto Research Center. They were not widely used, though, until implemented on the popular Apple Macintosh personal computer in the 1980s.

Sign-on Procedures

The first thing that your operating system will do is announce its presence and its readiness to accept commands. For example, the CP/M operating system makes an announcement that is something like this:

```
CP/M–86/80 Version 2.00 (1.1)
A>
```

The symbols A> are CP/M's *prompt*, an indication that CP/M is now ready to accept a command.

More elaborate operating systems than CP/M usually require you to go through some sort of sign-on procedure before you can continue. MS-DOS, for instance, announces itself like this:

```
MS-DOS  Version  2.05
Current  date  is  Sat  10-01-198>
Enter  new  date:
```

After the user enters a date in response to this prompt MS-DOS then responds:

```
Current  time  is  0:04:10.90
Enter  new  time:
```

When the user has entered a time, MS-DOS responds with the prompt:

```
A
```

The user is now signed on the MS-DOS system and can enter commands.

An operating system that uses windows, menus, and icons may announce its readiness to accept commands by producing a display such as that shown in figure 4-5. Menu headings are listed along the top of the screen, and labeled file folders show the files that are available for use.

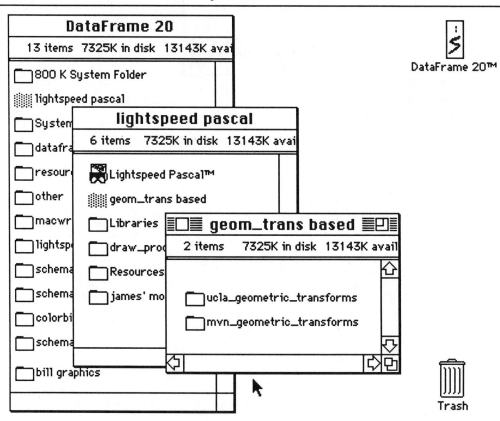

4-5. A display indicating that an operating system is ready to accept commands.

Multi-user operating systems usually require the user's name and a password to be entered. The operating system then checks these against a list of names and passwords stored in memory to determine whether the intending user is properly authorized before granting access. The procedure usually goes something like this:

```
Username: MITCHELL
Password:
Welcome to VAX/VMS version V3.4
$
```

The symbol $ is this particular operating system's prompt for a command. Notice that the user's password, typed in response to the prompt, is not displayed on the screen. This helps to preserve its confidentiality.

Getting Help

The user's manual for your operating system will list the commands that are available and describe their effects. Sometimes, though, the manual is not available, and you do not know what command to give next. Many operating systems provide a way out of this difficulty by allowing you to enter the command HELP (or some equivalent). CP/M, for example, will respond by displaying a list of topics and asking you to select one. When you reply, it will then display explanatory text. Most versions of Unix keep the Unix Programmer's Manual on the system, and you can display any part that you want by using the command MAN.

Commands

A typed command usually begins with a short English word, or a mnemonic, that specifies the action to be executed. Depressing special command keys, or selecting commands from menus, as allowed by some operating systems, are alternative ways to specify actions. Simple operating systems, such as MS/DOS, can execute relatively few actions, so they have relatively short lists of available commands. Figure 4-6, for example, lists MS/DOS's commands. More elaborate operating systems, such as Unix, have much longer lists of commands. Other information must often be included in a typed command as well. If you want to delete a file, for example, you must specify the name of the file that is to be deleted. There will be a specified format for inclusion of such additional information, and this must be followed exactly. Exact spacing and punctuation are important. Where icons are used, the name of a file might be specified by pointing at the appropriate labeled file folder.

You should get to know the command syntax for the operating system that you will be using and study its list of available commands. Do not be intimidated by the technical complexities; you will find that with practice an operating system rapidly becomes familiar and easy to use.

Files

Most operating system commands act on files. The best way to begin to understand these commands is to compare a file of information stored on disk

Command

ASSIGN	Assign drive
ATTRIB	Attribute
BACKUP	Backup
[.BAT]	Batch file commands
BREAK	Break
CHDIR	Change directory
CHKDSK	Check disk
CLS	Clear screen
COMMAND	Secondary command processor
COMP	Compare files
COPY	Copy
CTTY	Change console
DATE	Date
DEL	Delete
DIR	Directory
DISKCOMP	Compare diskettes
DISKCOPY	Copy diskettes
ERASE	Erase
EXE2BIN	Convert .EXE file
FDISK	Prepare fixed disk
FIND	Find text string
FORMAT	Format
GRAFTABL	Load graphics table
GRAPHICS	Screen Print
JOIN	Join
KEYBxx	Load keyboard
LABEL	Volume label
MKDIR	Make directory
MODE	Mode
MORE	Display screen full of data
PATH	Set search directory
PRINT	Print
PROMPT	Set system prompt
RECOVER	Recover
RENAME	Rename
RESTORE	Restore
RMDIR	Remove directory
SELECT	Select
SET	Set environment
SHARE	Share
SORT	Sort text data
SUBST	Substitute
SYS	System
TIME	Time
TREE	Tree
TYPE	Type
VER	Version
VERIFY	Verify
VOL	Volume

4-6. List of commands available in the simple MS/DOS operating system.

in your computer to a file folder of information in a file cabinet by your desk. Icons that are used for file operations make this analogy explicit.

A file, whether in a cabinet or on disk, is a container into which you can put data (fig. 4-7). It must have a name by which it can be found and referred to in commands. It may be empty or it may have contents: text, numerical data, a program, or a picture.

In a file cabinet, a file is created and named by taking a folder and attaching a name tag. Similarly, an operating system provides a command for opening a new file; it has the effect of allocating some space on disk, which can be accessed by name, just as you access a file folder in a cabinet by its name tag. You can also open an existing file to work on it. You may want to rename files. This can be done by changing the name tag on a file folder; an operating system usually provides a command with analogous effect.

When a file has been opened, you can display its contents. There are also commands for performing operations on its contents: entering data; deleting data; and altering data. You can copy its contents, or combine its contents with those of another file. When you have finished work on a file, you must give a command to close it.

A file folder that is no longer needed can be removed from a cabinet and thrown in the trash. Similarly, an operating system provides a command for deleting files and freeing the disk space that they occupied (fig. 4-8). This command is potentially dangerous, since accidental deletion of a file can cause you to lose a lot of information, so operating systems usually require you to reconfirm that you want to delete a file before this is actually done.

Directories

A *directory* is a special type of file that lists the names of other files and contains information about them. By displaying the directory, you can find out what files you currently have in the system.

Figure 4-9, for example, illustrates an MS/DOS directory. In simple

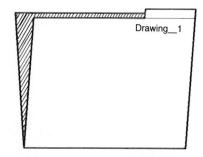

4-7. A file acts as a container with a name into which you can put data.

4-8. Graphic file deletion on the Macintosh personal computer—the icon representing the file to be deleted is dragged to the trash can.

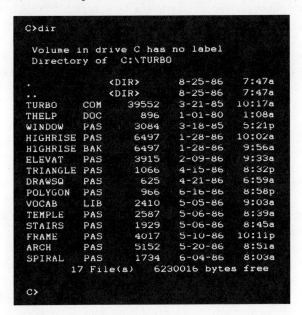

```
C>dir

   Volume in drive C has no label
   Directory of  C:\TURBO

   .            <DIR>      8-25-86    7:47a
   ..           <DIR>      8-25-86    7:47a
   TURBO    COM  39552     3-21-85   10:17a
   THELP    DOC    896     1-01-80    1:08a
   WINDOW   PAS   3084     3-18-85    5:21p
   HIGHRISE PAS   6497     1-28-86   10:02a
   HIGHRISE BAK   6497     1-28-86    9:56a
   ELEVAT   PAS   3915     2-09-86    9:33a
   TRIANGLE PAS   1066     4-15-86    8:32p
   DRAWSQ   PAS    625     4-21-86    6:59a
   POLYGON  PAS    966     6-16-86    8:58p
   VOCAB    LIB   2410     5-05-86    9:03a
   TEMPLE   PAS   2587     5-06-86    8:39a
   STAIRS   PAS   1929     5-06-86    8:45a
   FRAME    PAS   4017     5-10-86   10:11p
   ARCH     PAS   5152     5-20-86    8:51a
   SPIRAL   PAS   1734     6-04-86    8:03a
        17 File(s)   6230016 bytes free

   C>
```

4-9. A typical MS/DOS directory of files.

operating systems the directory just lists files. Most operating systems, however, allow directories to contain *subdirectory* files, which themselves may contain subdirectories, and so on for several levels (fig. 4-10). This allows information to be organized hierarchically, much as books in a library are arranged hierarchically under the Dewey decimal system.

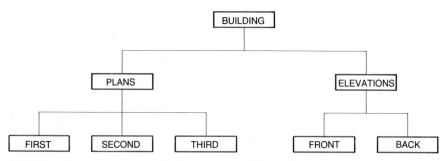

4-10. Hierarchical arrangement of a directory and subdirectories.

Text Editors

When entering information into a file, or modifying the contents of a file, you use the *text editor* provided by the operating system. This consists of a set of commands that allow you to enter text from the keyboard into a file, to browse through a file by displaying its contents on the screen, to find and change strings of text, and to perform various other textual operations.

Text editors vary widely in their styles of dialogue with the user, in their ease of use, and in the range of functions that they provide. Generally, though, they may be divided into *line* and *screen* editors. A line editor provides commands to operate on a line of text at a time. It can display a line, insert a line, delete a line, copy a line, move a line to a different place in the file, or change the contents of a line. A screen editor allows you to display a specified part of a file on the screen and move a cursor to indicate where you want to make changes. The cursor might be controlled by cursor keys or by a mouse (fig. 4-11).

The first practical computer skill that you must acquire is the ability to create, inspect, and edit text files using the editor provided by your operating system. You should read the documentation carefully and practice by entering and editing some short letters or memos.

This is the original text.

This is the ▮original▮ text.

This is the revised text.

4-11. A screen editor in use.

Writing a Program

The text editor allows you to produce programs by entering into a file text specifying what the computer is to do. In the early days of computing, programs were expressed in other ways, by setting switches, for example, or by punching them on cards. But text editors, operating on files stored on disk, are almost universally used for this purpose today.

What kinds of instructions might a program contain? The best way to answer this question is to observe that the purpose of the program is to control the operations of the various hardware elements. First, there may be *input instructions*, which cause data to be read or accepted from input devices. Then there will be instructions for organizing data in memory, usually known

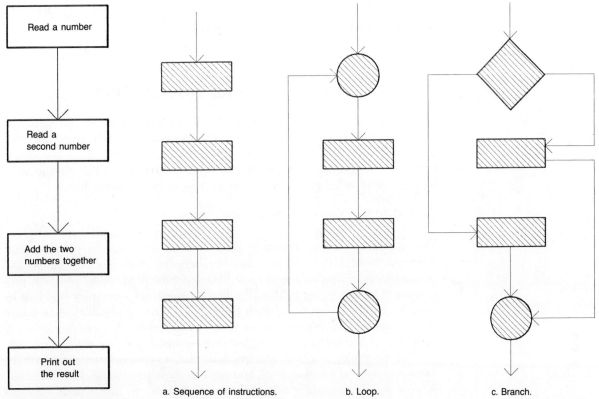

Read a number

Read a
second number

Add the two
numbers together

Print out
the result

a. Sequence of instructions.

b. Loop.

c. Branch.

4-12. The organization of instructions to perform some arithmetic on data.

4-13. The flow of control in a program.

as *data declarations*. There will be *arithmetic instructions*, which cause data to be retrieved from memory, loaded into the registers of the arithmetic and logical unit, and processed. Finally, there will be *output instructions*, which cause data to be retrieved from memory and sent to output devices. The organization of some instructions to read data, perform arithmetic on it, and output results is shown schematically in figure 4-12.

A computer, as we have noted, is a serial device; it executes instructions one by one, so the sequence of instructions in a program affects results. A simple way to define the required sequence is to write instructions one after the other. The flow of execution that results from this is shown in figure 4-13a. More complex programs may contain *loops* (fig. 4-13b) in which an instruction (or sequence of instructions) is repeated some specified number of times, or while some condition holds, or until some condition holds. They may also contain *branches* (fig. 4-13c), which cause either one instruction or another to be executed, depending on the result of some specified test. *Control instructions* in a program are used to define the flow that is required. Instructions specifying loops and branches are possible because the arithmetic and logical unit can perform not only arithmetic operations (addition, subtraction, multiplication, division) on numbers, but also the logical operation of *comparing* numbers to determine which is the greater.

In summary, a program consists of instructions that specify the nature of the input data (if any) and where to get it, the organization of data in memory, the operations that are to be performed, the nature of the output data and where to send it, and that also express some scheme for controlling the sequence in which instructions are executed.

Language Compilers and Interpreters

Any program can be expressed directly in terms of binary integers that designate memory locations containing data to be operated upon, together with binary integers that specify the operations (from the machine's instruction set) to be performed. You can think of each instruction as the settings for a long string of switches, expressed as a string of binary digits like:

00101000000000000000000000001100100

This is called *machine language* programming. It is not very convenient, however, to think in terms of binary numbers and elementary operations and to express programs in the cryptic binary notation. Machine language programming is like trying to describe how to construct a complex building by specifying the coordinates of each brick; it is better, if possible, to structure your thoughts and expressions in terms of higher-level, more immediately understandable constructs. Making use of an *assembler* is a step in this direction.

An assembler is a computer program that accepts instructions expressed more concisely, at a higher level, and decodes these into the machine language. A very simple assembler might allow you to refer to instructions by short mnemonics and to memory locations by decimal integers. Thus the machine language instruction shown above might be reexpressed:

CLA 100

This is called assembly language programming.

A further step in assembly language programming is to allow the use of convenient names to label memory locations, so that instructions can be written in a form like this:

CLA X

This introduces the important construct of a *named variable*, the *value* of which is the contents of the corresponding memory location.

The development of assembly language made it possible to write longer and more sophisticated programs for early computers than had been feasible in machine language, and assembly language is still used for specialized purposes today. But assembly language remains at too low a level for our purposes here, and we shall turn to a high-level *algorithmic language*, which provides a way to express instructions to the computer using English commands, convenient mnemonics, and elements of standard arithmetic and logical notation. Whereas machine language and assembly language are very close to the machine's instruction set, high-level algorithmic languages are much closer to the way that people generally express themselves verbally and mathematically. So it is much easier to write, read, and understand programs in these languages. Here, for example, are some instructions to add three numbers and print the result:

```
SUM := 1+2+3;
WRITE (SUM);
```

Ultimately, of course, a computer can only execute instructions expressed in its own machine language (which have unambiguous meanings in terms of its own instruction set). So a program written in a high-level algorithmic language must always be translated into the machine language of the particular computer on which it is to run.

One popular way to accomplish this is to use a *compiler* (fig. 4-14). A compiler is a special type of program that accepts as input a *source program* written in a high-level language and produces as output an *object program* expressed in the appropriate machine language. This process is called *compilation*. When a program has been compiled for a particular computer, it can then be executed on that computer.

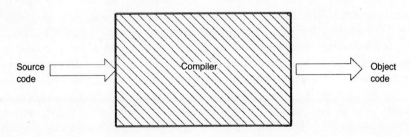

Source code → Compiler → Object code

4-14. The process of compilation.

An *interpreter* may be used instead of a compiler. Instead of translating the whole source program into machine language before execution, an interpreter accepts source code line by line, translates each line, then executes that line before going on to the next. Sometimes interpreters are implemented as software, and sometimes (especially in personal computers) they are permanently stored in ROM.

Compilation of a large program can be a lengthy process, but a source program need be compiled only once, and the object program can be executed repeatedly after that. Furthermore, a good compiler produces object code that executes very efficiently. Interpreted programs run much more slowly than compiled programs, since the translation of source code into object code must be repeated every time the program is executed.

Dozens of high-level algorithmic languages are in widespread use with associated compilers and interpreters for various computers. The oldest, and still one of the most popular, is Fortran. This was developed in the mid-1950s, primarily for use in engineering and scientific calculations. There are good Fortran compilers for virtually all mainframes and minicomputers as well as most of the more powerful microcomputers.

If you have had some experience with low-cost personal computers, you will also certainly have encountered Basic. This is much like a simplified version of Fortran and is very easy to learn. Indeed, it was developed in the mid-1960s for use by beginning students. Many personal computers provide built-in Basic interpreters stored in ROM.

In this book we shall introduce Pascal, which was developed by the Swiss computer scientist Niklaus Wirth around 1970. It is a more modern and elegant language than either Fortran or Basic, and it was specifically designed for teaching computer programming as a systematic discipline. It has become very popular; good Pascal interpreters or compilers are now available for most personal computers, minicomputers, and mainframes.

Pascal Systems

Some Pascal interpreters and compilers come with specialized text editors designed to facilitate input of correctly formatted Pascal code, plus other software tools for use in Pascal program development and execution. Such *Pascal systems* can be thought of as specialized operating systems, which can be invoked from the main operating system, and which provide commands for input, modification, translation, execution, and filing of Pascal programs. When you want to work with Pascal, you first instruct the main operating system to invoke the Pascal system.

A comprehensive Pascal system will provide you with the most convenient way to undertake the programming exercises given in later chapters. If a complete system is not available on the computer that you will be using, you will at least need a Pascal interpreter or compiler, which can then be used in conjunction with the text editor and file commands provided by the operating system. You should find out which Pascals are available for your computer. If you have a choice between several, choose one that is easy to use, adheres closely to the standards for the Pascal language (see Bibliography), and provides good graphics capabilities. Obtain and study a copy of its user documentation.

Running and Debugging Programs

If you use a compiler, there will be a command to compile a program contained in the file that you specify. The resulting object program will be stored in another file. You can then give a command to *run* the object program. If you use an interpreter, there is just one step; you give a command to run a source program.

Sometimes when you use a compiler the compilation process terminates before a complete, executable object program is produced. This happens when the compiler encounters a source statement that breaks the rules of Pascal syntax, or contains a typographic error, and therefore cannot be translated properly. In this case, the compiler outputs an *error message*. The message may be very general, like this:

SYNTAX ERROR

4-15. Icons for errors.

On some systems, an icon of a bug or bomb is displayed (fig. 4-15). Good compilers, though, will usually provide some additional diagnostic information; they will tell you precisely where the error is in your source code, make some suggestions about what might be wrong, and even suggest how to fix it. When compilation fails, you must find the error, correct it, and recompile. Sometimes it will take several attempts before compilation finally succeeds.

Succesful compilation does not guarantee that a program is completely free of errors. Some types of errors cannot be detected by a compiler, and show up only when you attempt to execute the compiled program. If you get an error message at this stage, you must, once again, correct the source code, recompile, and attempt to execute the new object program. The complete process of detecting and correcting errors at compilation and execution is diagramed in figure 4-16.

The computer can detect and report logical inconsistencies in the Pascal code that you write, but it cannot tell whether the code that you have written actually does what you intended it to do. After you have debugged the syntax of a program and it runs successfully, you must also carefully check the results that are produced.

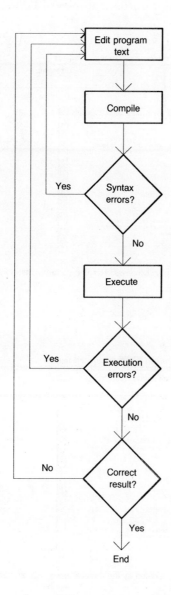

4-16. The process of detecting and correcting errors at compilation and execution.

When you use an interpreter to translate and execute a Pascal program line by line, the interpretation process will terminate with an error message whenever a line containing an error is encountered. After the line is corrected, interpretation may be reinitiated from the beginning. Thus each run gets you further along in the program until, finally, execution is successfully completed. This process is illustrated in figure 4-17.

Some Pascal systems make effective use of windows to help you follow the execution of your program and debug it. Macintosh Pascal, for instance, provides three windows (fig. 4-18). The Pascal code that is being interpreted is shown in one, text and numeric output is shown in another, and graphic output is shown in the third. Error messages appear at the top of the screen. You can either let the interpreter run the program at full speed, or else step through it slowly, watching what happens at each line. When an error is encountered, a thumbs-down icon is displayed beside the offending line.

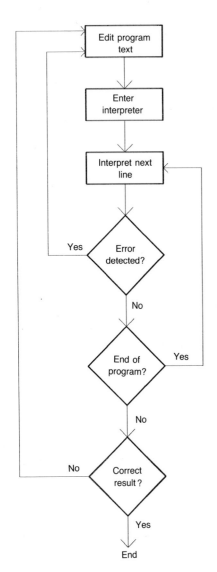

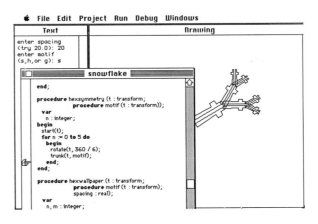

a. Program, text, and graphic windows. The line currently being interpreted is indicated by the pointing finger.

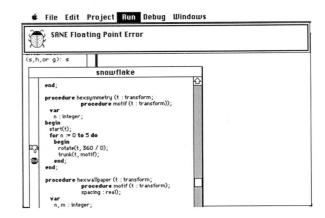

b. A line with an error is indicated by the thumbs down sign, and an error message appears at the top of the screen.

4-18. The use of windows in a Pascal system.

4-17. The process of debugging a program with an interpreter.

Signing Off

When you finish a work session on a personal computer with a single-user operating system, you can just close your files, eject your floppy disk, and switch the computer off. But a more sophisticated operating system requires you to enter a command indicating that you want to terminate work:

```
LOGOFF
```

In response, the computer performs necessary internal management functions and displays a farewell message.

Summary

There is much more to know about the process of writing, compiling, and executing a program, but you should learn this, as you need to, by reading the user documentation for your operating system, text editor, and Pascal system, as well as through practice. In the next chapter, we shall introduce the Pascal programming language and suggest exercises that you can undertake in order to become familiar with it.

Exercises

1. Obtain the introductory user documentation for your operating system. Follow the examples that are given and attempt the exercises that are suggested.

2. Using the available text editor, write a letter. Experiment with the commands for finding, modifying, and shifting strings of text. Print out your letter.

3. Obtain and read the introductory user documentation for the Pascal system that you will be using. Try the following Pascal program (exactly as it appears):

```
PROGRAM TEST;
    BEGIN
      WRITELN ('THIS TEST WAS SUCCESSFUL');
    END.
```

PART TWO
Elementary Graphics Programs

5.

The Pascal
Programming Language

What Is a Computer Program?

We have introduced computer programs as sequences of instructions that computers follow in order to produce useful results—much as a cook might follow a recipe, a musician a score, or a cab driver a sequence of directions. The remainder of this book will focus on how to write programs that, when executed by a computer, generate pictures on some kind of display or plotter. But before going into the details, we will describe more precisely what a computer program really is.

The Language

Any computer program is written in some particular *language*. The language (unlike a natural language such as English) has a precisely specified *vocabulary* and *syntax* that must be followed rigorously. The *semantic* properties are also well defined; any syntactically correct statement causes the computer to perform some specific action. Thus a programming language provides a very precise means of communication and requires you to express yourself exactly; there is no latitude for the vagueness, incompleteness, ambiguities, and errors that we tolerate in everyday speech.

Hundreds of computer languages have been developed for different types of applications, different styles of expression, and different types of computers. Ideas about computing have progressed over the years, so modern programming languages are often more sophisticated than older ones. Pascal belongs to a family of languages derived from, and having many features in common with, an influential early language called *Algol*. *Algol-68*, *Modula-2*, and *C* are some other modern languages in this family.

The names of some computer languages are acronyms or abbreviations: Algol stands for "algorithmic language"; Fortran for "formula translator"; and PL/1 for "programming language one." Others are named after pioneers of the field: *Euler* for the great mathematician; and *Ada* for Ada Augusta, Countess of Lovelace, Lord Byron's illegitimate daughter, friend of Charles Babbage, and the first computer programmer. Pascal is named for the remarkable Blaise Pascal (1623–62): mathematical prodigy, author of *The Geometric Spirit*, inventor of calculating machines (the first, at the age of nineteen, to help his father

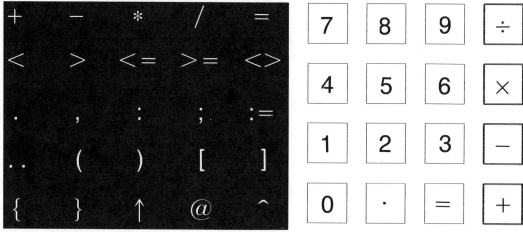

5-1. The symbols used in Pascal.

5-2. The keyboard of a four-function hand calculator, showing the four operator keys.

work out his tax), philosopher, theologian, and writer of breathtakingly lucid and elegant French prose. The name was chosen knowingly; Pascal syntax encourages an awareness of fundamental, computational principles, clarity and economy of expression, and a concern for logical elegance.

Notation and Vocabulary

Pascal, like any computer language, has a *vocabulary* of *symbols* and *reserved words* that are used to form meaningful *statements*. The symbols used in Pascal are shown in figure 5-1. They consist of *operators* and *delimiters*. The operators +, −, *, and / (add, subtract, multiply, and divide, respectively) are familiar to everybody who has worked with four-function hand calculators (fig. 5-2). Notice that the asterisk is used instead of a multiplication sign to denote multiplication; this avoids confusion with the letter x and is standard in programming languages. We will explain the other operators later in this chapter, as the need arises. The delimiters function much like punctuation marks in English sentences, or parentheses in mathematical expressions. For instance, a period signifies the end of a program, just as it signifies the end of a sentence. The reserved words used in Pascal are listed in figure 5-3. We will explain each of these as we proceed.

Pascal statements may contain not only symbols and reserved words, but also *identifiers*. These are names chosen by the programmer for programs, variables, and other entities to which a user must refer. For example, a program that draws a square might be called Square, and a variable might be called x. Think of memory as an array of pigeonholes containing entities that you will want to manipulate and identifiers as labels placed on the pigeonholes so that you can refer to them by name (fig. 5-4).

AND	MOD
ARRAY	NIL
BEGIN	NOT
CASE	OF
CONST	OR
DIV	PACKED
DO	PROCEDURE
DOWNTO	PROGRAM
ELSE	RECORD
END	REPEAT
FILE	SET
FOR	THEN
FORWARD	TO
FUNCTION	TYPE
GOTO	UNTIL
IF	VAR
IN	WHILE
LABEL	WITH

5-3. The Pascal reserved words.

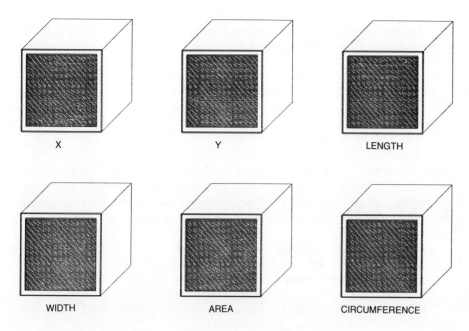

5-4. Identifiers are labels used to refer to entities stored in memory.

Under the conventions of Pascal, an identifier must begin with a letter, which may be followed by a string, of any length and in any sequence, of letters and digits. Some compilers recognize only the first eight characters, so if you are working with one of these, you must make sure that different identifiers are distinct in their first eight characters. Some versions of Pascal, however, recognize identifiers of up to thirty-one characters. Since use of longer identifiers often improves the readability of a program, we will use identifiers of up to sixteen characters in this book. Sometimes it is typographically convenient to insert a break in an identifer. Blank spaces are not allowed, however, so you must use an underscore thus: Villa_Malcontenta. The following are examples of acceptable identifiers:

```
X Y ROOT2 H20 TOM_KVAN TRIANGLE
VERY_VERY_VERY_LONG
```

The following are examples of unacceptable identifiers:

2ND	(begins with a numeral)
ROBIN LIGGETT	(contains a blank space)
SHEET.3	(contains a symbol)

Pascal also has some *standard identifiers*, which refer to entities predefined in Pascal (fig. 5-5). The list and form of standard identifiers may vary a little from compiler to compiler. In this book, we will use those shown; you should check them against the list for the compiler that you will be using. We shall return, later, to the uses of these standard identifiers. For the moment, you need only remember not to choose them as identifiers for anything other than the entities shown in figure 5-5.

ABS	PACK
ARCTAN	PAGE
BOOLEAN	PRED
CHAR	PUT
CHR	READ
COS	READLN
DISPOSE	REAL
EOF	RESET
EOLN	REWRITE
EXP	ROUND
FALSE	SIN
GET	SQR
INPUT	SQRT
INTEGER	SUCC
LN	TEXT
MAXINT	TRUE
NEW	TRUNC
ODD	UNPACK
ORD	WRITE
OUTPUT	WRITELN

5-5. Pascal standard identifiers.

THE PASCAL PROGRAMMING LANGUAGE **111**

Pascal statements may also contain *numbers*. We shall be concerned here with two *types* of numbers—*integers* written in the standard way, for example,

    1 23 992 1024 −10

and *real numbers* written in decimal notation thus:

    0.0 3.1412 1000.001 −10.0

At least one digit must precede the decimal point, where it is used, and one must follow it, but whole numbers may be written without the decimal point. Do not include commas when writing numbers, since Pascal uses commas as delimiters. The following are numbers written incorrectly in Pascal:

    .5   (no digit preceding the decimal point)
    5.   (no digit following the decimal point)
    1,000 (contains a comma)

It is allowable, and often convenient, to use another notation for very long real numbers. For example, the number

    123400000000000000000

may be expressed thus:

    1.234E20

E stands for *exponent* and means move the decimal point twenty places to the right. Similarly, the number

    0.00000000000000000001234

may be expressed:

    1.234E-20

Blanks and line breaks are used in Pascal as *separators*. At least one separator must be inserted between any pair of consecutive words or numbers, in order to avoid ambiguity. But separators cannot be inserted within words or numbers. Aside from these necessary restrictions, separators should be used freely to achieve typographic clarity in programs.

Standard Pascal allows the free use of both uppercase and lowercase characters for legibility and to accommodate stylistic preferences. Some Pascal programmers confine themselves to lowercase, others to uppercase, and some like to capitalize according to their own rules of typographic style. Here, in order to distinguish code clearly from other text, we will print it in uppercase and in a different typeface.

We shall also find it convenient to use **boldface** and *italic* as well as standard characters. In particular, Pascal reserved words and standard identifiers will be printed in boldface. Special text editors used for Pascal programming often do this automatically, which improves the legibility of a program. Interpreters and compilers ignore the distinction when processing Pascal code.

The following is an example of a simple Pascal statement that illustrates the conventions of notation and vocabulary that have now been introduced:

```
SUM := 2 + 3;
```

This means that the variable Sum is given the value of the result of adding the integers 2 and 3. The components of the expression are:

SUM	(name of a variable)
:=	(the assignment operator)
2	(integer number)
+	(the addition operator)
3	(integer number)
;	(delimiter, denoting end of statement)

Figure 5-6 illustrates the memory location denoted by Sum before and after execution of this statement. Here is another example:

```
CIRCUMFERENCE := DIAMETER * 3.1417;
```

In this case, the components are:

CIRCUMFERENCE	(name of a variable)
:=	(the assignment operator)
DIAMETER	(name of a variable)
*	(the multiplication operator)
3.1417	(real number)
;	(delimiter, denoting end of expression)

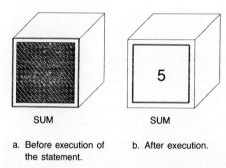

SUM   SUM

a. Before execution of the statement.   b. After execution.

5-6. Value stored in the memory location denoted by Sum.

Notice (fig. 5-7) that the value of the variable Circumference after execution of this statement will depend on the value of the variable Diameter before execution. Later, we shall make much use of statements like this:

```
SQUARE (X,Y,LENGTH);
```

This instructs the computer to draw a square of a specified Length at coordinates X, Y. Here the components are:

SQUARE	(name of a section of code that tells how to draw a square)
(	(delimiter)
X	(name of a variable)
,	(delimiter)
Y	(name of a variable)
,	(delimiter)
LENGTH	(name of a variable)
)	(delimiter)
;	(delimiter, denoting end of statement)

Syntax

The symbols, reserved words, identifiers, and numbers that constitute Pascal statements are put together according to certain rules of *syntax*. Rules of syntax also govern the ways in which statements themselves may be put

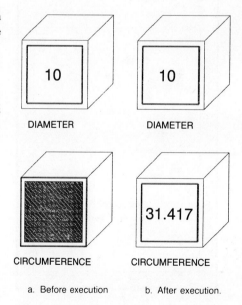

DIAMETER   DIAMETER

CIRCUMFERENCE   CIRCUMFERENCE

a. Before execution   b. After execution.

5-7. The result of execution of a statement.

together to form larger units of Pascal code. In other words, Pascal is a language, like English or French, with its own rules of grammar.

The rules of Pascal syntax are quite extensive and have numerous subtleties. These may either be expressed very rigorously and concisely using a notation system known as *BNF*, or else by means of *syntax diagrams*. The original definition of the Pascal language (Jensen and Wirth 1985) used these techniques.

BNF definitions and syntax diagrams are very clear and convenient for computer specialists, but they are intimidating and difficult to follow for the novice. We shall therefore introduce rules of syntax as we need them, and we shall illustrate each with examples that become increasingly complex and sophisticated as we progress—much in the manner of introductory French or Spanish texts. In this way you will gradually learn the structure and use of the language. You may eventually want to systematize your understanding by looking at the formal definition. We shall cover all the major features of Pascal syntax in this way, and if you work carefully through this book, including the exercises, you should become a competent Pascal programmer. However, we will not discuss all of the most esoteric details—particularly those that have only marginal relevance to graphics. For these you are referred to the original definition and to the Pascal texts listed in the Bibliography.

All of our examples will be programs and parts of programs that generate drawings on display devices or plotters, and we will approach programming from the viewpoint of the designer or graphic artist. That is, we shall analyze the logic of pictorial composition, then show how graphic compositional rules and principles correspond to constructs available in Pascal. You will learn to think about drawings in terms of these programming constructs—not only a useful technical skill, but profoundly illuminating in itself.

The General Organization of a Pascal Program

Any Pascal program has two essential parts: a description of the *data* to be operated upon, and a specification of the *actions* to be performed upon the data to achieve the desired result. Data are described by statements called *declarations* and *definitions*, whereas actions are specified by statements called *executable statements* or *commands*. In other words, declarations and definitions, like declarative English sentences, describe how something *is*. But executable statements, like imperative English sentences, specify something to be *done*. Both declarations and executable statements may be referred to, more generally, as *statements*.

A Pascal program is always divided into a *heading* and a *body*. The heading gives the program a name. The body, in turn, consists of a *declaration and definition part* followed by an *executable statement part*. Declarations and definitions are thus clearly segregated from executable statements. Figure 5-8 illustrates this organization.

The Heading

Here is an example of a heading:

```
PROGRAM TRIANGLE;
```

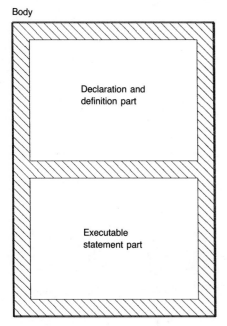

Heading

Name of program

Body

Declaration and definition part

Executable statement part

5-8. A Pascal program comprises a heading and a body. The body consists of the declaration and definition parts, followed by an executable statement part.

Headings consist of the reserved word **program**, followed by the chosen program name (in this case Triangle). A semicolon is used to denote that the heading is finished. You can name a program anything you like, but it is best to use clear, descriptive names.

To indicate that a program has **input** and **output**, or just **output** (fig. 5-9), some implementations of Pascal require a heading to look like this:

PROGRAM TRIANGLE (INPUT, OUTPUT);

or like this:

PROGRAM TRIANGLE (OUTPUT);

(A program with input but no **output** would not be very useful!) We will omit this here, and use the simpler form of heading.

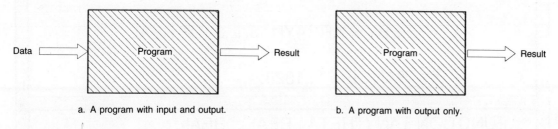

a. A program with input and output.   b. A program with output only.

5-9. Programs and data.

The Declaration and Definition Part

The declaration and definition part of a program, which immediately follows the heading, includes the following four subparts:

- constant definition part
- type definition part
- procedure and function declaration part
- variable declaration part

We shall usually follow the convention of giving the parts in this order. There are, however, some circumstances that require a different order; we shall discuss these as we encounter them. You do not always need all four parts in a given program, and you simply omit a part if it is not necessary.

Figure 5-10 illustrates the structure of the declaration and definition parts of a fairly complex program. Do not worry for the moment about what it all means. Just look at how the various parts are laid out.

The *constant definition part* looks like this:

CONSTANT PI = 3.1417;
         MODULE = 200;

```
PROGRAM BUILDING;

    USES GRAPHICS;
```

```
a. Constant definition part.
      CONST PI = 3.1417;
            MODULE = 200 ;
```

```
b. Type definition part.
      TYPE  GRAPHIC = RECORD
                VISIBLE : BOOLEAN;
                      X : REAL;
                      Y : REAL;
              END;


          THREEBY = ARRAY[1..3,1..3] OF REAL;


          XY_RANGE = 1..1023;
```

```
c. Procedure and function declaration part.
      FUNCTION TAN (THETA : REAL) : REAL;
          BEGIN
              TAN := SIN(THETA) / COS(THETA);
          END;


      PROCEDURE LINE (X1,Y1,X2,Y2 : INTEGER);
          BEGIN
              MOVE (X1,Y1);
              DRAW(X2,Y2);
          END;
```

```
      VAR X,Y,LENGTH : INTEGER;
          A,B : REAL;
```

d. Variable declaration part.

5-10. The structure of the declaration and definition parts of a program.

We use it when we want to establish constants (Pi and Module, in this case) for use in later calculations. It is omitted where there are no such constants. It begins with the reserved word **constant** (which can be abbreviated **const**), followed by any number of **constant** definitions. Each constant definition consists of a name, followed by the equality operator =, then an integer or real number, and finally the semicolon delimiter.

We shall defer discussion of the **type** definition part until later, as it will not be needed in our first, simple examples of Pascal programs. Procedures and functions are like miniature programs that can be invoked from within a program to perform a task. They must be defined in the *procedure and function declaration part* before they are used. We will come back to function declarations in chapter 6 and procedure declarations in chapter 7.

Every variable to be used in a Pascal program must be declared in a *variable declaration*, and this declaration must precede any use of the variable in the text of the program. Such variable declarations serve to reserve space in computer memory for values to be stored. In order to do this, we must specify not only the *name* of each variable, but also its *type*; for example, **integer** or **real** number. Thus the variable declaration part looks like this:

```
VAR  X,Y,LENGTH:  INTEGER;
     A,B:  REAL;
```

It begins with the reserved word **var**. Names of variables are then listed, separated by commas. A colon terminates the list, and this is followed by a reserved word that specifies type, then the semicolon delimiter.

Pascal Data Types

Pascal recognizes certain very specific types of data that may be stored in memory and operated upon by a program. We have already encountered the types **integer** and **real**. Let us now consider these in more detail.

The arithmetic of **integers** has certain rules, and these are reflected in the definitions of Pascal operators that can apply to **integers**. For example, the operators

*	multiply
+	add
−	subtract

always yield **integers** when applied to **integers**, but the operator

/   divide

will yield a **real** number. One way to assure an **integer** result from division, however, is to use:

DIV   divide and truncate

in place of /.

When at least one of the operands (numbers operated upon) of the multiply, add, or subtract operators is of type **real**, the result is always a **real** number. With the divide operator, the result is **real** even if both operands are **integers**, and the result turns out to be a whole number. Logical inconsistencies and errors follow if such rules (and there are many more of them, as we shall later see) are not rigorously followed. You will generate an error message if you attempt to inappropriately apply an operator.

Many personal computers represent **integers** by two bytes (sixteen bits) of information; this means that **integer** variables are limited to values from $-32,767$ to $+32,767$. Larger computers may use four bytes, or more, and so extend this range. Any version of Pascal has a built-in constant, called **maxint**, which represents the largest possible **integer** value.

Real numbers can have an indefinitely long decimal part, but can be represented only to a finite number of decimal places (that is, to finite *precision*) in a computer. Thus the value of

1.0/3.0

in Pascal is not the infinite sequence

0.333 . . .

but a finite sequence, the length of which may vary from computer to computer.

A third data type in Pascal is called **Boolean**. A variable of this type stores the logical values **false** and **true**. You cannot apply arithmetic operators, such as * and + to a **Boolean** variable, and of course you cannot give an **integer** or **real** value to a **Boolean** variable. But you can, for example, form expressions out of **Boolean** variables and logical operators such as:

AND   logical conjunction
OR   logical disjunction
NOT   logical negation

In other words, you can do **Boolean** logic in Pascal programs with **Boolean** variables—just as you can do **integer** arithmetic with **integer** variables and **real** arithmetic with **real** variables. We shall consider some interesting applications of **Boolean** variables and logical operators in chapter 11.

A fourth Pascal data type is **char** (character). A variable of this type stores a single text character. **Char** variables are used in programs that manipulate text. Since this book is mostly concerned with graphics, we will rarely use **char** variables.

There is much more to be said about Pascal data types, but this will suffice to introduce them. We will take up the topic again in chapter 13 when we consider the storage of drawings in data structures.

The Executable Statement Part

The *executable statement* part of a Pascal program begins with the reserved word **begin**, which is followed by at least one executable statement (that is, the computer must be instructed to do *something*), then the reserved word **end**—followed by a period, which terminates the program.

PROGRAM RECTANGLE;

```
{ This program calculates the area of a rectangle }

{ Variable definitions }
  VAR  LENGTH,WIDTH,AREA  :  INTEGER;

{ The executable statement part }
  BEGIN

    { Give values to length and width }
      LENGTH  : =  50;
      WIDTH  : =  20;

    { Calculate area }
      AREA  : =  LENGTH  *  WIDTH;

    { Print out the result }
      WRITELN  (AREA);

  END.
```

The statements between **begin** and **end** are executed by the computer in the sequence in which they are written. In our example, the first two executable statements give values to the variables Length and Width, respectively. The computer is then instructed to calculate the Area of the rectangle and print the results.

Note the way that the variables are handled. First they are named and typed in the declaration and definition part. This sets aside space in memory for storing values, but leaves values undefined. Within the executable statement part of a program, variables may be given values. When a variable is given a value, an **integer**, a **real** number, a **Boolean** value, or a **char** value (depending on the type of variable) is stored in the corresponding location. Once a variable has been given a value, this value may be used in executable statements. When a variable's value is used, the computer looks in the memory location identified by the variable name and retrieves the value stored at that location. Finally, in this example, the statement **writeln** (Area) causes the computer to look in the memory location labeled Area and print out what it finds there.

To understand our example program in these terms, imagine three empty memory locations:

The variable definition part of our program labels each one and specifies the type of data that can be stored there:

```
┌──────────┐ LENGTH  (integer)
├──────────┤ WIDTH   (integer)
└──────────┘ AREA    (integer)
```

Execution of the statement Length : = 50; generates the following result:

```
┌─── 5 0 ──┐ LENGTH  (integer)
├──────────┤ WIDTH   (integer)
└──────────┘ AREA    (integer)
```

Then execution of Width := 20; gives the result:

```
  5 0  LENGTH  (integer)
  2 0  WIDTH   (integer)
        AREA    (integer)
```

Next, execution of Area := Length * Width; gives the result:

```
    5 0  LENGTH  (integer)
    2 0  WIDTH   (integer)
1 0 0 0  AREA    (integer)
```

Some basic rules of program organization and use of variables have now been illustrated. They may be summarized as follows:

- A variable cannot be given a value or otherwise used in an executable statement until it has been named and typed in the declaration and definition part. If an attempt were made to use a value of a variable that had not yet been declared, the computer would not know where in memory to look for it. If an attempt were made to store a value of a variable that had not yet been declared, the computer would not know where to put it.
- The type of a variable cannot be changed; each variable declared in a program must have a single type throughout that program.
- A value of one type may not be given to a variable of another. This would be like putting a square peg in a round hole. If it were allowed, it would lead to logical inconsistencies.
- A variable may not be used in an executable statement unless the execution of the statement gives it a value, or unless it has already been given a value by the execution of a previous statement. If it were used without having been given a value, the computer would look in the memory location identified by the variable name and find nothing there.
- Certain rules, following from the logical properties of various types of data, must be followed in expressions that manipulate the values of variables.

Pascal is distinguished from many other programming languages by the comprehensiveness and rigor of its rules governing data types; it is a *strongly typed* language. This discipline can seem burdensome at first, but it provides a very effective way to eliminate programming errors. The compiler or interpreter can detect and report typographic errors in variable names (an extremely common source of problems in programs) by checking all variable names in the executable statement part against the declarations in the declaration and definition part. If a programmer attempts a meaningless operation, such as dividing an **integer** value by a **Boolean** value, this can also be detected and reported as a syntax error.

Assignment

Against this background, let us now look more carefully at the sorts of executable statements that appear in our example program. The most fundamental of all executable statements is the *assignment statement*, which assigns a value defined on the right side of the statement to the variable named on the left side. Here is an example:

```
LENGTH := 50;
```

We have, first, the name of a variable, followed by the *assignment operator* :=, then a number, and finally the semicolon delimiter.

The assignment operator := should not be confused with the equality operator =, which as we shall see later, has its uses in logical expressions. The assignment operator is pronounced *gets*, while the equality operator is pronounced *equals*.

In this example, an **integer** value is assigned to an **integer** variable. Similarly, a **real** value can be assigned to a **real** variable,

```
A_REAL := 3.14159;
```

a **Boolean** value can be assigned to a **Boolean** variable,

```
BEAUTIFUL := TRUE;
MAYBE := FALSE;
```

and a character can be assigned to a **char** variable,

```
ANSWER := 'Y';
```

Notice that the character must be delimited by single quotes, as shown.

Whereas declaration of a variable is like creating and labeling an empty pigeonhole, assignment is the operation of putting something in that pigeonhole. There must be a proper fit; types must match.

Arithmetic

Instead of a single number on the right side of an assignment statement, as in the examples above, there may be an *arithmetic expression* constructed using the arithmetic operators available in Pascal:

```
LENGTH := 3 + 4 - 5;
```

In this case, the expression is first *evaluated* by the computer, then the *result* is assigned to the variable. So this statement is equivalent to:

```
LENGTH := 2;
```

In general, an arithmetic expression is a rule for calculating a value by applying arithmetic operators according to the standard conventions of algebra. The most fundamental arithmetic operators in Pascal are those of a four-function calculator:

```
*     multiply
/     divide
+     add
-     subtract
```

To these Pascal adds divide and truncate (**div**), so that it can handle integer arithmetic. These operators are used, as shown below, to form expressions:

Expression	Value
2 + 3 * 4	14
3.785 / 9.001	0.421
2 * 3 − 4 * 5	−14
17 DIV 3 * 3	15
1 DIV 2	0

Another operator provided by Pascal, which we sometimes need in integer arithmetic, is **mod**. This function yields the integer division remainder, for example:

Expression	Value
33 MOD 4	1
22 MOD 10	2
10 MOD 11	10

Mixed mode arithmetic, in which some operands in an arithmetic expression are **integer** and some are **real**, is allowed in Pascal and is sometimes convenient. Here are the rules that govern:

Allowable operand types	Type of result
integer * integer	integer
integer * real	real
real * integer	real
real * real	real
integer / integer	real
integer / real	real
real / integer	real
real / real	real
integer + integer	integer
integer + real	real
real + integer	real
real + real	real
integer − integer	integer
integer − real	real
real − integer	real
real − real	real

These rules may seem arbitrary at first, but they follow directly from sound mathematical thinking. The **integer**s form a proper subset of the **real** numbers, so we can always use an **integer** as an operand. But you can only be sure of an **integer** result under certain circumstances. If it is not certain that a result will be an **integer**, then Pascal takes the safe position and presumes that the result is **real**.

Parentheses may be used, in the usual way, to group subexpressions— either where this is necessary to define how the expression is to be evaluated, or where it is not strictly necessary, but makes the expression easier to understand. Here are some examples:

Expression	Result
2 + (3 * 4)	14
(2 + 3) * 4	20
(2 + 3) − (4 * 5)	−15
2 * (3 − 4) * 5	−10
2 * ((3 − 4) + (5 * 6)) − 7	51

Certain conventions of *operator precedence* are followed in the evaluation of expressions. These may be summarized as follows:

- The computer scans the expression from left to right.
- Whenever an operand has an operator on both sides, for example, the number 2 in the expression 1 + 2 * 3, a priority scheme is applied. The multiplying operators *, /, and, **div** all have the same, highest priority. The adding operators + and − both have the same lower priority. Thus, the expression 1 + 2 * 3 is equivalent to 1 + (2 * 3).
- Parentheses may be used to remove ambiguity, or to change the priority that would result from the conventions of left-to-right evaluation and the priority scheme. For example, use of parentheses in the expression 1 + (2 * 3) merely removes ambiguity, whereas the use of parentheses in the expression (1 + 2) * 3 changes the priority.
- An expression enclosed within parentheses is evaluated independently of succeeding or preceding operators. Expressions with nested parentheses are evaluated from the inside out. Thus the expression:

$$2 * ((3 − 4) + (5 * 6)) − 7$$

is first reduced to:

$$2 * (−1 + 30) − 7$$

Next, it is reduced to:

$$2 * 29 − 7$$

Then, by left-to-right scanning and operator priority, we get:

$$58 − 7$$

Finally, subtraction yields the result:

$$51$$

This is illustrated by the tree diagram in figure 5-11.

- Consecutive multiplication and/or division operations are performed from left to right.
- Consecutive addition and/or subtraction operations are performed from left to right.

Novice programmers often confuse these rules. When in doubt, use parentheses for clarification. Never write an expression that leaves you unsure about how it will be evaluated. And never make the reader of a program puzzle about what an expression means.

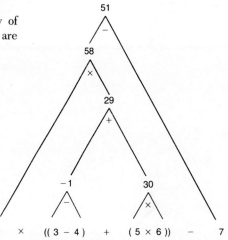

5-11. Evaluating an arithmetic expression according to the rules of operator precedence.

Provided that values have been assigned to them, variables may be used in arithmetic expressions, for example:

```
LENGTH * WIDTH
(X + Y) * 5
2 * PI * RADIUS
```

A name appearing in an expression may also be a **constant** that has previously been defined.

It is often clearer (and therefore better) to write a sequence of assignment statements with simple arithmetic expressions on the right-hand sides, rather than a single assignment statement with a complicated expression on the right-hand side. For example, we might write:

```
X := A + B − C;
Y := D * (E + F);
Z := (X + Y) * 5;
```

in place of the equivalent:

```
Z := ((A + B − C) + (D * (E − F))) * 5;
```

Where there are many parentheses, as in this last example, you have to make sure that they balance. Each left parenthesis must have a corresponding right parenthesis. An expression like the following, with unbalanced parentheses, infringes on the rules of Pascal syntax, has no clear meaning, cannot be evaluated, and generates an error message:

```
Z := ((A + B − C) + (D * E − F))) * 5;
```

In general, as a matter of good programming style, code describing arithmetic calculations should read easily and naturally and should explain itself to the reader. You should express well-known formulas in familiar ways, use parentheses judiciously, and break up complicated expressions.

So far we have, for clarity, used simple examples to illustrate the use of arithmetic expressions in Pascal. You do not need a computer to evaluate them. But the point, of course, is that a computer can evaluate even a very complex arithmetic expression extremely rapidly, and that it can repeatedly evaluate an expression for different values of the variables. Here, for example, is a program that does some fairly complicated arithmetic (fig. 5-12):

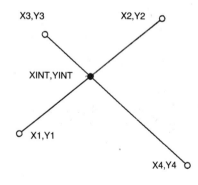

5-12. The intersection of two lines.

```
PROGRAM INTERSECT;
  { Finds the point of intersection of two straight
    lines defined by end point coordinates
    (X1, Y1), (X2, Y2) and (X3, Y3), (X4, Y4). }

  VAR X1,Y1,X2,Y2,X3,Y3,X4,Y4,
      A1,A2,B1,B2,XINT,YINT : REAL;

  BEGIN
    { Specify coordinates of endpoints of line. }
```

```
X1 := 100;
Y1 := 200;
X2 := 500;
Y2 := 500;
X3 := 200;
Y3 := 450;
X4 := 600;
Y4 := 100;

{ Determine slope of each line. }

B1 := (Y2 - Y1) / (X2 - X1);
B2 := (Y4 - Y3) / (X4 - X3);

{ Determine intercept of each line. }

A1 := Y1 - B1 * X1;
A2 := Y3 - B2 * X3;

{ Calculate coordinates of intersection. }

XINT := (A1 - A2) / (B2 - B1);
YINT := A1 + B1 * XINT;

WRITELN (XINT: 8:2; YINT: 8:2);

END.
```

To get a feel for the amount of work that the computer must do to execute this program, you should work through the code line by line using a hand calculator. Now imagine executing it thousands of times for different pairs of lines (that is, different initial values for the variables X1, Y1, X2, Y2, X3, Y3, X4, Y4).

It was a desire to eliminate the drudgery of routine, repetitive arithmetic calculations that motivated the nineteenth-century mathematician Charles Babbage to attempt to construct the first working computer. Draftsmen frequently have to perform routine arithmetic to find the correct coordinates for points and lines in drawings. In the past they used slide rules, now they mostly use pocket calculators. We shall see here how the powerful arithmetic capabilties of Pascal enable us to automate the draftsman's calculations needed to produce drawings.

Alphanumeric Output

Programs operate upon data in order to produce output that, as we have seen, can take many different forms: numbers displayed on a screen; printed text; drawings; audible speech; music; or even three-dimensional objects milled on numerically controlled machines. Ancient usage, revived in the computer era, made "output" a verb; originally (according to the *Oxford English Dictionary*) it meant to expel sinners from paradise. Now it means to transfer data from memory to an output device that displays or prints it. Programming languages, then, provide *output statements*.

The simplest form of output statement in Pascal looks like this:

```
WRITELN (X);
```

This writes out the value of the variable X. If X is an **integer** variable with a current value of 100, for example, the resulting output will look like this:

```
100
```

Often it is convenient to associate some text with an output value, so that we know what we are getting. This can be accomplished by including the required text, between single quotation marks, in the **writeln** statement. For example, the statement:

```
WRITELN ('THE VALUE OF X IS ', X);
```

generates the output:

```
THE VALUE OF X IS 100
```

To illustrate the use of simple output statements, here is an example of a program that performs some **integer** arithmetic and prints out the results:

```
PROGRAM SQUARE;
     VAR SIDE,AREA,PERIMETER : INTEGER;
    BEGIN
         SIDE := 5;
         AREA := SIDE * SIDE;
         PERIMETER := 4 * SIDE;

         WRITELN ('FOR A SQUARE OF SIDE ', SIDE);
         WRITELN ('THE AREA IS ', AREA);
         WRITELN ('THE PERIMETER IS ', PERIMETER);
    END.
```

You should be able to see that output from this program will look like this:

```
FOR A SQUARE OF SIDE 5
THE AREA IS 25
THE PERIMETER IS 20
```

Output of **real** numbers is slightly more complicated, since we must specify how many digits we want to follow the decimal point. The most convenient way to approach this is to write expressions of the following form:

```
WRITELN (X: 8:2);
```

Here X is the variable, the number 8 indicates that the value of X is to be printed (right justified) in an eight-column field, and 2 indicates that two digits follow the decimal point. Thus, according to the value of X, this **writeln** statement will produce output such as:

```
123.56
10.91
0.00
```

(Note, if two decimal places are required, the minimum field length is 4, since there must always be a column for a leading zero and one for the decimal point.)

Here, now, is an example of a Pascal program that does some **real** arithmetic and prints out the results:

```
PROGRAM CIRCLE;
    CONST PI = 3.1415;
    VAR RADIUS,AREA,CIRCUMFERENCE : REAL;

    BEGIN
        RADIUS := 5;
        AREA := PI * RADIUS * RADIUS;
        CIRCUMFERENCE := 2 * PI * RADIUS;

        WRITELN ('FOR A CIRCLE OF RADIUS', RADIUS: 8:2);
        WRITELN ('THE AREA IS', AREA: 8:2);
        WRITELN ('THE CIRCUMFERENCE IS',
                    CIRCUMFERENCE: 8:2);

    END.
```

A little work with a calculator will show you that the output will look like this:

```
FOR A CIRCLE OF RADIUS      5.00
THE AREA IS    78.54
THE CIRCUMFERENCE IS      31.42
```

If you wanted fewer leading blanks and more decimal places, you might change the formats from 8:2 to 7:3. This would give the following result:

```
FOR A CIRCLE OF RADIUS  5.000
THE AREA IS 78.537
THE CIRCUMFERENCE IS 31.415
```

This is hard to read, so you might insert the appropriate number of blanks between the quotes in the **writeln** statements to yield:

```
FOR A CIRCLE OF RADIUS  5.000
THE AREA IS              78.537
THE CIRCUMFERENCE IS  31.415
```

There is much more to be said about the output of numbers and text in Pascal. However, we shall be concerned essentially with graphic output in this book, so we shall not pursue further the topic of alphanumeric output. If you are interested in more details, most Pascal texts provide an extensive treatment.

Graphic Output

Standard Pascal does not include statements to generate graphic output, but many popular implementations of Pascal do. Since they are not standard, these statements take different forms in different implementations. In this book, we shall use graphic output statements of the form:

MOVE (X,Y);

This moves an electron beam or plotter pen invisibly to the position (X,Y). The statement

DRAW (X,Y);

draws a line from the current location of the beam or pen to the location (X, Y). We shall consider this again, in much more detail, in the next chapter.

Input

All of the programs that we have considered so far have output but no input. Programs may also be written to *process* data; these take data as input and operate on it to produce output (fig. 5-13).

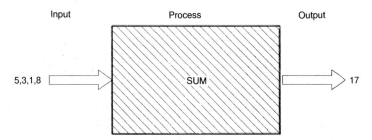

5-13. A program that processes data—a sequence of numbers is the input, and their sum is the output.

A Pascal input statement in its simplest form looks like this:

READLN (A,B,C);

The standard identifier **readln** is followed by a list of variables enclosed in parentheses. This is used to read numbers typed in a single line at a terminal. Here is an example of a program that reads in three **integer**s, adds them, and outputs the result:

```
PROGRAM SUMINTEGERS;
    VAR A,B,C,D : INTEGER;
    BEGIN
        WRITELN ('TYPE IN 3 INTEGERS');
        READLN (A,B,C);

        D := A + B + C;

        WRITELN ('THE SUM IS ', D);
    END.
```

A user of this program first sees displayed on the screen the message:

TYPE IN 3 INTEGERS

If he or she then types

100 25 3

the output will be:

THE SUM IS 128

The **readln** statement may also be used for input of **real** numbers. So we might rewrite our example program as follows:

```
PROGRAM SUMREALS;
    VAR A,B,C,D : REAL;
    BEGIN
        WRITELN ('TYPE IN 3 REAL NUMBERS');
        READLN (A,B,C);
        D := A + B + C;
        WRITELN ('THE SUM IS', D: 6:2);
    END.
```

Now a user of the program first sees displayed on the screen the message:

TYPE IN 3 REAL NUMBERS

If he or she then types

3.1415 99.999 83.1

the following output will result:

THE SUM IS 186.24

You can see from these examples how a computer might save a draftsman a great deal of work. Imagine, for instance, that an architectural draftsman is designing a series of elliptical rooms and must know the floor area and perimeter of each. The following program takes as input the lengths of the minor and major axes and prints out the area and perimeter:

```
PROGRAM ELLIPSE;
    CONST PI = 3.1415;
    VAR MINOR,MAJOR,AREA,PERIMETER : REAL;
    BEGIN
        WRITELN ('TYPE IN THE LENGTHS OF THE MAJOR ',
                 'AND MINOR AXIS OF THE ELLIPSE');
```

```
READLN  (MAJOR,MINOR);
AREA  :=  PI  *  MINOR  *  MAJOR;
PERIMETER  :=  2  *  PI  *  SQRT  ((SQR(MINOR)
                        +  SQR(MAJOR))  /  2);

WRITELN  ('THE  AREA  IS  ',  AREA:  10:2);
WRITELN  ('THE  PERIMETER  IS  ',  PERIMETER:  10:2);
END.
```

The draftsman can use this program, whenever needed, to perform the tedious, time-consuming, and error-prone process of evaluating the complex formula for each new set of input values.

In addition to the **readln** and **writeln** statements that we have introduced, standard Pascal also provides **read**, **write**, **get**, **put**, and **page**. You may need to use these if you want to program more elaborate input and output operations. They are discussed in detail in the Pascal texts listed in the Bibliography.

Proper Punctuation

We have now introduced enough of the basic features of Pascal to enable you to write simple programs. You should try a few to get the feel of programming; the exercises at the end of this chapter offer some suggestions. You must, however, make correct use of the symbols and words that function as delimiters in Pascal, or errors will result. Here are a few important rules to keep in mind:

- The word **program** at the start of a program must be matched by a period at the end.
- The word **begin** at the beginning of the executable statement part must be matched by the word **end** at the end.
- Left and right parentheses must balance, and parentheses must not be left open.
- The semicolon must always be used to end a declaration or an executable statement.
- Colons and commas are used much as they are used in English sentences. A colon usually keeps apart things of different kinds. Commas are used to separate elements in a list. Lists are often enclosed in parentheses.
- Do not include blank spaces and ends of lines where they are not allowed.

Explaining a Program with Comments

You will have noticed in our example programs lowercase text between curly brackets, like this:

{ *This is a comment.* }

Such text is known as a *comment*. The interpreter or compiler simply ignores everything between the delimiter { and the delimiter } when executing a program. This provides a way to insert explanatory English text into Pascal code. The following example shows how comments can be used to explain the purpose and logic of a program.

```
PROGRAM CONVERT; { Converts feet to meters. }
   VAR FEET,METERS : REAL;
   BEGIN

      { Obtain input in feet. }
         WRITELN ('ENTER MEASUREMENT IN FEET');
         READLN (FEET);

      { Apply conversion formula. }
         METERS := FEET * 0.3048;

      { Print output. }
         WRITELN ('VALUE IN METERS IS', METERS: 8:2);
   END.
```

Since comments are in English, not in Pascal, we shall follow the convention of using lowercase characters with normal English capitalization and printing them in italics to clearly distinguish them from Pascal code.

Some computers do not provide curly brackets, so Pascal implementations on them must use some other symbol for comment delimiters, for example:

```
(*This is a comment.*)
```

You should check the symbol used in your Pascal implementation.

A program should include enough comments to make it *self-documenting*. In other words, it should be possible to read a program and see immediately what it does and how.

Typographic Style

Pascal allows a great deal of freedom in the layout of a program on the page. You should take advantage of this to achieve maximum readability and typographic attractiveness. In particular, make use of blank lines and indentation (as in our examples here) to clarify the organization of your programs. A standard convention, which we have followed in our examples so far, is to indent **var**, **begin**, and **end** from the heading, then further indent the lines of code between. As we introduce additional programming constructs, we shall illustrate the associated indentation conventions.

If you work with a general purpose text editor, you must know the indentation conventions and take care to follow them. Some special editors for Pascal remove this burden by automatically indenting lines, inserting **end**s to correspond to **begin**s, and printing reserved words in boldface.

Clarity and Verifiability

Just as there are usually many ways to express the same thought in English, there are usually different but logically equivalent ways to write Pascal code. Some programmers delight in writing masses of complex, impressive-looking statements, the effects of which are almost impossible to decipher. This makes errors difficult to find and correct, causes considerable frustration to a reader trying to figure out what programs do and how they work, and is inconsiderate to those who may later have to work on your programs to modify or correct them. Complex statements should be avoided; a good programmer has a Zen-like reverence for perfect simplicity of expression.

A program must not only work correctly, you must also be able to demonstrate that it does so. To this end, a good general principle to follow is to break down the code into short, easily understandable and verifiable pieces, which reflect the logic of the computation that is to be carried out. Judicious use of functions and procedures—Pascal constructs that we shall introduce in later chapters—facilitates this.

Be particularly careful about the names you choose for programs, variables, constants, functions, and procedures. Wherever possible, names should be descriptive. (It is infuriating to attempt to read a program in which variable and other names make no sense.) Where there is any possibility of ambiguity in names, write comments to make things clear.

You may have heard from computer enthusiasts that programmers must spend a lot of time debugging—tracking down and eliminating errors in programs. Good programmers do not; they eliminate bugs by programming in a style that minimizes the possibility of errors and that makes finding and correcting any errors that do occur a quick and simple process. In programming, as in other crafts, good style pays off.

Summary

We have now introduced the basics of Pascal: how a program is set out; how variables and constants are declared; how numbers may be input; how arithmetic may be performed; and how results may be output. At this point you know enough to write a simple Pascal program. Try a few before going further to make sure that you understand the fundamentals. In the next chapter, we shall begin to consider programs that generate drawings.

Good luck!

Exercises

1. Write a program that, when executed, displays your name on the screen.

2. Write a program that assigns **integer** values to the Length, Width, and Height of a rectangular box, calculates Volume and Surface_area, and writes out the values of all five variables.

3. Modify this program to read in the values for Length, Width, and Height.

4. The area of a triangle is half its base multiplied by its height. Write a program that reads in **integer** values for these dimensions, uses the **div** function to calculate area, and writes out the result.

5. The formula for the volume of a sphere is $\frac{4}{3}\pi R^3$, where R is the radius, and π is 3.1415. The formula for surface area is $4\pi R^2$. Write a program that reads in a **real** number value for the radius and writes out values for volume and surface area.

6. Figure 5-14 shows the plan and two elevations of a *hip roof*, with associated design variables. Take the cost per square foot of roofing material as an additional variable. Write a program that reads in values for the variables and calculates the cost of a roof.

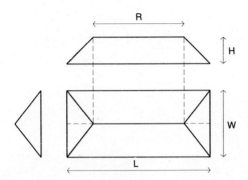

5-14. A hip roof.

6.

Programs to Generate
Simple Line Drawings

Now that you know the notational conventions of Pascal and the way to organize a Pascal program, you can write some elementary programs to generate drawings. We will begin with very simple, two-dimensional line drawings constructed from vectors in a screen coordinate system.

The Screen Coordinate System

In the discussions that follow (until chapter 14), we shall assume a screen coordinate system, in pixels, with the origin at the bottom-left corner (fig. 6-1). Note that this means that coordinates are always positive **integer**s.

For purposes of discussion, we shall assume that we are using a display with a resolution of 1,024 by 1,024 square pixels. This allows a coordinate to be specified with ten bits of information and has become standard. We will adopt the convention that a pixel is described by the coordinates of its bottom-left corner (fig. 6-2). Thus we begin numbering pixels at 0 and end at 1,023.

Not all displays follow these conventions. Some of the other screen formats used are shown in figure 6-3. A Tektronix storage tube uses a 1,024 by 780 coordinate system, for instance, and many low-cost personal computers have lower resolutions—typically 512 by 512, or 256 by 256. An Apple Macintosh has a 512 by 342 pixel system, with the origin at the top-left rather than the bottom-left corner. An IBM PC in high-resolution mode has 640 by 200 rectangular pixels with a top-left origin. Do not worry, though, if you will be using a display that is not 1,024 by 1,024 pixels. Later, in chapter 7, we will show you how to handle this.

If your system has windows for text and graphic output, think of the graphic window as the display surface, with the origin at its bottom-left corner (fig. 6-4). You will find it most convenient to use a square window and to make it as large as possible.

You will find it helpful when programming with a screen coordinate system to use a 1,024 by 1,024 graph-paper grid, with coordinate values marked along the axes, to sketch out your graphic ideas (fig. 6-5). You should make some copies and use these as required.

Origin

6-1. The origin of the coordinate system.

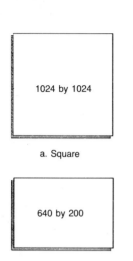

a. Square

1024 by 1024

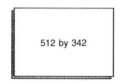

640 by 200

b. IBM PC, 640 by 200 rectangular pixels.

512 by 342

c. Apple Macintosh, 512 by 342.

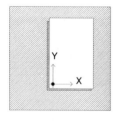

1024 by 780

d. Tektronix storage tube, 1,024 by 780.

6-3. Some display-screen formats.

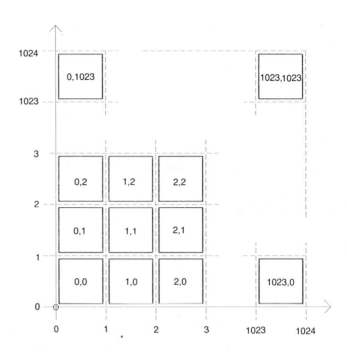

6-2. A pixel is described by the coordinates of its bottom-left corner.

Clipping to the Screen Boundaries

Some graphic compositions consist of motifs fully contained within the boundaries of the picture plane (fig. 6-6a), while others imply the existence of a larger whole by clipping motifs to the edges of the picture plane (figure 6-6b). When a screen coordinate system serves as the picture plane, clipped motifs have vectors with at least one endpoint off the screen (fig. 6-7). What actually happens when an attempt is made to draw off the screen varies from device to device. Some produce unpredictable, unwanted effects, whereas others automatically clip vectors to screen boundaries (fig. 6-8). You should check whether the device you will be using provides automatic clipping. If it does not, you will have to take special care in your programs never to start or end a vector outside the boundaries of the screen. In any case, you should always take care about the placement of your drawings relative to the screen boundary, just as you would carefully consider the positioning of a drawing on a sheet of paper.

If you are working with a device of lower resolution than 1,024 by 1,024, or with a screen of a different shape, you may find that some of the example programs that we discuss would draw vectors off your screen. You can easily adjust them to eliminate this difficulty.

Primitive Graphic Commands

We shall be using two commands called **move** and **draw** (fig. 6-9) to create drawings by moving a drawing instrument around in the screen coordinate system. To move the instrument invisibly from wherever it is to a position

6-4. A graphic window.

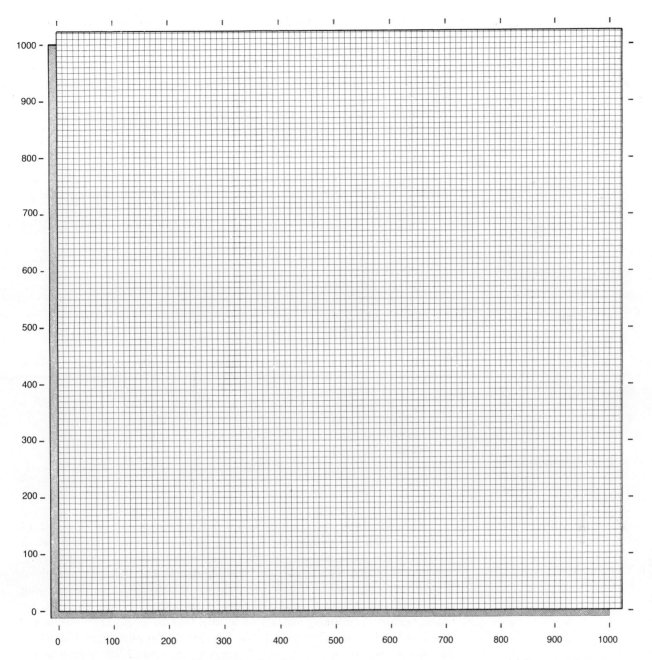

6-5. A 1,024 by 1,024 grid for use in sketching graphic ideas.

6-6. Clipping in graphic composition.

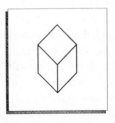

a. A motif fully contained within the boundaries of the picture plane.

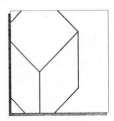

b. A motif clipped to the edges of the picture plane to imply the existence of a larger whole.

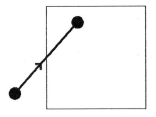

a. Begins off screen.

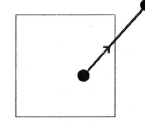

b. Ends off screen.

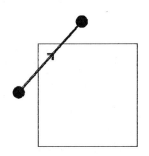

c. Begins and ends off screen.

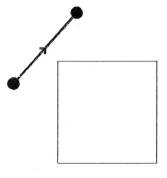

d. Exists entirely off screen.

6-7. Vectors drawn off the screen.

(X, Y) in the screen coordinate system, we write a statement of the form

   MOVE (X,Y);

where X is an **integer** in the range 0 to 1,023, and Y is an **integer** in the range 0 to 1,023.

To draw a vector from the current position of the drawing instrument to a position (X,Y), we write a statement of the form

   DRAW (X,Y);

where X is an **integer** in the range 0 to 1,023, and Y is an **integer** in the range 0 to 1,023.

Thus the sequence of statements to draw the square shown in figure 6-10 is written:

   MOVE (400,200);
   DRAW (700,200);
   DRAW (700,500);
   DRAW (400,500);
   DRAW (400,200);

The sequence of statements to draw the cross shown in figure 6-11 is written:

   MOVE (400,200);
   DRAW (700,500);
   MOVE (700,200);
   DRAW (400,500);

Move and **draw**, then, are *primitive marking operations*, much as a hand movement with the pencil raised, and a hand movement with the pencil lowered to the paper surface, are the primitive operations in making a pencil drawing. They allow us to construct a drawing directly out of graphic primitives; that is, vector by vector. If the output device is a storage tube, the drawing instrument controlled by **move** and **draw** commands is, in fact, the electron beam; vectors are actually traced out by the electron beam in the sequence specified by the code. With a refreshed vector display, the effect is to store data describing vectors in the display memory from which the screen image is generated and refreshed. If output is on a raster display, the effect is to write pixel values into the frame buffer, so that vectors mapped onto the raster grid are displayed. In any case, however, it is convenient to think of **move** and **draw** as commands for moving the point of a drawing instrument across the surface of the screen.

The **draw** command makes no provision for controlling line thickness, intensity, pattern, or color, and we will not introduce these additional graphic variables into our examples. You may, however, wish to do so in your programs, and the system you are using may allow this. You should consult the documentation for your system to see what capabilities are provided. In general, you should find that it is straightforward to elaborate programs in this way.

Starting and Finishing Drawings

With conventional graphic media there are certain preparations that you must make before you can actually start work on a drawing—setting up a drawing board, cleaning a blackboard, sharpening pencils, or cleaning brushes. Similarly there are certain things that you need to do when you finish a drawing—spraying it with fixative, perhaps, or making a print and cleaning up your work space.

It is the same with a computer graphics system; certain preparations might need to be made before you begin displaying vectors, and some things must be done when you have finished. We shall accomplish this by use of a command called **start_drawing**, which is given immediately before the first **move** or **draw** in a program, and another called **finish_drawing**, which is given immediately after the last **move** or **draw**. Thus the code to prepare for drawing our example square (see fig. 6-10), to draw it, then to clean up afterward, looks like this:

```
START_DRAWING;

    MOVE  (400,200);
    DRAW  (700,200);
    DRAW  (700,500);
    DRAW  (400,500);
    DRAW  (400,200);

FINISH_DRAWING;
```

The visible effect of **start_drawing** is to clear the screen, or open a graphic window, so that a clear working surface is available. You need not worry about how **start_drawing** and **finish_drawing** actually work. (If you have some technical background and are interested, this is discussed in the Appendix.) In any case, they will perform different tasks as needed in different computational environments. But you must always use them as indicated. If you do not, your program may run, but there is a danger of getting unexpected results.

Announcement of External Graphics Procedures

These basic graphic commands—**move**, **draw**, **start_drawing**, **finish_drawing**—are not part of the Pascal language itself. Technically they are known as *external procedures*, and any program that uses them must contain, immediately following the heading, the following announcement:

```
USES  GRAPHICS;
```

These external procedures must be implemented on your computer before you can use them in Pascal programs. This is done in different ways for different Pascal systems: the Appendix provides detailed implementation instructions.

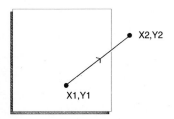

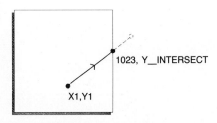

6-8. Automatic clipping of vectors to the screen boundaries.

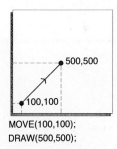

6-9. The use of **move** and **draw** commands to draw a vector between two points.

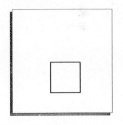

6-10. A square produced by **move** and **draw** operations.

6-11. A cross produced by **move** and **draw** operations.

A Complete Graphics Program

We are now in a position to write a very simple but complete graphics program. The following is our example. It announces the graphics tools that will be used (the external procedures), makes the necessary preparations to draw a picture, uses **moves** and **draws** to produce our example square (see fig. 6-10), and cleans up afterward.

```
PROGRAM SQUARE;

    { Include external graphic procedures }
    USES GRAPHICS;

    BEGIN

        START_DRAWING;

            MOVE (400,200);
            DRAW (700,200);
            DRAW (700,500);
            DRAW (400,500);
            DRAW (400,200);

        FINISH_DRAWING;

    END.
```

Using Variables in Move and Draw

There are no variables in this version of the program; coordinates are expressed directly, as **integer** numbers, in **move** and **draw** commands. Another way to write it is to declare **integer** variables X1, X2, Y1, and Y2, assign values to these variables, and give the appropriate variable names in the **move** and **draw** commands:

```
PROGRAM SQUARE;

    USES GRAPHICS;

    { Declare the coordinate variables }
    VAR X1,X2,Y1,Y2 : INTEGER;

    BEGIN
        { Assign coordinate values }
        X1 := 400;
        X2 := 700;
        Y1 := 200;
        Y2 := 500;

        { Draw the square }
        START_DRAWING;

            MOVE (X1,Y1);
            DRAW (X2,Y1);
            DRAW (X2,Y2);
            DRAW (X1,Y2);
            DRAW (X1,Y1);

        FINISH_DRAWING;

    END.
```

When the computer executes the **move** and **draw** commands in this program, it substitutes the values that have been assigned to the variables.

Reading in Coordinate Values

Instead of assigning values to our variables X1, X2, Y1, and Y2 by statements in the code of the program, we might choose to *read* in these values:

```
PROGRAM SQUARE;

    USES GRAPHICS;

    { Declare the coordinate variables }
    VAR X1,X2,Y1,Y2 : INTEGER;

    BEGIN

        { Prompt for and read in coordinates }
        WRITELN ('ENTER INTEGER FOR X1');
        READLN (X1);
        WRITELN ('ENTER INTEGER FOR X2');
        READLN (X2);
        WRITELN ('ENTER INTEGER FOR Y1');
        READLN (Y1);
        WRITELN ('ENTER INTEGER FOR Y2');
        READLN (Y2);

        { Draw the square }
        START_DRAWING;

            MOVE (X1,Y1);
            DRAW (X2,Y1);
            DRAW (X2,Y2);
            DRAW (X1,Y2);
            DRAW (X1,Y1);

        FINISH_DRAWING;

    END.
```

The significant difference here is that values are given to the coordinate variables at execution time, rather than by being specified in the code of the program. Figure 6-12 shows a screen with text and graphic windows;

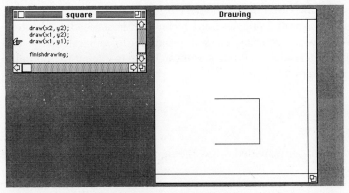

6-12. A data entry dialogue. The window headed "square" displays the Pascal program, the text window shows the data entry dialogue, and the corresponding square appears in the drawing window.

the dialogue by which coordinate values were entered appears in the text window, and the corresponding square appears in the drawing window. By reexecuting the program and entering different values for the four variables, the user can generate drawings of many different squares and rectangles.

The Three Essential Parts of a Graphic Program

It should now be clear that there are three essential parts of a graphic program. First, we must declare the variables that will appear in **move** and **draw** commands, so that space is set aside in memory to store the coordinate data needed to generate our drawing. Second, we must give values to all of these variables, which can either be done with assignment statements or by reading in values. Third, we use these values in **move** and **draw** commands enclosed between **start_drawing** and **finish_drawing** to generate the image.

For clarity and simplicity, we shall mostly give values to variables by means of assignments in our examples. But keep in mind that you can always replace the assignment statements by **readln** statements if you want to experiment with the effects of different values. You will find that it is more interesting in your own programming projects to allow for user input in this way. If your computer is equipped with a mouse or graphic tablet, you can probably use these devices for input of coordinate values, and you may want to explore this alternative to typing in numbers. If so, you should check the relevant documentation. In chapter 15, we will look in detail at the design of interactive dialogues for the construction of drawings.

Summary

You now know how to write the simplest kind of program to generate a line drawing. Before going on, you should do some of the suggested exercises. You will find that it is very tedious to program this way, and you may wonder whether it is worth it. If you know all the coordinates of a figure, why not just draw it yourself, instead of writing down a lot of **move**s and **draw**s?

The problem, here, is that there is a great deal of effort with little reward. It does *not* make very much practical sense to program this way; you have to write a relatively long program to generate a relatively simple figure. But, as you learn more sophisticated programming techniques in succeeding chapters, you will be able to write concise, elegant programs to generate large and complex drawings. When you can do this, you can begin to exploit the potential power of computer graphics.

Exercises

1. Using the gridded paper provided, draw the figures defined by the following **move**s and **draw**s:

- MOVE (200,200);
  DRAW (600,200);

```
        DRAW (300,300);
        DRAW (500,300);
        DRAW (200,200);
    •   MOVE (400,250);
        DRAW (200,200);
        DRAW (600,200);
        DRAW (400,250);
        DRAW (300,300);
        DRAW (500,300);
        DRAW (400,250);
```

2. Write a program to draw an equilateral triangle.

3. Write a program to draw your initials.

4. Write a program to read in the coordinates of the vertices of a triangle, then draw the triangle.

5. Figure 1-1e shows Paul Klee's "active line, limited in its movement by fixed points." Write a program to draw a line of this type.

7.

Coordinate Calculations

So far we have considered graphic programs in which coordinate values are either assigned directly or read in. As you will have found when doing the exercises, you must calculate coordinates to enter in **moves** and **draws**, or to type in when prompted, in order to produce a picture. Perhaps you used a pocket calculator to do this. You probably needed something a bit more sophisticated than a four-function calculator, since calculation of coordinates often requires evaluation of trigonometric functions such as sine and cosine, and perhaps others such as square root.

Consider, for example, the equilateral triangle of side length 200 shown in figure 7-1. In order to generate it using **moves** and **draws**, we must know its height to establish the Y coordinate of the apex. From the Pythagorean theorem, we know that the height will be the square root of 200 squared minus 100 squared, which comes to 173.2050. Alternatively, we can use a trigonometric function and calculate the height as 200 multiplied by the sine of 60 degrees.

Independent and Dependent Variables

An alternative to performing such calculations outside the program is to write code to perform them within the program. If we want to draw a square parallel to the coordinate axes, for example, we can give values to X1, Y1, and Side, then calculate all the other vertex coordinates from these (fig. 7-2). That is, we first assign or read in values for our independent variables,

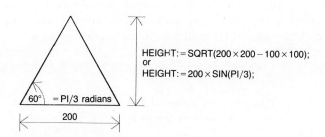

HEIGHT: = SQRT(200 × 200 − 100 × 100);
or
HEIGHT: = 200 × SIN(PI/3);

7-1. An equilateral triangle.

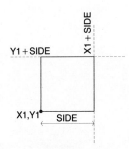

7-2. The vertex coordinates of a square as dependent variables.

145

then calculate values for dependent variables and finally use the values in **move** and **draw** commands. Here is an example of a simple program that does this:

```
PROGRAM SQUARE;

   USES GRAPHICS;

   VAR X1,Y1,X2,Y2,SIDE : INTEGER;

   BEGIN

      { Independent variables }
      X1 := 400;
      Y1 := 200;
      SIDE := 300;

      { Dependent variables }
      X2 := X1 + SIDE;
      Y2 := Y1 + SIDE;

      { Draw square }
      START_DRAWING;

         MOVE (X1,Y1);
         DRAW (X2,Y1);
         DRAW (X2,Y2);
         DRAW (X1,Y2);
         DRAW (X1,Y1);

      FINISH_DRAWING;

   END.
```

Standard Arithmetic Functions

In this example we used the Pascal arithmetic operators to obtain the desired result—much as we might use a four-function calculator. In addition to these, for use in more complex calculations, Pascal provides certain *standard arithmetic functions* analogous to those of a scientific calculator. For example, the square root function is called *sqrt*. To get the square root of 317.835 you write the statement:

```
HEIGHT := SQRT(317.835);
```

The result of taking the square root of 317.835 is thus assigned to Height.

Different implementations of Pascal may provide more or less extensive sets of standard arithmetic functions, but these are the basic ones that you will need and that should be available in any implementation:

ABS(X)	Computes the *absolute value* of X. The type of the result is the same as that of X.
SQR(X)	Computes the *square* of X; that is, X * X. The type of the result is the same as that of X.
SQRT(X)	Computes the *square root* of X. The type of the result is always real.

SIN(X)	Computes the *sine* of X, where X is specified in radians. The type of the result is always real.
COS(X)	Computes the *cosine* of X, where X is specified in radians. The type of the result is always real.
ARCTAN(X)	Computes the *arctangent* of X. The result is in radians, and its type is always real.

Rounding and Truncating

You will notice that, in many cases, these functions yield real results. Yet you always need an **integer** to substitute in a **move** or **draw**. Substitution of a **real** number will not work; it will simply generate an error.

A **real** number can be converted to an **integer** either by *truncating* it—throwing away the decimal part—or *rounding* it to the nearest whole number. To perform these operations, Pascal provides *transfer functions*:

TRUNC(X)	X must be a real number. The result is the greatest integer less than or equal to X where X is greater than or equal to 0, and the least integer greater than or equal to X for X less than 0.
ROUND(X)	X must be a real number. The result, of type integer, is the value of X rounded.

The relationship between these two functions can be expressed as follows:

$$ROUND(X) = TRUNC(X+0.5) \text{ for X greater than or equal to 0}$$

$$ROUND(X) = TRUNC(X-0.5) \text{ for X less than 0}$$

Here are some examples of rounding and truncating and their results:

Expression	Result
TRUNC(1.732)	1
TRUNC(−1.732)	−1
ROUND(1.732)	2
ROUND(−1.732)	−2
ROUND(1.01)	1
TRUNC(0.0)	0
ROUND(0.0)	0

Here is an example of a simple program that uses standard arithmetic functions to compute coordinate values and round the results.

```
PROGRAM TRIANGLE;
  { Draw an equilateral triangle }
  USES GRAPHICS;
  VAR X1,X2,X3,Y1,Y2,SIDE,HEIGHT : INTEGER;
  CONST RADIANS = 0.01745;
  BEGIN
    { Independent variables }
    X1 := 300;
```

```
Y1 := 300;
SIDE := 400;

{ Dependent variables }
X2 := X1 + SIDE;
X3 := (X1 + X2) DIV 2;
HEIGHT := ROUND(SIDE * SIN(60 * RADIANS));
Y2 := Y1 + HEIGHT;

{ Draw triangle }
START_DRAWING;

      MOVE (X1,Y1);
      DRAW (X2,Y1);
      DRAW (X3,Y2);
      DRAW (X1,Y1);

    FINISH_DRAWING;

END.
```

a. Real coordinates rounded to a raster grid.

b. Real coordinates truncated to a raster grid.

7-3. Enlargements of the apex of a triangle.

Note that in the above program, the Height of the equilateral triangle calculated to two decimal places is 346.41. Since we use an **integer** screen coordinate system, this is rounded to the closest raster unit (346) before plotting. In this case the same value results whether the Height is rounded or truncated. However, if the Side of the triangle were given as 300, the calculated Height would be 259.81. Rounding would give us 260 raster units, whereas truncating would result in a Height of 259. In low-resolution coordinate systems, rounding or truncating **real** values to the closest **integer** raster unit may lead to perceptible overlaps or gaps between line segments (fig. 7-3).

Writing Your Own Functions

If Pascal does not have the function that you need for a calculation, you can write it yourself. The following, for example, is a function that computes the cube of X:

```
FUNCTION CUBE (X : INTEGER) : INTEGER;
    BEGIN
        CUBE := X * X * X;
    END;
```

The first line is analogous to a program heading. It begins with the reserved word **function**, followed by the identifier (name) of the function—in this case Cube. The variable X is referred to as the *formal parameter* of this function, and its type is **integer**. The formal parameter is named and typed within the parentheses as shown. Then, following a colon, the type of the result produced by the function (in this case **integer**)is specified.

The code between **begin** and **end** specifies how the value of the function is to be calculated for a given value of the formal parameter. It must contain at least one assignment statement, assigning a value to the function identifier. Finally, the function terminates with a semicolon, rather than with a period as for a program.

A function must be *declared* in the procedure and function declaration part of a program before it is *invoked* in the program—just as a variable must be declared before it can be used in an executable statement. Here is an example of a simple program that calculates the volume of a cube of side length 3:

```
PROGRAM VOLUME;

    { Function declaration }
      FUNCTION CUBE (X : INTEGER) : INTEGER;
        BEGIN
            CUBE := X * X * X;
        END;

    { Variable declaration }
      VAR VOLUME : INTEGER;

    { Main program }
      BEGIN

          VOLUME := CUBE(3);
          WRITELN (VOLUME);

      END.
```

Notice how the function is invoked—in exactly the same way as Pascal's built-in functions such as **sin** and **cos**. When it is invoked, it calculates the Cube of 3. The result is substituted for the expression Cube(3) and assigned to Volume. Notice also the typographic convention; whereas the names of Pascal built-in functions are shown in boldface, the names of user-declared functions are not.

The value 3 in this program is referred to as the *actual parameter* of the function Cube. When Cube is invoked, this value is assigned to the formal parameter X. This is the way that the function is given an input value on which to operate.

The actual parameter need not be a value; it might be a variable to which a value has been assigned. This is illustrated in the following program, which reads in the side length of a cube then calculates the volume:

```
PROGRAM VOLUME;

    { Function declaration }
      FUNCTION CUBE (X : INTEGER) : INTEGER;
        BEGIN
            CUBE := X * X * X;
        END;

    { Variable declaration }
      VAR SIDE,VOLUME : INTEGER;

    { Main program }
      BEGIN

          { Read side length }
          WRITELN ('ENTER INTEGER FOR SIDE LENGTH');
          READLN (SIDE);

          { Calculate and print volume }
          VOLUME := CUBE(SIDE);
          WRITELN (VOLUME);

      END.
```

In essence, declaring a function in this way allows us to use a short, meaningful name in our program in place of a longer, more complex, and less meaningful expression. Once the function is declared, we can invoke it repeatedly in a program, without having to write it out in full each time, or to worry about the details of its internal operation. The construct of a function, then, provides us with a very powerful *abstraction* mechanism for use in programming.

Functions with Several Parameters

In computer graphics programming, we are often interested in functions that return an X coordinate or a Y coordinate of a point in a drawing. Consider, for example, the bisection of a line defined by its endpoints (X1, Y1) and (X2, Y2) (fig. 7-4). The following function, which computes the midpoint between any two **integer**s Low and High, might be used to find the midpoint coordinates:

```
FUNCTION  MIDPOINT (LOW,HIGH  :  INTEGER)  :  INTEGER;
    BEGIN
        MIDPOINT  := (LOW  +  HIGH)  DIV  2;
    END;
```

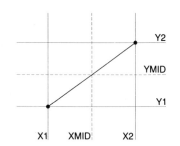

7-4. The bisection of a line defined by its endpoints.

The code to calculate the midpoint (Xmid,Ymid) using this function is as follows:

```
XMID  :=  MIDPOINT(X1,X2);
YMID  :=  MIDPOINT(Y1,Y2);
```

Notice that Midpoint has two formal parameters, Low and High, and that each invocation of Midpoint lists two actual parameters. A function may, in fact, have as many formal parameters as we wish. Whenever the function is invoked, there must be an actual parameter for each formal parameter. The correspondence is established by *position* in the parameter list; the value of the first actual parameter is assigned to the first formal parameter, that of the second actual parameter to the second formal parameter, and so on.

The following program illustrates use of this Midpoint function to draw a smaller triangle within a larger triangle (fig. 7-5):

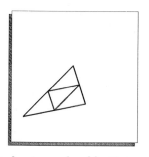

7-5. A drawing produced by Nest_triangles.

```
PROGRAM  NEST_TRIANGLES;

    USES  GRAPHICS;

    FUNCTION  MIDPOINT (LOW,HIGH  :  INTEGER)  :  INTEGER;
        BEGIN
            MIDPOINT  := (LOW  +  HIGH)  DIV  2;
        END;

    VAR  X1,Y1,X2,Y2,X3,Y3,
         X12,Y12,X23,Y23,X31,Y31  :  INTEGER;

BEGIN
    { Set coordinates of outer triangle }
        X1  :=  100;
        Y1  :=  200;
        X2  :=  500;
        Y2  :=  600;
```

```
    X3 := 600;
    Y3 := 300;

{ Calculate midpoints of sides }
    X12 := MIDPOINT(X1,X2);
    Y12 := MIDPOINT(Y1,Y2);
    X23 := MIDPOINT(X2,X3);
    Y23 := MIDPOINT(Y2,Y3);
    X31 := MIDPOINT(X3,X1);
    Y31 := MIDPOINT(Y3,Y1);

START_DRAWING;

    { Draw outer triangle }
      MOVE (X1,Y1);
      DRAW (X2,Y2);
      DRAW (X3,Y3);
      DRAW (X1,Y1);

    { Draw inner triangle connecting midpoints }
      MOVE (X12,Y12);
      DRAW (X23,Y23);
      DRAW (X31,Y31);
      DRAW (X12,Y12);

FINISH_DRAWING;

END.
```

Local Variables

Now consider the simple coordinate calculation problem illustrated in figure 7-6. We have a point (X1, Y1), an angle Theta, and a Length; we want to calculate the coordinates (X2, Y2). We know from elementary trigonometry that the Base of the triangle is given by the formula Length * **cos**(Theta), so a function to return X2 can be written as follows:

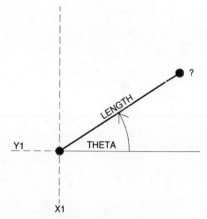

7-6. A coordinate calculation problem to find X2, given X1, Y1, Theta, and Length.

```
FUNCTION X2 (X1,LENGTH : INTEGER; THETA : REAL) : INTEGER;

    VAR BASE : REAL;

    BEGIN

      { Calculate real value for base }
      BASE := LENGTH * COS(THETA);

      { Round and add to X1 }
      X2 := X1 + ROUND(BASE);

    END;
```

Note that we are invoking functions from within a function; the Pascal standard functions **cos** and **round** are invoked from within X2. In this way, you can can also invoke functions that you have declared yourself.

Also note that since the angle Theta is expressed as a **real** number of radians, the function X2 has both **integer** and **real** formal parameters in its parameter list. The **cos** function returns a **real** value, and since the result of multiplying an **integer** by a **real** number is **real**, the value of the expression Length * **cos**(Theta) is **real**.

Finally, note that we have declared a **real** variable Base within the function. Whenever a variable is declared within a function, it is *local* to that function. In effect, it does not exist outside the function; it cannot be referenced from outside the function; its value is unknown outside the function; and in fact, it exists only during the time that the function is activated. After the function returns its result value and terminates, the program has no way of knowing that the local variable ever existed. The function's formal parameters are all local in this same sense.

If we wanted to eliminate the local variable Base, we could easily do so by rewriting the function like this:

```
FUNCTION  X2  (X1,LENGTH  :  INTEGER;  THETA  :  REAL)  :  INTEGER;
  BEGIN
      X2  :=  X1  +  ROUND(LENGTH  *  COS(THETA));
  END;
```

Here, instead of using the variable Base as the actual parameter in the invocation of the Pascal built-in function **round**, we have used the expression Length * **cos**(Theta). In general, we can use expressions as actual parameters when we invoke procedures. This is more concise, but it usually makes programs more difficult to follow. In most cases it is better to introduce local variables, break complicated expressions down into several separate lines, and provide explanatory comments at each step, as we did in our first version of this function.

You can now see that strict rules govern the use of functions. The list of formal parameters specifies the precise nature of the data that the function is to operate upon; the type of result to be returned must also be specified in the heading. The local nature of the formal parameters, and of variables declared within the function, ensures that nothing done to these variables during the execution of the function can have any effect on anything outside the function. That is, the internal workings of a function are completely insulated from the rest of the program. This discipline may seem restrictive, but you will find that it clarifies your programs and keeps you out of trouble.

To conclude, here is a program that uses functions X2 and Y2 to calculate coordinates, then draws a line of length Length at angle Theta from point (X1, Y1):

```
PROGRAM  LINE;

  USES  GRAPHICS;

  FUNCTION  X2  (X1,LENGTH  :  INTEGER;  THETA  :  REAL)  :
  INTEGER;
      VAR  BASE  :  REAL;

      BEGIN

          BASE  :=  LENGTH  *  COS(THETA);
          X2  :=  X1  +  ROUND(BASE);

      END;

  FUNCTION  Y2  (Y1,LENGTH  :  INTEGER;  THETA  :  REAL)  :
  INTEGER;
      VAR  HEIGHT  :  REAL;

      BEGIN
```

```
            HEIGHT  :=  LENGTH  *  SIN(THETA);
            Y2  :=  Y1  +  ROUND(HEIGHT);

        END;

    CONST  RADIANS  =  0.01745;
    VAR  X1,Y1,X,Y,ANGLE,LENGTH  :  INTEGER;
         THETA  :  REAL;

    BEGIN

        {  Set  variables  defining  line  }
            ANGLE  :=  45;
            X1  :=  300;
            Y1  :=  200;
            LENGTH  :=  400;

        {  Calculate  dependent  variables  }
            THETA  :=  ANGLE  *  RADIANS;
            X  :=  X2(X1,LENGTH,THETA);
            Y  :=  Y2(Y1,LENGTH,THETA);

        {  Draw  line  }
            START_DRAWING;

                MOVE  (X1,Y1);
                DRAW  (X,Y);

            FINISH_DRAWING;

        END.
```

Functions to Map between Screen Coordinate Systems

If you want to run the example programs given in this book using a display with a screen coordinate system different from the 1,024 by 1,024 one that we use, then you will find it useful to have a function that maps points from a 1,024 by 1,024 system to your own system (fig. 7-7).

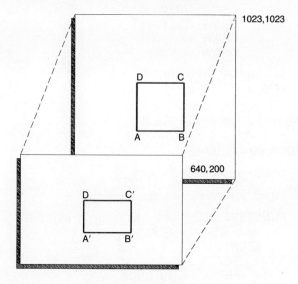

7-7. Mapping from one screen coordinate system to another.

Let us assume, for example, that you have an IBM PC with a 640 by 200 display, and the origin is at the top-left rather than the bottom-left. The coordinate conversion factors will be:

```
X  640/1024  =  0.6250  { In the X direction }
Y  200/1024  =  0.1953  { In the Y direction }
```

So the functions that you need are:

```
FUNCTION NEWX (X : INTEGER) : INTEGER;
    VAR REALX : REAL;
    BEGIN
        REALX := 0.6250 * X;
        NEWX := ROUND(REALX);
    END;
FUNCTION NEWY (Y : INTEGER) : INTEGER;
    VAR REALY : REAL;
    BEGIN
        REALY := 200.0 - 0.1953 * Y;
        NEWY := ROUND(REALY);
    END;
```

To illustrate the use of these functions, let us consider the conversion of the following program that draws a square on the 1,024 by 1,024 screen (fig. 7-8a):

```
PROGRAM SQUARE;

    USES GRAPHICS;

    BEGIN

        START_DRAWING;

            MOVE (400,200);
            DRAW (700,200);
            DRAW (700,500);
            DRAW (400,500);
            DRAW (400,200);

        FINISH_DRAWING;
    END.
```

The converted version looks like this:

```
PROGRAM SQUARE;

    USES GRAPHICS;

    { Coordinate conversion functions }
    FUNCTION NEWX (X : INTEGER) : INTEGER;
        VAR REALX : REAL;
        BEGIN
            REALX := 0.6250 * X;
            NEWX := ROUND(REALX);
        END;
```

```
FUNCTION NEWY (Y : INTEGER) : INTEGER;
    VAR REALY : REAL;
    BEGIN
        REALY := 200.0 − 0.1953 * Y;
        NEWY := ROUND(REALY);
    END;

{ Draw in IBM PC coordinates }
    BEGIN

        START_DRAWING;

            MOVE (NEWX(400),NEWY(200));
            DRAW (NEWX(700),NEWY(200));
            DRAW (NEWX(700),NEWY(500));
            DRAW (NEWX(400),NEWY(500));
            DRAW (NEWX(400),NEWY(200));

        FINISH_DRAWING;

    END.
```

a. On a 1,024 by 1,024 screen
coordinate system.

b. On a 512 by 342 screen
coordinate system.

7-8. A drawing produced by Square.

The resulting output is shown in fig. 7-8b. Note that due to the differing aspect ratios of the two coordinate systems and the differing shapes of the pixels, the square is distorted into a rectangle. Notice also how the use of functions shortens and clarifies this program. Instead of having to write a long and obscure expression each time that we convert a coordinate, we simply write NewX or NewY.

Global Variables

In architectural drafting, it is sometimes useful to take a figure with coordinates defined on the points of a fine grid and map these coordinates onto the nearest points of some coarser grid. This is often referred to as *snapping* to a grid. Let us assume that we have a figure defined on a one-unit square grid. The following function converts a coordinate Fine to the nearest coordinate Coarse of the coarser grid, where Size is an integer that specifies the resolution of the coarser grid:

```
FUNCTION COARSE (SIZE,FINE : INTEGER) : INTEGER;
    BEGIN
        COARSE := ROUND(FINE/SIZE) * SIZE;
    END;
```

We might take our example square, then, and snap it to, say, a twelve-unit grid as follows:

```
PROGRAM SNAP_SQUARE;

    USES GRAPHICS;

    FUNCTION COARSE (SIZE,FINE : INTEGER) : INTEGER;
       BEGIN
            COARSE := ROUND(FINE/SIZE) * SIZE;
       END;

  { Plot snapped drawing }
      BEGIN

      START_DRAWING;
          MOVE (COARSE(12,400),COARSE(12,200));
          DRAW (COARSE(12,700),COARSE(12,200));
          DRAW (COARSE(12,700),COARSE(12,500));
          DRAW (COARSE(12,400),COARSE(12,500));
          DRAW (COARSE(12,400),COARSE(12,200));

      FINISH_DRAWING;

    END.
```

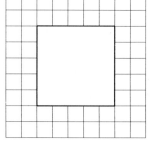

a. A figure defined in a one-unit grid.

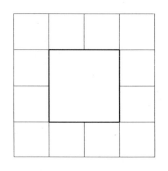

b. The same figure snapped to a coarser grid.

7-9. Snapping to a grid.

The effect is shown in figure 7-9.

This program looks and is unnecessarily cumbersome. Since the coarse grid has the same dimension whenever we invoke Coarse, we should need to specify this value only once. We can eliminate the redundancy by rewriting the program in the following way:

```
PROGRAM SNAP_SQUARE;

    USES GRAPHICS;
  { Define global variables }
    VAR SIZE : INTEGER;

    FUNCTION COARSE (FINE : INTEGER) : INTEGER;
       BEGIN
            COARSE := ROUND(FINE/SIZE) * SIZE;
       END;
  BEGIN

      WRITELN ('ENTER GRID SIZE');
      READLN (SIZE);

      START_DRAWING;

          MOVE (COARSE(400),COARSE(200));
          DRAW (COARSE(700),COARSE(200));
          DRAW (COARSE(700),COARSE(500));
          DRAW (COARSE(400),COARSE(500));
          DRAW (COARSE(400),COARSE(200));

      FINISH_DRAWING;

    END.
```

Here we have made Size into a *global variable* by declaring it before anything else is declared. Any function that follows, as well as the main program, can refer to and assign values to a global variable declared this way. The function Coarse has been rewritten with just one formal parameter, and a value is read in for the global variable Size before creating the drawing.

If there are no global variables in a program, an error in a function can have only two effects: either execution will terminate in the function when an illegal operation is attempted; or an erroneous value will be returned. Nothing that happens in the function can have other side effects. Where there are global variables, on the other hand, an error in a function can also potentially change the values of one or more of these, producing erroneous results when these values are later used elsewhere in the program. In other words, the barrier that otherwise isolates the internal workings of a function from other parts of the program is breached, and errors can propagate complex logical consequences. This makes debugging difficult.

Global variables are used legitimately, as in our example, to set a value once and thereafter make it available for repeated use by functions. In general, though, it is good practice to try to localize the potential effects of any errors in your code, and the syntax of Pascal is designed to encourage this. In particular, you should never use global variables where local variables will suffice. Sometimes programmers lazily declare a lot of global variables, instead of determining where local variables should be declared, how data should be passed into functions via parameters, and how values should be returned by functions; this is bad style. If we do not ever wish to change the value of **size**, we could declare it as a global constant instead of as a global variable. The declaration would precede the function declaration and would look like this:

```
CONSTANT SIZE = 12;
```

This is safer, since erroneous values cannot be propagated via a global constant, as they can via a global variable.

Scale Conversion Functions

It is sometimes convenient to specify coordinates in feet, inches, or centimeters, rather than in raster units, and then use a scale factor to convert these values to raster units. If we wanted to input coordinates in feet, for example, then draw at a scale of eight feet to one raster unit, we could use the following function to convert feet to raster units:

```
FUNCTION RASTER_UNITS (FEET : REAL) : INTEGER;
   BEGIN
      RASTER_UNITS: = ROUND(FEET/8);
   END;
```

It might then be invoked:

```
DRAW (RASTER_UNITS(X),RASTER_UNITS(Y));
```

For simplicity in our examples, we will mostly avoid introducing scale conversion functions. You can easily modify the code, if you wish, to produce drawings at particular scales.

Functions for Trigonometry and Analytic Geometry

In technical drafting it is often necessary to use theorems of trigonometry and analytic geometry in order to find points needed in construction of figures. If we want to write programs to find points automatically, it is useful to have at our disposal a library of functions to evaluate the relevant formulas. Only a few of those that we need are built into Pascal. You will recall, from the discussion earlier in the chapter, for example, that standard Pascal has only **sin**(X), **cos**(X), and **arctan**(X) as trigonometric functions (although some implementations may have more). You will probably need to write a few functions of your own for use later as building blocks of your graphic programs.

You may find it more convenient, for example, to specify angles in degrees rather than radians. A function to perform the conversion is:

```
FUNCTION RADIANS (DEGREES : REAL) : REAL;
    CONST PI = 3.1415;
    BEGIN
        RADIANS := DEGREES * 180 / PI;
    END;
```

You will often need a tangent function as well as sine and cosine. This is very simple and can be written as follows:

```
FUNCTION TAN (THETA : REAL) : REAL;
    BEGIN
        TAN := SIN(THETA) / COS(THETA);
    END;
```

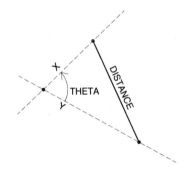

7-10. The principle of triangulation.

Here is an example of something a bit more complicated. Surveyors often find a distance by triangulation (fig. 7-10). They measure an angle Theta and distances X and Y to obtain data necessary to calculate Distance. The function needed to obtain Distance may be written:

```
FUNCTION DISTANCE (THETA,X,Y : REAL) : REAL;
    BEGIN
        DISTANCE := SQRT(SQR(X) + SQR(Y) - 2*X*Y*COS(THETA));
    END;
```

So a useful program to read in Theta (in degrees) and the distances X and Y can be written as follows:

```
PROGRAM TRIANGULATION;

    { Degrees to radians conversion }
    FUNCTION RADIANS (DEGREES : REAL) : REAL;
        CONST PI = 3.1415;
        BEGIN
            RADIANS := DEGREES * 180 / PI;
        END;

    { Distance calculation }
    FUNCTION DISTANCE (THETA,X,Y : REAL) : REAL;
```

```
        BEGIN
            DISTANCE  :=  SQRT(SQR(X) + SQR(Y)  − 2*X*Y*COS(THETA));
        END;

{ Variables }
    VAR  THETA,X,Y,Z  :  REAL;

BEGIN

    { Prompt  for  and  read  in  data }
        WRITELN ('ENTER  ANGLE  IN  DEGREES');
        READLN  (THETA);
        WRITELN ('ENTER  FIRST  LENGTH');
        READLN  (X);
        WRITELN ('ENTER  SECOND  LENGTH');
        READLN  (Y);

    { Convert  angle }
        THETA  :=  RADIANS(THETA);

    { Calculate  distance }
        Z :=  DISTANCE(THETA,X,Y);

    { Write  out  result }
        WRITELN ('DISTANCE  =  ',Z:  10:2);

END.
```

One subtle technical point should be noted here; the formal parameters Theta, X, and Y of Distance have the same identifiers as the corresponding actual parameters. However, the formal parameters are local to the procedure Distance and are not the same thing as the actual parameters. When Distance is invoked, the current values of the actual parameters are assigned to the corresponding formal parameters. But, if Distance assigned a value to one of its formal parameters, this would have no effect on the actual parameters; a function can never create a side effect by assigning values to its formal parameters. In other words, the formal parameters of a function are like valves that let data into a function, but do not let modified data back out.

Summary

We have seen, in this chapter, how Pascal standard functions and functions that you write yourself can be used to clarify, simplify, and shorten programs that carry out complicated calculations. You should make sure that you thoroughly understand the rules for declaration and invocation of functions as well as for the passing of data. You should structure your programs logically by breaking them down into short, easily understandable functions.

You will find that this modularization helps you to write correct programs and to quickly trace and fix errors that do occur. The insulation around a function localizes the effect of any error within it and prevents the propagation of mysterious side effects. You will also find that building up a library of carefully written, generalized functions provides you with reusable program modules that can serve as building blocks in later programs.

The functions that you build for calculating coordinates will become your tools for correctly sizing and placing elements of a graphic composition. As

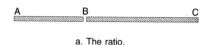

a. The ratio.

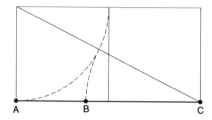

b. Its geometric construction.

7-11. A line divided in the golden ratio.

such, they will encode both technical knowledge (of how to calculate the tangent of an angle or the midpoint of a line, for example) and aesthetic rules—in particular, rules of proportion.

Exercises

1. Pascal does not have a function to calculate the reciprocal of an integer. Write one.

2. Pascal does not have an exponentiation function. Write one.

3. Write a function that calculates the area of a circle of specified radius.

4. Write a function that calculates the perimeter of a circle of specified radius.

5. Write a function to return the mean of two real numbers.

6. A line is divided into the so-called golden ratio when $AB/BC = BC/AC$ (fig. 7-11a). Figure 7-11b shows a geometric construction for dividing a line in this ratio. Write a function that accepts the coordinates of A and C, and returns the X coordinate of B. Write a second function to return the Y coordinate.

7. Consider the following function:

```
FUNCTION CHANGE_Y (Y: INTEGER): INTEGER;
   BEGIN
      CHANGE_Y := (1024 - Y) DIV 2;
   END;
```

What would be the effect of using Change_Y to change every Y coordinate of a drawing in a 1,024 by 1,024 screen coordinate system?

8.

Graphic Vocabularies

We began our discussion of line drawings by observing that they are composed of individual primitive marks, such as pencil or pen strokes. For our purposes here, we have taken the primitive mark to be a vector—a straight line segment defined by the coordinates of its endpoints.

A drawing is made by executing a *sequence* of primitive marking operations, such as movements of a pencil held in the hand. Thus you can specify a picture by giving a sequence of commands to execute primitive marking operations one after the other. This works, although it is very tedious—much like instructing, over the telephone, a draftsman who cannot understand any task more complicated than drawing a single line.

Pictures as Programs

We have now seen how a computer can be programmed in exactly the same laborious, step-by-step way to generate a picture composed of vectors. You write a sequence of **move** and **draw** commands. When the computer executes these commands, one after the other, the specified drawing is generated on the screen. In other words, a picture is encoded as a Pascal program that specifies the sequence of primitive marking operations (**move**s and **draw**s) needed to create it.

If we want to refer to a picture, we usually give it a name, such as *square*, *triangle*, *squiggle*, *north elevation*, or *Mona Lisa*. It makes sense to give the same name to the program that generates the picture. In Pascal, this name becomes the heading of the program.

In summary, then, we have seen that you can write a Pascal program to generate a line drawing as follows:

- Write the heading, which names the drawing that is to be generated.
- Declare the external procedures needed to produce a line drawing in a screen coordinate system by making the announcement:

  USES GRAPHICS;

  This is analogous to providing a draftsman with drawing board and pencil.
- Declare the constants, functions, and variables that will be needed, much as you might provide a draftsman with a scratchpad to jot down numbers and an electronic calculator with a useful array of function keys.
- **Begin** the executable statement part.

- Assign or read in values for the independent variables.
- Calculate values of any dependent variables.
- Initialize the graphics system (**start_drawing;**).
- Write **move** and **draw** commands to generate the picture.
- Cleanup (**finish_drawing;**).
- **End**.

You must always have values for independent variables before you can calculate values for dependent variables, and you must always have X and Y coordinate values before you can execute a **move** or **draw**. One logical way to organize code, then, is in three distinct steps, as in the following code to draw an equilateral triangle.

```
BEGIN

   { Assign values to independent variables }
     X1  :=  300;  { Bottom-left vertex coordinate }
     Y1  :=  300;  { Bottom-left vertex coordinate }
     SIDE  :=  400;  { Side length }

   { Calculate values of dependent variables }
     X2  :=  X1  +  SIDE;  { Bottom-right vertex coordinate }
     X3  :=  (X1+X2) DIV 2;  { Apex X-coordinate }
     HEIGHT  :=  ROUND (SIDE * SIN(60*RADIANS));
     Y2  :=  Y1  +  HEIGHT;  { Apex Y-coordinate }

   START_DRAWING;  { Triangle }

       MOVE  (X1,Y1);
       DRAW  (X2,Y1);
       DRAW  (X3,Y2);
       DRAW  (X1,Y1);

   FINISH_DRAWING;
END.
```

Another possibility is to calculate values just before they are needed.

```
BEGIN

   START_DRAWING;  { Triangle }

     { Move to bottom-left vertex }
       X1  :=  300;
       Y1  :=  300;
       MOVE  (X1,Y1);

     { Draw base }
       X2  :=  X1  +  SIDE;
       DRAW  (X2,Y1);

     { Draw side to apex }
       X3  :=  (X1  +  X2) DIV 2;
       HEIGHT  :=  ROUND(SIDE * SIN(60*RADIANS));
       Y2  :=  Y1  +  HEIGHT;
       DRAW  (X3,Y2);
       DRAW  (X1,Y1);

   FINISH_DRAWING;
END.
```

The choice between these alternatives, and among possible combinations of the two, is a matter of programming style, not of Pascal syntax. You should always choose the clearest, most expressive method.

Parts of Pictures and Parts of Programs

So far we have considered only very simple figures, composed of a few vectors. When we look at more complex pictures, we usually find that they have a number of distinct *parts*. Figure 8-1, for example, is composed of a triangle, a square, and a hexagon.

It is convenient to break down a graphic program to draw such a picture in corresponding distinct parts—one part of the program draws a triangle, one a square, and one a hexagon. The program then has an internal structure that reflects the structure of the image. (This mirroring of structure is a very important general principle, and we will come back to it later.) One way to do this is simply to insert appropriate *comment* statements between the **moves** and **draws** as follows:

8-1. A picture composed of three distinct parts: a triangle, a square, and a hexagon.

```
PROGRAM SHAPES;
  { Program to draw a triangle, square and hexagon }

  USES GRAPHICS;

  BEGIN

    START_DRAWING;

      { Draw a triangle }
      MOVE (100,200);
      DRAW (300,200);
      DRAW (200,400);
      DRAW (100,200);

      { Draw a square }
      MOVE (400,200);
      DRAW (600,200);
      DRAW (600,400);
      DRAW (400,400);
      DRAW (400,200);

      { Draw a hexagon }
      MOVE (758,200);
      DRAW (874,200);
      DRAW (932,300);
      DRAW (874,400);
      DRAW (758,400);
      DRAW (700,300);
      DRAW (758,200);

    FINISH_DRAWING;

  END.
```

Thus we can immediately see what each group of **moves** and **draws** does.

Procedures

A more sophisticated approach is to write a separate *procedure* for each part. A procedure in Pascal has the same organization as a program, with a heading, a declaration part, and an executable part enclosed between a **begin** and an **end**. For example, a procedure to draw a square looks very much like a program to draw a square:

```
PROCEDURE SQUARE;
   BEGIN

      MOVE  (400,200);
      DRAW  (600,200);
      DRAW  (600,400);
      DRAW  (400,400);
      DRAW  (400,200);

   END;
```

Note, however, that it terminates with a semicolon rather than a period. This reflects the fact that a procedure is a distinct part of a program, not a complete program in itself.

As you can see, procedures are similar to functions. (There are significant differences, too; we will go into these a little later.) Like functions, procedures are first declared, then used (invoked) within a program. The following example, in which the program Drawsquare invokes the procedure Square, illustrates the logical distinction between declaration and invocation:

```
PROGRAM DRAWSQUARE;

   USES GRAPHICS;

   PROCEDURE SQUARE;

      BEGIN

         MOVE  (400,200);
         DRAW  (600,200);
         DRAW  (600,400);
         DRAW  (400,400);
         DRAW  (400,200);

      END;

   BEGIN

      START_DRAWING;

         SQUARE;

      FINISH_DRAWING;

   END.
```

The procedure Square is declared by writing the code to draw a square and then invoked by name in the executable part of the program. There are a couple of rules to be followed here. Just as you cannot use a tool until you have it in your hand, you cannot invoke a procedure (just as you cannot invoke a function), unless you have already declared it. In our example, declaration of the procedure Square, in effect, makes a tool to draw a square available to the computer. Then, by giving the command Square in the executable part of the program, we instruct the computer to use this tool. Once a procedure has been declared, it may be invoked any number of times, just as a tool, once in hand, may be used over and over again.

To draw our example picture, now, we might declare procedures Square, Triangle, and Hexagon, then invoke them in the main program to create the picture:

```
PROGRAM SHAPES;

  { Program to draw a triangle, square and hexagon }

    USES GRAPHICS;

  { Draw a triangle }
    PROCEDURE TRIANGLE;
      BEGIN

              MOVE (100,200);
              DRAW (300,200);
              DRAW (200,400);
              DRAW (100,200);

      END;

  { Draw a square }
    PROCEDURE SQUARE;
      BEGIN

              MOVE (400,200);
              DRAW (600,200);
              DRAW (600,400);
              DRAW (400,400);
              DRAW (400,200);

      END;

  { Draw a hexagon }
    PROCEDURE HEXAGON;
      BEGIN

              MOVE (758,200);
              DRAW (874,200);
              DRAW (932,300);
              DRAW (874,400);
              DRAW (758,400);
              DRAW (700,300);
              DRAW (758,200);

      END;

  { Main program }
    BEGIN

        START_DRAWING;

            TRIANGLE;
            SQUARE;
            HEXAGON;

        FINISH_DRAWING;

    END.
```

The main program now consists of commands at a higher level than **move** and **draw**. Instead of specifying primitive marks (vectors) one by one, it specifies more complicated figures consisting of sets of primitive marks. The procedures that have been declared tell how these more complicated figures

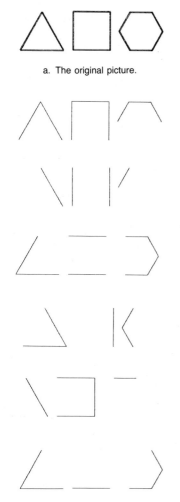

a. The original picture.

b. Several different ways to break it into distinct parts.

8-2. Alternative decompositions of a picture.

are put together out of primitive marks. In other words, the construct of a procedure provides us with an extremely powerful means of abstraction; we can associate a name with an arbitrarily complex arrangement of vectors.

Notice that the **start_drawing** and **finish_drawing** commands surround the procedure invocations in the main program, not the **move** and **draw** commands in the procedure declarations. This is because the computer does not execute a **move** or a **draw** at the point in the program text where we place the declaration of a procedure containing these commands, but at the point where this procedure is invoked by name. In general, **start_drawing** and **finish_drawing** surround the procedure invocations in the main program that generate the complete drawing. They never surround commands in a procedure that generate part of the drawing.

The Art of Abstraction

In the example that we have been discussing, we have broken our drawing down, in the most obvious way, into a triangle, a square, and a hexagon. But there are many other possible ways to separate this picture into parts. Figure 8-2 shows just a few of these possibilities. We could, of course, write a procedure to generate any one of these parts.

The crucial point here is that a way of breaking a picture down into parts is not somehow given, but represents a choice among alternatives—usually many of them. We choose the method that seems most natural and useful to us. In our example, we recognized familiar, closed, symmetrical figures that have well-known English names and did not consider the more bizarre possibilities.

Sometimes, however, the choice is not so obvious. Figure 8-3 shows a simple line figure and a variety of plausible and interesting ways of breaking it into parts. The method that is chosen is the result of artistic vision, not of the mechanics of computer technology. The structuring of a Pascal graphics program as a set of procedures merely reflects a commitment to a particular vision and makes it explicit.

Parameterization of Graphic Elements

If the unintelligent human draftsman that we considered at the beginning of this chapter at least understood the concepts of a triangle, square, and hexagon, we could give him concise telephone instructions that sound much like the main part of our program. We could say:

Start drawing;

Draw a triangle;
Draw a square;
Draw a hexagon;

Finish drawing;

But he would ask some questions:

• How big is the square?

• Where is it placed on the surface? etc.

The issue that emerges here is the distinction between the *essential* and *accidental* properties of an object. All squares share certain properties:

- Four straight sides
- Parallel and equal opposite sides
- 90-degree vertex angles

These properties are essential to a square; they define a square. But size and position are accidental properties; they may vary from square to square. So, if somebody tells you to draw a square, you know what shape to make it, but you must determine how big it will be and where to put it. In other words, the essential properties of an object are those that it shares with all others of the same *type*, whereas accidental properties may vary among the *instances* of the type and must be specified to identify a particular instance.

To depict a general type of graphic element (rather than one of its instances), a diagram that shows the essential properties is used. It is labeled with variable names and dimension lines, according to the standard conventions of technical drafting, to identify the accidental properties. Figure 8-4a, for example, diagrams a square with sides parallel to the coordinate axes and indicates that X and Y (coordinates of the bottom-left corner) as well as side Length are accidental properties. That is, the diagram stands for all the squares, of any size, that may be instantiated in the coordinate system. A particular instance of this type can be specified by substituting values for variable names (fig. 8-4b), as in an unscaled architectural drawing, or by redrawing the element to the correct scale as indicated by these values (fig. 8-4c).

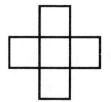

a. The original composition.

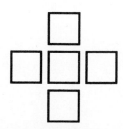

b. The composition viewed as four squares connected at their corners.

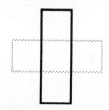

c. The composition viewed as two overlapping rectangles.

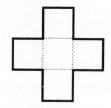

d. The composition viewed as a square superimposed on a cross.

8-3. A variety of ways to see the same composition.

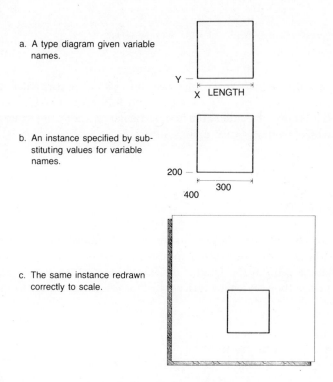

a. A type diagram given variable names.

Y —
X   LENGTH

b. An instance specified by substituting values for variable names.

200 —
400
300

c. The same instance redrawn correctly to scale.

8-4. A square with sides parallel to the axes of the coordinate system.

The type diagram depicts the spatial relations between vectors that characterize the type (that are essential and found in all instances). These relations are of *connection, direction,* and *length.* A pair of vectors may have any one of three connectivity relations (fig. 8-5). They may be connected end-to-end, intersect, or be disjoint. We also commonly recognize three possible relations of direction. Vectors may be parallel, perpendicular, or angled in relation to each other.

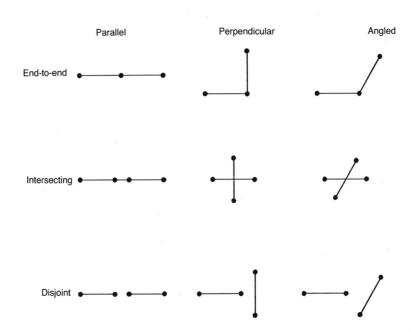

8-5. The relations of connectivity and angle between vectors.

The lengths of pairs of vectors may be related in particular ratios. The Pythagorean philosophers, for example, and following them Renaissance architects, like Andrea Palladio, attached particular aesthetic importance to ratios of small whole numbers such as in figure 8-6:

- 1:1 identity
- 1:2 octave
- 2:3 fifth
- 3:4 fourth

These ratios often govern Palladio's plans and elevations (fig. 8-7). Coordinates of endpoints may also be related in specified ratios (fig. 8-8). This amounts to specifying a ratio of the lengths of "invisible" vectors.

A square, then, is characterized by the following connectivity relations (fig. 8-9a):

- side 1 is connected to side 2
- side 2 is connected to side 3
- side 3 is connected to side 4
- side 4 is connected to side 1
- no sides intersect

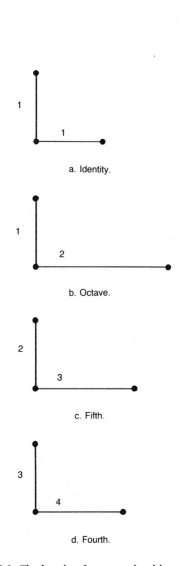

a. Identity.

b. Octave.

c. Fifth.

d. Fourth.

8-6. The lengths of vectors related by ratios of small whole numbers.

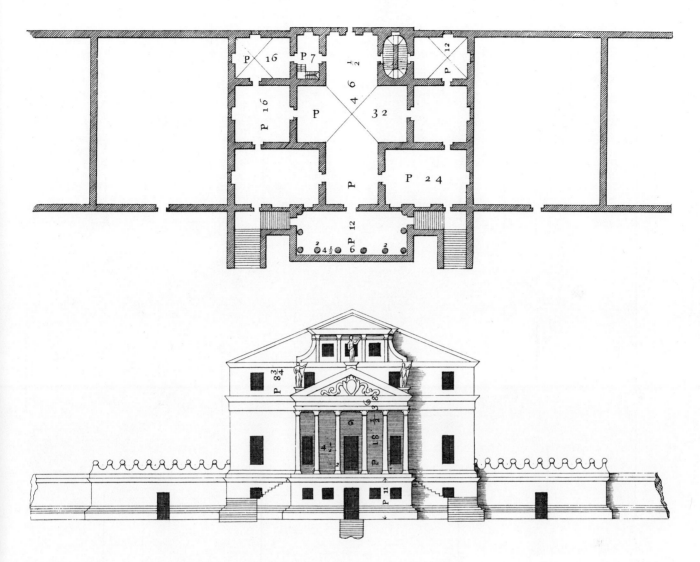

8-7. Plan and elevation of the Villa Malcontenta, from Isaac Ware's edition of Andrea Palladio's *Four Books of Architecture*. Important ratios of lengths are marked.

It also has the following relations of direction (fig. 8-9b):

- side 1 is parallel to side 3
- side 2 is parallel to side 4
- side 1 is perpendicular to side 2
- side 2 is perpendicular to side 3
- side 3 is perpendicular to side 4
- side 4 is perpendicular to side 1

Finally, the lengths of all sides are related in the ratio 1:1 (fig. 8-9c).

The variables associated with the diagram are called the *parameters* of the graphic element. Each parameter has a *name* (for example, Length), a *type* (for example, **integer** or **real** number), and a *range* (for example, **integers** from 0 to 1,000). A graphic element with parameters is called a *parameterized*

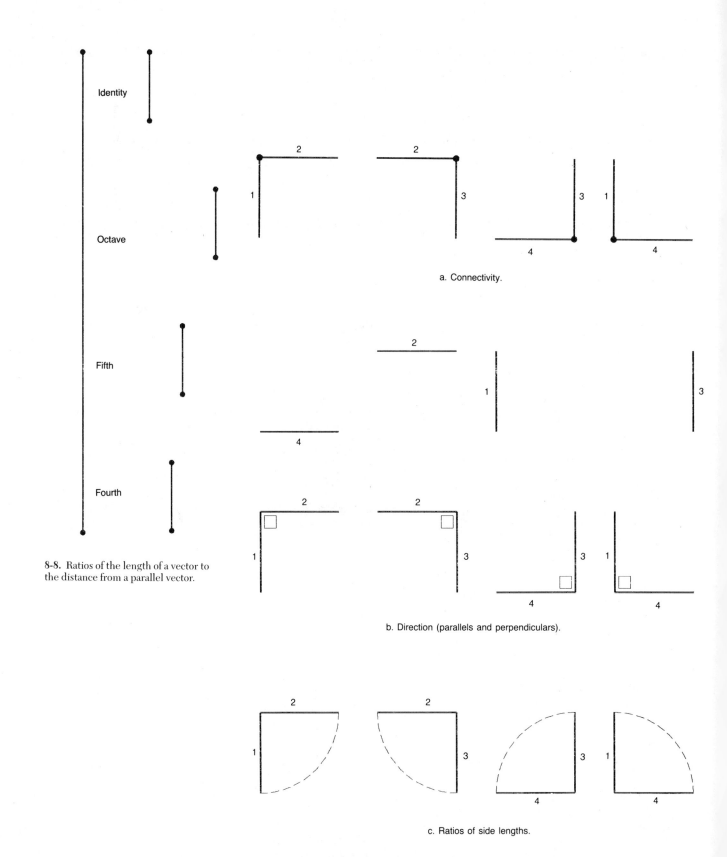

Identity

Octave

Fifth

Fourth

2

1

2

3

3

1

4

4

a. Connectivity.

2

1

3

4

8-8. Ratios of the length of a vector to the distance from a parallel vector.

2

1

2

3

3

1

4

4

b. Direction (parallels and perpendiculars).

2

1

2

3

3

1

4

4

c. Ratios of side lengths.

8-9. Relations of vectors that characterize a square.

or *parametric element*. When specific values from their ranges are assigned to the parameters, a particular instance is defined. Figure 8-10 illustrates some of the many possible instances of our square, all defined by assigning values to the parameters.

Composition of a motif can be understood, then, as a process of specifying essential relations of connectivity, direction, and ratio in a set of vectors. All instances of the same type of motif will consist of vectors related in the same way. This formalizes, in a fashion suitable for our purposes here, a famous definition of design given by the Renaissance architect and theorist Leon Battista Alberti in his *Ten Books on Architecture*: "the right and exact adapting and joining together of the lines and angles which compose and form the face of the building" (fig. 8-11).

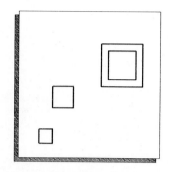

8-10. Squares instantiated within a screen coordinate system.

8-11. "A right and exact adapting and joining together the lines and angles which compose and form the face of the building": a composition of parallels, perpendiculars, simple whole number ratios, and instances of squares by Alberti.

Parameterized Procedures

Just as we used procedures Square, Triangle, and Hexagon earlier to generate the corresponding figures, we can use *parameterized* procedures to generate instances of parametric objects, such as our square (fig. 8-12).

The first step in writing a parameterized procedure is to list the formal parameters in parentheses after the procedure name and declare their types. For example, we might begin a parameterized procedure to draw a square:

```
PROCEDURE SQUARE (X,Y,LENGTH : INTEGER);
```

Note the convention that is used for declaring the types of the formal parameters; the list of formal parameters is terminated by a colon, then we specify that they all take **integer** values.

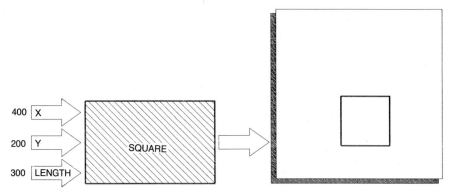

8-12. The action of a parameterized procedure to draw a square; parameter values are passed in, and the corresponding instance is passed out.

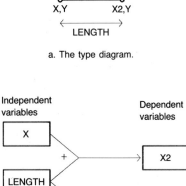

a. The type diagram.

b. Independent and dependent variables.

8-13. Vertex coordinates of a square expressed in terms of X, Y, and Length.

For the moment, we will keep things simple by assuming that all our formal parameters take **integer** values, and that they range over all the **integers**. Later we shall consider situations in which parameters are of different types (for example, both **integer** and **real**) and may have more restricted ranges.

Next we express our **move**s and **draw**s in terms of the three formal parameters (fig. 8-13). The coordinates X and Y are given directly by the formal parameters. The coordinate X2 is given by X + Length, and the cooordinate Y2 is given by Y + Length. Using these coordinate values, we can write the procedure as follows:

```
PROCEDURE SQUARE (X,Y,LENGTH : INTEGER);

    VAR X2,Y2 : INTEGER;

    BEGIN

        { Calculate values for X2 and Y2 }
        X2 := X + LENGTH;
        Y2 := Y + LENGTH;

        { Move to bottom left corner }
        MOVE (X,Y);

        { Draw the four sides of the square }
        DRAW (X2,Y);
        DRAW (X2,Y2);
        DRAW (X,Y2);
        DRAW (X,Y);

    END;
```

Notice that the code within this procedure produces *any* square with sides parallel to the coordinate axes, (as specified by the parameter values) and *only* such squares, so it expresses the essence of the type Square. This is done by means of arithmetic expressions and assignments that define the appropriate connectivity, direction, and ratio-of-length relations. Then each **draw** generates a vector that is spatially related in the appropriate way to its predecessors. The first **draw** produces a vector starting at point (X, Y), parallel to the X axis, and of the specified Length (fig. 8-14a). The second **draw** produces a second vector connected to the end of the first, perpendicular to it, and in a Length ratio of 1:1 (fig. 8-14b). The third **draw** produces a third vector, connected to the end of the second, perpendicular to it, and once again, in a Length ratio of 1:1 (fig. 8-14c). Finally, the fourth **draw** produces a fourth vector that connects the end of the third vector back to the beginning of the first (fig. 8-14d).

The formal parameter list, on the other hand, specifies whatever it is that we want to vary about squares—the accidental properties of squares that we want to control. If we want to make a composition out of squares, the formal parameters establish our graphic variables. In this case, the parameters are X, Y, and Length, corresponding to the variables shown on our diagram.

Once such a parameterized procedure has been declared, it may be invoked with defined parameter values to generate an instance. The following statements first assign values to X, Y, and Length, then invoke Square with these values as actual parameters to generate the corresponding instances:

```
X  :=  400;
Y  :=  200;
LENGTH  :=  300;
SQUARE  (X,Y,LENGTH);
```

Instead of using separate assignment statements, we can more concisely write:

```
SQUARE  (400,200,300);
```

That is, we can specify values for X, Y, and Length directly in the list of actual parameters.

If we repeatedly invoke Square, with different X, Y, and Length values, we produce a picture composed of many instances of squares. The following program, for example, generates the drawing shown in figure 8-15:

```
PROGRAM DRAWSQUARE;
  { Program to draw stack of shrinking squares }

  USES GRAPHICS;

  PROCEDURE SQUARE (X,Y,LENGTH : INTEGER);

    VAR X2,Y2 : INTEGER;

    BEGIN

      { Calculates values for X2 and Y2 }
      X2  :=  X  +  LENGTH;
      Y2  :=  Y  +  LENGTH;

      { Move to the bottom left corner }
      MOVE  (X,Y);

      { Draw the four sides of the square }
      DRAW  (X2,Y);
      DRAW  (X2,Y2);
      DRAW  (X,Y2);
      DRAW  (X,Y);

    END;
```

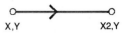

a. First vector drawn from point (X, Y), parallel to the X axis, and of specified Length.

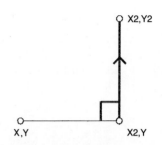

b. Second vector connected to end of first, perpendicular to it, and in ratio 1:1.

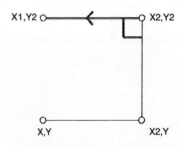

c. Third vector drawn in the same relationship to the second as the second is to the first.

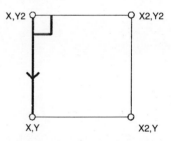

d. Fourth vector connects to the beginning of the first.

8-14. The procedure Square spatially relates four vectors.

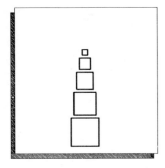

8-15. A stack of shrinking squares.

```
{ Start the main program to draw squares }
BEGIN

    START_DRAWING;

        SQUARE (400,  50,200);
        SQUARE (420,270,160);
        SQUARE (440,450,120);
        SQUARE (460,590, 80);
        SQUARE (480,690, 40);

    FINISH_DRAWING;

END.
```

We could produce exactly the same result with the following, which specifies each vector directly by a **draw**:

```
PROGRAM DRAWSQUARE;
    { Program to draw stack of shrinking squares }

    USES  GRAPHICS;

    BEGIN

        START_DRAWING;

            { Draw the first square with side  =  200 }
            MOVE (400,  50);
            DRAW (600,  50);
            DRAW (600,250);
            DRAW (400,250);
            DRAW (400,  50);

            { Draw the second square with side  =   160 }
            MOVE (420,270);
            DRAW (580,270);
            DRAW (580,430);
            DRAW (420,430);
            DRAW (420,270);

            { Draw the third square with side  =  120 }
            MOVE (440,450);
            DRAW (560,450);
            DRAW (560,570);
            DRAW (440,570);
            DRAW (440,450);

            { Draw the fourth square with side  =  80 }
            MOVE (460,590);
            DRAW (540,590);
            DRAW (540,670);
            DRAW (460,670);
            DRAW (460,590);

            { Draw the fifth square with side  =  40 }
            MOVE (480,690);
            DRAW (520,690);
            DRAW (520,730);
            DRAW (480,730);
            DRAW (480,690);

        FINISH_DRAWING;

    END.
```

But this program is lengthy and difficult to follow, and unlike the program that invokes the parameterized procedure Square, it does not take advantage of our knowledge that the picture is composed entirely of instances of squares with sides parallel to the coordinate axes. So the program that invokes Square is more concise and tells us more about the structure of the drawing that it generates.

Invoking Procedures

The concept of a parameterized graphic procedure and its uses should now be clear. Before going on, though, it will be useful to pause and summarize the rules that must be followed when invoking procedures. These are much like the rules that apply to the invocation of functions.

We have seen, first, that a procedure is invoked by giving its name and the actual parameters. This causes the values of the actual parameters to be assigned to the corresponding formal parameters. The procedure is then executed, and the computer returns to process the next statement following the procedure invocation. The values of the actual parameters can be specified directly in the list as

```
SQUARE (400,200,300);
```

or by assigning values to variables that are then listed as actual parameters, for example:

```
X  := 400;
Y  := 200;
LENGTH := 300;
SQUARE (X,Y,LENGTH);
```

In this latter case, these variables must be declared in the main program and are local to it. It is not necessary for these variables to have the same identifiers as the formal parameters of the procedure Square. For example, we might write:

```
X_CORNER := 400;
Y_CORNER := 200;
SIDE := 300;
SQUARE (X_CORNER,Y_CORNER,SIDE);
```

It is the *positions* these variables occupy in the actual parameter list that are important. In this case the value assigned to the variable X_corner will be passed to the formal parameter X; the value assigned to the variable Y_corner will be passed to the formal parameter Y; and the value assigned to Side will be passed to the formal parameter Length. The only requirement is that the type of the variable must match the type of the corresponding parameter. In this case X_corner, Y_corner, and Side must all be declared as **integer** variables.

The following program illustrates these points by showing yet another way to create the stack of squares in figure 8-15:

```
PROGRAM DRAWSQUARE;
  { Program to draw stack of shrinking squares }
```

```
USES GRAPHICS;
PROCEDURE SQUARE (X,Y,LENGTH : INTEGER);

    VAR X2,Y2 : INTEGER;

    BEGIN

        { Calculate values for X2 and Y2 }
        X2 := X + LENGTH;
        Y2 := Y + LENGTH;

        { Move to the bottom left corner }
        MOVE (X,Y);

        { Draw the four sides of the square }
        DRAW (X2,Y);
        DRAW (X2,Y2);
        DRAW (X,Y2)
        DRAW (X,Y);

    END;

{ Start the main program to draw squares }
VAR X_CORNER,Y_CORNER,SIDE,INCREMENT : INTEGER;

BEGIN

    X_CORNER := 400;
    Y_CORNER := 50;
    SIDE := 200;
    INCREMENT := 20;

    START_DRAWING;

        { Draw the first square }
        SQUARE (X_CORNER,Y_CORNER,SIDE);

        { Draw the second square }
        X_CORNER := X_CORNER + INCREMENT;
        Y_CORNER := Y_CORNER + SIDE + INCREMENT;
        SIDE := SIDE - 2 * INCREMENT;
        SQUARE (X_CORNER,Y_CORNER,SIDE);

        { Draw the third square }
        X_CORNER := X_CORNER + INCREMENT;
        Y_CORNER := Y_CORNER + SIDE + INCREMENT;
        SIDE := SIDE - 2 * INCREMENT;
        SQUARE (X_CORNER,Y_CORNER,SIDE);

        { Draw the fourth square }
        X_CORNER := X_CORNER + INCREMENT;
        Y_CORNER := Y_CORNER + SIDE + INCREMENT;
        SIDE := SIDE - 2 * INCREMENT;
        SQUARE (X_CORNER,Y_CORNER,SIDE);

        { Draw the fifth square }
        X_CORNER := X_CORNER + INCREMENT;
        Y_CORNER := Y_CORNER + SIDE + INCREMENT;
        SIDE := SIDE - 2 * INCREMENT;
        SQUARE (X_CORNER,Y_CORNER,SIDE);

    FINISH_DRAWING;
END.
```

Note that in order to draw a different set of stacked squares, one need change only the initially assigned values of the variables (X_corner, Y_corner, Side, and Increment). Notice also that several statements are repeated each time a square is drawn. In chapter 9, we will see how to eliminate this redundancy.

The Differences between Functions and Procedures

You now know the basic rules for declaring and invoking functions and procedures, and we have explored some of the uses of each. There are many similarities in the syntax, and both functions and procedures provide means of abstraction and modularization. But why do we distinguish between the two, and what are the important differences?

The essential difference is that a procedure can do anything that we can express in Pascal code, whereas a function performs one specific, very restricted kind of task. A function always returns a single value of a specified type (**integer**, **real**, **Boolean**, or **char**acter). Thus, you will recall, a function heading always specifies the function's type (as well as the types of the formal parameters), but the concept of data type does not apply to procedures, and procedure headings do not specify a data type. For the same reason, a function must always contain a statement that assigns a value (of the correct type) to the function identifier, but an attempt to do this to a procedure identifier would generate an error.

This logic leads to some important differences in the ways that functions and procedures are executed. In executable code, a function identifier always appears as part of an executable statement; a function identifier alone is not an executable statement. When a function is executed, its value is substituted for the function identifier in the expression containing that identifier. But a procedure identifier by itself is an executable statement. Its effect is like that of copying the statements of the procedure into the program text each place it appears.

In Pascal programming functions and procedures have a wide variety of uses, but in this book we shall use them to achieve very specific ends. We shall mostly use functions to return values that we need in coordinate calculations, and (for the moment) we shall use procedures to generate parts of drawings. Later, in Section Three, we shall transform drawings with procedures. Procedures and functions are the building blocks of programs to generate drawings; they encode knowledge of how to produce graphic motifs and of how to size and position these motifs on the drawing surface to create compositions.

Shape and Position Parameters

In the remainder of this chapter we shall assume that you have a sound grasp of parameterized procedures that generate a line figure, and we shall concentrate on the logic of parameterization. Specifically, how do you choose and express the parameters of a graphic element?

It is useful to begin by distinguishing between the *shape* and *position* parameters of a graphic element. Shape parameters control size, proportion, and other such properties, whereas position parameters control the location on the drawing surface. In Square, for example, Length is a shape parameter; X and Y are position parameters (fig. 8-16).

a. Shape parameter of a square.

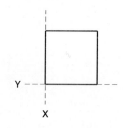

b. Position parameters of a square.

8-16. Shape and position parameters.

Alternative Parameterization Schemes

Usually there are different, though mathematically equivalent, ways to specify shape and position parameters. For example, we could locate a square by its center point, rather than its bottom-left corner (fig. 8-17) and rewrite procedure Square as follows:

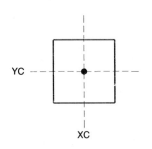

8-17. A square located by its center point.

```
PROCEDURE  SQUARE  (XC,YC,LENGTH  :  INTEGER);

    VAR  X1,X2,Y1,Y2  :  INTEGER;

    BEGIN

        { Calculate values for corners }
        X1  :=  XC  −  (LENGTH  DIV  2);
        X2  :=  X1  +  LENGTH;
        Y1  :=  YC  −  (LENGTH  DIV  2);
        Y2  :=  Y1  +  LENGTH;

        { Move to the bottom left corner }
        MOVE  (X1,Y1);

        { Draw the four sides }
        DRAW  (X2,Y1);
        DRAW  (X2,Y2);
        DRAW  (X1,Y2);
        DRAW  (X1,Y1);

    END;
```

Or we might want to specify squares by giving the coordinates of the top-right corner and the length of the diagonal (fig. 8-18). In this case, Square could be rewritten:

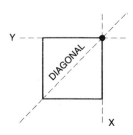

8-18. Another way to parameterize a square.

```
PROCEDURE  SQUARE  (X,Y,DIAGONAL  :  INTEGER);

    VAR  X2,Y2,SIDE  :  INTEGER;
         THETA  :  REAL;

    BEGIN

        { Given X,Y as the coordinates of the top right
          corner, calculate the values for X2 and Y2 }
        THETA  :=  45.0  ∗  0.01745;
        SIDE  :=  ROUND(DIAGONAL  ∗  SIN(THETA));
        X2  :=  X  −  SIDE;
        Y2  :=  Y  −  SIDE;

        { Move to the bottom left corner }
        MOVE  (X2,Y2);

        { Draw the four sides }
        DRAW  (X,Y2);
        DRAW  (X,Y);
        DRAW  (X2,Y);
        DRAW  (X2,Y2);

    END;
```

Choice of the parameterization scheme depends on the intended compositional use of the motif. If you intend to fit squares together with edges aligned (fig. 8-19a), you will probably find it convenient to specify position by corner coordinates and shape by side length. Concentric nesting (fig. 8-19b), on the other hand, is easier if position is specified by center coordinates. And corner-to-corner diagonal connection (fig. 8-19c) is easier if shape is specified by the length of the diagonal. If you intend to use a motif in several different ways, you may find it convenient to write a procedure for each.

Choosing Position Parameters

We can establish many or few position parameters to a graphic element, depending on the number of degrees of freedom that we want in positioning the element within the boundaries of the screen coordinate system. In Square we have used two position parameters, X and Y, so that we have two degrees of freedom, which enables us to move instances in directions parallel to the X and Y axes. But we could have fewer. In the following procedure, for example, Y is made a constant within the procedure, and the only position parameter is X:

```
PROCEDURE SQUARE (X,LENGTH : INTEGER);

    VAR X2,Y2 : INTEGER;
    CONST Y = 200;

    BEGIN

        { Given a constant value for Y,
          calculate values for X2 and Y2 }
        X2 := X + LENGTH;
        Y2 := Y + LENGTH;

        { Move to the bottom left corner }
        MOVE (X,Y);

        { Draw the four sides of the square }
        DRAW (X2,Y);
        DRAW (X2,Y2);
        DRAW (X,Y2);
        DRAW (X,Y);

    END;
```

In other words, a certain Y coordinate becomes an essential property of the element, and we have fewer design variables. We can invoke this procedure to generate compositions of aligned squares. The following statements, for example, generate the composition shown in figure 8-20:

```
SQUARE (150, 50);
SQUARE (250,100);
SQUARE (400,150);
SQUARE (600,200);
```

The next version of a procedure to draw a square has no position parameters:

```
PROCEDURE SQUARE (LENGTH : INTEGER);

    VAR X2,Y2 : INTEGER;
    CONST X = 200;
          Y = 300;
```

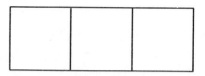

a. Edges of squares related.

b. Centers of squares related.

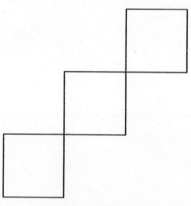

c. Diagonals of squares related.

8-19. Different parameterization schemes facilitate the formation of different relationships between squares.

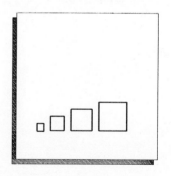

8-20. A composition of aligned squares.

```
BEGIN
  { Given constant values for X and Y,
    calculate values for X2 and Y2 }
  X2 := X + LENGTH;
  Y2 := Y + LENGTH;

  { Move to the bottom left corner }
  MOVE (X,Y);

  { Draw the four sides of the square }
  DRAW (X2,Y);
  DRAW (X2,Y2);
  DRAW (X,Y2);
  DRAW (X,Y);
END;
```

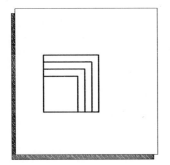

8-21. A composition in which squares are fixed at their bottom-left corner, but side lengths vary.

This procedure draws squares starting at a certain point, and Length is the only design variable. The following statements use it to generate the composition shown in figure 8-21:

```
SQUARE (250);
SQUARE (300);
SQUARE (350);
SQUARE (400);
```

Another possibility is to define not only X and Y as position parameters, but also an angle Theta of rotation from the X axis (fig. 8-22). It is thus no longer an essential property that a square has sides parallel to the coordinate axes, and we have an additional position variable to work with in design. The code of the procedure now becomes more complicated and involves use of some trigonometry:

```
PROCEDURE SQUARE (X,Y,LENGTH : INTEGER;
                  THETA : REAL);

  CONST K = 0.01745;
  VAR X2,X3,X4,Y2,Y3,Y4 : INTEGER;
      DIAGONAL : REAL;

BEGIN
  { Calculate values for other corners }
  X2 := X + ROUND(LENGTH * COS(THETA*K));
  Y2 := Y + ROUND(LENGTH * SIN(THETA*K));

  THETA := THETA + 45.0;
  DIAGONAL := SQRT(SQR(LENGTH) * 2);
  X3 := X + ROUND(DIAGONAL * COS(THETA*K));
  Y3 := Y + ROUND(DIAGONAL * SIN(THETA*K));

  THETA := THETA + 45.0;
  X4 := X + ROUND(LENGTH * COS(THETA*K));
  Y4 := Y + ROUND(LENGTH * SIN(THETA*K));

  { Move to the rotating corner }
  MOVE (X,Y);

  { Draw the four sides }
  DRAW (X2,Y2);
```

```
        DRAW (X3,Y3);
        DRAW (X4,Y4);
        DRAW (X,Y);

    END;
```

(Do not be too intimidated by this. Later we shall explore much more convenient ways to handle rotations.)

The following code assigns values to all three position parameters and the shape parameter Length, for each instance, and generates the composition shown in figure 8-23:

```
{ Outer square }
X1 := 200;
Y1 := 200;
LENGTH1 := 500;
SQUARE (X1,Y1,LENGTH1,0);

{ Rotated second square }
X2 := X1 + (LENGTH1 DIV 2);
LENGTH2 := ROUND(LENGTH1/SQRT(2.0));
SQUARE (X2,Y1,LENGTH2,45);

{ Third square }
X3 := X1 + (LENGTH1 DIV 4);
Y3 := Y1 + (LENGTH1 DIV 4);
LENGTH3 := ROUND(LENGTH2/SQRT(2.0));
SQUARE (X3,Y3,LENGTH3,0);

{ Rotated inner square }
LENGTH4 := ROUND(LENGTH3/SQRT(2.0));
SQUARE (X2,Y3,LENGTH4,45);
```

The effect of introducing additional position parameters is much like that of introducing additional drawing instruments. If you have only a parallel rule and a ninety-degree set square, you can only constuct squares parallel to the coordinate axes. But, if you introduce an adjustable drafting triangle, or a drafting machine, you can construct squares at any angle.

Choosing Shape Parameters

We can also establish many or few shape parameters, with corresponding degrees of freedom to vary the shapes of instances. By definition, a square has only one shape parameter, which we have taken to be Length. We might even eliminate this, as in the following procedure that draws squares of fixed size at different positions parallel to the coordinate axes:

```
PROCEDURE SQUARE (X,Y : INTEGER);

    VAR X2,Y2 : INTEGER;
    CONST LENGTH = 100;

    BEGIN
        { Given a constant value for LENGTH,
          calculate values for X2 and Y2 }
        X2 := X + LENGTH;
        Y2 := Y + LENGTH;
```

8-22. The introduction of Theta as a third position parameter.

8-23. A composition of rotated squares.

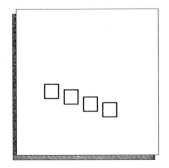

8-24. A composition in which the squares are of fixed size but vary in position.

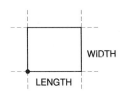

8-25. A rectangle with sides parallel to the coordinate axes. Length and Width are the two shape parameters.

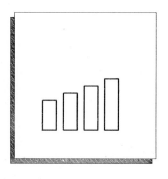

8-26. A simple composition of rectangles.

```
    { Move to the bottom left corner }
    MOVE (X,Y);

    { Draw the four sides of the square }
    DRAW (X2,Y);
    DRAW (X2,Y2);
    DRAW (X,Y2);
    DRAW (X,Y);

END;
```

Our only design decisions now are about values of the position parameters X and Y for each instance. The composition shown in fig. 8-24 was generated by the following statements, which assign values to these parameters for each instance:

```
SQUARE (200,400);
SQUARE (340,360);
SQUARE (480,320);
SQUARE (620,280);
```

A rectangle, by definition, has two shape parameters, which we usually think of as Length and Width (fig. 8-25). We can modify our Square procedure to become a Rectangle procedure:

```
PROCEDURE RECTANGLE (X,Y,LENGTH,WIDTH : INTEGER);

    VAR X2,Y2 : INTEGER;

    BEGIN

        { Calculate values for X2 and Y2 }
        X2 := X + LENGTH;
        Y2 := Y + WIDTH;

        { Move to the bottom left corner }
        MOVE (X,Y);

        { Draw the four sides }
        DRAW (X2,Y);
        DRAW (X2,Y2);
        DRAW (X,Y2);
        DRAW (X,Y);

    END;
```

Note that this represents a *generalization* of the idea of a square. Rectangle can still produce squares if we choose to relate Length and Width by assigning each the same value, but it can also produce rectangles that are not squares. In other words, the square is a specialized *subtype* (with a more restrictively defined essence) of the rectangle. The following statements, which invoke Rectangle, generate the composition shown in figure 8-26.

```
RECTANGLE (200,200,100,200);
RECTANGLE (350,200,100,250);
RECTANGLE (500,200,100,300);
RECTANGLE (650,200,100,350);
```

A rectangle with sides parallel to the coordinate axes can also be parameterized in terms of the coordinates of its diagonally opposite corners (fig. 8-27). The following procedure illustrates this approach:

```
PROCEDURE  RECTANGLE (X1,Y1,X2,Y2 :  INTEGER);

    BEGIN

        { Move to the bottom left corner }
        MOVE (X1,Y1);

        { Draw the four sides }
        DRAW (X2,Y1);
        DRAW (X2,Y2);
        DRAW (X1,Y2);
        DRAW (X1,Y1);

    END;
```

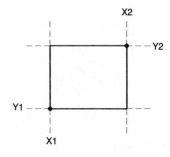

8-27. A rectangle parameterized by the coordinates of its diagonally opposite corners.

Introduction of the additional shape parameter Shear_angle (fig. 8-28) yields the type *parallelogram*. The following procedure draws parallelograms:

```
PROCEDURE  PARALLELOGRAM (X,Y,LENGTH,WIDTH :  INTEGER;
                                    SHEAR_ANGLE :  REAL);

    VAR X2,X3,X4,Y2 :  INTEGER;

    BEGIN

        { Calculate coordinates of corners }
        SHEAR_ANGLE := SHEAR_ANGLE * 0.01745;
        X2 := X + LENGTH;
        X4 := X + ROUND(WIDTH * COS(SHEAR_ANGLE));
        X3 := X4 + LENGTH;
        Y2 := Y + ROUND(WIDTH * SIN(SHEAR_ANGLE));

        { Move to the bottom left corner }
        MOVE (X,Y);

        { Draw the four sides }
        DRAW (X2,Y);
        DRAW (X3,Y2);
        DRAW (X4,Y2);
        DRAW (X,Y);

    END;
```

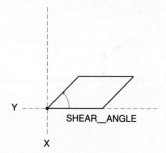

8-28. A parallelogram with two sides parallel to the X axis.

This represents another generalization. Parallelogram will draw rectangles when Shear is set to 90 degrees, and it will draw squares when Shear is 90 degrees and Length has the same value as Width.

Here, for the ambitious, is a procedure with X, Y, Theta, Length, Width, and Shear_angle (fig. 8-29) as parameters:

```
PROCEDURE  PARALLELOGRAM (X,Y,LENGTH, WIDTH :  INTEGER;
                                    SHEAR_ANGLE,THETA :  REAL);

    VAR ANGLE, DIAGONAL,XL,YL :  REAL;
        X1,X2,X3,Y1,Y2,Y3 :  INTEGER;

    BEGIN
```

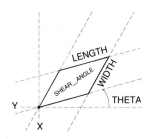

8-29. A rotated parallelogram.

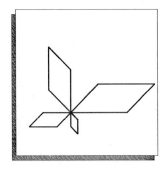

8-30. A composition of rotated parallelograms.

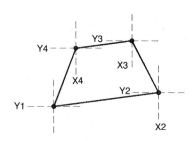

8-31. A quadrilateral.

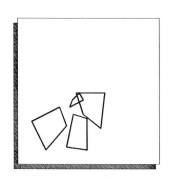

8-32. A composition of quadrilaterals.

```
SHEAR_ANGLE  :=  SHEAR_ANGLE  *  0.01745;
THETA  :=  THETA  *  0.01745;
XL  :=  WIDTH  *  COS(SHEAR_ANGLE);
YL  :=  WIDTH  *  SIN(SHEAR_ANGLE);
DIAGONAL  :=  SQRT(SQR(YL)  +  SQR(LENGTH + XL));
ANGLE  :=  ARCTAN(YL/(LENGTH + XL));
X1  :=  X  +  ROUND(LENGTH  *  COS(THETA));
Y1  :=  Y  +  ROUND(LENGTH  *  SIN(THETA));
X2  :=  X  +  ROUND(DIAGONAL  *  COS(THETA + ANGLE));
Y2  :=  Y  +  ROUND(DIAGONAL  *  SIN(THETA + ANGLE));
X3  :=  X  +  ROUND(WIDTH  *  COS(SHEAR_ANGLE + THETA));
Y3  :=  Y  +  ROUND(WIDTH  *  SIN(SHEAR_ANGLE + THETA));

  { Move to bottom left corner }
  MOVE  (X,Y);

  { Draw the four sides }
  DRAW  (X1,Y1);
  DRAW  (X2,Y2);
  DRAW  (X3,Y3);
  DRAW  (X,Y);

END;
```

This involves some fairly complicated trigonometry. The following statements invoke it to generate the composition of rotated parallelograms shown in figure 8-30:

```
PARALLELOGRAM  (400,300,400,200,45,0);
PARALLELOGRAM  (400,300,300,150,45,90);
PARALLELOGRAM  (400,300,200,100,45,180);
PARALLELOGRAM  (400,300,100,50,45,270);
```

The Maximum Possible Number of Parameters

We can generalize the idea of a four-sided figure to the ultimate by allowing the coordinates of each vertex to be set independently (fig. 8-31). Thus we have eight parameters, giving us eight degrees of freedom. The following program generates a composition of such figures (see fig. 8-32):

```
PROGRAM  FIGURES;

  USES  GRAPHICS;

  PROCEDURE  FOURSIDE (X1,Y1,X2,Y2,X3,Y3,X4,Y4  :  INTEGER);

    BEGIN

      { Move to one corner }
      MOVE  (X1,Y1);

      { Draw the four sides }
      DRAW  (X2,Y2);
      DRAW  (X3,Y3);
      DRAW  (X4,Y4);
      DRAW  (X1,Y1);

    END;

  { Begin main program }
  BEGIN
```

```
START_DRAWING;

    FOURSIDE  (200,100,350,275,300,400,100,300);
    FOURSIDE  (350,125,500,100,500,325,400,350);
    FOURSIDE  (600,250,625,500,425,500,475,450);
    FOURSIDE  (350,400,450,450,425,500,375,450);

  FINISH_DRAWING;
END.
```

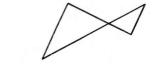

8-33. A "bow-tie" figure.

Notice that the procedure Fourside does not necessarily generate polygons. It can also generate "bow-tie" figures (fig. 8-33).

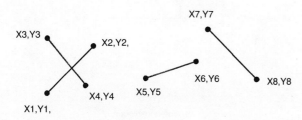

a. A figure composed of 4 vectors can have 4n = 16 parameters.

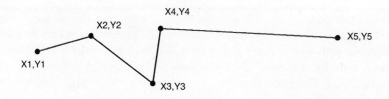

b. A chain of 4 vectors can have 2(n + 1) = 10 parameters.

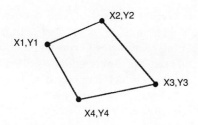

c. A 4-sided figure can have 2n = 8 parameters.

8-34. The maximum number of parameters for a figure composed of n vectors.

In general, the maximum number of parameters for a figure composed of n vectors is 4n (fig. 8-34a). If the vectors are connected head to tail (Klee's "active line, limited in its movement by fixed points") the maximum is 2(n + 1) (fig. 8-34b). If they are connected to form an n-sided figure, the maximum is 2n (fig. 8-34c). Our task in parameterizing a procedure to draw a figure composed of n vectors, therefore, is to choose some appropriate number of

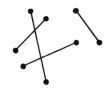

a. Composition of four vectors.

b. Four-sided figure.

c. Four-sided polygon.

d. Trapezoid.

e. Parallelogram.

f. Rectangle.

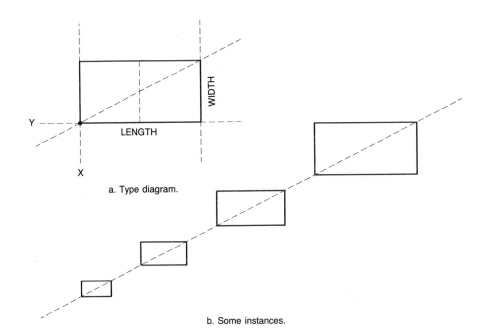

a. Type diagram.

b. Some instances.

8-36. A rectangle of proportion 2:1.

g. Square

8-35. A typical hierarchy of types and subtypes.

degrees of freedom between 0 and 4n, then to work out a convenient way to define the parameters and express the code of the procedure in terms of them.

Figures with few degrees of freedom are subtypes of figures with more. We have seen, for instance, that the square is a subtype of the rectangle, and the rectangle of the parallelogram. Thus hierarchies of types and subtypes emerge (fig. 8-35).

Rules of Proportion

Where there are n vectors and we choose d degrees of freedom for a figure, 4n-d coordinate values must be generated within the procedure. This can be done either by setting coordinates to constants, or by making coordinates dependent on the parameters. Such dependencies often express *rules of proportion*. For example, this procedure incorporates the rule:

```
WIDTH := LENGTH DIV 2;
```

and generates rectangles of proportion 2:1 (fig. 8-36).

```
PROCEDURE RECTANGLE (X,Y,LENGTH : INTEGER);

    VAR X2,Y2,WIDTH : INTEGER;

    BEGIN

        { Calculate width as function of length }
        WIDTH := LENGTH DIV 2;

        { Calculate values for X2 and Y2 }
        X2 := X + LENGTH;
        Y2 := Y + WIDTH;
```

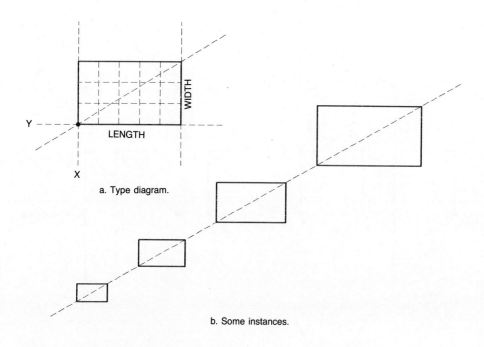

a. Type diagram.

b. Some instances.

8-37. A rectangle of proportion 5:3.

```
        { Move to the bottom left corner }
          MOVE (X,Y);

        { Draw the four sides }
          DRAW (X2,Y);
          DRAW (X2,Y2);
          DRAW (X,Y2);
          DRAW (X,Y);
      END;
```

The next procedure incorporates the rule:

```
      WIDTH := (3*LENGTH) DIV 5;
```

and generates rectangles of proportion 5:3 (fig. 8-37).

```
      PROCEDURE RECTANGLE (X,Y,LENGTH : INTEGER);

          VAR X2,Y2,WIDTH : INTEGER;

          BEGIN
            { Calculate width as function of length }
              WIDTH := (3*LENGTH) DIV 5;

            { Calculate values for X2 and Y2 }
              X2 := X + LENGTH;
              Y2 := Y + WIDTH;

            { Move to the bottom left corner }
              MOVE (X,Y);

            { Draw the four sides }
```

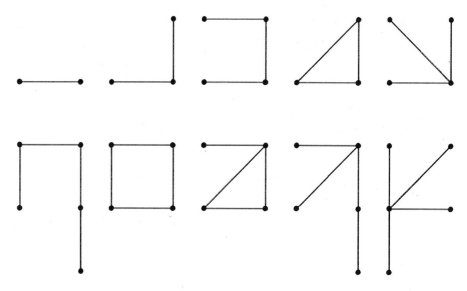

8-38. All the possible ways to connect four or fewer vectors.

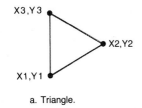

a. Triangle.

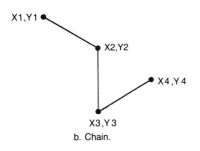

b. Chain.

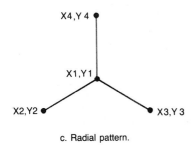

c. Radial pattern.

8-39. Patterns of three vectors.

```
DRAW  (X2,Y);
DRAW  (X2,Y2);
DRAW  (X,Y2);
DRAW  (X,Y);.
END;
```

Both of these procedures have the same parameters X, Y, and Length, but the different functions relating Length and Width make them different subtypes of the type Rectangle.

Ways to Connect Vectors

Types of motifs can be constructed systematically by considering all the different ways to make a connected figure out of n vectors (fig. 8-38). Two vectors can be connected end to end. There are three ways to connect three vectors. With four vectors the possibilities expand. There is, as one might expect, a combinatorial explosion as the number of vectors grows (see Harary 1969). The essential point, though, is that the number of possibilities for a given number of vectors is finite, and you can systematically enumerate all of them. If vectors are the atoms, these connected figures are the molecules of line drawings.

The pattern of connection of vectors in a graphic element is expressed in the generating procedure by the sequencing of **move**s and **draw**s. Let us consider, for example, the shapes composed of three vectors. Code for a triangle (fig. 8-39a) may be expressed:

```
MOVE  (X1,Y1);
DRAW  (X2,Y2);
DRAW  (X3,Y3);
DRAW  (X1,Y1);
```

Note that six variables are used here, indicating that there are six potential degrees of freedom. Code for a chain of three vectors (fig. 8-39b), which has eight potential degrees of freedom, may be expressed:

```
MOVE   (X1,Y1);
DRAW   (X2,Y2);
DRAW   (X3,Y3);
DRAW   (X4,Y4);
```

The only difference is that the last vector does not connect back to the point (X1, Y1), but ends at independently established coordinates (X4, Y4). Finally, code to draw the radial pattern (fig. 8-39c) may be expressed:

```
MOVE   (X1,Y1);
DRAW   (X2,Y2);
MOVE   (X1,Y1);
DRAW   (X3,Y3);
MOVE   (X1,Y1);
DRAW   (X4,Y4);
```

Once the pattern of connectivity is established, we might want to restrict ourselves to some subtype by introducing direction and ratio of length relations. In the triangular pattern, for example, we might require a pair of sides to be perpendicular, defining a right triangle (fig. 8-40a). Or we might require a pair of sides to be of equal length to produce an isosceles triangle (fig. 8-40b). If we require a pair of sides to be both perpendicular and of equal length, we obtain a right isosceles triangle (fig. 8-40c). And if we require all sides to be of equal length, we produce an equilateral triangle (fig. 8-40d).

Restricting the Ranges of Parameters

It does not always make sense to let *any* integer value be assigned to a parameter of a graphic element, since we know that some values are meaningless, or would generate errors. For example, our screen coordinate system ranges from 0 to 1,023 units, so it is meaningless to assign a value less than 0 or greater than 1,023 to a coordinate variable. The Pascal construct of a *subrange type* may be used to express this. The definition of an integer subrange type indicates the least and largest constant value in the subrange, where the lower bound must be less than the upper bound.

Until now we have defined variables in terms of predefined Pascal types—**integer** or **real**. It is possible to specify our own types, and by this means to limit the values that variables can take on. To declare a subrange type, you select an identifier (up to eight characters) and then explicitly specify the values that variables of the type may take on. For example,

```
TYPE SCREEN_COORDINATE = 0..1023;
```

can be declared at the beginning of the Pascal program. **Integer** variables that are to be limited to these values can be specified to be of this type rather than **integer**. For example, a procedure to draw a triangle that is guaranteed to be within the limits of the screen coordinate system might be written:

a. Right triangle.

b. Isosceles triangle.

c. Right isosceles triangle.

d. Equilateral triangle.

8-40. Subtypes of the triangle.

```
PROCEDURE TRIANGLE (X1,Y1,X2,Y2,X3,Y3 : SCREEN_COORDINATE);
BEGIN
      MOVE (X1,Y1);
      DRAW (X2,Y2);
      DRAW (X3,Y3);
      DRAW (X1,Y1);
END;
```

In most Pascal systems, an attempt to execute this procedure with inappropriate parameter values will generate an error message. The type of error message depends on the way values are assigned to the parameters. If they are passed as constants as in

```
TRIANGLE (700,800,1200,500,600,500);
```

you should be given a message, at compilation, that a constant is out of range. If the values of the parameters are calculated as follows,

```
X2 := 500 + K;
TRIANGLE (70,800,X2,500,600,500);
```

the error message should show up during execution of the program, indicating that upper or lower bounds of a variable have been exceeded.

In general, where we know the range of meaningful values that an **integer** parameter may take, it is good programming practice to declare this. First, it expresses our knowledge explicitly in the code. Second, it gives the compiler an opportunity to detect errors in a program. Third, it provides a way to detect inappropriate input values.

Subranges may also be used to restrict the dimensions that instances of some type of graphic element may take. The next procedure, for example, draws rectangles of side lengths between 20 and 100 units, on a 20-unit module and located in a 10-unit grid, within the limits of the screen coordinate system (fig. 8-41).

```
TYPE XY_RANGE  = 0..102;
     SIDE_RANGE  = 1..5;

PROCEDURE MODRECT (X1,Y1: XY_RANGE;
                   LENGTH,WIDTH  : SIDE_RANGE);
   CONST UNITS = 20;
         GRID  = 10;
   VAR XSTART,YSTART,LENGTH_UNITS,WIDTH_UNITS,
       X2,Y2 : INTEGER;

BEGIN
   { Calculate coordinates }
     XSTART := X1 * GRID;
     YSTART := Y1 * GRID;
     LENGTH_UNITS := LENGTH * UNITS;
     WIDTH_UNITS := WIDTH * UNITS;
     X2 := XSTART + LENGTH_UNITS;
     Y2 := YSTART + WIDTH_UNITS;
```

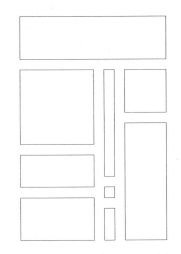

8-41. Modular rectangles in a modular grid.

```
{ Draw square }
   MOVE (XSTART,YSTART);
   DRAW (X2,YSTART);
   DRAW (X2,Y2);
   DRAW (XSTART,Y2);
   DRAW (XSTART,YSTART);

END;
```

Note that by declaring module size (20) and grid size (10) as **constants** within the procedure, we make them essential properties. It is also established as essential (by declaration of subranges) that dimensions of the rectangle vary between one and five modules, and that an instance can only be located within the limits of the screen coordinate system.

The concept of an **integer** subrange provides a way to calculate the number of instances of a type. Simply take the numbers of possible values for each parameter of the procedure and multiply these to obtain the *Cartesian product* of the subranges. If a procedure has three parameters, for example, each of which can take ten values, the number of instances is $10 \times 10 \times 10 = 1,000$. A vector in the screen coordinate system has four parameters (the coordinates of its endpoints), each of which has approximately 10^3 values, so the number of instances is approximately $10^{12} = 1,000,000,000,000$.

How Much Variation Is Needed?

How much variation should there be within a type? More precisely:

- How many degrees of freedom?
- How should these degrees of freedom be expressed in terms of parameters and dependencies?
- What should be the ranges of the parameters?
- What should be the increments of variation within these ranges?

At one extreme, a type might have only one instance. At the other extreme, for a figure of n vectors, there might be 4n parameters, each with a range of 1,024 values, yielding $1,024^{4n}$ instances. This, however, is a reduction to absurdity; we are back to having n independent vectors. Unless we can see some particular advantage in composing vectors n at a time, instead of one at a time, we do not gain anything.

The trade-off, then, is that if we write procedures with few shape and position parameters, we will have few graphic variables to manipulate in generating a composition, and we will be able to generate only highly structured, disciplined drawings of a very specific kind. But if we allow too many shape and position parameters, then the method of thinking in terms of types and instances begins to lose its power.

In fact, most of the drawings that we want to generate do turn out to be structured and disciplined in identifiable ways. The point is to recognize the rules that apply, or that we want to apply, and to express these rules concisely and elegantly in Pascal code. Conversely, you should avoid coding in restrictions that work against your graphic intentions. Once again, the fundamental issues here are not ones of computer technology, but of an artist's or a designer's stylistic choices.

Defining Vocabularies of Graphic Elements

So far we have considered examples of programs that generate compositions from one type of graphic element, such as a square, a rectangle, a trapezoid, or a triangle. But there is nothing to stop us from declaring procedures to draw several different types of graphic elements, then instantiating these to create a composition. The next program, for example, draws the composition of rectangles and triangles that is illustrated in figure 8-42.

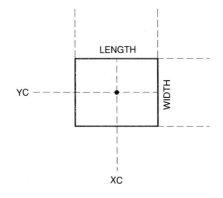

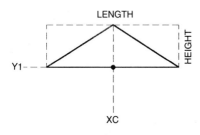

a. Vocabulary elements.

b. Composition of instances.

8-42. A composition of rectangles and triangles.

```
PROGRAM WINDOW;

    USES GRAPHICS;

    PROCEDURE RECTANGLE (XC,YC,LENGTH, WIDTH : INTEGER);

        { Draws rectangle centered around XC, YC }

        VAR X1,Y1,X2,Y2 : INTEGER;

        BEGIN

            { Calculate coordinates of corners }

            X1 : = XC − LENGTH DIV 2;
            X2 : = X1 + LENGTH;
            Y1 : = YC − WIDTH DIV 2;
            Y2 : = Y1 + WIDTH;

            { Move to the bottom left corner }
            MOVE (X1,Y1);

            { Draw the four sides }
            DRAW (X2,Y1);
            DRAW (X2,Y2);
            DRAW (X1,Y2);
            DRAW (X1,Y1);

        END;

    PROCEDURE TRIANGLE (XC,Y1,BASE,ALTITUDE : INTEGER);
        { Draws a triangle with center of base positioned at XC,Y1 }

        VAR X1,X2,Y2 : INTEGER;

        BEGIN

            X1 : = XC − (BASE DIV 2);
            X2 : = X1 + BASE;
            Y2 : = Y1 + ALTITUDE;

            { Move to bottom left corner }
            MOVE (X1,Y1);

            { Draw the three sides }
            DRAW (X2,Y1);
            DRAW (XC,Y2);
            DRAW (X1,Y1);

        END;

    { Begin main program }
    BEGIN
```

```
START_DRAWING;

    RECTANGLE (450,125,300,50);
    RECTANGLE (450,375,200,400);
    RECTANGLE (450,375,250,424);
    TRIANGLE (450,612,200,67);
    TRIANGLE (450,600,300,100);

FINISH_DRAWING;

END.
```

A *graphic vocabulary* may now be defined as a set of graphic element types that can be instantiated to generate drawings. Each element in the vocabulary is defined by the declaration of a parameterized procedure, and an instance is created whenever the procedure is invoked by name with appropriate actual parameters. In our example, then, we have a vocabulary consisting of rectangle and triangle.

We have seen that the parameters to a procedure that generates a vocabulary element establish the design variables associated with that element. There may be many or few of these, depending upon whether you want many features of an instance to be "given," or whether you want to be able to vary many features from instance to instance.

The code within a procedure that generates a vocabulary element defines the essential properties. **Moves** and **draws** express how vectors are connected. By setting constants and writing code that makes coordinate values dependent on the parameters, you establish essential dimensional properties. And, by declaring subranges, you make it essential to comply with certain limits.

We have also seen that you can take a systematic approach to defining a vocabulary element. First, decide how the vectors are connected. Next, decide what degrees of freedom you want in shaping and positioning instances, and develop a convenient scheme for expressing the shape and position parameters. Write expressions making coordinates in **moves** and **draws** dependent on these parameters. Finally, express any dimensioning discipline that you want to impose by means of constants and subranges.

Once the vocabulary has been declared, you can specify a composition by writing commands in the main program to create instances. The composition can very easily be modified by adding or deleting such commands or changing parameter values.

In summary, then, the structure of a simple Pascal graphic program that uses a graphic vocabulary to generate a composition is as follows:

```
program heading (describing what the program draws)
    USES GRAPHICS;
    declare constants
    declare global variables (if you must)
    declare coordinate calculation functions
    declare graphic procedures (establish vocabulary)
    declare variables local to main program
    BEGIN
        assign or read values for independent (design) variables
        calculate values of dependent variables
```

```
          START_DRAWING;
            invoke graphic procedures (generate drawing)
          FINISH_DRAWING;
      END.
```

There are several ways to organize the code between **begin** and **end**. You might first assign or read values for all the independent variables, then calculate values for all dependent variables, and finally **start_drawing** after you have established all the necessary parameter values. Alternatively, you might read and calculate parameter values immediately before you need to pass them into a graphics procedure, or you might use some combination of the two alternatives.

Each approach has its advantages and disadvantages. Strict segregation of the three steps keeps clear the logical distinction between independent and dependent design variables, but makes it more difficult to trace through the text of the program how a value is derived for a particular shape or position parameter. Conversely, calculation of values as needed usually makes it easier to trace the derivation of a parameter value, but obscures the distinction between independent and dependent variables. You must decide what is most important in a given program and choose an approach accordingly.

Examples of Graphic Vocabularies

A graphic vocabulary allows us to avoid writing long, tedious lists of instructions at the vector-by-vector level. It, instead, allows us to write instructions at the vocabulary element–by–vocabulary element level. We make use of our knowledge of the structure of the drawings that we want to produce in order to achieve this, and the structure of the program expresses this

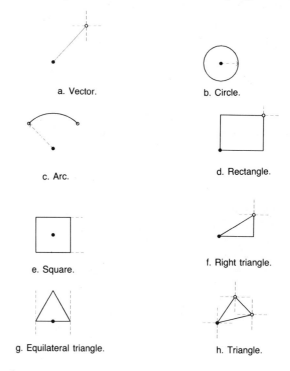

a. Vector. b. Circle.

c. Arc. d. Rectangle.

e. Square. f. Right triangle.

g. Equilateral triangle. h. Triangle.

8-43. A vocabulary for generating compositions of simple geometric figures.

knowledge. Thus the program becomes shorter, more elegant, more informative, and easier to change.

If you want to write graphics programs, then, one of the first steps is to put together an appropriate library of graphics procedures. These can be used as building blocks for producing programs very quickly.

You must, of course, think carefully about the kind of graphic vocabulary that you will need. It should be appropriate to your particular graphic purposes and extensive and flexible enough to allow you to accomplish the results that you want, yet it should not be too large. Let us consider some examples.

If you want to generate compositions of simple geometric figures, you might put together the following vocabulary (fig. 8-43):

```
LINE
CIRCLE
ARC
RECTANGLE
SQUARE
RIGHT_TRIANGLE
EQUILATERAL_TRIANGLE
SCALENE_TRIANGLE
```

At this point you can write procedures for all of these except Circle and Arc. We will introduce procedures for drawing circles and arcs in chapter 10.

To create lettering, you might define procedures to instantiate each element of an alphabet. You might allow only position parameters X and Y (fig. 8-44a); or you might allow size to be varied as well by introducing one shape parameter (fig. 8-44b). You might also allow compressed or extended versions by introducing a fourth parameter, allowing height and width to be varied independently (fig. 8-44c). Finally, you might allow the detailed adjustment of each character form (figure 8-44d).

Where the graphic task is to draw furniture layouts, you will need a vocabulary of furniture types: chairs, desks, tables, and so on. Or, where the task is to draw architectural elevations, you will need a vocabulary of architectural elements: doors, windows, columns, arches, and the like. You might develop different vocabularies for elevations in different architectural styles, such as classical or gothic. A landscape architect might develop a vocabulary of different types of trees. To draw people you might define a parameterized man, a parameterized woman, and a parameterized child.

When you establish a graphic vocabulary, the consideration of how instances will be put together to produce compositions will suggest appropriate parameterization schemes. An architect composing a floor plan, for example, usually wants to specify columns by center point (XC,YC) and Width (fig. 8-45a). It is usually most convenient to specify walls by start point (X1,Y1), endpoint (X2,Y2), and thickness T (fig. 8-45b). Windows in elevation are conveniently specified by Width, Height, center line XC, and sill height Sill (fig. 8-45c). And arch voussoirs might reasonably be specified by arch Radius, voussoir Thickness, voussoir Angle, and center-line angle Theta (fig. 8-45d).

Summary

We have introduced the fundamentally important idea of a graphic vocabulary expressed as a set of parameterized procedures. We have seen, too,

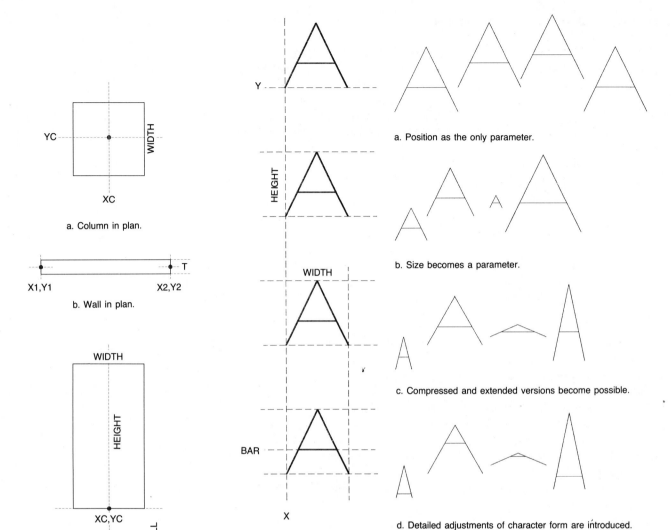

a. Position as the only parameter.

b. Size becomes a parameter.

c. Compressed and extended versions become possible.

d. Detailed adjustments of character form are introduced.

8-44. The parameterization of a character.

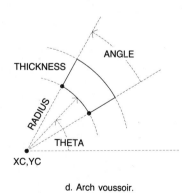

a. Column in plan.

b. Wall in plan.

c. Window in elevation.

d. Arch voussoir.

8-45. Parameterization schemes for some architectural vocabulary elements.

how such procedures may be invoked within a program to generate a composition. The nature and extent of your graphic vocabulary and appropriate schemes for parameterization of its elements are established by carefully analyzing the ways that the drawings you intend to produce can be decomposed, the ways that these parts can be classified into types according to their commonalities and differences, and the ways that instances are varied and related in compositions.

Exercises

1. Take the graphic programs that you have developed so far and create procedures from them, so the figures that they draw can be used as vocabulary elements. Put them together in a program that generates a simple composition.

2. The following procedure generates a simple line figure:

```
PROCEDURE CROSS_BOX (XC,YC,LENGTH,WIDTH : INTEGER);

    VAR X1,Y1,X2,Y2 : INTEGER;

    BEGIN

        X1 := XC − LENGTH DIV 2;
        Y1 := YC − WIDTH DIV 2;
        X2 := X1 + LENGTH;
        Y2 := Y1 + WIDTH;

        MOVE (X1,Y1);
        DRAW (X2,Y1);
        DRAW (X2,Y2);
        DRAW (X1,Y2);
        DRAW (X1,Y1);
        DRAW (X2,Y2);
        MOVE (X1,Y2);
        DRAW (X2,Y1);

    END;
```

The following invocations generate instances of this figure:

```
CROSS_BOX (450,50,200,50);
CROSS_BOX (400,200,100,200);
CROSS_BOX (500,200,100,200);
CROSS_BOX (400,400,100,100);
CROSS_BOX (500,400,100,100);
```

Using screen grid paper, draw these instances.

3. Many graphic artists and designers have been fascinated by the generation of highly disciplined but interesting compositions, using nothing more than a square as the vocabulary element. Think about the graphic variables that you might want to use in producing such a composition, and write a Square procedure with these as the formal parameters. Use this procedure in a program to generate a composition.

4. Repeat this exercise with progressively more general types of four-sided figures: rectangle, parallelogram, polygon.

5. Try the same exercise with triangles. Remember that there are four recognized subtypes: equilateral, right, isosceles, and scalene. Do you want to use all of these? Should they all be parameterized in the same way?

6. Consider the uppercase characters needed to draw your initials. How might these be parameterized to allow a wide variety of alternatives? Write the necessary procedures, and use them in programs to draw monograms.

7. Take one of your procedures to draw a graphic element, and use it in an interactive program that reads in values for the parameters, then displays the corresponding instance. Use the program to generate a series of variations of the motif.

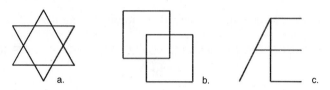

8-46. Some geometric figures to be decomposed.

8. The Star of David (fig. 8-46a) is a well-known two-dimensional line figure. We usually think of it as two superimposed triangles, but there are many less obvious ways to decompose it. Think of an interesting decomposition, write appropriately parameterized procedures to generate each of the parts, and use these in programs to generate variations on the Star of David. You may find it interesting to repeat this exercise for different decompositions and different parameterization schemes. Repeat the exercise for the line drawings shown in figures 8-46b and 8-46c.

9. Figure 8-47 shows four instances of a type. What properties are constant from instance to instance? What properties vary? Write a procedure to generate figures of this type.

10. Figure 8-48 shows a well-known floor plan by Mies van der Rohe. Write a parameterized procedure to generate the basic vocabulary element. Use this in a program to replicate the plan. Then use it in programs to produce variations on this theme.

8-47. Some instances of a type.

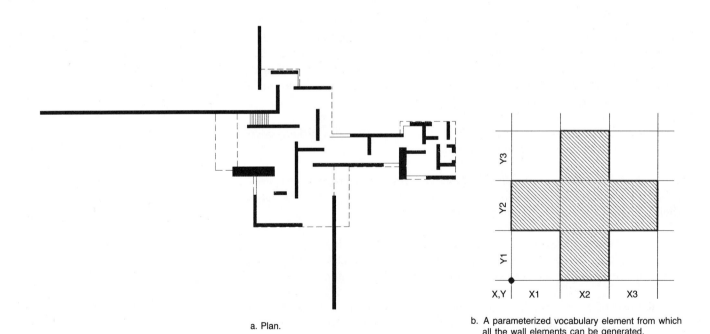

a. Plan.

b. A parameterized vocabulary element from which all the wall elements can be generated.

8-48. Mies van der Rohe's "Project for a Brick Country House," 1923.

11. Clothing designers often establish a motif, then produce a series of parametric variants to fit the motif to different figures. What are the usual parameters of hats, shirts, trousers, and shoes? What varies when a new value is given to one of these parameters? What remains constant? Other designed artifacts (for example, steel beams, bathtubs, and pen nibs) are also produced in series of parametric variants. Write an analysis of the role of parametric variation in design.

12. Donald Knuth's *Metafont* system for typographic design (Knuth 1986) is one of the most sophisticated explorations of the idea of parametric variation by computer yet to appear. Study its characteristics carefully, compare it to more traditional tools for typographic design, and write a critique.

9.

Repetition

We began by looking at pictures simply as sets of vectors, and we saw how they could be generated by sequences of **move** and **draw** operations. Then, in the last chapter, we saw that pictures may have more structure; they are often composed of instances of elements from some limited vocabulary of graphic types.

To write a Pascal program to draw a picture that is structured in this way, you must first declare the vocabulary elements that you intend to use. This is done by declaring a set of parameterized procedures in the declaration part of the program. Then, in the executable part of the program, you specify what vocabulary elements are to be instantiated (by giving procedure names) and the shape and location of each instance (by assigning values to the actual parameters of procedures). This is analogous to graphic design by first creating then using some vocabulary of templates or stencils, or to architectural design by first creating then using some kit of parts—an industrialized component building system, for example.

In other words, the procedure declarations establish the parts of the picture; the variable declarations to the main program establish the design variables that must be assigned values in order to create a picture; and the code between **start_drawing** and **finish_drawing** actually specifies how the parts are to be put together in a particular graphic composition. By varying this code, you can create different compositions from the same vocabulary.

Principles of Regular Composition

Now let us consider a particular kind of composition: the plan or elevation of a building (fig. 9-1). We can see immediately that, in this example, there is a limited vocabulary of standard columns, windows, and so on. Furthermore, the composition is not merely a random collection of instances. On the contrary, it is very highly ordered; it exhibits regular repetition of elements, consistencies of proportion, and numerous symmetries. Not all drawings are as highly ordered as this, but most do display at least some obvious regularities.

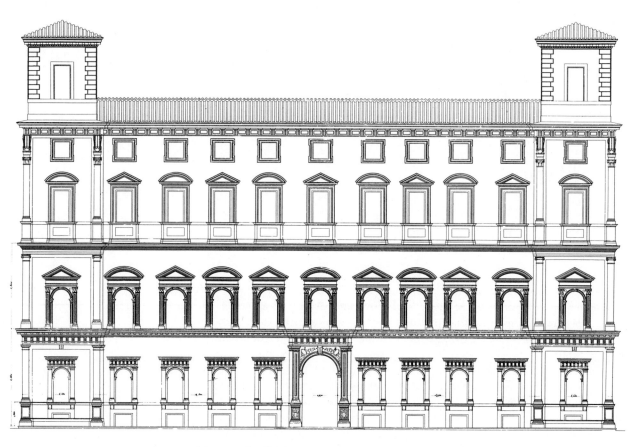

9-1. An ordered composition using a limited vocabulary. (Palace in the Piazza di Sora, Rome, as depicted in Paul Letarouilly's *Edifices de Rome Moderne*.)

Use of Control Structures to Express Compositional Rules

If we were to write a Pascal procedure to generate this drawing, we would need to express the regularities of the composition in the code, between **start_drawing** and **finish_drawing**, that specify the composition. How might this be done?

A good way to approach this problem is to consider how you might execute the drawing by hand, with pen on a piece of tracing paper. You could begin at the bottom-left corner and draw the lines one by one, until you reach the top-right corner—but you would not. Almost certainly (especially after reading the last chapter) you would begin by making templates for repeating vocabulary elements, such as windows and columns, so that these could be instantiated rapidly by tracing. Then you might recognize that whole bays repeat. This suggests first using the templates to create a bay, then slipping the bay along and tracing it repeatedly to produce the whole elevation. Probably you would first lay out regular grid lines to control placement. There are special conditions at the end bays and at the center, so you would have to handle these a little differently. You might notice, too, that many elements are bilaterally symmetrical. For these you need only a half template, which can be flipped over to produce a mirror image.

An important general principle emerges. Analyzing the principles of the composition's organization (its vocabulary, the nesting of smaller units within larger units, the regular repetition of units, the symmetries that appear, and the special conditions that must be handled) allows you to organize your work intelligently. This would enable you to produce the drawing much more quickly and easily than would otherwise be possible. Similarly, in writing the Pascal code to generate a graphic composition, we should take advantage of our insights into the principles of the composition in order to minimize our effort. The use of *control structures* available in Pascal enables us to do this very effectively.

The role of control structures in a program is to express the *flow of control*—the sequence in which operations (for example, instantiation of vocabulary elements) are executed. So far, without explicitly discussing it, we have been making use of the most elementary control structure—*textual sequence*. That is, operations are executed, one after another, in the sequence in which they are written in the text of the main program. If we want to change the sequence in which operations are performed, we simply change the sequence of statements in the main program.

More precisely, Pascal syntax provides the possibility of writing not just single statements, but *compound statements* as well. A compound statement begins with **begin** and ends with **end**, and the component statements within it are executed in the same sequence as they are written. This, for example, is a compound statement:

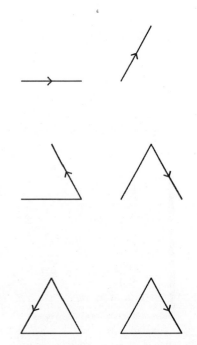

a. Counterclockwise from left vertex.   b. Clockwise from left vertex.

9-2. Sequences for drawing a triangle.

```
BEGIN

    MOVE  (100,100);
    DRAW  (500,100);
    DRAW  (300,300);
    DRAW  (100,100);

END;
```

The result is a triangle, with sides drawn in counterclockwise order (fig. 9-2a). If we were to flip the first and second **draw** statements, as follows, we would obtain the same triangle, but it would now be drawn in clockwise order (fig. 9-2b)·

```
BEGIN

    MOVE  (100,100);
    DRAW  (300,300);
    DRAW  (500,100);
    DRAW  (100,100);

END;
```

For typographic clarity, it is customary to align the components of a compound statement and indent them from their **begin** and **end**, as shown in the examples above. This enables us to read a compound statement easily as a sequence.

We can, then, always encode a picture as a compound statement containing **moves** and **draws** or invocations of procedures that instantiate vocabulary elements. Note, too, that the body of any Pascal program, any function, or any procedure takes the form of a single compound statement.

Pascal, however, provides several other very useful control structures in addition to the compound statement. We shall be concerned, in the next few chapters, with structures of *repetition*, *branching*, *nesting*, and *recursion* and with using these to express principles of regular graphic composition. Intelligent use of these structures not only enables us to write very concise and elegant graphic programs to generate large and apparently complicated compositions, but also to clearly portray the regularities of a composition in the text of its generating program.

Regular Repetition

Let us begin by considering the row of columns in plan, illustrated in figure 9-3. This is created by regular repetition of a vocabulary element, a specific number of times, along an axis.

To generate this composition, we might first declare a procedure to draw a square parallel to the coordinate axes, then invoke it in the main program the required number of times to generate the instances, arranged in the appropriate way. The program looks like this:

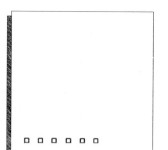

9-3. A row of six square columns (drawn in plan) in the screen coordinate system.

```
PROGRAM ROW_SQUARES;

    USES GRAPHICS;

    PROCEDURE SQUARE (X,Y,LENGTH : INTEGER);

        VAR X2,Y2 : INTEGER;

        BEGIN

            { Calculate values for X2 and Y2 }
            X2 := X + LENGTH;
            Y2 := Y + LENGTH;

            { Move to bottom left corner }
            MOVE (X,Y);

            { Draw the four sides of the square }
            DRAW (X2,Y);
            DRAW (X2,Y2);
            DRAW (X,Y2);
            DRAW (X,Y);

        END;

    { Main program }
    BEGIN

        START_DRAWING;

            SQUARE (100,100,30);
            SQUARE (200,100,30);
            SQUARE (300,100,30);
            SQUARE (400,100,30);
            SQUARE (500,100,30);
            SQUARE (600,100,30);

        FINISH_DRAWING;

    END.
```

It is not difficult to identify the textual redundancy in our main program. The only thing that changes in each successive statement is the value of the

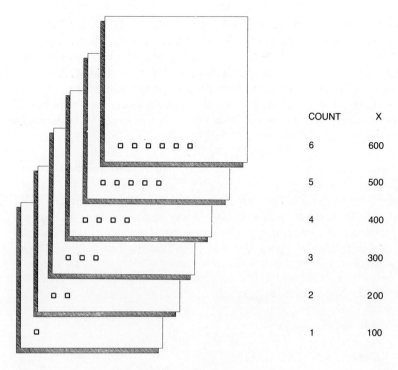

COUNT	X
6	600
5	500
4	400
3	300
2	200
1	100

9-4. States of the drawing, with values of Count and values of X at each iteration.

X parameter. It would be much more concise, elegant, and expressive of the composition's organization simply to say that the square is to be instantiated a specified number of times, starting X at a specified value and incrementing it by a specified amount at each successive step in the process.

The Counted Loop

Pascal provides a control structure that enables us to write the program in just this way. It is called the *counted loop* or the **for** statement. Here is our main program rewritten with a **for** statement:

```
{ Main program }
    VAR X,COUNT : INTEGER;

BEGIN

    START_DRAWING;

        X := 100;

        FOR COUNT := 1 TO 6 DO
        BEGIN

            SQUARE (X,100,30);
            X := X + 100;

        END;

    FINISH_DRAWING;

END.
```

The **for** statement begins with the reserved word **for**. This is followed by the name of the *control variable*—in this case Count. Next comes the assignment operator : =, followed by the *initial value* of the control variable. In this case, we begin counting at 1. The reserved word **to** follows, then the *final value* of the control variable (in this case 6) and the reserved word **do**. It all means: "**for** Count given an initial value of 1 and incrementing to 6 **do** the following compound statement." The compound statement then appears, enclosed by its **begin** and its **end**. The whole **for** statement is then terminated, like any other executable statement, by a semicolon. Everything between its **begin** and **end** is *within* the loop; everything else in the program is *outside* the loop.

The loop is controlled by the initial and final values specified for the control variable. For our purposes here, we shall assume that the control variable, the initial value, and the final value are always of type **integer**. (The control variable may, more generally, be of any *ordinal* data type, but we shall not make use of ordinal data types other than **integer**s in this context.) It usually makes sense to begin a count at 1, so that the **for** statement looks something like this:

FOR COUNT : = 1 **TO** 4 **DO**

But we could begin the count at 0:

FOR COUNT : = 0 **TO** 3 **DO**

We could even begin at a negative integer:

FOR COUNT : = −1 **TO** 2 **DO**

It is possible and often necessary to use variables like this:

FOR COUNT : = INITIAL **TO** FINAL **DO**

In this case, of course, Initial and Final must be declared of type **integer**, and they must be assigned values before the **for** loop is processed. It is even possible to use **integer**-valued expressions and functions in the following manner:

FOR COUNT : = A **DIV** B **TO** TRUNC(SIN(C)) **DO**

This can become very confusing, however, and we do not recommend it. Where such expressions are used, they are evaluated once when the loop commences.

Here is yet another variant:

FOR COUNT : = 10 **DOWNTO** 1 **DO**

In this case the count is **downto** a lower final value from a higher initial value. The usefulness of this will become apparent when we consider functions of the control variable.

What happens if, in counting **to** a value, the initial value is greater than the final value, or in counting **downto** a value, the initial value is less than the final value? In Pascal the loop is not executed in these cases.

Notice that the variable X in our example program is assigned an initial value outside the loop. It is then incremented the required amount by the following statement within the loop:

```
X := X + 100;
```

The initial value of X specifies where the first instance of square is to be placed, and the assignment within the loop controls the placement of each successive instance relative to its predecessor.

You should study figure 9-4 carefully. It traces the execution of this loop by showing, at each iteration, the values of the control variable Count and the position parameter X, and the state of the drawing.

In order to avoid confusion, you must pay careful attention to the values of variables such as Count and X on exit from the loop. The convention followed by Pascal is that the value of a control variable, such as Count, is undefined on exit from a **for** statement. This means that you cannot use the variable again before resetting its value. The value of X on exit is the last value that was assigned to it. You may use this value in subsequent parts of the program, or you may choose to reset it to another value.

Another rule that must be followed to avoid confusion is that the value of a control variable, such as Count, cannot be changed by a statement within a counted loop; the computer would lose track of where it was in the count. You can, however, use the value of the control variable within a counted loop, for example, in something like:

```
DISTANCE := COUNT * 100;
```

Finally, **for** loops that include only one statement may be written in simplified form:

```
FOR COUNT := 1 TO 10 DO
    WRITELN (COUNT);
```

The **begin** and **end** can be omitted here, since their absence does not cause any ambiguity about the scope of the loop.

Counted Loops within Procedures

A further refinement of our example program to draw a row of squares is to put the loop within a procedure, as follows:

```
PROCEDURE ROW_SQUARES (X_INITIAL,X_INCREMENT,Y,
                       LENGTH,NUM_SQUARES : INTEGER);

    VAR X,COUNT : INTEGER;

    BEGIN

        X := X_INITIAL;

        FOR COUNT := 1 TO NUM_SQUARES DO
        BEGIN

            SQUARE (X,Y,LENGTH);
            X := X + X_INCREMENT;

        END;

    END;
```

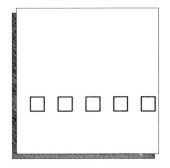

9-5. Another row of squares, produced by varying the parameters.

The effect here is to define a row of squares as a graphic type. Part of its essence is the compositional principle of regular repetition parallel to the X axis. Its parameters are the initial value of X, the X increment, the Y coordinate, the side length of the square, and the final value of Count. It is usually convenient to generalize in this way and to treat repetitive compositions as graphic types.

Here is a variant of our program, with the procedure to draw the row of squares now parameterized to produce drawings of the type shown in figure 9-5:

```
PROGRAM  DRAW_SQUARES;

    USES  GRAPHICS;

    PROCEDURE  SQUARE  (X,Y,LENGTH  :  INTEGER);

        VAR  X2,Y2  :  INTEGER;

        BEGIN

            { Calculate values for X2 and Y2 }
            X2  :=  X  +  LENGTH;
            Y2  :=  Y  +  LENGTH;

            { Move to bottom left corner }
            MOVE  (X,Y);

            { Draw the four sides of the square }
            DRAW  (X2,Y);
            DRAW  (X2,Y2);
            DRAW  (X,Y2);
            DRAW  (X,Y);

        END;

    PROCEDURE  ROW_SQUARES  (X_INITIAL,X_INCREMENT,Y,LENGTH,
                             NUM_SQUARES  :  INTEGER);

        VAR  X,COUNT  :  INTEGER;

        BEGIN

            X  :=  X_INITIAL;

            FOR  COUNT  :=  1  TO  NUM_SQUARES  DO
            BEGIN

                SQUARE  (X,Y,LENGTH);
                X  :=  X  +  X_INCREMENT;

            END;

        END;

    { Main program }
    BEGIN

        START_DRAWING;

            ROW_SQUARES  (100,200,300,100,5);

        FINISH_DRAWING;

    END.
```

The While Statement and Control Expressions

The use of a control variable to keep count of repetitions, as in a **for** statement, is not the only way to control a loop. Pascal provides two other possibilities: the **while** statement and the **repeat until** statement.

Here is an example of a loop (to draw a row of squares) that uses the **while** statement:

```
X := 100;
TOTAL_X := X + 30;
WHILE TOTAL_X <= 1023 DO
BEGIN
      SQUARE (X,300,30);
      X := X + 100;
      TOTAL_X := X + 30;
END;
```

The **while** statement consists of the reserved word **while**, followed by an expression, then the reserved word **do,** and finally the statement that is to be executed repeatedly.

Here it is the *control expression* Total_X <= 1,023 that controls the loop. This control expression is constructed using Pascal's *Boolean operators*:

and	conjunction
or	disjunction
not	negation
=	equal
< >	unequal
<	less
>	greater
<=	less or equal
>=	greater or equal

The syntax of the expression is the normal syntax used in Boolean logic. Here are some examples:

```
X = Y
X <> Y
X < Y
X >= Y
(X <= Y) OR (A > B)
```

Integer, real, Boolean, and **character** variables may all appear in these statements. However, you must be careful about type. It would be meaningless, for example, to state that a **real** variable is equal to a **character** variable. When such a control expression is evaluated, the result is a **Boolean** value: **true** or **false.** Thus we say that the type of the control expression is **Boolean.**

The variables in a control expression must all have defined values when the **while** statement is entered. The statement is evaluated before each iteration. If it is **true,** then the statement within the loop is executed, if it is **false,** the loop is exited. In other words, the loop is repeated **while** the control expression is **true.** To put this in yet another way, the loop is repeated until the control

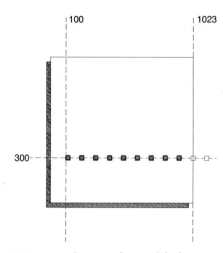

9-6. A row of squares drawn **while** there is still space on the screen.

expression is **false.** If the control expression is **false** at the beginning, then the loop is not executed at all.

This construct makes sense, of course, only if the control expression can (sometimes or always) be expected to be **true** at the beginning, and if something happens within the loop that can change the value of the control expression to **false.** If nothing within the loop can make the control expression **false,** the loop can never be exited. In our example, the control expression is:

```
TOTAL_X <= 1023
```

The value of Total_X is incremented within the loop, so we can be sure that it will eventually become equal to or greater than 1,023, resulting in exit from the loop. The effect of this is to draw a row of squares **while** we have space on the screen to do so; that is, *until* we run out of space at the right-hand edge of the screen (in this case drawing nine squares as shown in fig. 9-6).

When the **while** statement is evaluated for the tenth time the value of Total_X is 1,030, so the expression

```
TOTAL_X <= 1023
```

now evaluates to **false,** and the loop is exited. If the expression

```
X <= 1023
```

had been used to control the loop, it would have evaluated to **true** on the tenth iteration, and a tenth square intersecting the right-hand side of the screen would have been drawn.

The choice between using a **for** loop or a **while** loop depends on the information available when entering the loop. If we know the exact number or repetitions to be made, then the **for** loop is the appropriate construct. If we do not, but we do know a condition that we can use to establish when to exit the loop, then the **while** loop is appropriate. Sometimes it is possible to use either one. In this case, the choice should be made to achieve clarity and expressiveness.

In design applications, the choice becomes a matter of how we want to specify the essence of a repetitive graphic type, and how we want to parameterize it. If it is essential to repeat a vocabulary element some specified number of times, then we write a **for** loop in which the initial and final values of the control variable are fixed as constants:

```
FOR COUNT := 1 TO 10 DO
```

But, if we want to treat the number of repetitions as a design variable, then we write a **for** loop with variable names standing for the initial and final values:

```
FOR COUNT := INITIAL TO FINAL DO
```

On the other hand, if we want to make some limit part of the essence, we can write a **while** loop with a control expression in which the limit is set as a constant:

```
WHILE TOTAL_X <= 1023 DO
```

If we want to treat the limit as a design variable, though, we use a variable name like this:

WHILE TOTAL_X <= LIMIT **DO**

In design and graphics applications, we typically use a **while** loop when we want to fit a repetitive graphic type to some established context. In our example program, we fitted a row of squares to the display screen. Here is a slightly more complicated example:

```
PROCEDURE ROW_SQUARES (X_MIN,X_MAX,X_INCREMENT,
                        Y,LENGTH : INTEGER);

    VAR X,TOTAL_X : INTEGER;

    BEGIN
        X := X_MIN;
        TOTAL_X := X + LENGTH;

        WHILE TOTAL_X <= X_MAX DO
        BEGIN
            SQUARE (X,Y,LENGTH);
            X := X + X_INCREMENT;
            TOTAL_X := X + LENGTH;

        END;

    END;
```

In this case, parameters to the procedure that draws the row define the boundaries of a rectangle on the screen, the size of the square, and the spacing of squares. Figure 9-7 shows some results of executing this procedure with different parameter values.

The Repeat Until Statement

A third way to control a loop in Pascal is to use a **repeat until** statement. Here is an example of a loop to draw a row of squares controlled in this way (fig. 9-8):

```
X := 100;

REPEAT
    SQUARE (X,300,30);
    X := X + 100;
    TOTAL_X := X + 30;
UNTIL TOTAL_X > 1023;
```

The sequence of statements between the reserved words **repeat** and **until** is always executed at least once. Note that **repeat** and **until** bracket together the statements within the loop, so that they become a compound statement. It is unnecessary, but not incorrect, to bracket them with **begin** and **end** as well.

Execution of the loop is controlled by the Boolean expression that follows

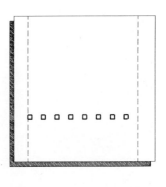

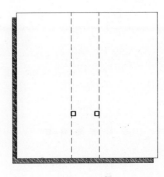

9-7. Rows of squares fitted within specified boundaries on the screen.

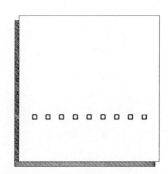

9-8. A row of squares drawn **until** there is no space left on the screen.

until. This is evaluated after every iteration. Initially we expect this expression to be **true.** Something happens within the loop that can make it **false.** When evaluation shows it to be **false,** the loop is exited.

It is generally feasible to write both a **while** and a **repeat until** version of a loop. (For example, the graphic result shown in fig. 9-6 for the **while** loop is identical to that shown in fig. 9-8 for the **repeat** loop.) Choice of one or another is a matter of clarity of expression, and of whether or not we want to guarantee that there will always be at least one iteration.

Notice that the control expressions used in our examples of **repeat until** and **while** loops must be evaluated at every iteration. In these examples, there are few iterations, and the control expression is simple, so the amount of computation required for this is insignificant. But it is possible to write very complex control expressions, and if there are many iterations, the amount of computation can then become significant. It is good programming practice, then, to keep control expressions as simple as possible.

Programs to Explore Variations

Code to read in parameter values and draw the corresponding instance of a motif may be placed within a **repeat until** loop as follows:

```
REPEAT

    { Prompt for and read in parameter values }

        START_DRAWING;
          { Draw the motif }
        FINISH_DRAWING;

        WRITELN ('SATISFACTORY?');
        WRITELN ('ANSWER Y OR N');
        READLN (SATISFACTORY);

UNTIL SATISFACTORY <> 'N';
```

Satisfactory must be declared as a **char** variable. The advantage of this arrangement is that a user of the program can keep cycling through the loop until a satisfactory variant of the motif is obtained.

You can always convert a program that generates a drawing of a motif into a program that allows you to explore variants of the motif by introducing a **repeat until** loop in this way. We suggest that from now on you do so in your own programming projects.

The Compositional Uses of Repetition

Now that we have established the three basic modes of repetition provided by Pascal, we can go on to consider various types of repetitive graphic compositions, and how these may be generated using loops.

We shall begin by considering compositions made by incrementing a single position parameter of a vocabulary element within a loop. Then we shall go on to consider incrementing two and three position parameters. Next, we shall look at incrementing a single shape parameter of a vocabulary element. Finally, we shall put all of this together and consider incrementing multiple

a. Horizontal row.

b. Vertical row.

c. Circle.

9-9. Simple compositions of squares generated by incrementing a single position parameter.

parameters of a vocabulary element within a loop. Various kinds of *mathematical progressions* (arithmetic progressions, geometric progressions, and so on) are frequently used to structure architectural and graphic compositions. We shall consider how such progressions may be constructed within loops. We shall ultimately look beyond single loops to see what happens when we combine loops. There are two cases of this: *compound* loops and *nested* loops.

Always, though, we shall be concerned with two basic compositional issues. What is it that remains constant in the repeating motif from instance to instance? And what is the pattern of change from instance to instance across the composition? In other words, what are the variables, and what are their increments?

Incrementing a Single Position Parameter

In all the examples provided so far, we have been incrementing a single position parameter—the X coordinate of the bottom-left corner of our column—within a loop. This produces a horizontal row of regularly spaced columns (fig. 9-9a). An obvious alternative is to keep the X coordinate constant, while incrementing the Y coordinate, to generate a vertical row (fig. 9-9b).

```
Y := 100;
FOR COUNT := 1 TO 6 DO
BEGIN
    SQUARE (300,Y,30);
    Y := Y + 100;
END;
```

A third possibility is to increment the rotation of the column about some specified center point to produce a regularly spaced ring of columns (fig. 9-9c). You can write code to do this, using trigonometric functions, but it will be better to defer detailed consideration of this kind of composition until after we have discussed circles and arcs (in the next chapter) and the rotation transformation (in chapter 14).

It is worth noting that the most ancient architectural compositions that we know are based on this elementary idea of incrementing a single position parameter—perhaps to create settings for processional rituals. The Megaliths of Carnac, in Brittany, are regular rows of stones (fig. 9-10a), and at Stonehenge, the stones are regularly spaced around circles (fig. 9-10b).

Architects have often made use of the device of regularly spaced rows of openings in wall planes. This shows up both in plan (fig. 9-11a) and in elevation (fig. 9-11b). The following procedure instantiates this architectural type. It takes as parameters the Y coordinate of the wall, its starting X coordinate, its ending X coordinate, the wall thickness, the number of openings, and the width of each opening (fig. 9-12a).

a. Rows of stones at Carnac, Brittany.

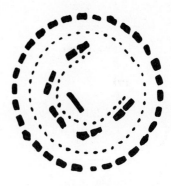

b. The circles of Stonehenge.

9-10. Megalithic compositions produced by the regular repetition of elements.

```
PROCEDURE WALL (Y,X_START,X_END,THICKNESS,
                WIDTH,NUM_OF_OPENINGS : INTEGER);

    VAR COUNT,X,WALL_SEGMENT : INTEGER;
        LENGTH,OPEN,SOLID : INTEGER;
```

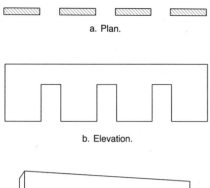

a. Plan.

b. Elevation.

c. Perspective.

9-11. A regularly spaced row of openings in a wall plane.

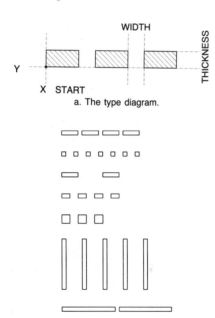

a. The type diagram.

b. Some instances.

9-12. A wall with regularly spaced openings.

```
BEGIN

  { Calculate length of wall segments }

    LENGTH := X_END - X_START;
    OPEN := WIDTH * NUM_OF_OPENINGS;
    SOLID := LENGTH - OPEN;
    WALL_SEGMENT := SOLID DIV
                        (NUM_OF_OPENINGS + 1);
    X := X_START;

  { Loop to draw wall segments }

    FOR COUNT := 1 TO (NUM_OF_OPENINGS+1) DO
    BEGIN

        RECTANGLE (X,Y,WALL_SEGMENT,THICKNESS);
        X := X + WALL_SEGMENT + WIDTH

    END;

END;
```

Notice how this procedure automatically calculates the X increment that is to be used at each step. Notice, too, the trouble that will be caused by invoking this procedure with parameter values that specify too many openings, or openings that are too wide so that they overlap. For the moment you will have to avoid such values. Later, in chapter 11, we shall see how to write code to check automatically for "illegal" parameter values and respond appropriately. Figure 9-12b shows some results generated by invoking this procedure with different parameters.

If you look closely at these results, you can discover an interesting change in the architectural meaning of the type as the values of the parameters vary. Where the voids are narrow relative to the solids, we interpret the object as a regularly pierced wall. Conversely, where the voids are wide relative to the solids, we interpret it as a colonnade—that is, as a regularly subdivided opening. If wall thickness is larger than the spacing of openings, we read parallel walls running in the perpendicular direction. There are also versions where the reading is ambiguous.

Another common architectural device, based upon the idea of incrementing a single position parameter, is that of the *enfilade*—a sequence of parallel wall planes with aligned openings. The following procedure takes the parameters defining a boundary rectangle, the wall thickness, the width of the opening, and the spacing between walls as parameters (fig. 9-13a) and fits an enfilade within the specified rectangle:

```
PROCEDURE ENFILADE (X_MIN,Y_MIN,X_MAX,Y_MAX,
                      THICKNESS,WIDTH,SPACING : INTEGER);

    VAR LENGTH,INC,X1,X2,Y : INTEGER;

    BEGIN

      { Calculate length of wall segment }
        LENGTH := ((X_MAX - X_MIN) - WIDTH) DIV 2;
        INC := THICKNESS + SPACING;
        X1 := X_MIN;
        X2 := X_MAX - LENGTH;
        Y := Y_MIN;
```

```
{ Loop to place parallel wall planes }
WHILE (Y + THICKNESS) <= Y_MAX DO
BEGIN

    RECTANGLE (X1,Y,LENGTH,THICKNESS);
    RECTANGLE (X2,Y,LENGTH,THICKNESS);
    Y := Y + INC;

END;

END;
```

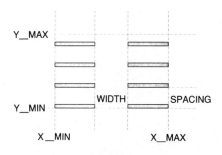

a. The type diagram.

The architectural logic followed here is that the last wall should occur just before the boundary of the rectangle is reached. Figure 9-13b illustrates some examples of enfilades specified by different sets of parameter values. (The boundary rectangle is not drawn by this procedure, but is shown for clarity in the illustrations. We have also added *poché* in the traditional manner.)

Notice that if the boundary rectangle is too small, no wall will be drawn. If we wanted to follow a different architectural logic, and guarantee that at least one wall would always be drawn, we could use a **repeat until** loop instead of a **while** loop. We might also handle the relation of the last wall thickness to the boundary rectangle in a different way, by substituting the control expression

$$Y <= Y\_MAX$$

for the control expression

$$Y + THICKNESS <= Y\_MAX$$

This allows the last wall to overlap the end of the boundary rectangle (fig. 9-14), but never to be completely outside the boundary rectangle.

Now consider a row of rectangular wall panels shown in elevation as illustrated in fig. 9-15. It is clear that you can control widths, numbers of repetitions, and the termination condition in several different ways, depending on what is the most appropriate architectural principle to follow. You can let width vary and have your procedure automatically fit a specified number of panels into the boundary rectangle using a **for** loop (fig. 9-15b). If you keep width constant, then you can use a **while** or **repeat until** loop, so that there is undershoot at the right side (fig. 9-15c). Alternatively, you can control the loop, so that there is an overshoot at the right side (fig. 9-15d). The procedure can be modified so that the undershoot is at the left side (fig. 9-15e), or so that the overshoot is at the left side (fig. 9-15f). A final pair of possibilities is to divide the necessary undershoot in half at both ends (fig. 9-15g), or to do the same with overshoot (fig. 9-15h).

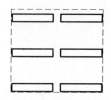

b. Instances of enfilades fitted within specified rectangles.

9-13. The use of a **while** loop to generate an enfilade.

High-rise office buildings typically consist of parallel, regularly repeated floor planes (fig. 9-16). These can be drawn in section by a procedure that takes location coordinates for the ground floor, floor length, floor thickness, floor-to-floor height, and the number of floors as the parameters (fig. 9-16a). Alternatively, an architect might find it more convenient to use floor-to-ceiling height as a parameter (fig. 9-16b). Should you start with a floor plane (fig. 9-16c), or with a floor-to-floor space (fig. 9-16d)? That is a question of architectural principle that you must resolve before writing the procedure. You must then express your resolution appropriately in the code. Similarly, should you count the last (top) plane as a floor (fig. 9-16e), or as a roof (fig. 9-16f)?

It is common for building codes to limit the heights of buildings by specifying the maximum angle Max_angle that can be formed at the center of a street (fig. 9-17). As an architect, you might be particularly interested in the maximum floor area that you can fit on a site. Let us assume that the floors of our building are rectangular. The following interactive program reads in values for floor Length and Width, Floor_to_floor height, and for the constraints Max_angle and Street_width, then draws the building section and displays the total floor area. Notice the use of two functions: raster, which

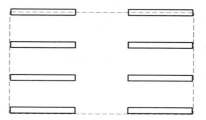

9-14. The use of a **repeat until** loop to generate an enfilade.

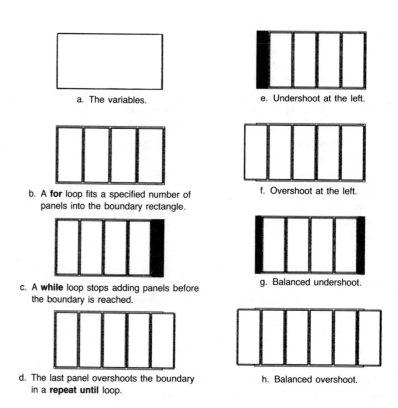

a. The variables.

b. A **for** loop fits a specified number of panels into the boundary rectangle.

c. A **while** loop stops adding panels before the boundary is reached.

d. The last panel overshoots the boundary in a **repeat until** loop.

e. Undershoot at the left.

f. Overshoot at the left.

g. Balanced undershoot.

h. Balanced overshoot.

9-15. A row of rectangular wall panels with different conditions governing termination.

converts feet to raster units so that the section can be drawn to appropriate scale on the screen; and Max_height, which calculates the maximum allowable height for given Street_width and Max_angle. Here is the complete code:

```
PROGRAM BUILDING;

  USES GRAPHICS;

{ Scale factor which turns feet to raster units }

  VAR FACTOR : REAL;

{ Function for converting feet to raster units }

  FUNCTION RASTER (FEET : REAL) : INTEGER;
    BEGIN
         RASTER := ROUND(FEET * FACTOR);
    END;

  PROCEDURE RECTANGLE (X,Y,LENGTH,WIDTH : INTEGER);

    VAR X1,Y1 : INTEGER;

    BEGIN

        X1 := X + LENGTH;
        Y1 := Y + WIDTH;

        MOVE (X,Y);
        DRAW (X1,Y);
        DRAW (X1,Y1);
        DRAW (X,Y1);
        DRAW (X,Y);

    END;

  FUNCTION MAX_HEIGHT (STREET_WIDTH,MAX_ANGLE : REAL)
                        : REAL;

{ Calculates maximum height given street width and maximum
  angle }

    CONST RADIANS = 0.01745;

    BEGIN

        MAX_ANGLE := MAX_ANGLE * RADIANS;
        MAX_HEIGHT := (STREET_WIDTH/2) /
                        COS(MAX_ANGLE)*SIN(MAX_ANGLE);

    END;

  PROCEDURE HIGH_RISE (X,Y : INTEGER;
                        LENGTH,THICKNESS,FLOOR_TO_FLOOR,
                        STREET_WIDTH,MAX_ANGLE : REAL);

{ Draws floors of highrise }

    VAR TOTAL_HEIGHT,HEIGHT : REAL;

    BEGIN

        { Calculate maximum height of building }

        TOTAL_HEIGHT := MAX_HEIGHT (STREET_WIDTH,
                        MAX_ANGLE) - THICKNESS;
```

```
                    HEIGHT := 0;
            { Loop to draw floors }
               WHILE HEIGHT <= TOTAL_HEIGHT DO
               BEGIN
                    RECTANGLE (X,Y,RASTER(LENGTH),
                              RASTER(THICKNESS));
                    HEIGHT := HEIGHT + FLOOR_TO_FLOOR;
                    Y := Y + RASTER(FLOOR_TO_FLOOR);
               END;
          END;
FUNCTION TOTAL_AREA (LENGTH,WIDTH : REAL; NUM_FLOORS :
                    INTEGER) : REAL;

          { Calculates total area of building given LENGTH and
          WIDTH of a floor and NUM_FLOORS }

     BEGIN
          TOTAL_AREA := LENGTH * WIDTH * NUM_FLOORS;

     END;

CONST X = 550;
      Y = 100;

VAR  LENGTH,WIDTH,THICKNESS,FLOOR_TO_FLOOR : INTEGER;
     STREET_WIDTH,NUM_FLOORS : INTEGER;
     MAX_ANGLE,AREA : REAL;
     SATISFACTORY : CHAR;

BEGIN
     REPEAT
     { Prompt for data }

          WRITELN ('ENTER LENGTH OF FLOOR : ');
          READLN (LENGTH);
          WRITELN ('ENTER WIDTH OF FLOOR : ');
          READLN (WIDTH);
          WRITELN ('ENTER THICKNESS OF FLOOR : ');
          READLN (THICKNESS);
          WRITELN ('ENTER FLOOR TO FLOOR HEIGHT : ');
          READLN (FLOOR_TO_FLOOR);
          WRITELN ('ENTER STREET WIDTH : ');
          READLN (STREET_WIDTH);
          WRITELN ('ENTER MAXIMUM ANGLE : ');
          READLN (MAX_ANGLE);
     { Set up feet to raster scale }

          WRITELN ('ENTER FEET TO RASTER SCALE FACTOR :');
          READLN (FACTOR);

          START_DRAWING;

               HIGH_RISE (X,Y,LENGTH,THICKNESS,FLOOR_TO_FLOOR,
                         STREET_WIDTH,MAX_ANGLE);

          FINISH_DRAWING;

          NUM_FLOORS := TRUNC((MAX_HEIGHT(STREET_WIDTH,
                         MAX_ANGLE) - THICKNESS) /
                         FLOOR_TO_FLOOR);
```

```
            AREA := TOTAL_AREA(LENGTH,WIDTH,NUM_FLOORS);
            WRITELN ('TOTAL FLOOR AREA IS : ',AREA : 8:1);
      WRITELN ('SATISFACTORY?');
      WRITELN ('ANSWER Y OR N');
      READLN (SATISFACTORY);
    UNTIL SATISFACTORY <> 'N';
  END.
```

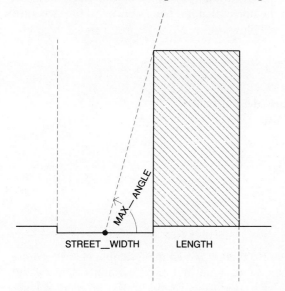

a. The type diagram.

b. Floor-to-ceiling height as a parameter.

c. Starting with a floor plane.

d. Starting with a floor-to-floor space.

e. Ending with a floor.

f. Ending with a roof.

9-16. A schematic section of a high-rise office building.

9-17. Max_angle and street_width as parameters controlling the height of a building.

```
ENTER LENGTH OF FLOOR:
200
ENTER WIDTH OF FLOOR:
150
ENTER THICKNESS OF FLOOR:
7
ENTER FLOOR_TO_FLOOR HEIGHT
35
ENTER STREET WIDTH:
300
ENTER MAXIMUM ANGLE:
56.5
TOTAL FLOOR AREA IS: 180000
```

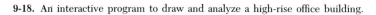

9-18. An interactive program to draw and analyze a high-rise office building.

Some typical output is illustrated in figure 9-18.

This program introduces an important new idea. There is a function called Total_area, which calculates the total floor area of a building and is invoked after the building is drawn. This is an *analysis* function and is executed to tell us something useful about the object that has been drawn. So the structure of our program is essentially as follows:

> declare functions, procedures, variables
>
> **BEGIN**
>
>> read values of independent variables
>> calculate values of dependent variables
>>
>> **START_DRAWING**;
>> draw the design
>> **FINISH_DRAWING**;
>>
>> perform analysis
>
> **END**.

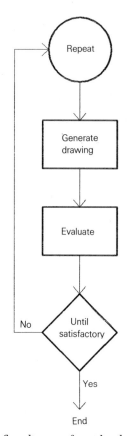

9-19. A flow diagram of a trial-and-error design process.

This is not just a graphics program, then; it is a simple example of a *computer-aided design* program. It assists the designer not only by rapidly drawing the building, but also by automatically performing some of the problem solving that is necessary *before* the building can be drawn, then by automatically performing some of the analysis that is necessary *after* the building has been drawn. This allows a very rapid trial-and-error design process, as shown by the flow diagram in figure 9-19.

We shall generally restrict our attention to computer graphics, rather than explore the much larger topic of computer-aided design. But it is useful to remember that, in practice, graphics procedures are often embedded in computer-aided design programs, and that the code of a computer-aided design program basically consists of problem-solving functions and procedures, graphics procedures, and analysis functions and procedures.

Incrementing Two Position Parameters

Figure 9-20 shows some section drawings of stairs. They were generated by the following procedure:

```
PROCEDURE  STAIRS  (X_INITIAL,Y_INITIAL,LENGTH,WIDTH,
                    X_INCREMENT,Y_INCREMENT,
                    NUM_OF_STEPS  :  INTEGER );

    VAR  COUNT,X,Y,  :  INTEGER;

    BEGIN

        X  :=  X_INITIAL;
        Y  :=  Y_INITIAL;

        FOR COUNT  :=  1  TO  NUM_OF_STEPS  DO
        BEGIN
            RECTANGLE  (X,Y,LENGTH,WIDTH);
            X  :=  X  +  X_INCREMENT;
            Y  :=  Y  +  Y_INCREMENT;

        END;

    END;
```

The parameters of this procedure specify a starting point, the dimensions of the tread, the X and Y increments at each step, and the number of stairs. That is, we now increment *two* position parameters at each iteration.

A number of important architectural variables are involved here. The principal ones are (fig. 9-21):

- tread length
- tread width
- number of treads
- number of risers
- tread increment
- riser increment
- tread/riser increment ratio
- angle formed with horizontal
- length of run
- floor-to-floor height

These are interrelated by functions in obvious ways, so not all of them can be taken as independent. You can parameterize a stair procedure in a variety of ways, then, depending on how you might want to use it in generating architectural drawings. You might reasonably assume, for example, that length of run and floor-to-floor height will usually be givens, so you would express

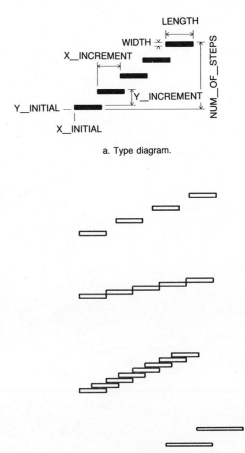

a. Type diagram.

b. Instances.

9-20. Section drawings of stairs.

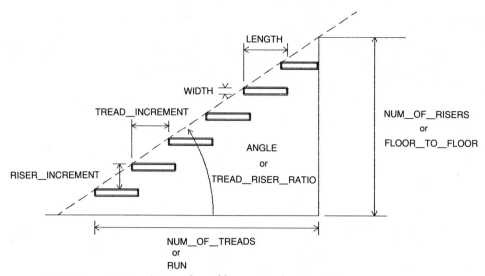

9-21. The principal architectural variables associated with a stair.

these as parameters. Then you might choose to take number of treads as an independent design variable, so this too would be a parameter to the procedure. These three parameters, together with tread length and width and starting coordinates, are sufficient to define fully an instance. Alternatively, you might take the number of risers, riser increment, and tread increment as parameters. There are other reasonable possibilities as well; in any case, there will be seven independent design variables, and others will become dependent.

Not only are there different ways to parameterize stair procedures, but also different ways to handle termination. Do you want to begin with a tread or with a riser? Similarly, do you want to end with a tread or with a riser? Figure 9-22 shows the four possible combinations of cases. The choices that

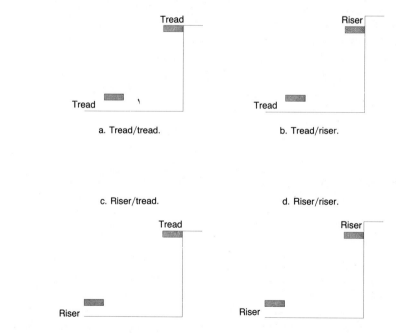

9-22. Possible starting and finishing conditions for a square.

you make will have implications for how the length of run and floor-to-floor height are defined and calculated. They will also determine whether you will always have an odd number of treads, or an even number, or whether you can get either one. The question can be of some architectural importance. It was a rule of Roman temple architecture, for example, that there should always be an odd number of steps. In the context of actual construction, the termination rules determine where the change of material from that used to construct the floors to that used to construct the treads takes place, which can have important structural and aesthetic consequences.

The risers in stairs should generally be exactly the same height and all the treads the same length. Anything else is dangerous. This means that you cannot end a stair with a short or long riser or tread in order to make it fit into a specified space. The implication for a stair procedure is that you will always have a **for** loop, rather than a **while** or a **repeat until** loop that can produce an undershoot or overshoot condition. The number of iterations of the **for** loop might be specified directly, or it might be calculated from information about length of run, floor-to-floor height, and either tread increment or riser increment.

There is an important lesson to be drawn from these detailed analyses of procedures to draw simple, repetitive architectural compositions. If you want to write really useful procedures to draw repetitive compositions, you must think very carefully about the logic of parameterization and about the desired end conditions. The Pascal distinction between **for, while,** and **repeat until** loops provides a useful framework for this and enables you to express the principles that you have chosen to follow in a clear and explicit way.

Incrementing a Single Shape Parameter

Another very interesting class of compositions can be generated by keeping position constant, but incrementing a single shape parameter at each iteration. The following procedure, for example, takes as parameters coordinates of a starting point, a starting side length, a length increment, and the number of repetitions; incorporates a **for** loop; and generates compositions of concentric squares as illustrated in figure 9-23.

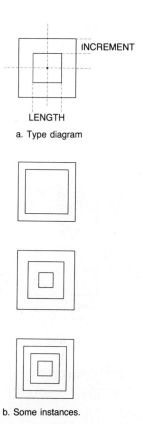

a. Type diagram

b. Some instances.

9-23. A composition of nested squares.

```
PROCEDURE SQUARE (X_CENTER,Y_CENTER,LENGTH : INTEGER);

    VAR X1,Y1,X2,Y2 : INTEGER;

    BEGIN

        { Calculate coordinates of corners }
        X1 := X_CENTER - LENGTH DIV 2;
        Y1 := Y_CENTER - LENGTH DIV 2;
        X2 := X1 + LENGTH;
        Y2 := Y1 + LENGTH;

        { Move to bottom left corner }
        MOVE (X1,Y1);

        { Draw the four sides }
        DRAW (X2,Y1);
        DRAW (X2,Y2);
        DRAW (X1,Y2);
        DRAW (X1,Y1);

    END;
```

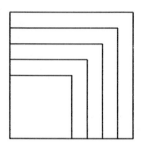

a. At a corner.

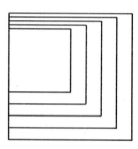

b. On an edge.

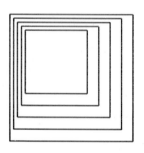

c. Inside.

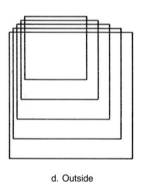

d. Outside

9-24. Compositions of squares about different fixed points.

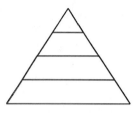

a. Equilateral triangles fixed at apex.

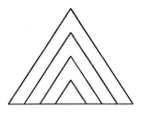

b. Equilateral triangles fixed at center of base.

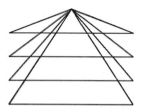

c. Isosceles triangles of constant width fixed at apex.

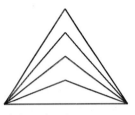

d. Isosceles triangles of constant width fixed at center of base.

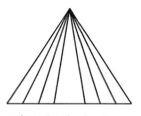

e. Isosceles triangles of constant height fixed at apex.

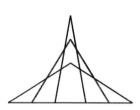

f. Height and width vary, with fixed point at center of base.

9-25. Compositions of triangles about different fixed points.

```
PROCEDURE NEST_SQUARES (X_CENTER,Y_CENTER,LENGTH,
                        INCREMENT,REPETITIONS : INTEGER);

   VAR COUNT : INTEGER;

   BEGIN
      FOR COUNT := 1 TO REPETITIONS DO
      BEGIN

         SQUARE (X_CENTER,Y_CENTER,LENGTH);
         LENGTH := LENGTH + INCREMENT * 2;

      END;

   END;
```

We have used here a procedure Square that locates a square by its center point, but the fixed point might be anywhere. Figure 9-24 illustrates examples of compositions of squares generated by taking the fixed point at a corner, at an arbitrary point along an edge, at an arbitrary point inside the initial square, and at an arbitrary point outside the square. Similar games can be played with triangles (fig. 9-25).

Incrementing Multiple Shape Parameters

We saw in chapter 8 that a figure can have not just one, but many shape parameters. Where there are multiple shape parameters, any number of these may be incremented within a loop.

We have seen, for instance, that a rectangle parallel to the coordinate axes has two shape parameters: Length and Width. The following iterative procedure takes as parameters an initial Length and Width, a Length and Width increment, and a lower limit on the value of Length:

```
PROCEDURE  CROSS_RECTANGLE  (X,Y,LENGTH,WIDTH,LENGTH_INC,
                              WIDTH_INC,LIMIT  :  INTEGER);

    VAR  X1,Y1  :  INTEGER;

    BEGIN
        X1  :=  X;
        Y1  :=  Y;

      { Loop  to  draw  rectangles }
        WHILE  LENGTH  >=  LIMIT  DO
        BEGIN

            RECTANGLE  (X1,Y1,LENGTH,WIDTH);
            X1  :=  X1  +  LENGTH_INC;
            Y1  :=  Y1  −  WIDTH_INC;
            LENGTH  :=  LENGTH  −  LENGTH_INC * 2;
            WIDTH  :=  WIDTH  +  WIDTH_INC * 2;

        END;

    END;
```

At each iteration, this procedure subtracts the increment from Length (that is, it decrements), and it adds the increment to Width. The control structure is a **while** loop, controlled by the lower bound on Length. It generates the kind of composition shown in figure 9-26.

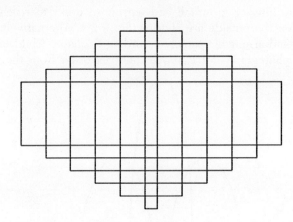

9-26. Composition produced by incrementing Length and Width of concentric rectangles.

Now consider the general four-sided object shown in figure 9-27a. It has eight shape parameters: the X and Y coordinates of the four vertices. We can associate an increment, which may be a positive or a negative number, with each of these. The following procedure with seventeen parameters (including a parameter controlling the number of iterations) changes all eight shape variables at each iteration:

```
PROCEDURE  NEST_FIGURE  (X1,Y1,X2,Y2,X3,Y3,X4,Y4,
                          X1_INC,Y1_INC,X2_INC,Y2_INC,
                          X3_INC,Y3_INC,X4_INC,Y4_INC,
                          REPETITIONS  :  INTEGER);
    VAR  COUNT  :  INTEGER;
```

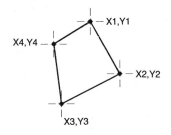

a. Parameters of the quadrilateral element.

b. Some instances.

9-27. Compositions produced by incrementing vertex coordinates of a quadrilateral.

```
BEGIN

  { Loop to draw 4-sided figures }
    FOR COUNT := 1 TO REPETITIONS DO
  BEGIN

      FOUR_SIDE (X1,Y1,X2,Y2,X3,Y3,X4,Y4);

      X1 := X1 + X1_INC;
      Y1 := Y1 + Y1_INC;
      X2 := X2 + X2_INC;
      Y2 := Y2 + Y2_INC;
      X3 := X3 + X3_INC;
      Y3 := Y3 + Y3_INC;
      X4 := X4 + X4_INC;
      Y4 := Y4 + Y4_INC;

    END;

  END;
```

Some of the many compositions that this procedure can generate are shown in figure 9-27b. Notice that, as the quadrilateral changes with each iteration, each vertex moves along a straight line. The angle of this line and the direction of movement are determined by the relation between the X and Y increments.

Incrementing Both Position and Shape Parameters

Sometimes in nature we find that the shapes of instances of some type of object vary systematically with position. In a grove of trees, for example, the trees in the interior grow tall and narrow in order to reach the light, whereas trees on the outside are shorter (fig. 9-28). Alternatively, instances may be sorted and arranged spatially according to shape. Children might be lined up for a photograph, for example, in strict order from the shortest to the tallest.

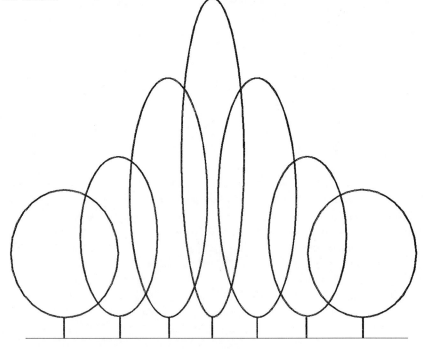

9-28. A grove of trees; interior trees grow taller and narrower in order to reach light.

In architecture it is very common for position and shape to vary regularly in a correlated way. A regular row of columns supporting a pitched roof must grow in height (fig. 9-29a). Structural logic suggests that columns will also become thicker as they get taller (fig. 9-29b).

The logic of this kind of composition can often be captured with a procedure that increments both shape and position parameters within a loop. The following simple procedure, for example, generates column rows of the type shown in figure 9-29b:

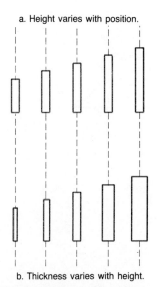

a. Height varies with position.

b. Thickness varies with height.

9-29. A row of columns supporting a pitched roof.

```
PROCEDURE  ROW_COLUMNS  (X,Y,HEIGHT,THICKNESS,SPACING,
                         HEIGHT_INC,THICKNESS_INC,
                         NUM_OF_COLUMNS : INTEGER);

    VAR COUNT : INTEGER;

    BEGIN

      { Loop to place row of columns }
        FOR COUNT := 1 TO NUM_OF_COLUMNS DO
        BEGIN

            COLUMN (X,Y,HEIGHT,THICKNESS);

            X := X + SPACING;

          { Change height and thickness of column }
            HEIGHT := HEIGHT + HEIGHT_INC;
            THICKNESS := THICKNESS + THICKNESS_INC;

        END;

    END;
```

Note that the parameters specify initial position and dimensions, center-to-center column spacing, number of columns, height increment, and thickness increment. You should be able to think of other, perhaps more convenient, parameterization schemes.

Here is an analogous procedure to draw a stepped pyramid in elevation:

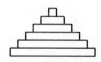

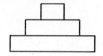

```
PROCEDURE PYRAMID (X,Y,LENGTH,WIDTH,LENGTH_INC : INTEGER);

    BEGIN

      REPEAT

          RECTANGLE (X,Y,LENGTH,WIDTH);

          X := X + LENGTH_INC DIV 2;
          Y := Y + WIDTH;
          LENGTH := LENGTH - LENGTH_INC;

      UNTIL (LENGTH <= 0);

    END;
```

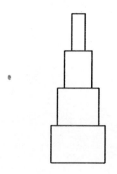

Here the parameters specify length, width and position of the lowest layer, and the amount by which the length of each successive layer is to be decremented. Iteration continues **until** the length of the layer becomes zero (fig. 9-30).

9-30. Stepped pyramids.

We considered, in chapter 7, a function to find the Midpoint of a line. We can use this function in the following iterative procedure that takes parameters specifying center point coordinates, an initial side length, and the total number

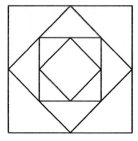

9-31. A pattern of nested squares.

of squares to be nested and produces compositions like the one shown in figure 9-31.

```
PROCEDURE NEST_SQUARES (X_CENTER,Y_CENTER,LENGTH,
                          NUM_SQUARES : INTEGER);

  VAR X1,Y1,X2,Y2,X3,Y3,X4,Y4 : INTEGER;
      NEW_X1,NEW_Y1,NEST : INTEGER;

BEGIN

  { Calculate coordinates of corners of square based on center
    point and side length }

  X1 := X_CENTER − (LENGTH DIV 2);
  Y1 := Y_CENTER − (LENGTH DIV 2);
  X2 := X1;
  Y2 := Y1 + LENGTH;
  X3 := X2 + LENGTH;
  Y3 := Y2:
  X4 := X3;
  Y4 := Y1;

  { Loop to nest squares }

  FOR NEST := 1 TO NUM_SQUARES DO
  BEGIN

    { Draw square }

    MOVE (X1,Y1);
    DRAW (X2,Y2);
    DRAW (X3,Y3);
    DRAW (X4,Y4);
    DRAW (X1,Y1);

    { Calculate midpoints of sides of square }

    NEW_X1 := MIDPOINT (X1,X2);
    NEW_Y1 := MIDPOINT (Y1,Y2);
    X2 := MIDPOINT (X2,X3);
    Y2 := MIDPOINT (Y2,Y3);
    X3 := MIDPOINT (X3,X4);
    Y3 := MIDPOINT (Y3,Y4);
    X4 := MIDPOINT (X4,X1);
    Y4 := MIDPOINT (Y4,Y1);
    X1 := NEW_X1;
    Y1 := NEW_Y1;

  END;

END;
```

Notice what happens if we specify too many squares; a square of side length 1 will be repeated until the loop terminates.

Another interesting way to look at this figure is as a square that is rotated through a quarter circle and scaled down by a factor of **sqrt** (2) at each iteration. That is, shape varies together with rotation, rather than with translation of the element, as in our earlier examples. The beautiful radial spiral shown in figure 9-32 is generated in a very similar way. Here a line with a fixed endpoint is rotated and lengthened by a fixed increment at each iteration.

Finally, figure 9-33 illustrates a type of floor plan very much like that of Le Corbusier's famous Spiral Museum. The repeating element is a 45-degree trapezoid. Plans of this type can be generated by a procedure that lengthens the element by an appropriate increment, translates its origin forward, and rotates it through a half circle at each iteration.

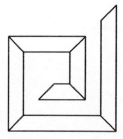

9-33. A spiral formed by repeating instances of a 45-degree trapezoid.

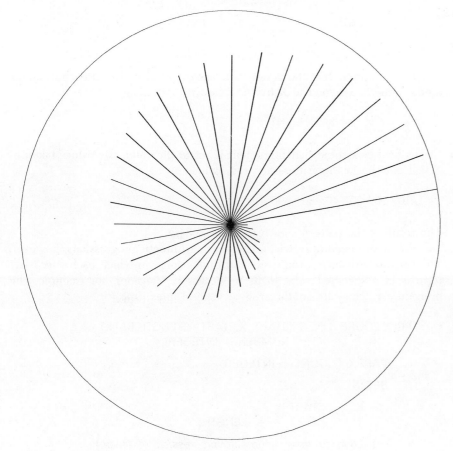

9-32. A radial spiral.

Constructing Mathematical Progressions

So far we have focused mostly on repetitive compositions in which an element dimension is changed by a specified increment or decrement at each iteration, or in which a line of elements is lengthened by a fixed amount whenever a new element is added. In these compositions, dimensions form *arithmetic* progressions. Here is a procedure, for example, that generates a row of equally spaced vertical lines:

```
PROCEDURE LINES (START_X,START_Y,LENGTH,INCREMENT,
                 NUMBER : INTEGER);

    VAR X,Y,COUNT : INTEGER;

    BEGIN

        X := START_X;
        Y := START_Y + LENGTH;
```

```
                           { Loop to draw arithmetic progression of lines }
                           FOR COUNT := 1 TO NUMBER DO
                           BEGIN

                               MOVE (X,START_Y);
                               DRAW (X,Y);
                               X := X + INCREMENT;

                           END;

                      END;
```

Let us assume that the initial value assigned to X is 10. At each iteration, a new value is assigned to X by the following statement:

```
        X := X + INCREMENT;
```

Let us further assume that Increment is set to the value 10. Values taken by X will now be in the arithmetic progression:

```
        10, 20, 30, 40, 50, 60, . . .
```

The result is the pattern shown in figure 9-34a.

We do not need to restrict ourselves to arithmetic progressions, however. We can use *geometric* progressions of dimensions, in which each successive term is in a specified *ratio* to its predecessor. Consider, for example, this procedure to generate another row of vertical lines:

```
        PROCEDURE LINES (START_X,START_Y,LENGTH,RATIO,
                          NUMBER : INTEGER);

        VAR X,Y,COUNT : INTEGER;

        BEGIN

            X := START_X;
            Y := START_Y + LENGTH;

            { Loop to draw geometric progression of lines }
            FOR COUNT := 1 TO NUMBER DO
            BEGIN

                MOVE (X,START_Y);
                DRAW (X,Y);
                X := X * RATIO;

            END;

        END;
```

Let us once again assume that the initial value assigned to X is 10. Now, at each iteration, a new value is assigned to X by the statement:

```
        X := X * RATIO;
```

Let us assume, further, that Ratio is set to the value 2. Values taken by X will now be in the geometric progression:

```
        10, 20, 40, 80, 160, 320, . . .
```

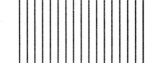

a. X coordinates form an arithmetic progression.

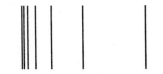

b. X coordinates form a geometric progression.

9-34. The spacing of parallel lines.

The result is the pattern shown in figure 9-34b.

In this example, Ratio is of type **integer.** But it is more generally useful to make it of type **real.** The assignment statement then becomes:

```
X := ROUND(X * RATIO);
```

The sizes of objects, too, may increase in either arithmetic or geometric progression. The next procedure, for example, generates concentric squares with side lengths forming an arithmetic progression (fig. 9-35a).

```
PROCEDURE NEST_SQUARES (X_CENTER,Y_CENTER,LENGTH,
                        INCREMENT,NUMBER : INTEGER);

    VAR COUNT : INTEGER;

    BEGIN

        { Loop to draw arithmetic progression of nested squares }
        FOR COUNT := 1 TO NUMBER DO
        BEGIN

            SQUARE (X_CENTER,Y_CENTER,LENGTH);
            LENGTH := LENGTH + INCREMENT;

        END;

    END;
```

Nest_squares can be modified slightly to generate concentric squares with side lengths forming a geometric progression (fig. 9-35b).

```
PROCEDURE NEST_SQUARES (X_CENTER,Y_CENTER,LENGTH,
                        RATIO,NUMBER : INTEGER);

    VAR COUNT : INTEGER;

    BEGIN

        { Loop to generate geometric progression of nested squares }
        FOR COUNT := 1 TO NUMBER DO
        BEGIN

            SQUARE (X_CENTER,Y_CENTER,LENGTH);
            LENGTH := LENGTH * RATIO;

        END;

    END;
```

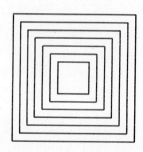

a. Side lengths in arithmetic progression.

Where the values of more than one parameter of some object are changed within a loop, different expressions may assign the successive values to each one of these. This produces *differential* change. In the following procedure, for example, different expressions assign values to X, Y, Length, and Width of a rectangle.

```
PROCEDURE VARY_RECTANGLES (X,Y,LENGTH,WIDTH,INC_X,INC_Y,
                           INC_LENGTH,INC_WIDTH,NUMBER
                           : INTEGER);

    VAR COUNT : INTEGER;
```

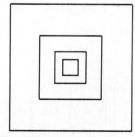

b. Side lengths in geometric progression.

9-35. Compositions of concentric squares.

```
BEGIN

    { Loop to place successive rectangles }
    FOR COUNT := 1 TO NUMBER DO
    BEGIN

        RECTANGLE (X,Y,LENGTH,WIDTH);
        X := X + INC_X;
        Y := Y + INC_Y;
        LENGTH := LENGTH + INC_LENGTH;
        WIDTH := WIDTH + INC_WIDTH;

    END;

END;
```

Figure 9-36 illustrates some results produced by the execution of this procedure.

In summary, the Pascal code to construct a sequence of instances of some type of object, with position or shape values forming arithmetic or geometric progressions, generally looks like this:

Assign initial values to position and shape variables.

Loop control statement (**FOR, WHILE,** or **REPEAT**)

    BEGIN

        Draw instance with current position and shape values.

        Assign new values to position and shape variables using incrementing variables.

    END;

Expressions Containing the Control Variable

When we employ an assignment of the form

```
X := X + INCREMENT;
```

within a loop to construct an arithmetic progression, or an assignment of the form

```
X := X * RATIO;
```

within a loop to construct a geometric progression, we make the position or the shape of each instance of the repeating element depend upon that of its predecessor. In other words, we directly specify how shape or position changes from one instance to the next. An alternative approach is to specify the nature of the change indirectly, by making the value of a position or shape variable depend upon the value of a **for** loop's control variable.

Where Count is the control variable of a **for** loop, we can, for example, generate arithmetic progressions by employing assignments of the form:

```
X := COUNT * INCREMENT;
```

We can make a value of a position or shape variable grow exponentially, rather than arithmetically or geometrically, by using assignments of the form:

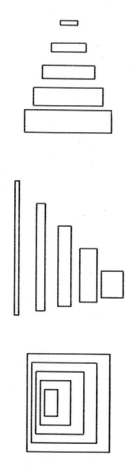

9-36. Some results produced by the procedure Vary_rectangles.

```
X := EXPONENT(COUNT,POWER);
```

where Exponent is an **integer** function that raises Count to the **integer** exponent
specified by Power. For example, if Count begins at 1, and Power is set at
2, successive values of X are:

```
COUNT   1   2   3   4 . . .
X       1   4   9  16 . . .
```

If Power is set at 3, then successive values of X are:

```
COUNT   1   2   3   4 . . .
X       1   8  27  64 . . .
```

The Exponent function can generate very large values even when Count is
small, so you must take care. If Power is 2, for example, Exponent will reach
a value of 32,768 when Count is 15; this is larger than the largest **integer**
representable in many Pascal systems.

More generally, we can specify exponential growth by means of expressions
of the form:

```
X := ROUND (EXPONENT ((COEFFICIENT*COUNT), POWER));
```

where Exponent is now a **real** rather than **integer** function, and Coefficient
is set to a **real** value.

Pascal, unlike some other languages (Fortran and Basic, for example),
does not have a built-in Exponent function. But you can easily write your
own:

```
FUNCTION EXPONENT (BASE : REAL; POWER : INTEGER) : REAL;

    VAR COUNT,N : INTEGER;
        E : REAL;

    BEGIN

        E := BASE;
        N := POWER - 1;

      { Loop to raise BASE to POWER }
        FOR COUNT := 1 TO N DO
        BEGIN

            E := E * BASE;

        END;

        EXPONENT := E;

    END;
```

Sometimes it is useful to use *periodic* functions of the control variable.
Consider, for example, a row of columns to support a sawtooth roof (fig. 9-
37). The following procedure employs the **mod** function to generate compositions
of this type:

```
PROCEDURE ROW_COLUMNS (X_START,Y,MIN_HEIGHT,THICKNESS,
                       HEIGHT_INC,SPACING,PERIOD,
                       NUM_OF_COLUMNS : INTEGER);

    VAR COUNT,HEIGHT,X : INTEGER;
```

```
BEGIN

    HEIGHT := MIN_HEIGHT;
    X := X_START;

    { Loop to place columns with heights incrementing in a
    periodic fashion }
    FOR COUNT := 1 TO NUM_OF_COLUMNS DO
    BEGIN

        COLUMN (X,Y,HEIGHT,THICKNESS);
        HEIGHT := MIN_HEIGHT + (COUNT MOD PERIOD)
                    * HEIGHT_INC;
        X := X + SPACING;

    END;

END;
```

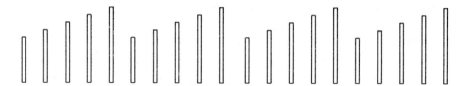

9-37. A row of columns, in a sawtooth pattern, generated with the **mod** function.

Note that the **mod** function is used to produce the remainder that results from dividing a dividend by a divisor. For example, the result of 5 **mod** 2 is 1—the remainder when dividing 5 by 2 is 1. In our example, we used the **mod** function to determine the start of a period.

In figure 9-38 the roof takes a sine curve rather than a sawtooth form. To generate this type of composition, we simply modify our procedure to employ the **sin** function:

```
PROCEDURE SINE_COLUMNS (X_START,Y,MIN_HEIGHT,THICKNESS,
                        HEIGHT_INC,SPACING,PERIOD,
                        NUM_OF_COLUMNS : INTEGER);

CONST RADIANS = 0.01745;

VAR COUNT,HEIGHT,X : INTEGER;
    THETA,ANGLE : REAL;

BEGIN

    ANGLE := 180.0 / PERIOD * RADIANS;
    THETA := 0.0;
    X := X_START;

    { Loop to place columns following a sine curve }
    FOR COUNT := 1 TO NUM_OF_COLUMNS DO
    BEGIN

        HEIGHT := ROUND (MIN_HEIGHT + ABS(HEIGHT_INC
                    * SIN(THETA)));
        COLUMN (X,Y,HEIGHT,THICKNESS);
        X := X + SPACING;
        THETA := COUNT * ANGLE;
```

```
        END;

    END;
```

9-38. A row of columns generated with the **sin** function.

Our earlier procedure for drawing a row of squares can be modified to make X dependent on the control variable Count. This allows us to draw portions of a row of squares by starting and finishing Count at different values. The parameters to this modified procedure now include the initial and final values of Count.

```
PROCEDURE ROW_SQUARES (X_INITIAL,X_INCREMENT,Y,
                       LENGTH,INITIAL,FINAL : INTEGER);

    VAR X,COUNT : INTEGER;

    BEGIN

        { Loop to draw portion or row of squares }
        FOR COUNT := INITIAL TO FINAL DO
        BEGIN

            X := X_INITIAL + (COUNT − 1) * X_INCREMENT;
            SQUARE (X,Y,LENGTH);

        END;

    END;
```

Figure 9-39a shows the resulting row of squares when the initial and final values of Count are set at 1 and 9 respectively. Figure 9-39b shows just a portion of the row when the loop is specified to go from 3 to 6.

Another alternative is to use a **downto** loop as shown in the following procedure:

```
PROCEDURE ROW_SQUARES (X_INITIAL,X_INCREMENT,Y,
                       LENGTH,INITIAL,FINAL : INTEGER);

    VAR X,COUNT : INTEGER;

    BEGIN

        { Loop to draw portion of row of squares }
        FOR COUNT := INITIAL DOWNTO FINAL DO
        BEGIN

            X := X_INITIAL + (COUNT − 1) * X_INCREMENT;
            SQUARE (X,Y,LENGTH);

        END;

    END;
```

Figure 9-40 traces the execution of this procedure.

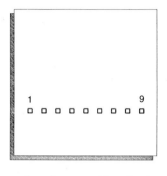

a. Count incremented from 1 to 9.

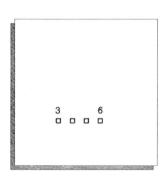

b. Count incremented from 3 to 6.

9-39. Rows of squares generated by the procedure Row_squares.

9-40. States of the drawing as it is generated by a **downto** loop, with values of Count and values of X at each iteration.

Should you add an increment to the value of X at each iteration (as in our original version of Row_squares), or should you make X depend on the value of the control variable Count (as in these modified versions)? If integer arithmetic is used to calculate the value of X, the choice is one of style. If real arithmetic is used, however, there is an important practical difference—roundoff errors will cumulate as increments are added to X at each iteration, but they will not if X depends on the value of Count. Just as a craftsman must watch out for cumulative error when fitting elements together in a row, we must do the same when writing programs to generate repetitive compositions.

A wide variety of expressions containing the control variable may be employed within loops to construct repetitive compositions. But the code always takes the same general form:

```
FOR COUNT : = INITIAL TO FINAL DO
    BEGIN

        Evaluate expressions containing Count to assign values to position
        and shape variables.

        Draw instance with current position and shape values.

    END;
```

Sequences of Loops

So far in this chapter we have considered repetitive compositions that are generated by single loops. But not all repetitive compositions can be produced in this way. The grid shown in figure 9-41a, for example, cannot. We can decompose it, however, into overlaid vertical and horizontal parallel lines (figs. 9-41b,c). Here is a simple procedure to generate parallel horizontal lines:

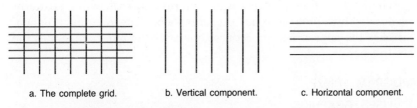

a. The complete grid.   b. Vertical component.   c. Horizontal component.

9-41. The decomposition of a grid of lines.

```
PROCEDURE HORIZONTALS (STARTX_H,STARTY_H,LENGTH_H,
                       SPACING_H,NUMBER_H : INTEGER);

    VAR X,Y,COUNT : INTEGER;

    BEGIN

        X := STARTX_H + LENGTH_H;
        Y := STARTY_H;

        { Loop to draw series of horizontal parallel lines }
        FOR COUNT := 1 TO NUMBER_H DO
        BEGIN

            MOVE (STARTX_H,Y);
            DRAW (X,Y);
            Y := Y + SPACING_H;

        END;
    END;
```

And here is a very similar procedure to generate parallel vertical lines:

```
PROCEDURE VERTICALS (STARTX_V,STARTY_V,LENGTH_V,
                     SPACING_V,NUMBER_V : INTEGER);

    VAR X,Y,COUNT : INTEGER;

    BEGIN

        X := STARTX_V;
        Y := STARTY_V + LENGTH_V;

        { Loop to draw series of parallel vertical lines }
        FOR COUNT := 1 TO NUMBER_V DO
        BEGIN

            MOVE (X,STARTY_V);
            DRAW (X,Y);
            X := X + SPACING_V;

        END;
    END;
```

If these are invoked one after the other,

```
HORIZONTALS (STARTX_H,STARTY_H,LENGTH_H,SPACING_H,
                     NUMBER_H);
VERTICALS (STARTX_V,STARTY_V,LENGTH_V,SPACING_V,
                     NUMBER_V);
```

then the horizontal lines will be drawn first, followed by the vertical lines.

Now consider the simple frieze pattern shown in figure 9-42. It can be decomposed into several simpler repeating patterns, and each of these patterns can be generated by a procedure that executes a loop. The following program, which invokes the appropriate procedures one after the other, generates the complete frieze:

```
PROGRAM  FRIEZE;

    USES  GRAPHICS;

    PROCEDURE  RECTANGLE (X,Y,LENGTH,WIDTH : INTEGER);

        VAR X2,Y2 : INTEGER;

        BEGIN

            { Calculate values for X2 and Y2 }
            X2 := X + LENGTH;
            Y2 := Y + WIDTH;

            { Move to the bottom left corner }
            MOVE (X,Y);

            { Draw the four sides }
            DRAW (X2,Y);
            DRAW (X2,Y2);
            DRAW (X,Y2);
            DRAW (X,Y);

        END;


    PROCEDURE  TRIANGLE (X1,Y1,BASE,ALTITUDE : INTEGER);

        VAR X2,X3,Y2 : INTEGER;

        BEGIN

            X2 := X1 + BASE;
            X3 := X1 + BASE DIV 2;
            Y2 := Y1 + ALTITUDE;

            { Move to the bottom left corner }
            MOVE (X1,Y1);

            { Draw the three sides }
            DRAW (X2,Y1);
            DRAW (X3,Y2);
            DRAW (X1,Y1);

        END;

    PROCEDURE  ROW_RECTANGLES (START_X,Y,LENGTH,WIDTH,
                                        SPACING,NUMBER : INTEGER);

        VAR X,COUNT : INTEGER;
```

```
BEGIN

    X := START_X;

    { Loop to draw row of rectangles }
    FOR COUNT := 1 TO NUMBER DO
    BEGIN

        RECTANGLE (X,Y,LENGTH,WIDTH);
        X := X + SPACING + LENGTH;

    END;

END;

PROCEDURE ROW_TRIANGLES (START_X,Y,BASE,ALTITUDE,
                         SPACING,NUMBER : INTEGER);

VAR X,COUNT : INTEGER;

BEGIN

    X := START_X;

    { Loop to draw row of triangles }
    FOR COUNT := 1 TO NUMBER DO
    BEGIN

        TRIANGLE (X,Y,BASE,ALTITUDE);
        X := X + SPACING + BASE;

    END;

END;

{ Begin main program }
BEGIN

    START_DRAWING;

        ROW_RECTANGLES (50,100,60,10,60,6);
        ROW_RECTANGLES (60,115,40,80,80,6);
        ROW_TRIANGLES (50,200,60,20,60,6);

    FINISH_DRAWING;
END.
```

Notice that the sequence in which the procedures are invoked controls the sequence in which the component patterns are actually drawn on the screen, but does not have any effect on the final drawing. If we were to change the sequence of procedure invocations in our program to the following,

```
ROW_TRIANGLES (50,200,60,20,60,6);
ROW_RECTANGLES (60,115,40,80,80,6);
ROW_RECTANGLES (50,100,60,10,60,6);
```

the effect would be to reverse the order in which the component patterns are drawn on the screen, but the end result would be exactly the same.

In this program, we have taken care that the overlaid rows of triangles and rectangles are in phase with each other. By passing different values for the parameter Spacing into the procedures Row_rectangle and Row_triangle, we can also generate compositions in which the rows are out of phase (fig. 9-42e).

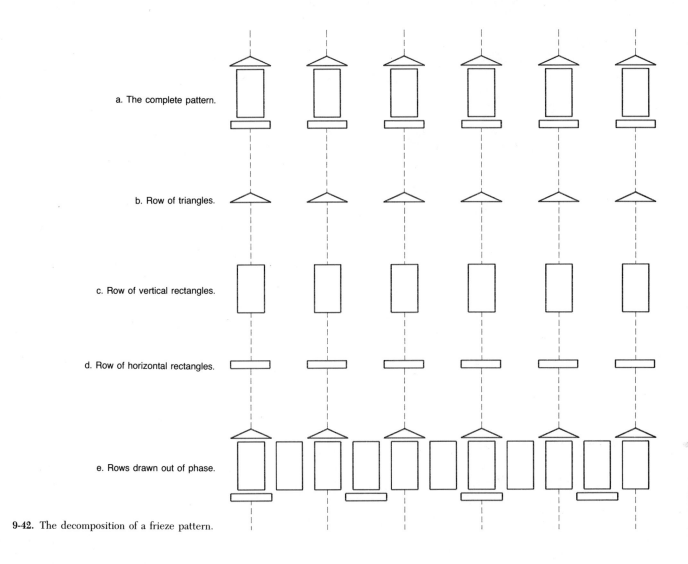

a. The complete pattern.

b. Row of triangles.

c. Row of vertical rectangles.

d. Row of horizontal rectangles.

e. Rows drawn out of phase.

9-42. The decomposition of a frieze pattern.

Nested Loops

Figure 9-43 illustrates a rectangular column grid, which often appears in plan drawings of buildings. To draw it, we might first write a procedure to generate a row of columns as follows:

```
PROCEDURE  ROW  (INITIAL_X,Y,DIAMETER,SPACING,
                        NUM_COLUMNS :  INTEGER);

      VAR  X,COUNT_COLUMNS :  INTEGER;

      BEGIN

          X  :=  INITIAL_X;

        { Loop to place row of columns }
          FOR  COUNT_COLUMNS  :=  1  TO  NUM_COLUMNS  DO
          BEGIN

              COLUMN  (X,Y,DIAMETER);
              X  :=  X  +  SPACING;
```

```
        END;

    END;
```

We might then invoke this procedure the requisite number of times.

```
ROW  (100,500,30,100,4);
ROW  (100,400,30,100,4);
ROW  (100,300,30,100,4);
```

The effect is to draw rows, one after the other.

A more concise way to express this, however, is to invoke the Row procedure from within a loop:

```
Y := 500;

FOR COUNT_ROWS := 1 TO 3 DO
BEGIN
    ROW (100,Y,30,100,4);
    Y := Y − 100;

END;
```

The effect is to *nest* one loop within another. The *inner* loop repeatedly invokes the procedure Column to produce horizontal rows, and the *outer* loop repeatedly invokes the procedure Row to produce the grid. Figure 9-44 shows the step-by-step construction of the grid along with the values that the counters of the inner and outer loops have at each step. You should study this carefully before going on.

Pascal allows an alternative way to express the nesting of loops by using **begin** and **end** statements to delimit the scope of the inner and outer loops and so to prevent any possible ambiguity. Following this approach, we could rewrite our code to generate the column grid in the following fashion:

```
Y := 500;

FOR COUNT_ROWS := 1 TO 3 DO
BEGIN

    X := 100;

    FOR COUNT_COLUMNS := 1 TO 4 DO
    BEGIN

        COLUMN (X,Y,30);
        X := X + 100;

    END;

    Y := Y − 100;

END;
```

It is good practice to indent as shown; this visually expresses the idea of nesting and clearly distinguishes the inner from the outer loop.

This second approach should be employed only when the inner loop does something very simple and straightforward. Usually it is clearer and more expressive to give a descriptive name to the figure generated by the inner

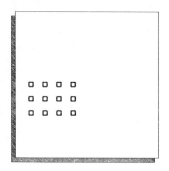

9-43. A grid of columns drawn in the screen coordinate system.

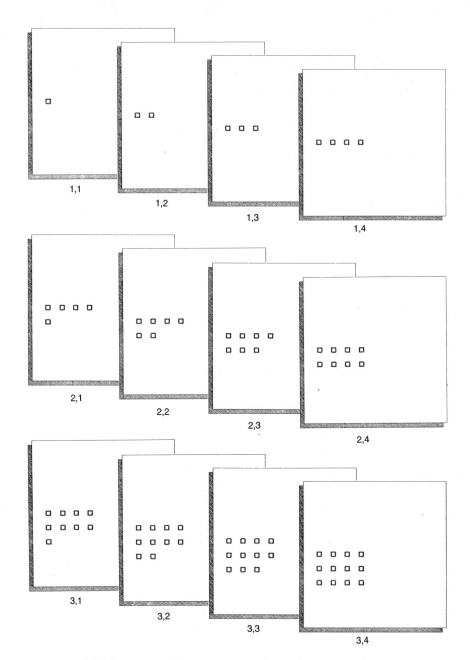

1,1

1,2

1,3

1,4

2,1

2,2

2,3

2,4

3,1

3,2

3,3

3,4

9-44. States of the drawing at each iteration, as it is generated by nested loops.

loop and to group the necessary statements under this name in a procedure.

We are now in a position to write a very general program to draw rectangular column grids. The design variables are shown in figure 9-45a.

The complete program is as follows:

```
PROGRAM GRID;
    USES GRAPHICS;
    PROCEDURE SQUARE (X,Y,SIDE : INTEGER);
        VAR X1,Y1,X2,Y2 : INTEGER;
```

```
BEGIN

    { Calculate coordinates of corners of the square }
    X1 := X - (SIDE DIV 2);
    Y1 := Y - (SIDE DIV 2);
    X2 := X1 + SIDE;
    Y2 := Y1 + SIDE;

    { Move to bottom left corner }
    MOVE (X1,Y1);

    { Draw the four sides of the square }
    DRAW (X2,Y1);
    DRAW (X2,Y2);
    DRAW (X1,Y2);
    DRAW (X1,Y1);

END;

{ Main program }

VAR X_CENTER,Y_CENTER,DIAMETER,BAYS_LONG,BAYS_WIDE,
    BAY_LENGTH,BAY_WIDTH : INTEGER;
    X_START,Y_START,X,Y : INTEGER;
    COUNT_COLUMNS,COUNT_ROWS : INTEGER;

BEGIN

    { Read in design variables }
    WRITELN ('ENTER X_COORDINATE OF CENTER OF GRID:');
    READLN (X_CENTER);
    WRITELN ('ENTER Y_COORDINATE OF CENTER OF GRID:');
    READLN (Y_CENTER);
    WRITELN ('ENTER COLUMN DIAMETER:');
    READLN (DIAMETER);
    WRITELN ('ENTER NUMBER OF BAYS LONG:');
    READLN (BAYS_LONG);
    WRITELN ('ENTER NUMBER OF BAYS WIDE:');
    READLN (BAYS_WIDE);
    WRITELN ('ENTER BAY LENGTH:');
    READLN (BAY_LENGTH);
    WRITELN ('ENTER BAY WIDTH:');
    READLN (BAY_WIDTH);

    { Calculate center of top left column of grid }

    X_START := X_CENTER - (BAY_LENGTH * BAYS_LONG
                DIV 2);
    Y_START := Y_CENTER - (BAY_WIDTH * BAYS_WIDE
                DIV 2);

    START_DRAWING;

    { Loop to draw column grid }
    Y := Y_START;
    FOR COUNT_ROWS := 1 TO BAYS_WIDE+1 DO
    BEGIN

        X := X_START;
        FOR COUNT_COLUMNS := 1 TO BAYS_LONG+1 DO
        BEGIN
            SQUARE (X,Y,DIAMETER);
            X := X + BAY_LENGTH;
```

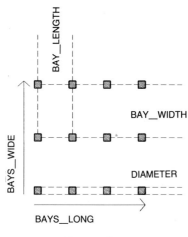

a. The type diagram.

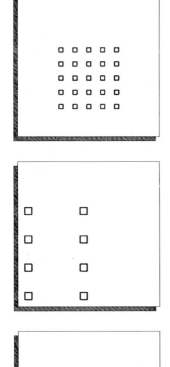

b. Some instances drawn in the screen co-ordinate system.

9-45. Rectangular grids of square columns.

```
        END;
    Y  :=  Y  +  BAY_WIDTH;
  END;
  FINISH_DRAWING;
END.
```

This program first prompts for and reads in values for the design variables, then executes the loops to draw the required number of columns of the specified size and at the appropriate locations. Some of the many possible results are illustrated (fig. 9-45b).

It is simple to modify this program to draw another type of column at the grid locations; it is only necessary to substitute a different procedure for Square. The following procedure, for example, draws a cross-shaped column:

```
PROCEDURE  CROSS (X,Y,LENGTH :  INTEGER);

  VAR  X0,Y0,X1,Y1,X2,Y2,X3,Y3,WIDTH  :  INTEGER;

  BEGIN
    { Calculate coordinates of corners }
    WIDTH  := LENGTH DIV 3;
    X0  :=  X  −  (LENGTH DIV 2);
    X1  :=  X0  +  WIDTH;
    X2  :=  X0  +  2 * WIDTH;
    X3  :=  X0  +  LENGTH;
    Y0  :=  Y  −  (LENGTH DIV 2);
    Y1  :=  Y0  +  WIDTH;
    Y2  :=  Y0  +  2 * WIDTH;
    Y3  :=  Y0  +  LENGTH;

    { Draw  cross }
    MOVE (X0,Y1);
    DRAW (X0,Y2);
    DRAW (X1,Y2);
    DRAW (X1,Y3);
    DRAW (X2,Y3);
    DRAW (X2,Y2);
    DRAW (X3,Y2);
    DRAW (X3,Y1);
    DRAW (X2,Y1);
    DRAW (X2,Y0);
    DRAW (X1,Y0);
    DRAW (X1,Y1);
    DRAW (X0,Y1);
  END;
```

If this is substituted in the column grid program, then the type of drawing shown in figure 9-46 is generated.

The object that is drawn at grid locations may itself be generated by a loop. Figure 9-47, for example, shows a grid of nested squares:

```
PROGRAM  GRID;

  USES  GRAPHICS;
```

```
PROCEDURE SQUARE (X,Y,SIDE : INTEGER);

    VAR X1,Y1,X2,Y2 : INTEGER;

    BEGIN

        { Calculate values for X1,Y1,X2,Y2 }
        X1 := X - (SIDE DIV 2);
        Y1 := Y - (SIDE DIV 2);
        X2 := X1 + SIDE;
        Y2 := Y1 + SIDE;

        { Move to bottom left corner }
        MOVE (X1,Y1);

        { Draw the four sides of the square }
        DRAW (X2,Y1);
        DRAW (X2,Y2);
        DRAW (X1,Y2);
        DRAW (X1,Y1);

    END;

PROCEDURE NESTED_SQUARES (X,Y,DIAMETER,INCREMENT,
                          NEST : INTEGER);

    VAR COUNT : INTEGER;

    BEGIN

        { Loop to nest squares centered around X,Y }
        FOR COUNT := 1 TO NEST DO
        BEGIN

            SQUARE (X,Y,DIAMETER);
            DIAMETER := DIAMETER - INCREMENT;

        END;

    END;

PROCEDURE ROW (INITIAL_X,Y,DIAMETER,INCREMENT,NEST,
               SPACING,NUM_COLUMNS : INTEGER);

    VAR X,COUNT_COLUMNS : INTEGER;

    BEGIN

        X := INITIAL_X;

        { Loop to place row of nested squares }
        FOR COUNT_COLUMNS := 1 TO NUM_COLUMNS DO
        BEGIN

            NESTED_SQUARES (X,Y,DIAMETER,INCREMENT,NEST);
            X := X + SPACING;

        END;

    END;

{ Main program }
VAR Y,COUNT_ROWS : INTEGER;

BEGIN

    START_DRAWING;

        Y := 500;
```

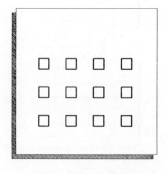

a. Grid of square columns.

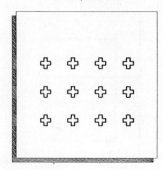

b. Cross-shaped columns substituted at the same locations.

9-46. Substitution of motifs within a loop.

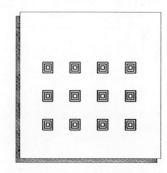

9-47. Patterns of nested squares repeated on a grid.

REPETITION   245

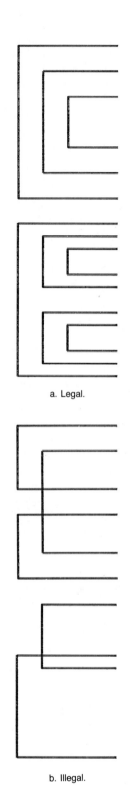

a. Legal.

b. Illegal.

9-48. Nesting of loops.

```
{ Loop to draw grid of nested squares }
  FOR COUNT_ROWS := 1 TO 3 DO
  BEGIN

      ROW (100,Y,60,20,3,200,4);
      Y := Y − 200;

  END;

  FINISH_DRAWING;

END.
```

The inner loop of this program invokes the procedure Square to generate nested squares. The middle loop invokes the procedure Nested_squares to generate rows of nested squares. Then the outer loop invokes the procedure Row to generate the grid. Alternatively (but less clearly), the nesting could be expressed using **begin** and **end** statements and indenting as follows:

```
Y_CENTER := 500;

FOR COUNT_ROWS := 1 TO 3 DO
BEGIN

    X_CENTER := 100;
    FOR COUNT_COLUMNS := 1 TO 4 DO
    BEGIN

        DIAMETER := 60;

        FOR COUNT_NEST := 1 TO 3 DO
        BEGIN

            SQUARE (X,Y,DIAMETER);
            DIAMETER := DIAMETER − 20;

        END;

        X := X + 200;

    END;

    Y := Y − 200;

END;
```

In general, you can nest loops as deeply as you want to generate repetitive compositions such as regular rows, stacks, nested objects, and combinations of these. The only restrictions are that successive loops cannot overlap, and an inner loop must always be contained completely within an outer loop. The syntactic conventions of Pascal make it difficult to write code that violates these rules. Figure 9-48a illustrates some examples of legal nesting, whereas figure 9-48b illustrates some examples of illegal nesting. They are illegal because they could result in ambiguous values of control variables or expressions.

Vocabulary Elements with Repetition Parameters

It should now be obvious that the use of loops allows us to declare graphic vocabulary elements that have not only position and shape parameters, but also repetition parameters. That is, the amount of repetition may vary from instance to instance. Consider our procedure Row, to generate a row of square columns in the program Grid. The position parameters are the coordinates of the starting point. There is a shape parameter controlling the diameter of the column. Then there is a repetition parameter—Num_columns—controlling the number of columns. Finally, there is a parameter controlling the spacing of columns.

Where **for** loops are employed, repetition parameters may specify initial and final values for the control variable. Where **while** or **repeat until** loops are employed, repetition parameters may specify values for variables that appear in the control expressions. Where an arithmetic progression is employed, the initial value may be treated as a design variable and so may the value of the increment. Similarly, the initial values and ratios that define geometric progressions may be treated as design variables. Where functions of the control variable are employed, the values of any coefficients may also be treated as design variables.

In summary, any or all of the following may be treated as design variables and represented as parameters of procedures that generate repetitive compositions:

- position of the entire composition
- shape variables of the repeating element
- initial and final values of control variables in **for** loops
- values for variables in control expressions for **while** and **repeat until** loops
- initial values and increments for arithmetic progressions
- initial values and ratios for geometric progressions
- values for coefficients appearing in functions of control variables

Summary

In this chapter we have made use of the knowledge that a composition may be generated not only from a limited vocabulary, but that there may also be regular repetition of vocabulary elements. Where this is the case, we do not need to explicitly specify each instance of the repeating element. It suffices to specify what element is repeated, where the repetition starts, what changes at each step, and where the repetition ends. We can do this by writing a loop from within which a procedure to generate the repeating element is invoked.

We have seen that Pascal provides three kinds of loops: the counted **for** loop, and the **while** and **repeat until** loops that are controlled by the evaluation of expressions. These can be used to write concise programs that generate simple repetitive compositions. More complicated repetitive compositions can be generated by writing loops that execute one after the other, or that are nested one within the other.

The first step in writing a program to generate a repetitive composition is to identify the repeating graphic element and declare an appropriately parameterized procedure to generate it. This procedure can then be invoked from within a loop (or a structure of nested loops). Consideration of how you want to control the way that the loop begins and ends and the number of iterations should indicate whether a **for,** a **while,** or a **repeat until** loop is most appropriate. You may want the successive values of the repeating element's shape and position parameters to form arithmetic or geometric progressions.

In this case, you can initialize values outside the loop and calculate new values from old values at each iteration. Alternatively, you may want successive values of the shape and position parameters to be functions of the control variable. In this case, you must evaluate these functions at each iteration.

Whereas Pascal provides concise, convenient ways to express rules of repetition, establishment of those rules is up to the designer, who must decide if there are practical or aesthetic reasons to repeat some elements within a composition, and if so, how the repeating pattern should be started and terminated, what shape or position properties should change at each iteration, and what should remain the same.

Exercises

1. Assume a procedure to draw a square positioned by X, Y at the bottom-left corner of side length Length. Execute the following code by hand. Record the value taken by each variable at each iteration, and draw the graphic output accurately on screen grid paper.

a.
```
X := 100;
Y := 100;
LENGTH := 10;

FOR COUNT := 1 TO 5 DO
BEGIN

    SQUARE(X,Y,LENGTH);
    X := X + 2*LENGTH;
    LENGTH := LENGTH*2;

END;
```

b.
```
X := 100;
Y := 100;
LENGTH := 200;

WHILE LENGTH > 20 DO
BEGIN

    SQUARE(X,Y,LENGTH);
    LENGTH := LENGTH DIV 2;
    X := X + LENGTH;
    Y := Y + LENGTH;

END;
```

c.
```
X_INITIAL := 100;
Y_INITIAL := 100;
LENGTH_INITIAL := 100;

FOR COUNT := 1 TO 3 DO
BEGIN

    X := X_INITIAL;
    Y := Y_INITIAL;
    LENGTH := LENGTH_INITIAL;

    REPEAT
        SQUARE(X,Y,LENGTH);
        LENGTH := LENGTH - 10;
```

```
        X := X + 5;
        Y := Y + 5;
    UNTIL (LENGTH < 10);

    X_INITIAL := X_INITIAL + 100;
    Y_INITIAL := Y_INITIAL + 100;

  END;
```

2. Assuming a Rectangle procedure positioned by X, Y at the bottom-left corner with Length and Width defining horizontal and vertical dimensions respectively, draw the picture that would be produced by the following code:

```
X_INITIAL := 100;
Y_INITIAL := 100;
LENGTH := 100;
WIDTH := 30;
NX := 8;

Y := Y_INITIAL;

REPEAT

    X := X_INITIAL;

    FOR COUNT_X := 1 TO NX DO
    BEGIN
        RECTANGLE (X,Y,LENGTH,WIDTH);
        X := X + LENGTH;

    END;
    NX := NX − 1;
    X_INITIAL := X_INITIAL + LENGTH DIV 2;
    Y := Y + WIDTH;

UNTIL NX = 0;
```

3. Write procedures to draw the types of grids of squares shown in figure 9-49.

4. Consider radial patterns of the type illustrated in figure 9-50. Write a general procedure to generate them.

5. Figure 9-51 illustrates some common types of building sections. Consider how each one should be parameterized, and write procedures to generate them.

9-49. Some grids of squares.

9-50. A radial pattern.

9-51. Some schematic sections for multistory buildings.

9-52. Some standard types of roof trusses.

6. There are various standard patterns for placement of the chords in a roof truss. Some of the most common are shown in figure 9-52. Choose one of these and, taking span, depth, and the number of subdivisions as parameters, write a procedure to lay out the chords correctly and draw the truss.

7. A standard method for determining the rake of an auditorium floor so that each row of seats has a clear view of the stage is illustrated in figure 9-53. Write an appropriately parameterized procedure that generates the profile of the floor according to this method.

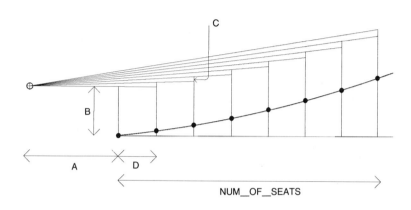

9-53. Construction of the dished profile of an auditorium floor.

8. Examine the leaves along a twig from a plant. Can you characterize the pattern that you see in terms of type and regular repetition? What changes from instance to instance? What kinds of arithmetic and geometric sequences are involved? Write a brief, illustrated analysis.

9. What are the practical reasons for regular repetition of elements in architectural compositions? Discuss.

10. It has often been argued that the aesthetic success of a composition is a matter of appropriate balance between "unity" (which may be established by regular repetition of a motif) and "variety" (which may be introduced by changing parameters from instance to instance). Test this proposition by generating repetitive compositions with different degrees of variation. Provide a critical analysis of your results.

10.

Curves

We have taken a straight line segment to be the primitive element of graphic composition; we have considered drawings as sets of straight line segments in the picture plane; and we have treated composition as the relation of straight line segments by connection, angle, ratio, and repetition. But this does not seem an adequate framework for analysis of a composition like Botticelli's *Birth of Venus* (fig. 10-1); the only straight line is the horizon (parallel to the X axis), and all the others are *curves*. Different types of curves are used to construct the shell, waves, hair, drapery, foliage, and outlines of human bodies, and the composition relates curves to each other and to the horizon line. Sharp inflections contrast with shallow sweeps; curves accompany each other or diverge; in the shell, there are waves and hair repetitions with variation from instance to instance.

Ezra Pound once wrote, with considerable scorn: "Give your draughtsman sixty-four stencils of 'Botticelli's most usual curves.' And will he make you a masterpiece?" We cannot guarantee the masterpiece, but we can approach the composition of curves by considering different types of curves, parameterized procedures to generate these types, and visually important relations between curves of various types.

The Approximation of Curves by Straight Segments

Consider the smooth curve shown in figure 10-2a. Since we have no primitive to draw a line of continuously varying slope, we cannot write a Pascal program to replicate it exactly. But we can approximate it, more or less closely, with sequences of vectors generated by **draw** commands. Here is a procedure that produces the coarse approximation illustrated in figure 10-2b:

251

10-1. Sandro Botticelli, *The Birth of Venus* c. 1480, Uffizi Gallery, Florence.

a. A smooth curve.

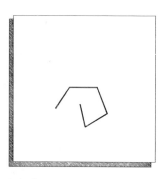

b. A coarse approximation with straight line segments.

c. A finer approximation with straight line segments.

10-2. Approximations of a curve.

```
PROCEDURE CURVE;
   BEGIN

         MOVE (481,354);
         DRAW (518,195);
         DRAW (677,290);
         DRAW (605,472);
         DRAW (404,471);
         DRAW (306,324);

   END;
```

And here is a procedure that produces the finer approximation illustrated in figure 10-2c:

```
PROCEDURE CURVE;
   BEGIN

         MOVE (481,354);
         DRAW (447,264);
         DRAW (518,195);
         DRAW (616,208);
         DRAW (677,290);
         DRAW (671,393);
         DRAW (605,472);
         DRAW (505,500);
         DRAW (404,471);
         DRAW (332,398);
         DRAW (306,324);

   END;
```

We can ultimately make the approximation as close as the resolution of our display device allows. How many points are needed for an adequate approximation? The answer will depend on the amount of information needed for recognition of the curve (fig. 10-3), the aesthetic importance of *smooth* curves, and the available resolution. You should experiment.

Fortunately, many of the types of curves of most interest to us—circles, arcs of circles, ellipses, parabolas, and so on—do not need to be described in this cumbersome, point-by-point fashion. It is possible to write loops that repeatedly invoke functions to generate X- and Y-coordinate values of successive, closely spaced points on the curve. These values can then be used in **draw** commands to generate a vector approximation of the curve. In this chapter, we shall explore this approach to generating the kinds of curves that we most often need in drawings.

10-3. The curve of a human profile represented by successively greater amounts of information.

Functions of X

In many cases, the Y coordinate of a point on a curve can simply be represented as a function of the X coordinate. A sequence of points can then be generated by a loop that increments the value of X through some range and invokes the appropriate function at each iteration to return the corresponding Y value. The following procedure uses the standard Pascal function **sqr** (which computes the square of a number) in this way to generate a parabolic curve:

```
PROCEDURE  PARABOLA  (X0,Y0,START_X,FINISH_X,N_SEGMENTS  :
                      INTEGER);

   { Calculates points of curve relative to 0,0 and then shifts origin
     to X0,Y0 to plot }

   VAR  X,Y,COUNT,X_INCREMENT  :  INTEGER;

   BEGIN

         X_INCREMENT  : =  (FINISH_X  −  START_X)  DIV
                           N_SEGMENTS;
         X  : =  START_X;
         Y  : =  SQR(X);
         MOVE  (X + X0,Y + Y0);

         FOR COUNT  : =  1  TO  N_SEGMENTS  DO
         BEGIN

             X  : =  X  +  X_INCREMENT;
             Y  : =  SQR(X);
             DRAW  (X + X0,Y + Y0);

         END;

   END;
```

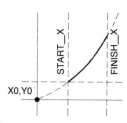

a. Type diagram.

b. Examples of instances.

10-4. A parabola generated using the function **sqr.**

Notice how this procedure is parameterized. There are parameters that specify the starting X coordinate, the finishing X coordinate, the location of the curve in the screen coordinate system, and the number of segments. Some examples of output are given in figure 10-4.

A very broad class of curves, which includes the straight line and the parabola, is the class of *polynomial* curves. A straight line is a polynomial of *degree one,* and a straight line composed of a specified number of segments is generated by this procedure (figure 10-5a):

```
PROCEDURE POLY_1 (A0,A1 : REAL; X0,Y0,START_X,FINISH_X,
                        N_SEGMENTS : INTEGER);

  { Calculates points of line relative to 0,0 and then shifts origin to
    X0,Y0 to plot }

  VAR X,Y,X_INCREMENT,COUNT : INTEGER;

  BEGIN

      X_INCREMENT := (FINISH_X − START_X) DIV
                            N_SEGMENTS;
      X := START_X;
      Y := ROUND(A0 + A1 ∗ X);
      MOVE (X+X0,Y+Y0);

      FOR COUNT := 1 TO N_SEGMENTS DO
      BEGIN

          X := X + X_INCREMENT;
          Y := ROUND(A0 + A1 ∗ X);
          DRAW (X+X0,Y+Y0);

      END;

  END;
```

The value of Y is assigned by the statement:

```
Y := ROUND(A0 + A1 ∗ X);
```

The value of A1 determines the *slope* of the line, and the value of A0 determines the *intercept* of the line with the Y axis.

This procedure is pointless (or rather, generates too many points) as it stands, because we could simply draw a vector from the first point to the last without generating those between. But it can easily be converted into a useful procedure to draw a dotted line (fig. 10-5b), as follows:

```
X := START_X;

FOR COUNT := 1 TO N_SEGMENTS+1 DO
BEGIN

    Y := ROUND(A0 + A1 ∗ X);
    MOVE (X+X0,Y+Y0);
    DRAW (X+X0,Y+Y0);
    X := X + X_INCREMENT;

END;
```

A parabola is a polynomial of *degree two* and is generated by the following procedure (fig. 10-5c):

```
PROCEDURE POLY_2 (A0,A1,A2 : REAL; X0,Y0,START_X,FINISH_X,
                  N_SEGMENTS : INTEGER);

{ Calculates points of curve relative to 0,0 and then shifts origin
  to X0,Y0 to plot }

    VAR X,Y,X_INCREMENT,COUNT : INTEGER;
    BEGIN

        X_INCREMENT := (FINISH_X - START_X) DIV
                       N_SEGMENTS;
        X := START_X;
        Y := ROUND(A0 + A1 * X + A2 * EXPONENT(X,2));

        MOVE (X+X0,Y+Y0);

        FOR COUNT := 1 TO N_SEGMENTS DO
        BEGIN

        X := X + X_INCREMENT;
        Y := ROUND(A0 + A1 * X + A2 * EXPONENT(X,2));
        DRAW (X+X0,Y+Y0);

        END;

    END;
```

a. Straight line (degree one).

Here the value of Y is assigned by the statement:

```
    Y := ROUND(A0 + A1 * X + A2 * EXPONENT(X,2));
```

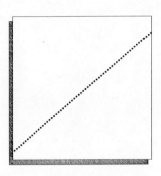

b. Dotted straight line.

Exponent is the exponentation function that was introduced in chapter 9. The coefficients A0, A1, and A2 determine the location in the coordinate system and the precise shape of an instance.

In similar fashion, a polynomial of *degree three* is generated by this next procedure (fig. 10-5d):

```
PROCEDURE POLY_3 (A0,A1,A2,A3 : REAL; X0,Y0,START_X,
                  FINISH_X,N_SEGMENTS : INTEGER);

{ Calculates points of curve relative to 0,0 and then shifts origin
  to X0,Y0 to plot }

    VAR X,Y,X_INCREMENT,COUNT : INTEGER;

    BEGIN

        X_INCREMENT := (FINISH_X - START_X) DIV
                       N_SEGMENTS;
        X := START_X;
        Y := ROUND(A0 + A1 * X + A2 * EXPONENT(X,2) +
             A3 * EXPONENT(X,3));

        MOVE (X+X0,Y+Y0);

        FOR COUNT := 1 TO N_SEGMENTS DO
        BEGIN

            X := X + X_INCREMENT;
            Y := ROUND(A0 + A1 * X + A2 * EXPONENT(X,2)
                 + A3 * EXPONENT(X,3));
            DRAW(X+X0,Y+Y0);

        END;
    END;
```

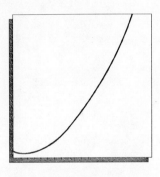

c. Parabola (degree two).

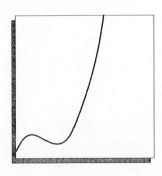

d. Cubic (degree three).

10-5. Type diagrams for polynomials.

In this case, the value of Y is assigned by the statement:

$$Y := \textbf{ROUND}(A0 + A1 * X + A2 * \text{EXPONENT}(X,2) + A3 * \text{EXPONENT}(X,3));$$

Now there are four coefficients: A0, A1, A2, and A3.

Similarly, for a fourth degree polynomial, we would have coefficients A0, A1, A2, A3, and A4 as well as a correspondingly expanded assignment statement. For a fifth degree polynomial we would have six such coefficients, and so on. Note that if some of the coefficients of a higher-degree polynomial are set to zero, a lower-order curve is generated. So we could, if we wished, employ one general polynomial procedure with n parameters to draw polynomial curves of any degree up to n. However, this would be inconvenient for use in drawing lower-order polynomials.

Polynomial procedures can be invoked from within loops to produce repetitive compositions of curves. The following procedure, for example, invokes Poly_2 to generate a pattern like Botticelli's waves (fig. 10-6).

10-6. A composition of parabolas like Botticelli's waves.

```
PROGRAM WAVE;

    USES GRAPHICS;

    PROCEDURE POLY_2 (A0,A1,A2 : REAL; X0,Y0,START_X,
                             FINISH_X,N_SEGMENTS : INTEGER);
    { Creates parabola around 0,0 and shifts to X0,Y0 to plot }

        VAR X,Y,X_INCREMENT, COUNT : INTEGER;

        BEGIN
            X_INCREMENT := (FINISH_X - START_X) DIV
                               N_SEGMENTS;
            X := START_X;
            Y := ROUND(A0 + A1 * X + A2 * EXPONENT(X,2));
            MOVE (X+X0,Y+Y0);

            FOR COUNT := 1 TO N_SEGMENTS DO
            BEGIN

                X := X + X_INCREMENT;
                Y := ROUND(A0 + A1 * X + A2 *
                           EXPONENT(X,2));
                DRAW (X+X0,Y+Y0);

            END;

        END;

    { Main program }
    VAR X0,Y0,COUNT,X_RANGE,START_X,FINISH_X : INTEGER;
        A0,A1,A2 : REAL;
    BEGIN
        START_DRAWING;
            A0 := 0;
            A1 := 0;
            A2 := 0.05;
            X_RANGE := 40;
            START_X := -X_RANGE DIV 2;
```

```
        FINISH_X  :=  +X_RANGE DIV 2;
        X0  :=  40;
        Y0  :=  10;

    { Loop  to  generate  waves }
        FOR COUNT  :=  1 TO 6 DO
        BEGIN

            POLY_2  (A0,A1,A2,X0,Y0,START_X,FINISH_X,20);
            X0  :=  X0  +  X_RANGE;

        END;

    FINISH_DRAWING;

  END.
```

A pattern like Botticelli's shell (fig. 10-7) is generated by:

10-7. A composition of parabolas like Botticelli's shell.

```
PROGRAM SHELL;

  USES GRAPHICS;

  PROCEDURE POLY_2 (A0,A1,A2 : REAL; X0,Y0,START_X,
                    FINISH_X,N_SEGMENTS : INTEGER);
    { Creates parabola around 0,0 and shifts to X0,Y0 to plot }

      VAR X,Y,X_INCREMENT,COUNT : INTEGER;

      BEGIN

          X_INCREMENT  :=  (FINISH_X  −  START_X) DIV
                          N_SEGMENTS;
          X  :=  START_X;
          Y  :=  ROUND (A0+A1 ∗ X+A2 ∗ EXPONENT(X,2));
          MOVE  (X+X0,Y+Y0);

          FOR COUNT  :=  1 TO N_SEGMENTS DO
          BEGIN

              X  :=  X  +  X_INCREMENT;
              Y  :=  ROUND (A0+A1 ∗ X+A2 ∗ EXPONENT (X,2));
              DRAW  (X+X0,Y+Y0);

          END;

      END;

  { Main program }

  VAR X0,Y0,COUNT,X_RANGE,START_X,FINISH_X,INC :
      INTEGER;
      A0,A1,A2 : REAL;

  BEGIN

      START_DRAWING;

      { Set starting values of parabola parameters }
          A0  :=  0;
          A1  :=  0;
          A2  :=  0.012;
          INC  :=  40;
          START_X  :=  −90;
          FINISH_X  :=  0;
          X0  :=  300;
          Y0  :=  10;
```

a. Sketch of an architectural motif, with several different types of curves related in complex ways.

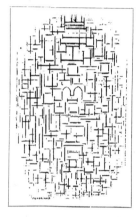

b. A later version consisting almost entirely of straight lines in †, L, and T relationships.

10-8. Levels of abstraction in the work of Piet Mondrian (1917).

```
{ Loop to generate curves }
FOR COUNT := 1 TO 5 DO
BEGIN

    POLY_2 (A0,A1,A2,X0,Y0,START_X,FINISH_X,20);

    START_X := START_X − INC;    {Increase range
                                     of x}

    INC := INC − 10;
    A2 := A2 * (1 − 1/(COUNT + 1)):    {Decrease
                                         slope
                                         of curve}

END;

FINISH_DRAWING;

END.
```

In the case of the waves, position varies from instance to instance, whereas shape remains constant. In the shell, position is the same, whereas shape varies.

Are polynomials adequate approximations of Botticelli's curves, or are they too "mechanical"? This depends on the desired level of abstraction. If you want to emphasize similarity, repetition, and the clear, simple relation of graphic elements, then simple polynomials, with few parameters, are appropriate. But if you want to inflect curves in complex ways and create subtle variation from instance to instance, you will need more complex polynomials with more parameters, giving you more degrees of freedom. The works of Piet Mondrian explore this issue; early paintings use a vocabulary of several different types of curves in a rich variety of relations, but later paintings reduce this to straight lines in just a few simple relations. At the same time, his early palette was wide and was developed to create complex relationships of tone, hue, and saturation. He then reduced his palette to black, white, and saturated primaries. Sometimes this process of simplification is illustrated particularly strikingly by successive versions of the same motif. The sketch of a church in figure 10-8a, for example, contains many curved lines, and there is considerable variation from line to line. The later version, shown in figure 10-8b, is reduced almost completely to a gridlike pattern of horizontal and vertical straight segments; fewer graphic variables are used and simpler relations are formed.

Polynomials are not the only kinds of functions that can be employed to generate curves. Trigonometric functions can also be used. Our next procedure illustrates this by drawing a sine curve (fig. 10-9), the coordinates of which are found by evaluating the Pascal **sin** function.

```
PROCEDURE SINE_CURVE (X0,Y0,START_X,FINISH_X,N_SEGMENTS,
                       HEIGHT,FREQUENCY,SHIFT,A0 :
                       INTEGER);

{ Calculates points of curve relative to 0,0 and then shifts origin
  to X0,Y0 to plot }

VAR X,Y,X_INCREMENT,COUNT : INTEGER;
     THETA : REAL;
CONST RADIANS = 0.01745;

BEGIN
```

```
    X_INCREMENT := (FINISH_X - START_X) DIV
                     N_SEGMENTS;
    X := START_X;
    THETA := (FREQUENCY * X + SHIFT) * RADIANS;
    Y := A0 + ROUND(HEIGHT * SIN(THETA));
    MOVE (X+X0,Y+Y0);

    FOR COUNT := 1 TO N_SEGMENTS DO
    BEGIN

        X := X + X_INCREMENT;
        THETA := (FREQUENCY * X + SHIFT) * RADIANS;
        Y := A0 + ROUND(HEIGHT * SIN(THETA));
        DRAW (X+X0,Y+Y0);

    END;

  END;
```

Here the value is assigned by the statement

```
    Y := A0 + ROUND(HEIGHT * SIN(THETA);
```

where

```
    THETA := (FREQUENCY * X + SHIFT)*RADIANS;
```

Height specifies the amplitude, Frequency specifies the number of cycles for a given range of X, Shift specifies the displacement from the origin (where a value of 0 gives a standard sine curve), and A0 is the vertical displacement of the origin.

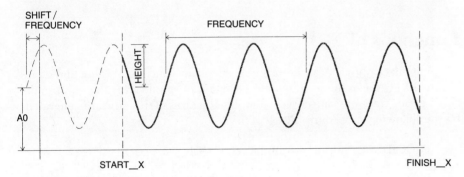

10-9. Type diagram for a sine curve.

The following code invokes Sine_curve within a loop to generate a repetitive composition:

```
VAR Y0,HEIGHT,COUNT : INTEGER;

BEGIN

    START_DRAWING;

        Y0 := 20;
        HEIGHT := 25;

    { Draws parallel sine curves with increasing heights }
```

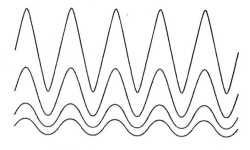

10-10. A repetitive composition of sine curves.

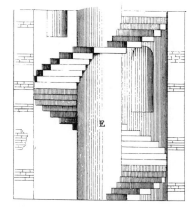

10-11. Circular spiral stairs, from Isaac Ware's edition of Andrea Palladio's *Four Books of Architecture*.

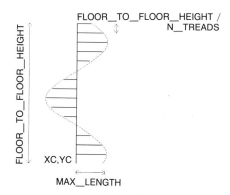

a. Type diagram.

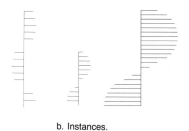

b. Instances.

10-12. Simplified spiral stairs.

```
    FOR COUNT := 1 TO 4 DO
    BEGIN

        SINE_CURVE (10,Y0,0,1000,100,HEIGHT,6,0,0);
        HEIGHT := HEIGHT * 2;
        Y0 := Y0 + HEIGHT;

    END;

        FINISH_DRAWING;

    END.
```

Figure 10-10 shows some output. The axes of the curves are parallel and evenly spaced, and they are all in phase, but height varies. More complex compositions could be produced by varying additional parameters within the loop.

As these examples illustrate, there is a general form for code to plot curves that are described as functions of X:

```
Assign initial value to X
Calculate Y as a function of X

MOVE (X,Y);

FOR COUNT := 1 TO N_SEGMENTS DO
BEGIN

    Increment X
    Calculate Y as a function of X

    DRAW (X,Y);

END;
```

Functions of Y

A similar approach can be taken to curves in which X is a function of Y. Figure 10-11, for example, shows an elevation of spiral stairs; the outer ends of the treads trace out sine curves. Simplified figures of this type are generated by the following procedure (fig. 10-12):

```
PROCEDURE SPIRAL_STAIR (XC,YC,FLOOR_TO_FLOOR_HEIGHT,
                        N_TREADS,MAX_LENGTH,FREQUENCY :
                        INTEGER);

VAR X,Y,Y_INCREMENT,COUNT : INTEGER;
    THETA : REAL;

CONST RADIANS = 0.01745;

BEGIN

  { Calculate distance between treads }
    Y_INCREMENT := FLOOR_TO_FLOOR_HEIGHT DIV
                   N_TREADS;
    Y := YC;

  { Trace out treads of spiral stair to follow sine curve }
    FOR COUNT := 1 TO N_TREADS DO
    BEGIN
```

```
THETA  :=  FREQUENCY  *  Y  *  RADIANS;
X  :=  XC  +  ROUND (MAX_LENGTH  *  SIN(THETA));

{ Draw vector to represent tread }
MOVE  (XC,Y);
DRAW  (X,Y);
Y  :=  Y  +  Y_INCREMENT;

          END;

        END;
```

Figure 10-13 shows a beautiful section drawing of an elliptical spiral stair by Paul Letarouilly. It is a composition of instances of vertical sine curves, contrasted with the regular horizontal rhythms of the treads and the vertical rhythms of columns and balusters. Its richness is generated by overlaying variations on the theme of the vertical sine curve.

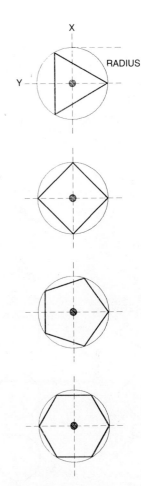

10-14. The parameterization of a regular polygon by center coordinates, radius, and number of sides.

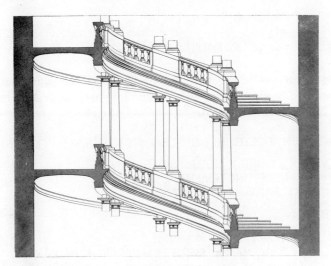

10-13. A section of the elliptical stair at the Barberini Palace, Rome, from Paul Letarouilly's *Edifices de Rome Moderne*.

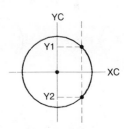

10-15. For any X coordinate on the circumference of a circle, there are two Y-coordinate values.

Regular Polygons and Circles

The most frequently used type of curve in architecture and most other fields of design is the circle. For our purposes, a circle may be regarded as a regular polygon with a sufficiently large number of sides to appear smooth. It is useful, then, to have a procedure that draws a regular polygon with any specified number of sides, of any specified radius, and centered at any specified point (X, Y) (fig. 10-14).

We cannot simply evaluate a function of X to find the Y coordinates of points on a circle, because for any given value of X there will always be two Y coordinates (fig. 10-15). We must therefore find some other approach.

Figure 10-16 illustrates the principle that we will employ. An Angle is measured from a vertical line. We know, from elementary trigonometry, that the X coordinate of a point on the circle is assigned by:

```
X_COORD  :=  XC  +  RADIUS  *  COS(ANGLE);
```

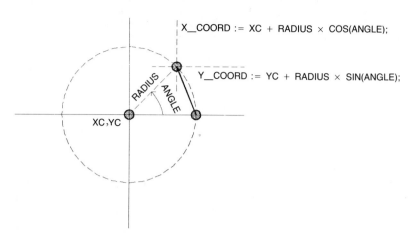

$$X\_COORD := XC + RADIUS \times COS(ANGLE);$$

$$Y\_COORD := YC + RADIUS \times SIN(ANGLE);$$

RADIUS

ANGLE

XC,YC

10-16. The geometric construction for drawing a regular polygon.

Similarly, the Y coordinate is assigned by:

$$Y\_COORD := YC + RADIUS * SIN(ANGLE);$$

So, to produce an n-sided regular polygon, we need a procedure that executes a loop from 1 to N_sides, calculates a value for Angle at each iteration, and calculates X_coord and Y_coord:

```
PROCEDURE POLYGON (XC,YC,RADIUS,N_SIDES : INTEGER);

    VAR X_COORD,Y_COORD,SIDES : INTEGER;
        ANGLE, INCREMENT : REAL;
    CONST RADIANS = 0.01745;

BEGIN

    { Determine angle increment }
    INCREMENT := (360.0 / N_SIDES) * RADIANS;
    ANGLE := 0.0;
    X_COORD := XC + RADIUS;

    { Move to starting point }
    MOVE (X_COORD,YC);

    FOR SIDES := 1 TO N_SIDES DO
    BEGIN

        { Calculate coordinates of each vertex }
        ANGLE := ANGLE + INCREMENT;
        X_COORD := XC + ROUND(RADIUS * COS(ANGLE));
        Y_COORD := YC + ROUND(RADIUS * SIN(ANGLE));

        { Draw to next vertex }

        DRAW (X_COORD,Y_COORD);

    END;

END;
```

10-17. Polygons with increasing numbers of sides that will eventually approximate a circle.

Some examples of output from this procedure are shown in figure 10-17. You should experiment with it to find how many sides you need to draw smooth-looking circles of various sizes. You should avoid specifying more sides than you really need, because this will result in unnecessary computation and will slow down the process of displaying a circle.

It is usually most convenient to specify a circle by its center point and radius, but you may want to specify a circle by the coordinates of three points on its perimeter (fig. 10-18). Here is a procedure that takes these coordinate values as parameters and invokes our previous circle procedure to generate the required result:

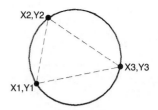

10-18. A circle specified by three points on its perimeter.

```
PROCEDURE  CIRCLE3 (X1,Y1,X2,Y2,X3,Y3,N_SIDES  :  INTEGER);

    VAR  TX2,TY2,TX3,TY3,XC,YC,RADIUS  :  INTEGER;

    BEGIN

      { Transfer points X1,Y1 back to origin and calculate new
        coordinates for points X2,Y2,X3,Y3 }

        TX2  :=  X2  −  X1;
        TY2  :=  Y2  −  Y1;
        TX3  :=  X3  −  X1;
        TY3  :=  Y3  −  Y1;

      { Set XC,YC to be the center of the circle, then
              SQR(0 −XC)  +  SQR(0 −YC)  =  SQR(RADIUS)
              SQR(TX2−XC)  +  SQR(TY2−YC)  =  SQR(RADIUS)
              SQR(TX3−XC)  +  SQR(TY3−YC)  =  SQR(RADIUS) }

        XC  :=  ROUND ((TY3 * (SQR(TX2) + SQR(TY2)) − TY2 *
                (SQR(TX3) + SQR(TY3))) / ((TX2 * TY3 − TX3 *
                TY2) /2));
        YC  :=  ROUND ((TX3 * (SQR(TX2) + SQR(TY2)) − TX2 *
                (SQR(TX3) + SQR(TY3))) / ((TY2 * TX3 − TY3 *
                TX2) / 2));
        RADIUS  :=  ROUND (SQRT (SQR(XC) + SQR(YC)));

      { Transfer center point back relative to X1,Y1 }
        XC  :=  XC  +  X1;
        YC  :=  YC  +  Y1;
        POLYGON (XC,YC,RADIUS,N_SIDES);

    END;
```

Because circles are perfectly symmetrical, we can create only simple relations between instances in compositions: ratios of diameters and relations of center points (fig. 10-19). Certain simple relations of the circle and the straight line are very common in architectural and graphic compositions (fig. 10-20): *diametrical, radial, chord,* and *tangential.* The combination of repeating straight line patterns and repeating circular patterns yields many common motifs, such as the radioconcentric web (fig. 10-21).

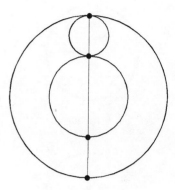

a. Simple ratios of diameters.

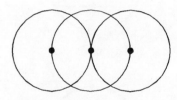

b. Simple relationships of center points.

Arcs

Our circle procedure can be generalized to create an arc. In figure 10-22a an arc is defined by specifying the center point and Radius, together with an angle Theta_1 degrees to specify where it starts and an angle Theta_2 to specify where it ends. To draw this arc, we can modify our circle procedure to go from Theta_1 to Theta_2 in appropriately sized increments, instead of from 0 degrees to 360 degrees, as follows:

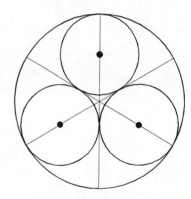

c. A more complex relationship of four circles.

10-19. Relationships of circles in compositions.

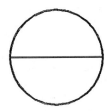

a. Diametrical.

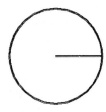

b. Radial.

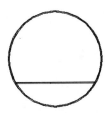

c. Chord.

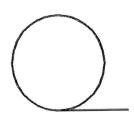

d. Tangential.

10-20. Common simple relationships of the circle and the straight line.

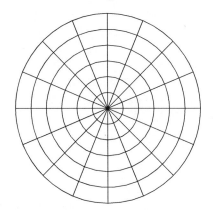

10-21. The radioconcentric web.

```
PROCEDURE ARC (XC,YC,RADIUS,N_SIDES : INTEGER;
                    THETA_1,THETA_2 : REAL);

   VAR X_COORD,Y_COORD,SIDES : INTEGER;
       ANGLE,INCREMENT : REAL;
   CONST RADIANS = 0.01745;

   BEGIN
       { Calculate angle increment }
       INCREMENT := (ABS(THETA_1 − THETA_2)/N_SIDES) *
                         RADIANS;
       ANGLE := THETA_1 * RADIANS;
       X_COORD := XC + ROUND(RADIUS * COS(ANGLE));
       Y_COORD := YC + ROUND(RADIUS * SIN(ANGLE));

       { Move to first point }
       MOVE (X_COORD,Y_COORD);

       { Loop to calculate and draw subsequent points on arc }
       FOR SIDES := 1 TO N_SIDES DO
       BEGIN

           ANGLE := ANGLE + INCREMENT;
           X_COORD := XC + ROUND(RADIUS * COS(ANGLE));
           Y_COORD := YC + ROUND(RADIUS * SIN(ANGLE));
           DRAW (X_COORD,Y_COORD);

       END;

   END;
```

Some examples of output for different values of the parameters Radius, Theta_1, Theta_2, and N_sides are shown in figure 10-22b.

Arcs have convex and concave sides and can vary in their curvature. A straight line segment may be considered a degenerate case of an arc with infinite radius and zero curvature. A common compositional principle, then, is to contrast convexity with concavity and high curvature with low. The Plaza of the Three Powers at Brasilia (fig. 10-23) is a simple relation of horizontal, vertical, concave, and convex, and Aldo van Eyck's Arnheim Pavilion plan (fig. 10-24) breaks parallel straight lines with semicircles, three-quarter circles, and complete circles of varying sizes.

Ellipses

Another generalization of our circle procedure is a procedure that generates an ellipse. This is analogous to the generalization of a square procedure to generate a rectangle. In both cases, we generalize by introducing more parameters.

As figure 10-25 shows, we no longer have a single Radius, but an X_Radius and a Y_radius. Coordinates are now assigned by the expressions:

```
X_COORD := XC + X_RADIUS * COS(ANGLE);
Y_COORD := YC + Y_RADIUS * SIN (ANGLE);
```

So the procedure now becomes:

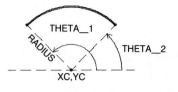

a. Type diagram.

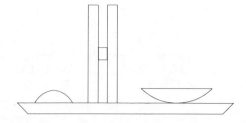

10-23. Plaza of the Three Powers, Brasilia, by Oscar Niemeyer, 1958–60.

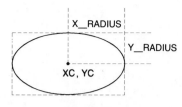

a. Type diagram.

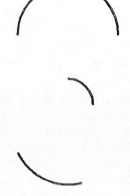

b. Some instances.

10-22. An arc specified by center coordinates, radius, angles, and number of sides.

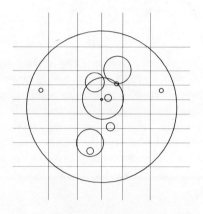

a. Relations of lines and circles.

b. Floor plan.

10-24. Aldo van Eyck, Arnheim Pavilion, 1966.

b. Some instances.

10-25. The ellipse.

```
PROCEDURE  ELLIPSE  (XC,YC,X_RADIUS,Y_RADIUS,N_SIDES  :
                 INTEGER);
      VAR  X_COORD,Y_COORD,SIDES  :  INTEGER;
           ANGLE, INCREMENT  :  REAL;
      CONST  RADIANS  =  0.01745;

      BEGIN

        { Calculate angle increment }
           INCREMENT  :=  (360.0 / N_SIDES) * RADIANS;
           ANGLE  :=  0.0;
           X_COORD  :=  XC + X_RADIUS;
```

```
{ Move to first point }
  MOVE (X,YC);

{ Loop to calculate and draw subsequent points }
  FOR SIDES := 1 TO N_SIDE DO
  BEGIN

    ANGLE := ANGLE + INCREMENT;
    X_COORD := XC + ROUND (X_RADIUS *
                  COS(ANGLE));
    Y_COORD := YC + ROUND (Y_RADIUS *
                  SIN(ANGLE));
    DRAW (X_COORD,Y_COORD);

  END;

END;
```

An ellipse, unlike a circle, has a major axis, two different dimensions, and two foci rather than a single centerpoint, so a richer variety of relations can be constructed in a composition of ellipses than in a composition of circles. Baroque architects realized and made extensive use of elliptical geometry in their plans, where their more classically inclined predecessors would have preferred the simplicity of the circle. Figure 10-26 shows a more recent exploitation of the complexities of the ellipse: Charles Moore's design for the Beverly Hills Civic Center.

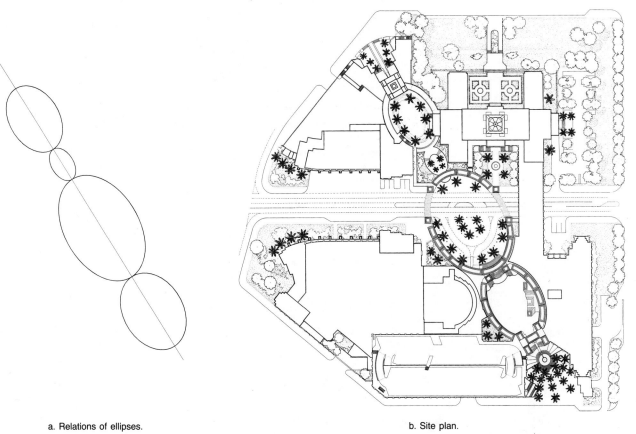

a. Relations of ellipses.

b. Site plan.

10-26. Charles Moore and Urban Innovations Group, Beverly Hills Civic Center, California.

Spirals

Yet another generalization of the circle procedure is a procedure that generates a spiral. In this case, we need to introduce parameters that specify a starting radius, an ending radius, and the number of revolutions. The procedure, then, is a slightly modified version of our arc procedure:

```
PROCEDURE SPIRAL (XC,YC,START_RADIUS,END_RADIUS,N_SIDES
                  : INTEGER; REVOLUTIONS : REAL);

    VAR TOTAL_SEGMENTS,X_COORD,Y_COORD,COUNT : INTEGER;
        DEGREE,ANGLE,RADIUS,RADIUS_INC : REAL;
    CONST RADIANS = 0.01745;

    BEGIN

      { Calculate angle increment }
      DEGREE := (360.0 / N_SIDES) * RADIUS;
      ANGLE := 0.0;

      { Calculate radius increment }
      TOTAL_SEGMENTS := ROUND(REVOLUTIONS *
                        N_SIDES);
      RADIUS_INC := (END_RADIUS - START_RADIUS) /
                    TOTAL_SEGMENTS;
      X_COORD := XC + START_RADIUS;

      { Move to starting point }
      MOVE (X_COORD,YC);

      { Loop to generate spiral }
      RADIUS := START_RADIUS;
      FOR COUNT := 1 TO TOTAL_SEGMENTS DO
      BEGIN

        { Increment radius and angle }
        RADIUS := RADIUS + RADIUS_INC;
        ANGLE := ANGLE + DEGREE;

        { Calculate and draw to next point }
        X_COORD := XC + ROUND (RADIUS * COS
                   (ANGLE));
        Y_COORD := YC + ROUND (RADIUS * SIN
                   (ANGLE));
                   DRAW (X_COORD,Y_COORD);

      END;

    END;
```

Figure 10-27 illustrates some examples of output.

The steps of an alternative way to construct a spiral, using quarter circles of successively greater radii, are shown in figure 10-28. The corresponding procedure runs thus:

```
PROCEDURE SPIRAL (XC,YC,START_RADIUS,REVOLUTIONS,
                  N_SIDES : INTEGER);

    VAR X,Y,SIDEX,SIDEY,SIGN,N_QUARTERS : INTEGER;
        COUNT : INTEGER;
        THETA1,THETA2 : REAL;
```

```
BEGIN
    { Draw first half circle from 0 to 180 degrees
      centered at XC,YC }
    ARC (XC,YC,START_RADIUS,N_SIDES,0,180);

    X  :=  XC;
    Y  :=  YC;
    SIDEX  :=  START_RADIUS;
    SIDEY  :=  START_RADIUS;
    SIGN  :=  1;
    THETA2  :=  180;
    N_QUARTERS  :=  (REVOLUTIONS * 4) DIV 2 − 1;

    FOR COUNT := 1 TO N_QUARTERS DO
    BEGIN
        { Find new center, radius and angles }
        X  :=  X + SIGN*SIDEX;
        SIDEX  :=  SIDEX + SIDEY;
        THETA1  :=  THETA2;
        THETA2  :=  THETA1 + 90;

        { Draw quarter circle }

        ARC (X,Y,SIDEX,N_SIDES,THETA1,THETA2);

        { Find new center, radius and angles }

        Y  :=  Y + SIGN*SIDEY;
        SIDEY  :=  SIDEY + SIDEX;
        THETA1  :=  THETA2;
        THETA2  :=  THETA1 + 90;

        { Draw quarter circle }

        ARC (X,Y,SIDEY,N_SIDES,THETA1,THETA2);

        SIGN  :=  −SIGN;
    END;
END;
```

Notice that the side lengths of successive squares in this construction
form a *Fibonacci sequence*:

1, 1, 2, 3, 5, 8, 13, 21, 34, 55, 89, 144 . . .

Each successive term is the sum of its two predecessors. As this sequence
grows, the ratio of successive terms approaches the golden ratio:

1:1	1.000
2:1	2.000
3:2	1.5000
5:3	1.6667
8:5	1.6000
13:8	1.6250
21:13	1.6154
34:21	1.6190
55:34	1.6176
89:55	1.6182
144:89	1.6180

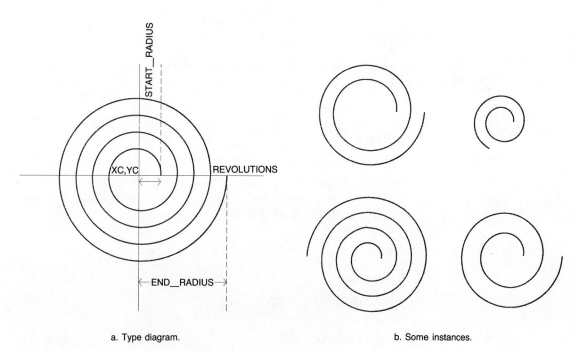

a. Type diagram.

b. Some instances.

10-27. The spiral as a generalization of the arc.

In other words, this spiral fills the golden rectangle.

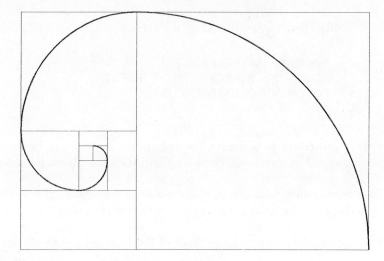

10-28. The construction of a spiral from quarter circles.

Summary

Curves are drawn by loops. Each iteration of a loop that draws a curve generates one straight segment, the beginning point and the end point of which lie on the mathematically defined curve. Coordinate values are returned by functions that are invoked from within the loop. We have seen how polynomial and sine curves can be generated by functions of X or of Y in this way and how circles, arcs, ellipses, and spirals can be generated by functions of Angle.

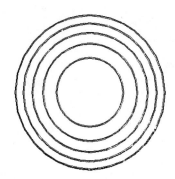

10-29. Fresnel circles; each larger circle encloses twice the area of its predecessor.

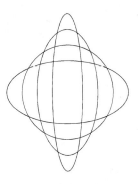

10-30. A composition of concentric ellipses.

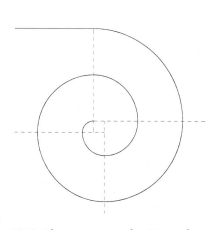

10-31. The construction of an Ionic volute from quarter circles.

Exercises

1. On screen grid paper, make accurate plots of the curves generated by the following code:

a.
```
X := 10;
Y := ROUND (10000 / X);
MOVE (X,Y);

WHILE X < 1023 DO
BEGIN

    X := X + 10;
    Y := ROUND(10000 / X);
    DRAW (X,Y);

END;
```

b.
```
MOVE (0,0);

FOR COUNT := 1 TO 10 DO
BEGIN

    X := 100 * COUNT;
    Y := ROUND(SQRT(X));
    DRAW (X,Y);

END;
```

c.
```
RADIUS := 300;

WHILE RADIUS > 10 DO
BEGIN

    POLYGON (500,500,RADIUS,4);
    RADIUS := ROUND(RADIUS / SQRT(2));
    POLYGON (500,500,RADIUS,8);

END;
```

2. Write a procedure to generate Fresnel circles as shown in figure 10-29. (The area enclosed by each larger circle is twice that enclosed by its predecessor.)

3. Write a procedure to generate compositions of concentric ellipses (fig. 10-30). Let the X_diameter and Y_diameter vary independently.

4. Write a procedure to generate curves of the type defined by the formula:

$$Y = X * SIN(X)$$

5. Generalizing the idea of a circular spiral, write an appropriately parameterized procedure to generate elliptical spirals.

6. The construction of a well-known ancient architectural motif, the Ionic volute, is illustrated in figure 10-31. Write a procedure to generate this curve.

7. Figure 10-32 illustrates the footprint of Alvar Aalto's Baker Dormitory at Massachusetts Institute of Technology. What are the important relations between straight lines and axes in this composition? How might you generate interesting variants on this theme? Write a parameterized procedure to do so.

8. Take the procedures that you have written to generate curves and use them to write simple interactive programs that prompt for and read in parameter values. Then invoke the procedures to generate the corresponding curve instance. Experiment with the effects of inputting different values.

9. Figure 10-33 shows how to construct the shape of an egg from four arcs. Write an appropriately parameterized procedure to draw eggs.

10-32. The footprint of Alvar Aalto's Baker Dormitory at Massachusetts Institute of Technology.

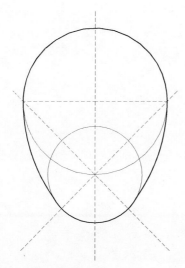

10-33. The construction of an egg from four arcs.

10. The schemata of four paintings by Georges Vantongerloo are shown in figure 10-34. What types of curves are used, and how are they related? Write procedures to generate the curves, and use them in programs to generate variations on Vantongerloo's theme.

10-34. Schemata of four paintings by Georges Vantongerloo from the 1930s.

11. In *The Stones of Venice*, John Ruskin discussed the abstraction of different types of lines from nature (fig. 10-35). How might each of these types be generated? What are the parameters? Investigate ways to write procedures to generate them.

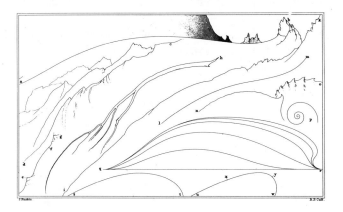

10-35. Some curves sketched by John Ruskin in *The Stones of Venice*.

11.

Conditionals

An artist or designer constantly chooses among sets of alternatives—colors from a palette, line weights provided by a set of pens, or shapes in a graphic vocabulary. Sometimes the designer makes choices such that the sizes, or shapes, or colors of elements in the composition are uniform. A *regular* composition results, and there is a danger that it will become boring. Conversely, the designer's choices may be entirely random or willful. The result, then, is an *irregular* composition, and there is a danger that it will become chaotic. Most interesting compositions, though, are neither uniform nor haphazard. Instead, the shapes, positions, and other attributes of the compositional elements vary *conditionally*, according to context. That is, variation is controlled by conditional *rules*.

Consider the three compositions of circles shown in figure 11-1. In the first, the circles are of uniform diameter and spacing, and it is easy to see that the composition can be generated by the execution of loops as follows:

```
Y := Y_START;
FOR COUNT_Y := 1 TO NY DO
BEGIN

    X := X_START;
    FOR COUNT_X := 1 TO NX DO
    BEGIN

        CIRCLE (X,Y,RADIUS);
        X := X + INCREMENT;

    END;

    Y := Y + INCREMENT;

END;
```

In the second, the circles are of random diameter and spacing, and the coordinates and diameter of each must be explicitly specified:

```
CIRCLE (250,850,175);
CIRCLE (350,680,100);
CIRCLE (600,600,225);
CIRCLE (425,250,175);
```

a. Uniform circles on a regular grid.

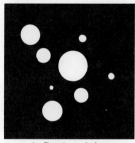
b. Random circles.

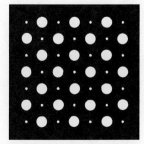
c. Variation according to a simple rule.

11-1. Unity and variety.

273

```
CIRCLE  (675,350,100);
CIRCLE  (400,400,25);
CIRCLE  (900,500,50);
CIRCLE  (700,800,60);
```

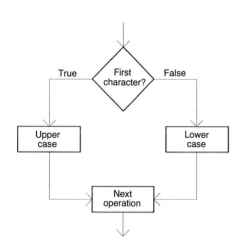

11-2. A flow diagram representing a choice between two branches in a program.

There is variation from circle to circle in the third composition, too, but it is according to rule, rather than random.

How can we write programs to generate compositions with conditional variations? We must be able to identify *conditions* that we want to respond to and specify what *response* to make when a condition is identified. In Pascal, **Boolean** expressions and **Boolean** functions can be evaluated to determine the existence of specific conditions of interest, and **if** and **case** statements (generally known as *conditionals*) can be used to relate conditions to responses. In this chapter, we shall discuss these constructs and explore their applications.

Two Alternatives: If . . . Then . . . Else

The simplest possible kind of design choice is between just two alternatives. Rules for making this kind of choice can conveniently be expressed in the following form:

> IF some condition is true THEN
> > choose the first alternative
> ELSE
> > choose the second

A typographer, for example, might follow this rule:

> IF this is the first character of a sentence THEN
> > uppercase
> ELSE
> > lowercase

We can represent this graphically, as illustrated in figure 11-2, as a choice between two *branches*. The proposition stated between **if** and **then** is either true or false. When it is **true**, the first branch is taken. When it is **false**, the second branch is taken.

Pascal provides the **if** . . . **then** . . . **else** statement for specifying that one of two alternative actions is to be chosen, depending upon the truth value of an expression in this way. It takes the form:

> IF Boolean expression THEN
> > Executable statement 1
> ELSE
> > Executable statement 2;

Here is a simple example:

```
IF  X  <  0  THEN
      WRITELN ('X  IS  NEGATIVE')
ELSE
      WRITELN ('X  IS  POSITIVE');
```

In executing this, the computer first evaluates the **Boolean** expression
X < 0. Depending on the value that has been assigned to the variable X, the
result will either be **true** or **false**. If the result if **true**, the message

```
X  IS  NEGATIVE
```

will be output. If the result is **false**, then the message:

```
X  IS  POSITIVE
```

will be output. The computer then goes on to execute the next statement in
the program in the normal way.

Note that there is no semicolon before the **else**. An **if** . . . **then** . . . **else**
statement always begins with **if** and ends with a semicolon following the second
statement. The delimiters **begin** and **end** are used where necessary like this:

```
IF Boolean expression THEN
      BEGIN
          Executable statement 1;
          Executable statement 2;
          . . .
      END
ELSE
      BEGIN
          Executable statement 3;
          Executable statement 4;
          . . .
      END;
```

It is usual to indent, according to the convention shown, for clarity.

The Evaluation of Boolean Expressions

As we have seen, an expression of type **Boolean** always appears between
if and **then** in an **if** . . . **then** . . . **else** statement. **True** and **false** are the only
two possible values for such expressions. When a **Boolean** expression is evaluated,
one of these values is substituted for the expression in the statement in which
it occurs. We have encountered such expressions before, particularly in our
discussions of **while** and **repeat until** loops, but only in their very simplest
form. It will now be useful, before we go further, to look at them in more
detail.

The simplest **Boolean** expression is a single **Boolean** variable. More complicated **Boolean** expressions consist of a constant, variable, or arithmetic or
Boolean expression on the left-hand side, followed by a *relational operator*
then a constant, variable, or arithmetic or **Boolean** expression on the right-
hand side. **Boolean** expressions are evaluated by comparing the left-hand side

to the right-hand side to see whether the specified relation holds (in which case the value is **true**) or does not (yielding a value **false**).

The relational operators, which are used to compare the left-hand side to right-hand side were introduced along with arithmetic and other operators in chapter 5. To refresh your memory, they are:

=	equal
<>	not equal
<	less than
>	greater than
<=	less or equal
>=	greater or equal

Here are some examples of their use in **Boolean** expressions:

```
X  <=  10
X  >=  Y
A+B  <>  SQR(X)
SIN(X)  <  COS(Y)
TRUNC(X)  =  0
```

The values of the left-hand side and the right-hand side must be of the same type, or the comparison would make no sense. We shall be concerned mostly with comparing **integer** values to **integer** values, but you can also compare **reals** to **reals**, **Booleans** to **Booleans** and **char**acters to **char**acters. You have to be particularly careful, incidentally, when using = and <> to compare **real** values to **real** values, since roundoff errors may generate unexpected results.

Compound **Boolean** expressions can be formed from simple **Boolean** expressions by using the *Boolean operators:*

NOT	negation operator
AND	conjunction operator
OR	disjunction operator

If you know a little elementary logic, you will be familiar with these. If you are not, you should study the following definitions carefully. Where P and Q are **Boolean** variables, the meaning and effects of the **Boolean** operators are defined as follows:

Expression	Value
NOT P	FALSE if P is TRUE TRUE if P is FALSE
P AND Q	TRUE if both P and Q are TRUE FALSE otherwise
P OR Q	FALSE if both P and Q are FALSE TRUE otherwise

Parentheses can, and sometimes must, be used to make compound **Boolean** expressions read unambiguously. Here are some examples of the use of **Boolean** operators to form compound **Boolean** expressions:

```
(X >= 0) AND (X <= 1023)
(Y < 0) OR (Y > 780)
(X < 10) AND (Y=500) AND P
```

Values of **Boolean** expressions can be assigned to **Boolean** variables in the same way that values of **integer** expressions can be assigned to **integer** variables, or values of **real** expressions to **real** variables:

```
ON_SCREEN := ((X >= 0) AND (X <= 1024));
             AND
             ((Y >= 0) AND (Y <= 1024));
```

Boolean Functions

Sometimes a considerable amount of code must be executed in order to determine the existence of some condition. In this case, it is usually clearest and most convenient to express that code as a *Boolean function*.

Consider, for example, the task of determining whether a specified **integer** is *prime*—that is, whether it is exactly divisible only by itself and 1. An obvious (though inefficient) way to do this is to attempt division by every **integer** from 2 to the specified number minus 1. The following **Boolean** function takes an **integer** argument Number, determines in this way whether Number is prime, and returns a value of **true** or **false** accordingly:

```
FUNCTION PRIME (NUMBER : INTEGER) : BOOLEAN;

    VAR DIVISOR : INTEGER;
        FLAG : BOOLEAN;

    BEGIN

    { Flag used to stop loop when a divisor is found }
    FLAG := TRUE;
    DIVISOR := 2;

    WHILE (FLAG = TRUE) AND (DIVISOR < NUMBER) DO
    BEGIN

        IF NUMBER MOD DIVISOR = 0 THEN
            FLAG := FALSE;
        DIVISOR := DIVISOR + 1;

    END;

    PRIME := FLAG;

    END;
```

Incidentally, there are many much cleverer ways to write this function. If you are interested, you should be able to discover some obvious improvements for yourself.

Boolean functions are employed in **if** . . . **then** . . . **else** statements in the obvious way:

```
IF PRIME (NUMBER) THEN
    WRITELN ('NUMBER IS PRIME')
ELSE
    WRITELN ('NUMBER IS NOT PRIME');
```

Pairs of Design Alternatives

Now that we have the means to express rules of choice between two alternatives in Pascal, let us return to the design and graphic issues. The primary use of **if** . . . **then** . . . **else** statements in graphics programs is to specify that either one graphics procedure or another is to be invoked, depending on circumstance, in order to instantiate either one or another graphic type. An architect drawing a floor plan, for example, might have a choice between square and circular columns and might express the rule of choice like this:

```
IF condition THEN
    SQUARE (X,Y,DIAMETER)
ELSE
    CIRCLE (X,Y,DIAMETER);
```

An artist or designer may take a great many things into consideration when choosing vocabulary elements to instantiate in a composition, but Pascal is much more limited. The universe that it can consider consists *only* of the variables that have been declared in the program and the values that have been assigned to them. Rules of choice must always be formulated in terms of these variables and must take the form of **Boolean** expressions constructed using the relational and **Boolean** operators. This seems and is very restrictive, but some surprisingly powerful and useful design rules can be expressed in this way.

In a graphics program (as we have seen in the examples considered so far) we will typically have variables describing the shapes, positions, and numbers of instances of various types of graphic elements in a composition. These variables, then, can be used in decision rules. It is often necessary, as well, to introduce additional variables specifically for the purpose of storing values that we want to use in decision rules, plus functions to assign values to these variables. Remember, Pascal cannot inspect a partially completed drawing in the way that you can when you are making a graphic decision; it can inspect only the values currently assigned to declared variables, evaluate functions of these, and compare values.

Odd or Even: Parity Conditions

Consider the row of columns shown in figure 11-3. Beginning at the left, the odd columns are square and the even columns circular. This composition can be generated by a loop that instantiates the required number of columns and chooses either a square or circular one at each iteration, depending on whether the count is odd or even. Pascal provides a built-in **Boolean** function **odd**(X), which takes an integer argument X and returns a value **true** when X is odd and **false** when X is even. Using this function, a procedure to generate the row of alternating square and circular columns can be written as follows:

11-3. A row of alternating square and circular columns.

```
PROCEDURE ROW (INITIAL_X,Y,DIAMETER,SPACING,
               N_COLUMNS : INTEGER);

   VAR X,COUNT : INTEGER;
   BEGIN
       X := INITIAL_X;
       FOR COUNT := 1 TO N_COLUMNS DO
       BEGIN
           IF ODD (COUNT) THEN
               SQUARE (X,Y,DIAMETER)
           ELSE
               CIRCLE (X,Y,DIAMETER);
           X := X + SPACING;

       END;
   END;
```

The zigzag illustrated in figure 11-4 can be generated in a very similar way. Here the decision rule is:

```
IF ODD(COUNT) THEN
    ZIG (COUNT*INCREMENT)
ELSE
    ZAG (COUNT*INCREMENT);
```

11-4. A zigzag.

Figure 11-5 shows the elevation of a Renaissance palace. You will notice that the window types alternate. (This was a very common device for enlivening the rhythms of what could otherwise be fairly static compositions.) The general form of the decision rule for such rows of windows is:

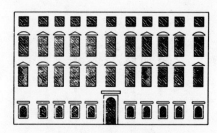

11-5. Schematic elevation of a renaissance palace with alternating window types.

```
IF ODD(COUNT) THEN
    WINDOW_1
ELSE
    WINDOW_2;
```

Exterior or Interior: End Conditions

Figure 11-6 illustrates another row of circular and square columns. Here square columns are at the ends, and circular columns are everywhere else. The decision rule needed to generate this type of composition can be expressed:

11-6. A row of circular columns terminated by square columns.

```
IF  END_CONDITION(COUNT,FIRST,LAST)  THEN
    SQUARE(X,Y,DIAMETER)
ELSE
    CIRCLE(X,Y,DIAMETER);
```

Count is the control variable of a **for** loop from First to Last, and
End_condition is the following **Boolean** function:

```
FUNCTION  END_CONDITION(COUNT,FIRST,LAST  :  INTEGER)  :  BOOLEAN;
    BEGIN
        END_CONDITION  :=  (COUNT=FIRST)  OR  (COUNT=LAST);
    END;
```

The procedure to generate the complete composition is:

```
PROCEDURE  ROW  (INITIAL_X,Y,DIAMETER,SPACING,N_COLUMNS
                    :  INTEGER);

    VAR  X,COUNT  :  INTEGER;

    BEGIN

        X  :=  INITIAL_X;

        FOR  COUNT  :=  1  TO  N_COLUMNS  DO
        BEGIN

            IF  END_CONDITION(COUNT,1,N_COLUMNS)  THEN
                SQUARE  (X,Y,DIAMETER)
            ELSE
                CIRCLE  (X,Y,DIAMETER);

            X  :=  X  +  SPACING;

        END;
    END;
```

Center or Side: Middle Conditions

Yet another type of row of square and round columns is shown in figure
11-7a. There is an odd number of columns, and the center column is round;
those on either side are square. The decision rule needed here is:

```
IF  CENTER_POINT(COUNT,FIRST,LAST)  THEN
    CIRCLE(X,Y,DIAMETER)
ELSE
    SQUARE(X,Y,DIAMETER);
```

The Boolean function Center_point is as follows:

```
FUNCTION  CENTER_POINT(COUNT,FIRST,LAST  :  INTEGER)  :  BOOLEAN;
    VAR  MIDDLE  :  INTEGER;
    BEGIN
        MIDDLE  :=  (LAST  +  FIRST)  DIV  2;
        CENTER_POINT  :=  (COUNT  =  MIDDLE);
    END;
```

Note that this function will work correctly only if the total number of columns
in the row is odd. If the total is even, there is no center point.

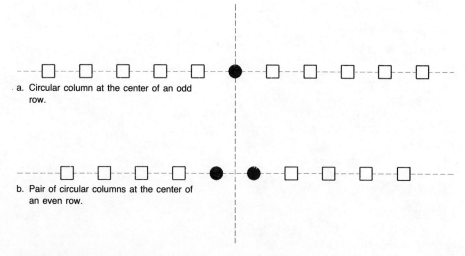

a. Circular column at the center of an odd row.

b. Pair of circular columns at the center of an even row.

11-7. The treatment of middle conditions.

The case of an even number of columns is illustrated in figure 11-7b. Here the rule is to make the middle *pair* of columns circular instead of square. The decision rule is:

```
IF  MIDDLE_PAIR(COUNT,FIRST,LAST)  THEN
     CIRCLE(X,Y,DIAMETER)
ELSE
     SQUARE(X,Y,DIAMETER);
```

The necessary **Boolean** function Middle_pair can be written:

```
FUNCTION MIDDLE_PAIR(COUNT,FIRST,LAST : INTEGER) : BOOLEAN;
     VAR LEFT,RIGHT : INTEGER;
     BEGIN
         LEFT := (LAST + FIRST) DIV 2;
         RIGHT := LEFT + 1;
         MIDDLE_PAIR := (COUNT = LEFT) OR (COUNT = RIGHT);
     END;
```

If we want a general procedure that will work for either an odd or an even number of columns, we can use a decision rule like this,

```
IF ODD(N_COLUMNS) THEN
     ODDROW  (X,Y,SPACING,DIAMETER,N_COLUMNS)
ELSE
     EVENROW  (X,Y,SPACING,DIAMETER,N_COLUMNS);
```

where Oddrow and Evenrow are procedures that draw odd and even rows of columns respectively.

The following is an interactive program that prompts for and accepts input specifying the starting coordinates of the row, the column spacing, the diameter, and the number of columns, then chooses whether to invoke Oddrow or Evenrow:

```
PROGRAM ROW_COLUMNS;

    USES GRAPHICS;

    FUNCTION CENTER_POINT (COUNT,FIRST,LAST : INTEGER)
                              : BOOLEAN;
        VAR MIDDLE : INTEGER;

        BEGIN
            MIDDLE := (LAST + FIRST) DIV 2;
            CENTER_POINT := COUNT = MIDDLE;
        END;
    FUNCTION MIDDLE_PAIR (COUNT,FIRST,LAST : INTEGER)
                              : BOOLEAN;
        VAR LEFT,RIGHT : INTEGER;

        BEGIN
            LEFT := (LAST + FIRST) DIV 2;
            RIGHT := LEFT + 1;
            MIDDLE_PAIR := (COUNT = LEFT) OR
                           (COUNT = RIGHT);
        END;
    PROCEDURE ODDROW (INITIAL_X,Y,DIAMETER,SPACING,
                      N_COLUMNS : INTEGER);

        VAR X,COUNT : INTEGER;

        BEGIN

            X := INITIAL_X;

            FOR COUNT := 1 TO N_COLUMNS DO
            BEGIN

                IF CENTER_POINT(COUNT,1,N_COLUMNS) THEN
                    CIRCLE (X,Y,DIAMETER)
                ELSE
                    SQUARE (X,Y,DIAMETER);

                X := X + SPACING;

            END;
        END;
    PROCEDURE EVENROW (INITIAL_X,Y,DIAMETER,SPACING,
                       N_COLUMNS : INTEGER);

        VAR X,COUNT : INTEGER;

        BEGIN

            X := INITIAL_X;

            FOR COUNT := 1 TO N_COLUMNS DO
            BEGIN

                IF MIDDLE-PAIR(COUNT,1,N_COLUMNS) THEN
                    CIRCLE (X,Y,DIAMETER)
                ELSE
                    SQUARE (X,Y,DIAMETER);

                X := X + SPACING;

            END;
    END;
```

```
{ Main Program }
   VAR X,Y,SPACING,DIAMETER,N_COLUMNS : INTEGER;

   BEGIN

        WRITELN ('ENTER X COORDINATE:');
        READLN (X);
        WRITELN ('ENTER Y COORDINATE:');
        READLN (Y);
        WRITELN ('ENTER COLUMN SPACING:');
        READLN (SPACING);
        WRITELN ('ENTER COLUMN DIAMETER:');
        READLN (DIAMETER);
        WRITELN ('ENTER NUMBER OF COLUMNS:');
        READLN (N_COLUMNS);

        START_DRAWING;

           IF ODD(N_COLUMNS) THEN
                ODDROW (X,Y,DIAMETER,SPACING,N_COLUMNS)
           ELSE
                EVENROW (X,Y,DIAMETER,SPACING,N_COLUMNS);

        FINISH_DRAWING;

    END.
```

Arbitrary Exceptions

Sometimes a designer wants to make an arbitrarily chosen element in a repetitive composition different from all the others. For example, an architect might want to make the nth column in a colonnade round instead of square. The following procedure takes N as one of its parameters and produces the required result:

```
    PROCEDURE ARBITRARY_ROW (INITIAL_X,Y,DIAMETER,SPACING,
                                N_COLUMNS,N : INTEGER);

    VAR X,COUNT : INTEGER;

    BEGIN

        X := INITIAL_X;

        FOR COUNT := 1 TO N_COLUMNS DO
        BEGIN

            IF COUNT = N THEN
                CIRCLE (X,Y,DIAMETER)
            ELSE
                SQUARE (X,Y,DIAMETER);

            X := X + SPACING;

        END;

    END;
```

Some examples of output are shown in figure 11-8.

Selecting Size and Spacing

An architect might want to vary not only the type of column according

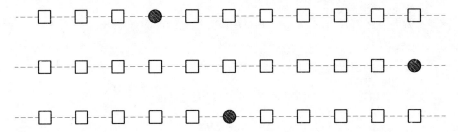

11-8. Rows with circular columns at arbitrarily chosen locations.

to rules based on the value of the **for**-loop control variable, but also the diameter and spacing. For example, odd and even columns might be of different diameters, end columns might be smaller, or middle columns might be larger (fig. 11-9a). Spacing might be handled in similar ways (fig. 11-9b).

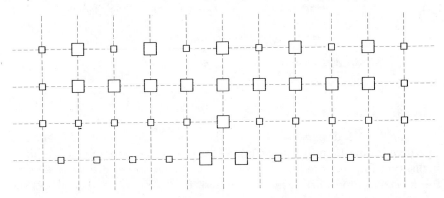

a. Size varied by parity, end, and center conditions.

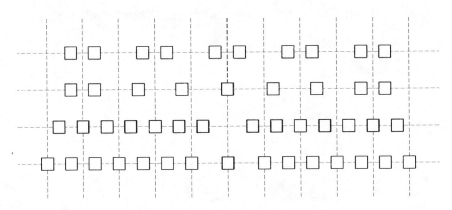

b. Spacing varied by parity, end, and center conditions.

11-9. Further variations by condition.

All this can be handled, straightforwardly, within the framework of **if** . . . **then** . . . **else** statements. Here, for example, is a rule to vary the type, size, and spacing of odd and even columns (fig. 11-10):

```
IF  ODD(COUNT)  THEN
    BEGIN
        CIRCLE  (X,Y,ODD_DIAMETER);
        X := X  +  ODD_SPACING;
```

```
        END
    ELSE
        BEGIN
            SQUARE   (X,Y,EVEN_DIAMETER);
            X  :=  X  +  EVEN_SPACING;
        END;
```

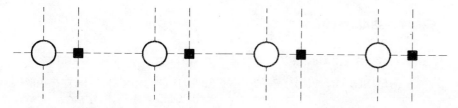

11-10. Type, size, and spacing vary by parity.

Choosing No Action: If . . . Then

Sometimes a designer must choose between the alternatives of doing
something and doing nothing. If walls are close together, for example, beams
can economically span a space with nothing in between to support them (fig.
11-11a). But if walls are further apart, intermediate columns must be introduced
(fig. 11-11b). The rule that applies here can be expressed:

```
IF  SPAN  <=  LIMIT  THEN
    { Do  nothing }
ELSE
        ROW  (X,Y,DIAMETER,SPACING,NCOLUMNS);
```

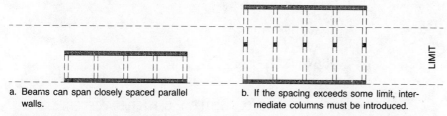

a. Beams can span closely spaced parallel
   walls.

b. If the spacing exceeds some limit, intermediate columns must be introduced.

11-11. The genesis of the hypostyle hall, as explained in Auguste Choisy's
Histoire de l'Architecture, 1899.

Span specifies the width of the space, and the value of Limit specifies when
the span is sufficiently great to require columns.

This is an unnecessarily clumsy way of expressing the rule, though. When
the decision to be made is whether to execute an action or not, Pascal allows
contracted **if** statements of the form:

```
    IF  Boolean expression  THEN
            Statement;
```

So our rule could be rewritten more clearly and cogently as:

```
    IF  SPAN  >  LIMIT  THEN
```

To illustrate the use of this rule, the following interactive program prompts for and reads in the length and span of a space, and the number of equally spaced beams that are to span between the walls. If the span is greater than the distance between beams, it introduces columns. There are also proportioning rules; walls and interior columns are one-fifth as wide as the distance between beams, and end columns are one-tenth as wide (since they support only half as much roof area as interior columns).

```
PROGRAM SUPPORT;
  { Program to draw roof support }

    USES GRAPHICS;

    FUNCTION END_CONDITION (COUNT,FIRST,LAST : INTEGER)
                                    : BOOLEAN;
      BEGIN
          END_CONDITION := (COUNT=FIRST) OR
                           (COUNT=LAST);
      END;

    PROCEDURE WALL (X,Y,LENGTH,WIDTH : INTEGER);

      { Procedure to draw a rectangular wall }

      VAR X1,Y1 : INTEGER;

      BEGIN

          { Calculate coordinates }
          X1 := X + LENGTH;
          Y1 := Y + WIDTH;

          { Move to the bottom left corner }
          MOVE (X,Y);

          { Draw the four sides }
          DRAW (X1,Y);
          DRAW (X1,Y1);
          DRAW (X,Y1);
          DRAW (X,Y);

      END;

    PROCEDURE SQUARE (X_CENTER,Y_CENTER,DIAMETER :
                      INTEGER);

      VAR X1,Y1,X2,Y2 : INTEGER;

      BEGIN

          { Calculate corners of square column }

          X1 := X_CENTER − DIAMETER DIV 2;
          Y1 := Y_CENTER − DIAMETER DIV 2;
          X2 := X1 + DIAMETER;
          Y2 := Y1 + DIAMETER;

          { Move to bottom left corner }
          MOVE (X1,Y1);

          { Draw sides of column }
          DRAW (X2,Y1);
          DRAW (X2,Y2);
          DRAW (X1,Y2);
```

```
            DRAW  (X1,Y1);
    END;
    PROCEDURE  ROW  (INITIAL_X,Y,DIAMETER,SPACING,N_COLUMNS
                     : INTEGER);
      { Draw a row of columns }
        VAR  X,COUNT,HALF_DIAMETER :  INTEGER;
        BEGIN
            X := INITIAL_X;
            HALF_DIAMETER := DIAMETER DIV 2;
            FOR COUNT := 1 TO N_COLUMNS DO
            BEGIN

              { End columns are drawn with half the diameter of
                interior columns }

              IF END_CONDITION(COUNT,1,N_COLUMNS) THEN
                  SQUARE  (X,Y,HALF_DIAMETER)
              ELSE
                  SQUARE  (X,Y,DIAMETER);

              X := X + SPACING;
            END;
        END;

{ Main program }
    VAR  LENGTH,SPAN,N_BEAMS,LIMIT,SPACING,DIAMETER,X,Y,Y1 :
        INTEGER;

    BEGIN
        WRITELN ('ENTER LENGTH OF SPACE:');
        READLN (LENGTH);
        WRITELN ('ENTER WIDTH OF SPACE:');
        READLN (SPAN);
        WRITELN ('ENTER NUMBER OF BEAMS:');
        READLN (N_BEAMS);

        SPACING := LENGTH DIV (N_BEAMS – 1);
        DIAMETER := ROUND(0.2 * SPACING);

        X := 100;
        Y := 100;
        Y1 := Y + SPAN + DIAMETER;

        START_DRAWING;

          { Draw outer walls }
          WALL (X,Y,LENGTH,DIAMETER);
          WALL (X,Y1,LENGTH,DIAMETER);

          { Draw row of columns if needed }
          IF SPAN > SPACING THEN
              BEGIN

                  Y := Y + SPAN DIV 2 + DIAMETER;
                  ROW (X,Y,DIAMETER,SPACING,N_BEAMS);

              END;
        FINISH_DRAWING;
    END.
```

Figure 11-12 shows some examples of output from this program.

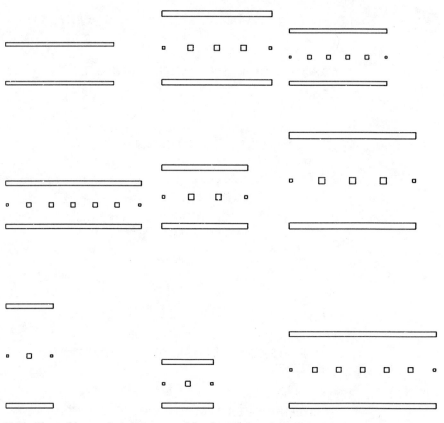

11-12. Plans of hypostyle halls generated by the program Support.

This program assumes that one central row of columns will suffice. A more general program might first determine how many rows were needed, then insert the required number. The following function takes Span and Limit as parameters and returns the required number of rows:

```
FUNCTION N_ROWS (SPAN,LIMIT : INTEGER) : INTEGER;
    BEGIN
        N_ROWS := (SPAN−1) DIV LIMIT;
    END;
```

Assuming equal spans, this next procedure now draws the required number of rows (fig. 11-13).

```
PROCEDURE ROWS(INITIAL_X,INITIAL_Y,SPAN,LIMIT,DIAMETER,
                SPACING,N_COLUMNS : INTEGER);

    VAR N,Y,Y_INCREMENT,COUNT : INTEGER;

    BEGIN

        N := N_ROWS(SPAN,LIMIT);
        Y_INCREMENT := SPAN DIV (N+1);
        Y := INITIAL_Y + DIAMETER,
```

11-13. Hypostyle hall with multiple rows of columns.

```
FOR COUNT := 1 TO N DO
BEGIN

    Y := Y + Y_INCREMENT;
    ROW (INITIAL_X,Y,DIAMETER,SPACING,N_COLUMNS);

END;

END;
```

We have now produced a program to generate a well-known plan type (found, for example, in ancient Egyptian architecture) known as the *hypostyle hall*. Figure 11-14a illustrates some instances of another familiar and very similar plan type, that of the *classical temple*. Here we have a column grid surrounding a *cella*, rather than parallel walls surrounding a column grid. Columns in an interior rectangle are left out to provide room for the cella.

The limits of the cella can be specified by values for X_start, X_finish, Y_start, Y_finish (fig. 11-14b). The following function is **true** for a grid point outside the cella and **false** for a grid point within it:

```
FUNCTION OUTSIDE (COUNT_X,COUNT_Y,X_START,X_FINISH,
                  Y_START,Y_FINISH : INTEGER) : BOOLEAN;
    BEGIN
        OUTSIDE := ((COUNT_X < X_START) OR
                    (COUNT_X > X_FINISH) OR
                    (COUNT_Y < Y_START) OR
                    (COUNT_Y > Y_FINISH));
    END;
```

The column grid can be drawn by a pair of nested loops (see chapter 9), and space for the cella can be left out of the center of the grid by application of the rule:

```
IF OUTSIDE (COUNT_X,COUNT_Y,X_START,X_FINISH,Y_START,
            Y_FINISH)

    THEN COLUMN (X,Y,DIAMETER);
```

Here is a complete procedure to draw column grids with appropriate space left for the cella (fig. 11-15).

```
PROCEDURE GRID (INITIAL_X,INITIAL_Y,DIAMETER,SPACING,NX,NY,
                X_START,X_FINISH,Y_START,Y_FINISH
                : INTEGER);

    VAR X,Y,COUNT_X,COUNT_Y : INTEGER;

    BEGIN

        Y := INITIAL_Y;

    { Loop to place grid rows }
        FOR COUNT_Y := 1 TO NY DO
        BEGIN

            X := INITIAL_X;

    { Loop to place grid columns }
            FOR COUNT_X := 1 TO NX DO
            BEGIN
```

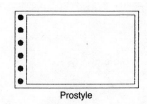

a. Type diagram for the column grid.

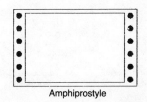

Prostyle

Amphiprostyle

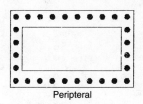

Peripteral

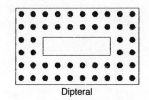

Dipteral

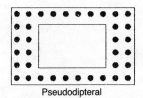

Pseudodipteral

b. Some traditional subtypes.

11-14. The classical temple plan.

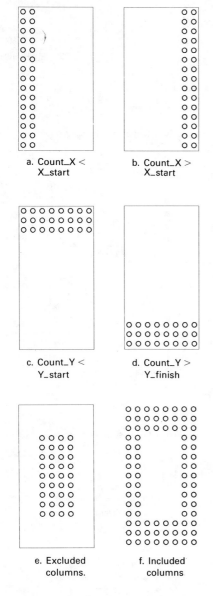

a. Count_X <
   X_start

b. Count_X >
   X_start

c. Count_Y <
   Y_start

d. Count_Y >
   Y_finish

e. Excluded
   columns.

f. Included
   columns

11-15. Column grid of the Temple of Apollo at Didyma, drawn by the procedure Grid.

```
{ Only place column if outside cella boundaries }
      IF OUTSIDE (COUNT_X,COUNT_Y,X_START,
                  X_FINISH,Y_START,Y_FINISH)
        THEN COLUMN (X,Y,DIAMETER);
      X := X + SPACING;
    END;
    Y := Y + SPACING;
  END;
END;
```

The nested loops enumerate column positions. The subset of positions at which columns are actually drawn is the union of the four subsets specified by the four conditions:

```
COUNT_X < X_START
COUNT_X > X_FINISH
COUNT_Y < Y_START
COUNT_Y > Y_FINISH
```

This is illustrated in figure 11-15.

Conditional Choices among Many Design Alternatives

There are often more than two design alternatives to choose from. **Else if** chains and the case statement are two ways to express rules for choosing from many alternatives.

Else If Chains

The following type of statement chooses one alternative from n possibilities:

```
IF Boolean expression 1 THEN
   Statement 1
ELSE IF Boolean expression 2 THEN
   Statement 2
ELSE IF Boolean expression 3 THEN
   Statement 3
   . . .
ELSE
   Statement n;
```

The computer evaluates each Boolean expression in order. **If** it finds a value of **true**, it executes the associated statement, then jumps to the statement following the **else if** chain.

When none of the Boolean expressions turns out to have a value of **true** the statement following the last **else** is executed. This last statement, then, specifies what happens in a none-of-the-above situation. The following code illustrates this:

```
IF COUNT = 1 THEN
    WRITELN ('ONE')
ELSE IF COUNT = 2 THEN
    WRITELN ('TWO')
ELSE IF COUNT = 3 THEN
    WRITELN ('THREE')
ELSE
    WRITELN ('NOT ONE OR TWO OR THREE');
```

The structure of this code is illustrated in figure 11-16.

If you want to do nothing when none of the Boolean expressions turns out to be **true**, you can simply omit the last **else** and the associated statement:

```
IF COUNT = 1 THEN
    WRITELN ('ONE')
ELSE IF COUNT = 2 THEN
    WRITELN ('TWO')
ELSE IF COUNT = 3 THEN
    WRITELN ('THREE');
```

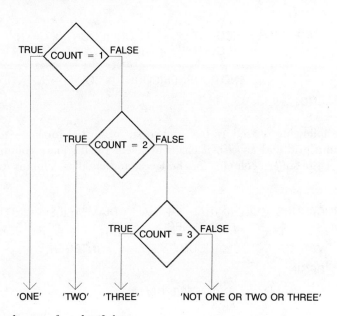

11-16. A flow diagram of an **else if** chain.

Conditions in a Column Grid

To illustrate the use of **else if** chains in graphics programs, let us consider the column grid shown in figure 11-17. One architect might make all the columns the same (fig. 11-17a). Another architect after more subtle effects might recognize that columns on the face support only half as much load as columns in the interior, and that columns at the corners support only a quarter as much. There are other architectural differences, too. Operating on the principle that form follows function, then, the second architect might respond to each of these conditions in a different way (fig. 11-17b). How can we write Pascal code to express the rules that are followed here?

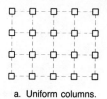

a. Uniform columns.

b. Corner, face, and interior columns take different forms.

11-17. The inflection of a column grid.

First, we need **Boolean** functions to identify the conditions that concern us. Here, then, is a function Corner:

```
FUNCTION  CORNER  (COUNT_X,COUNT_Y,NX,NY  :  INTEGER)
                    :  BOOLEAN;
     BEGIN
        CORNER  := ((COUNT_X  =  1)  AND  (COUNT_Y  =  1))
                                 OR
               ((COUNT_X  =  1)  AND  (COUNT_Y  =  NY))
                                 OR
               ((COUNT_X  =  NX)  AND  (COUNT_Y  =  1))
                                 OR
               ((COUNT_X  =  NX)  AND  (COUNT_Y  =  NY));
     END;
```

And here is a function Face:

```
FUNCTION  FACE  (COUNT_X,COUNT_Y,NX,NY  :  INTEGER)
                 :  BOOLEAN;

     BEGIN
        FACE  := ((COUNT_X  =  1)  OR  (COUNT_X  =  NX)  OR
                (COUNT_Y  =  1)  OR  (COUNT_Y  =  NY))
                            AND
               NOT(CORNER(COUNT_X,COUNT_Y,NX,NY));
     END;
```

The following procedure executes a pair of nested **for**-loops to generate the column grid and an **else if** chain to select small square columns for the corners, large square columns for the faces, and circular columns everywhere else:

```
PROCEDURE  GRID  (INITIAL_X,INITIAL_Y,DIAMETER,SPACING,NX,NY
                  :  INTEGER);

       VAR  X,Y,COUNT_X,COUNT_Y,DIAM4  :  INTEGER;

     BEGIN
        DIAM4  :=  DIAMETER  DIV  4;
        Y  :=  INITIAL_Y;

       { Loop to place rows of grid }
        FOR  COUNT_Y  :=  1  TO  NY  DO
        BEGIN

           X  :=  INITIAL_X;

          { Loop to place columns of grid }
           FOR  COUNT_X  :=  1  TO  NX  DO
           BEGIN

              IF  CORNER(COUNT_X,COUNT_Y,NX,NY)  THEN
                 SQUARE  (X,Y,DIAM4)
              ELSE IF  FACE(COUNT_X,COUNT_Y,NX,NY)  THEN
                 SQUARE  (X,Y,DIAMETER)
              ELSE
                 CIRCLE  (X,Y,DIAMETER);
```

```
            X  :=  X  +  SPACING;
        END;
            Y  :=  Y  +  SPACING;
    END;
END;
```

Some of the results generated by this procedure for different-sized grids are shown in figure 11-18.

This procedure is easily altered to associate different responses with the same conditions. The following **else if** chain, for example, places cross-shaped columns at the corners, circular columns along the faces, and square columns in the interior (fig. 11-19):

```
IF  CORNER(COUNT_X,COUNT_Y,NX,NY)  THEN
    CROSS  (X,Y,DIAMETER)
ELSE  IF  FACE(COUNT_X,COUNT_Y,NX,NY)  THEN
    CIRCLE  (X,Y,DIAM4)
ELSE
    SQUARE  (X,Y,DIAMETER);
```

We might be interested in responding to different conditions. The following procedure, for example, uses the built-in **Boolean** function **odd** to generate a checkerboard pattern of square and circular columns (fig. 11-20):

```
PROCEDURE  GRID  (INITIAL_X,INITIAL_Y,DIAMETER,SPACING,NX,NY
                    :  INTEGER);
    VAR  X,Y,COUNT_X,COUNT_Y  :  INTEGER;
    BEGIN
    Y  :=  INITIAL_Y;
    { Loop to place rows of grid }
    FOR  COUNT_Y  :  =  1  TO  NY  DO
    BEGIN
        X  :=  INITIAL_X;
        { Loop to place columns of grid }
        FOR  COUNT_X  :=  1  TO  NX  DO
        BEGIN
            IF  (ODD(COUNT_X)  AND  ODD(COUNT_Y))  OR
                (NOT(ODD(COUNT_X))  AND
                NOT  (ODD(COUNT_Y)))
            THEN
                SQUARE  (X,Y,DIAMETER)
            ELSE
                CIRCLE  (X,Y,DIAMETER);
            X  :=  X  +  SPACING;
        END;
            Y  :=  Y  +  SPACING;
    END;
END;
```

11-18. Column grids of various sizes with different corner, face, and interior columns.

11-19. Different responses associated with the same conditions in the grid.

11-20. A checkerboard pattern of square and circular columns.

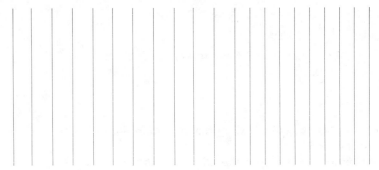

a. Two simple, regular rhythms.

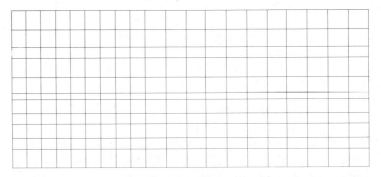

b. The grid becomes more complex.

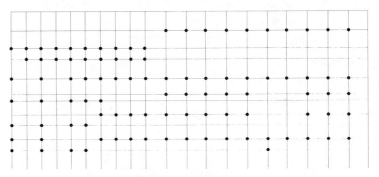

c. Columns occupy some, but not all, of the grid locations.

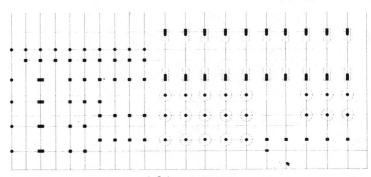

d. Column types vary.

11-21. Entrance-level plan of the editorial offices of the Turum Sanomat newspaper, Turku, Finland by Alvar Aalto, 1927/29.

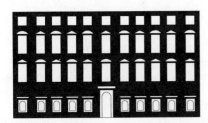

a. The complete composition.

b. Regular fenestration.

c. Bays on either side of the central axis widened.

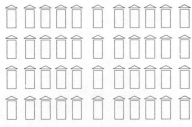

d. End bays widened.

e. Topmost story has square openings.

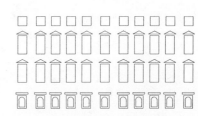

f. Ground floor has a special window type.

11-22. The compositional principles of a Renaissance palace facade.

Sophisticated designers sometimes use much more complex rules to inflect column grids than the elementary ones we have explored here. Consider, for example, Alvar Aalto's plan for the editorial offices of the Turum Sanomat in Turku (fig. 11-21). It begins as a regular grid, then some rows are eliminated and others are offset. Finally, circular, square, rectangular, and bullet-shaped columns are introduced according to relations with walls and stairs and use of the adjacent floor area.

Another Example: Conditions in an Elevation

Let us consider once again the organization of openings in a Renaissance palace facade (fig. 11-22a). The starting point is a regular grid (fig. 11-22b). However, the bays on either side of the central axis are wider than normal (fig. 11-22c) as are the end bays (fig. 11-22d). The topmost story, unlike all the others, has square openings (fig. 11-22e). The ground floor also has a special window type (fig. 11-22f). There is a door opening, instead of a window, at the center of the ground floor (fig. 11-22g). Alternate intermediate stories begin with triangular and round-pedimented windows (fig. 11-22h). Finally, at each intermediate level, triangular and round-pedimented windows alternate.

Let us assume that there will always be an odd number of openings horizontally. To draw such facades, we need **Boolean** functions to identify End, Center, and Odd openings along a story. We also need functions to identify Ground, Top, and Odd stories. To respond to these conditions by generating appropriate types of openings, we need procedures for Triangular_window, Round_window, Square_window, Ground_window, and Door. Finally, we must define values for the different widths—End_bay, Center_bay, and Normal_bay, and the different heights—Ground_floor, Top_floor, and Normal_floor.

g. Door opens at center.

h. Round and triangular pediments alternate in a checkerboard pattern.

```
        Y  :=  Y_INITIAL;
{ Loop  to  place  stories  of  building }
  FOR  FLOOR  := 1  TO  N_OF_FLOORS  DO
  BEGIN

        X  :=  X_INITIAL;

    { Loop  to  place  bays  across  a  story }
      FOR  BAY  := 1  TO  N_OF_BAYS +1 DO
      BEGIN

        { Ground  story }
          IF  GROUND(FLOOR)  THEN
            IF  CENTER(BAY,N_OF_BAYS + 1 ) THEN
              DOOR

          ELSE
              GROUND_WINDOW

        { Top  story }
          ELSE  IF  TOP(FLOOR,N_OF_FLOORS)  THEN
              SQUARE_WINDOW

        { Intermediate  stories }
          ELSE  IF  ODD(FLOOR + BAY)  THEN
              TRIANGULAR_WINDOW

          ELSE
              ROUND_WINDOW;

        { Vary  horizontal  spacing  depending  on  end  or  center
          bay }
          IF  END_CONDITION(BAY,N_OF_BAYS)  THEN
              X  :=  X  +  END_BAY
          ELSE  IF  CENTER  (BAY,N_OF_BAYS)  THEN
              X  :=  X  +  CENTER_BAY
          ELSE
              X  :=  X  +  NORMAL_BAY;
      END;

    { Vary  vertical  spacing  depending  on  ground  or  top  floor }
      IF  GROUND(FLOOR)  THEN
          Y  :=  Y  +  GROUND_FLOOR
      ELSE  IF  TOP(FLOOR,N_OF_FLOORS)  THEN
          Y  :=  Y  +  TOP_FLOOR
      ELSE
          Y  :=  Y  +  NORMAL_FLOOR;
  END;
```

This code could be elaborated, of course, by introducing additional parameters controlling dimensions and the spacing of elements. Proportioning rules, such as those typically followed by Renaissance architects, could be introduced by writing expressions or functions interrelating the values of these variables. Figure 11-23 shows some designs produced in this way. The extreme versions are particularly interesting; they show how a Renaissance palace may become a modest house, a factory, or a high-rise office building.

The Case Statement

In addition to **else if** chains, Pascal provides another way to choose among many alternatives:

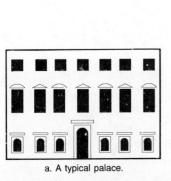
a. A typical palace.

b. A modest house.

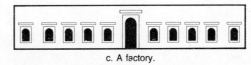
c. A factory.

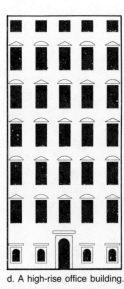
d. A high-rise office building.

11-23. Renaissance palaces with different numbers of bays, stories, and different proportions.

```
CASE COUNT OF
    1 : WRITELN ('ONE');
    2 : WRITELN ('TWO');
    3 : WRITELN ('THREE');
END;
```

This is called a **case** statement. To execute it, the computer first evaluates Count, then selects and executes the statement whose *label* (the integer to the left of the colon) is equal to the value of Count. Control then goes to the end of the **case** statement.

In our example, Count is the *selector* of the **case**. In general, the selector can be any variable or expression of type **integer**, **Boolean**, or **character**. It cannot, however, be of type **real**. Following **case . . . of** in a **case** statement, is a list of *labeled statements*. In each of these the label appears first, followed by a colon, then a statement terminated by a semicolon. The statement labels must be of the same type as the selector. Finally, a **case** statement is terminated by **end.**

Case statements should be used when choosing between mutually exclusive possibilities. There are a couple of important rules to observe in their use. First, Pascal considers it an error when the selector yields a value that is not equal to one of the statement labels, so you must make sure that this can never happen. Second, a given label can appear only once in a **case** statement. A labeled statement, however, can have more than one label:

```
CASE COUNT OF
    1,2 : WRITELN ('ONE OR TWO');
      3 : WRITELN ('THREE');
END;
```

In other words, a **case** statement can specify either a one-to-one or a many-to-one relationship of conditions to actions (fig. 11-24).

a. A one-to-one relationship.

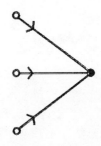
b. A many-to-one relationship.

11-24. The relation of conditions to actions by **case** statements.

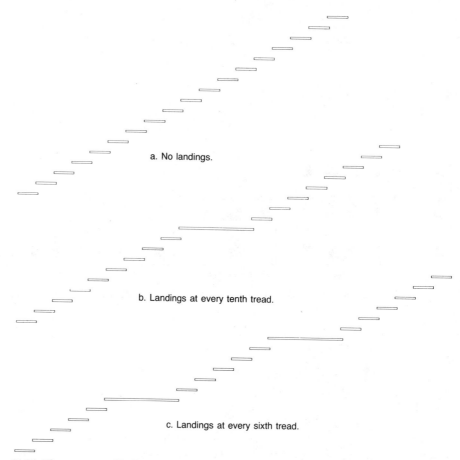

a. No landings.

b. Landings at every tenth tread.

c. Landings at every sixth tread.

11-25. The insertion of landings into stairs.

Case statements are most useful in graphics programs where we want to choose an alternative according to the value of some **integer** expression or function. Here we shall consider examples of its use in conjunction with the Pascal **mod** function and with functions that return random **integer**s.

Use of Modular Arithmetic to Generate Rhythms

Consider the very long stair shown in figure 11-25a. It needs landings; an architect might decide that a landing is to be inserted in place of every nth tread, where n is some specified positive integer. The Pascal **mod** function, which, as you will recall from chapter 5, computes the remainder of the division of two integer factors, provides a convenient way to accomplish this. The following procedure takes N as a parameter and computes the value of Count **mod** N to decide when to insert a landing:

```
PROCEDURE STAIRS (X_INITIAL,Y_INITIAL,DEPTH,WIDTH,
                  X_INCREMENT,Y_INCREMENT,
                  NUM_OF_STAIRS,N : INTEGER);

    VAR COUNT,X,Y,LANDING_DEPTH : INTEGER;
```

```
BEGIN
    LANDING_DEPTH := 2 * DEPTH;
    X := X_INITIAL;
    Y := Y_INITIAL;

    FOR COUNT := 1 TO NUM_OF_STAIRS DO
    BEGIN

        { Determine when to insert landing }
        IF COUNT MOD N = 0 THEN
            BEGIN
                RECTANGLE (X,Y,LANDING_DEPTH,WIDTH)
                    X := X + DEPTH;
            END
        ELSE
            RECTANGLE (X,Y,DEPTH,WIDTH);

        X := X + X_INCREMENT;
        Y := Y + Y_INCREMENT;

    END;

END;
```

11-26. The use of modular arithmetic to vary every nth window in a row.

Some typical results for different values of N are shown in figure 11-25b and c.

Similar logic might be followed in fenestration. Figure 11-26, for example, shows a row of square windows in which every nth square has been replaced by a larger, pedimented window. This is simply a generalization of the idea of alternating window types, which was discussed earlier.

A further generalization, familiar to musicians, is to consider the possibilities for *rhythms* of different *period*. The simplest possible rhythm of period 1 has the form:

AAA . . .

When the period is 2, an additional possibility emerges:

ABABAB . . .

A period of 3 gives us:

ABBABBABB . . .
ABCABCABC . . .

The possibilities now begin to multiply rapidly. Going to a period of 4 adds the possibilities:

ABBBABBBABBBABBB . . .
AABBAABBAABBAABB . . .
ABBCABBCABBCABBC . . .
ABCBABCBABCBABCB . . .
etc.

This enumeration can, of course, continue indefinitely.

Procedures to generate compositions that have complex rhythmic structures

11-27. A complex fenestration rhythm generated by using the **mod** function and a **case** statement.

can be written, very simply, using the **mod** function together with a **case** statement. The next procedure, for example, generates rows of triangular-pedimented, square, and rectangular windows in the following rhythm (of period 6):

ACBBCAACBBCAACBBCA . . .

Here is the code:

```
PROCEDURE  ROW_WINDOWS  (X,Y,WIDTH,HEIGHT,SPACING,
                              N_OF_WINDOWS  :  INTEGER);

     VAR  COUNT,X,Y_SQUARE  :  INTEGER;

  BEGIN

       Y_SQUARE  :=  Y  +  ((HEIGHT−WIDTH) DIV 2);

       FOR COUNT  :=  1 TO N_OF_WINDOWS  DO
       BEGIN

       { Select  window  type }
          CASE (COUNT MOD 6) OF

              0,1  :  TRIANGULAR_WINDOW  (X,Y,WIDTH,HEIGHT);
              2,5  :  SQUARE_WINDOW  (X,Y_SQUARE,WIDTH);
              3,4  :  RECTANGULAR_WINDOW  (X,Y,WIDTH,HEIGHT);

          END;

          X  :=  X  +  SPACING;

       END;

  END;
```

Notice that the value of Count **mod** 6 is computed at each iteration, and the result is then used to select a **case.** The **case** statement establishes the structure of the rhythm by associating a window type with each of the possible values (fig. 11-27).

Random Choice

Case statements also provide a way to have a program choose randomly from design alternatives. The following **case** statement, for example, randomly chooses between a circle, a cross, and a star:

```
CASE  RANDOM_NUMBER(SEED,1,3)  OF
   1  :  CIRCLE  (X,Y,DIAMETER);
   2  :  CROSS  (X,Y,DIAMETER);
   3  :  STAR  (X,Y,DIAMETER);
END;
```

Random_number is a kind of function called a *random number generator*. Here it used to return, at random, an integer between 1 and 3.

The Seed of the random number generator may be any integer. The other two parameters of Random_number define the range of integers from within which a particular value is to be selected at random. An initial value must be assigned to Seed before Random_number is called for the first time in a program. It is generally recommended that the seed be a large odd number. Thereafter, the last value returned by Random_number is used as the next value of Seed if the Seed is assigned the value of 0 when the procedure is next invoked. The following code, for example, generates and prints out a thousand random integers in the range 0 to 100;

```
SEED := 12347;
R := RANDOM_NUMBER(SEED,0,100);

FOR COUNT := 1 TO 1000 DO
BEGIN
    R := RANDOM_NUMBER(0,0,100);
    WRITELN (R);
END;
```

Different initial values for Seed will produce different sequences of random numbers. These sequences are random in the sense that if the sequence is long, each integer in the range from which values are selected will show up about the same number of times, but there will be no apparent regular pattern. This is acceptable as a random sequence:

> 2 1 1 3 2 2 1 3 3 3 1 2

But these are not:

> 1 1 1 1 2 2 2 2 3 3 3 3
> 3 1 1 1 1 1 1 1 1 2 1 1

The sequence generated meets statistical criteria for randomness, then, but it is not unpredictable; for a given Seed and range, the random number generator will always return the same value.

The technique for generating random numbers depends upon the computer hardware that is used, so we will not go into the details here. Most Pascal systems provide a random number generator that returns a **real** number between zero and one and has a single parameter Seed. Let us assume this function is called **random**. Our procedure Random_number can now be written:

```
FUNCTION RANDOM_NUMBER (SEED,MIN_VALUE,MAX_VALUE
                                : INTEGER) : INTEGER;
    VAR INTERVAL : INTEGER;

    BEGIN

        INTERVAL := MAX_VALUE − MIN_VALUE;
        RANDOM_NUMBER := MIN_VALUE +
                            ROUND(RANDOM(SEED*INTERVAL));

    END;
```

Our next procedure also accepts as input the initial Seed value for the random number generator and produces in response a random array of circles, crosses, and stars. It randomly chooses not only the type of element to place at each location, but also (within limits) the diameter of the element.

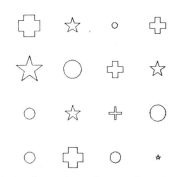

11-28. The random selection of circular, cross, and star columns for location in a grid.

```
PROCEDURE GRID (INITIAL_X,INITIAL_Y,SPACING,NX,NY,
                       MIN_DIAMETER,MAX_DIAMETER,SEED
                        : INTEGER);

    VAR X,Y,COUNT_X,COUNT_Y,FIRST : INTEGER;
        DIAMETER,COLUMN_TYPE : INTEGER;

BEGIN

    { Generate first random number }
    FIRST := RANDOM_NUMBER(SEED,1,100);

    Y := INITIAL_Y;
    FOR COUNT_Y := 1 TO NY DO
    BEGIN

        X := INITIAL_X;

        FOR COUNT_X := 1 TO NX DO
        BEGIN

            { Randomly select size of diameter }
            DIAMETER := RANDOM_NUMBER(0,
                        MIN_DIAMETER,MAX_DIAMETER);

            { Randomly select type of column }
            COLUMN_TYPE := RANDOM_NUMBER(0,1,3);

            CASE COLUMN_TYPE OF

                1: CIRCLE (X,Y,DIAMETER);
                2: CROSS (X,Y,DIAMETER);
                3: STAR (X,Y,DIAMETER);

            END;

            X := X + SPACING;

        END;

        Y := Y + SPACING;

    END;

END;
```

Figure 11-28 illustrates a typical result.

Random choice, as we noted earlier, is relatively rare in architecture; however, it does occasionly occur. Figure 11-29, for example, shows a traditional motif of Chinese garden architecture. Windows are regularly spaced in a row along a walkway wall, but there are several different window types, and the choices for each location do not fall into any regular pattern.

The next procedure draws this type of elevation. Parameters specify window diameter, window spacing, the number of windows, and a random number generator seed. The code is:

11-29. A Chinese garden-wall motif.

```
PROCEDURE ROW_WINDOWS (X_INITIAL,Y_INITIAL,DIAMETER,
                       SPACING,N_OF_WINDOWS,
                       N_OF_TYPES,SEED : INTEGER);

    VAR X,Y,COUNT,FIRST : INTEGER;

    BEGIN

        { Generate first random number }
        FIRST := RANDOM_NUMBER(SEED,1,N_OF_TYPES);

        X := X_INITIAL;
        Y := Y_INITIAL;

        FOR COUNT := 1 TO N_OF_WINDOWS DO
        BEGIN

            { Randomly select type of window }
            WINDOW_TYPE := RANDOM_NUMBER(0,1,
            N_OF_TYPES);

            CASE WINDOW_TYPE OF

                1: WINDOW1 (X,Y,DIAMETER);
                2: WINDOW2 (X,Y,DIAMETER);
                3: WINDOW3 (X,Y,DIAMETER);
                4: WINDOW4 (X,Y,DIAMETER);
                5: WINDOW5 (X,Y,DIAMETER);

            END;

            X := X + SPACING;

        END;

    END;
```

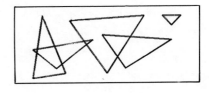

11-30. A composition of random triangles.

Random number generators can be used to choose not only between different vocabulary elements, but also to choose shape and position parameter values. The following program generates compositions of a specified number of random triangles within a specified rectangle on the screen (fig. 11-30):

```
PROGRAM RANDOM_TRIANGLES;

    USES GRAPHICS;

    PROCEDURE TRIANGLE (X1,Y1,X2,Y2,X3,Y3 : INTEGER);

        { Draw a triangle given coordinates of vertices }

        BEGIN

            MOVE (X1,Y1);
            DRAW (X2,Y2);
            DRAW (X2,Y3);
            DRAW (X1,Y1);

        END;

    VAR MIN_X,MAX_X,MIN_Y,MAX_Y,N,COUNT,SEED : INTEGER;
        X1,Y1,X2,Y2,X3,Y3 : INTEGER;

    { Main program }

    BEGIN

        { Read in boundaries of picture rectangle }
```

```
WRITELN ('ENTER MINIMUM X COORDINATE:');
READLN (MIN_X);
WRITELN ('ENTER MAXIMUM X COORDINATE:');
READLN (MAX_X);
WRITELN ('ENTER MINIMUM Y COORDINATE:');
READLN (MIN_Y);
WRITELN ('ENTER MAXIMUM Y COORDINATE:');
READLN (MAX_Y);

WRITELN ('HOW MANY TRIANGLES?');
READLN (N);

WRITELN ('ENTER RANDOM NUMBER SEED:');
READLN (SEED);
{ Generate first random number }
X1 := RANDOM_NUMBER(SEED,MIN_X,MAX_X);

START_DRAWING;

   { Loop to generate coordinates of random triangles }

   FOR COUNT := 1 TO N DO
   BEGIN

      X1 := RANDOM_NUMBER(0,MIN_X,MAX_X);
      X2 := RANDOM_NUMBER(0,MIN_X,MAX_X);
      X3 := RANDOM_NUMBER(0,MIN_X,MAX_X);
      Y1 := RANDOM_NUMBER(0,MIN_X,MAX_X);
      Y2 := RANDOM_NUMBER(0,MIN_X,MAX_X);
      Y3 := RANDOM_NUMBER(0,MIN_X,MAX_X);

      TRIANGLE (X1,Y1,X2,Y2,X3,Y3);

   END;

   FINISH_DRAWING;

END.
```

Other Applications of Conditionals

So far we have seen how to use **if** . . . **then** . . . **else** and **case** statements to choose between design alternatives. But they also have many other important uses. They can be used for error checking, in situations that arise with the construction of curves, and in programs that search for design alternatives that meet specified criteria.

Error Conditions

It is often useful to check the values assigned to variables to see if they make sense and if not, to report the existence of an *error condition*. When you work in a 1,024 by 1,024 screen coordinate system, for example, it does not make sense for a coordinate value to be less than 0 or greater than 1,023. The following code checks for and reports such errors:

```
IF X < 0 THEN
   WRITELN ('ERROR: X LESS THAN 0')
ELSE IF X > 1023 THEN
   WRITELN ('ERROR: X GREATER THAN 1023');
```

If there is no error, no message is printed out.

Sometimes, in addition to reporting an error condition, you will want the program to terminate execution immediately if an error exists. A standard way to approach this is to introduce an Error_code variable. This is initialized to 0, but is assigned a new value if an error is found:

```
ERROR_CODE := 0;
IF  X < 0 THEN
    BEGIN
        WRITELN ('ERROR: X LESS THAN 0');
        ERROR_CODE := 1;
    END
ELSE IF X > 1023 THEN
    BEGIN
        WRITELN ('ERROR: X GREATER THAN 1023');
        ERROR_CODE := 2;
    END;
```

The value of Error_code can then be tested to determine what to do next. The following code, for example, either draws a circle or terminates execution without drawing anything:

```
IF  ERROR_CODE = 0 THEN
    CIRCLE (X,Y,RADIUS);
```

It is often necessary to check values that are read in by a program, since you cannot control what a user of the program may enter in response to a prompt; it might be some absurd value. In this case, you probably want to give the user the chance to reenter a correct value. A **repeat until** loop can be used for this purpose:

```
REPEAT

    ERROR_CODE := 0;
    WRITELN ('ENTER VALUE FOR X');
    READLN (X);

    IF X < 0 THEN
        BEGIN
            WRITELN ('X LESS THAN 0: RE-ENTER');
            ERROR_CODE := 1;
        END
    ELSE IF X > 1023 THEN
        BEGIN
            WRITELN ('X GREATER THAN 1023: RE-ENTER');
            ERROR_CODE := 1;
        END;

UNTIL ERROR_CODE = 0;
```

Curves and Conditionals

Mathematical functions, like architectural compositions, often manifest special conditions (requiring special treatment) at their extremes. The following Pascal function, for example, computes the reciprocal of a number X:

```
FUNCTION RECIPROCAL (X : INTEGER) : REAL;
    BEGIN
        RECIPROCAL := 1 / X;
    END;
```

This function will work for any value of X except zero. When X is zero, the value of 1/X should be infinity, but an infinitely large **integer** cannot be represented in a finite memory location, so an attempt to execute Reciprocal when X is zero will generate an error. It is good practice, then, to test for a zero value of X before passing it into Reciprocal as follows:

```
IF X <> 0 THEN
    Y := RECIPROCAL (X)
ELSE
    WRITELN ('CANNOT TAKE THE RECIPROCAL OF 0');
```

The mathematical properties of curves make conditionals useful in some other contexts too. Consider, for instance, the task of drawing an arc through three specified points. Assume that points are specified in clockwise fashion as shown in figure 11-31a. The required construction is illustrated in figure 11-31b. The code to draw the arc this way must test to determine the quadrant of the circle into which the start angle falls and into which the finish angle falls. Here it is:

```
FUNCTION QUADRANT (ANGLE,X,Y : REAL) : REAL;
    { Modifies angle according to quadrant }
    BEGIN
        QUADRANT := ANGLE;
        IF X < 0 THEN
            IF Y > 0 THEN
                QUADRANT := 180.0 - ANGLE
            ELSE
                QUADRANT := 180.0 + ANGLE
        ELSE IF Y < 0 THEN
            QUADRANT := 360.0 - ANGLE;
    END;

PROCEDURE ARC3 (X1,Y1,X2,Y2,X3,Y3,NSIDES : INTEGER);
    { Draws arc clockwise through 3 points }
    VAR TX2,TY2,TX3,TY3,RXC,RYC,THETA1,THETA3 : REAL;
        XC,YC,RADIUS : INTEGER;
    CONST RADIANS = 0.01745;

    BEGIN
        { Determine center and radius of arc }
        TX2 := X2 - X1;
        TY2 := Y2 - Y1;
        TX3 := X3 - X1;
        TY3 := Y3 - Y1;
```

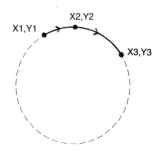

a. Any three points specify an arc.

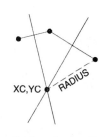

b. The construction of perpendicular bisectors of chords to find center, radius, and start and stop angles.

11-31. Drawing an arc through three specified points.

```
    RXC  :=  (TY3*(SQR(TX2)+SQR(TY2))  −
             TY2*(SQR(TX3)+SQR(TY3)))/
             ((TX2 * TY3 − TX3 * TY2) *2);

    RYC  :=  (TX3*(SQR(TX2)+SQR(TY2))  −
             TX2*(SQR(TX3)+SQR(TY3)))/
             ((TY2 * TX3 − TY3 * TX2) *2);

    RADIUS  :=  ROUND(SQRT(SQR(RXC)  +  SQR(RYC)));

    XC  :=  ROUND(RXC)  +  X1;
    YC  :=  ROUND(RYC)  +  Y1;

  { Determine start and stop angles }

    IF  X1  <>  XC  THEN
        THETA1  :=  ARCTAN(ABS((Y1−YC)/(X1−XC)))  /
                    RADIANS
    ELSE
        THETA1  :=  90;

    IF  X3  <>  XC  THEN
        THETA3  :=  ARCTAN(ABS((Y3−YC)/(X3−XC)))  /
                    RADIANS
    ELSE
        THETA3  :=  90;

  { Select appropriate quadrant }

    THETA1  :=  QUADRANT(THETA1,X1−XC,Y1−YC);
    THETA3  :=  QUADRANT(THETA3,X3−XC,Y3−YC);

    IF  THETA3  >  THETA1  THEN
        THETA1  :=  THETA1  +  360;

  { Draw arc }

        ARC  (XC,YC,RADIUS,NSIDES,THETA3,THETA1)
  END;
```

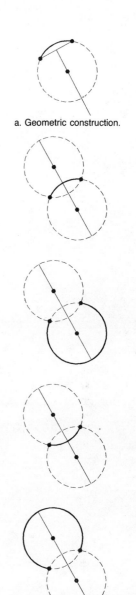

a. Geometric construction.

b. Two points and a radius specify four different arcs.

c. The required arc is drawn clockwise from the first point to the second, with the center on the right of the line connecting them.

11-32. Drawing an arc of specified radius between two points.

Note that this procedure invokes Arc, the procedure to draw an arc about a specified center point from a specified start angle to a specified finish angle (see chapter 10).

Another way to specify an arc is with two points and a radius (fig. 11-32a). This information is insufficient to specify an arc uniquely; four different arcs are consistent with it (fig. 11-32b). We need two additional items: which of the two center points to use; and which of the two arcs about the center point to draw. We can either specify these explicitly or rely on a convention to do so implicitly. Here we shall assume that the arc is drawn clockwise from the first point to the second, with the center to the right of the line connecting them (fig. 11-32c).

```
PROCEDURE  ARC2  (X1,Y1,X2,Y2,RADIUS,NSIDES  :  INTEGER);

  { Draw arc given 2 points and a radius }

  VAR  XC,YC,XMID,YMID,XINC,YINC,SIGNY  :  INTEGER;
       XL,YL,D2,ALPHA,H  :  REAL;
       THETA1,THETA2  :  REAL;
       CONST  RADIANS  =  0.01745;
```

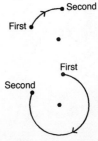

```
BEGIN
      { Determine center point of arc between X1,Y1 and X2,Y2 }
         XL := X2 − X1;
         YL := Y2 − Y1;
         D2 := SQRT(SQR(XL) + SQR(YL)) / 2;
         XMID := (X1 + X2) DIV 2;
         YMID := (Y1 + Y2) DIV 2;
         IF YL <> 0 THEN
            ALPHA := ARCTAN(ABS(XL/YL))
         ELSE
            ALPHA := 90 * RADIANS;

         H := SQRT(SQR(RADIUS*1.0) − SQR(D2));
         XINC := ROUND(H*COS(ALPHA));
         YINC := ROUND(H*SIN(ALPHA));

      { Determine direction of center point from line between points.
        Arc is drawn clockwise from the first point to the second
        with the center to the right of the line connecting them. }

         SIGNY := 1;
         IF (X1 < X2) AND (Y1 < Y2) THEN
            SIGNY := −1;
         IF (X1 > X2) AND (Y1 > Y2) THEN
            SIGNY := −1;

         XC := XMID + XINC;
         YC := YMID + SIGNY * YINC;

      { Determine start angle and stop angle for arc }

         IF X1 <> XC THEN
            THETA1 := ARCTAN(ABS((Y1−YC)/(X1−XC))) /
                      RADIANS
         ELSE
            THETA1 := 90;

         IF X2 <> XC THEN
            THETA2 := ARCTAN(ABS((Y2−YC)/(X2−XC))) /
                      RADIANS
         ELSE
            THETA2 := 90;

         THETA1 := QUADRANT(THETA1,X1−XC,Y1−YC);
         THETA2 := QUADRANT(THETA2,X2−XC,Y2−YC);

      { Draw arc }

         IF THETA1 > THETA2 THEN
            ARC (XC,YC,RADIUS,NSIDES,THETA2,THETA1)
         ELSE
            ARC (XC,YC,RADIUS,NSIDES,THETA2,THETA1+360);
END;
```

What happens if the specified radius is less than half the distance between the start and endpoints (fig. 11-33)? This makes the construction impossible, so it should be treated as an error. The following test for this condition can be added to the procedure so that termination with an error message results if it is found:

```
IF RADIUS < H THEN
    WRITELN ('ERROR – RADIUS LESS THAN HALF THE
             DISTANCE', 'BETWEEN THE 2 POINTS.')
ELSE
  BEGIN
      { Remainder of program }
  END;
```

Yet another way to specify an arc is by giving the starting point and endpoint, plus a *curvature* rather than radius (fig. 11-34):

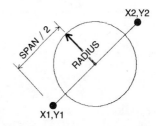

11-33. An error condition; the radius is less than half the distance between the starting point and endpoint.

```
PROCEDURE ARC_CURVE (X1,Y1,X2,Y2,CURVATURE,NSIDES :
                     : INTEGER);

  { Draw arc given two points and a curvature }

    VAR X3,Y3,XMID,YMID,XINC,YINC,SIGNX,SIGNY : INTEGER;
        XL,YL,ALPHA : REAL;
    CONST RADIANS = 0.01745;
    BEGIN
      { Determine third point of arc between X1,Y1 and X2,Y2 }

        XL := X2 – X1;
        YL := Y2 – Y1;
        XMID := (X1 + X2) DIV 2;
        YMID := (Y1 + Y2) DIV 2;
        IF YL <> 0 THEN
           ALPHA := ARCTAN(ABS(XL/YL))
        ELSE
           ALPHA := 90 * RADIANS;
        XINC := ROUND(CURVATURE*COS(ALPHA));
        YINC := ROUND(CURVATURE*SIN(ALPHA));

      { Determine direction of third point from line between points,
        short arc is always drawn clockwise between the two
        points }

        SIGNX := 1;
        SIGNY := 1;
        IF X1 > X2 THEN
           IF Y1 > Y2 THEN
              SIGNY := –1;
           ELSE BEGIN
              SIGNX := –1;
              SIGNY := –1;
              END
        ELSE IF Y1 < Y2 THEN
           SIGNX := –1;

        X3 := XMID + SIGNX * XINC;
        Y3 := YMID + SIGNY * YINC;

      { Draw arc }
        ARC3 (X1,Y1,X3,Y3,X2,Y2,NSIDES);

    END;
```

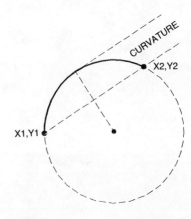

11-34. Drawing an arc of specified curvature between two points.

This procedure follows the same conventions as the earlier procedure for drawing an arc of specified radius between two points. If the specified curvature

a. The center point and angles are fixed, but radius varies from instance to instance.

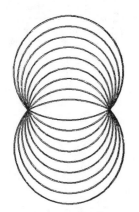

b. Endpoints are fixed, but curvature varies from instance to instance.

11-35. Compositions relating arcs in different ways.

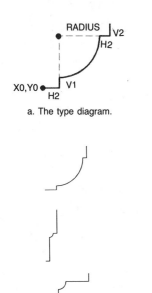

a. The type diagram.

b. Some instances.

11-37. The parametric variation of the ovolo.

is zero, it will draw a straight line.

Why do we need four different procedures to draw arcs? When we add an arc to a composition, we usually want to relate it in some definite way to existing elements by setting some of its parameters equal to known values of variables describing those elements. If we want to center the arc on some established point in the composition (fig. 11-35a), we need the procedure with center point coordinates as parameters. If we want to end the arc on two established points in the composition, as when we spring an arch from established abutments, we need one of the procedures with endpoint coordinates as parameters (fig. 11-35b). Each arc procedure allows the formation of different types of relations. Procedures for constructing profiles for architectural moldings clearly illustrate the uses of the different arc procedures. Most traditional moldings are composed from circular arcs and straight line segments (fig. 11-36). For example, the *ovolo* and its converse the *cavetto* are usually developed from quarter circles and are occasionally shallower. The *torus* and its converse the *scotia* are developed from semicircles. Similarly, the ¾ round and the ¾ hollow are developed from 270-degree arcs.

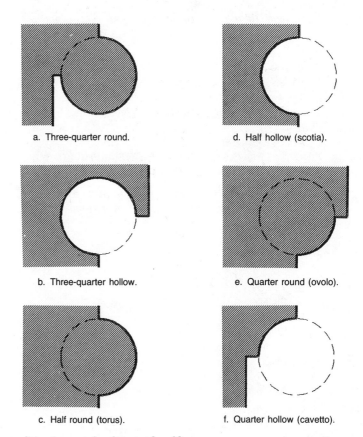

a. Three-quarter round.

d. Half hollow (scotia).

b. Three-quarter hollow.

e. Quarter round (ovolo).

c. Half round (torus).

f. Quarter hollow (cavetto).

11-36. Some traditional types of architectural molding.

In the design of a molding, an architect manipulates shape variables to create effects of light, shading, and shadow line. Increasing the depth of an overhang, for example, creates deeper shadows. Varying the curvature of an arc alters the shading. And appropriate balances of flat and curved surfaces, and of light and shade, must be achieved. Figure 11-37a shows how an ovolo profile might be parameterized to allow this kind of design exploration. The corresponding procedure, which invokes Arc, is as follows:

```
PROCEDURE  OVOLO  (X0,Y0,H1,V1,H2,V2,RADIUS,NSIDES : INTEGER);

    VAR XC,YC,X1,Y1,Y2 : INTEGER;

    BEGIN

        { Calculate center of arc and other coordinates of ovolo }
        XC := X0 + H1;
        Y1 := Y0 + V1;
        YC := Y1 + RADIUS;
        Y2 := YC + V2;
        X1 := XC + RADIUS + H2;

        { Draw ovolo with quarter circle arc }
        MOVE (X0,Y0);
        DRAW (XC,Y0);
        DRAW (XC,Y1);
        ARC  (XC,YC,RADIUS,NSIDES,270.0,360.0);
        DRAW (X1,YC);
        DRAW (X1,Y2);

    END;
```

We can introduce an additional degree of design freedom by allowing the Arc of the ovolo to be greater or less than a quarter circle. Now we need to invoke arc3 in the construction procedure:

```
PROCEDURE  OVOLO  (X0,Y0,X1,Y1,X2,Y2,X3,Y3,X4,Y4,NSIDES :
                        INTEGER);
    BEGIN
        { Draw ovolo given 3 points on arc }

        MOVE (X0,Y0);
        DRAW (X1,Y0);
        DRAW (X1,Y1);
        ARC3 (X3,Y3,X2,Y2,X1,Y1,NSIDES);
        DRAW (X4,Y3);
        DRAW (X4,Y4);

    END;
```

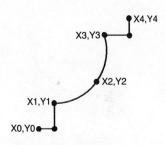

a. The type diagram.

Some examples of output generated by this procedure are shown in figure 11-38.

It may be more convenient to specify the curvature of an ovolo as illustrated in figure 11-39a. Further, if we allow the curvature to be negative (fig. 11-39b), we can produce cavetto profiles as well. Here is a procedure structured in this way:

```
PROCEDURE  OVOLO  (X0,Y0,X1,Y1,X2,Y2,X3,Y3,CURVATURE,NSIDES :
                        INTEGER);
    BEGIN

        { Draw ovolo given curvature of arc }
        MOVE (X0,Y0);
        DRAW (X1,Y0);
        DRAW (X1,Y1);
```

b. Some instances.

11-38. An ovolo with more degrees of design freedom.

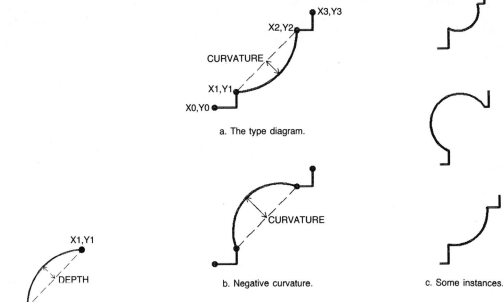

a. The type diagram.

b. Negative curvature.

c. Some instances.

11-39. Another parameterization of the ovolo.

```
IF  CURVATURE  >  0  THEN       { Draw  ovolo }
    ARC_CURVE (X2,Y2,X1,Y1,CURVATURE,NSIDES)
ELSE                            { Draw  cavetto }
    ARC_CURVE (X1,Y1,X2,Y2,−CURVATURE,NSIDES);

MOVE (X2,Y2);
DRAW (X3,Y2);
DRAW (X3,Y3);

END;
```

Figure 11-39c shows some typical output.

    More complex types of molding profiles are formed by fitting together several arcs. The S-shaped *cyma recta*, for example, is constructed as shown in figure 11-40a. Its converse is the *cyma reversa* (fig. 11-40b). Both the cyma recta and the cyma reversa can be constructed from equal arcs, or they can be *quirked* by using unequal arcs (fig. 11-40c). In any case, their intersection must be tangential.

Generate-and-Test Procedures

    Sometimes a designer knows conditions that an instance of some design element must satisfy, but does not know the parameter values that will generate a satisfactory instance. The problem, then, is to find these parameter values. A structural designer, for example, might intend to span a space with a rectangular wooden beam. The span and loading conditions are given, and the problem is to find satisfactory values for the height and width of the beam's cross section.

    There are often formulas that can be evaluated to yield the required value directly. In other cases, however, there is no alternative to engaging in a trial-and-error process of generating candidate sets of parameter values for consideration and testing these for compliance with the conditions. The flow

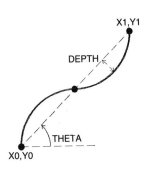

a. Cyma recta.

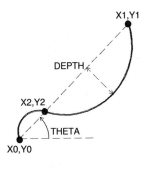

b. Cyma reversa.

c. Quirked cyma reversa.

11-40. Arcs connected at tangents.

diagram in figure 11-41 illustrates the general structure of this process.

As the diagram suggests, it is not difficult to write programs to perform this kind of search. You use loops to enumerate parameter values, **Boolean** expressions to describe the conditions that must be met, and a conditional to terminate the search when the required values are found.

The next program illustrates this. It finds satisfactory values for Length and Width of a rectangular room. It begins by prompting for and reading in values for:

- minimum acceptable Length
- maximum acceptable Length
- minimum acceptable Width
- maximum acceptable Width
- minimum acceptable Area
- maximum acceptable Area
- minimum acceptable Proportion (Length/Width)
- maximum acceptable Proportion
- minimum acceptable Perimeter
- maximum acceptable Perimeter

It then uses nested loops to enumerate values for Length and Width. At each iteration, it calculates values for Area, Proportion, and Perimeter. When it first finds Length and Width values that satisfy the requirements, it exits from the loop and draws the appropriately sized rectangle. If the requirements are impossible to satisfy, then it eventually exhausts all the possibilities and reports this. Here is the complete code:

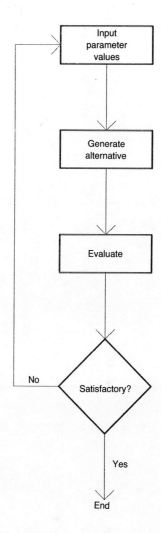

11-41. A flow diagram of a simple trial-and-error design process.

```
PROGRAM SEARCH;

  USES GRAPHICS;

  PROCEDURE RECTANGLE (X,Y,LENGTH,WIDTH : INTEGER);

    VAR X1,Y1 : INTEGER;

    BEGIN

      { Calculate coordinates of corners }
      X1 := X + LENGTH;
      Y1 := Y + WIDTH;

      { Move to bottom left corner }
      MOVE (X,Y);

      { Draw the four sides }
      DRAW (X1,Y);
      DRAW (X1,Y1);
      DRAW (X,Y1);
      DRAW (X,Y);

    END;


  { Main program }
  VAR MIN_LENGTH,MAX_LENGTH,MIN_WIDTH,MAX_WIDTH,
      MIN_AREA,MAX_AREA,MIN_PERIMETER,MAX_PERIMETER,
      LENGTH,WIDTH,AREA,PERIMETER : INTEGER;
      MIN_PROPORTION,MAX_PROPORTION,PROPORTION
      : REAL; SATISFIES : BOOLEAN;
```

```
BEGIN
    { Set design variables }
        WRITELN ('ENTER THE MINIMUM LENGTH :');
        READLN (MIN_LENGTH);
        WRITELN ('ENTER THE MAXIMUM LENGTH :');
        READLN (MAX_LENGTH);
        WRITELN ('ENTER THE MINIMUM WIDTH :');
        READLN (MIN_WIDTH);
        WRITELN ('ENTER THE MAXIMUM WIDTH :');
        READLN (MAX_WIDTH);
        WRITELN ('ENTER THE MINIMUM AREA :');
        READLN (MIN_AREA);
        WRITELN ('ENTER THE MAXIMUM AREA :');
        READLN (MAX_AREA);
        WRITELN ('ENTER THE MINIMUM PROPORTION :');
        READLN (MIN_PROPORTION);
        WRITELN ('ENTER THE MAXIMUM PROPORTION :');
        READLN (MAX_PROPORTION);
        WRITELN ('ENTER THE MINIMUM PERIMETER :');
        READLN (MIN_PERIMETER);
        WRITELN ('ENTER THE MAXIMUM PERIMETER :');
        READLN (MAX_PERIMETER);
    START_DRAWING;

    { Loop to generate alternatives to test }
        SATISFIES := FALSE;
        LENGTH := MIN_LENGTH - 1;

        WHILE NOT(SATISFIES) AND (LENGTH < MAX_LENGTH) DO
        BEGIN

            LENGTH := LENGTH + 1;
            WIDTH := MIN_WIDTH - 1;

            WHILE NOT(SATISFIES) AND (WIDTH < MAX_WIDTH) DO
            BEGIN

                WIDTH := WIDTH + 1;
                AREA := LENGTH * WIDTH;
                PROPORTION := LENGTH / WIDTH;
                PERIMETER := 2 * (LENGTH + WIDTH);

                IF (AREA >= MIN_AREA) AND
                   (AREA <= MAX_AREA) AND
                   (PROPORTION >= MIN_PROPORTION) AND
                   (PROPORTION <= MAX_PROPORTION) AND
                   (PERIMETER >= MIN_PERIMETER) AND
                   (PERIMETER <= MAX_PERIMETER)

                THEN SATISFIES := TRUE;
            END;
        END;

        IF SATISFIES THEN
            RECTANGLE (200,200,LENGTH,WIDTH)
        ELSE
            WRITELN ('CONDITIONS NOT SATISFIED.');
    FINISH_DRAWING;
END.
```

With the use of generate-and-test methods, you can build problem-solving intelligence into graphics programs. You should be careful, though, of the combinatorial explosion that results when the number of design variables, and the number of values possible for each, begins to grow. A computer can execute generate-and-test loops very rapidly, but each iteration does take a finite amount of time. When the number of iterations becomes very large, total execution time can easily become impractically great.

Notice that the execution of the Search program can be made more effective by adding logical conditions to the inner **while** loop. For example, once the Width reaches a value such that the calculated Area is greater than the maximum allowed, there is no reason to continue incrementing Width. In generate-and-test programs, it is important to take advantage of any available way to reduce the number of iterations. Where a motif is generated by a parameterized procedure, you can always generate sets of variants by invoking the procedure from within loops that increment parameter values. And you can always turn such enumeration procedures into generate-and-test procedures by testing, within the loop, for compliance with conditions.

Summary

In the simplest Pascal programs, the computer executes each successive statement once and only once (fig. 11-42a):

```
BEGIN
      Statement 1;
      Statement 2;
      Statement 3;
END;
```

It neither repeats nor skips a statement.

In chapter 9, we explored the use of loops that cause a sequence of statements to be repeated (fig. 11-42b):

```
FOR COUNT := 1 TO 10 DO
BEGIN
      Statement 1;
      Statement 2;
      Statement 3;
END;
```

In this chapter, we have learned how to use conditionals that cause statements to be skipped (fig. 11-42c):

```
CASE COUNT OF
      1: Statement 1;
      2: Statement 2;
      3: Statement 3;
END;
```

Whereas loops serve the graphic purpose of repeating instances of graphic elements in uniform patterns, conditionals allow us to break the uniformity of a pattern where appropriate, in order to adjust or inflect parts of a composition

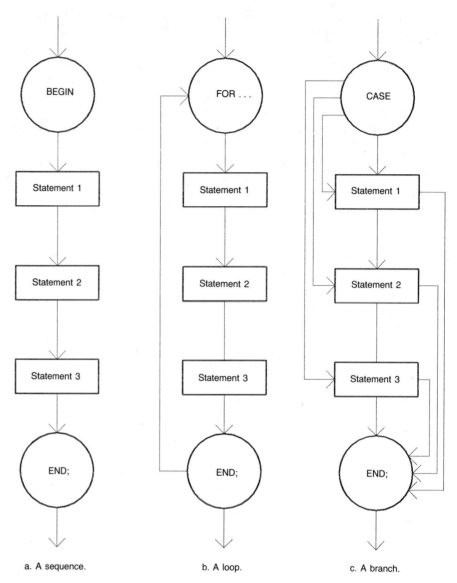

a. A sequence.   b. A loop.   c. A branch.

11-42. The control of action.

to respond to special conditions. We have illustrated this principle mostly by considering odd and even conditions, end conditions, interior conditions, and center conditions in rows and grids of architectural elements, but you should be able to think of many more ways in which parts of compositions are varied in response to existing conditions.

Uniformity is prized by some designers, and programs to generate work in their style will contain few conditionals. Much of classical architecture and of the work of Mies van der Rohe, for example, is like this (fig. 11-43a). Other designers, however, value the way that interest and meaning can be created within a composition by varying and inflecting elements in response to subtle contextual differences. Baroque architects were masters of this approach as was Alvar Aalto (fig. 11-43b). Programs to generate compositions of this sort will be rich in conditionals. Finally, some designers are interested in the startling effects of purely arbitrary variation. Programs to produce this kind of composition will incorporate random selection mechanisms. In any case, the code makes explicit answers to two basic aesthetic questions. Under what conditions should elements vary? And, under a given condition, what kind of variation should occur?

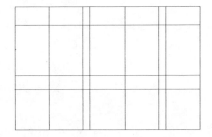

a. The column grid for Lake Shore Towers, Chicago, by Mies van der Rohe.

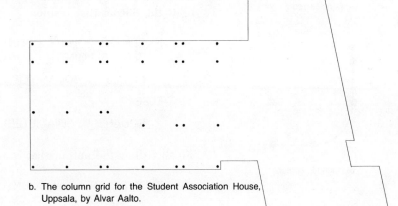

b. The column grid for the Student Association House, Uppsala, by Alvar Aalto.

11-43. Uniformity and variety.

Exercises

1. Assume there is a procedure to draw a Square, a procedure to draw a Circle, and the **Boolean** functions End_condition and Center_point as defined earlier. Execute the following code by hand and draw the graphic output on screen grid paper.

```
INITIAL_X := 100;
INITIAL_Y := 100;
NX := 5;
NY := 5;
DIAMETER := 25;
SPACING := 100;

Y := INITIAL_Y;
FOR Y_COUNT := 1 TO NY DO
BEGIN

    X := INITIAL_X;
    FOR X_COUNT := 1 TO NX DO
```

```
                    BEGIN
                        IF (END_CONDITION(Y_COUNT,1,NY)  AND
                            CENTER_POINT  (X_COUNT,1,NX))
                            OR
                            (END_CONDITION(X_COUNT,1,NX)  AND
                            CENTER_POINT  (Y_COUNT,1,NY))  THEN
                                CIRCLE  (X,Y,DIAMETER)
                        ELSE
                                SQUARE  (X,Y,DIAMETER);
                            X  :=  X  +  SPACING;
                    END;
                        Y  :=  Y  +  SPACING;
                END;
```

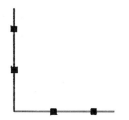

a. Cantilevered corner.

Keep the same loop structure, replace the conditional with the following, and draw the output that results.

```
        IF  CENTER_POINT(X_COUNT,1,NX))  AND
            CENTER_POINT(Y_COUNT,1,NY))  THEN
                CIRCLE  (X,Y,DIAMETER)
        ELSE
                SQUARE  (X,Y,DIAMETER);
```

b. Rounded corner.

Finally, draw the output that results when the conditional is replaced with:

```
        IF  (X_COUNT  =  Y_COUNT)  OR
            (X_COUNT  =  NY  −  Y_COUNT  +  1)  THEN
                CIRCLE  (X,Y,DIAMETER)
        ELSE
                SQUARE  (X,Y,DIAMETER);
```

c. Chamfered corner.

2. A common way to handle the corners in a high-rise office building is to leave out the corner columns and cantilever the floor (fig. 11-44a). This allows the outline of the floor to be shaped freely at the corners (fig. 11-44b, c, and d). Choose a way to shape the corner and write a general procedure to produce floor plans of this type.

3. In the floor plan shown in figure 11-45, a rectangular light well has been introduced. The reentrant corners of the light well constitute a special condition in the column grid. What architectural response might you make to this? Using conditionals, write a general procedure that generates a plan with a rectangular light well of arbitrary size and arbitrary location within the column grid and that handles the reentrant corners appropriately.

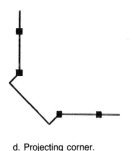

d. Projecting corner.

11-44. Corner treatments for a high-rise office building.

4. A scheme for the layout of an amphitheater is shown in fig. 11-46. Notice that concentric aisles for access alternate at regular intervals between the concentric rows of seating, and that a conditional rule governs placement of the radial lines of steps. Taking stage diameter, seating row width, aisle width, step width, number of rows of seating, and number of seating rows per aisle as parameters, and using conditionals, write a general procedure to draw layouts of this type.

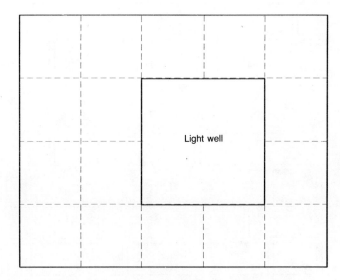

11-45. A floor plan with a square column grid and an interior light well.

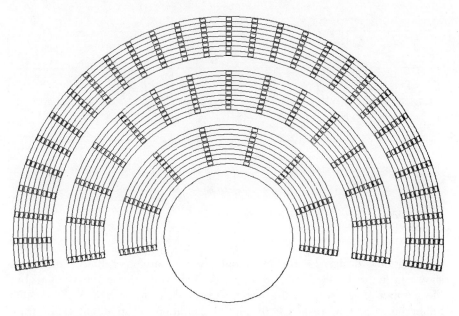

11-46. Type diagram for an amphitheater.

5. Figure 11-47 illustrates various traditional types of brickwork bonding. Choose one of these and consider the parameters that would be needed to control the position, size, and pattern of a rectangular panel in this bond. Using conditionals, write an appropriately parameterized procedure to generate such a panel.

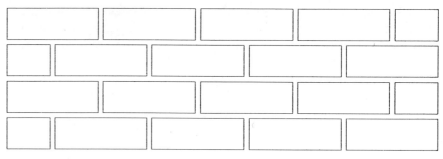

a. Running.

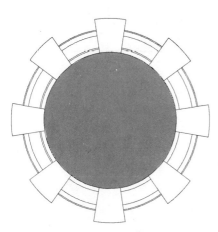

11-48. A circular window design from Batty Langley's *Builder's and Workman's Treasury of Designs*.

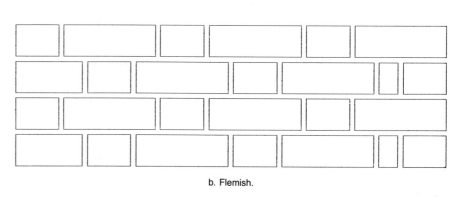

b. Flemish.

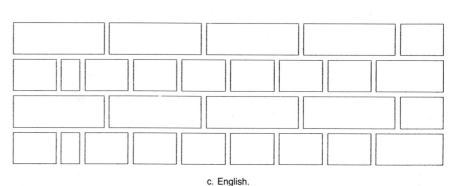

c. English.

11-47. Traditional types of brickwork bonding.

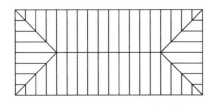

11-49. The layout of rafters in a hipped roof.

6. A window design by the eighteenth-century architect Batty Langley is shown in figure 11-48. There are eight identical voussoirs in this version, but the number of voussoirs might become a variable, and the shapes of voussoirs might be varied in response to special conditions. Top might differ from bottom, horizontal from vertical, odd from even, and so on. Write a procedure, incorporating conditionals, to generate variants.

7. A standard scheme for the layout of rafters in a hipped roof over a rectangular floor plan is shown in figure 11-49. Notice that if the rafters on the long side intersect the hip, they are short. Otherwise, they are of normal length. Write an appropriately parameterized procedure to lay out rafters in this fashion and draw the plan.

8. Figure 11-50 illustrates how the *parti* for a church, of the Florence Cathedral type, might be developed: this process can be understood as one of increasingly refined differentiation of an initially uniform design. Begin by writing a procedure to generate uniform designs of the type shown in figure 11-50a. Then, by successively introducing additional vocabulary elements and conditionals controlling their use, successively refine it into procedures to generate the more differentiated types.

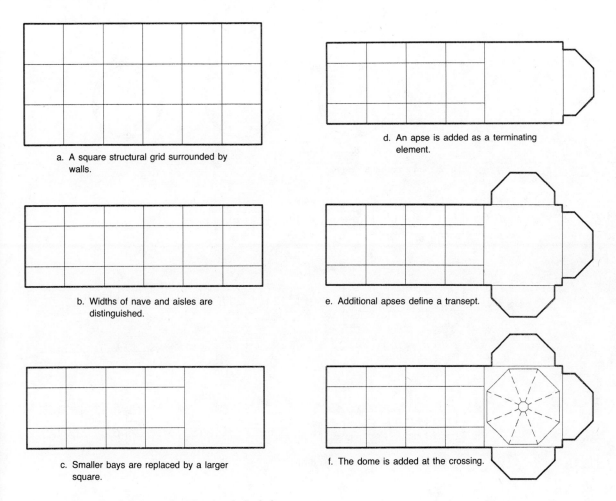

a. A square structural grid surrounded by walls.

b. Widths of nave and aisles are distinguished.

c. Smaller bays are replaced by a larger square.

d. An apse is added as a terminating element.

e. Additional apses define a transept.

f. The dome is added at the crossing.

11-50. Elaboration of the *parti* for Florence Cathedral.

9. Many town plans (fig. 11-51) consist of regular street grids interrupted at various points and in various ways. Examine some plans of this type. What are the conditions under which the grid is interrupted? Write a set of conditional rules that could be used to produce plans of this type, and discuss their effects.

10. Figure 11-52a illustrates a common motif of Gothic architecture, composed of circles and arcs and known as the *trefoil*. Similarly, a *quatrefoil* is shown in figure 11-52b. In general, we can have *multifoils*—any number of segments. What parameters are needed to control the position, size, segmentation, and shape of a multifoil? Write a general multifoil procedure.

11-51. The regular street grid of the French bastide Montpazier, interrupted by major public buildings.

11. Some typical Greek meander patterns are shown in figure 11-53. Write procedures, incorporating the **mod** function and a **case** statement, to generate some of these.

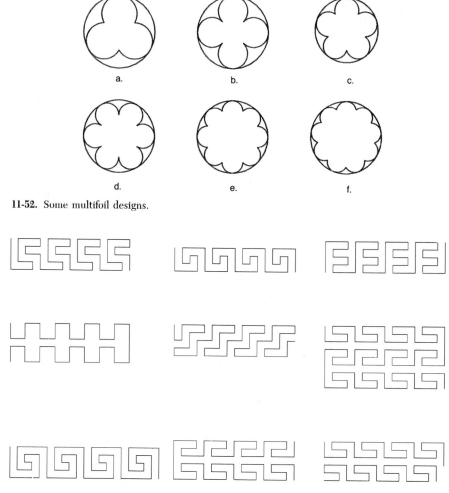

11-52. Some multifoil designs.

11-53. Some Greek meander patterns.

12.

Hierarchical Structure

Subsystems

Consider a composition consisting just of a square, generated by,

```
SQUARE (X_SQUARE,Y_SQUARE,SIDE);
```

and a circle, generated by,

```
CIRCLE (X_CIRCLE,Y_CIRCLE,DIAMETER);
```

Each procedure has three parameters (fig. 12-1), so there are six design variables in all. In other words, we have established a spatial relation with six degrees of freedom between the square and the circle.

We can reduce the degrees of freedom by making one of these six variables depend upon another:

```
SQUARE (X_SQUARE,Y_SQUARE,SIDE);
X_CIRCLE := X_SQUARE;
CIRCLE (X_CIRCLE,Y_CIRCLE,DIAMETER);
```

The circle can now move only on a vertical line through the center of the square (fig. 12-2). We have established a particular type of graphic subsystem, consisting of two vocabulary elements spatially related in a specific way.

Subtypes can be established by further reducing the degrees of freedom in the relation (fig. 12-3):

```
SQUARE (X_SQUARE,Y_SQUARE,SIDE);
X_CIRCLE := X_SQUARE;
Y_CIRCLE := Y_SQUARE − SIDE;
DIAMETER := SIDE*2;
CIRCLE (X_CIRCLE,Y_CIRCLE,DIAMETER);
```

A procedure to generate this subsystem can now be written:

```
PROCEDURE PANTHEON (X_SQUARE,Y_SQUARE,SIDE: INTEGER);

VAR X_CIRCLE,Y_CIRCLE,DIAMETER : INTEGER);
```

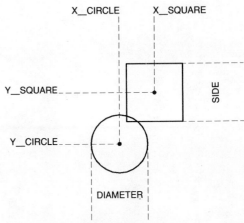

12-1. A composition of a square and circle, with six degrees of freedom.

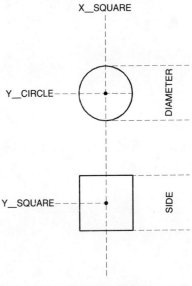

12-2. A composition with five degrees of freedom; the circle moves on a vertical line through the center of the square.

323

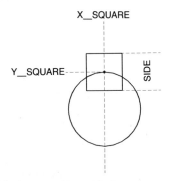

X_SQUARE

Y_SQUARE

SIDE

12-3. A composition with three degrees of freedom.

BEGIN

{ *Draw square* }
SQUARE (X_SQUARE,Y_SQUARE,SIDE);

{ *Relate circle to square* }
X_CIRCLE := X_SQUARE;
Y_CIRCLE := Y_SQUARE − SIDE;
DIAMETER := SIDE*2;

{ *Draw circle* }
CIRCLE (X_CIRCLE,Y_CIRCLE,DIAMETER),

END;

This gives the type of subsystem a name and specifies the relation between its constituent vocabulary elements.

The same vocabulary elements may be related in many different ways to form different types of subsystems. Figure 12-4 suggests some of the possibilities for a circle and a square.

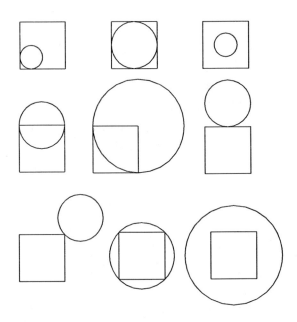

12-4. Some possible relationships between a circle and square.

Subsystems of Many Elements

A subsystem that is built up from available vocabulary elements placed in some specific spatial relationship need not consist of just two such elements. There may be any number. The following procedure, for example, interrelates a square, a circle, and a triangle:

PROCEDURE CLOCKFACE (X,Y,DIAMETER : INTEGER);

VAR HALF_DIAMETER,YT : INTEGER;

```
BEGIN

    HALF_DIAMETER := DIAMETER DIV 2;

    CIRCLE (X,Y,DIAMETER);
    SQUARE (X,Y,DIAMETER);

    YT := Y + HALF_DIAMETER;
    TRIANGLE (X,YT,DIAMETER);

END;
```

Some output is shown in figure 12-5.

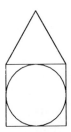

12-5. A subsystem consisting of a circle, a square, and a triangle.

Kinds of Spatial Relations

Vocabulary elements can be related to form subsystems in an infinite number of ways, but certain kinds of subsystems have always been of particular interest to architects and graphic designers. These can be characterized by their properties of symmetry.

Many vocabulary elements (circles, regular polygons, and the like) have symmetry about a point, and these are often related by making the symmetry points coincident. Figure 12-6, for example, shows some cases of a square and circle related in this way. In figure 12-6a they have the same diameter. This relationship characterizes Roman, Byzantine, and Ottoman building plans, where hemispherical domes are often placed over square spaces. In figure 12-6b the circle is much smaller than the square. We find this in the plan of Palladio's Villa Rotonda, for example, where a cylindrical central space is placed within an outer cubic mass. In figure 12-6c and d the diameters are similar but not the same, so that an interesting residual space is created between the inner and outer enclosures. Louis Kahn often used this relationship in his compositions.

It is usually convenient to parameterize procedures that draw point-symmetrical figures by the X and Y coordinates of the center point, plus a radius. Thus a concentric relationship of two such elements is established by making their center point coordinates the same, and perhaps by specifying a ratio of the two radii as well. Our next procedure, for example, draws a concentrically related pair of regular polygons. Parameters are X and Y, the numbers of sides of each polygon, and the radius of each polygon:

a. A dome over a square space.

b. A circular room at the center of a square building.

c. Residual space outside the circle.

```
PROCEDURE TWO_POLYGONS (X,Y,RADIUS_1,RADIUS_2,
                        NSIDES_1,NSIDES_2 : INTEGER);

    BEGIN

        POLYGON (X,Y,RADIUS_1,NSIDES_1);
        POLYGON (X,Y,RADIUS_1,NSIDES_2);

    END;
```

Figure 12-7 shows some output.

Where vocabulary elements have symmetry about one or more axes, they are frequently related by making the axes coincident. Figure 12-8 shows a plan composed of squares, circles, and ovals related in this way. Architects have often extended this principle by stringing many bilaterally symmetrical spaces along a circulation axis. Classical and neoclassical architects tended to

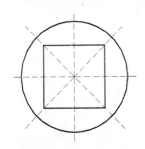

d. Residual space outside the square.

12-6. Coincident symmetry points.

keep the constituent spaces disjoint (fig. 12-9a). Baroque architects, on the other hand, often let them intersect in complex ways (fig. 12-9b).

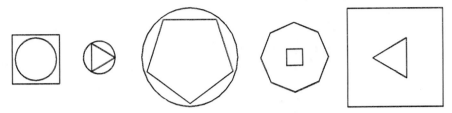

12-7. Pairs of concentric regular polygons.

Procedures that draw bilaterally symmetrical figures often take the X coordinate of the axis of symmetry as a parameter. Thus bilaterally symmetrical figures can be coaxially related by invoking their procedures with the same X value. The following procedure, for example, draws an isosceles triangle:

```
PROCEDURE ISOSCELES (X,Y,BASE,HEIGHT : INTEGER);

    VAR X1,X2,Y1 : INTEGER;

    BEGIN

        X1 := X − (BASE DIV 2);
        X2 := X1 + BASE;
        Y1 := Y + HEIGHT;

        MOVE (X1,Y);
        DRAW (X2,Y);
        DRAW (X,Y1);
        DRAW (X1,Y);

    END;
```

The next procedure invokes Isosceles three times to draw three coaxially related isosceles triangles (fig. 12-10a):

```
PROCEDURE THREE_TRIANGLES (X,Y1,Y2,Y3,BASE_1,BASE_2,BASE_3,
                           HEIGHT_1,HEIGHT_2,HEIGHT_3
                           : INTEGER);

    BEGIN

        ISOSCELES (X,Y1,BASE_1,HEIGHT_1);
        ISOSCELES (X,Y2,BASE_2,HEIGHT_2);
        ISOSCELES (X,Y3,BASE_3,HEIGHT_3);

    END;
```

This relationship of triangles was explored by Palladio in his church elevations (figs. 12-10b, c).

Another common way to relate elements is to align their edges. Consider the relationship of a large and a small square window in elevation. As shown in figure 12-11, the edges of the large window establish four axes, which divide the surrounding wall plane into eight quadrants. The small window might intersect any one of these axes on either side to yield eight possible relations.

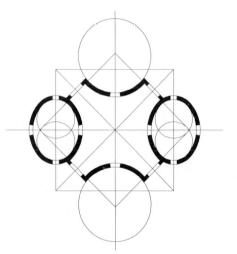

12-8. Axial relations of circles and squares in a sketch for a Lustgartengebäude in Vienna by J.B. Fischer von Erlach.

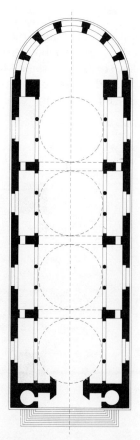

a. Classical space—clearly separated circles and squares in Schinkel's Church for the Werderschen Market in Berlin.

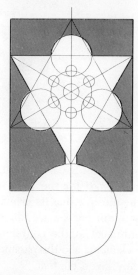

b. Baroque space—overlapping triangles, hexagons, circles, and rectangles in Borromini's S. Ivo Sapienza, Rome.

12-9. Bilaterally symmetrical figures strung along an axis.

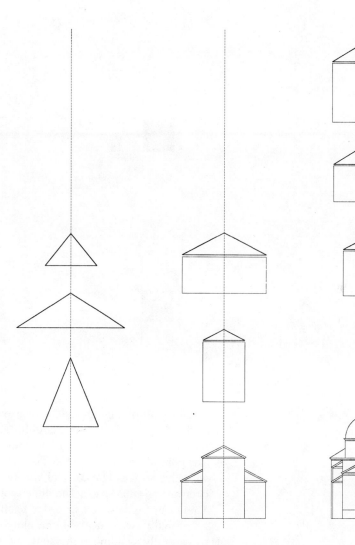

a. The principle of coaxial composition.

b. S. Giorgio Maggiore, Venice.

c. Il Redentore, Venice.

12-10. Coaxial isosceles triangles in two church elevations by Palladio.

Or the small window might be contained wholly within any one of the quadrants to yield eight more possibilities. Within any one of the quadrants, the top, bottom, or side of the small window might be on an axis; another sixteen possibilities emerge from this. If we allow the windows to touch at their edges, we obtain twelve more possibilities. And, if we allow them to touch just at their corners, we obtain another four. Finally, we might make the diagonal axes coincident.

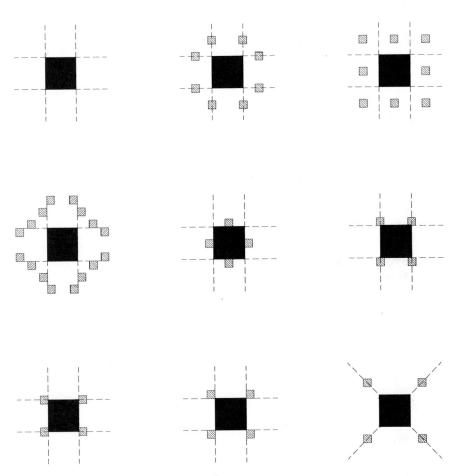

12-11. Relating a small to a large square window.

Instead of aligning edges or axes, we can choose to intersect them at an angle. Figure 12-12, for example, shows a common *parti* for the plan of a mosque. The large rectangle, forming the body of the mosque, has its principal axis pointing toward Mecca. The small rectangle is an entrance space, aligned with the street. The axes of the two rectangles intersect at the center of a circular transition space. The dimensions of the three elements and the parameter Theta can be adjusted in order to fit the plan to any given context.

Finally, we can place one element in a "floating" relationship to another by carefully avoiding coincidence of important points or alignment of axes and edges. A square, for instance, has four edges and four axes of symmetry, dividing the plane into sixteen regions outside the square and eight within it (fig. 12-13a). We can float a circle in relation to this square by placing it so

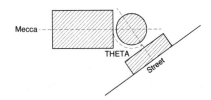

12-12. The arrangement of a mosque in relation to Mecca and to the street.

that its center point falls within any one of these regions and not on one of their boundaries, and also so that its circumference is not tangent to any one of these boundaries (fig. 12-13b). We might go further and require that the circumference does not pass through any of the intersections of axes and edge lines.

Sometimes designers make the relationships of vocabulary elements in a composition explicit by showing axes, grids, circles, and other construction lines on their drawings. Le Corbusier called these *tracés regulateurs,* and they show up on many of his early projects (fig. 12-14).

Interfaces

Now consider the column shown in figure 12-15a. It consists of a base, a shaft, and a capital (fig. 12-15b, c, d). Procedures to draw these elements might be written as follows:

```
PROCEDURE  BASE (X,Y,TOP_WIDTH  :  INTEGER);

    VAR  X1,X2,X3,X4,Y1  :  INTEGER;
         BOTTOM_WIDTH,HEIGHT,Y_TOP  :  INTEGER;

    BEGIN

        BOTTOM_WIDTH  :=  ROUND(TOP_WIDTH  *  1.5);
        HEIGHT  :=  ROUND(TOP_WIDTH  *  0.3);

        X1  :=  X  −  (BOTTOM_WIDTH  DIV  2);
        X2  :=  X1  +  BOTTOM_WIDTH;
        X3  :=  X  −  (TOP_WIDTH  DIV  2);
        X4  :=  X3  +  TOP_WIDTH;
        Y1  :=  Y  +  ROUND(HEIGHT  *  0.8);
        Y_TOP  :=  Y  +  HEIGHT;
```

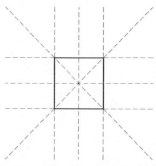

a. Axes of symmetry and edge lines.

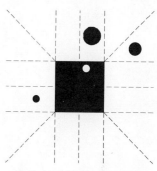

b. Circles fall between the lines.

12-13. Circles in floating relationship to a square.

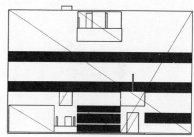

12-14. Regulating lines of Le Corbusier's Villa Garches (north elevation).

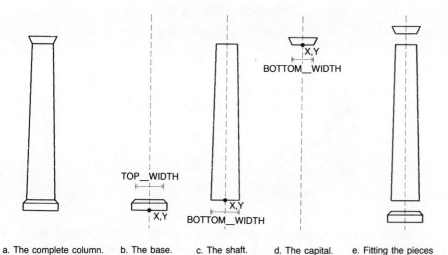

a. The complete column.   b. The base.   c. The shaft.   d. The capital.   e. Fitting the pieces together.

12-15. A column consisting of base, shaft, and capital.

```
          MOVE  (X1,Y);
          DRAW  (X2,Y);
          DRAW  (X2,Y1);
          DRAW  (X4,Y_TOP);
          DRAW  (X3,Y_TOP);
          DRAW  (X1,Y1);
          DRAW  (X1,Y);
          MOVE  (X1,Y1);
          DRAW  (X2,Y1);

       END;

PROCEDURE  SHAFT  (X,Y,BOTTOM_WIDTH  :  INTEGER);

   VAR  X1,X2,X3,X4  :  INTEGER;
        TOP_WIDTH,HEIGHT,Y_TOP  :  INTEGER;

   BEGIN

          TOP_WIDTH  :=  ROUND(BOTTOM_WIDTH  *  0.6);
          HEIGHT  :=  ROUND(BOTTOM_WIDTH  *  6.0);
          Y_TOP  :=  Y  +  HEIGHT;

          X1  :=  X  −  (BOTTOM_WIDTH  DIV  2);
          X2  :=  X1  +  BOTTOM_WIDTH;
          X3  :=  X  −  (TOP_WIDTH  DIV  2);
          X4  :=  X3  +  TOP_WIDTH;

          MOVE  (X1,Y);
          DRAW  (X3,Y_TOP);
          MOVE  (X4,Y_TOP);
          DRAW  (X2,Y);

       END;

PROCEDURE  CAPITAL  (X,Y,BOTTOM_WIDTH  :  INTEGER);

   VAR  X1,X2,X3,X4  :  INTEGER;
        TOP_WIDTH,HEIGHT,Y_TOP  :  INTEGER;

   BEGIN

          TOP_WIDTH  :=  ROUND(BOTTOM_WIDTH  *  2.0);
          HEIGHT  :=  ROUND(BOTTOM_WIDTH  *  0.7);

          X1  :=  X  −  (BOTTOM_WIDTH  DIV  2);
          X2  :=  X1  +  BOTTOM_WIDTH;
          X3  :=  X  −  (TOP_WIDTH  DIV  2);
          X4  :=  X3  +  TOP_WIDTH;
          Y_TOP  :=  Y  +  HEIGHT;

          MOVE  (X1,Y);
          DRAW  (X2,Y);
          DRAW  (X4,Y_TOP);
          DRAW  (X3,Y_TOP);
          DRAW  (X1,Y);

       END;
```

In the complete column, the base, the shaft, and the capital are in a particular spatial relation (fig. 12-15e). They are stacked on top of each other, and their axes of symmetry are coincident.

What information is needed to draw the three elements in the correct relation? To draw the base, it is necessary first to establish position and size. Then, to draw the shaft, it is also necessary to know the height and width of the base. Finally, to draw the capital, it is necessary to know the height of the shaft and (since it tapers) its width at the top. This presents a problem, since the height of the base is calculated within the procedure Base and is therefore inaccessible outside that procedure. Similarly, the height and top width of the shaft are calculated inside the procedure Shaft, and are inaccessible outside that procedure.

Variable Parameters

The need here is for a means to pass values *out* of a procedure; the converse of using the parameter list to pass values in. Pascal provides the construct of a *variable parameter* for passing the result of a computation out of a procedure. The rules for use of variable parameters are simple. First, the actual parameter must be a variable; it cannot be a number, a constant, or any other kind of expression. Second, the corresponding formal parameter must be preceded by the word **var**. Any operation within the procedure on this formal parameter will then be performed directly upon the actual parameter.

Here, now, are the headings of procedures Base, Shaft, and Capital, modified by the incorporation of variable parameters as required:

```
PROCEDURE  BASE (X,Y,TOP_WIDTH  :  INTEGER;
                  VAR  Y_TOP  :  INTEGER);

PROCEDURE  SHAFT (X,Y,BOTTOM_WIDTH  :  INTEGER;
                   VAR  Y_TOP,TOP_WIDTH  :  INTEGER);

PROCEDURE  CAPITAL (X,Y,BOTTOM_WIDTH  :  INTEGER;
                     VAR  Y_TOP,TOP_WIDTH  :  INTEGER);
```

The inputs and outputs of these three procedures now are as shown in figure 12-16.

The Syntax of a Composition

In general, the formal parameters of a procedure to draw a graphic element or a subsystem define the *interface* between that element or subsystem and the rest of the composition. The spatial relations of instances of this element or subsystem with other parts of a composition can be defined *only* in terms of these parameters. Values passed *in* to the procedure, to specify an instance, establish the spatial relations of that instance to existing parts of the composition, and values passed *out* provide information that will be needed, later, to add instances of other elements or subsystems in the required spatial relations.

Arithmetic expressions and assignments relating the values passed into procedures establish spatial relations (for example, of relative size, of spacing, of alignment, or of coincidence) between the resulting instances. The *syntax* of a composition is defined in this way.

Here, now, is a complete program to read in values for the design variables and draw a column (fig. 12-17):

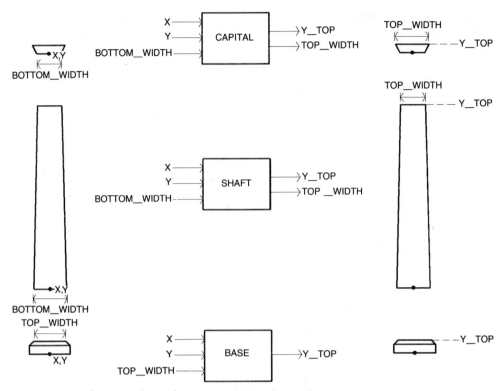

12-16. Inputs and outputs of procedures Base, Shaft, and Capital.

```
PROGRAM  BUILD;
    USES  GRAPHICS;
PROCEDURE  BASE (X,Y,TOP_WIDTH : INTEGER;
                      VAR Y_TOP : INTEGER);

    VAR  X1,X2,X3,X4,Y1 : INTEGER;
         BOTTOM_WIDTH,HEIGHT : INTEGER;

BEGIN
    BOTTOM_WIDTH := ROUND(TOP_WIDTH * 1.5);
    HEIGHT := ROUND(TOP_WIDTH * 0.4);

    X1 := X − (BOTTOM_WIDTH DIV 2);
    X2 := X1 + BOTTOM_WIDTH;
    X3 := X − (TOP_WIDTH DIV 2);
    X4 := X3 + TOP_WIDTH;
    Y1 := Y + ROUND(HEIGHT * 0.8);
    Y_TOP := Y + HEIGHT;

    MOVE (X1,Y);
    DRAW (X2,Y);
    DRAW (X2,Y1);
    DRAW (X4,Y_TOP);
    DRAW (X3,Y_TOP);
    DRAW (X1,Y1);
    DRAW (X1,Y);
    MOVE (X1,Y1);
    DRAW (X2,Y1);
END;
```

12-17. A column drawn by the procedure Column.

```
PROCEDURE  SHAFT  (X,Y,BOTTOM_WIDTH  :  INTEGER;
                        VAR  Y_TOP,TOP_WIDTH  :  INTEGER);
VAR  X1,X2,X3,X4  :  INTEGER;
     HEIGHT  :  INTEGER;

BEGIN
     TOP_WIDTH  :=  ROUND(BOTTOM_WIDTH  *  0.6);
     HEIGHT  :=  ROUND(BOTTOM_WIDTH  *  6.0);
     Y_TOP  :=  Y  +  HEIGHT;

     X1  :=  X  −  (BOTTOM_WIDTH  DIV  2);
     X2  :=  X1  +  BOTTOM_WIDTH;
     X3  :=  X  −  (TOP_WIDTH  DIV  2);
     X4  :=  X3  +  TOP_WIDTH;

     MOVE  (X1,Y);
     DRAW  (X3,Y_TOP);
     MOVE  (X4,Y_TOP);
     DRAW  (X2,Y);

END;

PROCEDURE  CAPITAL  (X,Y,BOTTOM_WIDTH  :  INTEGER;
                        VAR  Y_TOP,TOP_WIDTH  :  INTEGER);

     VAR  X1,X2,X3,X4  :  INTEGER;
          HEIGHT  :  INTEGER;

BEGIN
     TOP_WIDTH  :=  ROUND  (BOTTOM_WIDTH  *  2.0);
     HEIGHT  :=  ROUND  (BOTTOM_WIDTH  *  0.7);

     X1  :=  X  −  (BOTTOM_WIDTH  DIV  2);
     X2  :=  X1  +  BOTTOM_WIDTH;
     X3  :=  X  −  (TOP_WIDTH  DIV  2);
     X4  :=  X3  +  TOP_WIDTH;
     Y_TOP  :=  Y  +  HEIGHT;

     MOVE  (X1,Y);
     DRAW  (X2,Y);
     DRAW  (X4,Y_TOP);
     DRAW  (X3,Y_TOP);
     DRAW  (X1,Y);

END;

PROCEDURE  COLUMN  (X,Y,DIAMETER  :  INTEGER;
                        VAR  HEIGHT,TOP_WIDTH  :  INTEGER);

     VAR  Y_BASE,Y_SHAFT,Y_CAPITAL  :  INTEGER;
          TOP_SHAFT,TOP_CAPITAL  :  INTEGER;

BEGIN
     { Place column base centered at bottom around X,Y }
     BASE  (X,Y,DIAMETER,Y_BASE);

     { Place shaft centered on top of base }
     SHAFT  (X,Y_BASE,DIAMETER,Y_SHAFT,TOP_SHAFT);

     { Place capital centered on top of shaft }
     CAPITAL  (X,Y_SHAFT,TOP_SHAFT,Y_CAPITAL,
               TOP_CAPITAL);
```

```
                HEIGHT  := Y_CAPITAL;
                TOP_WIDTH := TOP_CAPITAL;

        END;

    { Main program }

        VAR  X,Y,DIAMETER,TOP_WIDTH,HEIGHT : INTEGER;

    BEGIN

            WRITELN ('ENTER COLUMN DIAMETER: ');
            READLN (DIAMETER);

            WRITELN ('ENTER X,Y COORDINATES OF BASE: ',
                        'CENTERLINE: ');
            READLN (X,Y);

            START_DRAWING;

                COLUMN (X,Y,DIAMETER,HEIGHT,TOP_WIDTH);

            FINISH_DRAWING;

    END.
```

Notice how the Pascal principle of declaring something before it can be used is followed here. Specifically, procedures must be declared before they are invoked. Where procedures are invoked from within other procedures, this means that the invoked procedure must appear, in the text of the program, before the procedure that does the invoking.

Notice also that procedure Column has two variable parameters: the height of the column and the width of the top of the capital. These are necessary if the column is to be placed in a more complex composition.

Declaration of Procedures within Procedures

Here is another way to structure our Column procedure:

```
PROCEDURE COLUMN (. . .);

        PROCEDURE BASE (. . .);
                .
                .
                .
        END;
        PROCEDURE SHAFT (. . .);
                .
                .
                .
        END;
        PROCEDURE CAPITAL (. . .);
                .
                .
                .
        END;
    BEGIN
                .
                .
                .
    END;
```

The difference here is that the procedures Base, Shaft, and Capital are declared *within* the procedure Column. The effect, as when a variable is declared within a procedure, is to make them local to that procedure. They can be invoked only from within the procedure in which they are declared. They are not accessible from outside, and any attempt to invoke them from outside will result in an error.

When should you declare graphic procedures locally, and when should you declare them globally? It depends on the specialization of the graphic element. A shaft, for example, might never appear in a composition except as part of a column. It is more expressive of the nature of this element, then, to declare procedure Shaft within procedure Column. But an arc might appear in a composition in many different contexts—as part of several different types of arches in an elevation, for example. So it makes sense to declare procedure Arc globally, so it is accessible from the different procedures that draw the various types of arches.

Hierarchies of Subsystems

Figure 12-18a illustrates a composition of two columns supporting a lintel. Each column can be thought of as a subsystem of the composition, and these subsystems have a particular spatial relationship to each other. They are of the same dimensions, and their bases are aligned along the same horizontal line. We might reasonably take the distance between the columns to be a parameter of the relationship. The next procedure, then, invokes procedure Column twice to generate a pair of columns in the appropriate relationship (fig. 12-18b):

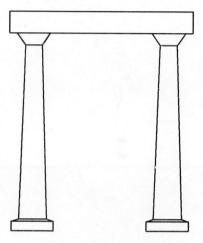

a. The complete system Frame.

```
PROCEDURE  COLUMN_PAIR  (X,Y,DIAMETER,SPACING  :  INTEGER;
                         VAR HEIGHT,TOP_WIDTH  :  INTEGER);

    VAR  BOTTOM_X,BOTTOM_Y :  INTEGER;

    BEGIN

        BOTTOM_X  :=  X  −  (SPACING  DIV  2);
        BOTTOM_Y  :=  Y;

        COLUMN  (BOTTOM_X,BOTTOM_Y,DIAMETER,HEIGHT,
              TOP_WIDTH);

        BOTTOM_X  :=  BOTTOM_X  +  SPACING;

        COLUMN  (BOTTOM_X,BOTTOM_Y,DIAMETER,HEIGHT,
              TOP_WIDTH);

    END;
```

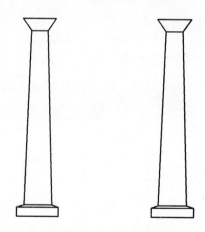

b. The Column_pair subsystem.

We can now go a step further and think of the whole composition as two subsystems, a pair of columns and a lintel related in a particular way. The lintel sits on top of the columns. Let us take the span of the lintel as a parameter and assume that depth is always one-eighth of the span (fig. 12.18c). A procedure to draw lintels of this type may be written:

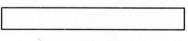

c. The Lintel subsystem.

```
PROCEDURE  LINTEL  (X_START,X_END,HEIGHT  :  INTEGER);

    VAR  DEPTH,Y :  INTEGER;
```

12-18. A system of two columns supporting a lintel.

```
BEGIN

    DEPTH := (X_END  −  X_START) DIV 8;
    Y := HEIGHT + DEPTH;

    MOVE (X_START,HEIGHT);
    DRAW (X_END,HEIGHT);
    DRAW (X_END,Y);
    DRAW (X_START,Y);
    DRAW (X_START,HEIGHT);

END;
```

Assuming the overhang of the lintel at either end is half the width of a column top, the complete composition can be generated by a procedure that invokes Column_pair and Lintel as follows:

```
PROCEDURE FRAME (X,Y,DIAMETER,SPACING : INTEGER);

  VAR X_START,X_END,HEIGHT,TOP_WIDTH : INTEGER;

  BEGIN

    { Place columns }

    COLUMN_PAIR (X,Y,DIAMETER,SPACING,HEIGHT,TOP_WIDTH);

    { Place lintel }

    X_START := X − (SPACING DIV 2) − TOP_WIDTH;
    X_END := X + (SPACING DIV 2) + TOP_WIDTH;

    LINTEL (X_START,X_END,HEIGHT);

END;
```

Notice that the heights of the columns and the widths of the tops, which are required to position the lintel correctly, are communicated from the Column procedure through the Column_pair procedure to Frame, which can then pass the values of these variables on to the Lintel procedure.

This procedure expresses rules for composing frames, using a particular vocabulary of architectural elements and a particular syntax. A designer using Frame has only to choose values for two shape variables, Diameter and Spacing, and the rules take care of everything else. The procedure Base produces a correctly proportioned base. Shaft fits a shaft correctly on top and chooses a proper height. Capital adds a correctly proportioned capital. Column_pair produces identical left and right columns, on a common baseline, the specified distance apart. Lintel generates a lintel of the required length and proportion. Finally, Frame places the lintel symmetrically on top of the columns.

A frame of this kind, governed by specific proportioning rules, is traditionally known as an architectural *order*. Figure 12-19 illustrates the proportions (as specified by Vignola) of the Tuscan, Doric, Ionic, and Corinthian orders. The procedure Frame can be modified to produce any one of these simply by altering the arithmetic expressions that define proportions. We could also substitute procedures to draw more specialized types of capitals, shafts, and so on.

The hierarchy of elements and subsystems that we have now developed is illustrated by the tree diagram in figure 12-20. Each vertex corresponds to a procedure that defines a spatial relationship between lower-level subsystems or elements. In other words, the organization of the program into procedures expresses our interpretation of the composition as a hierarchy of elements and subsystems.

Structure and Meaning

The way that we parse a graphic composition into elements and subsystems determines the *meaning* of the composition, just as the way that we parse a

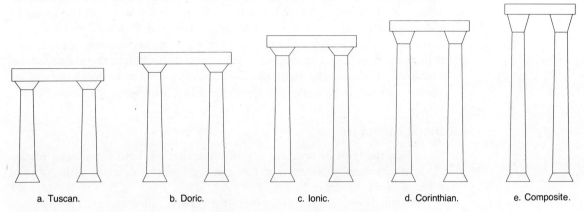

a. Tuscan.   b. Doric.   c. Ionic.   d. Corinthian.   e. Composite.

12-19. Examples of frames with a variety of proportions as specified by Vignola.

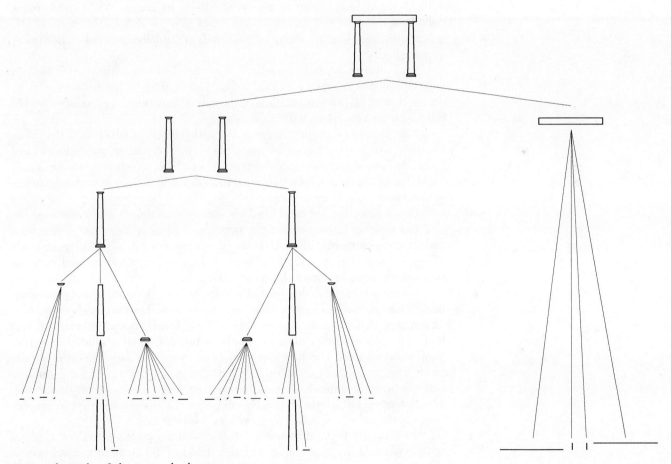

12-20. A hierarchy of elements and subsystems.

sentence determines its meaning. Individual vectors carry little specific meaning. When vectors are spatially related in particular ways, though, we can interpret them as components of bases, shafts, capitals, and lintels, and we express those interpretations in the names given to procedures: Base, Shaft, Capital, Lintel. When base, shaft, and capital are stacked coaxially, we can interpret the result as a column. When columns are paired, we can interpret the result as a subsystem capable of supporting a lintel. When the lintel is added in the correct relation, we recognize that we have a frame. In other words, the hierarchy of elements and subsystems determines the way that the meaning of the complete composition is built up from the meanings of its parts, just as the hierarchy of phrases determines the way that the meaning of a sentence is built up from the meanings of words. Procedures define the vocabulary of a graphic language, the hierarchy and interfacing of procedures defines its syntax, and the names given to procedures begin to define its semantics.

Block Structure

The principles of program organization that we have introduced in this chapter may now be summarized and generalized by describing the general rules of *block structure* in Pascal.

A Pascal program is a collection of segments called *blocks*. The program as a whole is a block. Each procedure is a block, and each function is a block. A block has a *heading*, so it can be identified by name. Within each block (following the heading) constants and types may be *defined;* then variables, procedures, and functions may be *declared,* and finally, program *actions* may be specified.

Since functions and procedures may be declared within any block, it follows that blocks may be nested within blocks. That is, procedures may be declared within procedures, functions within functions, procedures within functions, and functions within procedures.

A definition or declaration is *local* to the block in which it is declared. In other words, the names of constants, types, variables, procedures, and functions have significance only within the blocks in which they are declared. The *scope* of significance of a definition or declaration is from its first appearance to the end of the block.

Communication between blocks is strictly disciplined. The *parameter list* of a block defines the connections between a block (procedure or function) and its environment. Different kinds of parameters establish different kinds of connections. *Value parameters* allow values to be passed in, and *variable parameters* allow results to be passed out.

Where a variable is declared in a block *before* the function and procedure declarations in that block, it is *global* relative to those functions and procedures. This means that its value is accessible to these functions and procedures, and that execution of one of these functions or procedures may modify its value. Such a modification is called a *side effect* of execution. Side effects generally make a program difficult to understand, can propagate errors, and tend to make debugging difficult. It is therefore best to avoid the global declaration of variables except where absolutely necessary. Communication via parameter lists, on the other hand, keeps interfaces well defined.

To illustrate these principles, let us consider a program to draw classical temple plans of the type shown in figure 12-21a. The element and subsystem hierarchy that we shall adopt is shown in figure 12-21b. The basic vocabulary elements are Circle and Rectangle. A Column is composed of a Circle and a Rectangle. A Column_grid is composed of Columns. A Plinth is composed of Rectangles. The Cella consists of two Rectangles. The Temple consists of a Plinth, a Column_grid, and a Cella, all concentrically related.

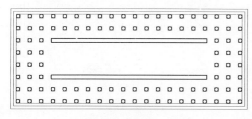

a. Type diagram.

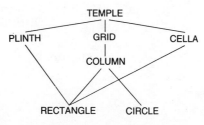

b. Hierarchy of elements and subsystems.

12-21. A classical temple plan.

Here is the complete code of the program:

```
PROGRAM DRAW_TEMPLE;

    USES GRAPHICS;

    PROCEDURE RECTANGLE (X,Y,LENGTH,WIDTH : INTEGER);

        { Draws a rectangle centered at X,Y }

        VAR X1,X2,Y1,Y2 : INTEGER;

        BEGIN

            { Calculate corner coordinates }
            X1 := X - LENGTH DIV 2;
            Y1 := Y - WIDTH DIV 2;
            X2 := X1 + LENGTH;
            Y2 := Y1 + WIDTH;

            { Draw sides of rectangle }
            MOVE (X1,Y1);
            DRAW (X2,Y1);
            DRAW (X2,Y2);
            DRAW (X1,Y2);
            DRAW (X1,Y1);

        END;

    PROCEDURE CIRCLE (XC,YC,DIAMETER : INTEGER);

        VAR DEGREES,THETA : REAL;
            X,Y,SIDES,RADIUS : INTEGER;
        CONST RADIANS = 0.01745;
              NSIDES = 40;

        BEGIN

            RADIUS := DIAMETER DIV 2;

            { Calculate angle increment in radians }
            DEGREES := (360.0 / NSIDES) * RADIANS;

            THETA := 0;
```

```
                { Move to starting point }
                  MOVE  (XC + RADIUS,YC);

                { Draw sides of circle }
                  FOR SIDES := 1 TO NSIDES DO
                  BEGIN

                       THETA := THETA + DEGREES;
                       Y := ROUND(RADIUS * SIN(THETA)) + YC;
                       X := ROUND(RADIUS * COS(THETA)) + XC;

                       DRAW (X,Y);

                  END;

            END;


    PROCEDURE  COLUMN (X,Y,DIAMETER : INTEGER);

        BEGIN

            { Creates column by placing a circle inside a square }

                RECTANGLE (X,Y,DIAMETER,DIAMETER);
                CIRCLE (X,Y,DIAMETER);

        END;

    PROCEDURE  PLINTH (X,Y,LENGTH,WIDTH,STEPS,STEP_SIZE :
                           INTEGER);

        VAR COUNT : INTEGER;

        BEGIN

            { Creates steps by nesting rectangles }

                FOR COUNT := 1 TO STEPS DO
                BEGIN

                     RECTANGLE (X,Y,LENGTH,WIDTH);
                     LENGTH := LENGTH + STEP_SIZE;
                     WIDTH := WIDTH + STEP_SIZE;

                END;

        END;


    PROCEDURE  CELLA (X,Y,LENGTH,DIAMETER,WIDTH : INTEGER);

        BEGIN

            { Creates a cella of two rectangles }

                RECTANGLE (X,Y,LENGTH,DIAMETER);
                Y := Y + WIDTH;
                RECTANGLE (X,Y,LENGTH,DIAMETER);

        END;

    PROCEDURE  GRID (X_INITIAL,Y_INITIAL,SPACING,
                       DIAMETER,NX,NY,X_START,X_FINISH,
                       Y_START,Y_FINISH : INTEGER);

        FUNCTION  OUTSIDE (COUNT_X,COUNT_Y,X_START,
                             X_FINISH,Y_START,Y_FINISH :
                               INTEGER) : BOOLEAN;
```

```
        BEGIN
            OUTSIDE := ((COUNT_X < X_START) OR
                       (COUNT_X > X_FINISH) OR
                       (COUNT_Y < Y_START) OR
                       (COUNT_Y > Y_FINISH));
        END;

    VAR X,Y,COUNT_X,COUNT_Y : INTEGER;

    BEGIN

      { Draws grid of columns with interior left empty as
        defined by X_START,X_FINISH,Y_START, and Y_FINISH }

        Y := Y_INITIAL;

        FOR COUNT_Y := 1 TO NY DO
        BEGIN

            X := X_INITIAL;

            FOR COUNT_X := 1 TO NX DO
            BEGIN

                IF OUTSIDE (COUNT_X,COUNT_Y,X_START,
                           X_FINISH,Y_START,Y_FINISH)
                THEN COLUMN (X,Y,DIAMETER);

                X := X + SPACING;

            END;

            Y := Y + SPACING;

        END;
    END;

PROCEDURE TEMPLE (X,Y,SPACING,DIAMETER,NX,NY,X_START,
                 X_FINISH,Y_START,Y_FINISH,STEPS,
                 STEP_SIZE : INTEGER);

  { Draws temple composed of grid, plinth and cella }

    VAR LENGTH,WIDTH,X_INITIAL,Y_INITIAL : INTEGER;

    BEGIN
      { Calculate dimensions of plinth }
        WIDTH := (NY-1)*SPACING + DIAMETER;
        LENGTH := (NX-1)*SPACING + DIAMETER;

        PLINTH (X,Y,LENGTH,WIDTH,STEPS,STEP_SIZE);

      { Place grid of columns inside plinth }
        X_INITIAL := X - (NX-1)*SPACING DIV 2;
        Y_INITIAL := Y - (NY-1)*SPACING DIV 2;

        GRID (X_INITIAL,Y_INITIAL,SPACING,DIAMETER,NX,NY,
             X_START,X_FINISH,Y_START,Y_FINISH);

      { Place cella in open space in grid }
        WIDTH := (Y_FINISH - Y_START) * SPACING;
        LENGTH := (X_FINISH - X_START) * SPACING +
                 DIAMETER;
        Y_INITIAL := Y - WIDTH DIV 2;
        CELLA (X,Y_INITIAL,LENGTH,DIAMETER,WIDTH);
    END;
```

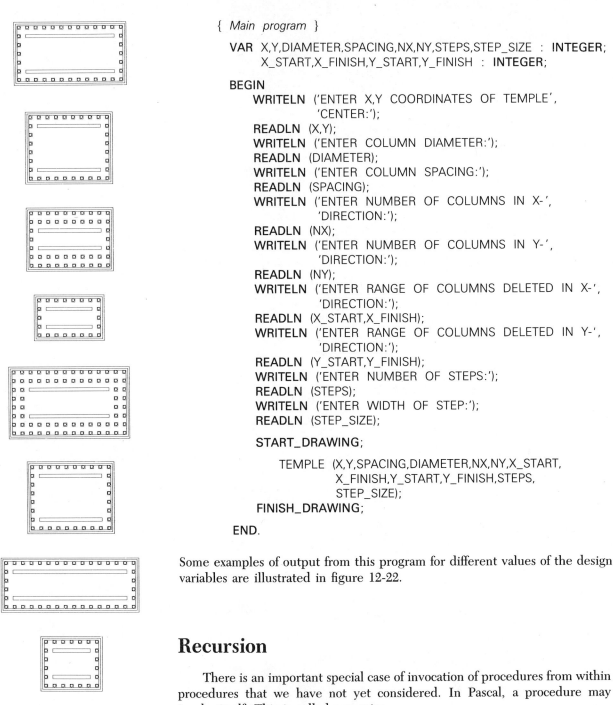

```
{ Main program }
    VAR  X,Y,DIAMETER,SPACING,NX,NY,STEPS,STEP_SIZE : INTEGER;
         X_START,X_FINISH,Y_START,Y_FINISH : INTEGER;

BEGIN
    WRITELN ('ENTER X,Y COORDINATES OF TEMPLE',
             'CENTER:');
    READLN (X,Y);
    WRITELN ('ENTER COLUMN DIAMETER:');
    READLN (DIAMETER);
    WRITELN ('ENTER COLUMN SPACING:');
    READLN (SPACING);
    WRITELN ('ENTER NUMBER OF COLUMNS IN X-',
             'DIRECTION:');
    READLN (NX);
    WRITELN ('ENTER NUMBER OF COLUMNS IN Y-',
             'DIRECTION:');
    READLN (NY);
    WRITELN ('ENTER RANGE OF COLUMNS DELETED IN X-',
             'DIRECTION:');
    READLN (X_START,X_FINISH);
    WRITELN ('ENTER RANGE OF COLUMNS DELETED IN Y-',
             'DIRECTION:');
    READLN (Y_START,Y_FINISH);
    WRITELN ('ENTER NUMBER OF STEPS:');
    READLN (STEPS);
    WRITELN ('ENTER WIDTH OF STEP:');
    READLN (STEP_SIZE);

    START_DRAWING;

        TEMPLE (X,Y,SPACING,DIAMETER,NX,NY,X_START,
                X_FINISH,Y_START,Y_FINISH,STEPS,
                STEP_SIZE);
    FINISH_DRAWING;

END.
```

Some examples of output from this program for different values of the design variables are illustrated in figure 12-22.

Recursion

There is an important special case of invocation of procedures from within procedures that we have not yet considered. In Pascal, a procedure may invoke itself. This is called *recursion*.

Let us begin by considering a very simple example. The following program draws patterns of concentric squares (fig. 12-23a).

```
PROGRAM NEST;

    USES GRAPHICS;

    PROCEDURE SQUARE (X,Y,SIDE : INTEGER);

        VAR X1,X2,Y1,Y2 : INTEGER;
```

12-22. Instances of classical temple plans.

```
            BEGIN
                { Draw square centered at X,Y }
                X1 := X − SIDE DIV 2;
                Y1 := Y − SIDE DIV 2;
                X2 := X1 + SIDE;
                Y2 := Y1 + SIDE;

                    MOVE (X1,Y1);
                    DRAW (X2,Y1);
                    DRAW (X2,Y2);
                    DRAW (X1,Y2);
                    DRAW (X1,Y1);

            END;
    PROCEDURE NESTED_SQUARE (X,Y,SIDE : INTEGER);
        BEGIN

            { Draw the shape }
            SQUARE (X,Y,SIDE);

            { Apply the construction rule }
            SIDE := SIDE DIV 2;

            { Test whether to stop }
            IF SIDE > 4 THEN
                NESTED_SQUARE (X,Y,SIDE);

        END;
    { Main program }
        BEGIN

            START_DRAWING;

                NESTED_SQUARE (512,512,512);

            FINISH_DRAWING;

        END.
```

a. The complete pattern.

b. The initial shape.

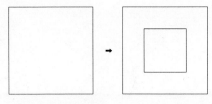

c. The construction rule.

12-23. A recursively constructed pattern of concentric squares.

Notice how the procedure Nested_square invokes itself.

A recursive graphic procedure, such as Nested_square, is best understood in terms of its *initial shape*, its *construction rule*, and its *limit*. In our example, the initial shape is a square centered at 512,512, of side length 512, as specified by the actual parameters passed into Nested square (12-23b). The construction rule is to place a square of half its predecessor's size concentrically within its predecessor (fig. 12-23c). This spatial relationship is expressed, within Nested_square, by the statement:

```
SIDE := SIDE DIV 2;
```

The limit tells when to stop applying the construction rule. In this case the limit is specified in the code of Nested_square by the **Boolean** expression:

```
SIDE > 4
```

What actually happens when the recursive procedure Nested_square executes? Let us trace the execution step by step. When Nested_square is first invoked, Side has the initial value of 512, and the initial shape is drawn.

The construction rule is then applied, so the value of Side becomes 256. Since this is greater than 4 (the limit), Nested_square invokes itself. The second invocation of Nested_square draws a square with Side of 256, then applies the construction rule to reduce Side to 128, tests against the limit, and invokes Nested_square. This process continues, as follows:

Invocation number	From	Value of Side
1	NEST	512
2	NESTED_SQUARE 1	256
3	NESTED_SQUARE 2	128
4	NESTED_SQUARE 3	64
5	NESTED_SQUARE 4	32
6	NESTED_SQUARE 5	16
7	NESTED_SQUARE 6	8

Finally, Nested_square is invoked with a value of 8 for Side. Application of the construction rule then reduces the value of Side to 4, the limit is reached, and this seventh invocation ends. Control then passes back to the sixth invocation, which ends, and so on, all the way back to the first invocation. This ends, and control passes back to Nest.

Another nonrecursive way to generate the same composition of nested squares is to use a **while** loop:

```
PROCEDURE NESTED_SQUARE (X,Y,SIDE : INTEGER);

    BEGIN

        WHILE SIDE > 4 DO
        BEGIN

            SQUARE (X,Y,SIDE);
            SIDE := SIDE DIV 2;

        END;

    END;
```

The program using recursion and the program using the **while** loop are are both clear and concise. There are, however, many situations in which use of recursion provides the clearest, shortest, and most natural way to express the logic of a graphic composition.

Trees

Generally, you should consider use of recursion when you can see that a complex composition can be generated by the application of a simple construction rule to some initial shape. Look at the branching tree shown in figure 12-24, for example. The initial shape is a **V**-shaped pair of branches. The construction rule is simply to add a **V**-shaped pair of branches to each preceding branch. Thus branches divide and grow at their tips, much as real trees grow. Here is a simple recursive procedure to generate trees in this way:

```
PROCEDURE BRANCH (X,Y,LENGTH,START_ANGLE,ANGLE,
                  MINIMUM : INTEGER;
                  RATIO : REAL);
```

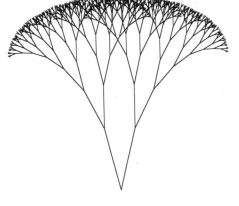

12-24. A symmetrical recursively constructed tree.

```
VAR  X1,X2,Y1,Y2 : INTEGER;
     START_LEFT,START_RIGHT : INTEGER;
     THETA1,THETA2 : REAL;
CONST RADIANS = 0.01745;

BEGIN

  { Calculate endpoints of branches }
    THETA1 := START_ANGLE − ANGLE;
    X1 := X + ROUND(LENGTH * COS(THETA1*RADIANS));
    Y1 := Y + ROUND(LENGTH * SIN (THETA1*RADIANS));
    THETA2 := START_ANGLE + ANGLE;
    X2 := X + ROUND(LENGTH * COS(THETA2*RADIANS));
    Y2 := Y + ROUND(LENGTH * SIN (THETA2*RADIANS));

  { Draw V-shaped branch }
    MOVE (X1,Y1);
    DRAW (X,Y);
    DRAW (X2,Y2);

  { Branch }
    LENGTH := ROUND(LENGTH * RATIO);
    IF LENGTH > MINIMUM THEN
      BEGIN

        START_LEFT := START_ANGLE − ANGLE;
        BRANCH (X1,Y1,LENGTH,START_LEFT,ANGLE,
                MINIMUM,RATIO);

        START_RIGHT := START_ANGLE + ANGLE;
        BRANCH (X2,Y2,LENGTH,START_RIGHT,ANGLE,
                MINIMUM,RATIO);

      END;

  END;
```

The design variables here are Length of the initial branches, Angle of the **V**, Ratio of a branch's length to its predecessor's length, and Minimum size for a branch (to establish the limit). By entering different values for these design variables, you can generate a very wide variety of trees.

The trees generated by this procedure are too regular to look entirely natural. This can be remedied to some extent by allowing the lengths and angles of the two sides of a **V** to vary independently (fig. 12-25). Here is the corresponding modified procedure:

```
PROCEDURE BRANCH (X,Y,LENGTH1,LENGTH2,START_ANGLE,
                  ANGLE1,ANGLE2,MINIMUM : INTEGER;
                  RATIO : REAL) ;

VAR  X1,X2,Y1,Y2 : INTEGER;
     START_LEFT,START_RIGHT : INTEGER;
     THETA1,THETA2 : REAL;
CONST RADIANS = 0.01745;

BEGIN

  { Calculate endpoints of branches }
    THETA1 := START_ANGLE − ANGLE1;
    X1 := X + ROUND(LENGTH1 * COS(THETA1*RADIANS));
    Y1 := Y + ROUND(LENGTH1 * SIN (THETA1*RADIANS));
```

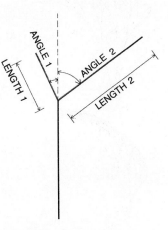

12-25. The independent variation of branch lengths and angles.

```
THETA2 := START_ANGLE + ANGLE2;
X2 := X + ROUND(LENGTH2 * COS(THETA2*RADIANS));
Y2 := Y + ROUND(LENGTH2 * SIN (THETA2*RADIANS));

{ Draw V-shaped branch }
MOVE (X1,Y1);
DRAW (X,Y);
DRAW (X2,Y2);

{ Branch }
LENGTH1 := ROUND(LENGTH1 * RATIO);
LENGTH2 := ROUND(LENGTH2 * RATIO);
IF (LENGTH1 > MINIMUM) AND (LENGTH2 > MINIMUM)
   THEN BEGIN

        START_LEFT := START_ANGLE − ANGLE1;
        BRANCH (X1,Y1,LENGTH1,LENGTH2,START_LEFT,
                ANGLE1,ANGLE2,MINIMUM,RATIO);

        START_RIGHT := START_ANGLE + ANGLE2;
        BRANCH (X2,Y2,LENGTH1,LENGTH2,START_RIGHT,
                ANGLE1,ANGLE2,MINIMUM,RATIO);

        END;

   END;
```

Figure 12-26 shows some typical results for different values of the parameters.

A further improvement can be made by allowing random choice (within limits) of lengths and angles for branches. We can use the random number generator that was introduced in chapter 11:

```
PROCEDURE  BRANCH (X,Y,MIN_LENGTH,MAX_LENGTH,
                   START_ANGLE,MIN_ANGLE,MAX_ANGLE,
                   MINIMUM : INTEGER;
                   RATIO : REAL);

VAR X1,X2,Y1,Y2 : INTEGER;
    LENGTH1,LENGTH2,ANGLE1,ANGLE2 : INTEGER;
    START_LEFT,START_RIGHT : INTEGER;
    THETA1,THETA2 : REAL;
CONST RADIANS = 0.01745;

BEGIN

  { Randomly select branch angles and lengths }

  LENGTH1 := RANDOM_NUMBER(0,MIN_LENGTH,
                           MAX_LENGTH);
  LENGTH2 := RANDOM_NUMBER(0,MIN_LENGTH,
                           MAX_LENGTH);
  ANGLE1 := RANDOM_NUMBER(0,MIN_ANGLE,MAX_ANGLE);
  ANGLE2 := RANDOM_NUMBER(0,MIN_ANGLE,MAX_ANGLE);

  { Calculate endpoints of branches }
  THETA1 := START_ANGLE − ANGLE1;
  X1 := X + ROUND(LENGTH1 * COS(THETA1*RADIANS));
  Y1 := Y + ROUND(LENGTH1 * SIN (THETA1*RADIANS));
  THETA2 := START_ANGLE + ANGLE2;
  X2 := X + ROUND(LENGTH2 * COS(THETA2*RADIANS));
  Y2 := Y + ROUND(LENGTH2 * SIN (THETA2*RADIANS));
```

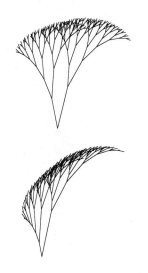

12-26. Instances of recursively constructed asymmetrical trees.

```
{ Draw V-shaped branch }
    MOVE (X1,Y1);
    DRAW (X,Y);
    DRAW (X2,Y2);

{ Branch }
    MIN_LENGTH := ROUND(MIN_LENGTH * RATIO);
    MAX_LENGTH := ROUND(MAX_LENGTH * RATIO);
    IF  MIN_LENGTH > MINIMUM
        THEN
        BEGIN

            START_LEFT := START_ANGLE − ANGLE1;
            BRANCH (X1,Y1,MIN_LENGTH,MAX_LENGTH,
                    START_LEFT,MIN_ANGLE,MAX_ANGLE,
                    MINIMUM);
            START_RIGHT := START_ANGLE + ANGLE2;
            BRANCH (X2,Y2,MIN_LENGTH,MAX_LENGTH,
                    START_RIGHT,MIN_ANGLE,MAX_ANGLE,
                    MINIMUM);

        END;

    END;
```

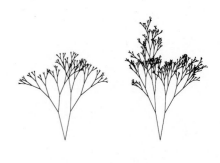

Each time that Branch is invoked, Length1, Angle1, Length2, and Angle2 have different, randomly chosen, values. Pascal automatically keeps track of these values. In a nonrecursive version you would have to declare variables to record them. Branching terminates when a value for Length1 or for Length2 that is less than or equal to the specified minimum is generated. Figure 12-27 shows some results.

12-27. Trees generated by a recursive procedure incorporating a random number generator.

Recursive Subdivision

Figure 12-28 introduces another type of composition that can be generated by means of a recursive procedure. It is a slightly simplified plan of the famous garden of the Taj Mahal (as it existed originally). This type of plan is produced by recursively subdividing a square into four squares by paths in the form of a +. Here is a procedure to generate such plans:

```
PROCEDURE DIVIDE (X_CENTER,Y_CENTER,DIAMETER,WIDTH,
                  MINIMUM : INTEGER;
                  RATIO : REAL);

VAR X1,Y1,X2,Y2,X3,Y3,X4,Y4 : INTEGER;
    HALF_DIAMETER,HALF_WIDTH,D4 : INTEGER;
    NEW_DIAMETER : INTEGER;

BEGIN

    HALF_DIAMETER := DIAMETER DIV 2;
    HALF_WIDTH := WIDTH DIV 2;

{ Draw path }

    X1 := XCENTER − HALF_DIAMETER;
    X2 := XCENTER − HALF_WIDTH;
    X3 := X_CENTER + HALF_WIDTH;
    X4 := X_CENTER + HALF_DIAMETER;
```

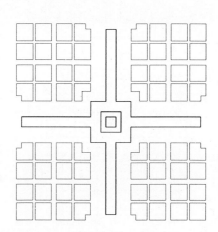

12-28. A schematic plan of the garden of the Taj Mahal, Agra.

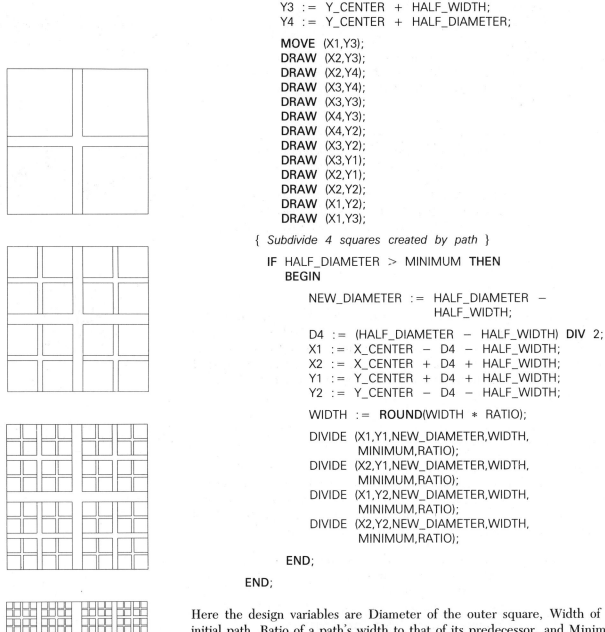

```
Y1 := Y_CENTER − HALF_DIAMETER;
Y2 := Y_CENTER − HALF_WIDTH;
Y3 := Y_CENTER + HALF_WIDTH;
Y4 := Y_CENTER + HALF_DIAMETER;

MOVE (X1,Y3);
DRAW (X2,Y3);
DRAW (X2,Y4);
DRAW (X3,Y4);
DRAW (X3,Y3);
DRAW (X4,Y3);
DRAW (X4,Y2);
DRAW (X3,Y2);
DRAW (X3,Y1);
DRAW (X2,Y1);
DRAW (X2,Y2);
DRAW (X1,Y2);
DRAW (X1,Y3);

{ Subdivide 4 squares created by path }

IF HALF_DIAMETER > MINIMUM THEN
  BEGIN

    NEW_DIAMETER := HALF_DIAMETER −
                    HALF_WIDTH;

    D4 := (HALF_DIAMETER − HALF_WIDTH) DIV 2;
    X1 := X_CENTER − D4 − HALF_WIDTH;
    X2 := X_CENTER + D4 + HALF_WIDTH;
    Y1 := Y_CENTER + D4 + HALF_WIDTH;
    Y2 := Y_CENTER − D4 − HALF_WIDTH;

    WIDTH := ROUND(WIDTH * RATIO);

    DIVIDE (X1,Y1,NEW_DIAMETER,WIDTH,
            MINIMUM,RATIO);
    DIVIDE (X2,Y1,NEW_DIAMETER,WIDTH,
            MINIMUM,RATIO);
    DIVIDE (X1,Y2,NEW_DIAMETER,WIDTH,
            MINIMUM,RATIO);
    DIVIDE (X2,Y2,NEW_DIAMETER,WIDTH,
            MINIMUM,RATIO);

  END;

END;
```

Here the design variables are Diameter of the outer square, Width of the initial path, Ratio of a path's width to that of its predecessor, and Minimum size for a square. Figure 12-29 shows a few of the possible outputs.

Notice the very close similarity in organization of the procedures that generate the tree and Taj Mahal garden. Although the types of objects that they generate look very different, the underlying constructive logic is much the same.

12-29. Recursively generated garden plans of the Taj Mahal type.

Alternative Structures

So far in our examples we have chosen obvious and natural ways to break drawings down into hierarchies of elements and subsystems. But it is important to remember that there are always alternative ways to define this hierarchy, and that different spatial relations of elements and subsystems may be taken to be the essential ones. Consider the plan *parti* shown in figure 12-30. We might reasonably interpret the central part as "a circle nested within a square"; there are two elements, and the essential relationship between them is of concentricity and equality of diameter. The design variables become the X and Y coordinates of the center point and Diameter.

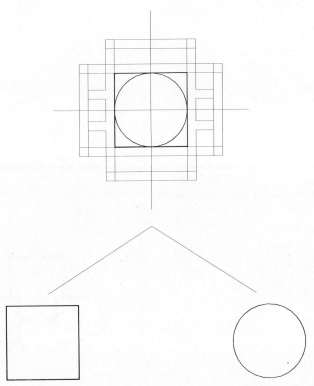

12-30. One obvious way to parse a simple composition (after a *parti* by J.N.L. Durand).

Another way to parse this composition is shown in figure 12-31. Now there are two different subsystems, each consisting of two elements, and the design variables are X, Y, Top_width, Top_height, Bottom_width, Bottom_height, Arc_diameter, and Arc_spacing; we can generate variants such as those illustrated in figure 12-32.

Some English sentences may also be parsed in alternative ways, and each alternative yields a different interpretation. A famous example is:

> Time flies like an arrow.

It seems most natural to take "flies" as the verb, but you can also take "like" as the verb, to yield a sentence describing the dietary preferences of "time flies," or you can take "time" as the verb, to yield an imperative. Similarly, in graphic compositions, parsing in different ways yields different interpretations. Since even simple graphic compositions can be parsed in alternative ways, the semantic properties of graphic languages are rich and complex. By committing ourselves to a particular hierarchy of elements and subsystems, expressed as a hierarchy of named procedures, we radically simplify and clarify the semantics.

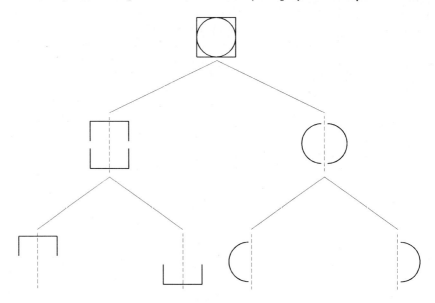

12-31. An alternative way to parse the composition.

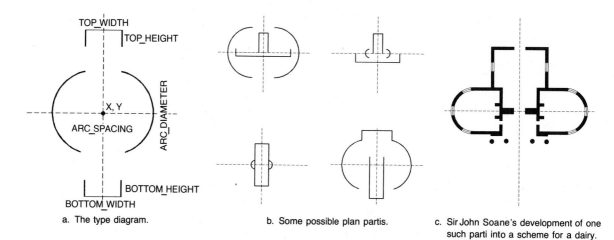

a. The type diagram.

b. Some possible plan partis.

c. Sir John Soane's development of one such parti into a scheme for a dairy.

12-32. Variants generated according to the alternative method of parsing the composition in figure 12-30.

Top-Down Programming

When you write a program to generate a complex composition of elements and subsystems, it is usually best to work *top-down*. Begin with a procedure that puts together the whole thing from two or more major subsystems. Within this top-level procedure, define the names of the major subsystems, their parameters, and their spatial relations. Write very schematic, "dummy" versions of the procedures to generate these major subsystems (draw them just as rectangles, for example), and make sure that this version of your program runs correctly.

Next, write fully developed versions of the procedures to generate the major subsystems. Within these, define the names and parameters of the lower-level subsystems from which they are composed, and establish the spatial relations of the lower-level subsystems. Using "dummy" versions of the procedures for the lower-level subsystems, check that this elaborated version of your program works correctly. Now repeat the process for the lower-level subsystems, and so on through a sequence of increasingly refined versions of your program, until you reach the procedures to draw the lowest-level vocabulary elements.

This parallels the common design strategy of working down to the details from an initial, rough sketch of the whole. It has several important advantages. You always have a running program, and you can always see the whole composition. Design variables are introduced one by one in a systematic way. And you can, at any point, choose not to refine any further.

Summary

In this chapter we have explored the ways in which graphic compositions can usefully be broken down into hierarchies of elements and subsystems. We have seen how such hierarchies are expressed directly in the block structures established by procedure declarations in graphics programs. The value parameters of procedures allow position and shape information to be passed in to blocks, and the variable parameters allow position and shape information to be passed out. This information is used to relate elements and subsystems correctly to each other; the spatial relations of the elements and subsystems of a composition are specified by means of arithmetic expressions and assignments relating the values of parameters.

Exercises

1. All of the elements and subsystems of the Doric order have names (fig. 12-33). Draw a tree diagram that depicts this hierarchy. Then write a program, structured in the same way, that generates the order. (Simplify the details where necessary to reduce the task to manageable proportions.)

2. The elements and subsystems of traditional Chinese timber construction also have standard names (fig. 12-34). Draw the corresponding tree diagram; write a program that expresses this structure to generate a drawing of the section of such a building. Take advantage of the recursive pattern of the bracket system. (Once again, simplify the details as necessary.)

3. An example of gothic tracery, as drawn by Eugène Viollet-le-Duc, is illustrated in figure 12-35. Work out a reasonable way to break this design down into a hierarchy of elements and subsystems, and draw the tree diagram. Write a program, structured in this way, that generates a single-line diagram of the design. Then, if you want to go further, elaborate it to show the thickness and detailing of the tracery members.

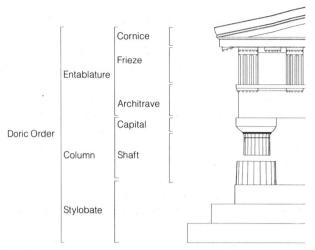

12-33. Well-defined hierarchy of elements and subsystems—all with traditional names—in the Doric order.

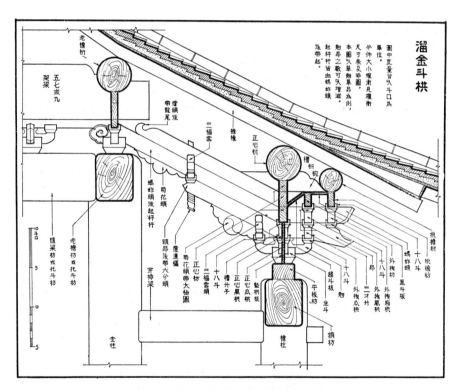

12-34. Named elements and subsystems in traditional Chinese timber construction.

4. The French architectural theorist Jean Nicholas-Louis Durand produced many beautiful plates demonstrating how architectural compositions could be understood as "combinations" built up from lower-level vocabulary elements. Figure 12-36 shows an example. Select one of Durand's combinations for careful analysis. What are the parts and subparts? What are the essential spatial relations? What are the design variables? On the basis of your analysis, write a program that generates an interesting series of variants on this architectural theme. Use a top-down programming strategy that parallels the sequence of refinement steps by Durand.

12-35. The analysis of gothic tracery by Viollet-le-Duc.

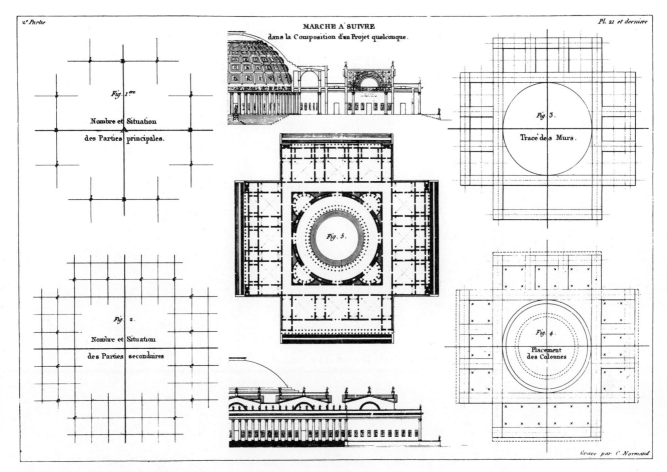

MARCHE A SUIVRE
dans la Composition d'un Projet quelconque.

Pl. 21 et dernière

Fig. 1.ᵉʳ

Nombre et Situation

des Parties principales.

Fig. 3.

Tracé des Murs.

Fig. 2.

Nombre et Situation

des Parties secondaires

Fig. 5.

Fig. 4.

Placement
des Colonnes

Gravé par C. Normand.

12-36. The combination of vocabulary elements, as illustrated by Durand.

5. Another of Durand's plates is shown in figure 12-37. This one shows a set of plan *partis*—"skeletons" of axes and simple geometric figures that are used to establish the essential spatial relations in a plan. Select one of these *partis* and, using a simple vocabulary of wall and column elements, write a program that generates variant plans based on it.

6. Figure 12-38 illustrates a tree drawn in plan. Write a recursive procedure that generates trees of this type. Make the depth of the recursion (the number of levels of branching) one of the design variables.

7. Gothic tracery is often recursive (fig. 12-39). That is, a large pointed arch is subdivided into two smaller pointed arches, each of which is further subdivided in the same way, and so on. Write a recursive procedure to generate such tracery designs.

8. We have seen how principles of architectural and graphic composition can be expressed in terms of the control constructs of Pascal: block structure, conditionals, repetition, and recursion. An alternative approach is to express rules of composition as productions organized in a production system (Stiny 1980). Compare the advantages and disadvantages of the two approaches.

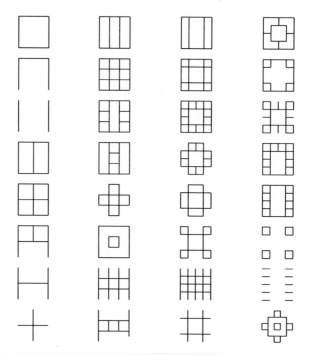

12-37. Plan partis, as illustrated by Durand.

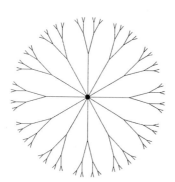

12-38. A tree in plan.

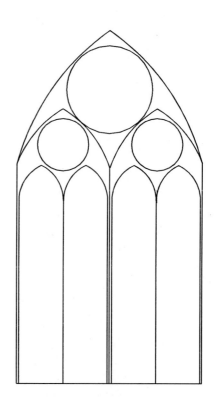

12-39. Gothic window tracery.

PART THREE
Advanced Techniques

13.

Storing Pictures:
Data Structures

Scalar, Structured, and Pointer Data Types

Until now all of the programs, procedures, and functions that we have considered have operated on variables that store either a single **integer** value, a single **real** value, a single **Boolean** value, or a single character. **Integer**, **real**, **Boolean**, and **character** are called the standard *unstructured* or *scalar* data types of Pascal. We have also seen that special scalar data types may be defined in the type definition part of a program. A scalar variable is much like a labeled pigeonhole, which stores a single item. The label is the variable's name, and the single item stored is its value.

Often, though, we store many data items together in some organized or structured way. A dictionary, for example, lists words and their definitions in alphabetical order. A table of distances between cities arrays numbers in rows and columns. A shopping list has a sequence of entries.

Similarly, it is often convenient to make use of structured data types in computer programming. Just as structured statements (compound statements, loops, and conditionals) are composed of more elementary statements, structured data types are composed of more elementary data types. Different structured data types are characterized, then, by the types of their components and by their structuring methods.

Pascal provides a rich variety of structured data types: **arrays**, **records**, **files**, and **sets**, plus a class of structures created using **pointers**. A Pascal program can operate on both scalar variables and on structures of these various types. Structures, like scalar variables, are first declared, then used.

In this chapter we shall introduce and then explore some uses in graphics of each of the Pascal structured data types.

Arrays

One-dimensional arrays are the simplest of all the structured data types. An **array** is a structure with a fixed number of components. The number of components is defined when the **array** is declared. You use **arrays**, then, when you know how many individual values you want to store.

Each component of an **array** is a variable in its own right. It may be assigned a value, and it may be referenced. All the components of an **array** are of the same type. So, for example, we can have **integer arrays**, **real arrays**, and **Boolean arrays**. The type of the components is defined when the **array** is declared.

Components are distinguished from each other and referred to by means of their *indexes*. A one-dimensional **array** is much like a row of serially numbered pigeonholes (fig. 13-1). The number of each pigeonhole (array component) is its index.

Here we shall always use subranges of the **integers** (1 . . 12 in our example) as indexes of **arrays**. Pascal does allow other possibilities, however; you can look these up in the Pascal texts listed in the Bibliography. The indexes, like the number and type of components, are specified when the **array** is declared.

Here, then, is the declaration for the one-dimensional **array** shown in figure 13-1:

RAINFALL : **ARRAY**[1..12] **OF INTEGER**;

An alternative approach is to define an **array** type, then declare a variable of that type:

TYPE TWELVE = **ARRAY** [1..12] **OF INTEGER**;
VAR RAINFALL : TWELVE;

This **array** stores rainfall figures for the twelve months of the year. The declaration first gives the **array** name, in this case Rainfall, followed by a colon. The word **array** then appears. Next comes a specification of the indexes that are to be used to reference components of the **array**; that is, the integers in the range 1 . . 12. This also establishes that there are twelve components in the **array**. Finally, it is specified that the components are all of type **integer**.

Note that square brackets are used in this declaration. Square brackets are not available on all computers, however, so some Pascal compilers accept the alternative:

RAINFALL : **ARRAY**(.1..12.) **OF INTEGER**;

Values may be assigned to **array** components in the same way that they are assigned to scalar variables, for example:

RAINFALL[3] := 5;

This specifies a value of 5 for the Rainfall in month 3. The index, between square brackets, selects the individual component to which the value is to be assigned.

Array components may, like scalar variables, appear in expressions, for example:

FIRST_QUARTER := RAINFALL[1] + RAINFALL[2] + RAINFALL[3];

Here the indexes select the individual components to be accessed.

To illustrate the use of this **array**, here is a simple program that reads in rainfall figures for the twelve months, stores them in Rainfall, sums them, and prints out the total:

PROGRAM RAIN;

```
    VAR RAINFALL: ARRAY [1..12] OF INTEGER;
        MONTH,SUM : INTEGER;
BEGIN
    FOR MONTH := 1 TO 12 DO
    BEGIN
        WRITELN ('ENTER RAINFALL FOR MONTH: ',MONTH);
        READLN (RAINFALL[MONTH]);
    END;
    SUM := 0;
    FOR MONTH :=1 TO 12 DO
        SUM := SUM + RAINFALL[MONTH];
    WRITELN ('TOTAL RAINFALL FOR 12 MONTHS IS', SUM :
            8:0);
END.
```

Here, now, is a graphic example. This program reads in rainfall figures, then draws a bar chart of them:

```
PROGRAM BARCHART;
    USES GRAPHICS;
    PROCEDURE BAR (X,Y,BAR_WIDTH,BAR_HEIGHT : INTEGER);
    VAR X1,Y1 : INTEGER;
    BEGIN
        X1 := X + BAR_WIDTH;
        Y1 := Y + BAR_HEIGHT;
        { Draw bar of specified height and width }
        MOVE (X,Y);
        DRAW (X1,Y);
        DRAW (X1,Y1);
        DRAW (X,Y1);
        DRAW (X,Y);
    END;
{ Main program }
VAR RAINFALL : ARRAY[1..12] OF INTEGER;
    MONTH,MAX_RAIN,X,Y : INTEGER;
    BAR_WIDTH,BAR_HEIGHT : INTEGER;
    SCALE : REAL;
BEGIN
    { Read in monthly rainfall values }
    FOR MONTH := 1 TO 12 DO
    BEGIN
        WRITELN ('ENTER RAINFALL FOR MONTH: ',MONTH);
        READLN (RAINFALL[MONTH]);
    END;
    { Determine maximum value }
```

```
MAX_RAIN := 0;
FOR MONTH := 1 TO 12 DO
    IF RAINFALL[MONTH] > MAX_RAIN THEN
        MAX_RAIN := RAINFALL[MONTH];
```

{ Set scale factor for bar chart }

```
SCALE := 500.0 / MAX_RAIN;
```

{ Draw bar chart }

```
START_DRAWING;
    X := 100;
    Y := 100;
    BAR_WIDTH := 50;

    FOR MONTH := 1 TO 12 DO
    BEGIN

        BAR_HEIGHT := ROUND(RAINFALL[MONTH] * SCALE);
        BAR (X,Y,BAR_WIDTH,BAR_HEIGHT);
        X := X + 75;

    END;

FINISH_DRAWING;
END.
```

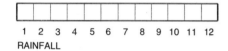

1 2 3 4 5 6 7 8 9 10 11 12
RAINFALL

13-1. A one-dimensional **array.**

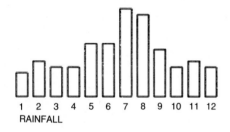

1 2 3 4 5 6 7 8 9 10 11 12
RAINFALL

13-2. A bar chart drawn by the program Bar-chart, with values as shown in figure 13-1.

Figure 13-2 shows some output.

Notice in these examples how **for** loops are used for **array** manipulation. First, a **for** loop counting from 1 to 12 is used to read in the 12 values. **For** loops are then used to step through the **array** to add up the values and to draw the bars. Since **for** loops and **arrays** use indexes in analogous ways, they go together naturally.

The program to add up rainfall figures served to introduce the idea of an **array**, but you may have noticed that it was not strictly necessary to use an **array** in this program. We could simply have kept a running total as we went along:

```
PROGRAM RAIN;

    VAR MONTH,RAINFALL,SUM : INTEGER;

BEGIN

    SUM := 0;

    FOR MONTH := 1 TO 12 DO
    BEGIN

        WRITELN ('ENTER RAINFALL FOR MONTH: ',MONTH);
        READLN (RAINFALL);
        SUM := SUM + RAINFALL;

    END;

    WRITELN ('TOTAL RAINFALL FOR 12 MONTHS IS', SUM);

END.
```

In the program to draw the bar graph, however, it was necessary to have an **array**, since we wanted to complete the input process and set a scale factor before drawing the graph. All twelve values therefore had to be available after exit from the input loop.

An **array** is generally convenient, or even essential, when two conditions are met. First, an array is useful when we must keep all of the components of some sequence of values available for use in later computations—rainfall figures for successive months, heights for successive points along a topographic section, or widths of successive windows across an elevation. Second, it is appropriate to store these values in an **array** when it is difficult or impossible to simply recompute them when needed. Rainfall figures vary arbitrarily; there is no formula by which we can calculate, say, Rainfall[9] as needed. We must therefore store Rainfall values. But we would not store successive values of some simple function of X, say **sqrt**(X), because we can easily obtain them by executing the statement,

    Y := SQRT(X);

within a **for** loop, whenever they are needed.

Two-dimensional Arrays

Figure 13-3a illustrates a line of evenly spaced rectangular windows of varying heights and widths. How might you store these height and width values? It is natural to use a table (fig. 13-3b). Each *row* of the table corresponds to an instance of the window. The first *column* stores widths, and the second column stores heights. This is a simple example of a *two-dimensional array*.

Here is a program that reads values for height and width into a two-dimensional **array**, then draws the corresponding line of windows:

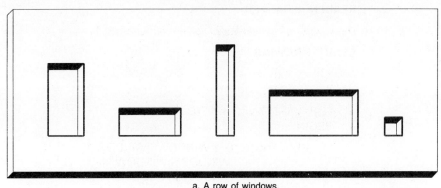

a. A row of windows.

	WIDTH	HEIGHT
1	50	100
2	80	40
3	20	120
4	120	60
5	20	20

b. Widths and heights stored in a two-dimensional **array**.

13-3. The use of a two-dimensional array.

```
PROGRAM  WINDOWS;
    USES  GRAPHICS;
    PROCEDURE  RECTANGLE (X,Y,LENGTH,WIDTH : INTEGER);
        VAR X1,Y1 : INTEGER;
        BEGIN
            X1 := X + LENGTH;
            Y1 := Y + WIDTH;

            MOVE (X,Y);
            DRAW (X1,Y);
            DRAW (X1,Y1);
            DRAW (X,Y1);
            DRAW (X,Y);

        END;

    VAR WINDOWS : ARRAY[1..5,1..2] OF INTEGER;
        WINDOW,X,Y,SPACING : INTEGER;
    BEGIN
      { Read in table of window dimensions }
        FOR WINDOW := 1 TO 5 DO
        BEGIN
            WRITELN ('ENTER WIDTH AND HEIGHT OF WINDOW:',
                    WINDOW);
            READLN (WINDOWS[WINDOW,1],WINDOWS[WINDOW,2]);
        END;
      { Read in spacing between windows }
        WRITELN ('ENTER SPACING BETWEEN WINDOWS:');
        READLN (SPACING);
      { Draw row of windows of given dimensions }
        START_DRAWING;
            X := 100;
            Y := 100;

            FOR WINDOW := 1 TO 5 DO
            BEGIN
                RECTANGLE (X,Y,WINDOWS[WINDOW,1],
                        WINDOWS[WINDOW,2]);
                X := X + WINDOWS[WINDOW,1] +
                SPACING;

            END;

        FINISH_DRAWING;
    END.
```

Notice that the two-dimensional **array** is declared as follows:

WINDOWS : **ARRAY**[1..5,1..2] **OF INTEGER;**

This specifies that there are five rows in the **array** (corresponding to the five windows), and that each row has two columns. As the form of the declaration implies, a two-dimensional **array** may be thought of as an **array** of one-dimensional **arrays**—just as a pair of nested loops is a loop of loops.

Two-dimensional **arrays** with two columns are particularly useful, in graphics programs, for storing arbitrary curves. Each row defines a point; the first column stores the X coordinate, and the second column stores the Y coordinate. Here is a program that reads in twenty points, then connects successive points to draw the corresponding arbitrary curve:

```
PROGRAM CURVE;

    USES GRAPHICS;

    VAR COORDINATE: ARRAY[1..20,1..2] OF INTEGER;
        POINT : INTEGER;

    BEGIN

      { Read in list of X,Y coordinates }

      FOR POINT := 1 TO 20 DO
      BEGIN
          WRITELN ('ENTER X,Y COORDINATES OF POINT: ',
                  POINT);
          READLN (COORDINATE[POINT,1],COORDINATE[POINT,2]);
      END;

    { Draw curve }

      START_DRAWING;

        { Move to first point }

        MOVE (COORDINATE[1,1],COORDINATE[1,2]);

        { Draw to subsequent points }

        FOR POINT := 2 TO 20 DO
            DRAW (COORDINATE[POINT,1],COORDINATE[POINT,2]);

      FINISH_DRAWING;

    END.
```

Figure 13-4a shows an example of values in the **array**, and figure 13-4b illustrates the corresponding curve.

The next program stores then draws an arbitrary composition of triangles. Since it takes six values to define a triangle, there are six columns in the **array**. The code is as follows:

```
PROGRAM TRIANGLES;

    USES GRAPHICS;

    VAR COORDINATE: ARRAY[1..5,1..6] OF INTEGER;
        TRIANGLE,POINT : INTEGER;

    BEGIN

        FOR TRIANGLE := 1 TO 5 DO
        BEGIN

            WRITELN ('TRIANGLE: ',TRIANGLE);

            FOR POINT := 1 TO 3 DO
            BEGIN
                WRITELN ('ENTER X,Y COORDINATES OF POINT: ',
                        POINT);
```

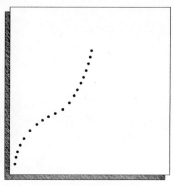

	X	Y
1	40	60
2	50	100
3	60	120
4	80	180
5	100	220
6	140	260
7	180	300
8	220	330
9	260	360
10	300	380
11	340	400
12	380	440
13	420	480
14	440	520
15	460	560
16	470	600
17	480	640
18	490	680
19	500	720
20	505	760

a. An **array** of coordinate values.

b. The corresponding curve.

13-4. Storing a curve in an array.

```
                  READLN (COORDINATE[TRIANGLE,(POINT − 1)*2 + 1],
                          COORDINATE[TRIANGLE,(POINT − 1)*2 + 2]);

            END;

        END;

        START_DRAWING;

            FOR TRIANGLE := 1 TO 5 DO
            BEGIN
                MOVE (COORDINATE[TRIANGLE,1],
                      COORDINATE[TRIANGLE,2]);
                DRAW (COORDINATE[TRIANGLE,3],
                      COORDINATE[TRIANGLE,4]);
                DRAW (COORDINATE[TRIANGLE,5],
                      COORDINATE[TRIANGLE,6]);
                DRAW (COORDINATE[TRIANGLE,1],
                      COORDINATE[TRIANGLE,2]);

            END;

        FINISH_DRAWING;

    END.
```

An example of the **array** with values assigned to all components is shown in figure 13-5a and the corresponding drawing in figure 13-5b.

	1	2	3	4	5	6
1	128	336	256	448	272	240
2	224	352	576	432	736	176
3	768	400	896	416	784	288
4	192	96	272	176	336	106
5	736	112	880	208	880	244

a. Vertex coordinates stored in an **array**.

b. The corresponding composition of triangles.

13-5. Storing an arbitrary composition of triangles.

The general principle illustrated by these examples is that a two-dimensional **array** is a natural mechanism for storing compositions of elements of the same type. Each row of the **array** describes an instance, and there are as many columns as the graphic type has parameters. The **array** is interpreted as a drawing by a loop in which the appropriate graphic procedure is invoked.

Storing Complete Drawings

Perhaps the most important use of two-dimensional **array**s in graphics programming is to store complete drawings in point-by-point fashion (fig. 13-6). A simple drawing is shown in figure 13-6a, and the **move** and **draw**

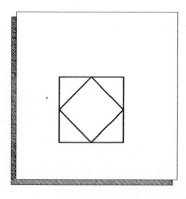

		X	Y
1	0	275	225
2	1	675	225
3	1	675	625
4	1	275	625
5	1	275	225
6	0	475	225
7	1	675	425
8	1	475	625
9	1	275	425
10	1	475	225

```
MOVE(275,225);
DRAW(675,225);
DRAW(675,625);
DRAW(275,625);
DRAW(275,225);
MOVE(475,225);
DRAW(675,425);
DRAW(475,625);
DRAW(275,425);
DRAW(475,225);
```

a. The drawing.

b. Representation by a sequence of **move** and **draw** commands.

c. Representation by an **array** of coordinates.

13-6. Alternative ways to represent a drawing.

commands needed to generate it are listed in figure 13-6b. Each **move** or **draw** command conveys three pieces of information:

- **Move** or **draw** specifies whether movement to the next point is to be made invisibly or visibly.
- The first parameter specifies the X coordinate.
- The second parameter specifies the Y coordinate.

Figure 13-6c shows a three-column **integer array** that stores exactly the same information:

- A value of 0 in the first column specifies that movement to the next point is to be made invisibly, and a value of 1 specifies that movement is to be made visibly.
- The value in the second column specifies the X coordinate.
- The value in the third column specifies the Y coordinate.

The sequence of **move** and **draw** commands encodes the drawing procedurally, as a sequence of actions (marking operations). The **array** encodes the drawing in a data structure as a sequence of values.

The **array** must be interpreted as a sequence of marking operations to actually produce a drawing. The following loop does it:

```
FOR POINT := 1 TO 10 DO
    IF POINTS[POINT,1] = 0 THEN
        MOVE (POINTS[POINT,2],POINTS[POINT,3])
    ELSE
        DRAW (POINTS[POINT,2],POINTS[POINT,3]);
```

Conversely, any graphics program can be modified to fill up an **array** with coordinate values, rather than to generate a drawing directly. Here, for example, is a simple program that executes **move** and **draw** commands to generate the drawing in figure 13-6a:

```
PROGRAM NEST_SQUARES;

    USES GRAPHICS;

BEGIN

    START_DRAWING;

        MOVE (275,225);
        DRAW (675,225);
        DRAW (675,625);
        DRAW (275,625);
        DRAW (275,225);
        MOVE (475,225);
        DRAW (675,425);
        DRAW (475,625);
        DRAW (275,425);
        DRAW (475,225);

    FINISH_DRAWING;

END.
```

A modified version first fills up the **array** of Points, then interprets this **array** to generate the drawing:

```
PROGRAM NEST_SQUARES;

    USES GRAPHICS;

    VAR POINTS : ARRAY [1..10,1..3] OF INTEGER;
        POINT : INTEGER;

BEGIN

    { Fill up array of points }
        POINTS[1,1] := 0;
        POINTS[1,2] := 275;
        POINTS[1,3] := 225;
        POINTS[2,1] := 1;
        POINTS[2,2] := 675;
        POINTS[2,3] := 225;
        POINTS[3,1] := 1;
        POINTS[3,2] := 675;
        POINTS[3,3] := 625;
        POINTS[4,1] := 1;
        POINTS[4,2] := 275;
        POINTS[4,3] := 625;
        POINTS[5,1] := 1;
        POINTS[5,2] := 275;
        POINTS[5,3] := 225;
        POINTS[6,1] := 0;
        POINTS[6,2] := 475;
        POINTS[6,3] := 225;
        POINTS[7,1] := 1;
        POINTS[7,2] := 675;
        POINTS[7,3] := 425;
        POINTS[8,1] := 1;
        POINTS[8,2] := 475;
        POINTS[8,3] := 625;
```

```
POINTS[9,1]  :=  1;
POINTS[9,2]  :=  275;
POINTS[9,3]  :=  425;
POINTS[10,1]  :=  1;
POINTS[10,2]  :=  475;
POINTS[10,3]  :=  225;
```

{ *Generate drawing* }

```
START_DRAWING;
    FOR  POINT  :=  1  TO  10  DO
        IF  POINTS[POINT,1]  =  0  THEN
            MOVE  (POINTS[POINT,2],POINTS[POINT,3])
        ELSE
            DRAW  (POINTS[POINT,2],POINTS[POINT,3]);
FINISH_DRAWING;

END.
```

The two versions of the program are functionally equivalent; they produce exactly the same output. So why go to all the trouble of creating and interpreting the **array**?

In this case, there is, in fact, no need for the **array**. But we do need the **array** if we want to operate on the drawing in some way before displaying it. For example, we might want to map all of the coordinates of a drawing onto the nearest points in a grid of some specified, coarser resolution. The following program first fills up the **array** of points, then reads in a value of grid resolution, and reinterprets the data structure to produce a new drawing to coarser resolution:

```
PROGRAM  COARSE_GRID;

    USES  GRAPHICS;

  { Global  data  structure }

    VAR  POINTS  :  ARRAY[1..10,1..3]  OF  INTEGER;
         POINT  :  INTEGER;

    FUNCTION  COARSE  (SIZE,FINE  :  INTEGER)  :  INTEGER;
        BEGIN
            COARSE  :=  ROUND(FINE/SIZE)  *  SIZE;
        END;

    PROCEDURE  FILL;

      { Fills  up  array  of  points }

        BEGIN

            POINTS[1,1]  :=  0;

                    .

                    .

                    .

        END;

    PROCEDURE  DISPLAY  (SIZE  :  INTEGER);

      { Displays  set  of  points  for  value  of  grid  resolution }

        VAR  X,Y  :  INTEGER;
```

```
BEGIN
    FOR  POINT  : =  1  TO  17  DO
    BEGIN
            X  : =  COARSE(SIZE,POINTS[POINT,2]);
            Y  : =  COARSE(SIZE,POINTS[POINT,3]);
            IF  POINTS[POINT,1]  =  0  THEN
                MOVE  (X,Y)
            ELSE
                DRAW  (X,Y);
    END;
END;
{ Main program }
    VAR  SIZE  :  INTEGER;
BEGIN
    { Fill array of points }
    FILL;
    { Read in value for grid resolution }
    WRITELN ('ENTER GRID RESOLUTION:');
    READLN (SIZE);
    START_DRAWING;
        { Display drawing at new resolution }
        DISPLAY (SIZE);
    FINISH_DRAWING;
END.
```

a. As defined initially in a 4 by 4 grid.

b. Mapped onto a 5 by 5 grid.

c. Mapped onto a 6 by 6 grid.

d. Mapped onto a 7 by 7 grid.

13-7. A drawing displayed at different grid resolutions.

Some examples of output for various values of resolution are shown in figure 13-7.

This type of program can be very useful in the design of architectural floor plans and elevations, because it allows you to explore how a plan or elevation type appears when it is mapped onto planning grids of different dimensions.

Arrays with Arbitrary Numbers of Entries

Sometimes we do not know how many points there will be in a drawing, so we do not know the dimension of the **array** needed to store it. In this case, we can simply declare a large **array** and fill up as much as we need. However, we must then keep a count of the number of entries, so that we can appropriately control the loops that operate on and interpret the **array**.

To illustrate these techniques, here is a program that reads in the vertex coordinates for an irregular polygon with an arbitrary number of sides, then draws the polygon:

```
PROGRAM POLYGON;

    USES GRAPHICS;

    VAR POINTS : ARRAY[1..100,1..2] OF INTEGER;
        POINT,N_POINTS ; INTEGER;

    BEGIN

        { Input coordinates of polygon }

            WRITELN ('ENTER NUMBER OF SIDES OF POLYGON:');
            READLN (N_POINTS);

            FOR POINT := 1 TO N_POINTS DO
            BEGIN
                WRITELN ('ENTER X,Y COORDINATES OF VERTEX:
                        POINT);
                READ (POINTS[POINT,1],POINTS[POINT,2]);

            END;

        { Close polygon }

            N_POINTS := N_POINTS +1;
            POINTS[N_POINTS,1] := POINTS[1,1];
            POINTS[N_POINTS,2] := POINTS[1,2];

        { Draw polygon }

            START_DRAWING;

                MOVE (POINTS[1,1]POINTS[1,2]);

                FOR POINT := 2 TO N_POINTS DO
                    DRAW (POINTS[POINT,1],POINTS[POINT,2]);

            FINISH_DRAWING;

    END.
```

Figure 13-8 shows a polygon drawn by this program, together with the corresponding state of the **array**. Notice that a third column of the **array**, indicating the distinction between **move** and **draw**, is not necessary, since an invisible **move** is made only to the first vertex of the polygon.

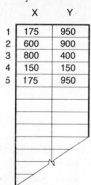
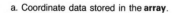

a. Coordinate data stored in the **array**.

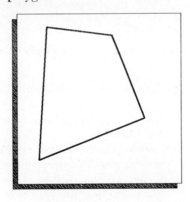

b. The corresponding polygon.

13-8. A polygon drawn by program Polygon.

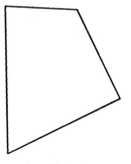

a. An unfilled polygon.

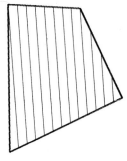

b. A polygon filled with hatching.

13-9. The polygon fill operation.

If the dimensions of the **array** are made too large, then memory space will be wasted. But, if the dimensions are made too small, then the **array** may overflow, generating an error in the execution of the program. This suggests that an **array** may not be the best data structure to use when it is difficult to tell what the dimensions should be. Later in this chapter we shall consider other structures that can be used instead.

Simple Polygon Filling Using Arrays

Once we have a graphic entity, such as a polygon, stored in an **array**, we can operate on it in many different ways. One useful operation on a polygon, for example, is to fill it with hatching (fig. 13-9). There is a simple way to do this, and it will be worthwhile to examine it in detail.

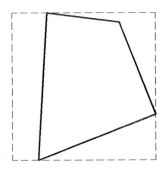

a. Find the bounding rectangle.

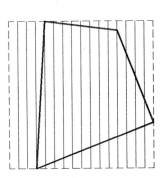

b. Use a loop to hatch.

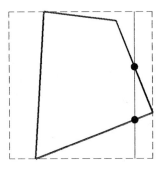

c. Find intersections with edges.

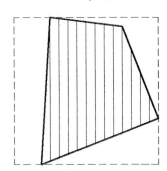

d. Draw only the portions of hatch lines that are inside the polygon.

13-10. The basic steps in a polygon fill procedure.

The basic steps are illustrated in figure 13-10.

- Scan through the polygon's coordinate **array** to find its bounding rectangle (fig. 13-10a).
- Use a loop to "hatch" the bounding rectangle. The hatching may be horizontal, vertical, or at an angle; the spacing can vary (fig. 13-10b).
- Within this loop, find all of the intersections of a given hatch line with the edges of the polygon (fig. 13-10c). Where the hatch line goes through a vertex, it is counted as two intersections.
- When drawing the hatch line, **move** to the first intersection, **draw** to the second intersection, then **move** to the third intersection, then **draw** to the fourth intersection, and so on (fig. 13-10d).

These steps are analogous to those that a draftsman might perform using a parallel rule.

The code for a procedure to find the bounding rectangle of a polygon is as follows:

```
PROCEDURE BOUND (VAR MIN_X,MAX_X,MIN_Y,MAX_Y :
                      INTEGER);

  { Finds the minimum and maximum X,Y values of the
    bounding rectangle of polygon defined by points }
  BEGIN

    { Set bounds equal to coordinates of first point }
      MIN_X := POINTS[1,1];
      MAX_X := POINTS[1,1];
      MIN_Y := POINTS[1,2];
      MAX_Y := POINTS[1,2];

      FOR POINT := 2 TO N_POINTS DO
      BEGIN

        IF POINTS[POINT,1] < MIN_X THEN
          MIN_X := POINTS[POINT,1]
        ELSE IF POINTS[POINT,1] > MAX_X THEN
          MAX_X := POINTS[POINT,1];
        IF POINTS[POINT,2] < MIN_Y THEN
          MIN_Y := POINTS[POINT,2]
        ELSE IF POINTS[POINT,2] > MAX_Y THEN
          MAX_Y := POINTS[POINT,2];

      END;

  END;
```

A loop to hatch this bounding rectangle with vertical lines now looks like this:

```
X := MIN_X + SPACING;

WHILE X < MAX_X DO
BEGIN

    MOVE (X,Y_MIN);
    DRAW (X,Y_MAX);
    X := X + SPACING;

END;
```

To hatch with horizontal rather than vertical lines, the Y coordinate rather than the X coordinate can be incremented. It is not difficult to generalize so that the hatching is at an arbitrary angle Theta.

If the polygon to be hatched is actually a rectangle with sides parallel to the coordinate axes, then there are no further steps to perform. The following program, then, reads in the dimensions and location of such a rectangle, together with Spacing and Theta, and draws a hatched rectangle:

```
PROGRAM HATCH;

  USES GRAPHICS;

  VAR MIN_X,MAX_X,MIN_Y,MAX_Y,SPACING : INTEGER;
```

```
                X,Y,LENGTH,WIDTH,X1,Y1,X2,Y2 : INTEGER;
                THETA,SLOPE,A : REAL;
        CONST RADIANS = 0.01745;
        BEGIN
            WRITELN ('ENTER X,Y COORDINATES OF BOTTOM,LEFT ',
                     'CORNER OF RECTANGLE:');
            READLN (X,Y);

            WRITELN ('ENTER LENGTH AND WIDTH OF RECTANGLE:');
            READLN (LENGTH,WIDTH);

            WRITELN ('ENTER ANGLE OF HATCHING:');
            READLN (THETA);

            WRITELN ('ENTER SPACING OF HATCHING:');
            READLN (SPACING);
          { Calculate X,Y boundaries of rectangle }
            MIN_X := X;
            MAX_X := X + LENGTH;
            MIN_Y := Y;
            MAX_Y := Y + WIDTH;
          { Make sure theta is between 0 and 90 }
            IF THETA >= 180 THEN THETA := THETA - 180;
            IF THETA > 90 THEN THETA := THETA - 90;

            START_DRAWING;
          { Draw Rectangle }
            RECTANGLE (X,Y,LENGTH,WIDTH);
          { Horizontal hatching }
            IF THETA = 0 THEN
            BEGIN
                Y := MIN_Y + SPACING;
                WHILE Y < MAX_Y DO
                BEGIN
                    MOVE (MIN_X,Y);
                    DRAW (MAX_X,Y);
                    Y := Y + SPACING;
                END;
            END
          { Vertical hatching }
            ELSE IF THETA = 90 THEN
            BEGIN
                X := MIN_X + SPACING;

                WHILE X < MAX_X DO
                BEGIN
                    MOVE (X,MIN_Y);
                    DRAW (X,MAX_Y);
                    X := X + SPACING;
                END;
            END
```

```
{ Angle of hatch between 0 and 90 }
  ELSE BEGIN
    { Calculate slope of hatch lines }
      SLOPE := SIN(THETA*RADIANS) /
               COS(THETA*RADIANS);
    { Calculate intercept of first line }
      A := MAX_Y − SLOPE * MIN_X;
    { Calculate intersection with bottom of rectangle }
      X := ROUND((MIN_Y − A) / SLOPE);
      X := X + SPACING;
    WHILE X < MAX_X DO
    BEGIN
        A := MIN_Y − SLOPE*X;
      { Calculate endpoints of hatch line }
        X1 := X;
        Y1 := MIN_Y;
      { If point X1,Y1 outside rectangle, clip }
        IF X1 < MIN_X THEN
          BEGIN
              X1 := MIN_X;
              Y1 := ROUND(A + SLOPE*X1);
          END;
        X2 := ROUND(MAX_Y − A) / SLOPE);
        Y2 := MAX_Y;
      { If point X2,Y2 outside rectangle, clip }
        IF X2 > MAX_X THEN
          BEGIN
              X2 := MAX_X;
              Y2 := ROUND(A + SLOPE*X2);
          END;
      { Draw line }
        MOVE (X1,Y1);
        DRAW (X2,Y2);
        X := X + SPACING;
    END;
  END;
  FINISH_DRAWING;
END.
```

Figure 13-11 shows some results.

    Where the polygon has a more complex shape, so that steps three and four of the method for filling must be executed, the procedure becomes considerably more complicated. We will come back to this later, when the more advanced data-structuring techniques that we must use have been introduced.

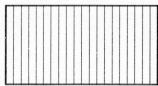

13-11. Hatched rectangles.

Arrays of Three and More Dimensions

The idea of an **array** may be generalized still further. A three-dimensional **array** is an **array** of **arrays** of **arrays**. It may be thought of as a box, in which each cubical cell stores a value (fig. 13-12).

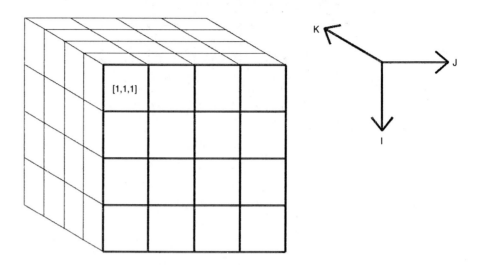

13-12. A three-dimensional **array**.

The declaration of the **array** illustrated takes the following form:

THREE_D : **ARRAY**[1..4,1..4,1..4] **OF INTEGER**;

Four-dimensional **arrays**, and so on, can be declared in analogous fashion. We shall mostly be concerned, here, with one- and two-dimensional **arrays** and shall not find uses for **arrays** of three or more dimensions. If you are interested, most standard Pascal programming texts provide extensive discussions.

PERSON

NAME	AGE	WEIGHT
JANE DOE	22	130.5

13-13. An example of a **record**.

Records

An **array** is a *homogeneous* data structure; all of the components, as we have seen, must be of the same data type. An obvious generalization is a structure that allows components to be of different data types. The Pascal **record** structure provides for this. A **record** is something like a one-dimensional **array** (fig. 13-13), except that the components can be of different types. Some components might be **integer**, some might be **real**, and others might be **Boolean** or **character**.

The components of a **record** are called its *fields*. Fields do not have indexes as do **array** components. They have, instead, *field identifiers*, which are like variable or procedure names. You cannot compute the field identifier as you can compute an array index; you must specify it directly.

A **record** must be defined as a new data type in the type definition part of a program, function, or procedure. The definition must specify a type identifier, as well as a field identifier and type for each field. The **record** illustrated in figure 13-13, for example, is called Person, and it has fields for Name, Age, and Weight. Its definition is as follows:

```
TYPE  PERSON  =
     RECORD
          NAME    : ARRAY[1..16] OF CHAR;
          AGE     : INTEGER;
          WEIGHT : REAL
     END;
```

Note the syntax. The type identifier Person comes first, followed by =. Fields are defined, in sequence, between the delimiters **record** and **end**. Each field is specified by its identifiers (for example, Name), followed by a colon, then the data type.

Once a **record** type has been defined in the type definition part, any number of variables of this type may be declared in the variable declaration part:

```
VAR  MAN,WOMAN,CHILD  :  PERSON;
```

It is often useful to have an **array** of **record**s:

```
VAR  EMPLOYEES  :  ARRAY[1..100] OF PERSON;
```

A field of a **record** is denoted by the **record** variable identifier, followed by a period, then the field name. So an assignment is written like this:

```
MAN.AGE  :=  39;
```

Or an arithmetic expression might be written:

```
TOTAL  :=  MAN.WEIGHT  +  WOMAN.WEIGHT;
```

Let us consider an example of a different nature. The following definition establishes a **record** type called Screen_point:

```
TYPE  SCREEN_POINT  =
     RECORD
          X  :  0..1023;
          Y  :  0..1023
     END;
```

The types of the components are subranges of **integer**, and each **record** of type Screen_point represents a point in our integer screen coordinate system.

Refer to the earlier example of a program to read coordinate values into an **array** of type **integer**, and draw out the corresponding curve. Here is a revised version of that program, using an **array** called Coordinate of type Screen_point:

```
                PROGRAM CURVE;

                    USES GRAPHICS;

                    TYPE SCREEN_POINT =
                        RECORD
                            X ; 0..1023;
                            Y : 0..1023
                        END;

                    VAR COORDINATE : ARRAY [1..20] OF SCREEN_POINT;
                        POINT : INTEGER;

                BEGIN

                    { Read in list of X,Y coordinates }

                    FOR POINT := 1 TO 20 DO
                    BEGIN

                        WRITELN ('ENTER X,Y COORDINATES OF POINT: ',
                                    POINT);
                        READLN (COORDINATE[POINT].X,COORDINATE[POINT].Y);

                    END;

                    { Draw curve }

                    START_DRAWING;

                        { Move to first point }

                        MOVE (COORDINATE[1].X,COORDINATE[1].Y);

                        { Draw to subsequent points }

                        FOR POINT := 2 TO 20 DO
                            DRAW (COORDINATE[POINT].X,
                                    COORDINATE[POINT].Y);

                    FINISH_DRAWING;

                END.
```

This version has two advantages. First, the more extensive use of descriptive names makes it clearer and easier to read. Second, the Pascal system, at execution, automatically checks that values assigned to Coordinate are within the allowable range and gives an appropriate error message if they are not.

The With Statement

The Pascal **with** statement can be used to simplify references to record fields, as illustrated in this revision of the program Curve.

```
                PROGRAM CURVE;

                    USES GRAPHICS;

                    TYPE SCREEN_POINT =
                        RECORD
                            X : 0..1023;
                            Y : 0..1023
                        END;

                    VAR COORDINATE : ARRAY [1..20] OF SCREEN_POINT;
                        POINT : INTEGER;
```

```
BEGIN
   { Read in list of X,Y coordinates }
      FOR POINT := 1 TO 20 DO
      BEGIN
         WRITELN ('ENTER X,Y COORDINATES OF POINT: ',
                  POINT);
         WITH COORDINATE[POINT] DO READLN (X,Y);
      END;
   { Draw curve }
      START_DRAWING;
         { Move to first point }
            WITH COORDINATE[1] DO MOVE (X,Y);
         { Draw to subsequent points }
            FOR POINT := 2 TO 20 DO
               WITH COORDINATE[POINT] DO DRAW (X,Y);
      FINISH_DRAWING;
END.
```

The **with** applies to the statement that follows it. The effect is to establish a reference to each **record** variable listed after the reserved word **with**, and this reference exists during execution of the statement that follows.

Our earlier example program to draw nested squares can also be rewritten to use **record**s instead of **array**s. It had an integer array called Points, which was used to store X and Y coordinates, together with codes of 0 or 1 to specify whether movements to the next point were to be visible or invisible. Each row of this **array** might be replaced by a **record**, defined as follows:

```
TYPE GRAPHIC =
   RECORD
      VISIBLE : BOOLEAN;
      X : 0..1023;
      Y : 0..1023
   END;
```

Points now becomes an **array** of **record**s of type Graphic. Here, then, is a new version of our program that fills up an array of points and then interprets Points as a drawing:

```
PROGRAM NEST_SQUARES;
   USES GRAPHICS;
   TYPE GRAPHIC =
      RECORD
         VISIBLE : BOOLEAN;
            X : 0..1023;
            Y : 0..1023
      END;
   VAR POINTS : ARRAY [1..10] OF GRAPHIC
       POINT : INTEGER;
```

```
PROCEDURE FILL (CODE : BOOLEAN; X_COORD,
                Y_COORD,POINT : INTEGER);
    BEGIN

      { Add one point to array of points }
        WITH POINTS[POINT] DO
        BEGIN
            VISIBLE := CODE;
            X := X_COORD;
            Y := Y_COORD;

        END;

    END;

{ Main Program }

BEGIN

  { Fill up array of points }
    FILL (FALSE,275,225,1);
    FILL (TRUE,675,225,2);
    FILL (TRUE,675,625,3);
    FILL (TRUE,275,625,4);
    FILL (TRUE,275,225,5);

    FILL (FALSE,475,225,6);
    FILL (TRUE,675,425,7);
    FILL (TRUE,475,625,8);
    FILL (TRUE,275,425,9);
    FILL (TRUE,475,225,10);

    START_DRAWING;

    { Draw vectors stored in array points }
        FOR POINT := 1 TO 10 DO
            WITH POINTS[POINT] DO
                IF VISIBLE THEN
                    DRAW (X,Y)
                ELSE
                    MOVE (X,Y);

    FINISH_DRAWING;

END.
```

There is much more to be said about **record**s and the sophisticated data structures that you can create with them. We have, however, introduced enough of the basic ideas about **record**s to serve our immediate purposes here. Many of the Pascal texts listed in the Bibliography give more extended treatments.

Advanced Polygon Filling Using Records

Procedures for filling nonrectangular polygons with hatching provide an interesting illustration of the use of **record** structures. You will recall, from our earlier discussion, that it is necessary to find the intersections of hatch lines with the edge lines of the polygon. To do this, we must know the slope and intercept of the edge line under consideration (fig. 13-14). So it becomes convenient to represent an edge line (redundantly) by its endpoint coordinates, slope, and intercept stored in a **record** called Edges and defined as follows:

```
TYPE  EDGES  =
   RECORD
      X1  :  INTEGER;
      Y1  :  INTEGER;
      X2  :  INTEGER;
      Y2  :  INTEGER;
      SLOPE  :  REAL;
      INTERCEPT  :  REAL
   END;
```

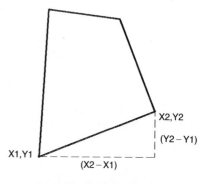

SLOPE := (Y2−Y1)/(X2−X1);
INTERCEPT := Y1−SLOPE×X1;

13-14. The slope and intercept of a polygon edge.

Then the following declarations establish that the polygon is represented by an **array** of **record**s of type Edges:

```
VAR  EDGE  :  ARRAY [1..20] OF  EDGES;
     N_EDGES  :  INTEGER;
```

If we assume an **array** called Points, containing the vertex coordinates of the polygon, we can now fill Edge from it by the following procedure:

```
PROCEDURE  CREATE_EDGES (VAR  MIN_Y,MAX_Y  :  INTEGER);

   VAR  TEMP  :  INTEGER;

   BEGIN

      { Initialize minimum and maximum values of Y }

      MIN_Y := 10000;
      MAX_Y := 0;

      { Set number of edges equal to one less than the length of
        the points array }

      N_EDGES := N_POINTS − 1;

      { Loop through the points array creating the edge data
        structure }

      FOR POINT := 1 TO N_EDGES DO
      BEGIN

            WITH  EDGE[POINT] DO
            BEGIN
               X1  :=  POINTS[POINT,1];
               X2  :=  POINTS[POINT+1,1];
               Y1  :=  POINTS[POINT,2];
               Y2  :=  POINTS[POINT+1,2];

            { Calculate slope of the line }

            IF  X1 <> X2 THEN
               SLOPE  :=  (Y1  −  Y2)/(X1  −  X2);

            { Calculate intercept of the line }

            IF  X1 <> X2 THEN
               INTERCEPT  :=  Y1  −  SLOPE*X1;

            { Store minimum X value in X1 }
```

```
                    IF  X1  >  X2  THEN
                        BEGIN
                            TEMP  :=  X1;
                            X1  :=  X2;
                            X2  :=  TEMP;
                        END;

                  { Store  minimum  Y  value  in  Y1 }
                    IF  Y1  >  Y2  THEN
                        BEGIN
                            TEMP  :=  Y1;
                            Y1  :=  Y2;
                            Y2  :=  TEMP;
                        END;

                  { Determine  minimum  and  maximum  Y  values  to  pass
                    to  hatching  procedure }
                    IF  Y1  <  MIN_Y  THEN  MIN_Y  :=  Y1;
                    IF  Y2  >  MAX_Y  THEN  MAX_Y  :=  Y2;

                END;

            END;

        END;
```

In order to find the polygon edges with which a horizontal hatch line intersects, the **array** Edge must be sorted according to the lowest Y value of the two endpoints of each edge. (If hatching is in the vertical direction, the edges should be sorted by the minimum X value of the two endpoints.) The sort procedure is:

```
PROCEDURE SORT_EDGES;

  { Sort  edges  in  ascending  order  according  to  the  maximum  Y
    value  of  the  edge }

    VAR  TEMP  :  EDGES;
         N1,I,I1,J  :  INTEGER;

BEGIN

    N1  :=  N_EDGES  −  1;

  { Loop  through  edges }

    FOR  I  :=  1  TO  N1  DO
    BEGIN

        I1  :=  I  +  1;
        FOR  J  :=  I1  TO  N_EDGES  DO

          { Exchange  edges }

            IF  EDGE[I].Y2  >  EDGE[J].Y2  THEN
                BEGIN
                    TEMP  :=  EDGE[I];
                    EDGE[I]  :=  EDGE[J];
                    EDGE[J]  :=  TEMP;
                END;

    END;

END;
```

We can now use the sorted **array** Edge in a procedure to hatch arbitrary convex polygons with horizontal lines, as follows:

```
PROCEDURE INTERSECT (Y,EDGE1,EDGE2 : INTEGER;
                          VAR X_MIN,X_MAX : INTEGER;

    { Determine X values where hatch line intersects edges }

    VAR TEMP : INTEGER;

    BEGIN
        WITH EDGE[EDGE1] DO
            IF X1 <> X2 THEN
                X_MIN := ROUND((Y - INTERCEPT)/SLOPE)
            ELSE
                X_MIN := X1;

        WITH EDGE[EDGE2] DO
            IF X1 <> X2 THEN
                X_MAX := ROUND((Y - INTERCEPT)/SLOPE)
            ELSE
                X_MAX := X1;

        IF X_MIN > X_MAX THEN
            BEGIN
                TEMP := X_MIN;
                X_MIN := X_MAX;
                X_MAX := TEMP;
            END;

    END;

PROCEDURE HORIZONTAL_HATCH (MIN_Y,MAX_Y,SPACING :
                                INTEGER);

    VAR ACTIVE : ARRAY [1..2] OF INTEGER;
        Y,X_MIN,X_MAX,MIN_EDGE,E : INTEGER;
        N_INTERSECTIONS : INTEGER;

    BEGIN
        MIN_EDGE := 1;
        Y := MIN_Y + SPACING;

    { For each hatch line }

        WHILE Y < MAX_Y DO
        BEGIN

            N_INTERSECTIONS := 0;
            E := MIN_EDGE;

        { Determine two edges of intersection }

            BEGIN
                IF (Y >= EDGE[E].Y1) AND (Y < EDGE[E].Y2)
                THEN
                    BEGIN
                        N_INTERSECTIONS := N_INTERSECTIONS + 1;
                        ACTIVE[N_INTERSECTIONS] := E;
                    END;
                E := E + 1;
            END;
```

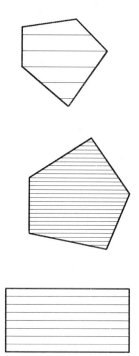

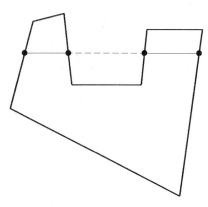

```
        INTERSECT (Y,ACTIVE[1],ACTIVE[2],X_MIN,X_MAX);

      { Draw hatch lines }

        MOVE (X_MIN,Y);
        DRAW (X_MAX,Y);
        Y := Y + SPACING;

      { Increment edge subscript so that loop will not test for
        intersections with edges with Y values below hatch line }

        WHILE Y > EDGE[MIN_EDGE].Y2 DO
              MIN_EDGE := MIN_EDGE + 1;

    END;

  END;
```

Some examples of output are illustrated in figure 13-15.

Note how the restriction to convex polygons keeps things simple by allowing us to assume, safely, that only two intersections per hatch line need to be computed. If we were to allow nonconvex polygons (fig. 13-16), then a hatch line might intersect more edges. Note, too, how the sorting of edges by the minimum Y value limits the number of edges that must be tested for intersection with each hatch line.

Further generalizations can be achieved at the cost of increasing the complexity both of the data structure and of the procedures that operate on it. We might, for example, allow polygons with holes (fig. 13-17). These cannot now be represented by a straightforward **array** of type Edges; we must devise some arrangement for representing the edges that bound the hole.

We might also want to hatch with lines at any angle. In this case, it is necessary to create an **array** of all edges with which a particular hatch line intersects, then sort this **array** in order of increasing value of the X intercept with the hatch line. This **array** is then used to draw the hatch line by executing a **move** to the first intersection, then a **draw** to the second, a **move** to the third, a **draw** to the fourth, and so on. Figure 13-18 shows some output from a fully generalized polygon hatching procedure.

The procedure can also be adapted to hatch everything *except* a specified polygon (fig. 13-19). We simply reverse the parity convention. That is, **draw** to the first intersection, **move** to the second, **draw** to the third, **move** to the fourth, and so on.

If we have a generalized procedure for hatching polygons, we can take an approach to graphics in which the hatched polygon, rather than the vector, is used as the primitive. This is rather like working with polygons cut out of sticky-backed mechanical screen and allows the creation of complex layering and transparency effects (fig. 13-20).

What would the data structure to store such a picture look like? Let us assume that a polygon can have up to ten edges, and that there are no holes. For each polygon we must represent the vertices, the edges, the angle of the hatching, and the spacing of the hatching. We might, then, use a rather long and complex **record**, defined like this;

13-15. Hatched convex polygons.

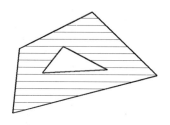

13-16. A hatch line may intersect more than two edges of a nonconvex polygon.

13-17. A polygon with holes.

```
        TYPE POLYGON =
        RECORD
              POINTS : ARRAY[1..10] OF GRAPHIC;
              EDGE : ARRAY[1..10] OF EDGES;
              N_POINTS : INTEGER;
```

```
        THETA : REAL;
      SPACING : INTEGER
  END;
```

Then, we might represent the complete picture as an **array** of such records, thus:

```
VAR PICTURE : ARRAY[1..100] OF POLYGON;
```

The organization of this data structure is depicted graphically in figure 13-21.

Similar data structures are often used in raster graphics, where color-filled polygons are taken as primitives. Procedures for filling a polygon with pixels of a specified color are similar to the procedure for horizontal hatching.

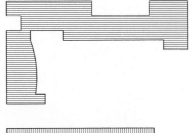

13-19. Hatching around a polygon.

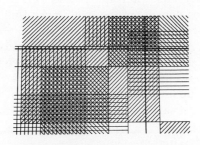

13-20. A composition of hatched polygons. Paul Klee, *Five-part Polyphony.*

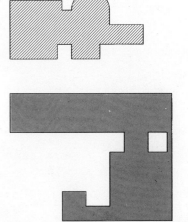

13-18. Examples of output from a fully generalized polygon fill procedure.

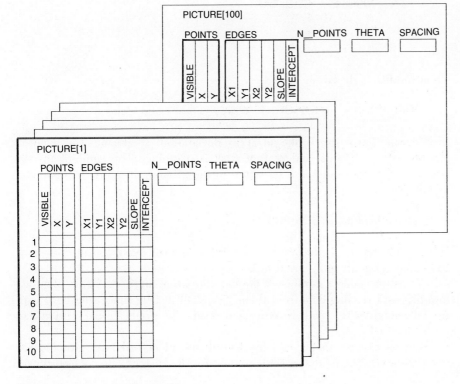

13-21. Records to store hatched polygons.

Reading and Writing Files

So far in this chapter we have seen how to store drawings in **arrays** that exist while a program is executing. These data structures have a temporary existence. But what if you want to store a drawing permanently in auxiliary storage? Pascal **files** provide a way to do this.

You can most easily understand **files** by imagining that they are being written onto and read from magnetic tape. This is not unrealistic; magnetic tape is frequently used as an auxiliary storage medium. Where disk is used as the medium, the Pascal code for reading and writing files looks exactly the same.

Magnetic tape is a strictly sequential medium. You reach a given part of the tape by scanning through it sequentially. If you want to read the one-hundredth item on a tape, for example, you must scan through the preceding ninety-nine. Similarly, a Pascal **file** is a sequential data type; it is a *sequence* of components of the same type. Unlike an **array**, the length of a file is not fixed by the **file** type definition.

Another difference is that an **array** is a *random* access data structure. As we have seen, **array** components have indexes by which they can be accessed directly. But **file** components do not; they can be accessed only by scanning the **file** until the required component is found.

An easy and convenient way to store drawings is to create **files** of Graphic **record**s. As we saw in our last example program, a Graphic **record** type may be declared as follows:

```
TYPE GRAPHIC =
   RECORD
      VISIBLE : BOOLEAN;
      X : 0..1023;
      Y : 0..1023
   END;
```

Then the **file** is declared:

```
VAR POINTS : FILE OF GRAPHIC;
```

This declaration is much like an **array** declaration. It specifies the name of the **file** (that is, Points) and its type (that is, Graphic). The name of any **file** used in a program must also be stated in the program heading, for example, as follows:

```
PROGRAM POLYGON(POINTS);
```

When a **file** has been declared, but nothing has yet been written into it, it has no components and is said to be *empty*.

Pascal provides a number of *file operators* that are used for writing data into **files** and reading data from them. We shall just be concerned here with the following: **write**, **read**, **rewrite**, and **reset**. The predicate **eof** (end of file) is also needed.

Let us assume that a variable Coordinate of **record** type Graphic has been declared. The following statement writes the current value of Coordinate into Points:

WRITE (POINTS,COORDINATE);

Conversely, a value is read from Points and assigned to Coordinate by the following:

READ (POINTS,COORDINATE);

Since a **file** is sequential, it is always read or written through a *window*, which gives access to one and only one component (fig. 13-22a). If the window is moved beyond the end of the file (fig. 13-22b), the value of the predicate **eof** (Points) is **true**. Otherwise it is **false**. A **write** statement first advances the window, then writes the new component into the **file**. Similarly, a **read** statement first advances the window, then reads the component where the window currently is.

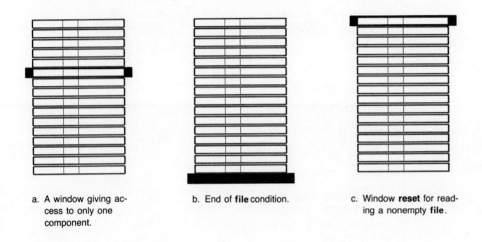

a. A window giving access to only one component.

b. End of **file** condition.

c. Window **reset** for reading a nonempty **file**.

13-22. Reading and writing **files**.

A **file** can be in a *write mode*, during which values can be written into it, or in a *read mode*, during which values can be read from it. Like an audio tape recorder, which can either record or play back, but not do both at once, a **file** cannot be in read and write modes simultaneously. To begin writing values into a **file**, then, you must:

- Put the **file** into write mode.
- Replace the current value of the **file** with **empty**.
- Position the window at the beginning of the **file**, ready to write the first component.
- Assign a value of **true** to the predicate **eof** for this **file**.

The following statement does all of this for a **file** called Points:

REWRITE (POINTS);

To begin reading a **file** you must:

- Put the **file** into read mode.
- Position the window at the beginning of the **file**, ready to read the first component.

This is accomplished for a **file** called Points by the statement:

RESET (POINTS);

When **reset** is executed, the predicate **eof** becomes **false** (fig. 13-22c) if the **file** is not empty; otherwise it is **true**.

Modifying Graphics Programs to Write Files

It is not difficult to modify any of the graphics programs that we have considered here to write a Points **file** rather than draw a picture. Simply declare Points, and use **write** commands in place of **move** and **draw** commands. Here, for example, is a very simple graphics program that draws a four-sided polygon:

```
PROGRAM POLYGON_4;
    USES GRAPHICS;
    BEGIN
        { Draws a 4-sided polygon }
        START_DRAWING;
            MOVE (350,50);
            DRAW (625,325);
            DRAW (350,600);
            DRAW (75,325);
            DRAW (350,50);
        FINISH_DRAWING;
    END.
```

The graphic output is illustrated in figure 13-23a. Here is the modified version:

```
PROGRAM POLYGON_4(POINTS);
    TYPE GRAPHIC =
        RECORD
            VISIBLE : BOOLEAN;
                X : 0..1023;
                Y : 0..1023
        END;
    VAR POINTS : FILE OF GRAPHIC;
    PROCEDURE MARK (VISIBLEC : BOOLEAN;
                        XC,YC: INTEGER);
        { Write coordinates of one point to the file }
        VAR COORDINATE : GRAPHIC;
```

```
        BEGIN
            WITH  COORDINATE  DO
            BEGIN
                VISIBLE  : =  VISIBLEC;
                X  : =  XC;
                Y  : =  YC;
            END;

            WRITE  (POINTS,COORDINATE);

        END;

    BEGIN

        REWRITE  (POINTS);

        { Write coordinates defining a 4-sided figure to a file }

        MARK  (FALSE,350,50);
        MARK  (TRUE,625,325);
        MARK  (TRUE,350,600);
        MARK  (TRUE,75,325);
        MARK  (TRUE,350,50);

    END.
```

The **file** output is depicted in figure 13-23b.

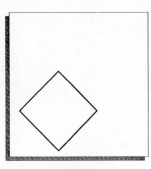

FALSE	350	50
TRUE	625	325
TRUE	350	600
TRUE	75	325
TRUE	350	50

a. A polygon.   b. Representation using a Points **file**.

13-23. The representation of pictures by files.

It is sometimes useful to produce both graphic output and a **file**. This can be accomplished by including a **move** or **draw** command with the **write** command. Thus the procedure Mark, from our last program, might be revised:

```
PROCEDURE MARK (VISIBLEC : BOOLEAN;
                XC,YC: INTEGER);

    { Execute a move or draw and record point in file }

    VAR COORDINATE : GRAPHIC;

    BEGIN
```

```
        IF VISIBLEC THEN
            DRAW (XC,YC)
        ELSE
            MOVE (XC,YC)
    WITH COORDINATE DO
    BEGIN
        VISIBLE := VISIBLEC;
        X := XC;
        Y := YC;
    END;
        WRITE (POINTS,COORDINATE);
    END;
```

Another approach is first to construct an **array** of coordinate data, then execute different procedures first to draw the corresponding picture, then write it into a **file**. Here, for example, is a program that generates the coordinate data for an n-sided regular polygon, stores the results in an **array**, executes a procedure to interpret the **array** as a drawing, and finally writes the **array** into a **file**:

```
PROGRAM POLYGON_N(POINTS);

    USES GRAPHICS;

  { Declare global variables, arrays and files }

    TYPE GRAPHIC =
        RECORD
            VISIBLE : BOOLEAN;
                X : 0..1023;
                Y : 0..1023
        END;

    VAR COORDINATE : ARRAY [1..100] OF GRAPHIC;
        POINTS : FILE OF GRAPHIC;
        N_POINTS,POINT : INTEGER;

    PROCEDURE POLYGON (XC,YC,RADIUS,N_SIDES : INTEGER);

        VAR X,Y,SIDES : INTEGER;
            THETA, INCREMENT : REAL;
        CONST RADIANS = 0.01745;

        BEGIN

          { Generate points of n-sided polygon and store in
            coordinate array }

            INCREMENT := (360.0/N_SIDES) * RADIANS;
            THETA := 0.0;

            WITH COORDINATE[1] DO
            BEGIN
                VISIBLE := FALSE;
                X := XC + RADIUS;
                Y := YC;
            END;
```

```
        FOR SIDES := 1 TO N_SIDES DO
        BEGIN
            THETA := THETA + INCREMENT;
            WITH COORDINATES[SIDES+1] DO
            BEGIN
                VISIBLE := TRUE;
                X := XC + ROUND(RADIUS * COS(THETA));
                Y := YC + ROUND(RADIUS * SIN(THETA));
            END;
        END;
    END;
PROCEDURE DISPLAY_DRAWING;
    BEGIN
    { Execute moves and draws stored in coordinate array }
        FOR POINT := 1 TO N_POINTS DO
            WITH COORDINATE[POINT] DO
                IF VISIBLE THEN
                    DRAW (X,Y)
                ELSE
                    MOVE (X,Y);
    END;
PROCEDURE WRITE_FILE;
    BEGIN
    { Write coordinate array into a file }
        REWRITE (POINTS);
        FOR POINT := 1 TO N_POINTS DO
            WRITE (POINTS,COORDINATE[POINT]);
    END;
{ Main program }
    BEGIN
        START_DRAWING;
        POLYGON (500,500,200,8);
        DISPLAY_DRAWING;
        WRITE_FILE;
        FINISH_DRAWING;
    END.
```

The **array**, drawing, and **file** that result for specified input data are shown in figure 13-24.

Graphics Programs that Read Files

A converse program reads a **file** called Points, consisting of Graphic **records**, into an **array**, then generates the corresponding drawing:

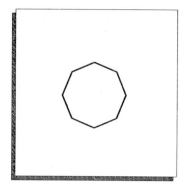

a. A regular polygon.

	1	2	3
	0	700	500
	1	640	640
	1	500	700
	1	360	640
	1	300	500
	1	360	360
	1	500	300
	1	640	360
	1	700	500

b. An **array** representation.

VISIBLE	X	Y
FALSE	700	500
TRUE	640	640
TRUE	500	700
TRUE	360	640
TRUE	300	500
TRUE	360	360
TRUE	500	300
TRUE	640	360
TRUE	700	500

c. A **file** representation.

13-24. Alternative representations of a picture.

```
PROGRAM  DRAWING(POINTS);

    USES  GRAPHICS;

    TYPE  GRAPHIC  =
        RECORD
            VISIBLE  :  BOOLEAN;
                  X  :  0..1023;
                  Y  :  0..1023
        END;

    VAR  COORDINATE ;  ARRAY [1..100] OF  GRAPHIC;
         POINTS  :  FILE  OF  GRAPHIC;
         N_POINTS,POINT  :  INTEGER;

    PROCEDURE  READ_FILE;

        BEGIN

            { Reads file of points into array coordinate }
                RESET  (POINTS);

                POINT  :=  0;

                WHILE  NOT(EOF(POINTS))  DO
                BEGIN

                    POINT  :=  POINT  +  1;
                    READ  (POINTS,COORDINATE[POINT]);

                END;

                N_POINTS  :=  POINT;

        END;

PROCEDURE  DISPLAY_DRAWING;

    BEGIN

        { Execute moves and draws stored in coordinate array }

            FOR  POINT  :=  1  TO  N_POINTS  DO

                WITH  COORDINATE[POINT]  DO
                    IF  VISIBLE  THEN
```

```
                DRAW  (X,Y)
         ELSE
                MOVE  (X,Y);
  END;
{ Main program }
  BEGIN
      READ_FILE;
      START_DRAWING;
          DISPLAY_DRAWING;
      FINISH_DRAWING;
  END.
```

Note the structure of the procedure that reads the **file** called Points. It is a **while** loop, controlled by the predicate **eof** (Points), that scans through the **file** in **record**-by-**record** fashion.

We now have two ways to store drawings permanently on disk. One method is to store a program that generates the drawing, then execute it when we want a display. The second method is to store a **file** of coordinate data, then use a program like the one above to read such **file**s and generate displays. Both have their advantages and disadvantages and are appropriate techniques on different occasions. It is usually convenient to store a drawing procedurally (as a program) when it can be generated by concise code that executes quickly and probably will not need to be altered. Storage as a **file** is usually more appropriate when these conditions are not met.

A great deal more can be done with **file**s than we have considered here. The topic of **file** manipulation is, in fact, a large and complex one. But the basic idea of reading and writing to a Points **file** will suffice for our immediate purposes. If you want to know more, you should consult one of the Pascal texts listed in the Bibliography.

Sets

Pascal provides one more structured data type: the **set**. This type is useful when we are concerned with efficient performance of operations on small sets of values of the same ordinal type. We will not use it here but, if you are interested, you will find it covered in the Pascal texts listed in the Bibliography.

Dynamic Data Structures

Arrays and **file**s are extremely useful and widely used structures, but they have severe limitations. In each case, the components are all of the same type. Furthermore their structures are simple and static. The size and organization of an **array** are determined when it is declared and cannot be changed. A **file** is of variable length, but it can only have a strictly sequential organization. Some applications require structures whose size can expand and contract and whose organization can be altered while a program is being executed. Pascal provides the facility to construct such *dynamic* data structures by using a Pointer data type and two built-in procedures—**new** and **dispose**.

A pointer tells you where to find something. A building directory, for example, contains pointers that indicate the floors and rooms where certain people can be found. If a person moves to a new location, the pointer must be updated to keep track. If a person leaves, the pointer must be deleted. A Pascal Pointer works in much the same way; it indicates the location of a value in memory.

Structures Created by Pointers

Here is an example of a **record** in which the last field is a variable of type Pointer:

```
TYPE GRAPHIC =
    RECORD
        VISIBLE : BOOLEAN;
        X : 0..1023;
        Y : 0..1023;
        NEXT : POINTER
    END;
```

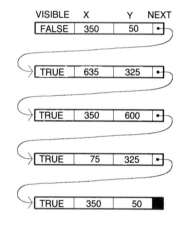

13-25. A linked list.

Values of Next are locations in memory of the next **record**s in the structure. Thus **record**s of type Graphic may be *linked* by pointers.

It is a standard convention to depict **record**s in dynamic structures by means of boxes and Pointer values by means of arrows. A structure of **record**s of type Graphic drawn in this way is shown in figure 13-25. This is called a *linked list*, or a *list*. Note that you do not want to have to specify the actual location of the next **record**. You just want Pascal to put it somewhere (anywhere) in memory and use a Pointer to keep track of it. This is what the value stored in the Pointer field accomplishes.

Pascal allows a **record** to be declared with any number of Pointer variables. This allows structures to be organized in many different ways. Figure 13-26 shows a few of the possibilities: (a) trees; (b) rings; and (c) two-way lists.

The elements of such structures do not have to be **record**s. They might, for example, be **integer** or **real** variables. But there are many practical advantages to the custom of always using **record**s as elements. For all practical purposes, then, we shall assume that a Pointer variable is a field in a **record** whose value points to some other **record** in a structure.

Declaration of Pointer Variables

Before variables of type Pointer can be used to create such structures, the Pointer type must be defined, and Pointer variables must be declared:

```
TYPE
    POINTER = ^GRAPHIC;
    GRAPHIC =
        RECORD
            VISIBLE : BOOLEAN;
            X : 0..1023;
            Y : 0..1023;
            NEXT : POINTER
        END;
VAR FIRST,PTR,SELECT,LAST : POINTER;
```

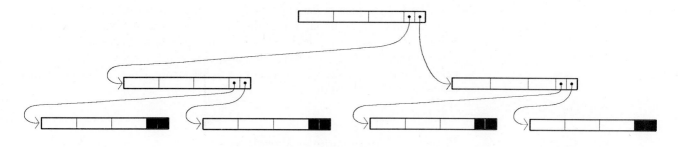

a. A tree.

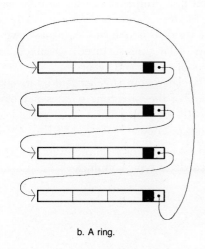

b. A ring.

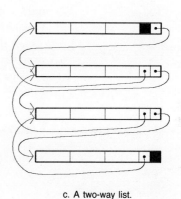

c. A two-way list.

13-26. Some structures created with pointers.

We have defined here a **record** of type Graphic. The first three fields store graphic data as in earlier examples. The last field stores a variable of type Pointer to be used to link these **record**s to form lists. Four additional variables of type Pointer have also been declared. These are First, Ptr, Select, and Last. We shall use these when manipulating lists.

The expression ^Graphic indicates that variables of type Pointer are *bound* to **record**s of type Graphic. That is, they always point to such **record**s. You must always specify what the variables of type Pointer are bound to; a pointer must point to something, and we must specify the data type to be indicated. If by error a variable of type Pointer is set to point to something else, then the compiler can detect the error.

The circumflex (^) may be read "points to." Some Pascal systems use the upward arrow (↑) for this. And others use the "at" symbol (@). You should check which convention is followed by the system that you are using.

Pointer is not a standard Pascal identifier, so we could have used another identifier in the type declaration:

    LINK = ^GRAPHIC;

Pointer, however, is a very common term, so we will continue to use it here.

The legal values of variables of type Pointer are locations of **record**s of type Graphic. In addition, **nil** is always a legal value of a variable of type Pointer. This indicates that the variable is pointing to no element. A Pointer variable with value **nil** is not the same thing as a Pointer variable with undefined value. When we consider some examples of list manipulation we shall see the importance of this distinction.

Dynamic Generation of Variables

In order to describe how a Pointer-implemented structure is created and accessed we must draw a distinction between *static* and *dynamic* variables.

A static variable is declared in a program. The declaration has the effect of allocating space in memory to store the variable's value. The name given to the variable is subsequently used to denote it. Until now, we have dealt only with static variables. The scalar (unstructured) variables are all static variables as are the components of arrays and **record**s.

A dynamic variable is not declared, but is *generated* by invocation of the procedure **new** during execution of the program. It does not have a name, so it cannot be referenced directly by name like a static variable. It may be referenced, instead, by following pointers.

The idea is best illustrated by means of a simple example. The following loop generates a list of ten **record**s of type Graphic:

```
{ Assign an initial value to FIRST }
  FIRST := NIL;
{ Begin the loop }
  FOR COUNT := 1 TO 10 DO
  BEGIN
    { Read in data }
      READLN (VISIBLEC);
      READLN (XC);
      READLN (YC);
    { Generate new graphic record }
      NEW (PTR);
    { Store data in record }
      WITH PTR^ DO
      BEGIN
        VISIBLE := VISIBLEC;
        X := XC;
        Y := YC;
        { Assign value to pointer field }
        NEXT := FIRST;
      END;
    { Assign new value to first }
      FIRST := PTR
  END;
```

Figure 13-27 illustrates the growth of the list and the states of the Pointer variables Next, First, and Ptr at successive iterations.

First is a Pointer variable that points to the beginning of the list. Before the list is created, it is initialized to the value **nil**, indicating that it does not point to anything.

Invocation of the Pascal standard procedure **new**, in the expression

```
NEW (PTR);
```

creates a new dynamic **record** of type Graphic and assigns to the variable Ptr the location of that **record**.

The expression Ptr^ may be read as "the **record** pointed to by the current value of Ptr^." Thus, for example, Ptr^.X indicates the field X of the **record**. Expressions of this form are used in the assignments of values to the data fields in the **record**.

After values are assigned to the data fields, a value is assigned to the Pointer field, thus:

```
PTR^.NEXT := FIRST;
```

Note that the value assigned to the first Pointer field to be created, in other words the Pointer field of the last record in the list, will be **nil**—pointing to nothing.

Finally, the current value of Ptr is assigned to First, thus:

```
FIRST := PTR;
```

This assures that the first **record** points to the second, the second to the third, and so on. When the loop terminates, First is left pointing at the first **record** in the list—that is, the last to be created.

This sort of list is much like a stack of cafeteria trays. Each successive element is added to the top, and we access elements in the reverse order of their creation. This is appropriate for many computational purposes, but there are other occasions (both in life and in computation) when we want to access things in the order that they were created. The structure that we need, then, is a queue rather than a stack. To put this in technical jargon, we must decide whether we want a last in first out (LIFO) or first in first out (FIFO) list.

If we want a FIFO structure, or queue, for our list of ten Graphic **record**s, we modify the code to create it as follows:

```
{ Assign an initial value to first }
FIRST := NIL;

{ Begin loop }
FOR COUNT := 1 TO 10 DO
BEGIN

{ Read in data }
READLN (VISIBLEC);
READLN (XC);
READLN (YC);

{ Generate new graphic record }
```

FIRST ■

PTR ■

Step 0

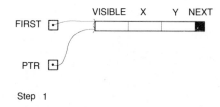

Step 1

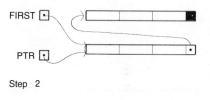

Step 2

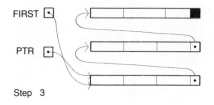

Step 3

13-27. The growth of a list, with the states of the pointer variables Next, First, and Ptr at each step.

```
          NEW (PTR);

       { Assign value to pointer field of the previous record }

          IF FIRST <> NIL THEN
             LAST^.NEXT := PTR;

       { If 1st record, assign pointer value to FIRST }

          IF FIRST = NIL THEN
             FIRST := PTR;

       { Store data in record }

          WITH PTR^ DO
          BEGIN
             VISIBLE := VISIBLEC;
             X := XC;
             Y := YC;
          END;

       { Points to previous record }

          LAST := PTR;

       END;

       { Set last record pointer to NIL }

          LAST^.NEXT := NIL;
```

Accessing Elements of Dynamic Structures

The following loop steps through our list (the queue, or **FIFO** version) and draws the figure that it stores:

```
       { Let SELECT point to the first element }

          SELECT := FIRST;

       { Begin loop }

          FOR COUNT := 1 TO 10 DO
          BEGIN

          { Draw }

             WITH SELECT^ DO
                IF VISIBLE THEN
                   DRAW (X,Y)
                ELSE
                   MOVE (X,Y);

          { Let SELECT point to the next element }

             SELECT := SELECT^.NEXT

       END;
```

This is satisfactory if we know that the list contains exactly ten elements. In general, though, the length of a list may be unknown, so we must control the loop in a different way. Since the value of the pointer field of the last record will be **nil**, we can test for this as follows:

```
       SELECT := FIRST;

       WHILE SELECT <> NIL DO
```

```
BEGIN
    WITH  SELECT^  DO
        IF  VISIBLE  THEN
            DRAW  (X,Y)
        ELSE
            MOVE  (X,Y);

    SELECT  : =  SELECT^.NEXT
END;
```

Graphics Programs Using Lists

So far we have considered three ways to write graphics programs. In the earlier chapters, we saw how to use **move** and **draw** commands to generate drawings directly. In this chapter, we have seen how to write programs that first fill an **array** with coordinate data, then step through the **array** to interpret it as a drawing. Similarly, we have seen how to write programs that first produce a **file** of graphic data, then read the **file** and interpret it as a drawing. Now we are in a position to write graphic programs that first create a list of **record**s of type Graphic, then step through the list to interpret it as a drawing. Here is an example:

```
PROGRAM  DRAWING(POINTS);

    USES  GRAPHICS;

    TYPE
        POINTER  =  ^GRAPHIC;
        GRAPHIC  =
            RECORD
                VISIBLE  :  BOOLEAN;
                    X  :  0..1023;
                    Y  :  0..1023;
                NEXT  :  POINTER
            END;

    TYPE
        COORDINATES  =
            RECORD
                VISIBLE  :  BOOLEAN;
                    X  :  0..1023;
                    Y  :  0..1023
            END;

    VAR  POINTS  :  FILE  OF  COORDINATES;

    PROCEDURE  READ_FILE  (VAR  FIRST  :  POINTER);

        VAR  POINT  :  COORDINATES;
            PTR,LAST  :  POINTER;

    BEGIN

        RESET  (POINTS);
        FIRST  : =  NIL;

        WHILE  NOT(EOF(POINTS))  DO
```

```
                          BEGIN

                              { Read record of data from file points }
                              READ (POINTS,POINT);

                              { Generate new graphic record in list }
                              NEW (PTR);

                              { Assign value to pointer field of previous record }
                              IF  FIRST <> NIL THEN
                                  LAST^.NEXT := PTR;

                              { If 1st record, assign pointer value to FIRST }
                              IF  FIRST := NIL THEN
                                  FIRST := PTR;

                              { Store data in record }
                              WITH  PTR^  DO
                              BEGIN
                                  VISIBLE := POINT.VISIBLE;
                                  X := POINT.X;
                                  Y := POINT.Y;
                              END;

                              { Point to previous record }
                              LAST := PTR;

                          END;

                          { Set last record pointer to NIL }
                          LAST^.NEXT := NIL;

                      END;
PROCEDURE DISPLAY_DRAWING (FIRST : POINTER);
        VAR SELECT : POINTER;
        BEGIN
                SELECT := FIRST;

                WHILE SELECT <> NIL DO
                BEGIN
                    { Draw }
                        WITH SELECT^ DO
                            IF VISIBLE THEN
                                DRAW (X,Y)
                            ELSE
                                MOVE (X,Y);

                    { Let SELECT point to the next element }
                        SELECT := SELECT^.NEXT;
                END;

        END;
{ Main program }
    VAR FIRST : POINTER;
```

```
BEGIN
    READ_FILE (FIRST);
    START_DRAWING;
        DISPLAY_DRAWING (FIRST);
    FINISH_DRAWING;
END.
```

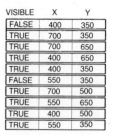

VISIBLE	X	Y
FALSE	400	350
TRUE	700	350
TRUE	700	650
TRUE	400	650
TRUE	400	350
FALSE	550	350
TRUE	700	500
TRUE	550	650
TRUE	400	500
TRUE	550	350

a. An input **file** for the program Drawing.

Figure 13-28 shows an input file, the corresponding list, and the drawing that results.

Notice the formal parameters of the procedures in this program. Values of Pointer variables are passed in to give procedures access to list elements. Notice, too, that the **file** is of unknown length, so the length of the list that will be created is also unknown.

The Insertion and Deletion of Records in Lists

It is easy to insert a new **record** between two **record**s in a list by resetting pointers (fig. 13-29). For example, a procedure Insert—to insert a new **record**

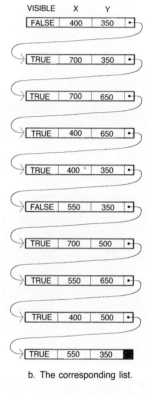

VISIBLE	X	Y
FALSE	400	350
TRUE	700	350
TRUE	700	650
TRUE	400	650
TRUE	400	350
FALSE	550	350
TRUE	700	500
TRUE	550	650
TRUE	400	500
TRUE	550	350

b. The corresponding list.

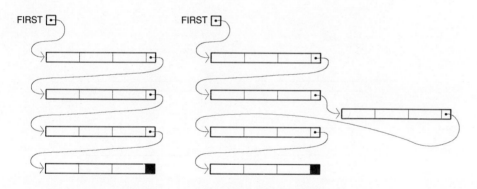

a. A list of four **record**s.   b. A new record inserted between the second and third **record**s.

13-29. Inserting a **record** in a list by resetting pointers.

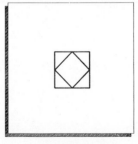

c. The output drawing.

13-28. The storage of a drawing in a list.

of type Graphic after the **record** currently being pointed to runs as follows:

```
PROCEDURE INSERT (XC,YC : INTEGER; P : POINTER);
    VAR PTR : POINTER;

    { Inserts new record of X,Y coordinates after the record that is
      addressed by the pointer variable P }

    BEGIN
        { Generate new graphic record }
```

```
NEW (PTR);

WITH PTR^ DO
BEGIN
    X := XC;
    Y := YC;
    NEXT := P^.NEXT;

END;

{ Modify pointer of record prior to inserted record }
    P^.NEXT := PTR;

END;
```

The converse operation of deleting a **record** is also straightforward (fig. 13-30). Here is a procedure Delete, which deletes the **record** currently indicated.

```
PROCEDURE DELETE (P : POINTER);

    VAR PTR : POINTER;

{ Delete record that is pointed to be P^.NEXT }

    BEGIN

        PTR := P^.NEXT;
        P^.NEXT := PTR^.NEXT;

    END;
```

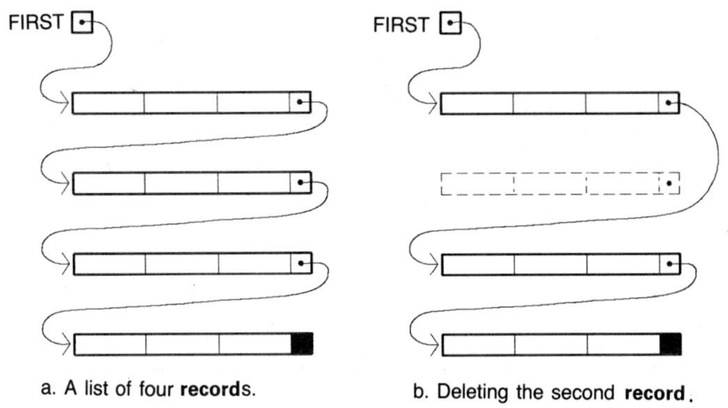

a. A list of four **record**s.   b. Deleting the second **record**.

13-30. Deleting a **record** from a list by resetting pointers.

These procedures might be used, for example, to modify the shape of a polygon by inserting or deleting coordinate points. Procedures to insert and delete vectors in arbitrary drawings are slightly more complicated, since values in the field Visible must be adjusted

Combining Lists

You can also combine two dynamic structures. Let us assume, for example, that a drawing is stored in a list of **record**s of type Graphic indicated by the value of the Pointer variable First, and that another such drawing is stored in a list indicated by the Pointer variable Second. You can append the second list to the first by resetting the last pointer in the first list from **nil** to Second

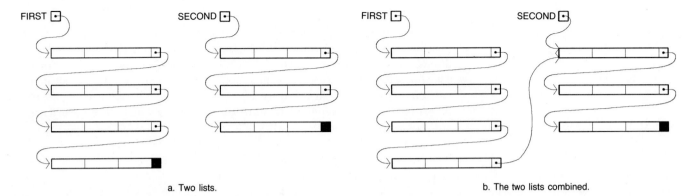

a. Two lists.   b. The two lists combined.

13-31. Combining lists by resetting pointers.

(fig. 13-31). Here is a procedure Append to do it:

```
PROCEDURE APPEND (FIRST,SECOND : POINTER);
    VAR SELECT,LAST : POINTER;
    BEGIN
      { Find last pointer in first list }
        SELECT := FIRST;
        WHILE SELECT <> NIL DO
        BEGIN
            LAST := SELECT;
            SELECT := SELECT^.NEXT;
        END;
      { Point last record in first list to first record in second list }
        LAST^.NEXT := SECOND;
    END;
```

The use of the procedure Append is the computational equivalent of the traditional technique of collage; existing drawings are combined to make new ones.

Disposing of Lists

Once a static structure, like an **array**, is declared, memory space remains allocated while the block in which it is declared is executing. But you can eliminate dynamic structures as soon as you have finished with them and free the memory space that they occupy. This is accomplished by use of the Pascal standard procedure **dispose** as follows:

```
DISPOSE (FIRST);
```

This has the effect of disposing of the structure indicated by the value of the Pointer variable First.

Representation of Arbitrary Curves by Lists of Points

An important application of lists in computer graphics is the representation of arbitrary curves that cannot be generated by the evaluation of formulas, as discussed in chapter 10. Such curves can be described only in terms of the coordinates of closely spaced points along them. Since the number of points needed to represent an arbitrary curve in this way cannot usually be pre-determined, it is convenient to store the coordinates in lists of **record**s that are structured as follows:

```
CURVEPOINT  =
    RECORD
            X  :  INTEGER;
            Y  :  INTEGER;
        NEXT  :  POINTER
    END;
```

Here is a program that prompts for and reads in points along a curve and stores them in a list:

```
PROGRAM CURVE;

    TYPE POINTER  =  ^CURVEPOINT;
        CURVEPOINT  =
            RECORD
                    X  :  INTEGER;
                    Y  :  INTEGER;
                NEXT  :  POINTER
            END;

    VAR N_POINTS,POINT  :  INTEGER;
        FIRST,PTR  :  POINTER;

    BEGIN
        { Read in number of points in curve }

        WRITELN ('ENTER NUMBER OF POINTS ON CURVE:');
        READLN (N_POINTS);

        { Assign initial value to first }

        FIRST  :=  NIL;

        { Loop to read points on curve }

        FOR POINT  =  1 TO N_POINTS DO
        BEGIN

            { Generate new graphic record }

            NEW (PTR);

            WITH PTR^ DO
            BEGIN
                WRITELN ('ENTER X,Y COORDINATES OF
                            POINT:',POINT);
                READLN (X,Y);
                NEXT  :=  FIRST;
            END;

            { Assign new value to FIRST }
```

```
        FIRST := PTR;
    END;
  END.
```

Curve Smoothing

Once we have a curve stored in this fashion, we can operate on the list to transform the curve in various ways. We might, for example, want to smooth it. One simple way to do this is illustrated in figure 13-32. Each straight segment is first divided into three equal parts; the third points are then connected. The same operation is then performed on the result. This operation is repeated as many times as is necessary to achieve the desired degree of smoothness.

This can be accomplished with a procedure that steps through the points list, deletes each successive point, and inserts two new points in its place. This procedure invokes Insert and Delete, which we introduced earlier. Here is the code:

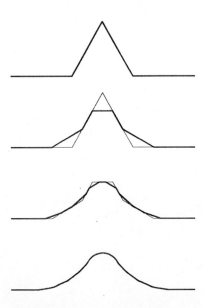

13-32. Third-point construction for smoothing a curve.

```
    PROCEDURE SMOOTH (MINIMUM : INTEGER; FIRST : POINTER);

      { Procedure to interatively smooth a curve so that each line
        segment is less than MINIMUM }

      FUNCTION DIS (X1,Y1,X2,Y2 : INTEGER) : INTEGER;

        { Calculates the straight line distance between 2 points }

        BEGIN

          DIS := ROUND(SQRT(SQR(X1−X2) + SQR(Y1−Y2)));

        END;

      PROCEDURE DIVIDE (N1,N2 : INTEGER; VAR N12 : INTEGER);

        VAR DIS,SIGN : INTEGER;

        { Divide interval between two numbers N1 and N2 into 3
          equal parts and set N12 equal to value of point closest to
          N1 }

        BEGIN

          DIS := ABS(N1−N2) DIV 3;
          SIGN := 1;
          IF N1 > N2 THEN SIGN := −1;
          N12 := N1 + SIGN*DIS;

        END;

      { Variables local to SMOOTH }

      VAR P1,P2,P3,LAST : POINTER;
          X12,Y12,X23,Y23 : INTEGER;
          AGAIN : BOOLEAN;

    BEGIN

      AGAIN := TRUE;

      { Reiterate through the points on the curve until all segments
        are less than MINIMUM }
```

```
WHILE  AGAIN  DO
BEGIN

    AGAIN  : =  FALSE;

{ Select  first  two  points  on  the  curve }

    P1  : =  FIRST;
    P2  : =  P1^.NEXT;
    LAST  : =  P1;

    WHILE  P2^.NEXT<>  NIL  DO
    BEGIN

        { Find  new  points  on  either  side  of  point  now  on  the
          curve }

        P3  : =  P2^.NEXT;
        DIVIDE  (P2^.X,P1^.X,X12);
        DIVIDE  (P2^.Y,P1^.Y,Y12);
        DIVIDE  (P2^.X,P3^.X,X23);
        DIVIDE  (P2^.Y,P3^.Y,Y23);

        { If  distance  between  points  is  greater  than
          MINIMUM,  delete  old  point  and  insert  two  new
          points }

        IF  DIS  (X12,Y12,X23,Y23)  >  MINIMUM  THEN
        BEGIN

            DELETE  (LAST);
            INSERT  (X12,Y12,LAST);
            LAST  : =  LAST^.NEXT;
            INSERT  (X23,Y23,LAST);

            { Flag  to  indicate  new  points  have  been  added
              this  iteration }

            AGAIN  : =  TRUE;
        END;
        { Increment  to  next  point }

        LAST  : =  LAST^.NEXT;
        P1  : =  P2;
        P2  : =  P3;

    END;

END;

END.
```

Fractals

A converse process is to *decrease* the smoothness of the curve (fig. 13-33). Once again, we divide each straight segment into three equal parts. Instead of connecting the third points, though, we construct an equilateral triangle over the central third of each segment, then delete the base. This process is repeated as often as necessary to achieve the desired degree of jaggedness.

Here we need a procedure that steps through the points list and inserts three new points between each existing pair of points. The code is as follows:

```
PROCEDURE FRACTAL (MINIMUM : INTEGER; FIRST : POINTER);
```

```
PROCEDURE TRIANGLE (X1,Y1,X2,Y2 : INTEGER;
                    VAR TX1,TY1,TX2,TY2,TX3,TY3 :
                    INTEGER);
```

{ *Determines points of equilateral triangle centered on line*
  segment defined by points X1,Y1 and X2,Y2 }

```
    VAR D,D2,X_DIS,Y_DIS,THETA,H : REAL;
        X_INC,Y_INC,X_MID,Y_MID,SIGNX,SIGNY : INTEGER;
    CONST RADIANS = 0.01745;
    BEGIN
```

    { *Divide line segment into thirds to determine base of the*
    triangle }

```
        X_DIS := ABS(X1 − X2) / 3;
        Y_DIS := ABS(Y1 − Y2) / 3;

        SIGNX := 1;
        IF X1 > X2 THEN SIGN := −1;
        TX1 := X1 + ROUND(SIGNX * X_DIS);
        TX2 := TX1 + ROUND(SIGNX * X_DIS);

        SIGNY := 1;
        IF Y1 > Y2 THEN SIGN := −1;
        TY1 := Y1 + ROUND(SIGNY * Y_DIS);
        TY2 := TY1 + ROUND(SIGNY * Y_DIS);
```

    { *Calculate 3rd point of equilateral triangle* }

```
        X_DIS := TX2 − TX1;
        Y_DIS := TY2 − TY1;

        D := SQRT(SQR(X_DIS) + SQR(Y_DIS)); { Side length }
        D2 := D/2;
        H := SQRT(SQR(D) − SQR(D2));          { Altitude }

        X_MID := (TX1 + TX2) DIV 2;
        Y_MID := (TY1 + TY2) DIV 2;

        IF Y_DIS <> 0 THEN
            THETA := ARCTAN(ABS(X_DIS/Y_DIS))
        ELSE
            THETA := 90 * RADIANS;

        X_INC := ROUND(H * COS(THETA));
        Y_INC := ROUND(H * SIN(THETA));
```

    { *Determine side of line to insert triangle* }

```
        SIGNX := 1;
        SIGNY := 1;
        IF TX1 < TX2 THEN
            IF TY1 < TY2 THEN
                SIGNY := −1
            ELSE BEGIN
                SIGNX := −1;
                SIGNY := −1
                END
        ELSE IF TY1 > TY2 THEN
            SIGNX := −1;

        TX3 := X_MID + SIGNX * X_INC;
        TY3 := Y_MID + SIGNY * Y_INC;
    END;
```

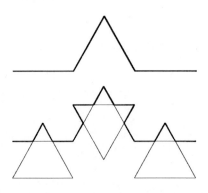
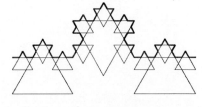
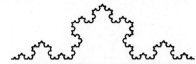

13-33. Third-point construction for
roughening a curve.

```
PROCEDURE JAG (X1,Y1,X2,Y2 : INTEGER; P1 : POINTER;
                  MINIMUM : INTEGER);

{ Inserts 3 new points between an existing pair of points
  X1,Y1,X2,Y2. This procedure continues recursively until
  distance between two points is less than MINIMUM }

VAR TX1,TY1,TX2,TY2,TX3,TY3 : INTEGER;
    P2,P3,P4 : POINTER;

BEGIN

  { Determine coordinates of 3 new points }

  TRIANGLE (X1,Y1,X2,Y2,TX1,TY1,TX2,TY2,TX3,TY3);

  { Insert new points }

  INSERT (TX1,TY1,P1);
  P2 := P1^.NEXT;
  INSERT (TX3,TY3,P2);
  P3 := P2^.NEXT;
  INSERT (TX2,TY2,P3);
  P4 := P3^.NEXT;

  { Test distance }

  IF DIS (TX1,TY1,TX2,TY2) > MINIMUM THEN
  BEGIN

    { Jag line segments formed by the addition of new
      points }

    JAG (X1,Y1,TX1,TY1,P1,MINIMUM);
    JAG (TX1,TY1,TX3,TY3,P2,MINIMUM);
    JAG (TX3,TY3,TX2,TY2,P3,MINIMUM);
    JAG (TX2,TY2,X2,Y2,P4,MINIMUM);

  END;

END;

{ Variables local to PROCEDURE FRACTAL }

VAR P1,P2 : POINTER;

BEGIN

  { Iterate through line segments of curve to jag }

  P1 := FIRST;
  WHILE P1^.NEXT <> NIL DO
  BEGIN

    P2 := P1^.NEXT;
    JAG (P1^.X,P1^.Y,P2^.X,P2^.Y,P1,MINIMUM);
    P1 := P2;

  END;

END;
```

We do not have to use equilateral triangles. We might produce even
more irregular curves by dividing segments into three unequal parts and
erecting triangles of varying shape (fig. 13-34).

Curves produced in this way belong to the class of geometric objects
known as *fractals*. There are many different kinds of fractal figures. They have
been extensively studied and have found many applicatiions in computer

13-34. An irregular fractal.

graphics—particularly in the rendering of topographic and plant forms (Mandelbrot 1982).

Construction Lines

Figure 13-35a shows a line composed of straight segments, as illustrated by Paul Klee in his *Pedagogical Sketchbook*. In figure 13-35b it has been smoothed, using procedure Smooth, and in figure 13-35c it has been turned into a fractal line, using procedure Fractal. Those procedures, then, replicate the traditional artist's technique of first laying out a simple construction line, then creating a more complex line from it.

Sometimes an artist contrasts the construction line with its offspring (fig. 13-35d, e). More subtly, two superimposed lines might suggest the form of the common construction line from which they were both derived (fig. 13-35f). As we saw in chapter 1 (fig. 1-1), Klee introduced all of these principles to his students. The architect Louis Sullivan also explored this idea with great subtlety. In his *System of Architectural Ornament* (fig. 13-36), he demonstrated how a simple line can be taken as an "axis" over which complex linear ornament may be developed.

a. A simple line from Paul Klee's *Pedagogical Sketchbook*.

b. The line smoothed, using Smooth.

c. The line converted to a fractal, using Fractal.

d. The original line contrasted with a smoothed version.

e. The original line contrasted with a fractal version.

f. Smooth and fractal lines combined.

13-35. Use of construction lines.

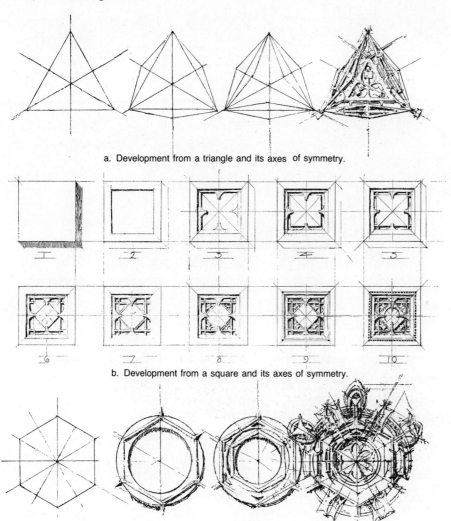

a. Development from a triangle and its axes of symmetry.

b. Development from a square and its axes of symmetry.

c. Development from a hexagon and its axes of symmetry.

13-36. The construction of architectural ornament, as illustrated by Louis Sullivan.

Hierarchical Data Structures

In chapter 12 we saw how the hierarchy of elements and subsystems in a graphic composition can be expressed by the block structure of the program that generates it. If we store such a drawing as a simple list of Graphic **record**s, the data structure does not reflect this hierarchy. As we noted earlier, though, pointers may be used not only to implement lists but also tree structures. Figure 13-37, for example, shows a tree structure to store a Frame composed of Column_pair and Lintel. The Column_pair consists of two instances of Column, and each Column consists of a Base, a Shaft, and a Capital. The

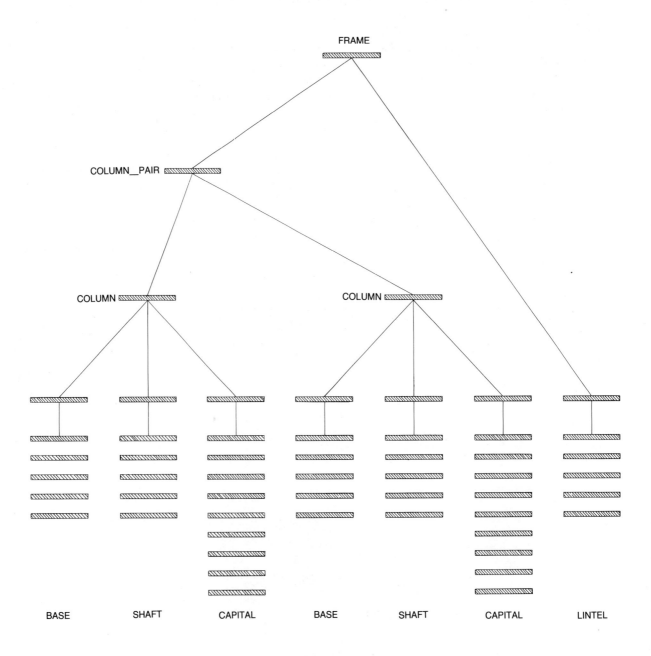

13-37. A hierarchical data structure for storing a drawing.

lowest-level elements are represented, finally, as lists of Graphic **record**s,
(Compare this with figure 12-10.)

For our purposes here, simple **arrays**, **file**s, and lists will be adequate.
But sophisticated interactive graphics programs often have elaborate data structures that express the structures of the drawings that they store.

Summary

Figure 13-38 illustrates the general organization of a graphics program
that employs a data structure to store coordinate data. The structure might
be an **array**, a **file**, or some kind of dynamic structure implemented using
Pointer variables, depending on what you want to do with the data.

Different structures are appropriate for different purposes. The possibilities
range from very simple but very limited and inflexible structures to very
flexible structures that require more sophisticated programming. The simplest,
but most rigid Pascal structure is a one-dimensional **array** of scalar variables.
We have seen that two-dimensional **arrays** have many uses, and that you can,
in fact, have **arrays** of as many dimensions as you need. Introducing **record**s
provides a way to handle data that is not homogeneous. Then, if you include
Pointer fields in **record**s, you can create enormously flexible dynamic structures.

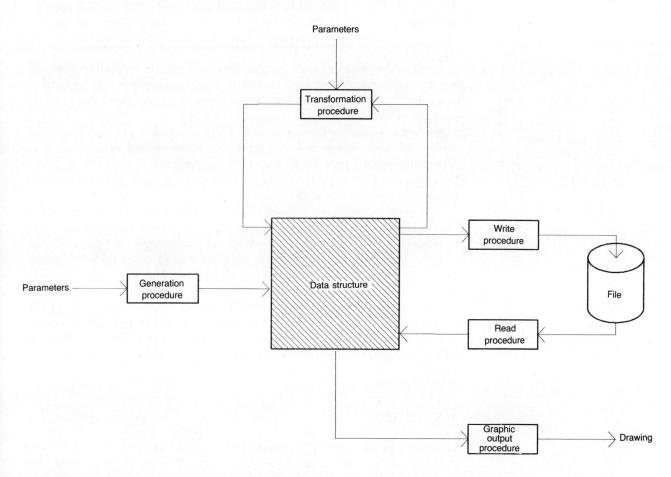

13-38. The general organization of a graphics program that uses a data structure to store
coordinate data.

You will generally find that it is feasible to use several different data structures for a given purpose; the choice is a matter of programming style. Often you will find that use of a sophisticated structure simplifies the procedures that operate upon the data, whereas use of a simpler structure requires more complicated procedures to accomplish the same thing. In other words, you can either express the logical structuring of a task in the organization of program actions, or in the organization of data.

Where some kind of data structure is at the heart of a graphics program, it will be surrounded by some or all of the following:

- procedures to *generate* graphic data
- procedures to *operate* on graphic data
- procedures to *read* and *write* graphic data on disk **files**
- procedures to *interpret* the data as displayed or plotted drawings

Procedures to generate graphic data take parameter values that specify an instance of some type of graphic element as input. Instead of executing **move** and **draw** commands, as in the graphic procedures discussed in earlier chapters, they store coordinate data in the data structure. In our examples, a **record** of type Graphic expresses the same thing as a **move** or **draw** command.

We have considered several examples of procedures to operate on graphic data—for instance, a procedure to hatch a polygon and a procedure to combine two drawings (stored in lists) into one. In chapters 14 and 15 we shall consider many more examples of procedures that operate on graphic data for various purposes.

Procedures that generate graphic data may write directly into a **file**. Or you can have procedures that step through data structures and write their contents into disk **files**. Conversely, you may need procedures that read the contents of **files** into main memory.

Graphic output can be generated, finally, by means of a procedure that reads a **file** and interprets the graphic data as **move** and **draw** operations. Alternatively, as figure 13-38 implies, you can have procedures that step through **arrays** or other data structures in main memory and interpret the graphic data as **move** and **draw** commands.

The interpretation of a **file** of graphic data by a procedure to generate a picture is analogous to the use of an engraved plate, or a photographic negative, to produce a print. As with printmaking and photography, the procedure (or its parameters) can be varied to produce different results from the same source. Computer graphics can therefore be seen as an extension of the aesthetic tradition of the reproducible picture, which began with seals and has extended to woodcut, engraving, etching, lithography, photography, and video. Future art historians may be as concerned to trace the histories of great data structures and the plots and displays that were made from them as they have been to follow great printmakers' plates and the various impressions that were pulled from them.

Exercises

1. Write a program that prompts for and reads in an **integer** specifying line thickness, then reads a **file** containing coordinate data for a drawing, and displays the drawing in the specified line thickness.

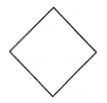

a. In simple straight lines.

b. In dashed lines.

c. In zigzag lines.

13-40. A primary line accompanied by a secondary line.

13-39. Three versions of a drawing.

2. Modify this program to display the drawing in dashed or zig-zag lines (fig. 13-39). What parameters will you need to control line character? Prompt for and read in values for these.

3. Paul Klee's *Pedagogical Sketchbook* discusses how a "primary line" in a composition may be "accompanied" by a "secondary line" (fig. 13-40). Write a program that allows you to enter a sequence of coordinates describing a primary line of some character and then constructs a secondary line to accompany it.

4. Write a program that converts a line drawing into a "reverse" image on a hatched ground (fig. 13-41).

5. Counterchange, the reversal of tone or color when a line is crossed, is a common graphic design principle (fig. 13-42). Write a program that applies horizontal counterchange hatching to an arbitrary drawing.

6. Write a program to hatch an arbitrary polygon with lines radiating from an arbitrary point in the interior (fig. 13-43). (This is easier than hatching with parallel lines.)

7. Write a program that converts a single-line polygon (fig. 13-44a) into a double-line polygon (fig. 13-44b).

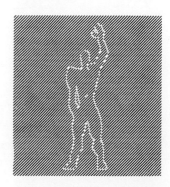

13-41. The figure/ground reversal of a line drawing.

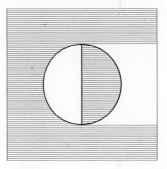

13-42. Horizontal counterchange hatching.

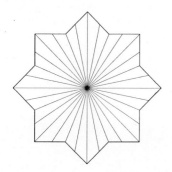

13-43. The radial hatching of a polygon.

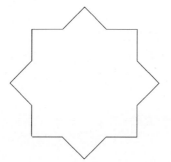

13-44. Converting a polygon from single to double line.

8. Write a program that smooths an arbitrary polygon into a closed curve (fig. 13-45).

9. Write a program that fractalizes an arbitrary polygon (fig. 13-46).

10. Combine programs that smooth and fractalize polygons into a program that produces a closed smooth curve accompanied by a fractal polygon (fig. 13-47). Explore variations on this theme by beginning with different polygons and by varying the parameters that control degrees of smoothing and fractalization.

11. A human profile can be represented as a single smooth curve, generated by smoothing a chain of straight line segments. Write a program that generates profiles in this way. Treat the positions of certain vertices in the underlying figure as variables. Generate different profiles by assigning different values to these variables.

12. When two convex polygons, A and B, intersect (fig. 13-48), they define the additional polygons:

- A union B
- A intersection B
- A minus B
- B minus A

Design procedures that will operate on data structures storing A and B to find and draw these four additional polygons. When you have established a viable general approach, consider whether you will be able to handle special cases such as:

- A and B do not intersect
- A is fully enclosed by B
- A touches B only at a single vertex
- A and B have an edge in common
- A is identical to B

How will your procedures be affected if you generalize and allow nonconvex polygons? What about holes?

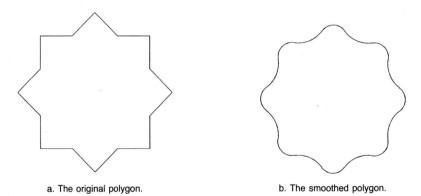

a. The original polygon.   b. The smoothed polygon.

13-45. Using a recursive construction to smooth a polygon.

412 ADVANCED TECHNIQUES

a. The original polygon.

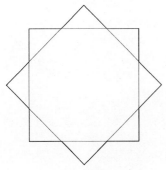

b. First step.

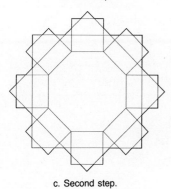

c. Second step.

13-46. Using a recursive construction to roughen a polygon.

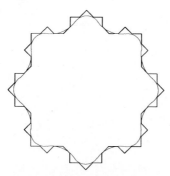

13-47. Smoothed and roughened versions of a polygon overlaid.

a. Overlapping convex polyhedra.

b. Union.

c. Intersection.

d. A minus B.

e. B minus A.

13-48. Union and intersection operations on convex polyhedra.

14.

Transformations

A *transformation* carries an object from one state to another. For example, you can transform a polygon from the unshaded to the shaded state (fig. 14-1a). (We discussed a procedure to do this in the last chapter.) Or you can transform its edges from solid to dashed (fig. 14-1b). You might transform its position by translating or rotating it (fig. 14-1c), or its size by scaling it (fig. 14-1d). Yet again, you might transform its shape by distorting it in some way (fig. 14-1e).

In this chapter we shall see how to write Pascal programs that transform drawings by translating, rotating, reflecting, and scaling them within coordinate systems. Such programs work by transforming a graphic data structure from an initial state that represents the initial state of the drawing to a new state that represents the new state of the drawing.

Geometric Transformations of a Point

Let us begin by considering a single point with coordinates (X, Y) in some coordinate system (fig. 14-2a). Translation of this point through a distance Tx parallel to the X axis (fig. 14-2b) is represented by the assignment:

    X := X + TX;

Similarly, translation through a distance Ty parallel to the Y axis (fig. 14-2c) is represented by:

    Y := Y + TY;

Since any translation can be resolved into a component Tx and a component Ty, a translation in general (fig. 14-2d) is represented by the pair of assignments:

    X := X + TX;
    Y := Y + TY;

The variables involved here (X, Y, Tx, and Ty) might either be **integer** or **real**. In general, it is most convenient to perform transformation calculations upon **real** variables, then to round the results back to **integer** values for display

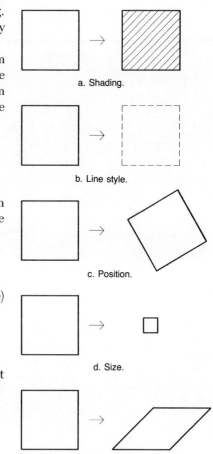

a. Shading.

b. Line style.

c. Position.

d. Size.

e. Shape.

14-1. Some transformations of a polygon.

415

in a screen coordinate system. This will become increasingly evident as we go along.

Rotations can be represented in a similar way. A rotation of angle Theta clockwise about the origin of the coordinate system (fig. 14-2e) is represented by:

```
X :=   X * COS(THETA) + Y * SIN(THETA);
Y := −X * SIN(THETA) + Y * COS(THETA);
```

Scaling is represented by multiplication by a scale factor Scale_F (fig. 14-2f) as follows:

```
X := X * SCALE_F;
Y := Y * SCALE_F;
```

If Scale_F is an integer variable, you can enlarge by any integer factor. If Scale_F is a real variable, you can enlarge by some real factor, or you can reduce by using a factor between 0 and 1. If Scale_F has a value of 0, the point is shifted to the origin of the coordinate system.

Unequal scaling (stretch) is represented by using two different scale factors as follows:

```
X := X * SCALE_X;
Y := Y * SCALE_Y;
```

If Scale_F is an **integer** variable, you can enlarge by any **integer** factor. If Scale_F is a **real** variable, you can enlarge by some **real** factor, or you can

Transformations on Graphic Data Structures

A geometric transformation applied to a drawing transforms every point (X, Y) in the original drawing to some new point (New_X, New_Y) in the transformed drawing. So it might seem that we would have to operate on every point in our screen coordinate system in order to transform a drawing.

This, fortunately, is not the case. First, translation, rotation, reflection, and scaling all transform straight lines into straight lines. Second, we represent straight lines by their endpoints. So we have only to apply transformations to the endpoints of each line in a drawing, then draw lines between the transformed endpoints in the usual way (fig. 14-3).

Consider, for example, the simple drawing shown in figure 14-4a. Using the technique that we discussed in the last chapter, we might store it in a one-dimensional **array** or a **file** of **records** of type Graphic. You will recall that Graphic is declared as follows:

```
TYPE GRAPHIC =
   RECORD
      VISIBLE : BOOLEAN;
      X : 0..1023;
      Y : 0..1023
   END;
```

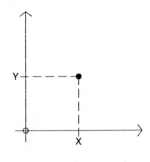

a. A point at coordinates (X,Y).

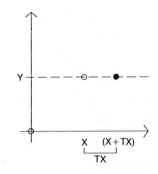

b. A translation parallel to the X axis.

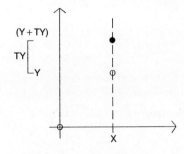

c. A translation parallel to the Y axis.

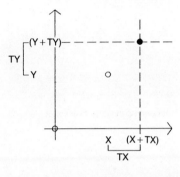

d. A translation with X and Y components.

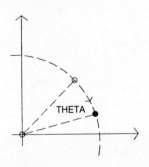

e. A rotation about the origin of the coordinate system.

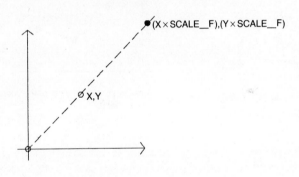

f. Scaling.

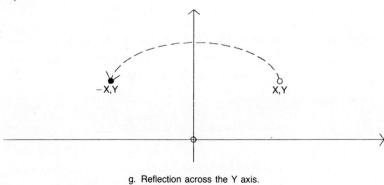

g. Reflection across the Y axis.

14-2. Geometric transformations of a point.

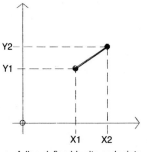

a. A line defined by its endpoints.

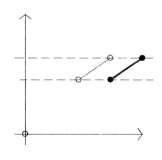

b. Translation parallel to the X axis.

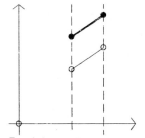

c. Translation parallel to the Y axis.

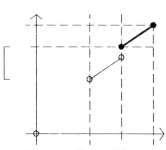

d. Translation with X and Y components.

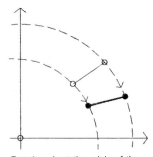

e. Rotation about the origin of the coordinate system.

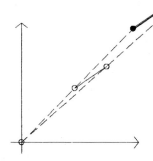

f. Scaling.

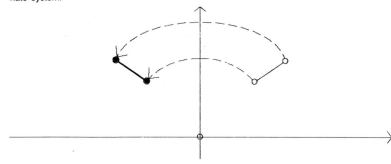

g. Reflection across the Y axis.

14-3. Transformations of a straight line.

The first field specifies whether a line is to be drawn, or whether an invisible movement is to be made; this remains unaffected by a transformation. The second and third fields specify an endpoint coordinate. Our purpose here, though, is not to store a completed drawing in screen coordinates, but a state of a drawing that is to be transformed to another state. So it is most appropriate to use **real** coordinates as follows (fig. 14-4b)·

```
TYPE  GRAPHIC  =
    RECORD
        VISIBLE : BOOLEAN;
        X  :  REAL;
        Y  :  REAL
    END;
VAR  POINTS :  ARRAY  [1..100]  OF  GRAPHIC;
```

Since every endpoint must be operated on, we need a loop to step through the data structure. The following code, for example, translates the drawing a distance of 500 in the X direction and 600 in the Y direction:

```
TX  :=  500;
TY  :=  600;

FOR  POINT  :=  1  TO  4  DO
    WITH  POINTS[POINT]  DO
    BEGIN
        X  :=  X  +  TX;
        Y  :=  Y  +  TY;
    END;
```

Figure 14-4c shows the transformed state of the drawing, and figure 14-4d shows the transformed state of the data structure.

Transformation Procedures

Just as we have used functions to name and perform certain kinds of coordinate calculations and procedures to name and generate graphic vocabulary elements, it is a useful abstraction to use procedures to name and perform geometric transformations. In general, a *transformation procedure* accepts as input a data structure representing a drawing (such as Points), together with *transformation parameters* (such as $Tx, Ty, Theta$, and $Scale\_F$), and produces as output the transformed data structure. This process is diagramed in figure 14-5.

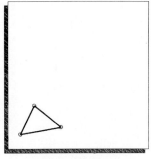

a. A simple line drawing.

FALSE	100.0	100.0
TRUE	400.0	150.0
TRUE	200.0	300.0
TRUE	100.0	100.0

b. Representation by a data structure.

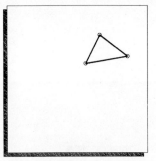

c. Transformed state of the drawing.

FALSE	600.0	700.0
TRUE	900.0	750.0
TRUE	700.0	900.0
TRUE	600.0	700.0

d. Transformed state of the data structure.

14-4. Transformations of drawings and data structures.

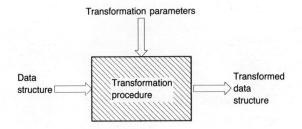

14-5. A transformation procedure.

An invocation of a procedure to translate a drawing might look like this:

TRANSLATE (POINTS,TX,TY);

Before execution of this statement, Points is in its initial state. After execution of this statement, Points is in its transformed state.

If the drawing is stored in a one-dimensional **array**, and we know exactly how many **record**s must be processed (in this example, 4), the procedure Translate will look something like this:

```
PROCEDURE TRANSLATE (VAR POINTS : FOUR; TX,TY : REAL);

    VAR POINT : INTEGER;

    BEGIN

        FOR POINT := 1 TO 4 DO
        WITH POINTS[POINT] DO
        BEGIN
            X := X + TX;
            Y := Y + TY;
        END;

    END;
```

Notice that the formal parameter list does not establish that Points is an **array**, or specify the size of the **array**. This must first be done, in the program that invokes Translate, by defining an **array** type, then declaring Points as a variable of that type:

```
TYPE FOUR = ARRAY [1..4] OF GRAPHIC;
VAR POINTS: FOUR;
```

Also notice that Points is declared as a variable parameter of Translate, so that the original drawing can be passed into the procedure, and the transformed drawing can be passed back out. It is also efficient to pass **arrays** as variable parameters; if they are passed as value parameters, a copy must be created by the compiler when the procedure is invoked.

Another useful way to parameterize a translation procedure is by direction and distance (fig. 14-6). The invocation looks like this:

TRANS_DD (POINTS,DIRECTION,DISTANCE);

The procedure Trans_DD can easily be built using Translate:

```
PROCEDURE TRANS_DD (VAR POINTS : FOUR;
                        DIRECTION,DISTANCE : REAL);

    VAR TX,TY : REAL;
    CONST RADIANS = 0.01745;

    BEGIN

        TX := DISTANCE * COS(DIRECTION*RADIANS);
        TY := DISTANCE * SIN(DIRECTION*RADIANS);

        TRANSLATE (POINTS,TX,TY);

    END;
```

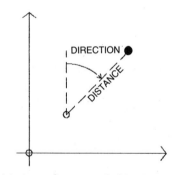

14-6. A translation specified by direction and distance.

It is generally unrealistic to assume that we will know exactly how many **records** must be processed by Translate. We are more likely to store Graphic **records** in a long **array** and keep count of the number of values that have been filled in by means of a variable N. It is then necessary to define a type and declare a variable as follows:

```
TYPE LONG_ARRAY = ARRAY [1..100] OF GRAPHIC;
VAR POINTS : LONG_ARRAY;
```

A more general procedure to translate, then, might be invoked as follows:

```
TRANSLATE (POINTS,N,TX,TY);
```

Here is the correspondingly modified version of the procedure:

```
PROCEDURE TRANSLATE (VAR POINTS : LONG_ARRAY;
                          N : INTEGER;
                          TX,TY : REAL);

    VAR POINT : INTEGER;

    BEGIN

        FOR POINT := 1 TO N DO
            WITH POINTS[POINT] DO
            BEGIN
                X := X + TX;
                Y := Y + TY;
            END;

    END;
```

Another possibility is that Points is a **file** of Graphic **records**. In this case, the **file** type must be defined:

```
TYPE GRAPHIC_FILE = FILE OF GRAPHIC;
```

Here is a version of Translate to operate on this:

```
PROCEDURE TRANSLATE (VAR POINTS : GRAPHIC_FILE; TX,TY :
                        REAL);

    VAR COORDINATE : ARRAY [1..100] OF GRAPHIC;
        POINT,N ; INTEGER;

    BEGIN
      { Read file of points }
        RESET (POINTS);
        N := 0;

        WHILE NOT(EOF(POINTS)) DO
        BEGIN
            N := N + 1;
            READ (POINTS,COORDINATE[N]);
        END;
      { Perform translation on coordinates }
        FOR POINT := 1 TO N DO
```

```
                    WITH  COORDINATE[POINT]  DO
                    BEGIN
                        X  :=  X  +  TX;
                        Y  :=  Y  +  TY;
                    END;
             { Rewrite  of  points }
                 REWRITE  (POINTS);
                 FOR  POINT  :=  1  TO  N  DO
                    WRITE  (POINTS,COORDINATE[POINT]);
         END;
```

Yet again, Points might be a Pointer variable indicating a list of Graphic records. So here is another version of Translate:

```
         PROCEDURE  TRANSLATE  (POINTS  :  POINTER;
                                TX,TY  :  REAL);

             BEGIN

                 WHILE  POINTS  <>  NIL  DO
                    WITH  POINTS^  DO
                    BEGIN
                        X  :=  X  +  TX;
                        Y  :=  Y  +  TY;
                        POINTS  :=  NEXT;
                    END;

             END;
```

Since this gives us the greatest flexibility, we shall use such list data structures in our examples from now on, unless otherwise indicated.

Here is a procedure Rotate, to rotate about the origin of the coordinate system:

```
         PROCEDURE  ROTATE  (POINTS  :  POINTER;  THETA  :  REAL);

             VAR  XC,ANGLE  :  REAL;
             CONST  RADIANS  =  0.01745;

             BEGIN

                 ANGLE  :=  THETA  *  RADIANS;

                 WHILE  POINTS  <>  NIL  DO
                    WITH  POINTS^  DO
                    BEGIN
                        XC  :=  X  *  COS(ANGLE)  +  Y  *  SIN(ANGLE);
                        Y  :=  -X  *  SIN(ANGLE)  +  Y  *  COS(ANGLE);
                        X  :=  XC;
                        POINTS  :=  NEXT;
                    END;

             END;
```

Note its close similarity to Translate.

Finally, here is a procedure Scale, based on the same principles as Translate and Rotate:

```
PROCEDURE SCALE (POINTS : POINTER;
                        SCALE_X,SCALE_Y : REAL);
    BEGIN
        WHILE POINTS <> NIL DO
            WITH POINTS^ DO
            BEGIN
                X := X * SCALE_X;
                Y := Y * SCALE_Y;
                POINTS := NEXT;
            END;
    END;
```

To provide a simple illustration of the use of these procedures, here is a program that first stores a drawing in the list indicated by Points, then reads in a value for a scale factor Scale_F, uses Scale to transform the coordinate list, then generates the scaled drawing:

```
PROGRAM DRAWING (DATA);
    USES GRAPHICS;
    TYPE
        POINTER = ^GRAPHIC;
        GRAPHIC =
            RECORD
                VISIBLE : BOOLEAN;
                     X : REAL;
                     Y : REAL;
                  NEXT : POINTER
            END;
    TYPE
        COORDINATE =
            RECORD
                VISIBLEC : BOOLEAN;
                      XC : REAL;
                      YC : REAL
            END;
    VAR DATA : FILE OF COORDINATE;
        POINT : COORDINATE;
PROCEDURE READ_FILE (VAR POINTS : POINTER);
    VAR LAST,PTR : POINTER;
    BEGIN
        RESET (DATA);
        POINTS := NIL;

        WHILE NOT (EOF(DATA)) DO
        BEGIN
            { Read record of data from file DATA }

            READ (DATA,POINT);

            { Generate new graphic record }

            NEW (PTR);
```

```
{ Assign value to pointer field of previous record }
  IF POINTS <> NIL THEN
      LAST^.NEXT := PTR;

{ If 1st record, assign pointer to POINTS }
  IF POINTS := NIL THEN POINTS := PTR;

{ Store data in record }
  WITH PTR^ DO
  BEGIN
      VISIBLE := POINTS.VISIBLEC;
      X := POINTS.XC;
      Y := POINTS.YC;

  END;

{ Point to previous record }
  LAST := PTR;

END;

{ Set last record pointer to NIL }
LAST^.NEXT := NIL;

END;
PROCEDURE SCALE (POINTS : POINTER;
                 SCALE_X,SCALE_Y : REAL);

BEGIN

  WHILE POINTS <> NIL DO
      WITH POINTS^ DO
      BEGIN
          X := X * SCALE_X;
          Y := Y * SCALE_Y;
          POINTS := NEXT;
      END;

END;
PROCEDURE DISPLAY_DRAWING (POINTS : POINTER);
  VAR SELECT : POINTER;
      XC,YC : INTEGER;
BEGIN

  SELECT := POINTS;

  WHILE SELECT <> NIL DO
      BEGIN

      { Retrieve a point from the list }
          XC := ROUND(SELECT^.X);
          YC := ROUND(SELECT^.Y);

      { Draw }
          IF SELECT^.VISIBLE THEN
              DRAW (XC,YC)
          ELSE
              MOVE (XC,YC);
```

```
          { Let SELECT point to the next element }
                SELECT := SELECT^.NEXT;
            END;

        END;

{ Main program }
    VAR POINTS : POINTER;
        SCALE_F : REAL;

    BEGIN
        READ_FILE(POINTS);

        WRITELN ('ENTER SCALE FACTOR:');
        READLN (SCALE_F);

        START_DRAWING;

            SCALE (POINTS,SCALE_F,SCALE_F);
            DISPLAY_DRAWING (POINTS);

        FINISH_DRAWING;

    END.
```

Notice how **real** coordinate values stored in the coordinate list are rounded to **integer** values before the drawing is displayed.

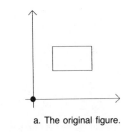

a. The original figure.

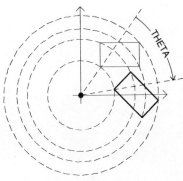

b. Each vertex rotates around the origin.

14-7. A figure rotated about the origin of the coordinate system.

Concatenation of Transformations

How could you rotate the drawing about its center point, rather than (as performed by Rotate) about the origin of the coordinate system (fig. 14-7)? A sequence of transformations is required to accomplish this. First translate the drawing's center point to the origin of the coordinate system (fig. 14-8a). Then rotate it about the origin by the required amount (fig. 14-8b). Finally, translate the drawing back to the original position (fig. 14-8c).

More generally, how could you rotate the drawing about any arbitrary point (Cx, Cy)? The required sequence of transformations is illustrated in figure 14-9. It can be executed by the following sequence of invocations of transformation procedures:

```
TRANSLATE (POINTS, – CX, – CY);
ROTATE (POINTS,THETA);
TRANSLATE (POINTS,CX,CY);
```

Rotation about an arbitrary point (Cx, Cy) is a very common operation, so it would be convenient to have a procedure to perform it. This would be invoked as follows:

```
ROTATE_XY (POINTS,CX,CY,THETA);
```

The procedure is easy to write using Translate and Rotate thus:

```
PROCEDURE ROTATE_XY (POINTS : POINTER;
                     CX,CY,THETA : REAL);
```

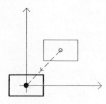

a. Translate to the origin.

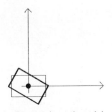

b. Rotate about the origin.

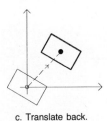

c. Translate back.

14-8. Steps in rotation of a figure about its center point.

```
BEGIN
    TRANSLATE  (POINTS, – CX, – CY);
    ROTATE  (POINTS,THETA);
    TRANSLATE  (POINTS,CX,CY);
END;
```

This simple example illustrates an important theoretical point. *Any* sequence of translation, rotation, reflection, and scaling transformations can be regarded as a single transformation that carries an object from an initial state to the final state, which results from the last transformation in the sequence. The combination of transformations, in this way, is known as *concatenation*. The concatenated transformation may be given a name, such as Rotate_XY, and can be executed by a procedure, in the same way that we named the elementary transformations (for example, Translate) and wrote procedures to perform them.

Here is another, more complicated example of concatenation. A *glide reflection* across an arbitrary axis parallel to the X axis is illustrated in figure 14-10. It is a concatenation of reflection and translation and is specified by the Y coordinate of the axis and the X translation. A glide reflection procedure, then, is invoked like this:

```
GLIDE  (POINTS,AXIS_Y,TRANS_X);
```

The procedure is as follows:

```
PROCEDURE GLIDE (POINTS : POINTER;
                 AXIS_Y,TRANS_X  :  REAL);
    BEGIN
        TRANSLATE  (POINTS,0, – AXIS_Y);
        SCALE  (POINTS,1, – 1);
        TRANSLATE  (POINTS,TRANS_X,AXIS_Y);
    END;
```

There are much more efficient ways to perform concatenated transformations than to perform component transformations in sequence, as for example, in our procedures Rotate_XY and Glide. In particular, you can use a *concatenated transformation matrix*. We need not concern ourselves with this technique here, but if you are interested, it is explained in detail in several of the computer graphics texts listed in the Bibliography.

The Order of Transformations

The result of performing two translations like

```
TRANSLATE  (POINTS,100, – 100);
TRANSLATE  (POINTS, – 200, – 50);
```

is the same as that of performing them in reverse order (fig. 14-11):

```
TRANSLATE  (POINTS, – 200, – 50);
TRANSLATE  (POINTS,100, – 100);
```

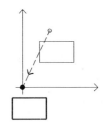

a. Translate the center of rotation to the origin.

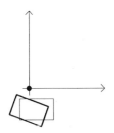

b. Rotate about origin.

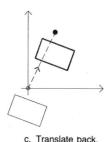

c. Translate back.

14-9. Steps in rotation of a figure about an arbitrary point.

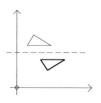

14-10. Glide reflection across an arbitrary axis parallel to the X axis.

However, the result of this sequence of transformations

```
TRANSLATE  (POINTS,0, – 150);
ROTATE  (POINTS,90);
```

is not the same as that of its reverse:

```
ROTATE  (POINTS,90);
TRANSLATE  (POINTS,0, – 150);
```

Figure 14-12 compares the two results. In general, then, the order of transformations matters. To achieve the results that you want, you must apply transformations in the appropriate sequence.

Types of Geometric Operators

The transformation procedures that we have considered may be regarded as *geometric operators*, just as $+$, $-$, and **sqrt** are arithmetic operators. The name of the transformation procedure specifies the type of geometric operation that it performs (translation, glide reflection, and so on). The first parameter (Points, in our examples) specifies the object to be operated upon. Then come the parameters that specify the specific instance of this type of transformation that is to be applied—for example, a translation specified by Tx and Ty.

These procedures, you will notice, are similar to those that generate graphic vocabulary types. Just as you can build up a vocabulary out of which to construct graphic compositions, you can build up a "toolbox" of geometric operators for manipulating compositions. In both cases, you must abstract to determine the types that you will need, name these types, define their essences in the code of procedures, and define the parameters that specify instances.

Framing

When you apply geometric operators to a data structure describing some drawing, you may generate a new state of the data structure, which now describes a drawing that no longer fits on the screen. You might translate or rotate the drawing too far; you might reflect it to a position off the screen; or you might scale it too large (fig. 14-13a). How should this be handled?

Clipping

The standard way to handle this problem is to perform the geometric operation of *clipping* the drawing to the boundaries of some rectangle that will fit (fig. 14-13b). This is much like clipping a drawing with scissors to fit a frame of a given size. A clipping operator might be invoked as follows, where Xc and Yc specify the center of the rectangle that the drawing is to be clipped to, and Length and Width specify its dimensions (fig. 14-14):

```
CLIP (POINTS,XC,YC,LENGTH,WIDTH);
```

If you would like to keep both the unclipped and clipped versions of the drawing, the invocation should look like this, where Points_in indicates a list

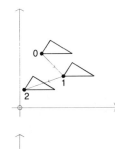
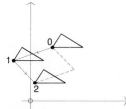

14-11. The same translations performed in different orders produce the same result.

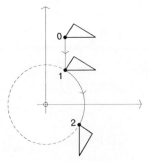

a. Translation first.

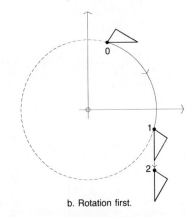

b. Rotation first.

14-12. The same translations and rotations performed in different orders produce different results.

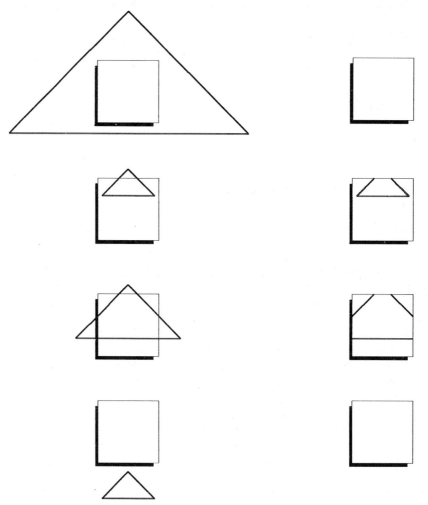

a. Some cases of a drawing that no longer fits the screen.

b. Effects of clipping to the screen boundaries.

14-13. Clipping a drawing.

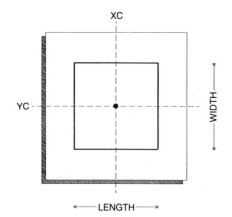

14-14. The clipping rectangle on the screen is defined by center coordinates (XC, YC), Length, and Width.

storing the unclipped drawing, and Points_out indicates a list storing the clipped drawing:

CLIP (POINTS_IN,POINTS_OUT,XC,YC,LENGTH,WIDTH);

Clipping can be accomplished by means of a surprisingly simple and elegant recursive procedure. We shall not go into the details here, since these are covered in standard technical texts on computer graphics (see Newman and Sproull 1979). Here, though, is the code of a clipping operator adapted from Newman and Sproull:

```
PROCEDURE CLIP (POINTS : POINTER;
                XC,YC,LENGTH,WIDTH : REAL);

VAR CLIPXL,CLIPXR,CLIPYB,CLIPYT : REAL;

PROCEDURE CLIP_LINE (VAR ON_SCREEN : BOOLEAN;
                     X1,Y1,X2,Y2 : REAL);
```

```
TYPE EDGE = (LEFT,RIGHT,BOTTOM,TOP);
     OUTCODE = SET OF EDGE;
VAR C,C1,C2 : OUTCODE;
    X,Y : REAL;
LABEL LEAVE;

PROCEDURE CODE (X,Y : REAL; VAR C : OUTCODE);

    BEGIN

      { Determine where point falls in relation to clipping
        boundary }

        C := [ ];
        IF X < CLIPXL THEN
           C := [LEFT]
        ELSE IF X > CLIPXR THEN
           C := [RIGHT];
        IF Y < CLIPYB THEN
           C := [BOTTOM]
        ELSE IF Y > CLIPYT THEN
           C := C + [TOP];

    END;

BEGIN

    ON_SCREEN := TRUE;
    CODE (X1,Y1,C1);
    CODE (X2,Y2,C2);

    WHILE (C1 <> []) OR (C2 <> []) DO
    BEGIN
        IF C1*C2 <> [] THEN
           BEGIN
               ON_SCREEN := FALSE;
               GOTO LEAVE;
           END;

        C := C1;
        IF C := [ ] THEN C := C2;

        IF LEFT IN C THEN { Crosses left side }
        BEGIN
            Y := Y1 + (Y2-Y1)*(CLIPXL-X1)/(X2-X1);
            Y := CLIPXL;
        END
        ELSE
        IF RIGHT IN C THEN { Crosses right edge }
           BEGIN
               Y := Y1 + (Y2-Y1)*(CLIPXR-X1)/(X2-X1);
               X := CLIPXR
           END
        ELSE
        IF BOTTOM IN C THEN { Crosses bottom edge }
           BEGIN
               X := X1 + (X2-X1)*(CLIPYB-Y1)/(Y2-Y1);
               Y := CLIPYB
           END
           ELSE
           IF TOP IN C THEN { Crosses top edge }
```

```
                               BEGIN
                                   X  :=  X1  +  (X2-X1)*(CLIPYT-Y1)/(Y2-Y1);
                                   Y  :=  CLIPYT
                               END;

                      IF  C  =  C1  THEN
                               BEGIN
                                   X1  :=  X;
                                   Y1  :=  Y;
                                   CODE  (X,Y,C1);
                               END

                      ELSE
                               BEGIN
                                   X2  :=  X;
                                   Y2  :=  Y;
                                   CODE  (X,Y,C2)
                               END;

                          END;

    LEAVE:  END;

    VAR  SELECT,LAST  :  POINTER;
         X1,Y1,X2,Y2  :  REAL;
         ON_SCREEN  :  BOOLEAN;
    BEGIN

      { Determine clipping boundaries }

      CLIPXL  :=  XC  -  LENGTH/2;
      CLIPXR  :=  XC  +  LENGTH/2;
      CLIPYB  :=  YC  -  WIDTH/2;
      CLIPYT  :=  YC  +  WIDTH/2;

      { Loop through list of points }

      SELECT  :=  POINTS;
      WHILE  SELECT^.NEXT  <>  NIL  DO
      BEGIN

         { Determine endpoints of a line }

         LAST  :=  SELECT;
         SELECT  :=  SELECT^.NEXT;
         IF  SELECT^.VISIBLE  THEN
            BEGIN
                X1  :=  LAST^.X;
                Y1  :=  LAST^.Y
            END
         ELSE
            BEGIN
                X1  :=  SELECT^.X;
                Y1  :=  SELECT^.Y;
                SELECT  :=  SELECT^.NEXT
            END;
         X2  :=  SELECT^.X;
         Y2  :=  SELECT^.Y;

         { Clip to boundaries }
```

```
CLIP_LINE  (ON_SCREEN,X1,Y1,X2,Y2);

{ Draw clipped line if within boundaries }

IF  ON_SCREEN  THEN
    BEGIN
        MOVE  (ROUND(X1),ROUND(Y1));
        DRAW  (ROUND(X2),ROUND(Y2));
    END;

    END;

END;
```

Viewing Transformations

It is possible to extend the idea of transformation further to gain a great deal of additional flexibility. Consider a coordinate system for defining a drawing, with the origin placed anywhere that is convenient, and with coordinates expressed in any units (inches, feet, miles, meters, or microns) that are most appropriate. Let us call this our *world coordinate system*, since it is used to describe the real world, and let us assume that a list of Graphic **record**s storing a drawing in this coordinate system is indicated by Points. When we are ready to display the drawing stored in Points, we simply apply some transformation to convert world coordinate values to screen coordinate values, clip to the screen boundaries, and display (fig. 14-15).

The transformation that converts world coordinates into screen coordinates is called the *viewing transformation*, and the parameters that control it are called *viewing parameters*. Viewing transformations and viewing parameters are best understood by comparing them to camera operations. In effect, we must be able to *pan* (translate) the screen up and down across the drawing in order to see different parts. We also must be able to *zoom* in and out (change scale), and *tilt* (rotate) the screen relative to the drawing.

To specify a pan, we need to say where the origin of the screen coordinate system is to be located within the world coordinate system. This can be done by giving a pair of world coordinates (X, Y) (fig. 14-16). To specify a zoom, we must say how many screen coordinates should equal one world coordinate. We can do this by specifying a Factor (fig. 14-17). A tilt may be defined as a clockwise rotation of the drawing around the location of the origin of the screen coordinate system and is specified by an angle Theta (fig. 14-18).

We may not always want to use the entire screen to display a drawing. We might, instead, define a rectangular *viewport* (fig. 14-19), and leave the rest of the screen free to display text or other drawings. The viewport is defined by specifying its location and dimensions. The effect of specifying a viewport is much like that of changing the format of a camera, say from two inch square to 35 mm rectangular.

A *viewing transformation procedure*, which performs specified pan, zoom, and tilt operations and displays a drawing within a specified viewport on the screen, might be invoked as follows:

```
VIEW  (POINTS,VP_X,VP_Y,VP_WIDTH,VP_HEIGHT,X,Y,
       FACTOR,THETA);
```

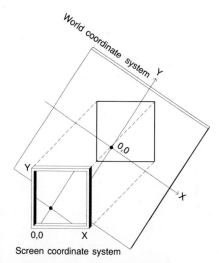

14-15. The viewing transformation maps a drawing in the world coordinate system onto the display screen.

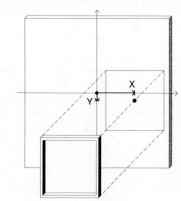

14-16. Parameters specifying a pan.

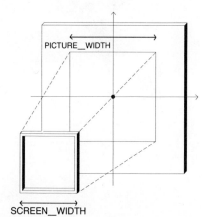

PICTURE_WIDTH := SCREEN_WIDTH/FACTOR;

14-17. Parameters specifying a zoom.

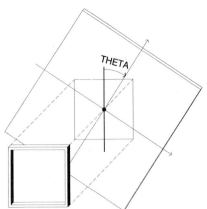

14-18. Parameters specifying a tilt.

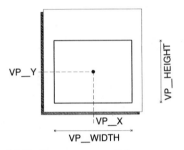

14-19. Parameters specifying a rectangular viewport on the screen allow variation in the drawing format.

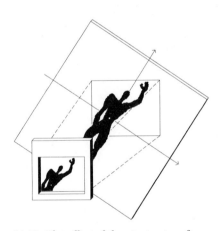

14-20. The effect of the viewing transformation procedure.

The parameters are:

POINTS	pointer to list containing the drawing to be displayed
VP_X,VP_Y	location, in screen coordinates, of the center of the viewport
VP_WIDTH	width of viewport in screen coordinates
VP_HEIGHT	height of viewport in screen coordinates
X, Y	location, in world coordinates, of point (VP_X,VP_Y)
FACTOR	scale factor (Factor screen coordinates = 1 world coordinate)
THETA	clockwise rotation, in degrees, of the drawing around X, Y

The effect is to map a rectangular portion of the drawing onto the viewport, clip it to the viewport boundaries, and display it (fig. 14-20).

The following viewing transformation procedure invokes the Translate, Rotate, Scale, and Clip procedures that we have already introduced. The code is:

```
PROCEDURE VIEW (POINTS : POINTER;
                VP_X,VP_Y,VP_WIDTH,VP_HEIGHT: INTEGER;
                X,Y,FACTOR,THETA : REAL);

   BEGIN
      { Translate point X,Y to origin }
         TRANSLATE (POINTS,-X,-Y);
      { Scale }
         SCALE (POINTS,FACTOR,FACTOR);
      { Rotate }
         ROTATE (POINTS,THETA);
      { Translate origin to screen point VP_X,VP_Y }
         TRANSLATE (POINTS,VP_X,VP_Y);
      { Clip and display }
         CLIP (POINTS,VP_X,VP_Y,VP_WIDTH,VP_HEIGHT);
   END;
```

To illustrate the use of this procedure, here is code that stores a drawing in the coordinate list, applies transformations, and displays the transformed picture. In this example, the program prompts for and reads in the viewing parameters, applies the **view** operator, and finally displays the result:

```
{ Main program }

VAR POINTS : POINTER;
    X,Y,FACTOR,THETA : REAL;
    VP_X,VP_Y,VP_WIDTH,VP_HEIGHT : INTEGER;
```

```
BEGIN

    READ_FILE (POINTS);

    WRITELN ('ENTER X,Y COORDINATES OF CENTER ',
             'OF DRAWING TO BE DISPLAYED:');

    READLN (X,Y);

    WRITELN ('ENTER SCALE FACTOR:');
    READLN (FACTOR);

    WRITELN ('ENTER ANGLE OF ROTATION:');
    READLN (THETA);

    WRITELN ('ENTER X,Y COORDINATES OF CENTER ',
             'OF SCREEN VIEWPORT:');
    READLN (VP_X,VP_Y);

    WRITELN ('ENTER WIDTH AND HEIGHT OF VIEWPORT:');
    READLN (VP_WIDTH,VP_HEIGHT);

    START_DRAWING;

        VIEW (POINTS,VP_X,VP_Y,VP_WIDTH,VP_HEIGHT,
              X,Y,FACTOR,THETA);

    FINISH_DRAWING;

END.
```

Figure 14-21 shows some examples of output.

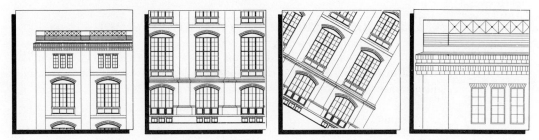

14-21. Some results produced by a viewing program.

Figure 14-22 summarizes the viewing transformation. A rectangle in the world coordinate system is specified by the parameters X, Y, Factor, and Theta. The viewing transformation maps this onto a similarly proportioned rectangle, specified by the parameters Vp_X, Vp_Y, Vp_height, and Vp_width in the screen coordinate system. All world coordinate system parameters are **real**, and all screen coordinate system parameters are **integer**.

Aesthetics of the Frame

In earlier chapters, we took the frame of the screen coordinate picture plane as a given starting point, and built up graphic compositions by relating elements to this frame and to each other, much as a stage director might compose a scene within the frame of a proscenium stage. Artists have often been concerned with the effects of differently formatted frames and the relations of graphic elements of different types to them. It was traditional, for instance, to compose portrait paintings within upright rectangles and landscape paintings within horizontal rectangles. In *Point and Line to Plane*, Kandinsky explored

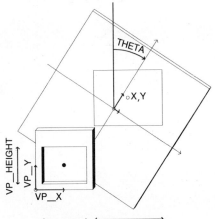

PICTURE_WIDTH := VP_WIDTH/FACTOR;

14-22. A summary of the parameters of the viewing transformation.

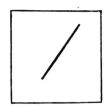

a. "In the first instance it lies freely. Its proximity to the border gives it a pronounced, heightened tension toward the upper right, with a resulting decrease in tension at its lower end."

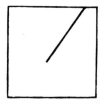

b. "In the second instance it collides with the border and, as a result, immediately forfeits its upward tension, while the downward tension is increased, expressing something sickly, almost despairing."

14-23. Kandinsky's analysis in *Point and Line to Plane* of the relation between a line and the frame.

the effects of relating a graphic element to the frame in different ways (fig. 14-23).

Now, by using viewing operations, we can first create a larger "world," independent of any frame, then select and frame a fragment of it. This is more closely analogous to work of a photographer, or cinematographer, and raises a new set of aesthetic issues. How, for example, might a close-up be framed (fig. 14-24) to suggest the larger whole of which it is a part?

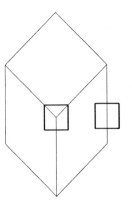
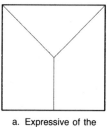
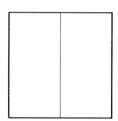

a. Expressive of the larger whole.

b. More ambiguous.

14-24. Two close-ups of a cube.

A Transformation and Viewing System

Now that transformation, clipping, and viewing operators are familiar, we shall introduce a library of such operators for use in subsequent examples and exercises. The components of this library are:

Graphic primitives:
MOVE
DRAW

Delimiting operators:
START
FINISH

Transformation operators:
TRANSLATE
ROTATE (about origin)
REFLECT_Y (across Y-axis)
SCALE

Viewing operators:
START_DRAWING
VIEW
FINISH_DRAWING

If the library has been installed on the system that you are using, you can make use of it in your programs by announcing

USES ADVANCED_GRAPHICS;

in place of the announcement that we have been using until now:

```
USES  GRAPHICS;
```

Under **advanced_graphics**, the primitives **move** and **draw** are invoked in the familiar way:

```
MOVE  (X,Y);
DRAW  (X,Y);
```

However, they now take **real** X and Y values in a world coordinate system, rather than **integer** X and Y values in a screen coordinate system as was the case under **graphics**.

The delimiting operators **start** and **finish** define the scopes of transformations in much the same way that **begin** and **end** define the scopes of variables. Transformations are always performed like this:

```
START;
    Transformation  operator  invocations
    Graphic  procedure  invocations
FINISH;
```

The transformation operators that follow a **start** command apply to all the graphic elements that are generated by graphic primitives or invocations of graphic procedures before the next **finish**. Every **start** must be matched by a **finish**. **Start** and **finish** pairs may be nested within each other like **begin** and **end** pairs, or within left and right parentheses.

The transformation operators are invoked as follows:

```
TRANSLATE  (TX,TY);
ROTATE  (THETA);
REFLECT_Y;
SCALE  (SX,SY);
```

Note that **reflect_Y** reflects across the Y axis and does not require a parameter. There is no need for a **reflect_X** operator, as reflections across the X axis can be accomplished by reflecting across the Y axis and rotating.

You can invoke as many transformation operators as you want and in any sequence that you want. You can also construct your own operators out of the primitive operators that are given. For example, you might want an operator for rotation about an arbitrary point invoked thus:

```
ROT_XY  (X,Y,THETA);
```

The code for this is as follows:

```
PROCEDURE ROT_XY (X,Y,THETA : REAL);
    BEGIN

        TRANSLATE  (−X,−Y);
        ROTATE  (THETA);
        TRANSLATE  (X,Y);

    END;
```

Earlier we saw how complex drawings can be built up, in a hierarchy of elements and subsystems, from simple parts. Now we have also seen how complex operators can be built up, in the same hierarchical way, from simpler operators.

Drawings are always finally displayed (usually in the main program) by a sequence of code like this:

```
START_DRAWING;
   { Graphic procedure invocation }
      VIEW (VP_X,VP_Y,VP_WIDTH,VP_HEIGHT,
            X,Y,FACTOR,THETA);
FINISH_DRAWING;
```

The effect of this is to display, within a viewport specified by Vp_X,Vp_Y, Vp_width, and Vp_height, a specified portion of the drawing that is created by the graphic procedure invoked after **start_drawing**. The viewport is positioned at location (X, Y), the scale is controlled by Factor, and the tilt of the viewport is controlled by Theta. Invocation of the graphic procedure must precede invocation of **view**, since **view** operates on the list of Graphic **record**s created by the graphic procedure.

The graphic primitives **move** and **draw** enter coordinate data into Graphic **record**s (as discussed earlier in this chapter), so that the data structure stores a drawing described in the world coordinate system. The transformation operators act on this data structure. You do not have to worry about declaring the data structure, however; this is handled by the procedures in the library.

To illustrate use of this library, the following program declares a simple graphic vocabulary, applies transformation operators to put together a composition of transformed instances of vocabulary elements, and uses **view** to display the result:

```
PROGRAM WINDOW;
   USES ADVANCED_GRAPHICS;
   PROCEDURE SQUARE;
      { Creates a unit square centered at origin }
   BEGIN
         MOVE (-0.5,-0.5);
         DRAW (0.5,-0.5);
         DRAW (0.5,0.5);
         DRAW (-0.5,0.5);
         DRAW (-0.5,-0.5);
   END;
   PROCEDURE TRIANGLE;
      { Creates an equilateral triangle of side length 1 with base
        centered at origin }
      BEGIN
            MOVE (-0.5,0.0);
            DRAW (0.0,0.866);
```

```
            DRAW  (0.5,0.0);
            DRAW  (−0.5,0.0);
        END;
    PROCEDURE  WINDOW;
        BEGIN
            { Place  rectangular  sill }
                START;
                    SCALE  (3.0,0.5);
                    TRANSLATE  (0.0,0.25);
                    SQUARE;
                FINISH;
            { Place  rectangular  opening }
                START;
                    SCALE  (2.0,3.5)
                    TRANSLATE  (0.0,2.5);
                    SQUARE;
                FINISH;
            { Place  triangular  top }
                START;
                    SCALE  (3.0,0.75);
                    TRANSLATE  (0.0,4.5);
                    TRIANGLE;
                FINISH;
        END;
    { Main  program }
        BEGIN
            START_DRAWING;
                WINDOW;
                VIEW  (512,512,1023,1023,0.0,2.5,150,0);
            FINISH_DRAWING;
        END.
```

Transformations and Hierarchical Structure

The hierarchical structure of the resulting drawing, as defined by the nesting of **start** and **finish** pairs, is illustrated in figure 14-25. And figure 14-26 illustrates what finally appears on the screen.

In chapter 12 we saw how to express the hierarchical structure of a graphic composition in the block structure of a program; each part (element or subsystem) was given a name, and a procedure of that name specified the lower-level components and how these were spatially related. Then, in chapter 13, we saw how the same structure might be reflected in the hierarchical organization of a data structure, Now we can also describe structure in terms of the nesting of geometric transformations. A part is now defined as a set of lower-level

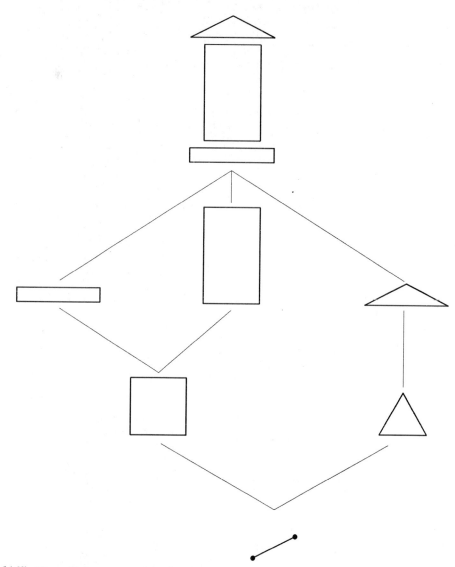

14-25. Hierarchical structure of the drawing generated by Window.

components grouped together between a **start** and a **finish**. This part can then be moved and scaled as a whole by assigning different values to the transformation procedures. You assemble a drawing, using transformations, much as you might assemble a complex piece of furniture, by building up subassemblies. Usually there are many ways to assemble a drawing (as there are to assemble a piece of furniture). You should choose an assembly sequence that is simple, clear, and expressive.

An analogy with industrial production may be helpful here. You can think of a parameterized graphic procedure as a machine for producing parts of a particular type. Adjusting the controls (varying the parameters) produces variation in those parts. You can, next, think of the code between a **start** and a **finish** as an assembly instruction that might be given to an assembly line worker or robot. It specifies the parts that are to constitute a subassembly and where to place that subassembly. As in a factory, you must give careful attention to the hierarchical organization of production and assembly operations.

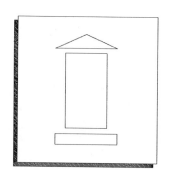

14-26. Screen display produced by Window.

Graphic Vocabularies Revisited

The use of a world coordinate system and transformation operators requires modification of the approach to parameterization of graphic procedures that was introduced in chapter 7. We no longer need position parameters, since translations, rotations, and reflections are used to position instances in the composition. Neither do we need size parameters, since elements can be scaled up and down. We will, however, still frequently need parameters that control shape and repetition.

It will generally be most convenient to define graphic vocabulary elements with their center at the origin of the world coordinate system and with their most characteristic dimension set at unity. This makes it easy to scale an instance to the correct size, rotate it to the correct orientation, then translate it to the required position. Here, for example, is a procedure to generate a square of unit length, centered at the origin of the world coordinate system:

```
PROCEDURE SQUARE;

    { Creates a unit square centered at origin }

    BEGIN

        MOVE (−0.5,−0.5);
        DRAW (0.5,−0.5);
        DRAW (0.5,0.5);
        DRAW (−0.5,0.5);
        DRAW (−0.5,−0.5);

    END;
```

Scaling to size, rotation, and location, then, are accomplished thus:

```
START;
    SCALE (500,500);
    ROTATE (30);
    TRANSLATE (300,200);
    SQUARE;
FINISH;
```

These stages are illustrated in figure 14-27.

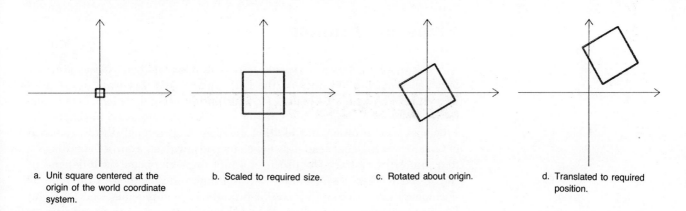

a. Unit square centered at the origin of the world coordinate system.

b. Scaled to required size.

c. Rotated about origin.

d. Translated to required position.

14-27. Stages in sizing and positioning a square.

Storage versus Computation

The transformation and viewing system that we have introduced stores a drawing as a list or **array** of Graphic **record**s, as discussed in chapter 13. This has the advantage of making a data structure available to be operated upon, but it imposes a limitation on the size of drawings that can be handled, since only a limited amount of memory is available. On a large machine, this limitation may not be particularly troublesome, but it can be severe on a small personal computer.

An alternative approach to implementation of the transformation and viewing system, which avoids this difficulty, is to parameterize the transformation operators like this:

```
TRANSLATE (T,TX,TY);
ROTATE (T,THETA);
REFLECT_Y (T);
SCALE (T,SX,SY);
```

T is a data structure (specifically, a 3-by-3 **array**) that describes the scale and position of the graphic element to which the transformation applies. T is passed as a variable parameter. Its value before execution of the transformation specifies the scale and position of the graphic element before it is transformed, and the value after execution specifies the scale and position resulting from application of the transformation. T must also be a parameter of graphic procedures, thus:

```
SQUARE (T);
```

Values of T are finally used, directly, to control **move** and **draw** operations, and no list or **array** of Graphic **record**s is required. Code for this alternative implementation is also given in the appendix.

This approach places the emphasis on computation rather than storage, so it has advantages where storage is particularly limited and where access to a list or **array** of Graphic **record**s is not needed for other purposes. In the code examples that follow, we will not introduce the parameter T, but they can easily be modified to do so if you wish to use this alternative implementation of the transformation and viewing system.

Filing and Printing

The transformation and viewing system, as described here, makes provision only for displaying drawings on the CRT screen. You may want to extend it by writing additional procedures for filing and printing drawings. Techniques for reading and writing **file**s of Graphic **record**s were discussed in chapter 13. Procedures for printing and plotting drawings step through the list or **array** of Graphic **record**s and send drawing commands, with appropriate coordinates, to a printer or plotter. The precise form of these commands will depend on the device and Pascal system that you are using; you should check the relevant documentation. Printing and plotting procedures require parameters to specify the viewing transformation from the world coordinate system to the appropriate device coordinate system.

Transformations, Loops, and Symmetry

When transformation operators are applied repeatedly within loops, symmetrical patterns result. The graphic element to which they are applied becomes the repeating element of the pattern, and different kinds of symmetry result from using different combinations of transformation operators.

To investigate this, let us define an asymmetrical vocabulary element, as follows:

```
PROCEDURE  TRIANGLE;
    BEGIN

        MOVE  (0.0,0.0);
        DRAW  (0.25,0.75);
        DRAW  (0.0,1.0);
        DRAW  (0.0,0.0);

    END;
```

This is illustrated in figure 14-28.

14-28. An asymmetrical vocabulary element.

There are four kinds of plane symmetry: *rotational, dihedral, frieze,* and *wallpaper.* We shall consider these in turn.

Rotational Symmetry

The following procedure has only one parameter, the Number of repetitions, and generates patterns with rotational symmetry:

```
PROCEDURE  CYCLIC (NUMBER :  INTEGER);
    VAR INCREMENT, ANGLE :  REAL;
        COUNT :  INTEGER;
    BEGIN
        INCREMENT : = 360.0/NUMBER;
        ANGLE := 0;
        FOR COUNT := 1 TO NUMBER DO
        BEGIN

            START;
                ROTATE (ANGLE);
                TRIANGLE;
            FINISH;

            ANGLE := ANGLE + INCREMENT;

        END;
    END;
```

Some typical output is illustrated in figure 14-29. Notice the effects of varying values for Number.

By substituting different procedures for Triangle in this code, we can produce different figures with rotational symmetry. Figure 14-30, for example, shows a floor plan that was generated this way.

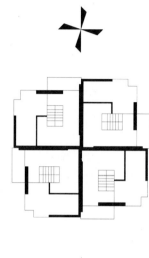

14-30. A floor plan with rotational symmetry of the Suntop Homes, by Frank Lloyd Wright, generated by substituting another procedure for Triangle in the code of Cyclic.

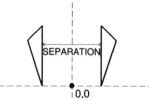

14-31. Bilateral symmetry.

Bilateral Symmetry

Bilateral symmetry results from the reflection of a motif across an axis (fig. 14-31). The human body has (approximate) bilateral symmetry, as do many buildings and architectural elements. The following code generates patterns with bilateral symmetry:

```
PROCEDURE BILATERAL (SEPARATION : REAL);

  BEGIN

    { Draw right-hand side }

      START;
        TRANSLATE (SEPARATION,0);
        TRIANGLE;
      FINISH;

    { Draw left-hand side }

      START;
        TRANSLATE (SEPARATION,0);
        REFLECT_Y;
        TRIANGLE;
```

14-29. Some patterns with rotational symmetry generated by Cyclic.

FINISH;

END;

Note the introduction of a parameter Separation, controlling the distance of the motif from the axis.

By substituting different procedures for Triangle, we can produce a wide variety of compositions with bilateral symmetry. Figure 14-32 shows an architectural example.

14-32. A floor plan of Montmorency Palace with bilateral symmetry, generated by substituting another procedure for Triangle in the code of Bilateral.

Dihedral Symmetry

If we rotate a motif with bilateral symmetry, we can produce figures with dihedral symmetry. So a procedure to generate patterns with dihedral symmetry can be produced by modifying our procedure Cyclic to invoke Bilateral instead of Triangle:

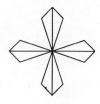

```
PROCEDURE DIHEDRAL (SEPARATION : REAL;
                    NUMBER : INTEGER);

    VAR INCREMENT,ANGLE : REAL;
        COUNT : INTEGER

BEGIN

        INCREMENT := 360.0/NUMBER;
        ANGLE := 0;

        FOR COUNT := 1 TO NUMBER DO
        BEGIN

            START;
                ROTATE (ANGLE);
                BILATERAL (SEPARATION);
            FINISH;

            ANGLE := ANGLE + INCREMENT;

        END;

    END;
```

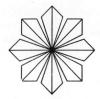

Figure 14-33 shows some examples of output. Note that when the parameter

14-33. Some patterns with dihedral symmetry.

Number is set to 1, a figure with bilateral symmetry results. This illustrates that bilateral symmetry is properly regarded as a limiting special case of dihedral symmetry.

A standard method of plan composition in architecture is to begin with

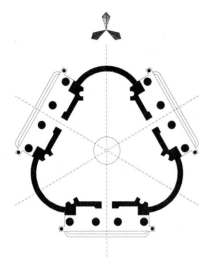

a. A sepulchral church by Sir John Soane.

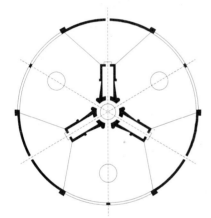

b. Kennels by Sir John Soane.

14-34. Floor plans with dihedral symmetry, generated by substituting other procedures for Triangle in the code of Dihedral.

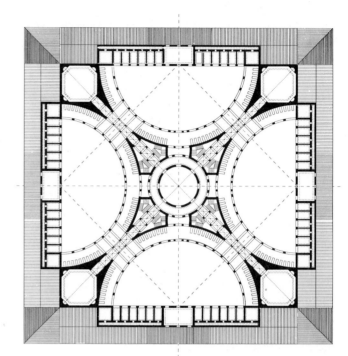

a. Project by Ledoux. (Image by Carlos Dell Acqua.)

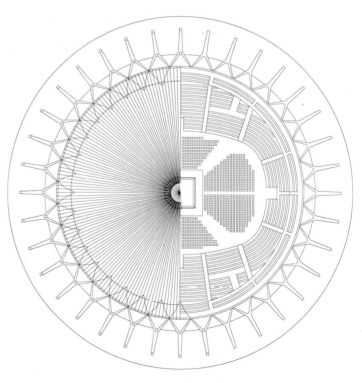

c. A sports stadium by Pier Luigi Nervi. (Image by Ehud Rapoport.)

14-35. Plan construction over axes passing through a point.

axes passing through a point (fig. 14-34), then to construct a plan with dihedral symmetry over this skeleton. Such plans can be produced by substituting procedures that generate appropriate motifs for Triangle in our dihedral symmetry procedure. Figure 14-35 illustrates some examples of plans produced this way.

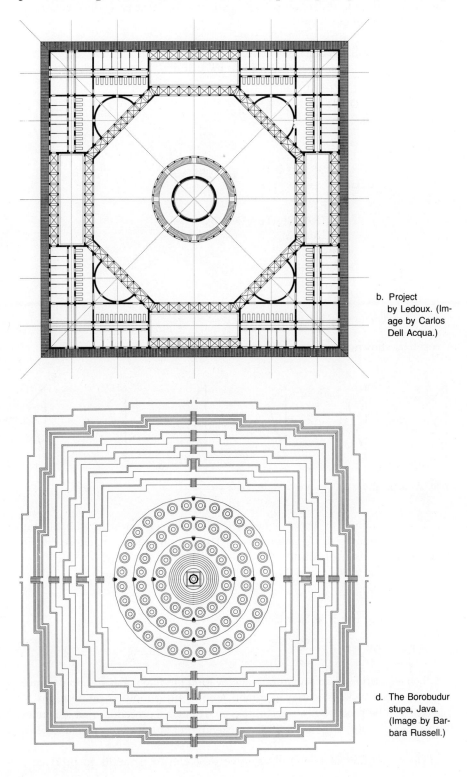

b. Project by Ledoux. (Image by Carlos Dell Acqua.)

d. The Borobudur stupa, Java. (Image by Barbara Russell.)

Frieze Symmetry

There are just seven different kinds of frieze symmetrical patterns. They can be generated by repeated applications of translation along one axis, rotation, reflection, and glide reflection transformations. This next procedure generates the simplest of them:

```
PROCEDURE FRIEZE (SPACING : REAL;
                    NUMBER : INTEGER);

    VAR TX : REAL;
        COUNT : INTEGER;

    BEGIN

        TX := 0;

        FOR COUNT := 1 TO NUMBER DO
        BEGIN

            START;
                TRANSLATE (TX,0.0);
                TRIANGLE;
            FINISH;

            TX := TX + SPACING;

        END;

    END;
```

A result is shown in figure 14-36.

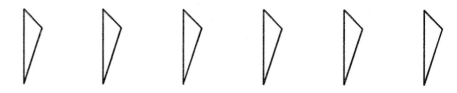

14-36. A simple frieze pattern produced by Frieze.

The remaining six frieze symmetries can be generated by substituting different procedures for Triangle. We get the result shown in figure 14-37a if, for example, we substitute:

CYCLIC (2);

And we get the result shown in figure 14-37b if we substitute:

BILATERAL (0);

The repetition of an asymmetrical elevation motif along an axis to produce a continuous facade is a very common architectural motif. Compositions of this type can be produced by substituting for Triangle a procedure that generates the required motif. Figure 14-38 is an example of an elevation produced this way.

The repetition of bilaterally symmetrical elevation motifs to produce a

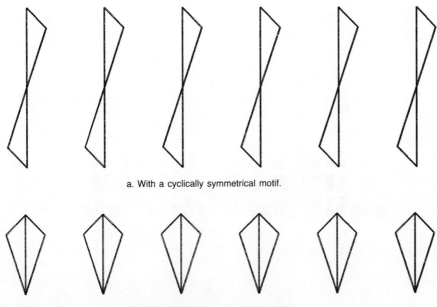

a. With a cyclically symmetrical motif.

b. With a bilaterally symmetrical motif.

14-37. More complex frieze patterns.

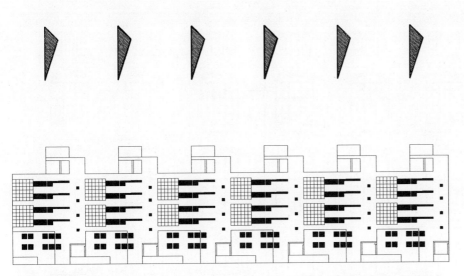

14-38. A facade of asymmetrical elements produced by Frieze. (Richard Meier's Am Karlsbad Housing, Berlin.)

different kind of frieze symmetry is also common. Figure 14-39 illustrates some examples of elevations produced using our Bilateral and Frieze procedures.

In the layout of housing units, frieze patterns with glide reflection are sometimes used. The following code generates layouts of this type:

```
PROCEDURE FRIEZE (X_SEPARATION,Y_SEPARATION,SPACING :
                  REAL; NUMBER : INTEGER);

    VAR TX : REAL;
```

a. A housing scheme by J.P. Oud.

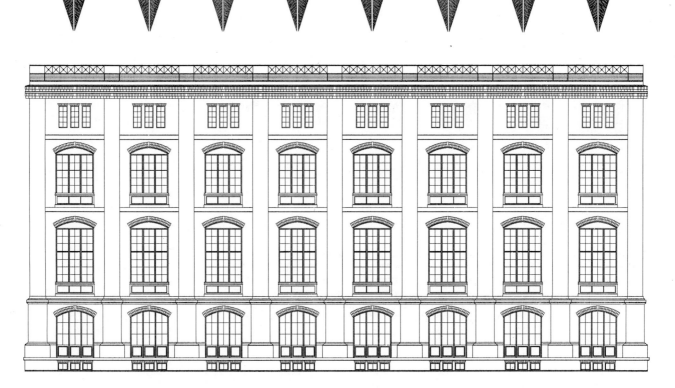

b. An elevation of the Allgemeine Bauschule, Berlin, by Karl Friedrich Schinkel.
   (Note how end conditions are handled, so that frieze symmetry is combined with bilateral symmetry.
   Conditionals are introduced into Frieze to produce the effect.)

14-39. Facades of bilaterally symmetrical elements produced by Frieze.

448   ADVANCED TECHNIQUES

```
        COUNT : INTEGER;
BEGIN
    TX := 0;
    FOR COUNT := 1 TO NUMBER DO
    BEGIN
        { Reflect unit around X_axis and glide }
            START;
                REFLECT_Y;
                ROTATE (180);
                TRANSLATE (TX + X_SEPARATION,
                           −Y_SEPARATION);
                TRIANGLE;
            FINISH;
        { Non-reflected unit }
            START;
                TRANSLATE (TX,0.0);
                TRIANGLE;
            FINISH;
            TX := TX + SPACING;
    END;
END;
```

The three parameters that control the spacing of the units in such layouts become critically important design variables. A layout produced by Frieze is shown in figure 14-40.

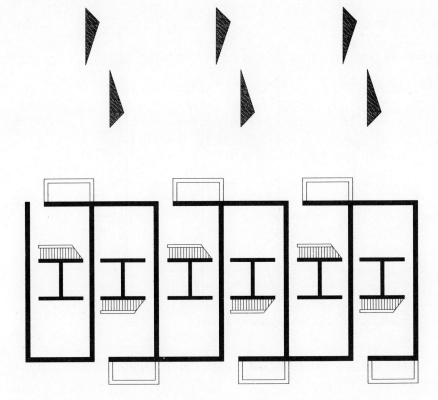

14-40. A housing layout in a frieze pattern with glide reflection. (Le Corbusier's terrace housing at Pessac).

Wallpaper Symmetry

There are just seventeen different kinds of wallpaper symmetrical patterns generated by translations in two directions, rotations, reflections, and glide reflections. Here is a procedure to generate one of them:

```
PROCEDURE SQUARE_GRID (SPACING : REAL;
                       H_NUMBER,V_NUMBER : INTEGER);
    VAR TX,TY : REAL;
        H_COUNT,V_COUNT : INTEGER;
BEGIN
    TY := 0;
    FOR V_COUNT := 1 TO V_NUMBER DO
    BEGIN
        TX := 0;
        FOR H_COUNT := 1 TO H_NUMBER DO
        BEGIN
            START;
                TRANSLATE (TX,TY);
                TRIANGLE;
            FINISH;
            TX := TX + SPACING;
        END;
        TY := TY + SPACING;
    END;
END;
```

The effect is to lay out triangles in a square grid (fig. 14-41).

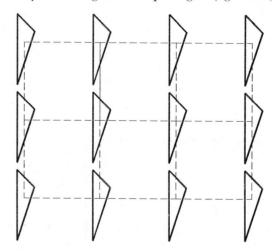

14-41. A pattern of triangles laid out in a square grid.

This next procedure lays out triangles in an equilateral triangular grid (fig. 14-42):

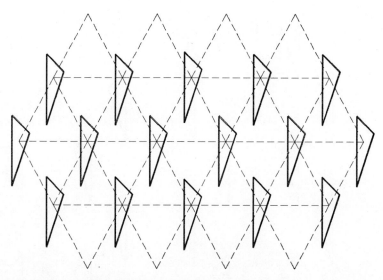

14-42. Pattern generated by placement in an equilateral triangular grid.

```
PROCEDURE TRI_GRID (SPACING : REAL;
                    H_NUMBER,V_NUMBER : INTEGER);
    VAR TX,TY,H : REAL;
        H_COUNT,V_COUNT : INTEGER;
    BEGIN
        { Determine vertical spacing as altitude of triangle }
        H := SQRT(SQR(SPACING) → SQR(SPACING/2));
        TY := 0;

        FOR V_COUNT := 1 TO V_NUMBER DO
        BEGIN
            TX := 0;

          { Shift odd numbered rows }

            IF V_COUNT MOD 2 = 1 THEN
                TX := TX + SPACING/2;

            FOR H_COUNT := 1 TO H_NUMBER DO
            BEGIN
                START;
                    TRANSLATE (TX,TY);
                    TRIANGLE;
                FINISH;

                TX := TX + SPACING;

            END;

            TY := TY + H;

        END;

    END;
```

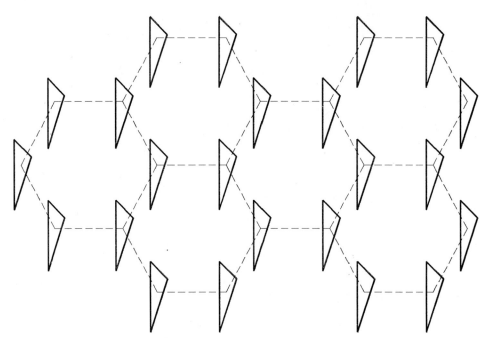

14-43. Pattern generated by placement in a hexagonal grid.

Another possibility is to lay the triangles out in a regular hexagonal grid (fig. 14-43). The following procedure accomplishes this:

```
PROCEDURE  HEX_GRID  (SPACING  :  REAL;
                        H_NUMBER,V_NUMBER  :INTEGER);

    VAR  TX,TY,H  :  REAL;
         H_COUNT,V_COUNT,SUM  :  INTEGER;

BEGIN
    { Determine vertical spacing—horizontal SPACING is the radius
      of the hexagonal grid }

    H  :=  SQRT(SQR(SPACING)  −  SQR(SPACING/2));
    TY  :=  0;

    FOR  V_COUNT  :=  1  TO  V_NUMBER  DO
    BEGIN

        TX  :=  0;

      { Indent for odd rows }

        IF  V_COUNT  MOD  2  =  1  THEN
            TX  :=  TX  +  SPACING/2;

        FOR  H_COUNT  :=  1  TO  H_NUMBER  DO
        BEGIN

            START;
                TRANSLATE  (TX,TY);
                TRIANGLE;
            FINISH;

          { Increment  horizontal  spacing }
```

```
        SUM := V_COUNT MOD 2 + H_COUNT MOD 2;
        CASE SUM OF
            0,2: TX := TX + SPACING;
              1: TX := TX + 2*SPACING;
        END;
    END;

    TY := TY + H;

  END;

END;
```

All of the wallpaper symmetries can be produced by laying out motifs with different degrees of rotational and reflective symmetry, and motifs produced by glide reflection, in square, equilateral triangular, and regular hexagonal grids. Thus they can be generated by making substitutions for Triangle in one or another of our grid-generating procedures. For example, substitution of

```
DIHEDRAL (SEPARATION,6);
```

in Hex_grid yields symmetrical wallpaper patterns of the type shown in figure 14-44. Variants can be produced by changing values for the parameters Spacing

14-44. Variants of a symmetrical pattern with the same elementary motif and the same symmetry.

and Separation. Considerable complexity results when the values assigned to these parameters result in overlap of the triangular elements.

Procedural and Functional Parameters

Let us summarize a general approach to the generation of symmetrical patterns. You begin with a library of procedures to generate elementary motifs. You can then generate patterns with rotational symmetry by invoking such procedures from within Cyclic, patterns with bilateral symmetry by invoking them from within Bilateral, and patterns with dihedral symmetry by invoking them from within Dihedral. Regular frieze patterns can be produced by invoking procedures to generate motifs with no symmetry, rotational symmetry, and dihedral symmetry from within Frieze. In addition, you can use motifs that have glide symmetries across the X and Y axes. Finally, you can produce patterns with wallpaper symmetry by invoking procedures to generate repeating motifs from within Square_grid, Tri_grid, and Hex_grid. The repeating motifs may have no symmetry, or they may, themselves, be generated by the rotation, reflection, and glide reflection of more elementary motifs.

By manipulating the scale of the repeating motif in a pattern, and the various parameters that control spacing of instances of the motif, you can vary proportions and figure/ground relationships. Very complex effects can be produced by scaling motifs and setting spacing parameters so that overlaps occur.

A symmetry group is a type of spatial organization that, as we have seen, can be generated by an appropriate procedure. Different instances can be produced not only by varying the parameters, but also by using the procedure to arrange different elementary motifs in the same type of spatial organization.

It is cumbersome, however, to change the code of a symmetry-generating procedure whenever we want it to repeat a different elementary motif. Pascal allows use of *procedural parameters* and *functional parameters* (in addition to value and variable parameters with which we are already familiar), and the use of procedural parameters resolves this difficulty.

Procedures and functions can be passed as parameters to other procedures and functions. In the formal parameter list, procedure and function parameters have the same syntax as procedure and function headings. Whenever a formal procedure or function is referenced, the corresponding actual parameter is activated. In the following symmetry-generating program, for example, Motif is a procedural parameter. This allows procedures that draw different figures to be passed in, so that symmetrical patterns of different figures can be drawn.

```
PROCEDURE CYCLIC (NUMBER : INTEGER; PROCEDURE MOTIF);

    VAR INCREMENT,ANGLE : REAL;
        COUNT : INTEGER;

    BEGIN

        INCREMENT := 360.0/NUMBER;
        ANGLE := 0;

        FOR COUNT := 1 TO NUMBER DO
        BEGIN

            START;
                ROTATE (ANGLE);
```

```
                { Invoke selected figure }
                    MOTIF;
                FINISH;

                ANGLE := ANGLE + INCREMENT;

            END;

        END;
```

Symmetrical patterns illustrate the use of procedural parameters particularly clearly, but any graphic procedure may be parameterized in this way. We might, for example, pass different line types into a procedure to draw a polygon, different window types into a procedure to fenestrate an elevation, and so on. This generalizes the idea of type of graphic motif that we have used until now; the essence of the type is simply a spatial organization. Instances might vary not only in shape and position, but also in the nature of their components.

Some Pascal systems do not support procedural and functional parameters. You should check the documentation of the particular system that you are using.

Repetition of Scale Transformations

So far in this chapter, we have considered the repetition of rotations, reflections, and translations to generate regular figures. We can also use our **scale** operator this way. This next procedure, for example, generates the pattern of nested squares shown in figure 14-45:

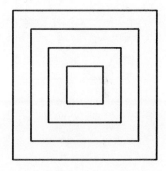

14-45. A pattern of nested squares.

```
PROCEDURE NEST_SQUARES (INCREMENT : REAL;
                            REPETITIONS : INTEGER);

    { Nest squares inside a unit square }

    VAR SIDE : REAL;
        COUNT : INTEGER;

    BEGIN

        SIDE := 1;

        FOR COUNT := 1 TO REPETITIONS DO
        BEGIN

            START;
                SCALE (SIDE,SIDE);
                SQUARE;
            FINISH;

            SIDE := SIDE - INCREMENT;

        END;

    END;
```

You will recall from earlier chapters the pattern of rotating and diminishing squares shown in figure 14-46. Now that we have **scale** and **rotation** operators at our disposal, we can express the procedure to generate it thus:

```
    PROCEDURE NEST_SQUARES (REPETITIONS : INTEGER);
```

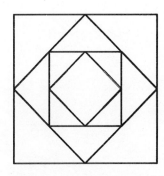

14-46. A pattern of rotating and diminishing squares.

```
{ Nest rotated squares inside a unit square }
  VAR SIDE,ANGLE : REAL;
      COUNT : INTEGER;
BEGIN
    SIDE := 1;
    ANGLE := 0;

    FOR COUNT := 1 TO REPETITIONS DO
    BEGIN
        START;
            SCALE (SIDE,SIDE);
            ROTATE (ANGLE);
            SQUARE;
        FINISH;
        SIDE := SQRT(SQR(SIDE)/2);
        ANGLE := ANGLE + 90;
    END;
END;
```

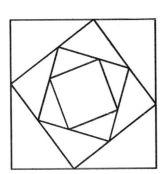

14-47. A variant pattern of rotating and diminishing squares, in which 3, 4, 5 rational triangles appear.

A variant, in which 3, 4, 5 rational triangles instead of root two triangles are generated, is shown in figure 14-47. The procedure to generate this is:

```
PROCEDURE NEST_SQUARES (REPETITIONS : INTEGER);

  { Nest rotated squares inside a unit square }

  VAR SIDE,ANGLE : REAL;
      COUNT : INTEGER;

BEGIN
    SIDE := 1;
    ANGLE := 0;

    FOR COUNT := 1 TO REPETITIONS DO
    BEGIN
        START;
            SCALE (SIDE,SIDE);
            ROTATE (ANGLE);
            SQUARE;
        FINISH;
        SIDE := SIDE * 5.0/7.0;
        ANGLE := ANGLE + 60;
    END;
END;
```

The "tree" composed of triangles (fig. 14-48) is a motif taken from the notebooks of Paul Klee. The repeating element is an equilateral triangle to which translation and unequal scale transformations are applied. The procedure for this is:

```
PROCEDURE TREE (SPACING,SX,SY,SX_INC,SY_INC : REAL;
                REPETITIONS : INTEGER);

  { Tree generated by scaling and translation of equilateral triangles }
```

```
    VAR TY : REAL;
        COUNT : INTEGER;
BEGIN
    TY := 0;
    FOR COUNT := 1 TO REPETITIONS DO
    BEGIN
        START;
            SCALE (SX,SY);
            TRANSLATE (0.0,TY);
            TRIANGLE;
        FINISH;
        SX := SX - SX_INC;
        SY := SY + SY_INC;
        TY := TY + SPACING;
    END;
END;
```

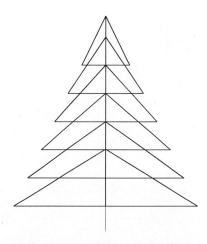

14-48. A tree motif (from the *Notebooks of Paul Klee*) generated by translation and unequal scaling of an equilateral triangle.

Different combinations of values for the parameters controlling the translation increment and the two scale increments produce variants with different characters.

Some architectural compositions are constructed according to a similar logic. The pagoda in figure 14-49 was generated this way. Both the tree and the pagoda can, in fact, be produced by the same procedure if we introduce a procedural parameter. Much architectural form can be understood, in the same way, as the result of abstracting a spatial organization from nature and substituting a new motif within that organization.

Motifs Constructed from Arcs

Many traditional architectural and decorative motifs are constructed by using compasses to strike arcs of specified radius about a specified center. In computer graphics, it is often convenient to strike the arc about the origin of the coordinate system, then to use transformations to locate the motif in the composition.

An arch can be constructed from arcs in this way. If only one arc is used in the construction, then there are three basic types (fig. 14-50): the flat arch, in which the radius is greater than half the span; the round arch, in which the radius is exactly half the span; and the bulging arch, in which the center-point is higher than the springing point.

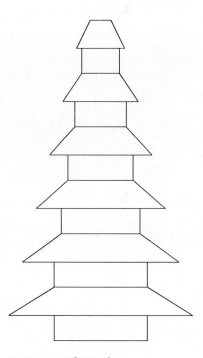

14-49. A pagoda motif.

There are many reasonable ways to parameterize arches, depending on how an architect might want to fit them into a composition. With a semicircular arch, we know that the bounding rectangle will have a proportion of 2:1. Thus we probably would choose to specify the width of the bounding rectangle (that is, the span of the arch) as the single parameter (fig. 14-51).

Using our transformation system, it is convenient to center the arch at the origin and set the span equal to one world unit. It can then be scaled to the appropriate size and translated to the desired position with the **scale** and **translate** transformation procedures.

If we assume that the arch can either be flat, semicircular, or bulging, then span is disconnected from height to yield an additional parameter (fig. 14-52).

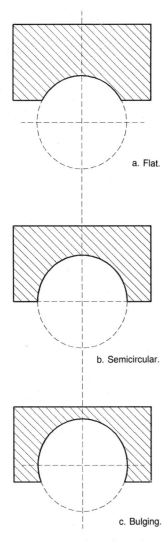

a. Flat.

b. Semicircular.

c. Bulging.

14-50. Basic types of circular arches.

Since the structural logic of a uniformly loaded arch dictates bilateral symmetry of form, we need only draw half an arch, then reflect it to get the other half. Here, then, is a generalized arch procedure based on this principle, with a single parameter, Height, that represents the ratio of height to span. (The additional parameter N_segments is required by the Arc procedure, but does not concern us here.)

```
PROCEDURE ARC (XC,YC,RADIUS,
               START_ANGLE,STOP_ANGLE : REAL;
               N_SEGMENTS : INTEGER);

  { Draw arc of unit diameter centered at 0,0 }

    VAR DEGREES,THETA,X,Y : REAL;
        SIDES : INTEGER;
    CONST RADIANS = 0.01745;

    BEGIN

      { Calculate angle increment in radians }

        DEGREES := (STOP_ANGLE - START_ANGLE)/
                   N_SEGMENTS * RADIANS;

        THETA := START_ANGLE * RADIANS;
      { Draw segments of arc }

        FOR SIDES := 1 TO N_SEGMENTS+1 DO
        BEGIN
            Y := YC + RADIUS * SIN(THETA);
            X := XC + RADIUS * COS(THETA);
            IF SIDES = 1 THEN
                MOVE (X,Y)
            ELSE
                DRAW (X,Y);
            THETA := THETA + DEGREES;

        END;

END;
PROCEDURE HALF_ARCH (HEIGHT : REAL;
                     N_SEGMENTS : INTEGER);

VAR HALF_SPAN,RADIUS,XC,YC,THETA,
    START_ANGLE,STOP_ANGLE : REAL;
CONST RADIANS = 0.01745;
BEGIN

  { Assuming a unit span, half the span = 0.5 }

    HALF_SPAN := 0.5;

  { Calculate radius and center of arc }

    RADIUS := (SQR(HALF_SPAN) + SQR(HEIGHT))/
              (2*HEIGHT);
    XC := 0.0;
    YC := HEIGHT - RADIUS;
    STOP_ANGLE := 90;

  { Semi-circular arch }
```

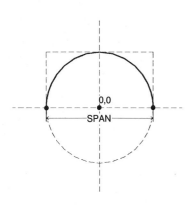

0,0

SPAN

14-51. The parameterization of a semi-circular arch.

```
        IF  HEIGHT  =  RADIUS  THEN
            START_ANGLE  :=  0
    { Flat  or  bulging  arch }
        ELSE
            START_ANGLE  :=  ARCTAN((RADIUS  −  HEIGHT)/
                            (HALF_SPAN))/RADIANS;

    { Draw  arc }
            ARC  (XC,YC,RADIUS,START_ANGLE,STOP_ANGLE,
                N_SEGMENTS);
        END:
PROCEDURE  ARCH  (HEIGHT :  REAL ;  N_SEGMENTS :  INTEGER);

    { Draws  full  arch  by  reflecting  HALF_ARCH }
        BEGIN
        { Right  half }
            HALF_ARCH  (HEIGHT,N_SEGMENTS);
        { Left  half }
            START;
                REFLECT_Y;
                HALF_ARCH  (HEIGHT,N_SEGMENTS);
            FINISH;
        END;
```

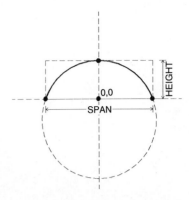

14-52. The parameterization of an arch with variable height and span.

A closely related architectural motif is the arcade. Here the architect has three additional choices to make: the number of arches; the spacing between arches; and the space above the arch (fig. 14-53a). Figure 14-53b shows some variants of the type. They were generated by the following program:

```
PROCEDURE  HALF_ARCADE  (HEIGHT,SPACING,SPACE_ABOVE :  REAL;
                        N_ARCHES,N_SEGMENTS :  INTEGER);

    { Creates  half  an  arcade  which  can  be  reflected  to  make  a
      complete  arcade }
    VAR  SPAN,HALF_SPAN,X,Y,TX :  REAL;
         N,COUNT :  INTEGER;

BEGIN
        SPAN  :=  1;
        HALF_SPAN  :=  SPAN/2;

    { Odd  number  of  arches }
        IF  N_ARCHES  MOD  2  =  1  THEN
        BEGIN

            HALF_ARCH  (HEIGHT,N_SEGMENTS);
            MOVE  (HALF_SPAN,0.0);
            X  :=  SPACING  +  HALF_SPAN;
            DRAW  (X,0.0);
            TX  :=  SPAN  +  SPACING;

        END
    { Even  number  of  arches }
        ELSE
            BEGIN
```

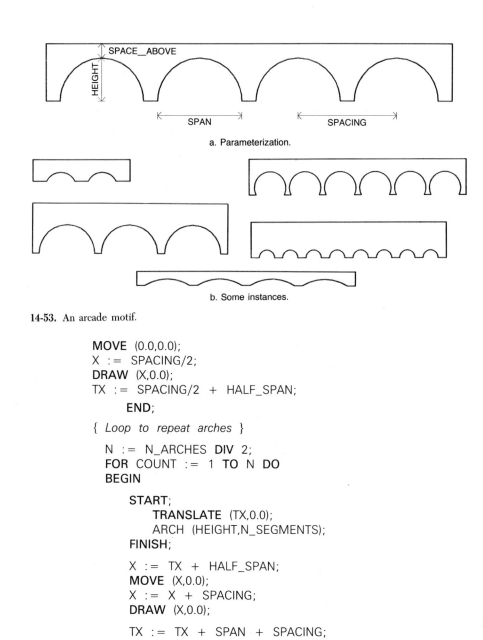

a. Parameterization.

b. Some instances.

14-53. An arcade motif.

```
MOVE (0.0,0.0);
X := SPACING/2;
DRAW (X,0.0);
TX := SPACING/2 + HALF_SPAN;
      END;

{ Loop to repeat arches }

  N := N_ARCHES DIV 2;
  FOR COUNT := 1 TO N DO
  BEGIN

      START;
          TRANSLATE (TX,0.0);
          ARCH (HEIGHT,N_SEGMENTS);
      FINISH;

      X := TX + HALF_SPAN;
      MOVE (X,0.0);
      X := X + SPACING;
      DRAW (X,0.0);

      TX := TX + SPAN + SPACING;

  END;

{ Draw end and top of arcade }

  Y := HEIGHT + SPACE_ABOVE;
  DRAW (X,Y);
  DRAW (0.0,Y);

END;
```

Now, a right triangle may be inscribed within a semicircular arch (fig. 14-54a). This suggests another way to generalize and introduce additional degrees of design freedom; we can let the height of the triangle become greater than half the base, and we can let the radii of the two half arcs be offset (fig. 14-54b), so that we obtain five degrees of design freedom. This new type is the *pointed* arch, used in gothic architecture.

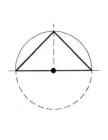

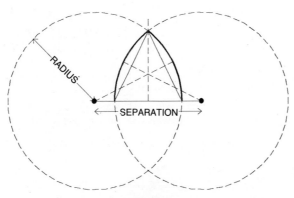

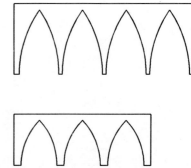

a. A right triangle inscribed within
a semicircular arch.

b. Parameterization.

14-54. The pointed arch.

Figure 14-55 illustrates some arcades of pointed arches, such as we might find in the nave of a gothic cathedral. Notice how the parameterization of the pointed arch allows achievement of the soaring verticality that is characteristic of gothic architecture. Compare this with the horizontal rhythms of semicircular arcades, which we considered earlier.

Another possibility is to base the arch on the form of the oval. Such arches are called *ogees*. The oval is visually almost indistinguishable from the ellipse, but is constructed from circular arcs of different radii. There are two standard subtypes: one is drawn from three centers (fig. 14-56); and the other is drawn from five centers (fig. 14-57). A three-centered ogee is generated by:

14-55. Arcades of pointed arches.

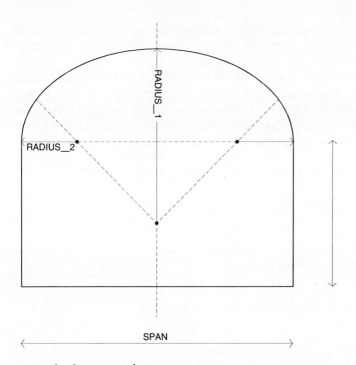

14-56. The three-centered ogee.

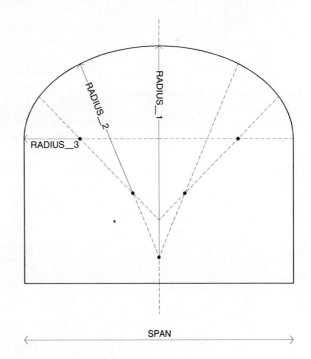

14-57. The five-centered ogee.

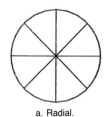

a. Radial.

b. Concentric.

c. Radioconcentric.

d. Parallel.

14-58. Methods for subdividing circles.

```
PROCEDURE OVAL (A,B : REAL; N_SEGMENTS : INTEGER);

   VAR D,XC1,YC1,XC2,YC2,RADIUS1,RADIUS2 : REAL;
       START_ANGLE,STOP_ANGLE : REAL;

BEGIN

   { Quarter oval based on 3-centered arc construction }
   { A is radius of major axis }
   { B is radius of minor axis }

      D := SQRT (2*SQR(A−B))/2;

   { Construct first arc }

      XC1 := A − B + D;
      YC1 := 0;
      RADIUS2 := B − D;
      START_ANGLE := 0;
      STOP_ANGLE := 45;

      ARC (XC1,YC1,RADIUS 2,START_ANGLE,STOP_ANGLE,
           N_SEGMENTS);

   { Construct second arc }

      XC2 := 0.0;
      YC2 := −XC1;
      RADIUS1 := RADIUS2 + SQRT (2*SQR(XC1));
      START_ANGLE := 45;
      STOP_ANGLE := 90;

      ARC (XC2,YC2,RADIUS1,START_ANGLE,STOP_ANGLE,
           N_ SEGMENTS);

   END;
```

Once an arch has been constructed, another classic architectural problem often arises. How can we subdivide it by window panes? More generally, what principles can we adopt for subdividing the circle?

One commonly used principle is subdivision by regularly spaced radial lines (fig. 14-58a). Another is subdivision by concentric circles (fig. 14-58b). These can be combined to yield a radioconcentric pattern (fig. 14-58c). Yet another possibility is subdivision by parallel straight lines (fig. 14-58d).

One parameter for any of these types of constructions will obviously be the number of subdivisions. The following procedure, for example, radially divides a specified circle into a specified number of equal parts:

```
PROCEDURE RADIAL (N_PARTS : INTEGER);

   { Divides a circle of unit diameter into N_PARTS }

   VAR ANGLE,INCREMENT : REAL;
       PART : INTEGER;

BEGIN

   { Generate a unit circle centered at origin }

      CIRCLE;

      INCREMENT := 360.0/N_PARTS;
      ANGLE := 0;
```

```
{ Using a horizontal line of unit length, with left endpoint
  positioned at the origin, scale and rotate it to divide circle }

FOR PART := 1 TO N_PARTS DO
BEGIN

    START;
        SCALE (0.5,1.0);
        ROTATE (ANGLE);
        LINE;
    FINISH;

    ANGLE := ANGLE + INCREMENT;

END;

END;
```

Figure 14-59 shows some output.

In the case of concentric subdivision, we must consider how to space the circles. The simplest approach is to subdivide the radius of the outer circle into a specified number of equal parts. This is accomplished with the following procedure:

```
PROCEDURE CONCENTRIC (N_PARTS : INTEGER);

    { Set of concentric circles inside a unit circle }

    VAR SPACING,DIAMETER : REAL;
        PART : INTEGER;

    BEGIN

        DIAMETER := 1.0;
        SPACING := DIAMETER / N_PARTS;

        FOR PART := 1 TO N_PARTS DO
        BEGIN

            START;
                SCALE (DIAMETER,DIAMETER);
                CIRCLE;
            FINISH;

            DIAMETER := DIAMETER - SPACING;

        END;

    END;
```

14-59. Radial division of a circle into equal parts.

Some examples of output are shown in figure 14-60.

Another possibility is a so-called *Fresnel* subdivision into annular regions of equal area. This requires a rather more complex procedure:

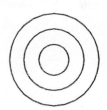

```
PROCEDURE FRESNEL (N_PARTS : INTEGER);

    { Set of concentric circles inside a unit circle with annular regions
      of equal area }

    VAR SPACING,DIAMETER,S : REAL;
        PART : INTEGER;
```

14-60. Evenly spaced concentric subdivision.

14-61. Fresnel subdivision.

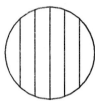

a. Equal spacing.

b. Equal areas.

14-62. Subdivision by parallel lines.

```
BEGIN
    S := 1;
    SPACING := S/N_PARTS;

    FOR PART := 1 TO N_PARTS DO
    BEGIN
        DIAMETER := 1.0 * SQRT(S);
        START;
            SCALE (DIAMETER,DIAMETER);
            CIRCLE;
        FINISH;

        S := S - SPACING;

    END;

END;
```

As the example of output in figure 14-61 illustrates, Fresnel circles become more closely spaced as they become larger.

Similar approaches can be taken to subdivision by parallel lines. The lines may be equally spaced, or they may divide the circle into equal areas (fig. 14-62).

The subdivided semicircular window, or *fanlight*, is a closely related architectural type. The subdivision by mullions and transoms may be radial, or radioconcentric, or divided by parallel vertical lines (fig. 14-63).

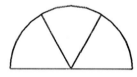

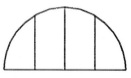

a. Methods of subdivision.

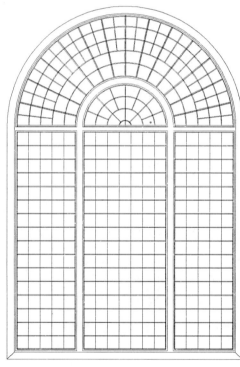

b. An elaborate arched window by Sir Christopher Wren.

14-63. Fanlight motifs.

The construction shown in figure 14-64 is another variant on the principle of radioconcentric subdivision. It might be used for the layout of wedge-shaped rooms in a plan, or the layout of the voussoirs of an arch. A reasonable parameterization is by the inner radius, outer radius, start angle, finish angle, and number of divisions. The following procedure produces patterns of this type:

```
PROCEDURE RADIOCONCENTRIC (INNER_RADIUS,OUTER_RADIUS,
                           START_ANGLE,FINISH_ANGLE :
                           REAL; N_PARTS : INTEGER);

    VAR LINE_LENGTH,INCREMENT,ANGLE : REAL;
        N,PART : INTEGER;

BEGIN

    LINE_LENGTH := OUTER_RADIUS - INNER_RADIUS;
    INCREMENT := (START_ANGLE - FINISH_ANGLE) /
                 N_PARTS;
    ANGLE := START_ANGLE;
    N := N_PARTS + 1;

    { Using a horizontal line of unit length with left end positioned
      at the origin, scale, translate and rotate }

    FOR PART := 1 TO N DO
    BEGIN

        START;
            SCALE (LINE_LENGTH,1.0);
            TRANSLATE (INNER_RADIUS,0.0);
            ROTATE (ANGLE);
            LINE;
        FINISH;

        ANGLE := ANGLE + INCREMENT;

    END;

END;
```

14-64. The voussoir motif.

Various examples of output are shown in figure 14-65.

Using the Arc and Radioconcentric procedures to generate an *intrados* (inner curve of an arch), radial subdivisions, and an *extrados* (outer curve), we can develop a general procedure for construction of arches of any thickness, with any specified number of voussoirs. The parameterization is as shown in figure 14-66a, and the code runs as follows:

14-65. Some output from Radioconcentric.

```
PROCEDURE ARCH (INNER_RADIUS,OUTER_RADIUS : REAL;
                N_PARTS : INTEGER);

BEGIN

    { Inner curve }

    ARC (0.0,0.0,INNER_RADIUS,0.0,180.0,N_PARTS);

    { Outer curve }

    ARC (0.0,0.0,OUTER_RADIUS,0.0,180.0,N_PARTS);

    { Voussoirs }

    RADIOCONCENTRIC (INNER_RADIUS,OUTER_RADIUS,0.0,
                     180.0,N_PARTS);

END;
```

An **array** of variant arches that were generated by this procedure is illustrated in figure 14-66b.

If the intrados and extrados are created with straight line segments, rather than arcs, a subtly different array of instances emerges (fig. 14-67). Further varieties can be produced by introducing procedural parameters to allow variation of intrados and extrados profiles (fig. 14-68).

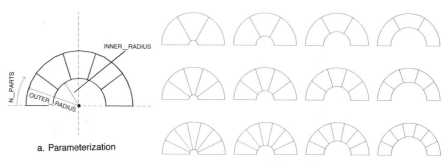

a. Parameterization

b. Some variants.

14-66. An arch with voussoirs.

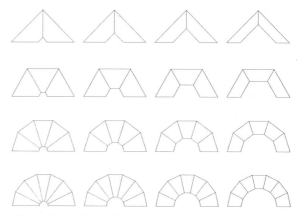

14-67. Arches with intrados and extrados formed by straight line segments.

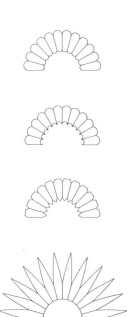

14-68. More arches, produced by allowing variation of intrados and extrados profiles.

Compositions with Mixed Symmetry

Many compositions contain parts with different symmetries. Consider, for example, the classical temple elevation in figure 14-69. The whole thing has bilateral symmetry, and the colonnade has frieze symmetry.

The plan (fig. 14-69) has a rather more complex combination of symmetries. The overall rectangle has symmetry about two axes. The details of the plan, however, distinguish between front and back and so reduce this to bilateral symmetry. The column grid sets up a wallpaper symmetry, but this is broken by insertion of the cella.

In general, the various symmetries that can be discovered within a composition suggest an appropriate way to break the composition down into a hierarchy of elements and subsystems. The elementary motifs can then be put together by a corresponding hierarchy of transformations that expresses the various symmetries that are involved. Broken symmetries can be handled with conditionals. Figure 14-70 shows an elevation by Sir Christopher Wren broken down in this way. In classical architecture, generally, there is symmetry of each element, symmetry of each subsystem, and symmetry of the whole. Early modern architects, on the other hand, often arranged symmetrical elements to form asymmetrical overall compositions (fig. 14-71). In Japanese stone gardens (Ryoan-ji, for example), asymmetrical elements form asymmetrical wholes.

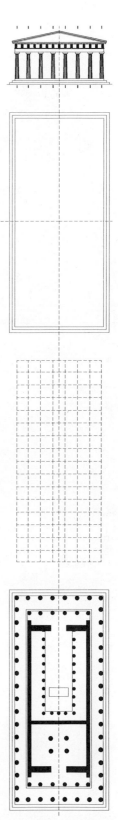

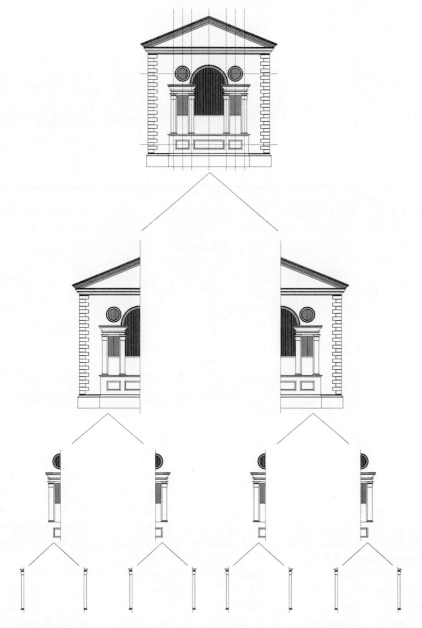

14-70. Hierarchy of symmetries in an elevation by Sir Christopher Wren (St. Olave's, Jewry).

14-69. The symmetries of a classical temple in elevation and plan.

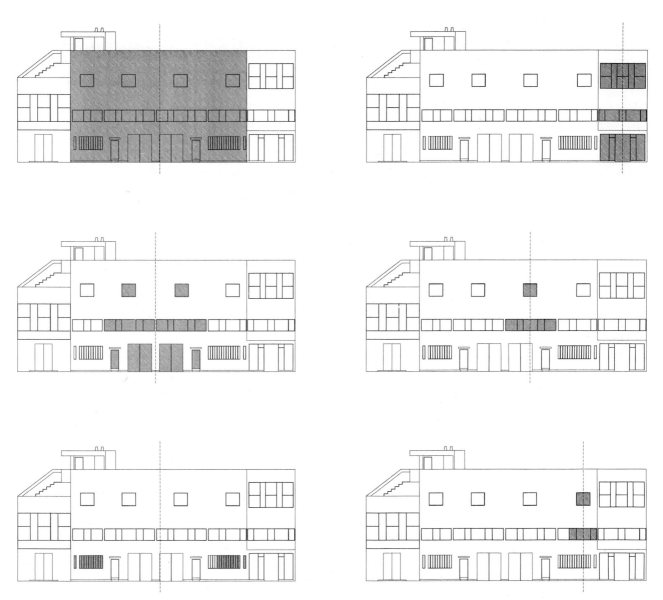

14-71. Early modern architectural composition; symmetrical elements form an asymmetrical whole. (Le Corbusier's Villa Garches, north elevation.)

Summary

In this chapter we have explored the use of operators to transform drawings stored in data structures. We have seen that you can build up a toolbox of graphic operators, implemented as Pascal procedures, in much the same way that you can build up a vocabulary of graphic elements. Graphic operators can then be applied to graphic vocabulary elements to put together graphic compositions.

In particular, we have focused on operators to perform the basic geometric transformations: translation, rotation, reflection, and scaling. Use of these operators led us to the use of a world coordinate system and viewing operators to display a selected part of the drawing on a selected part of the screen.

A library of transformation and viewing operators, based on these concepts,

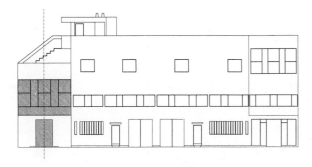

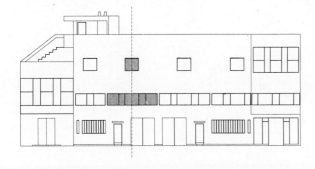

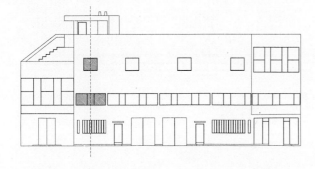

has been introduced. When this library is used, the delimiting operators **start** and **finish** control the application of transformations to parts of the drawing and define the hierarchical structure of the drawing.

This library can be used, along with the ideas of graphic vocabulary, repetition, conditionals, and hierarchical structure that were introduced earlier, to produce short, elegant programs that generate large and complicated compositions. To do this, though, you must have a sophisticated understanding of the structure of the drawing that you want to produce, particularly its symmetries.

Figure 14-72 shows some examples of architectural elevations that were generated by carefully structured Pascal programs employing our library of operators. Examine them and try to understand the structuring principles that were used.

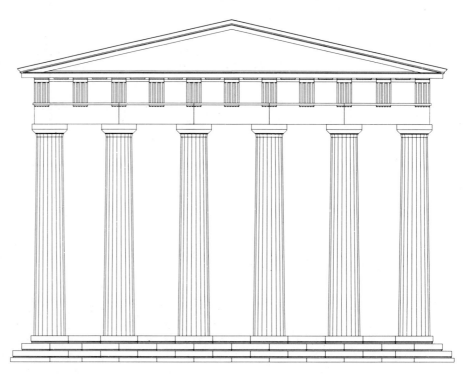

14-72. Examples of architectural elevations generated by Pascal programs. (Images [through page 475] by Manuel Bernar, Marty Borko, Roger Cantrell, Jan Darst, Jim LeFever, Alex Maxim, Pat Polk, Michael Poss.)

Exercises

1. The procedure Square generates a square of unit diameter, centered at the origin of the world coordinate system, with sides parallel to the coordinate axes. Draw on graph paper, in the world coordinate system, the result produced by the following sequence of code:

a.

```
PROCEDURE SHIFT_SQUARE;
    BEGIN
        START;
            TRANSLATE (0.6,0.6);
            SQUARE;
        FINISH;
    END;
```

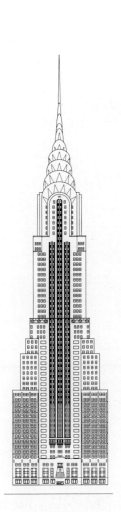 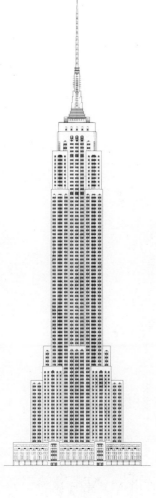 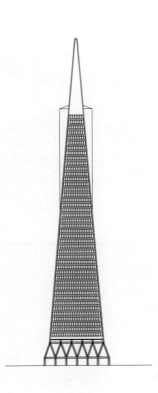

```
PROCEDURE TWO_SQUARES;

    BEGIN

    SHIFT_SQUARE;

    START;
        ROTATE (180);
        SHIFT_SQUARE;
    FINISH;

END;

PROCEDURE FOUR_SQUARES;

    BEGIN

        TWO_SQUARES;

        START;
            REFLECT_Y;
```

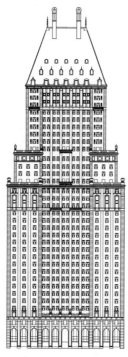 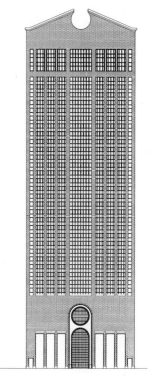

```
            TWO_SQUARES;
        FINISH;

    END;


PROCEDURE ROTATE_SQUARES;

    BEGIN

        START;
            ROTATE (45);
            FOUR_SQUARES;
        FINISH;

    END;

    { Invoked in main program }

    ROTATE_SQUARES;

b.

PROCEDURE DIAMOND (SPACING,SY : REAL);

    VAR TY : REAL;

    BEGIN

        TY := SQRT(2) + SPACING;

        START;
```

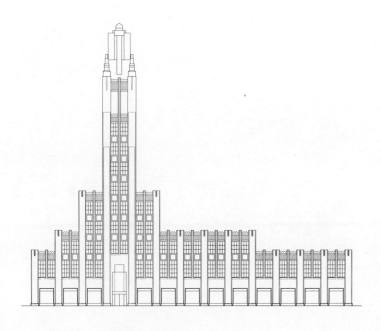

```
                SCALE  (SY,SY);
                ROTATE  (45);
                TRANSLATE  (0.0,TY);
                SQUARE;
            FINISH;

    END;

PROCEDURE  CYCLIC  (SPACING,SY  :  REAL;
                       N  :  INTEGER);

    VAR  ANGLE,INCREMENT  :  REAL;
         COUNT  :  INTEGER;

    BEGIN

        INCREMENT  :=  360.0  /  N;
        ANGLE  :=  0.0;

        FOR  COUNT  :=  1  TO  N  DO
        BEGIN

            START;
                ROTATE  (ANGLE);
                DIAMOND  (SPACING,SY);
            FINISH;

            ANGLE  :=  ANGLE  +  INCREMENT;
```

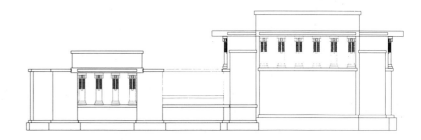

```
        END;

      END;

    { Invoked in main program }
      CYCLIC (0.1,1.0,4);


  c.


      CYCLIC (0.0,2.0,2);
```

2. Figure 14-73 shows a square located in a world coordinate system. Assuming that you are working with a 1,024 by 1,024 screen coordinate system, draw the screen displays produced by the following viewing transformations:

VIEW (500,500,1000,1000,0.0,0.0,1000.0,0.0);

VIEW (500,500,1000,1000, − 0.5, − 0.5,500,0.0)

VIEW (300,300,100,100,1.0,0.0.100.0,45.0);

3. Using the transformation operators that are provided in **advanced_ graphics**, write new transformation operators to perform:

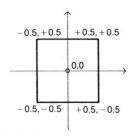

14-73. A square located in a world coordinate system.

- rotation about an arbitrary point
- reflection across the X axis

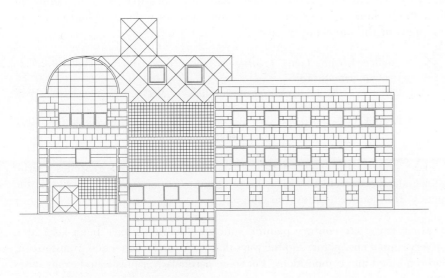

- glide reflection across the X axis
- glide reflection across the Y axis

4. Write a procedure to generate a regular polygon of unit diameter, centered on the origin of the world coordinate system, with the number of sides as a parameter. Using translation, rotation, and reflection to position instances, unequal scaling to vary size and proportion, and variation in the number of sides, explore the kinds of compositions that can be produced using this motif.

5. Figure 14-74 shows the schema of a villa plan from Andrea Palladio's *Four Books of Architecture*. It is composed of just a few different types of polygons. Using procedures that generate such polygons, write a program to generate this plan.

6. Numerous examples of rotational, dihedral, frieze, and wallpaper patterns are shown in:

- Dye, Daniel Sheets. *Chinese Lattice Designs*. New York: Dover, 1974. (Reprint of the original 1937 edition.)
- Grünbaum, Branko, and G. C. Shepherd. *Tilings and Patterns*. New York: W.H. Freeman, 1987.

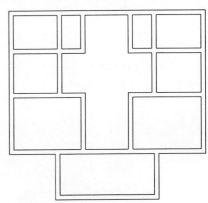

14-74. Schema of a villa plan from Andrea Palladio's *Four Books of Architecture*.

- Jones, Owen. *The Grammar of Ornament*. New York: Van Nostrand Reinhold, 1982. (Reprint of the original 1856 edition.)

Write procedures to generate some of those.

7. Choose a simple geometric motif; write a procedure to generate it; and use it to produce patterns with rotational, dihedral, frieze, and wallpaper symmetry. Experiment with effects that result from scaling the motif, varying the spacing parameters, and overlapping. Using procedural parameters, experiment with substituting different motifs.

8. The French neoclassical architects C. N. Ledoux, Etienne Louis Boullée, and J. N. L. Durand produced plans and elevations that are remarkable for their strictly limited vocabulary and rigorous symmetry. You can find numerous examples in the following treatises:

- Boullée, Etienne Louis. *Treatise on Architecture*, edited by Helen Rosenau. London: Tiranti, 1953.
- Durand, J. N. L. *Architecture*. Nordlingen: Verlag Dr. Alfons Uhl, 1985. (Reprint of *Précis des Leçons d'Architecture*, 1819.)
- Ledoux, C. N. *L'Architecture*. Princeton: Princeton Architectural Press, 1983. (Reprint of the original 1804 edition.)

Choose one of these compositions and, using **advanced_graphics**, write a program to generate it. Make the program as concise and expressive of the logic of the composition as you can.

9. Many twentieth-century painters and graphic artists have been fascinated by very simple line motifs, and the ways that these can be generated, transformed, and combined into compositions. For some particularly sophisticated explorations see:

- Albers, Josef. *Despite Straight Lines*. New Haven, CT: Yale University Press, 1977.
- Klee, Paul. *Notebooks*. 2 vols. London: Lund Humphries, 1961.

Take some of the motifs of Klee or Albers, and write parameterized procedures to generate them. Use the transformation operators provided by **advanced_graphics** to combine them into compositions. By varying values for transformation parameters, study the effects of varying distances, rotations, and scales of motifs relative to each other.

10. The plan and elevation compositions of the modern architectural masters Le Corbusier, Frank Lloyd Wright, and Alvar Aalto rarely display rigid axial symmetry in the classical manner. But, on careful inspection, they can usually be found to display less obvious symmetries and carefully broken symmetries. Take a composition that interests you, and see if you can discover the underlying principles of symmetry, and the exceptions and distortions that are used to break symmetry. Using the insights that you gain from this analysis, write a concise, expressive program to generate the composition.

15.

Simple Drawing Editors

If you have been doing the exercises at the end of each chapter, you will be thoroughly familiar with the process of editing a text file using a text editor. Such editors allow you, at least, to insert and delete text, to file and retrieve text, and to select text with which you want to work. Some are very sophisticated and perform many additional functions. The process of working with a text editor is a highly interactive one. The computer issues a prompt, you respond by entering a command or data, the computer responds appropriately then prompts again, and so on (fig. 15-1).

A drawing editor allows you to manipulate a drawing (stored in some kind of graphic data structure) in a similar way. It enables you to insert, delete, and alter graphic elements in a drawing and to file and retrieve drawings. Drawing editors can become extremely complex, and a full discussion would take us far beyond the scope of this book. In this chapter, though, we shall introduce the basic ideas and discuss the implementation of some simple types of drawing editors.

Input Devices

The first step in implementating a drawing editor is to consider the form of the dialogue to take place between a user and the computer. What graphic input devices will you place at the user's disposal? At the very least there will be a keyboard. You may also want to use a light pen or a mouse for pointing at items on the screen, a graphic tablet for digitizing coordinates from an existing drawing, a voice input device for verbal commands, and so on. The list of possibilities is long (see chapter 3), and it continues to grow.

Here we shall be concerned with very simple drawing editors that serve to demonstrate basic principles and that can be implemented on almost any graphics terminal or personal computer; we shall not assume the availability of any specialized input devices. We shall restrict ourselves to use of a standard keyboard, together with some device (which might be nothing more than cursor keys) for positioning the cursor on the screen.

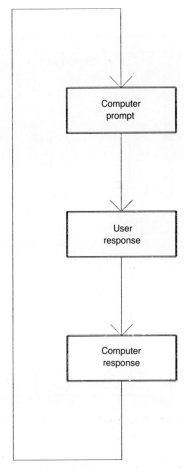

15-1. Dialogue with a text editor.

477

Giving Commands

How might you give commands that specify graphic operations?

One possibility is to design a system that requires a user to type in *single-word* commands. This is simple to implement, but places a burden of learning the commands on the user.

Another option is to design a system that displays text or graphic *menus* of commands and requires the user to select one. This places less burden on the user, but usually requires more elaborate and extensive programming. Furthermore, menus take up screen space and take time to display, so a menu-driven system can become unacceptably slow and cumbersome.

Yet another possibility is to design a *command language* (much like a simplified, special-purpose programming language) and to implement a command language interpreter for user commands. Command languages are potentially very flexible and powerful and can be very convenient and efficient in the hands of skilled, experienced users. But it requires considerable technical sophistication to design and implement a good command language interpreter, and command languages can be difficult and intimidating for the user.

Clearly, then, some trade-offs must be evaluated in order to choose the style of command that is most appropriate in a given context. Here, for simplicity, we shall use very simple text menus that are displayed on the screen.

Screen Organization

When you use an interactive graphics program, the screen usually displays at least three things: the drawing on which you are working, prompts or menus, and commands or data that you have entered. The code of your program might be displayed as well. You do not want text to be written over your drawing, and you do not want the screen to become a confused mess as your dialogue progresses. How then, should you organize the display of text and graphics on the available screen area?

Fixed Windows

A traditional approach is to divide the screen into fixed *windows* for the display of different kinds of information. Figure 15-2, for example, shows a screen layout that might reasonably be used for a simple interactive graphics program. On the right is a window for displaying the drawing being worked on, and on the left is an area for the display of prompts and input of typed commands and data. Storage tube screens are commonly organized in this way.

At least two special procedures are needed to handle this type of layout. The first, Set_up, organizes the screen for the beginning of a dialogue. It might, for example, clear the screen, draw the border of the graphics window (which will function as the viewport onto the drawing), and position the cursor at the top-left corner of the text area (fig. 15-3).

Graphic operations may affect the position of the cursor—leaving it at the end of the last vector drawn, for example. If this is the case on the system that you are using, you will need a procedure Return_cursor to return the cursor to a position below the last line of text (fig. 15-4), so new text will be displayed at that point.

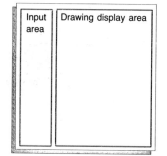

15-2. A layout for a storage-tube screen.

15-3. Result produced by the procedure Set_up.

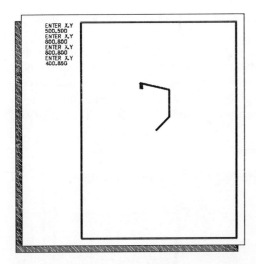

a. The cursor is left at the end of the last vector drawn.

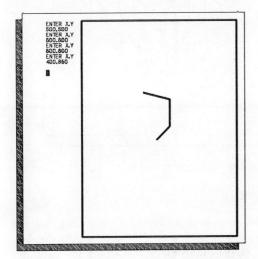

b. Return_cursor repositions it below the last line of text.

15-4. The effect of Return_cursor.

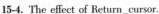

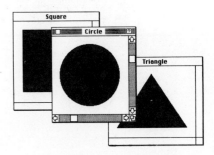

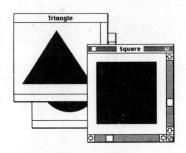

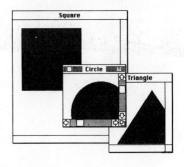

15-5. Dynamic windows on a raster display.

It is generally easy to implement Set_up and Return_cursor. The exact details, however, will depend on the hardware that you are using and the conventions of screen layout that you have adopted, so we will not go into them here.

Dynamic Windows

The use of fixed windows does clarify screen organization, but this technique has some severe disadvantages. First, it is very inflexible. It would be much better to allow the various windows to expand, contract, move around on the display surface, and perhaps to disappear temporarily, as appropriate at different stages in the dialogue. Second, fixed windows are usually very cumbersome to program. You need Set_up and Return_cursor functions, and you have to be careful to invoke them, as needed.

Dynamic windows become feasible and attractive when a raster display is used (particularly if a mouse is also available), and they have become increasingly standard on personal computers. You can think of them as sheets of paper laid out on a drawing board (fig. 15-5). They can be expanded, contracted, moved around, and overlaid as required. This can be done interactively, with a mouse, or under program control.

Windows may be organized in different ways for different purposes, but Pascal systems intended for use with windows typically devote one window to display of Pascal code, a second window to display of text input and output, and a third window to display of graphic output (fig. 15-6). In addition, windows that display menus can be temporarily "pulled down" from the top of the screen as required.

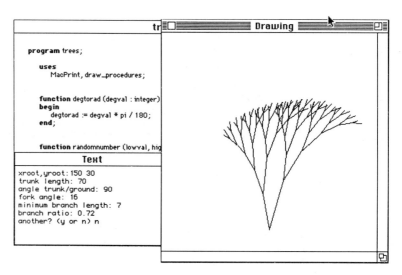

15-6. Windows on a personal computer display.

Standard Pascal does not provide built-in procedures for controlling dynamic windows, but Pascal systems intended for use with windows usually do. You should consult the documentation. In the examples discussed in the remainder of this chapter, we shall assume that dynamic windows are available and that a procedure Set_up (which invokes your particular Pascal system's special procedures for controlling windows) is used to size and position a graphic window.

Prompts and Responses

When a computer is waiting for text input, it displays the cursor in the text window. This gives the user little indication of what is expected, so it is usually best to display a prompt immediately before each **readln** command in the program.

At the very least, a prompt should indicate the type of value that is expected—for example an **integer**, a **real** number, or **char**acter data. Where a value for an **integer** variable is to be read, for instance, the following statements might be used.

```
WRITELN ('INTEGER:');
READLN (X);
```

Thus the prompt, followed by a user response, will look something like this:

```
INTEGER:
300
```

Some further explanation might be necessary as well:

```
WRITELN ('ENTER X COORDINATE...');
WRITELN ('INTEGER 0..1023:');
READLN (X);
```

Now the prompt and response look like this:

```
ENTER X COORDINATE...
INTEGER 0..1023
300
```

In general, prompts should be as concise as possible, but should not leave the user in doubt as to the nature of the expected response.

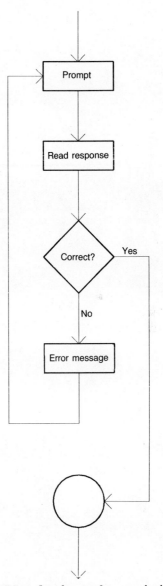

Detecting and Responding to Input Errors

It is inevitable that users of an interactive program will sometimes enter incorrect values. Wherever possible, then, the program should check the values immediately upon entry, and if an error is detected, inform the user and provide an opportunity for correction.

We know, for example, that an X screen coordinate must be in the range 0..1023, so the program can test for the conditions X < 0 and X > 1023. If either of these conditions is **true**, the program can write an appropriate message and prompt for entry of a new value. Code for this is as follows:

```
REPEAT;
    WRITELN ('ENTER X COORDINATE...');
    WRITELN ('INTEGER 0..1023:');
    READLN (X);

    IF (X < 0) OR (X > 1023) THEN
        WRITELN ('ILLEGAL VALUE - TRY AGAIN');
UNTIL (X >= 0) AND (X <= 1023);
```

A typical dialogue generated by this code looks like this:

```
ENTER X COORDINATE...
INTEGER 0..1023
2000
ILLEGAL VALUE - TRY AGAIN
ENTER X COORDINATE...
INTEGER 0..1023
1000
```

The essential logic is depicted by the flow diagram in figure 15-7.

15-7. A flow diagram for error-checking code.

Note that the only way to exit from the loop is to enter a value in the correct range. Note, also, that not all possible errors will be trapped within the loop. If the user enters **char**acter data, for example, the program will crash with a type error.

You can write much more elaborate and comprehensive error-detection code if you wish. This process is sometimes known as *bullet-proofing*. It may be justified in commercial applications, where a high level of user knowledge cannot safely be assumed, and where 100 percent reliability is critical. However, it is not worth the trouble in simple programs that will mostly be used by the programmer. The combination of informative prompting with some elementary input error checking will generally suffice to achieve adequate reliability.

Data Input Procedures

It is usually convenient to group the prompts, reads, and error checks for common kinds of input data into input procedures. For example, a procedure to read a pair of screen coordinates might be invoked like this:

```
READ_XY (X,Y);
```

The procedure is as follows:

```
PROCEDURE READ_XY (VAR X,Y : INTEGER);
  BEGIN

      WRITELN ('NEW POINT...');

      REPEAT;

          WRITELN;
          WRITELN ('ENTER X COORDINATE...');
          WRITELN ('INTEGER 0..1023:');
          READLN (X);

          IF (X < 0) OR (X > 1023) THEN
              WRITELN ('ILLEGAL VALUE - TRY AGAIN');

      UNTIL (X >= 0) AND (X <= 1023);

      REPEAT;

          WRITELN;
          WRITELN ('ENTER Y COORDINATE...');
          WRITELN ('INTEGER 0..1023:');
          READLN (Y);

          IF (Y < 0) OR (Y > 1023) THEN
              WRITELN ('ILLEGAL VALUE - TRY AGAIN');

      UNTIL (Y >= 0) AND (Y <= 1023);
  END;
```

The prompts that it produces look like this:

NEW POINT...

ENTER X COORDINATE...
INTEGER 0..1023:
1000

ENTER Y COORDINATE...
INTEGER 0..1023:
300

Notice that this procedure uses **var** parameters, since its role is to return values for X and Y to the procedure or program from which it is invoked.

Unit Conversions

Any necessary unit conversions may be carried out in input procedures. In architectural drafting applications, for example, it is often convenient to enter dimensions in feet and inches, both expressed as **integers**. But for computational purposes, we want **real** numbers of feet. The following input procedure, then, reads a dimension expressed in feet and inches and returns a **real** number of feet:

```
PROCEDURE READ_DIMENSION (VAR DIMENSION : REAL);
    VAR FEET,INCHES : INTEGER;

    BEGIN
        WRITELN ('DIMENSION...');
        WRITELN;
        WRITELN ('ENTER NUMBER OF FEET...');
        WRITELN ('INTEGER:');
        READLN (FEET);

        WRITELN;
        WRITELN ('ENTER NUMBER OF INCHES...');
        WRITELN ('INTEGER:');
        READLN (INCHES);

        DIMENSION := FEET + INCHES/12.0;

    END;
```

The prompts that it produces are as follows:

DIMENSION...

ENTER NUMBER OF FEET...
INTEGER:
12

ENTER NUMBER OF INCHES...
INTEGER:
6

If we wanted this procedure to return a **real** number of meters, we could modify it as follows:

DIMENSION := (FEET + INCHES/12.0) * 0.3048;

The prompts remain the same here, but a different value is recorded in the data structure.

It is usually easiest to enter angles in degrees, but Pascal trigonometric functions require them to be expressed in radians. So it is useful to have a procedure that reads an angle expressed in degrees and returns a value in radians as follows:

```
PROCEDURE READ_ANGLE (VAR ANGLE : REAL);
    VAR DEGREES : REAL;
    CONST RADIANS = 0.01745;

  BEGIN

    WRITELN ('ANGLE...');
    WRITELN;
    WRITELN ('ENTER NUMBER OF DEGREES...');
    WRITELN ('REAL 0..360:');

    READLN (DEGREES);

    ANGLE := DEGREES * RADIANS;

  END;
```

The prompts look like this:

```
ANGLE

ENTER NUMBER OF DEGREES...
REAL 0..360:
36.75
```

Input of Vectors

An input procedure to enter a vector defined by its endpoints in the world coordinate system can be written as follows:

```
PROCEDURE READ_VECTOR (VAR START_X,START_Y,END_X,END_Y :
                            REAL);
  BEGIN

    WRITELN ('VECTOR...');
    WRITELN;
    WRITELN ('ENTER START X...');
    WRITELN ('REAL:');
    READLN (START_X);

    WRITELN;
    WRITELN ('ENTER START Y...');
    WRITELN ('REAL:');
    READLN (START_Y);
```

```
            WRITELN;
            WRITELN ('ENTER  END  X...');
            WRITELN ('REAL:');
            READLN  (END_X);

            WRITELN;
            WRITELN ('ENTER  END  Y...');
            WRITELN ('REAL:');
            READLN  (END_Y);

      END;
```

This data input procedure generates the following prompts:

```
VECTOR...

ENTER  START  X...
REAL:
10.3

ENTER  START  Y...
REAL:
7.45

ENTER  END  X...
REAL:
−84.9

ENTER  END  Y...
REAL:
100
```

If, instead, we wanted to enter vectors by starting point, direction, and distance, we could use a procedure like this:

```
PROCEDURE  READ_VECTOR  (VAR  START_X,START_Y,DIRECTION,
                              DISTANCE  :  REAL);
      BEGIN

            WRITELN ('VECTOR...');

            WRITELN;
            WRITELN ('ENTER  START  X...');
            WRITELN ('REAL:');
            READLN  (START_X);

            WRITELN;
            WRITELN ('ENTER  START  Y...');
            WRITELN ('REAL:');
            READLN  (START_Y);

            WRITELN;
            WRITELN ('ENTER  DIRECTION...');
            WRITELN ('REAL  0..360:');
            READLN  (DIRECTION);

            WRITELN;
            WRITELN ('ENTER  DISTANCE...');
            WRITELN ('REAL:');
            READLN  (DISTANCE);

      END;
```

Now the prompting is as follows:

```
VECTOR...

ENTER  START  X...
REAL:
108.91

ENTER  START  Y...
REAL:
18.5

ENTER  DIRECTION...
REAL  0..360:
45

ENTER  DISTANCE...
REAL:
1000
```

Typing in coordinates from a keyboard is, of course, an extremely laborious way to enter vectors, so it is usually much more effective to use a mouse, graphic tablet, or another device that returns a pair of coordinate values. If you have access to such a device, you can replace Read_vector with an input procedure that takes advantage of the capabilities of this device. But the essential role of your new procedure remains exactly the same; it gets and returns the coordinate values required to specify a vector.

Menu Procedures

In addition to procedures that read in data, we may need procedures that read in user commands. If single-word commands are used, for example, we need a procedure to read in a text string and check that this corresponds to one of the acceptable commands. If a command language is employed, we need a procedure to read in a text string and perform a syntax check on it.

Here we shall use the very simple technique of displaying a menu of numbered options and requiring the user to enter an integer to specify one of these. So we need input procedures that display the menu, read an integer, and check that the integer entered is in the correct range. Here, for example, is a menu procedure for choosing between Yes and No:

```
PROCEDURE YES_NO (VAR CHOICE : INTEGER);
    BEGIN
        WRITELN ('CHOOSE BETWEEN...');
        WRITELN ('1. YES');
        WRITELN ('2. NO');

        REPEAT;
            WRITELN;
            WRITELN ('INTEGER 1..2:');
            READLN (CHOICE);

            IF (CHOICE < 1) OR (CHOICE > 2) THEN
                WRITELN ('ILLEGAL CHOICE - TRY AGAIN');

        UNTIL (CHOICE = 1) OR (CHOICE = 2);
    END;
```

This procedure displays a menu as follows:

```
CHOOSE BETWEEN...
1. YES
2. NO

INTEGER 1..2:
```

This next procedure is for choosing among the elements of a simple graphic vocabulary. It displays the following menu:

```
CHOOSE BETWEEN...
1. VECTOR
2. ARC
3. CIRCLE
4. SQUARE
5. RECTANGLE

INTEGER 1..5:
```

Here is the procedure:

```
PROCEDURE VOCABULARY (VAR CHOICE : INTEGER);
    BEGIN
        WRITELN ('CHOOSE BETWEEN...');
        WRITELN ('1. VECTOR');
        WRITELN ('2. ARC');
        WRITELN ('3. CIRCLE');
        WRITELN ('4. SQUARE');
        WRITELN ('5. RECTANGLE');

    REPEAT;
        WRITELN;
        WRITELN ('INTEGER 1..5:');
        READLN (CHOICE);

        IF (CHOICE < 1) OR (CHOICE > 5) THEN
            WRITELN ('ILLEGAL CHOICE - TRY AGAIN');
    UNTIL (CHOICE > = 1) AND (CHOICE <= 5);
    END;
```

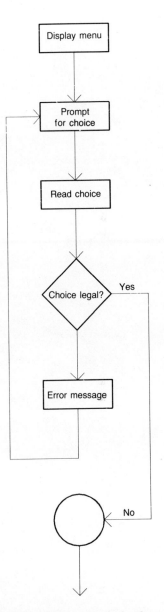

15-8. A flow diagram of code for choosing among vocabulary elements.

The essential logic is illustrated by the flow diagram in figure 15-8.

As far as the program that invokes a menu procedure is concerned, the role of the menu procedure is to return a single integer value. The invoking program has no knowledge of how this integer value was attained. So, if you wanted to employ a more sophisticated menu style (a pull-down menu from which items are picked with a mouse, for example) you could simply replace Vocabulary with a procedure that was quite different internally but in the end still returned an integer value for the parameter Choice.

Branching According to User Command

Menu procedures are typically used in conjunction with **case** statements that select a branch for the program to take. For example, our graphic vocabulary menu might be used to choose between input procedures for the various vocabulary elements as follows:

```
VOCABULARY (CHOICE);

CASE CHOICE OF

    1 : VECTOR  (X1,Y1,X2,Y2);
    2 : ARC  (X,Y,RADIUS,START,FINISH);
    3 : CIRCLE  (X,Y,RADIUS);
    4 : SQUARE  (X,Y,LENGTH);
    5 : RECTANGLE  (X,Y,LENGTH,WIDTH);

END;
```

A menu procedure offering the choice between Yes and No can be used to control exit from a loop. A typical structure is as follows:

```
CHOICE  :=  1;

REPEAT;

    ...
    ...
    ...

    WRITELN('DO YOU WANT TO GO AGAIN?');
    YES_NO(CHOICE);

UNTIL CHOICE  =  2;
```

In these examples, the branching of the program is controlled by tests of the user's inputs. Menus are displayed whenever a branch point is reached and indicate to the user the branches that are available. For each menu that the user sees, there is a corresponding conditional statement somewhere in the program to interpret the choice. That is, the conditional statement establishes the semantics of the menu.

A Program for Viewing Drawings

Let us now consider the use of data input procedures and menu procedures in a simple program that reads a **file** of graphic data, prompts the user to specify viewing parameters, and displays the appropriate portion of the drawing on the specified window on the screen. Here is the code for the input procedures:

```
PROCEDURE MENU (VAR CHOICE : INTEGER);

BEGIN

    WRITELN ('CHOOSE BETWEEN...');
    WRITELN ('1. PAN');
    WRITELN ('2. ZOOM');
    WRITELN ('3. ROTATE');
    WRITELN ('4. END');

    REPEAT;

        WRITELN;
        WRITELN ('INTEGER 1..4:');
        READLN (CHOICE);
```

```
            IF (CHOICE < 1) OR (CHOICE > 4) THEN
                WRITELN ('ILLEGAL CHOICE - TRY AGAIN');

        UNTIL (CHOICE >= 1) AND (CHOICE <= 4);

    END;

    PROCEDURE READ_PAN (VAR X_COORDINATE,Y_COORDINATE :
                            REAL);

        BEGIN

            WRITELN;
            WRITELN ('PAN PARAMETERS...');
            WRITELN;
            WRITELN ('X COORDINATE...');
            WRITELN ('REAL:');
            READLN (X_COORDINATE);

            WRITELN;
            WRITELN ('Y COORDINATE...');
            WRITELN ('REAL:');
            READLN (Y_COORDINATE);

        END;

    PROCEDURE READ_ZOOM (VAR FACTOR : REAL);

        BEGIN

            WRITELN;
            WRITELN ('ZOOM PARAMETER...');
            WRITELN;
            WRITELN ('SCALE FACTOR...');
            WRITELN ('REAL:');
            READLN (FACTOR);

        END;

    PROCEDURE READ_ROTATE (VAR ANGLE : REAL);

        BEGIN

            WRITELN;
            WRITELN ('ROTATE PARAMETER...');
            WRITELN;
            WRITELN ('ANGLE...');
            WRITELN ('REAL 0..360');
            READLN (ANGLE);

        END;
```

Code to read a **file** of Graphic records, display the menu, read display parameters, and display the drawing can now be written like this:

```
    { Main program }
    VAR CHOICE :INTEGER;
        X_COORDINATE,Y_COORDINATE,FACTOR,ANGLE : REAL;

    BEGIN

        READ_FILE;

        { Set default display values }
```

```
                    X_COORDINATE := 0;
                    Y_COORDINATE := 0;
                    FACTOR := 1;
                    ANGLE := 0;

               REPEAT;

                    MENU (CHOICE);

                    IF CHOICE < 4 THEN

                         BEGIN

                              CASE CHOICE OF

                                   1: READ_PAN (X_COORDINATE,
                                                Y_COORDINATE);
                                   2: READ_ZOOM (FACTOR);
                                   3: READ_ROTATE (ANGLE);

                              END;

                              START_ DRAWING;

                                   VIEW (512,512,1024,1024,
                                        X_COORDINATE,Y_COORDINATE,
                                        FACTOR,ANGLE);

                              FINISH_DRAWING;

                         END;

                    UNTIL (CHOICE = 4);

               END.
```

When execution begins, the origin of the world coordinate system is placed at the origin of the graphics area on the screen, and one unit in the world coordinate system becomes Factor units in the screen coordinate system. The user is then presented with the following menu:

```
CHOOSE BETWEEN...
1. PAN
2. ZOOM
3. ROTATE
4. END

INTEGER 1..4:
```

If the pan option is chosen, the following data input prompting is given:

```
PAN PARAMETERS...

X-DISTANCE...
REAL:
187.96

Y-DISTANCE...
REAL:
99.7
```

If the zoom option is chosen, the prompting is:

```
ZOOM PARAMETER...

SCALE FACTOR...
```

REAL:
2.5

If the rotate option is chosen, then the user sees:

ROTATE PARAMETER...

ANGLE...
REAL 0..360:

After any of these, the appropriate version of the drawing is displayed, and the menu is presented once again. A session is terminated by choosing the end option.

A Program for Interactive Parametric Variation

Figure 15-9 depicts a parameterized column, defined in a world coordinate system. Our next example program allows the user to choose between two actions: altering values of the design variables or altering values of the viewing parameters. After execution of the chosen input procedure, the new picture is displayed. The code for the input procedures is as follows:

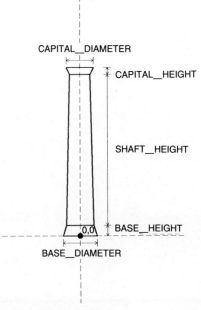

15-9. A parameterized column.

```
PROCEDURE MAIN_MENU (VAR CHOICE : INTEGER);

    BEGIN

        WRITELN;
        WRITELN ('CHOOSE BETWEEN...');
        WRITELN ('1. VIEW');
        WRITELN ('2. DESIGN');
        WRITELN ('3. END');

        REPEAT;

            WRITELN;
            WRITELN ('INTEGER 1..3:');
            READLN (CHOICE);

            IF (CHOICE < 1) OR (CHOICE > 3) THEN
                WRITELN ('ILLEGAL CHOICE - TRY AGAIN');
        UNTIL (CHOICE >= 1) AND (CHOICE <= 3);
    END;
PROCEDURE VIEW_MENU (VAR X_COORDINATE,Y_COORDINATE,
                        FACTOR,ANGLE : REAL);

    VAR CHOICE : INTEGER;

    BEGIN

        WRITELN ('CHOOSE BETWEEN...');
        WRITELN ('1. PAN');
        WRITELN ('2. ZOOM');
        WRITELN ('3. ROTATE');
        WRITELN ('4. END');

        REPEAT;

            WRITELN;
```

```
                    WRITELN ('INTEGER 1..4:');
                    READLN (CHOICE);
                    IF (CHOICE >= 1) AND (CHOICE <= 3) THEN
                        CASE CHOICE OF
                            1: READ_PAN (X_COORDINATE,
                                         Y_COORDINATE);
                            2: READ_ZOOM (FACTOR);
                            3: READ_ROTATE (ANGLE);

                        END;

                UNTIL CHOICE = 4;
            END;

        PROCEDURE DESIGN_MENU (VAR BASE_DIAMETER,BASE_HEIGHT,
                               SHAFT_HEIGHT,CAPITAL_DIAMETER,
                               CAPITAL_HEIGHT : REAL);
            VAR CHOICE : INTEGER;
            BEGIN
                REPEAT;
                    WRITELN;
                    WRITELN ('CHOOSE BETWEEN...');
                    WRITELN ('1. BASE DIAMETER');
                    WRITELN ('2. BASE HEIGHT');
                    WRITELN ('3. SHAFT HEIGHT');
                    WRITELN ('4. CAPITAL DIAMETER');
                    WRITELN ('5. CAPITAL HEIGHT');
                    WRITELN ('6. END');
                    WRITELN;
                    WRITELN ('INTEGER 1..6:');

                    READLN (CHOICE);

                    IF (CHOICE >= 1) AND (CHOICE <=5) THEN
                      CASE CHOICE OF
                        1: BEGIN
                               WRITELN;
                               WRITELN ('BASE DIAMETER...');
                               WRITELN ('REAL:');
                               READLN (BASE_DIAMETER);
                           END;

                        2: BEGIN
                               WRITELN;
                               WRITELN ('BASE HEIGHT...');
                               WRITELN ('REAL:');
                               READLN (BASE_HEIGHT);
                           END;

                        3: BEGIN
                               WRITELN;
                               WRITELN ('SHAFT HEIGHT...');
                               WRITELN ('REAL:');
                               READLN (SHAFT_HEIGHT);
                           END;
```

```
         4: BEGIN
               WRITELN;
               WRITELN ('CAPITAL  DIAMETER...');
               WRITELN ('REAL:')
               READLN (CAPITAL_DIAMETER);
            END;
         5: BEGIN
               WRITELN;
               WRITELN ('CAPITAL  HEIGHT...');
               WRITELN ('REAL:');
               READLN (CAPITAL_HEIGHT);
            END;
      END;

   UNTIL (CHOICE  =  6);

END;
```

Code to display the menus, read input data, and generate a display of the column can now be written:

```
{ Main program }
VAR CHOICE : INTEGER;
    X_COORDINATE,Y_COORDINATE,FACTOR,ANGLE  :  REAL;
    BASE_DIAMETER,BASE_HEIGHT,SHAFT_HEIGHT,
    CAPITAL_DIAMETER,CAPITAL_HEIGHT : REAL;

BEGIN
   REPEAT;
      MAIN_MENU (CHOICE);
      IF CHOICE <> 3 THEN
         CASE CHOICE OF
            1: VIEW_MENU (X_COORDINATE,
                          Y_COORDINATE,
                          FACTOR,ANGLE);

            2: DESIGN_MENU (BASE_DIAMETER,
                            BASE_HEIGHT,
                            SHAFT_HEIGHT,
                            CAPITAL_DIAMETER,
                            CAPITAL_HEIGHT);
         END;
      START_DRAWING;
         COLUMN (BASE_DIAMETER,BASE_HEIGHT,
              SHAFT_HEIGHT,CAPITAL_DIAMETER,
              CAPITAL_HEIGHT);
         VIEW (512,512,1024,1024,
              X_COORDINATE,Y_COORDINATE,
              FACTOR,ANGLE);
      FINISH_DRAWING;
   UNTIL (CHOICE  =  3);
END.
```

The first menu that the user of this program sees is:

```
CHOOSE  BETWEEN...
1.  VIEW
2.  DESIGN
3.  END

INTEGER  1..3:
```

If the view option is chosen, the following menu appears:

```
CHOOSE  BETWEEN...
1.  PAN
2.  ZOOM
3.  ROTATE
4.  END

INTEGER  1..4:
```

If the design option is chosen, however, the user is required to choose between design variables:

```
CHOOSE  BETWEEN...
1.  BASE  DIAMETER
2.  BASE  HEIGHT
3.  SHAFT  HEIGHT
4.  CAPITAL  DIAMETER
5.  CAPITAL  HEIGHT
6.  END

INTEGER  1..6:
```

Then a value for the chosen variable may be entered, for example, as follows:

```
BASE  DIAMETER...
REAL:
10.3
```

Some examples of results generated by this program are shown in figure 15-10. You can see how it allows very rapid exploration of design alternatives.

15-10. Examples of columns designed by interactive parametric variation.

Note that this program has a two-level menu structure (fig. 15-11). The first-level menu enables the user to choose between the view and design menus, or to end execution. The second-level menus enable the user to choose which data input procedure to invoke, or to end and return to the first level.

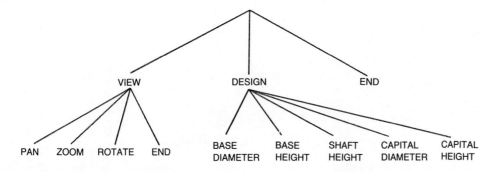

15-11. A two-level menu structure.

In general, programs may have multilevel menu structures, establishing trees of options (fig. 15-12). A sequence of choices takes the user down a branch of the tree. Usually, too, one of the choices on a lower-level menu will be to return to some higher level, so that a different branch can be taken.

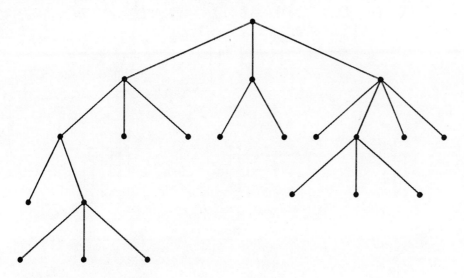

15-12. A tree of options defined by a multilevel menu structure.

More Sophisticated Interactive Parametric Variation

If you want to explore variations on some other theme, you can easily modify this program to do so. Simply replace the menu and data input procedures as well as the graphic procedure for the column by menu, data input, and graphic procedures for your new object. Figure 15-13, for example, shows a series of variations on another column, which were produced this way. A window motif by Charles Rennie Macintosh is varied in figure 15-14, and some surprising variations on the famous end elevation of Peter Behrens's AEG Turbine Factory are shown in figure 15-15.

One way to organize an interactive program to generate such variants would be to prompt for the value of each variable in turn. But this would be

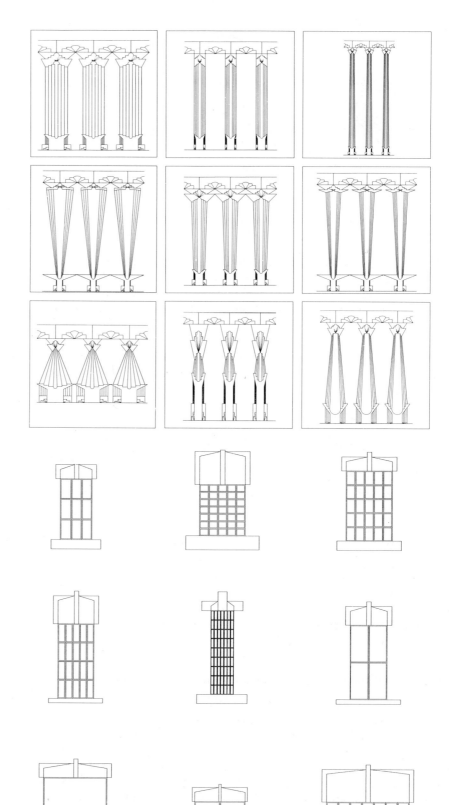

15-13. Versions of a column motif by Charles Jencks, produced by interactive parametric variation.

15-14. Variations on a window motif by Charles Rennie Macintosh. (Images by Eric Silver.)

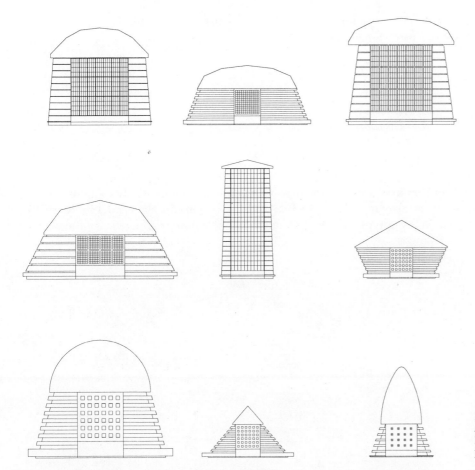

15-15. Variations on the elevation of the AEG Turbine Factory (Peter Behrens, Berlin, 1908). (Images by Brooke Fabricant.)

extremely tedious since, in most cases, the user will want to change only the values of a few of the variables to produce a new version. It is, then, time consuming and redundant to reenter values for the other variables. A better approach is first to display a menu of all the variable names. The user can then select the variable that is to be altered and enter the new value.

A Program for Exploring Combinations

Our next example program is again used to design columns. However, it allows not only the variation of dimensions, but also a choice among different types of bases, shafts, and capitals.

The first-level menu presents the following choice:

```
CHOOSE BETWEEN...
1. VIEW
2. DESIGN
3. END

INTEGER 1..3:
```

If the design option is chosen, the user is prompted for values of the design variables of the base, the shaft, and the capital in turn. For each of those elements, the user must first choose among the available types. The menu for the base, for example, is:

```
CHOOSE BETWEEN...
1. CONICAL
2. STEPPED
3. CONCAVE
4. CONVEX
5. END

INTEGER  1..5:
```

These options are illustrated in figure 15-16a. Similarly, the options for the shaft are shown in figure 15-16b, and the options for the capital in figure 15-16c. When a type has been selected, the program prompts for its dimensions as follows:

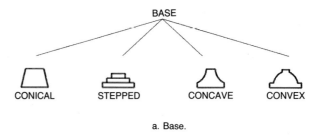

a. Base.

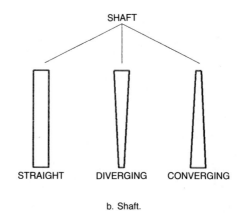

b. Shaft.

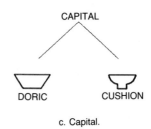

c. Capital.

15-16. Options for column elements.

```
CONICAL BASE...

BOTTOM WIDTH...
REAL:
36.5

HEIGHT...
REAL:
15

TOP WIDTH...
REAL:
18.25
```

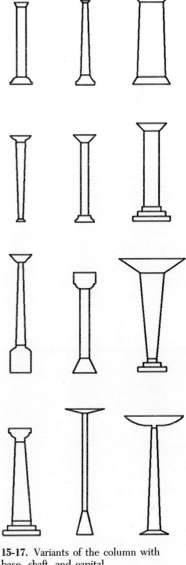

When base, shaft, and capital types have all been chosen, and values have been assigned to the parameters of each, the complete column is then drawn. Some examples of columns that were designed and drawn using this program are illustrated in figure 15-17. Here are the menu and data input procedures:

```
PROCEDURE BASE_MENU (VAR BASE_TYPE : INTEGER;
                     VAR BASE_DIAMETER,BASE_HEIGHT :
                     REAL);

  BEGIN

    WRITELN;
    WRITELN ('BASE TYPE...');

    WRITELN;
    WRITELN ('CHOOSE BETWEEN...');
    WRITELN ('1. CONICAL');
    WRITELN ('2. STEPPED');
    WRITELN ('3. CONCAVE');
    WRITELN ('4. CONVEX');

    REPEAT;

      WRITELN;
      WRITELN ('INTEGER 1..4:');
      READLN (BASE_TYPE);

      IF (BASE_TYPE < 1) OR (BASE_TYPE > 4) THEN
        WRITELN ('ILLEGAL CHOICE - TRY AGAIN');

    UNTIL (BASE_TYPE >= 1) AND (BASE_TYPE <= 4);

    WRITELN;
    WRITELN ('BASE DIAMETER...');
    WRITELN ('REAL:');
    READLN (BASE_DIAMETER);

    WRITELN;
    WRITELN ('BASE HEIGHT...');
    WRITELN ('REAL:');
    READLN (BASE_HEIGHT);

  END;

PROCEDURE SHAFT_MENU (VAR SHAFT_TYPE : INTEGER;
                      VAR SHAFT_HEIGHT : REAL);
```

15-17. Variants of the column with base, shaft, and capital.

```
    BEGIN

        WRITELN;
        WRITELN ('SHAFT TYPE...');
        WRITELN;
        WRITELN ('CHOOSE BETWEEN ...');
        WRITELN ('1. STRAIGHT');
        WRITELN ('2. DIVERGING');
        WRITELN ('3. CONVERGING');

        REPEAT;
            WRITELN;
            WRITELN ('INTEGER 1..3:');
            READLN (SHAFT_TYPE);

            IF (SHAFT_TYPE < 1) OR (SHAFT_TYPE > 3) THEN
                WRITELN ('ILLEGAL CHOICE - TRY AGAIN');

        UNTIL (SHAFT_TYPE >= 1) AND (SHAFT_TYPE <= 3);

        WRITELN;
        WRITELN ('SHAFT HEIGHT...');
        WRITELN ('REAL:');
        READLN (SHAFT_HEIGHT);

    END;
    PROCEDURE CAPITAL_MENU (VAR CAPITAL_TYPE: INTEGER;
                            VAR CAPITAL_DIAMETER,
                            CAPITAL_HEIGHT : REAL);

    BEGIN

        WRITELN;
        WRITELN ('CAPITAL TYPE...');
        WRITELN;
        WRITELN ('CHOOSE BETWEEN...');
        WRITELN ('1. DORIC');
        WRITELN ('2. CUSHION');

        REPEAT;
            WRITELN;
            WRITELN ('INTEGER 1..2:');
            READLN (CAPITAL_TYPE);

            IF (CAPITAL_TYPE < 1) OR (CAPITAL_TYPE > 2) THEN
                WRITELN ('ILLEGAL CHOICE - TRY AGAIN');

        UNTIL (CHOICE >=1) AND (CHOICE <= 3);

        WRITELN;
        WRITELN ('CAPITAL DIAMETER...');
        WRITELN ('REAL:');
        READLN (CAPITAL_DIAMETER);

        WRITELN;
        WRITELN ('CAPITAL HEIGHT...');
        WRITELN ('REAL:');
        READLN (CAPITAL_HEIGHT);

    END;
```

```
PROCEDURE DESIGN_MENU (VAR BASE_DIAMETER,BASE_HEIGHT,
                           SHAFT_HEIGHT,CAPITAL_DIAMETER,
                           CAPITAL_HEIGHT : REAL);

    VAR CHOICE : INTEGER;

    BEGIN

        REPEAT;

            WRITELN;
            WRITELN ('CHOOSE BETWEEN...');
            WRITELN ('1. BASE');
            WRITELN ('2. SHAFT');
            WRITELN ('3. CAPITAL');
            WRITELN ('4. END');
            WRITELN;
            WRITELN ('INTEGER 1..4:');

            READLN (CHOICE);

            IF (CHOICE >= 1) AND (CHOICE <= 3) THEN

                CASE CHOICE OF

                    1: BASE_MENU (BASE_TYPE,BASE_DIAMETER,
                                    BASE_HEIGHT);

                    2: SHAFT_MENU (SHAFT_TYPE,SHAFT_HEIGHT);

                    3: CAPITAL_MENU (CAPITAL_TYPE,
                                    CAPITAL_DIAMETER,
                                    CAPITAL_HEIGHT);

                END;

        UNTIL CHOICE = 4;

    END;
```

The following code displays the menus, obtains input data, and draws the specified version of the column:

```
{ Main program }
    VAR CHOICE : INTEGER;
        X_COORDINATE,Y_COORDINATE,FACTOR,ANGLE : REAL;
        BASE_DIAMETER,BASE_HEIGHT,SHAFT_HEIGHT,
        CAPITAL_DIAMETER,CAPITAL_HEIGHT : REAL;

    BEGIN

        REPEAT;

            MAIN_MENU (CHOICE);

            IF CHOICE <> 3 THEN

                CASE CHOICE OF

                    1: VIEW_MENU (X_COORDINATE,Y_COORDINATE,
                                    FACTOR,ANGLE);
```

```
          2:  DESIGN_MENU  (BASE_TYPE,SHAFT_TYPE,
                            CAPITAL_TYPE,
                            BASE_DIAMETER,
                            BASE_HEIGHT,SHAFT_HEIGHT,
                            CAPITAL_DIAMETER,
                            CAPITAL_HEIGHT);

        END;
      START_DRAWING;
        COLUMN  (BASE_TYPE,SHAFT_TYPE,CAPITAL_TYPE,
                 BASE_DIAMETER,BASE_HEIGHT,
                 SHAFT_HEIGHT,  CAPITAL_DIAMETER,
                 CAPITAL_HEIGHT);

        VIEW  (512,512,1024,1024,
               X_COORDINATE,Y_COORDINATE,
               FACTOR,ANGLE);

      FINISH_DRAWING;
    UNTIL (CHOICE  =  3);
  END.
```

Summary

All the examples that we have considered in this chapter are of highly specialized drawing editors; they enable you to manipulate one very particular type of object. However, they illustrate the basic principles of all drawing editors.

First, there must be some convenient and unambiguous way for the user to indicate graphic elements that are to be operated on—that is, to establish the reference of a graphic command. This is accomplished either by naming the elements, or by pointing at them in some way. The elements may be instances located in a composition, or they may be available on some menu but not yet located in the composition.

Second, there must be a way to specify the operation to be performed upon the indicated elements. Lists of available operations are often given in menus. They may include the insertion of an element into a composition, deletion of an element from the composition, transformation of an element in various ways, and combination of elements to create new elements. Finally, there must be ways to input necessary parameter values. We may be concerned with shape, size, position, and other types of parameters.

Basically, sophisticated interactive drawing editors differ from the simple editors that we have considered here in the generality of the graphic type that is handled. For example, an editor might be built to handle all possible drawings composed of vectors and arcs within an integer Cartesian coordinate system of specified extent. There is generally a fairly complex data structure, providing for large drawings to be stored, retrieved, and efficiently manipulated. A sophisticated editor will, in addition, usually provide fast and convenient ways to indicate graphic elements, wide ranges of available operations, and convenient methods for the input of parameter values.

Exercises

1. Write an interactive program to accept values for the hour and minute, and draw a clock face with the hands in the correct positions.

2. Write an interactive program to draw a human face. (It can be as simple or as complex as you wish.) What variables control expression (smiling, frowning, and so on)? Provide for the input of values for these variables, and use your program to produce a series of faces wearing different expressions.

3. Write an interactive program to show a human stick figure. What variables must you introduce to show different actions (running, jumping, dancing, and so on)? Provide for the input of values for these variables. Use your program to produce a series of drawings of the figure in action.

4. Write an interactive program to draw a tree, using the recursive techniques that were discussed in chapter 12. What variables do you need in order to show different ages and species of trees? Provide for input of values for these, and use your program to produce a series of trees.

5. Leaves can also be constructed and drawn recursively. Write an appropriate interactive program, and use it to produce a series of drawings of different types of leaves.

6. Examine some examples of sea shells. What types of curves might you use to draw them? What variables would you need to introduce in order to draw shells of different types? Write an appropriate interactive program, and use it to produce a series of drawings of shells.

7. Consider the architectural motif of an arched window. What variables must you introduce in order to allow adaptation of this motif for use in a wide variety of contexts? Write an interactive window design program, and use it to generate a series of windows.

8. The motif shown in figure 15-18 is known as a *Necker cube*. It is a well-known example of a spatially ambiguous figure. Think about possible ways to parameterize it, and write an interactive program to generate variants. Experiment with the production of such variants, and explore the variety of different spatial readings that you can produce. Try the same thing with other spatially ambiguous figures.

9. Architects often produce elevation compositions that are divided vertically into three parts: a base (steps, basement, or plinth), a middle part (walls or columns) and a top (roof or dome). Write an interactive program that provides a choice of different types of base, middle, and top as well as variations of each type.

10. Figure 15-19 shows typical compositions of rectangular forms by Piet Mondrian. Examine Mondrian's compositions carefully. How are the rectangles related to each other? Write an interactive program based on your analysis that enables you to generate rectangular compositions in the manner of Mondrian.

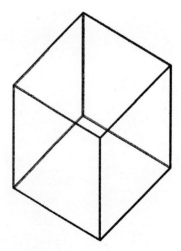

15-18. A Necker cube.

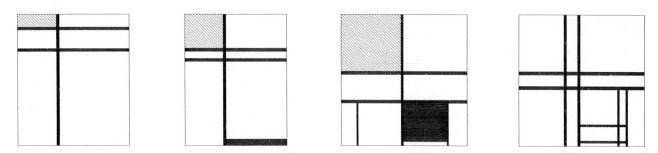

15-19. Some compositions of rectangular forms, created by Piet Mondrian in the 1930s.

11. Figure 15-20 illustrates typical suprematist compositions by Kasimir Malevich. Study Malevich's compositions. What types of elements does he include in his vocabulary? How are these elements parameterized? How are they related to each other in the composition? Write an interactive program based on your analysis that allows you to generate compositions in the manner of Malevich.

 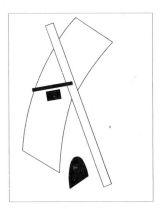

15-20. Two compositions from Kasimir Malevich's *Suprematism: Thirty-four Drawings*.

16.

Going On from Here

Chapter 15 concluded our introduction to fundamental computational ideas as they are implemented in the Pascal language and discussion of the processes of graphic composition in computational terms. We began by considering drawings as sets of vectors, and we saw how they could be generated by executing sequences of **move** and **draw** commands. Then we introduced the idea of a graphic vocabulary and saw how this could be implemented by means of procedure declarations and invocations. Next we examined the role of repetition in design and graphic composition and discussed the use of loops to generate repetitive drawings, then went on to consider designers' responses to special conditions, and how various forms of conditionals may be used to express the rules that govern this. We completed our discussion of the control of action in Pascal programs by showing how the hierarchical block structure of a program expresses the hierarchical structure of the drawing that it generates.

Turning from control structures to data structures, we next considered how drawings may be stored in **arrays**, **file**s, and various kinds of dynamic structures. We then introduced geometric transformations (by the transformation of data structures) and interactive drawing editing (by inserting, deleting, and changing values in data structures). We shall now suggest some directions for further study and practical work.

Graphics Packages and Standards

If you want to go beyond the simple examples that we have discussed here and write more sophisticated graphics programs, you will find that an appropriate *graphics package* provides the best starting point. A graphics package is a library of procedures and functions that can be used as building blocks for graphics programs. In this book we have introduced a very simple graphics package, which provides you with procedures to display vectors, apply transformations, and perform clipping and windowing. However, very much more extensive and sophisticated packages are available and can save a great deal of programming time and effort in the development of more advanced graphics programs.

Many early graphics packages were developed by hardware manufacturers, who supplied them for use with their own equipment. A well-known example is Plot-10, developed by Tektronix and supplied for use with storage tube terminals. Such packages are *device dependent;* they do not allow programs using them to run on other kinds of devices—at least not without considerable alteration.

As the computer graphics industry has developed, there has been growing interest in *device-independent* graphics packages, which allow much greater portability of graphics programs. This, in turn, has led to the development of standards for device-independent graphics packages. These standards are still evolving. The first standard to gain wide acceptance was CORE, developed by the ACM SIGGRAPH Graphics Standards Planning Committee. The first version was published in 1977, and a revised and refined version in 1979 (Graphic Standard Planning Committee 1979).

CORE is concerned primarily with line drawings. The graphic primitives that it recognizes are lines, markers (points), text strings, and polygons. Among its primitive graphic operations are **move_absolute**, which corresponds to our **move**, and **line_absolute**, which corresponds to our **draw**. It deals with transformations, windowing and clipping, and with various forms of interactive input/output processes. Many commercially available graphics packages now follow CORE, and so do some widely used technical texts on computer graphics (see Foley and van Dam 1983).

A second important standard is the Graphical Kernel System (GKS) (Hopgood, Duce, Gallop, Sutcliffe 1986). It is the result of a long, complex international process, principally involving the Deutsches Institut fur Normung (DIN), and the International Organization for Standards (ISO). In many respects, GKS grew out of CORE and is essentially identical to it in the way that it handles simple two-dimensional line graphics. However, there are also some important differences: it handles raster graphics in a more satisfactory way than CORE and deals with the difficult issue of how to display the same drawing on several different devices—something that CORE does not do. GKS now appears to be gaining broader support than CORE and is being followed increasingly in commercial graphics packages, and in technical texts (see Enderle, Kansy, and Pfaff 1984).

Interactive Graphics Systems

If you are more interested in becoming a sophisticated user of computer graphics than in developing computer graphics software yourself, you will need to select one of the available interactive graphics systems. For convenience here, these can be divided into four broad classes of two-dimensional systems:

- business graphics systems
- paint systems
- structured drawing systems
- drafting systems

plus four more classes of three-dimensional systems:

- wire-frame systems
- polygon-modeling systems
- curved surface-modeling systems
- solid-modeling systems

Finally, there are animation systems (both two-dimensional and three-dimensional), which deal with moving viewpoints and objects.

All of these provide the user with some kind of graphic vocabulary, some set of graphic operations, and some kind of interactive interface through which operations are applied and results displayed. We shall consider the various classes of systems in turn, paying particular attention to how they are structured, and to how their structures determine what they can do.

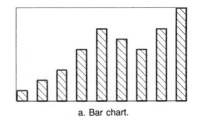

a. Bar chart.

Two-dimensional Systems

Two-dimensional interactive graphics systems are sophisticated versions of the simple drawing editors that we discussed in chapter 15. They vary in the types of drawings that they are designed to handle, the size and complexity of these drawings, the classes of computers on which they run, and the kinds of input and output devices that they use.

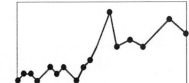

b. Line graph.

Business Graphics Systems

A business graphics system is designed to turn numerical data into graphs, bar charts, pie charts, and other standard diagrams. A business graphics system provides a fixed vocabulary of standard diagram types (fig. 16-1). The user of the system can select a diagram type and set parameter values to establish the size and layout of the diagram on the display surface. Appropriate labels for axes, and so on, can also be input. The parameters controlling such properties as the heights of bars in a bar chart, or the widths of slices in a pie chart, are then set to the data values that are to be displayed. The result is a diagram depicting these values. Figure 16-2, for instance, illustrates the display of different data values in a bar chart.

The simplest business graphics systems run on low-cost personal computers. These have restricted capabilities and are designed to be easy to use and to respond to the limitations of low-resolution displays. More advanced systems are intended for the production of publication-quality artwork and exploit the capabilities of high-quality output devices. These generally provide the user with a lot more control and are correspondingly more complex to use.

In general, then, business graphics systems represent a straightforward development of the basic concepts of vocabularies and parametric variation, which we introduced in chapter 8. They enable a user to produce standard types of drawings very quickly and easily.

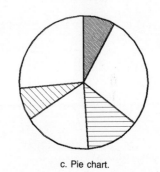

c. Pie chart.

16-1. A vocabulary of standard diagram types.

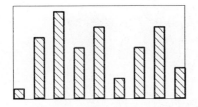 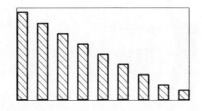 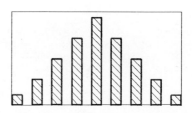

16-2. Bar charts produced by different data values.

Paint Systems

A paint system turns a raster display screen into a surface for freehand drawing. A moving cursor is used as the marking instrument, and the user controls this with a mouse or graphic tablet (fig. 16-3). As the cursor moves, the system senses its successive locations on the raster grid and displays a corresponding sequence of marks. A paint system represents a drawing internally in the simplest possible way—as an array of pixel values or as some compressed equivalent. This allows enormous flexibility, since almost any drawing can be represented reasonably satisfactorily in this format.

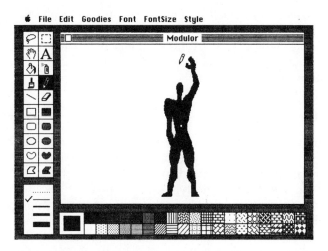

16-3. The screen layout for a paint system.

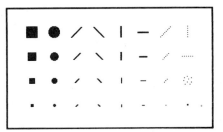

16-4. A menu of pen shapes to generate different line styles.

The combination of mouse or tablet interaction with this method of representation also allows the implementation of a wide variety of graphic input methods. To begin with, most paint systems allow the input of straight lines, curves of various types, and freehand lines. By pointing at a menu displayed on the screen, the user can select from a range of different line styles. These usually imitate the effects of familiar manual instruments: pens and pencils of various thicknesses, brushes, crayons, airbrushes, and so on (fig. 16-4).

Many paint systems also provide the capability to fill areas with various patterns and textures, in imitation of the use of mechanical screens (fig. 16-5). An appropriate pattern is selected by pointing at a menu displayed on the screen, then pointing at the area to be filled. (Fill procedures are analogous

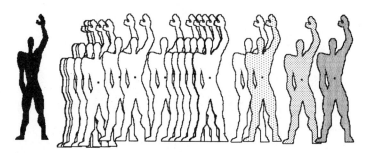

16-5. A composition produced using edge outline, copy, and area-fill operations.

to the polygon-hatching procedures that we considered in chapter 13.)

A figure is erased by changing the values of its pixels to the value of the background pixels (fig. 16-6). An "eraser" can be dragged across the picture plane to achieve this, or a rectangle on the screen may be specified and all pixels within the rectangle assigned the same value.

a. A frieze of figures.   b. The frieze after applying the erase operation.

16-6. The erase operation.

Manual cut-and-paste methods of picture construction are often imitated by allowing the user to specify a rectangle on the screen, then to replicate its contents at another specified position on the screen. More sophisticated systems may allow arbitrary nonrectangular areas to be "cut out," then translated, rotated, and scaled to fit in another part of the picture (fig. 16-7).

Another common operation is figure/ground reversal of a picture, or of a specified part of a picture. Black pixels are changed to white, and white to black (fig. 16-8). This is yet another graphic transformation, accomplished by a procedure that transforms a data structure.

16-7. Limbs are rearranged by using cut-and-paste operations.

16-8. The figure/ground reversal operation.

Since pictures are represented as arrays of pixel values, it is easy to provide the capability to zoom in to a portion of the picture and inspect the enlarged pixels. These enlarged pixels may then be manipulated one by one. This provides a way to produce textures and construct gradations (in effect, by manual dithering). A typical result is illustrated in figure 16-9.

Since scanners produce arrays of pixel values, and a paint system stores and allows operation on such arrays, it is natural to use paint systems to operate on pictures input by scanners. Figure 16-10, for example, shows some variations on a simple sketch that were produced by scanning the original, then employing the area-fill capabilities of a simple paint system.

16-9. Rendering shade and texture by operating on enlarged pixels.

16-10. Variations on a sketch by the Constructivist architect, Iakov Chernikhov, produced by scanning the original then using area- fill operations.

The designers of paint systems usually try to avoid typed commands and to make effective use of windows and icons wherever possible. When a graphic tool, such as a "brush" or "eraser," is selected, the cursor changes into the icon for that tool. Available colors and textures are set out in a "palette" (fig. 16-11).

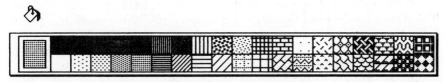

16-11. A palette of textures for a paint system.

The simplest paint systems operate on low-cost personal computers with low- to medium-resolution bilevel displays. However, the wide variety of line styles, patterns, and textures that they provide offsets these limitations, and a skilled user can produce remarkably good results with them (fig. 16-12). The best paint systems use full-color high-resolution displays. Their software includes the capability to "mix" colors, construct and display palettes, and select colors from palettes for lines and polygons. They can replicate a very wide range of traditional graphic media.

The major advantages of paint systems are that they are extremely easy and natural to use (since they directly replicate familiar manual methods), and that they offer a wide range of graphic effects. Their basic limitation is that they do not have any way to represent the *structure* of a drawing; everything is reduced to an array of pixel values. There may be operations to insert higher-level graphic entities such as vectors, circles, polygons, and instances of vocabulary elements into pictures, but these objects lose their identities once they are stored in the pixel array and cannot subsequently be the objects of graphic commands. There cannot, for example, be a command to construct a line parallel or perpendicular to an existing line, since the system (unlike the system's user) cannot recognize that line's existence.

Their simplicity and close imitation of manual techniques have made paint systems very popular among users of personal computers, who just need a convenient way to produce simple drawings. They serve as the graphic counterparts to simple word processors. In more advanced applications, paint systems are best suited for the final adjustment of pictures that have been scanned or generated by some other kind of graphic software—a process closely analogous to retouching a photograph or coloring a print by hand.

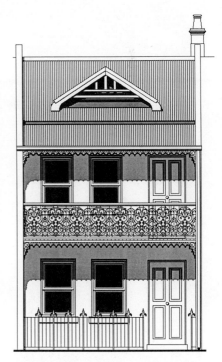

16-12. A building elevation sketched using a simple paint system.

Structured Drawing Systems

Just as a paint system replicates freehand drawing operations within an electronic environment, so a structured drawing system replicates technical drafting using instruments such as parallel rules, triangles, compasses, and stencils. The primitive is a vector, and there is a vocabulary of elementary geometric figures such as circles and arcs, squares, rectangles, and triangles. The user can interactively insert and delete vectors and instances of vocabulary elements to compose a picture on the screen. Objects can also be translated, rotated, reflected, and scaled.

The most fundamental difference between a paint system and a structured drawing system, however, is in the method of storing images. A structured drawing system internally represents a line drawing not as an array of pixel values, but as a list of vectors or some equivalent data structure (see chapter 13). Furthermore, the list may be segmented to divide the drawing into different "layers" of information, or into a hierarchy of graphic objects and subobjects.

A structured drawing system, unlike a paint system, thus recognizes the hierarchical structure of drawings (see chapter 12). This means that graphic objects such as vectors, arcs, polygons, instances of architectural vocabulary elements, and so on, can retain their identity within the system and can be the objects of graphic commands. So structured drawing systems can, and usually do, have numerous commands to construct lines parallel and perpendicular to existing lines, bisectors and fillets to existing angles, and so on. Many simple structured drawing systems are available for low-cost personal computers and are suitable for the production of simple diagrams. One of the first to gain wide popularity was the Macdraw system for the Macintosh personal computer.

Drafting Systems

A drafting system is a sophisticated version of a structured drawing system, with the capability to support architectural, engineering, cartographic, and other professional drafting applications. A good drafting system is designed for speed, efficiency, versatility, reliability, and the capacity to handle large and complex drawings (fig. 16-13).

Some drafting systems are marketed as software systems, designed to run on widely available standard hardware. Others are *turnkey* systems—integrated packages of hardware and software, often incorporating specialized hardware components. Drafting systems have been designed for a wide variety of applications and markets, so it is not surprising to find that they vary enormously in cost, versatility, and performance level. The simplest and cheapest systems run on sixteen-bit personal computers. Their limitations usually show up in relative slowness and clumsiness of operation and in restrictions on the size and complexity of drawings that can be handled. Faster, more sophisticated systems require thirty-two-bit processors, large hard-disk capacity, and usually cost more.

The drafting system industry has grown rapidly and chaotically and is highly competitive. As a result there are few standards, either officially adopted or de facto, and no two drafting systems provide exactly the same capabilities. However, most provide facilities for at least the following:

- establishing world coordinate systems in various units
- setting up grids as well as other location and dimension references
- selecting line styles
- inserting, deleting, extending, and trimming vectors and arcs
- adding hatching to a drawing
- lettering a drawing
- dimensioning a drawing
- using built-in menus of standard graphic elements, and establishing such menus for later use in the assembly of drawings
- selecting, scaling, and locating graphic elements to construct drawings

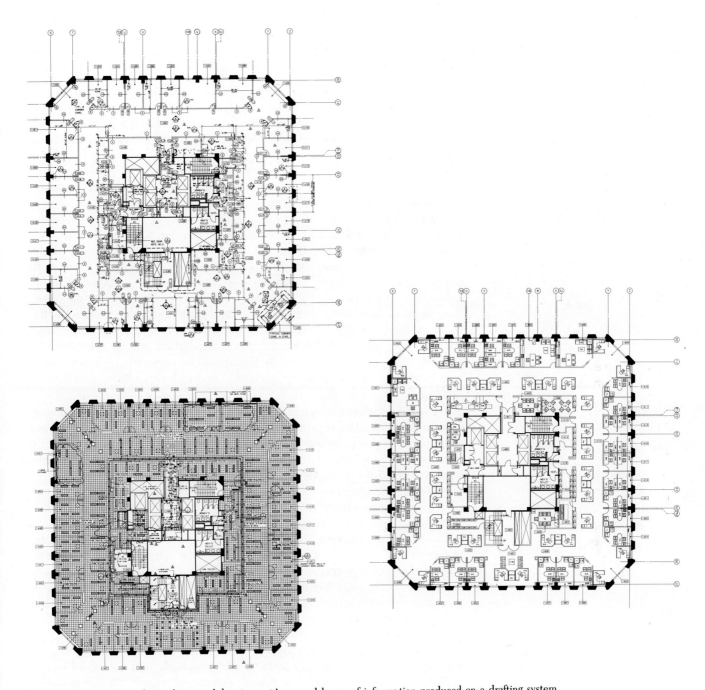

16-13. A large and complex architectural drawing, with several layers of information produced on a drafting system.

- executing geometric constructions, and performing geometric calculations as required in composing a drawing
- structuring drawings in layers or in hierarchies of parts
- viewing a specified part of a drawing, at a specified scale, with specified layers of information
- taking off areas and quantities and producing schedules, bills of materials, and so on

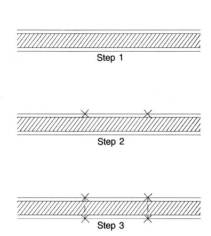

Step 1

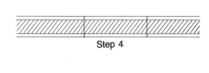

Step 2

Step 3

Step 4

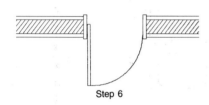

Step 5

Step 6

16-14. Steps in a door insertion operation.

- storing and retrieving drawings on disk
- plotting finished drawings
- archiving drawings that are no longer in active use

In addition to these general capabilities, many drafting systems also provide specialized software for use in particular applications, such as architectural drafting, mechanical engineering drafting, cartography, integrated circuit layout, and so on. Such software provides an appropriate specialized menu of parameterized graphic elements. Architectural software, for example, might provide a menu of wall and column elements, door swings, window elements, and the like, whereas a system for electronic circuit layout might provide a menu of standard electronic components.

Where there is a specialized menu, there are usually specialized operations for inserting and deleting elements as well. Consider, for example, the construction of an architectural floor plan out of standard wall and door elements. A sequence of operations must be executed to insert a door into a wall with correct detailing (fig. 16-14). A converse sequence must be executed to delete a door and close the gap. If a special door insertion operation is provided, then the user need only specify the position of the opening in the wall, the width, and the direction of swing, and the necessary sequence of lower-level operations on vectors is performed. Similarly, with a special door deletion operation, the user need only specify the door to be removed. Such specialized, high-level operations, suited to particular areas of application, can make a drafting system very efficient.

These specialized operations are, in fact, procedures that invoke lower-level procedures. (We explored the same technique in chapter 14, when we built up more complex geometric operations from simpler ones.) Many drafting systems provide interfaces to programming languages, so that you can write your own specialized high-level operations.

Where drafting systems are in widespread use, it becomes increasingly attractive, in principle, to transfer graphic data in electronic rather than hard-copy form. Thus an architect might send files containing floor plan drawings to a mechanical engineer. The engineer might then employ his own drafting system to add ductwork layouts and send the new file back to the architect. Finally, the architect might send files containing complete working drawings to the contractor, who would then produce plots at appropriate scales, with appropriate layers of information, as required for various purposes in the construction process. In practice there are some problems. Different drafting systems use different data structures, so direct transfer of drawing files from one system to another is usually not possible. This difficulty has motivated considerable interest in graphic data transfer standards, and a standard known as IGES (Smith et al. 1983) has gained widespread support. IGES defines a "neutral" format for graphic data files (fig. 16-15). An IGES translator for a drafting system is a piece of software that translates drawing files produced by the drafting system into the IGES neutral format, and conversely, translates files back from the IGES format. Thus, drafting systems equipped with IGES translators can communicate with each other, though some information may be lost in the process.

In general, the functions of a drafting system correspond directly to those of manual drafting. The graphic workstation corresponds to the drawing board and is used for the construction and editing of drawings. Disk filing capabilities correspond to the traditional plan chest, and electronic transfer of graphic

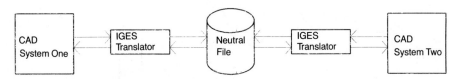

16-15. The operation of an IGES translator.

data replaces physical dissemination of drawings on paper.

The aim of this replacement of manual procedures and traditional tools by electronic technology is usually to achieve higher productivity in drafting tasks, and drafting system salespeople are fond of quoting the impressive productivity ratios that are possible. But productivity cannot be achieved unless a drafting system is used intelligently. You can always, for example, use a drafting system to construct a drawing in vector-by-vector fashion, just as you can write Pascal code to do so. Obviously this is slow, cumbersome, and confers little advantage over manual drafting. To use a drafting system in an efficient and productive way, you must think about how to construct a drawing by using as few commands as possible, just as you might try to write a concise Pascal program to produce it. Indeed, a sequence of drafting system commands *is* a program—expressed in the command language of the drafting system rather than Pascal, and interpreted command by command rather than compiled.

The fundamental principles of graphics programming that we have introduced here remain applicable whether you are writing code to be compiled and executed or interactively entering commands to be interpreted. You must first analyze the drawing in terms of the vocabulary to be used. In Pascal, the vocabulary is expressed in the procedure declarations, and in a drafting system it is expressed in the menu. In Pascal you put together a drawing by invoking procedures, and in a drafting system you do so by selecting and inserting elements from the menu. In both cases you must think carefully about the structure of the drawing in terms of repetition, conditionals, the hierarchy of parts, and the use of transformations; and the structure of the Pascal code or sequence of drafting system commands must reflect this.

Three-dimensional Systems

So far we have confined our attention to two-dimensional graphics. A *three-dimensional* graphics system allows you to model the geometry of a three-dimensional object in a three-dimensional world coordinate system, then project various different views onto the two-dimensional coordinate system. Thus the viewing transformation involves performance of orthographic, perspective, isometric, or some other kind of projective transformation. Techniques for accomplishing this are extensions of the simple, two-dimensional viewing transformation techniques that we discussed in chapter 14 (Penna and Patterson 1986).

Wire-frame Systems

The simplest kind of three-dimensional graphics system is a straightforward extension of two-dimensional vector graphics. A vector in a three-dimensional

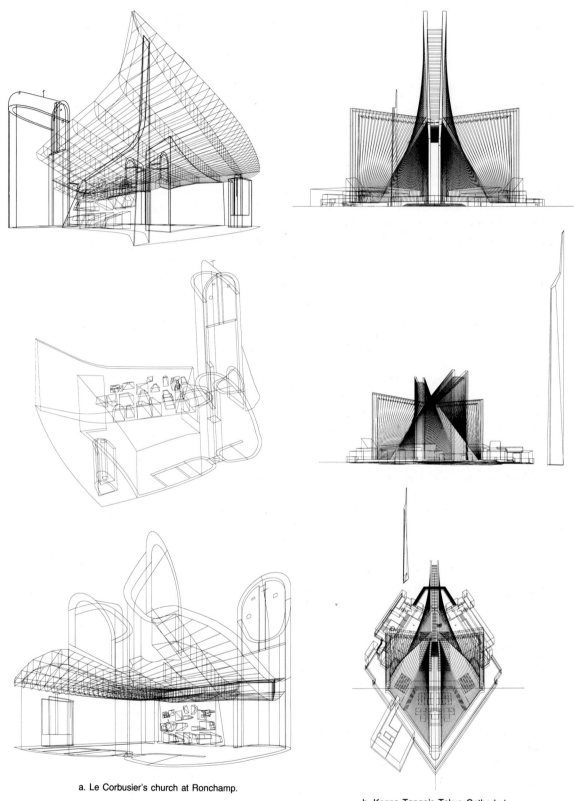

a. Le Corbusier's church at Ronchamp.

b. Kenzo Tange's Tokyo Cathedral.

16-16. Some examples of wire-frame images.

Cartesian coordinate system is the primitive, and a three-dimensional object is represented as a set of such vectors. Each vector is described by the X, Y, and Z coordinates of its endpoints.

When a three-dimensional object is modeled in this way, no information about the color or opacity of its surfaces is recorded. It follows, then, that the surfaces cannot be depicted when a projected view is generated, and that vectors that would be hidden by opaque surfaces will show up. The result is a wire-frame image (figure 16-16).

All of the programming techniques that we have introduced for generating two-dimensional vector drawings can be extended to three-dimensional wire-frame models. Similarly, many drafting systems provide software to extend their basic two-dimensional vector graphics capabilities to three dimensions by allowing input of three-dimensional coordinate data, the execution of three-dimensional translation, rotation, reflection, and scaling transformations, the specification of three-dimensional viewing parameters, and the generation of the corresponding projections.

Polygon-modeling Systems

Just as a vector may be represented by its endpoint coordinates, so a closed polygon may be represented by its vertex coordinates. And just as information specifying thickness and line style may be associated with a vector, so information specifying surface opacity or transparency, color, reflectivity, and texture may be associated with a polygon. Three-dimensional objects can thus be modeled as sets of polygons.

When an object is modeled as a collection of polygonal facets, instead of as a collection of vectors, it can be rendered as an opaque solid with hidden lines and surfaces removed. Renaissance artists were familiar with this technique. Sebastiano Serlio, for example, spoke in his *Five Books of Architecture* (English edition, 1611) of the "open frame" (fig. 16-17a), then went on to discuss making "the solid body thereof" (fig. 16-17b). The solid body "is the same that is before shewed, both form and measure, but all the lines which cannot outwardly be seen, are hidden." Similar drawings, with hidden edge lines of polygons deleted, can be produced with appropriate software (fig. 16-18). Alternatively, on a raster display, a shaded surface rendering with hidden polygonal surfaces removed can be generated (fig. 16-19).

In the real world, the appearance of a polygonal facet of a solid object is determined both by its surface properties and by lighting conditions. Thus, in the generation of shaded raster displays from polygon models, it is necessary to make some assumptions about lighting conditions. The simplest possibility is to assume uniform ambient light from all directions, so that the appearance of a polygonal facet is determined entirely by its surface properties. This produces a very flat-looking image, however (fig. 16-20a). It is usually much more effective, and involves very little additional calculation and software complexity, to assume diffuse light from a particular direction, then to calculate surface illuminations according to the well-known cosine law from elementary physics. This results in the types of images shown in figures 16-20b and c.

Surfaces that are to be smooth-shaded can either be approximated by polygonal facets (just as we have approximated curved lines by short straight segments), or represented accurately by mathematical formulas. The former approach is simpler and is adequate for many applications, but accurate surface

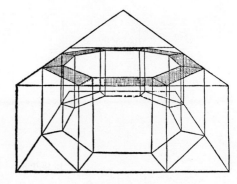

a. Wire-frame view.

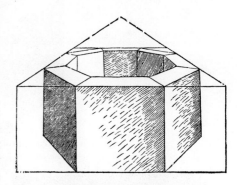

b. Hidden lines removed.

16-17. Perspective renderings of an octagonal well from Sebastiano Serlio's *Five Books of Architecture*, 1611.

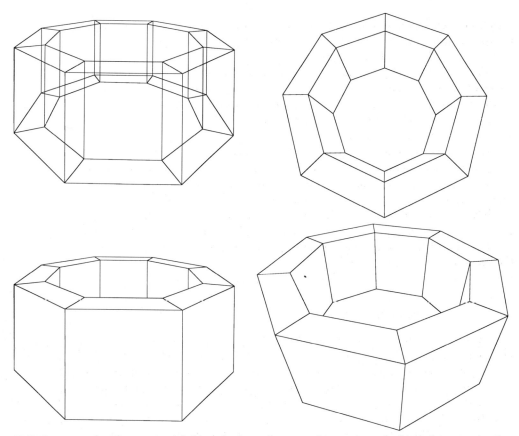

16-18. Perspective line drawings, with hidden edge lines of opaque polygons removed, of Serlio's octagonal well.

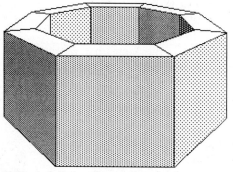

16-19. A shaded-surface rendering with hidden polygonal surfaces removed.

a. A high level of ambient light flattens the image.

16-20. Effects of varying lighting parameters.

b. A combination of ambient and directional light produces strong three-dimensional modeling, while preserving details in the shadows.

c. A high-contrast image is produced with no ambient light; all details in the shadows are lost.

modeling is necessary in applications such as automobile and aircraft body design.

Curved Surface–modeling Systems

The rendering of curved surfaces by smooth shading was an issue that preoccupied Western painters from Giotto to the French neoclassicists. These painters sought to understand the laws of shading, to achieve smoothness by blending pigment on the picture plane, and to suggest, in this way, the solidity and mass of three-dimensional objects. With a raster display, smooth-shading software can be used to produce similar results (fig. 16-21).

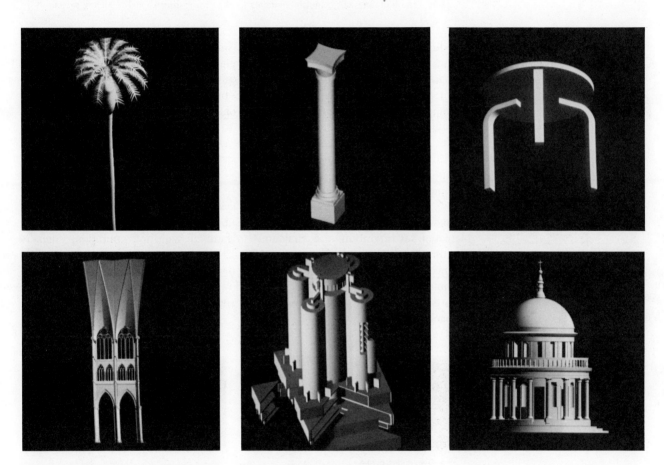

16-21. Smoothly shaded renderings, on a raster display, of objects with curved surfaces.

Solid-modeling Systems

So far we have seen how a vector is bounded and thus defined by its endpoints (fig. 16-22b), and similarly, how a closed plane polygon is bounded and defined by vectors (fig. 16-22c). By extension of the same principle, a closed polyhedron is bounded and defined by polygons (fig. 16-22d). The idea can be generalized to allow, as well, for solids with nonplanar faces, such as

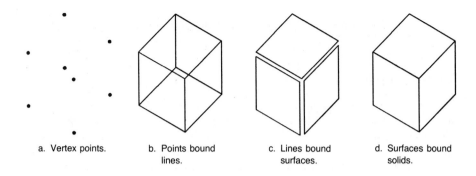

a. Vertex points.   b. Points bound   c. Lines bound   d. Surfaces bound
                         lines.   surfaces.   solids.

16-22. The hierarchy of geometric elements used in three-dimensional modeling systems.

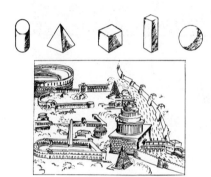

16-23. A drawing by Le Corbusier from *Vers une Architecture*, showing how architectural compositions can be produced by combining primitive solids.

cylinders, spheres, and cones. Once a solid has been defined in this way, it can be assigned properties such as weight, density, centroid location, and material. Thus we can model a three-dimensional composition not just as a set of vectors, or as a set of surfaces, but also as a set of closed solids. A computer system to handle this type of model is usually known as a *solid-modeling* system.

A solid-modeling system provides a vocabulary of primitive solids, together with commands for dimensioning instances, locating them in space, and combining them to produce more complex solids. The idea would have been congenial to Le Corbusier (fig. 16-23).

To combine solids, solid-modeling systems usually provide the *spatial set* operations of union, intersection, and subtraction (relative complement). The spatial set operations are analogous to familiar sculpting operations such as gluing, drilling, and carving (fig. 16-24). But they are much more powerful, since they are not subject to gravity, or to the limitations of physical tools and materials, and they can be executed rapidly. Thus they allow very complex three-dimensional compositions to be produced with short sequences of commands (figs. 16-25; 16-26).

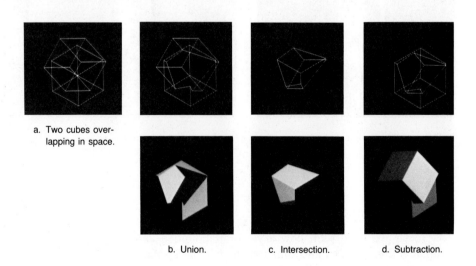

a. Two cubes over-
   lapping in space.

b. Union.   c. Intersection.   d. Subtraction.

16-24. The spatial set operations on solids.

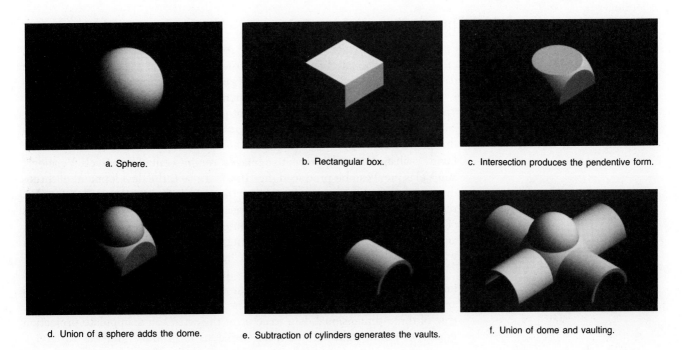

a. Sphere.

b. Rectangular box.

c. Intersection produces the pendentive form.

d. Union of a sphere adds the dome.

e. Subtraction of cylinders generates the vaults.

f. Union of dome and vaulting.

16-25. The generation of a volumetric composition using a solid modeler.

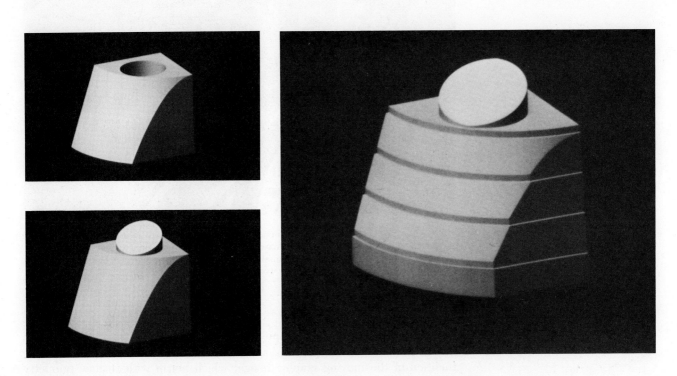

16-26. Construction of the form of the State of Illinois Center, Chicago, using a solid modeler.

Images from Data Structures

So far we have considered only the representation of geometric properties of three-dimensional objects in data structures and the generation from such data structures of monochrome line drawings or shaded images. A further step is to store data describing surface properties: reflectivity, color, and texture. Yet another step is to represent ambient properties of atmosphere (mist, dust, and so on) and optical properties of transparent and translucent solids. With this information, appropriate software, and sufficient computational resources, highly realistic colored perspective images (reminiscent of Van Eyck, Vermeer, and Velasquez) can be produced (fig. 16-27). In fact, the development of three-dimensional computer graphics from the mid-1960s to the mid-1980s has recapitulated the development of European painting from Giotto to the masters of the seventeenth and eighteenth centuries; an early concern with perspective, and the rendering of solidity by shading, has been followed by a fascination with the realistic rendition of complex light falling on complex scenes.

As we noted in chapter 13, it is possible to generate many different images from a single data structure, just as different prints may be made from an engraved plate or a photographic negative. This is even more strikingly true of three-dimensional data structures; the artist can manipulate projection type, viewpoint, lighting, and other variables to produce limitless variety.

16-27. A realistic image of sunset reflections on the hood of a black automobile, generated by application of sophisticated rendering software to a detailed, three-dimensional geometric model. (Digital Scene Simulation by Omnibus Simulation, Inc. Copyright © 1984, 1985 by Omnibus Simulation, Inc. All rights reserved.)

Animation

We have considered computer graphics primarily as a continuation of the traditions of still painting and drawing. However, it also extends the tradition of the moving graphic image, which began with shadow puppetry and has flowered spectacularly in the twentieth century with the emergence of film and video.

One of the most laborious aspects of the traditional animation technique is the manual production of successive frames. With a suitable computer graphics system, however, it takes only a little more effort to produce a sequence of animation frames than it does to produce a single, still image.

Animation is best understood as an extension of the concept of graphic repetition, which we introduced in chapter 9. An animation program is structured as a loop, each iteration of which results in the production of a new frame. One way to do this is to increment the position parameters of an object; this produces the illusion of movement. A second possibility is to increment size or shape parameters, so that the object appears to grow, shrink, or change shape. Third, the viewing parameters may be incremented, so that the "camera" appears to pan, zoom, or track.

Actions may be more complex than shape and position transformations of simple objects at uniform rates. When an automobile moves, for instance, the body translates relative to the road, while the wheels rotate relative to the body, and accelerations take place. When a yacht unfurls a sail, the shape of the sail transforms while the whole craft translates, pitches, yaws, and rolls. Puppetry is largely an art of articulated motion, and the construction of puppets establishes the kinds of motions that the puppeteer can compose. Dance may involve articulated motions of several dancers, coordinated in complex and subtle ways. The animation of such complex actions, to produce compositions in time as well as in space, has become known as *motion choreography*.

Motion choreography may be approached by extending the concepts of structured composition that we have developed here from space to time. The outer loop of an animation program, which increments frames, marks off units of time, just as a loop may construct a regular row or grid of points in space. The parameters of graphic elements establish what aspects of their shapes and positions may change over time. The hierarchical structure of the object to be animated establishes how the shape and position transformations of the various parts of the object are related to each other. The assignment of values within loops controls rates of shape and position change of the various parts. And conditionals may be employed to construct complex rhythms and to specify special actions at special points in time.

Real-time Animation

Where a dynamic display (such as a refreshed vector or raster CRT) is available, backed by a sufficiently powerful processor to perform the necessary computations sufficiently rapidly, real-time animation of screen displays becomes feasible. That is, successive frames may be computed and displayed at a rate of thirty or more per second, to produce the illusion of continuous motion. This motion may be controlled by devices such as joysticks.

Real-time translation of very simple two-dimensional figures can be handled even by eight-bit or sixteen-bit microprocessor chips. This technique is employed in the simplest kinds of video games. Rotation is more difficult, since it requires the relatively time-consuming evaluation of sine and cosine functions.

The ability to execute real-time two-dimensional pans and zooms is extremely useful in drafting systems when large and complex drawings must be handled via a screen of necessarily limited size and resolution; some of the more advanced drafting systems offer this. Usually it is accomplished through use of special-purpose processors, which rapidly execute the calculations required to perform the necessary geometric transformations.

Real-time translation and rotation of three-dimensional wire-frame objects, and real-time panning, zooming, and tracking, are available on some more advanced models of refreshed vector displays. Once again, special-purpose processors are usually employed. The principal applications have been in aircraft flight simulators and in high-performance computer-aided design systems.

The real-time animation of three-dimensional color raster images requires considerably more computation, since hidden surfaces must be removed and shading must be calculated. But this is also now feasible, through the use of special-purpose processors, and is finding increasing application in simulators, in computer-aided design systems, and in the animation industry.

In the past, the special-purpose processors required for real-time animation systems were extremely costly to fabricate, so the applications of real-time graphics were correspondingly limited. However, advances in VLSI technology are rapidly reducing the costs of designing and producing specialized processor chips, and this is making real-time graphics much more feasible in many contexts.

The Future

This brings us to the end of our brief survey of the types of computer graphics systems that are available today. But what of the future?

It is impossible to predict the precise course of development of computer graphics technology, since this is affected by often unexpected innovations and by complex market forces. Some general trends seem clear, though.

There is little doubt that the continued development of VLSI technology, leading to the availability at low cost of increasingly powerful processor chips, of increasingly capacious memory chips, and of a wide variety of special-purpose processors, will continue to reduce the cost of high-performance displays. As a result, we can expect high-resolution, full-color raster displays with real-time dynamics to become increasingly commonplace even on low-cost personal computers.

Ongoing research and development, and growth in the market for computer graphics software products, should lead to the availability of increasingly versatile and sophisticated graphics software. In particular, there will be growing integration of capabilities. Just as we have seen the combination of word processors, spreadsheet programs, and data-base packages into integrated systems (accessible via a consistent interface on a personal computer) so we can expect to see a trend toward integrated graphics systems that offer paint, two-dimensional drafting, three-dimensional modeling, and other capabilities that were available only separately in the past. Furthermore, graphics software will often be integrated closely with other kinds of software, particularly word-processing and data-base management systems.

When it is viewed in a broad cultural perspective, computer graphics seems still to be at a stage, characteristic of infant media, in which the development of technique has far outstripped the ability of artists to understand its true potentials and to use it in a mature way. There are early Greek cut stone buildings that imitate the forms of still earlier wooden constructions, there are early photographs that imitate oil paintings, and there are early films that imitate stage plays. Similarly, in the pioneering days of computer graphics, we have seen paint systems used in imitation of manual sketching, drafting systems in imitation of traditional technical drawing, and three-dimensional perspective rendering systems in imitation of photography and cinematography. Even the names given to graphic systems (*paint*, and *drafting*, for example) reflect this, as the term *horseless carriage* so quaintly reveals the way that the automobile was first understood. Yet we are at least beginning to understand how computer graphics may reveal new dimensions of visual experience to us, and open up new domains for artists and designers to explore. An aesthetic adventure is just beginning.

APPENDIX
Implementation Details

The procedures **move, draw, start_drawing,** and **finish_drawing** are needed for the examples and exercises (using screen coordinates) through to the end of chapter 13. For the examples and exercises in and following chapter 14 (using world coordinates and transformations), a library of procedures called **advanced_graphics** is needed. Here we give the code of these procedures, together with implementation instructions for two popular Pascal systems for personal computers: Turbo Pascal for the IBM PC; and Macintosh Pascal. Implementation for most other Pascal systems should also be possible with only minor changes.

Some Pascal systems do not support the statements:

```
USES GRAPHICS;
USES ADVANCED_GRAPHICS;
```

If the system that you are using does not, you will have to copy the relevant library of procedures in to the beginning of each of your programs. Other systems use different, nonstandard statements to announce external procedures. You should check the relevant documentation.

Screen Coordinate Graphics for the Turbo Pascal Compiler

Although standard Pascal does not provide graphics operations, many Pascal compilers and interpreters have built-in graphics procedures. The popular Turbo Pascal compiler, for example, provides:

DRAW (X1,Y1,X2,Y2);   Draw a line from points X1,Y1 to X2,Y2. (This procedure assumes an origin in the upper-left corner of the screen.)

GRAPHCOLORMODE;   Invokes low-resolution graphics color mode (320 x 200).

TEXTMODE;   Returns the screen to text mode.

These procedures can be used to create procedures **moveto**, **drawto**, **start_drawing**, and **finish_drawing** as needed for the examples and exercises in chapters 5 through 13. (Note that our **move** and **draw** are renamed **moveto** and **drawto**, respectively, to avoid confusion with the built-in **draw** provided by Turbo Pascal. The code of our examples must be modified accordingly.) You will need the following Pascal procedures:

```
PROCEDURE PLOT (X2,Y2 : INTEGER; VISIBLE : BOOLEAN);

  { This procedure saves the last point which was moved to or
    drawn to so that the basic TURBO drawing procedure can be
    invoked with both line endpoints }

  { X1 and Y1 are given ABSOLUTE addresses so their values can
    be remembered from one invocation of PLOT to the next }

  VAR X1 : INTEGER ABSOLUTE $0000:$00EE;
      Y1 : INTEGER ABSOLUTE $0000:00F0;
      Y1S,Y2S : INTEGER;

BEGIN

    { If MOVETO is invoked, then coordinates are stored for the
      next DRAWTO invocation }

    IF NOT(VISIBLE) THEN
      BEGIN
          X1 := X2;
          Y1 := Y2;
      END

    { If DRAWTO is invoked, transform Y values from TURBO
      origin to origin in the bottom-left corner and DRAW line
      using new and saved set of coordinates }

    ELSE BEGIN
          Y1S := 200 − Y1;
          Y2S := 200 − Y2;
          DRAW (X1,Y1S,X2,Y2S,1);
          X1 := X2;
          Y1 := Y2;
      END;

END;
```

```
PROCEDURE MOVETO (X,Y : INTEGER);
    BEGIN
        PLOT (X,Y,FALSE);
    END;
PROCEDURE DRAWTO (X,Y : INTEGER);
    BEGIN
        PLOT (X,Y,TRUE);
    END;
PROCEDURE START_DRAWING;
    BEGIN
        GRAPHCOLORMODE; { Invoke low resolution color mode }
    END;
PROCEDURE FINISH_DRAWING;
    BEGIN
        REPEAT UNTIL KEYPRESSED;
        TEXTMODE;           { Return to text mode }
    END;
```

The **repeat until keypressed** statement in **finish_drawing** should be noted. When **textmode** is invoked, the picture you have drawn will be erased. The **repeat** statement leaves the picture on the screen until you press any key, indicating you are ready to return to text mode.

These four procedures should be entered and stored in a file called **graphics.lib.** They are then included in your programs by replacing the **uses graphics** statement discussed in the text by the following:

```
{$I GRAPHICS.LIB}
```

For example, the following is the simple program to draw a square given in chapter 6 (the coordinates have been modified to fit on the 320 x 200 screen):

```
PROGRAM SQUARE;

    { Include external graphic procedures }
    {$I GRAPHICS.LIB }

    BEGIN
        START_DRAWING;

            MOVETO (40,20);
            DRAWTO (70,20);
            DRAWTO (70,50);
            DRAWTO (40,50);
            DRAWTO (40,20);

        FINISH_DRAWING;

    END.
```

Screen Coordinate Graphics for Macintosh Pascal

The Macintosh Pascal system provides a sophisticated editor for Pascal code, an interpreter, convenient debugging facilities, and access to the *QuickDraw* library of graphics routines. In many respects it is an ideal environment for exploring the examples and undertaking the exercises that we have introduced.

QuickDraw resides in ROM and provides extensive graphics capabilities. Drawings are displayed in a graphics window, with the origin at the top-left. The size and position of this window can be varied. A default graphics window, of 200 by 200 raster units, is established by invoking the **showdrawing** procedure. **Moveto** and **drawto** correspond to the **move** and **draw** procedures used in chapters 5 through 13. No procedure corresponding to our **finish_drawing** is needed, since text and graphics windows are shown simultaneously on the screen.

Quickdraw procedures can be used to create procedures **movexy, drawxy, start_drawing,** and **finish_drawing** as needed for the examples and exercises in chapters 5 through 13. (Note that our **move** and **draw** are renamed **movexy** and **drawxy**, respectively, to avoid confusion with the **move** routine provided by *QuickDraw*. The code of our examples must be modified accordingly.) You will need the following Pascal procedures:

```
PROCEDURE MOVEXY (X,Y : INTEGER);
    BEGIN
        MOVETO (X,200-Y);              { Origin at bottom-left corner }
    END;

PROCEDURE DRAWXY (X,Y : INTEGER);
    BEGIN
        LINETO (X,200-Y);              { Origin at bottom-left corner }
    END;

PROCEDURE START_DRAWING;
    BEGIN
        SHOWDRAWING;                   { Invoke default graphic window }
    END;

PROCEDURE FINISH_DRAWING;
    BEGIN
                                       { Dummy routine which does nothing }
    END;
```

The procedures **movexy** and **drawxy** shift the origin from the top-left to the bottom-left to comply with the convention followed in this book. The procedure **start_drawing** sets the default 200 by 200 graphics window. (If you like, you can write a more sophisticated **start_drawing**, with parameters to control size and position of the window.) The procedure **finish_drawing** does nothing, but is included for the sake of consistency. (Otherwise, all code invoking **finish_drawing** would have to be modified.)

The Advanced_Graphics Library for Turbo Pascal and Macintosh Pascal

The Pascal code for the **advanced_graphics** library, used from chapter 14 onward, is given below. Modifications needed to adapt the general code to Turbo Pascal or Macintosh Pascal are noted in starred comments, thus:

```
{ * Comment * }

{ ADVANCED_GRAPHICS Procedures }
{ Global data structure }
TYPE
    GRAPHIC = RECORD
        X : REAL;
        Y : REAL;
        VISIBLE : BOOLEAN;
    END;

TYPE THREEBY = ARRAY [1..3,1..3] OF REAL;

CONST LIMIT = 2000;              { Max allowable points in picture }

VAR PCOORD : ARRAY [0.LIMIT] OF GRAPHIC;
                                { Picture data structure }
    FCOORD : ARRAY [1..100] OF GRAPHIC;
                                { Element data structure }
    TLIST : ARRAY [1..100] OF THREEBY;
                                { Transformation data structure }
    NEST,NP,NC,START_CALL : INTEGER;


{ ********************************************** }
{ * Insert set of graphic procedures required by specific     * }
{ * implementation - TURBO PASCAL                             * }
{ * or MACINTOSH PASCAL                                       * }
{ ********************************************** }


{ Procedures to store untransformed data points }
    PROCEDURE MOVE (X_COORD,Y_COORD : REAL);

{ * Rename MOVETO in TURBO Pascal * }
{ * Rename MOVEXY in Macintosh Pascal * }

        BEGIN
            IF NEST < 0 THEN
                WRITELN ('ERROR - ATTEMPT TO MOVETO ',
                         'WITHOUT START');

            IF (X_COORD < −20000.0) OR (X_COORD > 20000.0)
            THEN
                    WRITELN ('ERROR - UNINITIALIZED X INPUT TO',
                             ' MOVE');
```

```
            IF (Y_COORD < −20000.0) OR (Y_COORD > 20000.0)
            THEN
                    WRITELN ('ERROR - UNINITIALIZED Y INPUT TO',
                                ' MOVE');

            IF NP = 100 THEN        { A maximum of 100 points can
                                        be added }
                BEGIN               { to element data structure
                                        before they }
                    NP := −NP;      { must be transformed and
                                        stored in }
                        FINISH;     { the picture data structure }
                END;

            NP := NP + 1;

            WITH FCOORD[NP] DO      { Add point to element data
                                        structure }
            BEGIN
                X := X_COORD;
                Y := Y_COORD;
                VISIBLE := FALSE;
            END;

        END;


PROCEDURE DRAW (X_COORD,Y_COORD : REAL);

{ * Rename DRAWTO in TURBO Pascal * }
{ * Rename DRAWXY in Macintosh Pascal * }

    BEGIN
            IF NEST < 0 THEN
                WRITELN ('ERROR - ATTEMPT TO DRAWTO ',
                            'WITHOUT START');

            IF (X_COORD < −20000.0) OR (X_COORD > 2000.0)
            THEN
                    WRITELN ('ERROR - UNINITIALIZED X INPUT TO',
                                ' DRAW');

            IF (Y_COORD < −20000.0) OR (Y_COORD > 20000.0)
            THEN
                    WRITELN ('ERROR - UNINITIALIZED Y INPUT TO',
                                ' DRAW');

            IF NP = 100 THEN
                BEGIN
                    NP := −NP;
                        FINISH;
                END;

            NP := NP + 1;

            WITH FCOORD[NP] DO      { Add point to element data
                                        structure }
            BEGIN
                X := X_COORD;
                Y := Y_COORD;
                VISIBLE := TRUE;
            END;
```

```
            END;

{ Matrix multiplication }
    PROCEDURE MMULT (AMAT,BMAT: THREEBY; VAR CMAT :
                    THREEBY);

        VAR I,J : INTEGER;

        BEGIN

            FOR I := 1 TO 3 DO
                FOR J := 1 TO 3 DO
                    CMAT[I,J] := AMAT[I,1]*BMAT[1,J]
                               + AMAT[I,2]*BMAT[2,J]
                               + AMAT[I,3]*BMAT[3,J];

        END;

{ Initialize to identity matrix }
    PROCEDURE MINIT (VAR MAT : THREEBY);

        VAR I,J, : INTEGER;

        BEGIN

            FOR I := 1 TO 3 DO
            BEGIN

                FOR J := 1 TO 3 DO
                    MAT[I,J] := 0;

                MAT[I,I] := 1;
            END;

        END;

{ Concatenate transformation matrices }
    PROCEDURE CONCAT (VAR T1 : THREEBY);

        VAR T2 : THREEBY;
            K : INTEGER;

        BEGIN

            MINIT (T1);

            FOR K = NEST DOWNTO 1 DO
            BEGIN

                MMULT (T1,TLIST[K],T1);

            END;

        END;

{ Rotation transformation }
    PROCEDURE ROTATE (ROT : REAL);

        VAR T2 : THREEBY;
            ANGLE : REAL;

        BEGIN

            IF (ROT < -10000.0) OR (ROT > 10000.0) THEN
                WRITELN ('ERROR - BAD ROTATION ANGLE );
```

```
            ANGLE  :=  ROT*3.14159/180.0;
            MINIT (T2);
            T2[1,1] := COS(ANGLE);
            T2[1,2] := −SIN(ANGLE);
            T2[2,1] := SIN(ANGLE);
            T2[2,2] := COS(ANGLE);

          { Multiply concatenated transformation matrix by rotation
          matrix }

            MMULT (TLIST[NEST],T2,TLIST[NEST]);

        END;

  { Scale transformation }
      PROCEDURE SCALE (X_SCALE,Y_SCALE : REAL);

        VAR T2 : THREEBY;

        BEGIN

            IF (X_SCALE < 0) OR (X_SCALE > 10000) OR
               (Y_SCALE < 0) OR (Y_SCALE > 10000) THEN
                   WRITELN ('ERROR - BAD SCALE FACTOR');

            MINIT(T2);
            T2[1,1] := X_SCALE;
            T2[2,2] := Y_SCALE;

          { Multiply concatenated transformation matrix by scale
          matrix }

            MMULT (TLIST[NEST],T2,TLIST[NEST]);

        END;

  { Reflection transformation }
      PROCEDURE REFLECT_Y;

        VAR T2: THREEBY;

        BEGIN

            MINIT (T2);
            T2 [1,1] := −1;

          { Multiply concatenated transformation matrix by reflection
          matrix }

            MMULT (TLIST[NEST],T2,TLIST[NEST]);

        END;

  { Translation transformation }
      PROCEDURE TRANSLATE (TRANS_X,TRANS_Y : REAL);

        VAR T2 : THREEBY;

        BEGIN

            IF (TRANS_X < −10000.0) OR (TRANS_X > 10000.0) OR
               (TRANS_Y < −10000.0) OR (TRANS_Y > 10000.0)
               THEN
                   WRITELN ('ERROR - BAD TRANSLATION FACTOR');
```

```
            MINIT  (T2);
            T2[3,1]  :=  TRANS_X;
            T2[3,2]  :=  TRANS_Y;

         {  Multiply concatenated transformation matrix by translation
            matrix }

            MMULT  (TLIST[NEST],T2,TLIST[NEST]);

      END;


      {  Delineates end of scope of set of transformations }

PROCEDURE  FINISH;

      LABEL  99;
      VAR  T1  :  THREEBY;
            K  :  INTEGER;

      BEGIN

            IF  NP  =  0  THEN  GOTO  99;      {  No points }

            START_CALL  :=  1;
            IF  NP  <  0  THEN                 {  STARTS are nested
                                                  so that a set of }
                  BEGIN                        {  points are generated
                                                  between two }
                        NP  :=  −NP;           {  STARTS without an
                                                  intervening FINISH }
                        START_CALL  :=  0;
                  END;

            CONCAT  (T1);                      {  Concatenate
                                                  transformations }

            FOR  K  :=  1  TO  NP  DO          {  Transform points in
                                                  element data }
            BEGIN                              {  structure and add to
                                                  picture data }
                                               {  structure }

                  IF  (NC  =  0)  OR  FCOORD[K].VISIBLE  OR
                  PCOORD[NC].VISIBLE  THEN
                  NC  :=  NC  +  1;

                  IF  NC  >  LIMIT  THEN
                        WRITELN ('ERROR - YOUR PICTURE HAS ',
                                 'EXCEEDED THE MAXIMUM ',
                                 'NUMBER OF ALLOWABLE ',
                                 'POINTS: ',LIMIT);
                  PCOORD[NC].X  :=  FCOORD[K].X  ∗  T1[1,1]  +
                                    FCOORD[K].Y  ∗  T1[2,1]  +  T1[3,1];
                  PCOORD[NC].Y  :=  FCOORD[K].X  ∗  T1[1,2]  +
                                    FCOORD[K].Y  ∗  T1[2,2]  +  T1[3,2];
                  PCOORD[NC].VISIBLE  :=  FCOORD[K].VISIBLE;

            END;

99:         NEST  :=  NEST  −  START_CALL;
            NP  :=  0;

      END;
```

```
{ Invoked to delineate start of transformations }
PROCEDURE START;
    BEGIN
        IF NEST > 200 THEN
            WRITELN ('ERROR - MAXIMUM NUMBER OF ',
                    'STARTS EXCEEDED');

        IF NP <> 0 THEN
            BEGIN
                NP := -NP;
                FINISH;
            END;

        NEST := NEST + 1;      { Increase level of transformation
                                nesting }
        MINIT (TLIST[NEST]);   { Initialize transformation matrix
                                to identity }

    END;

{ Display picture on screen }
PROCEDURE VIEW (VP_X,VP_Y,VP_WIDTH,VP_HEIGHT : INTEGER;
                X,Y,FACTOR,THETA : REAL);

    VAR CLIPXL,CLIPXR,CLIPYB,CLIPYT : REAL;

    PROCEDURE CLIP_LINE (VAR ON_SCREEN : BOOLEAN;
                        VAR X1,Y1,X2,Y2 : REAL);

        TYPE EDGE = (LEFT,RIGHT,BOTTOM,TOP);
            OUTCODE = SET OF EDGE;
        VAR C,C1,C2 : OUTCODE;
            X,Y : REAL;
        LABEL 9999;

        { Determine where point lies with respect to clipping
        window }

        PROCEDURE CODE (X,Y : REAL; VAR C : OUTCODE);
            BEGIN

                C := [ ];
                IF X < CLIPXL THEN
                    C := [LEFT]
                ELSE IF X > CLIPXR THEN
                    C := [RIGHT];
                IF Y < CLIPYB THEN
                    C := C + [BOTTOM]
                ELSE IF Y > CLIPYT THEN
                    C := C + [TOP];
            END;
        BEGIN

            ON_SCREEN := TRUE;
            CODE (X1,Y1,C1);
            CODE (X2,Y2,C2);

            { Clip to borders of clipping window }
```

```
{ If line endpoints are off screen, either C1 or C2 is
  not empty }
WHILE (C1 <> [ ]) OR (C2 <> [ ]) DO
BEGIN
    { If the intersection of C1 and C2 is not empty,
      then line is completely off the screen }
    IF (C1*C2) <> [ ] THEN
        BEGIN
            ON_SCREEN := FALSE;
            GOTO 9999;
        END;
    C := C1;
    IF C = [ ] THEN C := C2;
    IF LEFT IN C THEN
        BEGIN
            Y := Y1 +
                    (Y2 - Y1)*(CLIPXL - X1)/(X2 - X1);
            X := CLIPXL;
        END
    ELSE
    IF RIGHT IN C THEN
        BEGIN
            Y := Y1 +
                    (Y2 - Y1)*(CLIPXR - X1)/(X2 - X1);
            X := CLIPXR;
        END
    ELSE
    IF BOTTOM IN C THEN
        BEGIN
            X := X1 +
                    (X2 - X1)*(CLIPYB - Y1)/(Y2 - Y1);
            Y := CLIPYB
        END
    ELSE
    IF TOP IN C THEN
        BEGIN
            X := X1 +
                    (X2 - X1)*(CLIPYT - Y1)/(Y2 - Y1);
            Y := CLIPYT;
        END;
    IF C = C1 THEN
        BEGIN
            X1 := X;
            Y1 := Y;
            CODE (X,Y,C1);      { Update status of 1st
                                  endpoint }
        END
    ELSE
        BEGIN
            X2 := X;
            Y2 := Y;
            CODE (X,Y,C2);      { Update status of 2nd
                                  endpoint }
        END;
```

```
                    END;

            9999:  END;


                    VAR  X1,Y1,X2,Y2 : REAL;
                         ON_SCREEN,TWO_POINTS : BOOLEAN;
                         K : INTEGER;
                         T1 : THREEBY;

                    BEGIN
                      { Create transformation matrix that will
                        transform points in world coordinate system
                        to window in screen coordinate system }

                      NEST := 0;
                      START;
                      TRANSLATE (−X,−Y);
                      SCALE (FACTOR,FACTOR);
                      ROTATE (THETA);
                      TRANSLATE (VP_X,VP_Y);
                      T1 := TLIST[NEST];

                      CLIPXL := VP_X − VP_WIDTH DIV 2;
                      CLIPXR := VP_X + VP_WIDTH DIV 2;
                      CLIPYB := VP_Y − VP_HEIGHT DIV 2;
                      CLIPYT := VP_Y + VP_HEIGHT DIV 2;

                      { Draw rectangle around screen window }

        { * Delete the next five lines for Macintosh implementation * }
                      OFF (ROUND(CLIPXL),ROUND(CLIPYB));
                      ON (ROUND(CLIPXR),ROUND(CLIPYB));
                      ON (ROUND(CLIPXR),ROUND(CLIPYT));
                      ON (ROUND(CLIPXL),ROUND(CLIPYT));
                      ON (ROUND(CLIPXL),ROUND(CLIPYB));

                      K := 1;

                      { Loop through points in picture, transform to
                        screen coordinate system, clip to screen
                        window, and display }

                      WHILE K < NC DO
                      BEGIN

                        TWO_POINTS := FALSE;

                        REPEAT;

                          IF PCOORD[K+1].VISIBLE THEN
                          BEGIN
                            X1 := PCOORD[K].X*T1[1,1] +
                                  PCOORD[K].Y*T1[2,1] +
                                  T1[3,1];
                            Y1 := PCOORD[K].X*T1[1,2] +
                                  PCOORD[K].Y*T1[2,2] +
                                  T1[3,2];
                            X2 := PCOORD[K+1].X*T1[1,1] +
                                  PCOORD[K+1].Y*T1[2,1] +
                                  T1[3,1];
                            Y2 := PCOORD[K+1].X*T1[1,2] +
```

```
                              PCOORD[K + 1].Y*T1[2,2]  +
                              T1[3,2];
                       TWO_POINTS  :=  TRUE;
                END;
                K  :=  K  +  1;

            UNTIL  TWO_POINTS;

            CLIP_LINE  (ON_SCREEN,X1,Y1,X2,Y2);

            { Draw  line  if  visible  on  screen  window }

            IF  ON_SCREEN  THEN
               BEGIN
                  OFF  (ROUND(X1),ROUND(Y1));
                  ON  (ROUND(X2),ROUND(Y2));
               END;

         END;

      END;
```

Modifications for Turbo Pascal

Insert the following set of procedures in the beginning of the general code where marked and store as **grafx.lib**:

```
PROCEDURE PLOT (X2,Y2 : INTEGER; VISIBLE : BOOLEAN);

   { This procedure saves the last point which was moved to or
     drawn to so that the basic TURBO drawing procedure can be
     invoked with both line endpoints }

   { X1 and Y1 are given ABSOLUTE addresses so their values can
     be remembered from one invocation of PLOT to the next }

   VAR X1 : INTEGER ABSOLUTE $0000:$00EE;
       Y1 : INTEGER ABSOLUTE $0000:$00F0;
       Y1S,Y2S : INTEGER;

BEGIN

   { If MOVETO is invoked, then coordinates are stored for the
     next DRAWTO invocation }

   IF NOT(VISIBLE) THEN
      BEGIN
         X1 := X2;
         Y1 := Y2;
      END

   { If DRAWTO is invoked, transform Y values from TURBO
     origin to origin in the bottom-left corner and DRAW line
     using new and saved set of coordinates }

   ELSE BEGIN
         Y1S := 200 − Y1;
         Y2S := 200 − Y2;
         DRAW (X1,Y1S,X2,Y2S,1);
         X1 := X2;
         Y1 := Y2;
      END;
```

```
                END;
          PROCEDURE OFF (X,Y : INTEGER);
                BEGIN
                    PLOT (X,Y,FALSE);
                END;
          PROCEDURE ON (X,Y : INTEGER);
                BEGIN
                    PLOT (X,Y,TRUE);
                END;
          PROCEDURE START_DRAWING;
                BEGIN

                    GRAPHCOLORMODE;        { Invoke low resolution color mode }

                    NC := 0               { Initialize counters }
                    NP := 0;
                    NEST := 0;

                END;
          PROCEDURE FINISH_DRAWING;
                BEGIN

                    REPEAT UNTIL KEYPRESSED;
                    TEXTMODE;              { Return to text mode }

                END;
```

The only other change required in the general code is to rename the
move and **draw** procedures **moveto** and **drawto**. This set of procedures is
then included in your program by replacing the **uses advanced_graphics**
statement by the following:

`{$I GRAFX.LIB}`

The sample program for drawing rotated nested squares would then become:

```
          PROGRAM TEST;
          {$I GRAFX.LIB}
          PROCEDURE SQUARE;
              { Creates a unit square centered at origin }
                BEGIN

                    MOVETO (-0.5,-0.5);
                    DRAWTO (0.5,-0.5);
                    DRAWTO (0.5,0.5);
                    DRAWTO (-0.5,0.5);
                    DRAWTO (-0.5,-0.5);
                END;

          PROCEDURE NESTED_SQUARES;
              BEGIN

                  { Draw outer unit square }

                  SQUARE;
```

```
        { Draw  inner  square  with  side = SQRT(2),  rotated  45  deg }
            START;
                SCALE  (SQRT(2),SQRT(2));
                ROTATE  (45);
                SQUARE;
            FINISH;

        END;

{ Main  program }
    BEGIN

        START_DRAWING;

            NESTED_SQUARES;

            { Set  up  viewing  parameters  to  center  200×200  window
              on  320×200  screen }

                VIEW  (160,100,200,200,0.0,0.0,50,0);

        FINISH_DRAWING;

    END.
```

Modifications for Macintosh Pascal

When working in the Macintosh Pascal environment, the following procedures should be inserted where specified in the general code:

```
PROCEDURE OFF (X,Y : INTEGER);
    BEGIN
        MOVETO (X,200-Y);    { Origin  at  bottom-left  corner }
    END;
PROCEDURE ON (X,Y : INTEGER);
    BEGIN
        LINETO (X,200-Y);      { Origin  at  bottom-left  corner }
    END;
PROCEDURE START_DRAWING;
    BEGIN
        SHOWDRAWING;        { Invoke  default  graphic  window }

        NC := 0;              { Initialize  counters }
        NP := 0;
        NEST := 0;

    END;
PROCEDURE FINISH_DRAWING;
    BEGIN
                              { Dummy  routine  which  does  nothing }
    END;
```

In addition, the **move** and **draw** procedures should be renamed **movexy** and **drawxy.**

The following program uses the Macintosh version of **advanced_graphics** to draw nested squares.

```
            PROGRAM TEST;

              USES ADVANCED_GRAPHICS;

              PROCEDURE SQUARE;

            { Creates a unit square centered at origin }
                  BEGIN
                        MOVEXY (−0.5,−0.5);
                        DRAWXY (0.5,−0.5);
                        DRAWXY (0.5,0.5);
                        DRAWXY (−0.5,0.5);
                        DRAWXY (−0.5,−0.5);

                  END;

              PROCEDURE NESTED_SQUARES;

              BEGIN

            { Draw outer unit square }

                  SQUARE;

            { Draw inner square with side = SQRT(2), rotated 45 deg }

                  START;
                        SCALE (SQRT(2),SQRT(2));
                        ROTATE (45);
                        SQUARE;
                  FINISH;

              END;

            { Main program }
              BEGIN

                  START_DRAWING;

                    NESTED_SQUARES;

            { Set up viewing parameters for 200×200 window }
                        VIEW (100,100,200,200,0.0,0.0,50,0);

                  FINISH_DRAWING;

              END.
```

An Alternative Implementation of Advanced_Graphics

The following is an alternative implementation of **advanced_graphics**, called **mvns_transforms**, by Mark Van Norman of the Harvard Graduate School of Design. It does not use an **array** or list of Graphic **record**s; instead, it passes a 3-by-3 transformation matrix to transformation and graphics procedures, and eventually uses concatenated transformation matrices to control **move_to** and **draw_to** operations. The transformation matrix T is concatenated whenever **start** is invoked at the beginning of a graphic procedure. No **end** is required. Implementation is for Lightspeed Pascal by Think Technologies on a 512K Macintosh. A print procedure for the Laserwriter laser printer is included, and an example program, Snowflake, follows the library of graphic procedures.

This approach minimizes use of memory, and results in fast execution. It is highly recommended for use with small personal computers, and where access to a **list** or **array** of Graphic records is not required for other purposes.

```
UNIT  MVNS_TRANSFORMS;

INTERFACE

    USES
        MACPRINT;

    CONST
        INSIDEDRAWINGDIM  =  300;
        PRINT_SCALE_FACTOR  =  1.8414;

                        { Controls degree of enlargement of
                          printed copies over screen }

    TYPE

        THREEBY  =  ARRAY[1..3,1..3]  OF  REAL;

        TRANSFORM  =  RECORD

                        { Transforms hold two transformation
                          matrices, a local (.l) and a global (.g).
                          The global is passed into a procedure
                          and the local records all transformations
                          performed inside a procedure }

            L  :  THREEBY;
            G  :  THREEBY;
        END;   { Transform }

    VAR
        DRECT, TRECT, OUTRECT : RECT;
        VP_X, VP_Y : INTEGER;
        WX_CEN, WY_CEN, SCALE_FACTOR : REAL;
        T : TRANSFORM;

                        { T is a global identity threeby matrix
                          used to start the program }

        UNITTHREEBY : THREEBY;

                        { Another identity matrix, used for setting
                          matrices to the identity }

        ISPRINTING : BOOLEAN;
        C : CURSHANDLE;
        HPRINT : THPRINT;
        CURPRINTER : TPRINT;
        PRINTPORT : TPPRPORT;
        PRSTATUS : TPRSTATUS;
        SAVEPORT : GRAFPTR;

                        { Variables used in printing to the
                          laserwriter. Note that the chooser must
                          be set correctly before calling this unit }
```

PROCEDURE START_DRAWING (PRINTERORSCREEN : **CHAR**;
SVP_X, SVP_Y : INTEGER;
SWX_CEN, SWY_CEN, SSCALE_FACTOR : **REAL**);

> { *This procedure takes the place of view in other systems. It sets up screen coordinates and the scale relationship between screen and world. The meaning of the parameters is as follows:*
>
> *printerorscreen determines whether printing goes on at screen or printer. 'p' sets to printer, 's' to screen*
>
> *svp_x and svp_y determine the coordinates of the center of the view coordinate system in the drawing window. Range is 0->391 for svp_x and 0->300 for svp_y*
>
> *swx_cen and swy_cen determine the world coordinates located at the center of the screen. Range is not limited.*
>
> *sscale is the ratio of world to screen units. A figure of 8.0 means that one world unit will be mapped into 8 pixels onscreen. This should be used once as the first statement of your program.* }

PROCEDURE START (**VAR** T : TRANSFORM);

> { *Start takes a transform consisting of a global and local threeby array, places the result of t.l × t.g in t.g, and sets t.l to the identity threeby matrix. This permits successive use of local transformations in a single procedure without concatenating them with the global transform more than once. Use start as the first statement of any procedure invoking transforms, but you need not use it for procedures calling only move_to and draw_to.* }

PROCEDURE TRANSLATE (**VAR** T : TRANSFORM;
TRANS_X, TRANS_Y : **REAL**);

> { *Translates a motif by (trans_x,trans_y) world units. Note required parameter of type transform.* }

PROCEDURE ROTATE (**VAR** T : TRANSFORM;
THETA : REAL);

> { *Rotates a motif by theta degrees. Note required parameter of type transform.* }

PROCEDURE SCALE (**VAR** T : TRANSFORM;
X_SCALE, Y_SCALE : **REAL**);

> { *Scales a motif by (x_scale, y_scale). Note required parameter of type transform.* }

```
PROCEDURE (REFLECT_Y (VAR T : TRANSFORM);

                    { Reflects a motif about the y axis, but
                      does not make another instantiation.
                      Note required parameter of type
                      transform }

PROCEDURE MOVE_TO (T : TRANSFORM;
            X_COORD, Y_COORD : REAL);

                    { Moves to the coordinates x_coord,
                      y_coord. Note the required transform
                      parameter t. }

PROCEDURE DRAW_TO (T : TRANSFORM;
            X_COORD, Y_COORD : REAL);

                    { Moves to the coordinates x_coord, y_
                      coord. Note the required transform
                      parameter t. }

PROCEDURE FINISH_DRAWING;

                    { Must be the last statement of every
                      program. Finish_drawing shuts down the
                      printer if the output is being printed }

IMPLEMENTATION

FUNCTION MMULT (AMAT, BMAT : THREEBY) : THREEBY;
    VAR
        I,J : INTEGER;
        CMAT : THREEBY;
BEGIN
    FOR I := 1 TO 3 DO
    FOR J := 1 TO 3 DO
        CMAT[I,J] := AMAT[I,1] * BMAT[1,J] + AMAT[I,2] *
        BMAT[2,J] + AMAT[I,3] * BMAT[3,J];
  MMULT := CMAT;
END;

FUNCTION MINIT : THREEBY;
    VAR
        I,J : INTEGER;
        MAT : THREEBY;
BEGIN
    FOR I := 1 TO 3 DO
        BEGIN
            FOR J := 1 TO 3 DO
                MAT[I,J] := 0;
            MAT[I,I] : = 1;
        END;
    MINIT := MAT;
END;

PROCEDURE DRAW (X,Y : INTEGER);
BEGIN
    CASE ISPRINTING OF
        TRUE:
            LINETO(TRUNC(Y * PRINT_SCALE_FACTOR),
                    TRUNC(X * PRINT_SCALE_FACTOR));
        FALSE:
            LINETO(X, -Y + INSIDEDRAWINGDIM);
```

```
            END;
    END;
    PROCEDURE MOVE (X,Y : INTEGER);
    BEGIN
        CASE ISPRINTING OF
            TRUE:
                MOVETO(TRUNC(Y * PRINT_SCALE_FACTOR),
                TRUNC(X TRUNC(X * PRINT_SCALE_FACTOR));
            FALSE:
                MOVETO(X, - Y + INSIDEDRAWINGDIM);
        END;
    END;

    PROCEDURE STARTPRINTER;
    BEGIN
        PROPEN;
        HPRINT := THPRINT(NEWHANDLE(SIZEOF(TPRINT)));
        PRINTDEFAULT(HPRINT);
        IF (PRJOBDIALOG(HPRINT) = TRUE) THEN
            BEGIN
                ISPRINTING := TRUE;
                GETPORT(SAVEPORT);
                PRINTPORT := PROPENDOC(HPRINT,NIL,NIL);
                PROPENPAGE(PRINTPORT,NIL);
            END
    END;

    PROCEDURE START_DRAWING;
    BEGIN
        ISPRINTING := FALSE;
        UNITTHREEBY := MINIT;
        SETRECT(DRECT,134,40,525,355);
        SETRECT(TRECT,2,40,130,340);
        SETDRAWINGRECT(DRECT);
        SETTEXTRECT(TRECT);
        SHOWTEXT;
        SHOWDRAWING;
        SHOWPEN;
        IF (PRINTERORSCREEN IN ['p','P']) THEN
            STARTPRINTER;
        VP_X := SVP_X;
        VP_Y := SVP_Y;
        WX_CEN := SWX_CEN;
        WY_CEN := SWY_CEN;
        SCALE_FACTOR := SSCALE_FACTOR;
        T.L := UNITTHREEBY;
        T.G := UNITTHREEBY;
    END;

    PROCEDURE START;
    BEGIN
        T.G := MMULT(T.L,T.G);
        T.L := UNITTHREEBY;
    END;

    PROCEDURE TRANSLATE;
        VAR
            T2 : THREEBY;
    BEGIN
```

```
      IF (TRANS_X < -10000.0) OR (TRANS_X > 10000.0) OR
         (TRANS_Y < -10000.0) OR (TRANS_Y > 10000.0) THEN
         BEGIN
            WRITELN('ERROR - TRANSLATION OUT OF RANGE ');
         END;
      T2 := UNITTHREEBY;
      T2[3,1] := TRANS_X;
      T2[3,2] := TRANS_Y;
      T.L := MMULT(T.L, T2);
END;
PROCEDURE ROTATE;
   VAR
      T2 : THREEBY;
      ANGLE : REAL;
BEGIN
   IF (THETA < -10000.0) OR (THETA > 10000.0) THEN
      BEGIN
         WRITELN('ERROR - ROTATION OUT OF RANGE');
      END;
   ANGLE := THETA * PI / 180;
   T2 := UNITTHREEBY;
   T2[1,1] := COS(ANGLE);
   T2[1,2] := -SIN(ANGLE);
   T2[2,1] := SIN(ANGLE);
   T2[2,2] := COS(ANGLE);
   T.L := MMULT(T.L,T2);
END;
PROCEDURE SCALE;
   VAR
      T2 : THREEBY;
BEGIN
   IF (X_SCALE < 0.0) OR (X_SCALE > 10000.0) OR
      (Y_SCALE < 0.0) OR (Y_SCALE > 10000.0) THEN
      BEGIN
         WRITELN('ERROR - BAD SCALE FACTOR');
      END;
   T2 := UNITTHREEBY;
   T2[1,1] := X_SCALE;
   T2[2,2] := Y_SCALE;
   T.L := MMULT(T.L,T2);
END;
PROCEDURE REFLECT_Y;
   VAR
      T2 : THREEBY;
BEGIN
   T2 := UNITTHREEBY;
   T2[1,1] := -1;
   T.L := MMULT(T.L,T2);
END;
PROCEDURE MOVE_TO;
   VAR
      X1,Y1 : REAL;
BEGIN
   START(T);
   T.L := T.G;
```

```
          IF  (X_COORD  <  −20000.0)  OR  (X_COORD  >  20000.0)
               THEN  WRITELN('ERROR - UNINITIALIZED  X  INPUT  TO
                               'MOVE_TO');
          IF  (Y_COORD  <  −20000.0)  OR  (Y_COORD  >  20000.0)
               THEN  WRITELN('ERROR - UNINITIALIZED  Y  INPUT  TO
                               'MOVE_TO');
          X1  :=  X_COORD  *  T.L[1,1]  +  Y_COORD  *  T.L[2,1]  +
                  T.L[3,1];
          Y1  :=  X_COORD  *  T.L[1,2]  +  Y_COORD  *  T.L[2,2]  +
                  T.L[3,2];

          X1  :=  X1  −  WX_CEN;  { Viewing  transformations }
          Y1  :=  Y1  −  WY_CEN;
          X1  :=  X1  *  SCALE_FACTOR;
          Y1  :=  Y1  *  SCALE_FACTOR;
          X1  :=  X1  +  VP_X;
          Y1  :=  Y1  +  VP_Y;

          MOVE(TRUNC(X1),  TRUNC(Y1));
     END;

     PROCEDURE  DRAW_TO;
        VAR
           X1,Y1  :  REAL;
     BEGIN
        START(T);
        T.L  :=  T.G;
        IF  (X_COORD  <  −20000.0)  OR  (X_COORD  >  20000.0)
             THEN   WRITELN('ERROR - UNINITIALIZED  X  INPUT  TO
                             'MOVE_TO');
        IF  (Y_COORD  <  −20000.0)  OR  (Y_COORD  >  20000.0)
             THEN  WRITELN('ERROR - UNINITIALIZED  Y  INPUT  TO
                             'MOVE_TO');

        X1  :=  X_COORD  *  T.L[1,1]  +  Y_COORD  *  T.L[2,1]  +
                T.L[3,1];
        Y1  :=  X_COORD  *  T.L[1,2]  +  Y_COORD  *  T.L[2,2]  +
                T.L[3,2];

        X1  :=  X1  −  WX_CEN;  { Viewing  transformations }
        Y1  :=  Y1  −  WY_CEN;
        X1  :=  X1  *  SCALE_FACTOR;
        Y1  :=  Y1  *  SCALE_FACTOR;
        X1  :=  X1  +  VP_X;
        Y1  :=  Y1  +  VP_Y;

        DRAW(TRUNCX1),  TRUNC(Y1));
     END;

     PROCEDURE  FINISH_DRAWING;
     BEGIN
        IF  (ISPRINTING)  THEN
           BEGIN
               PRCLOSEPAGE(PRINTPORT);
               PRCLOSEDOC(PRINTPORT);
               PRPICFILE(HPRINT,NIL,NIL,NIL,PRSTATUS);
               SETPORT(SAVEPORT);
               PRCLOSE;
               ISPRINTING  :=  FALSE;
           END;
```

```
    END;
END. { Unit geometric_transforms }
PROGRAM SNOWFLAKE;
    USES
        MACPRINT, MVNS_TRANSFORMS;
    VAR
        WHICH :CHAR;
        SPACING : REAL;
        N : INTEGER;
    PROCEDURE STEM (T : TRANSFORM);

    BEGIN
        MOVE_TO (T, -0.3,0);
        DRAW_TO (T, -0.3,6);
        DRAW_TO (T, -0.8,6);
        DRAW_TO (T, -0.8,5);
        DRAW_TO (T, -1.5,5);
        DRAW_TO (T, -1.5,4);
        DRAW_TO (T, -0.8,4);
        DRAW_TO (T, -1,0);
        DRAW_TO (T, -0.3,0);
    END;
    PROCEDURE GUND (T : TRANSFORM);
    BEGIN
        MOVE_TO (T, -1,0);
        DRAW_TO (T, -2.5,0);
        DRAW_TO (T, -2.5,1.5);
        DRAW_TO (T, -3.5,1.5);
        DRAW_TO (T,0.3,8);
        DRAW_TO (T,1,8);
        DRAW_TO (T,1,3);
        DRAW_TO (T,0,3);
        DRAW_TO (T,0,1.5);
        DRAW_TO (T, -1,1.5);
        DRAW_TO (T, -1,0);
    END;

    PROCEDURE MIRROR (T : TRANSFORM;
                PROCEDURE MOTIF (T : TRANSFORM));
    BEGIN
        START(T);
        MOTIF(T);      { First, place motif }
        REFLECT_Y(T);     { Then, reflect it in y }
        MOTIF(T);
    END;

    PROCEDURE BRANCHMOTIF (T : TRANSFORM;
                PROCEDURE MOTIF (T : TRANSFORM);
                DONE : BOOLEAN);

    BEGIN
        DONE := NOT DONE;
        START (T);
        SCALE (T,0.666,0.666);
        ROTATE (T, -30.0);
```

```
                    TRANSLATE(T,0, 6.0);
                    MIRROR(T,MOTIF);
                    IF (NOT DONE) THEN
                        BRANCHMOTIF(T,MOTIF,DONE)

                    TRANSLATE(T,0, − 6.0);
                    ROTATE(T,60.0);
                    TRANSLATE(T,0,6.0);
                    MIRROR(T,MOTIF);
                    IF (NOT DONE) THEN
                        BRANCHMOTIF(T,MOTIF,DONE);
                END;

                PROCEDURE TRUNK (T : TRANSFORM;
                            PROCEDURE MOTIF (T : TRANSFORM));
                BEGIN
                    START (T);
                    MIRROR(T,MOTIF);
                    BRANCHMOTIF(T,MOTIF,TRUE);
                END;

                PROCEDURE HEXSYMMETRY (T : TRANSFORM;
                            PROCEDURE MOTIF (T : TRANSFORM));
                    VAR
                        N : INTEGER;
                BEGIN
                    START (T);
                    FOR N : = 0 TO 5 DO
                        BEGIN
                            ROTATE (T,360 / 6);
                            TRUNK(T,MOTIF);
                        END;
                END;

            BEGIN { main program }
                START_DRAWING ('p',180,150,0.0,0.0,10.0);
                    HEXSYMMETRY(T,GUND);
                FINISH_DRAWING;
            END. { main program }
```

Acknowledgments

Several of our students and former students produced graphics for this book using a Computervision system at the UCLA Graduate School of Architecture and Urban Planning. We wish, particularly, to acknowledge the assistance of Carlos Dell Acqua, Yi-Mei Fan, Wade Hokoda, Chung-Chien Hsu, Chia-yin Sheu, and Eric Silver.

Bibliography

Albers, Josef. *Despite Straight Lines*. Cambridge, MA: MIT Press, 1977.

Albers, Josef. *Interaction of Color*. New Haven, CT: Yale University Press, 1971.

Alberti, L. B. *Ten Books on Architecture*. Edited by J. Rykwert. Translated by J. Leoni. London: Tiranti, 1955.

Baglivo, Jenny A., and Jack E. Graver. *Incidence and Symmetry in Design and Architecture*. Cambridge, England: Cambridge University Press, 1983.

Booth, Kellogg S. *Tutorial: Computer Graphics*. Long Beach, CA: IEEE Computer Society, 1979.

Boullée, Etienne Louis. *Treatise on Architecture*. Edited by Helen Rosenau. London: Tiranti, 1953.

Chasen, Sylvan H. *Geometric Principles and Procedures for Computer Graphic Applications*. Englewood Cliffs, NJ: Prentice-Hall, 1978.

Chuan, Chieh Tzǔ Yüan Hua. *The Mustard Seed Manual of Painting*. Edited by Mai-Mai Sze. Princeton, NJ: Princeton University Press, 1956.

Conrac Corporation. *Raster Graphics Handbook*. New York: Van Nostrand Reinhold, 1985.

Cooper, Doug. *Standard Pascal*. New York: W. W. Norton and Company, 1983. (The International Standards Organization's standard for Pascal is introduced and discussed in detail.)

Cooper, Doug, and Michael Clancy. *Oh! Pascal!* 2d. ed. New York: W. W. Norton and Company, 1985. (One of the best of the general Pascal texts.)

Deken, Joseph, ed. *Computer Images*. New York: Stewart, Tabori and Chang, 1983.

Durand, J..N. L. *Architecture*. Reprint. Nordlingen: Verlag Dr. Alfons Uhl, 1985.

Dye, Daniel Sheets. *Chinese Lattice Designs*. Reprint. New York: Dover, 1974.

Foley, James D., and Andries van Dam. *Fundamentals of Interactive Computer Graphics*. Reading, MA: Addison-Wesley, 1982.

Freeman, Herbert, ed. *Tutorial and Selected Readings in Interactive Computer Graphics*. Long Beach, CA: IEEE Computer Society, 1980.

Gombrich, E. H. *Art and Illusion*. Princeton, NJ: Princeton University Press, 1960.

Goodman, Nelson. *Languages of Art*. 2d ed. Indianapolis: Hackett, 1976.

Graphic Standards Planning Committee. "Status Report of the Graphics Standards Planning Committee." *Computer Graphics*. vol. 11, no. 3 (Aug. 1977), and vol. 13, no. 13, no. 3 (Aug. 1979).

Grunbaum, Branko, and G. C. Shephard. *Tilings and Patterns*. New York: W. H. Freeman, 1987.

Hopgood, F. R. A., D. A. Duce, J. R. Gallop, and D. C. Sutcliffe. *Introduction to the Graphical Kernel System (GKS)*. 2d ed. London: Academic Press, 1981.

Jarvis, J. F., C. N. Judice, and W. H. Ninke. "A Survey of Techniques for the Display of Continuous Tone Pictures on Bi-level Displays." *Computer Graphics and Image Processing*. vol. 5, no. 1 (March 1976): 13–40.

Jensen, Kathleen, and Niklaus Wirth. *Pascal User Manual and Report*. 3d ed. New York: Springer-Verlag, 1985. (This text is the original, definitive reference on the Pascal language.)

Jones, Owen. *The Grammar of Ornament*. Reprint. New York: Van Nostrand Reinhold, 1982.

Kandinsky, Wassily. *Punkt und Linie zur Flache*. Munich, 1926. Translated as "Point and Line to Plane," in Kenneth C. Lindsay and Peter Vergo. *Kandinsky: Complete Writings on Art*. Boston: G. K. Hall, 1982.

Klee, Paul. *Notebooks*. 2 vols. London: Lund Humphries, 1961.

Klee, Paul. *Pedagogiche Skizzenbuch*. Munich, 1925. Translated as *Pedagogical Sketchbook*. London: Faber, 1953.

Knuth, Donald E. *The METAFONT Book*. Reading, MA: Addison Wesley, 1986.

Langley, Batty. *The City and Country Builder's and Workman's Treasury of Designs*. London: S. Harding, 1750.

Ledoux, C. N. *L'Architecture*. Reprint. Princeton, NJ: Princeton Architectural Press, 1983.

Letarouilly, Paul Marie. *Edifices de Rome Moderne*. Reprint. Princeton, NJ: Princeton Architectural Press, 1982.

Malevich, Kasimir. *Suprematism: Thirty-Four Drawings*. Vitelsk, 1920. Reprint, Lausanne, Editions des Massons, 1974.

March, Lionel, and Philip Steadman. *The Geometry of Environment*. Cambridge, MA: MIT Press, 1971.

Mandelbrot, Benoit B. *The Fractal Geometry of Nature*. San Francisco: W. H. Freeman, 1982.

Newman, William M., and Robert F. Sproull. *Principles of Interactive Computer Graphics*. 2d ed. New York: McGraw-Hill, 1979.

Palladio, Andrea. *The Four Books of Architecture*. Translated by Isaac Ware. New York: Dover, 1965.

Peitgen, H. O., and P. H. Richter. *The Beauty of Fractals*. Berlin: Springer-Verlag, 1986.

Penna, Michael A., and Richard R. Patterson. *Projective Geometry and Its Applications to Computer Graphics*. Englewood Cliffs, NJ: Prentice-Hall, 1986.

Rogers, David F. *Procedural Elements for Computer Graphics*. New York: McGraw-Hill, 1985.

Rogers, David F., and J. A. Adams. *Mathematical Elements for Computer Graphics*. New York: McGraw-Hill, 1976.

Ruskin, John. *The Elements of Drawing*. London, 1857. Reprint, New York: Dover, 1971.

Ruskin, John. *The Stones of Venice*. Edited by Jan Morris. Boston: Little, Brown, 1981.

Smith, Bradford, et al. Initial Graphic Exchange Specification (EDGES). Version 2.0, National Bureau of Standards, Department of Commerce, Washington, D.C., February, 1983.

Shubnikov, A. V., and V. A. Koptsik. *Symmetry in Science and Art*. New York: Plenum, 1974.

Sullivan, Louis H. *A System of Architectural Ornament*. New York: Press of the American Institute of Architects, 1924.

Stiny, George. "Introduction to Shape and Shape Grammars." *Environment and Planning B*. vol. 7, no. 3 (1980).

Venciolo, Federico. *Renaissance Patterns for Lace, Embroidery and Needlepoint*. New York: Dover, 1971.

Weyl, Hermann. *Symmetry*. Princeton, NJ: Princeton University Press, 1952.

Index

Aalto, Alvar, 295
ABS (absolute value) function, 146
Accuracy, of pen plotters, 14
Ada (language), 109
Addressable points, 6
Advanced graphics library
    alternative implementation of,
        542–50
    for Turbo Pascal and Macintosh
        Pascal, 531–42
Aesthetics of frame, 433–34
Aliasing (jaggies; pixel resolution), 44
    antialiasing techniques for, 45
    scan conversion methods for, 47
Albers, Josef, 18
Alberti, Leone Battista, 171
Algol (language), 109
Algorithmic languages, 100, 101
Alphanumeric displays, 83
Alphanumeric output, in Pascal,
        125–27
Altair computer, 80
Analytic geometry functions, 158–59
AND Boolean operator, 276
Angles
    in arcs, 263–64
    in regular polygons and circles,
        261–62
Animation systems, 522–24
Anodes, 4
Antialiasing, 45
Apple Macintosh computer
    graphics capabilities of, 80
    icons used by, 93
    Macdraw system on, 512
    screen resolution of, 135
Apple Paris computer, 46
Applications programs, 90
Arcades, 459–60
Arches, 457–62

Architecture
    of arches, 457–62
    arcs used in, 310
    building heights in, 216–20
    design in, 171
    drafting systems for, 514
    ellipses used in, 266
    enfilades in, 214–15
    frieze patterns in, 238–39
    of high-rise office buildings, 215
    ratios in, 168
    repetition of single position
        parameter in, 213
    stairs in, 221–23
    symmetries in, 325–26
Arcs, 263–64. *See also* Curved lines
    conditional statements to generate,
        306–12
    motifs constructed from, 457–66
    spirals, 267–69
ARCTAN (arctangent) function, 147
Arithmetic and logic units, 74
Arithmetic functions, 146–47
Arithmetic instructions, 99
Arithmetic progressions, 229
Arithmetic statements, in Pascal,
        121–25
Arpnet, 84–85, 86
Arrays, 357–61
    with arbitrary numbers of entries,
        368–70
    complete drawings stored as,
        364–68
    polygon filling using, 370–74
    as random-access data structures,
        384
    of records, 375
    of three or more dimensions, 374
    two-dimensional, 361–64
Assemblers, 100

Assembly languages, 100
Assignment statements, in Pascal, 120–21
Audio outputs, 83
Augusta, Ada, 109
Auxiliary memory, 82–83

Babbage, Charles, 109, 125
Bar codes, 67
Basic (language), 101
Batch operating systems, 91
Begin statement, in Pascal, 118
    for compound statements, 203
    in nested loops, 241
    in procedures, 164
Behrens, Peter, 495
Bilateral symmetry, 326, 442–43
    dihedral symmetry and, 443–45
Bilevel pictures, 48–49
Binary arithmetic, 74
Bitmaps (display memory), 36
Bitplanes, 37–38
    for color, 40–42
Bits (binary digits), 37, 73
Bits per second (bps), 84–85
Black Square (painting, Malevich), 31
Blocks, 338
Block structure, in Pascal, 338–42
BNF notation, 114
Bodies, in Pascal, 114
Boolean algebra, 41, 74
Boolean data, 118
    in while loops, 209–10
Boolean expressions
    in chained conditional statements, 290–91
    in if...then...else conditional statements, 275–77
    in repeat until loops, 211–12
    in while loops, 209–10
Boolean functions, 277
Boolean operators, 209
Boolean variables, 277
Botticelli, Sandro, 251
Branches, 99, 274
    in drawing editors, 487–88
Buildings
    heights of, 216–20
    high-rise office, 215
Bullet-proofing, 482
Business graphics systems, 507
Bytes, 73, 81

Calligraphy, 18–20
Cameras
    for photographic screens, 60
    video, for computer inputs, 68
Cartesian products, 191
Case statement, 296–98
Cathode ray tubes (CRTs), 3–4
    classes of images displayed on, 46–55
    cursors on, 71
    line intensity on, 21
    line thickness on, 18
    photographic output from, 58–60
    raster displays of line drawings on, 9–11
    raster units on, 15–16
    refreshed vector displays and, 8–10
    resolution of, 44
    storage tube displays and, 4–7
    touch screens and light pens used with, 69
Cathodes, 4
Cavetto, 310
CDC 6600 (computer), 77
Cellas, 289
Center conditions, 280–83
Central processing units (CPUs), 64, 72–74. *See also* Processors
    development of, 76–79
    instruction cycles in, 75
    measurement of performance of, 79–82
Chained if...then...else conditional statements, 290–91
Channels capacity, 84–86
Character data, in Pascal, 118
    in repeat until loops, 212
Characters, 56
    lettering, 24–26
    magnetic ink and optical recognition of, 68
Circles, 261–63. *See also* Arcs
    displays of, distorted by pixel resolution, 44
    displays of, distorted by pixel shape, 42
    subdividing, 462–66
Circuit boards, 79
Circumflexes (ˆ), 393
Classical temples, 289
Clipping of screen boundaries, 136, 427–31

Clocks (in computers), 74
Color
    continuous, 31
    in full-color pictures, 55
    in line drawings, 51–53
    for lines, 21–22
    in patterns, 52–53
    of pixels, 39–42
    of solid polygons, 52
Color video monitors, 35
Columns
    elements of 329–31, 334–35
    hierarchies of subsystems for,
        335–37
    program for exploring combinations
        in design of, 497–502
Combinations, program for exploring,
    497–502
Combining lists, 400–401
Command languages, 478
Commands, 90, 92, 95
    under Advanced_graphics, 435
    in drawing editors, 478, 487–88
    executed via menus and icons, 93
    graphic, primitive, 136–38
    in Pascal, 114
    to start and finish drawing, 139
Comments, in Pascal programs,
    130–31, 163
Communications, 84–86
Compatibility of hardware, 84
Compilation (of programs), 90, 101
    debugging and, 102–3
Compilers, 100–102
Composition
    control expressions and while
        statements in, 209–11
    control structures in, 201–4
    counted loops in, 205–8
    regular and irregular, 273–74
    regular repetition in, 204–5
    repeat until statements in, 211–12
    repetition used in, 212–29
    structure and meaning in, 337–38
    syntax of, 331–34
Compound Boolean expressions, 276
Compound statements, 203
Computer-aided design and drafting
    (CADD) systems, 51
Computer-aided design (CAD)
    programs, 220
Computers

auxiliary memory for, 82–83
CPUs and memory developed for,
    76–79
future of, 524
input devices for, 68–71
input media for, 65–68
inputs to, processes in, and outputs
    from, 63–64
networks of and data
    communications between, 84–86
operating systems for, 90–98
output devices for, 83–84
processor performance in, 79–82
processors for, 72–75
sign-off procedures for, 105
sign-on procedures for, 93–95
starting, 89–90
Concatenated transformation matrixes,
    426
Concatenation of transformations,
    425–26
Concentric shapes, 223–24
Conditionals, 273–74
    applications of, 304–15
    Boolean expressions in, 275–77
    in choosing among many design
        alternatives, 290–304
    in choosing among two design
        alternatives, 278–90
    if…then…else, 274–75
Connecting vectors, 188–89
Constants, 115–17
Construction lines, 407
Control cards, 91
Control expressions
    for repeat until statement, 211–12
    repetition parameters for, 247
    for while statement, 209–11
Control instructions, 99
Control structures
    for compositional rules, 201–5
    counted loops in, 205–8
    repeat until statement, 211–12
    while statement, 209–11
Control units, 74
Control variables, 205–6
    form for loops containing, 236
    in mathematical progressions,
        232–36
Conversions, of units, 483–84
Coordinate systems, 15–16
    arithmetic functions in, 146–47

functions to map between, 153–55
global variables in, 155–57
independent and dependent
    variables in, 145–46
local variables in, 151–53
parameters for functions in, 150–51
rounding and truncating in, 147–48
scale conversion functions in, 157
for screens, 135
in three-dimensional wire-frame
    systems, 517
trigonometric and analytic functions
    in, 158–59
user-written functions for, 148–50
world, 431, 439
CORE (graphics standard), 506
Core memory, 78
Corners, in line drawings, 18–20
COS (cosine) function, 147
Counted loops, 205–7
within procedures, 207–8
CP/M operating system, 93
Crosshair devices, 70
Cursors, 71
Curved lines, 251
approximated by straight segments,
    251–53
arcs, 263–64
circles and regular polygons, 261–63
conditional statements for
    generating, 305–12
ellipses, 264–66
fractals and, 404–7
for functions of X, 253–60
for functions of Y, 260–61
on pen plotters, 14
represented by lists of points, 402–3
smoothing of, 403–4
spirals, 267–69
stored in two-dimensional arrays,
    363
vectors for, 17
Curved surface–modeling systems,
    519
Cyma recta, 312
Cyma reversa, 312

Data
dynamic structures of, 391–97
hierarchical structures of, 408–9
inputting to drawing editors, 482–86
storage in memory of, 73

Data bus, 74
Data communications, 84–86
Data declarations, 99
Data types, in Pascal, 117–18
in Boolean expressions, 276
dynamic data structures, 391–97
hierarchical, 408–9
in records, 374–75
scalar, structured and pointer, 357
sets, 391
in while loops, 209–10
David, Jacques-Louis, 51
Debugging, 90, 102–4, 132
Declarations, in Pascal, 114–17, 338
for procedures, 164
for procedures called by other
    procedures, 334
for static variables, 394
for user-written functions, 148–50
Definitions, in Pascal, 114–17
Deflection plates, 4
Degrees (of angles), 158
Delimiters, in Pascal, 110
under Advanced_graphics, 435
Dependent variables, 145–46
Design
in architecture, 171
conditional statements
    (if…then…else) to pick among,
    278–304
interfaces in, 329–35
Device coordinate systems, 15–16
Device drivers, 84
Digital-to-analog converters (DACs),
    10, 11
Dihedral symmetry, 443–45
Direct input devices, 68
Directories, 97–98
Disk drives, 67
Display buffers, 8
Display controllers, 8
Display generators, 36–37
for personal computers, 46–47
Display memory, 36
Displays. *See also* Images; Raster
    displays; Screens
cathode ray tubes for, 3–4
classes of images, 46–55
logical and physical resolutin of, 42
photographing, 58–60
raster, of line drawings, 9–11
refreshed vector, 8–9

resolution of, 44–45
screen coordinate systems for, 135
of shapes, 45
storage tube, 4–7
windows, menus, and icons used on, 92–93
Dispose procedure, 401
Division, 117–18
Document readers, 67–68
Dot-matrix printers, 57
Dot screens, 22–24
Downto loops, 235
Drafting
line color in, 21–22
trigonometric and analytic functions for, 158
Drafting systems, 512–15
Draw command, 128, 136–38
under Advanced_graphics, 435
curves approximated by, 251–52
in graphic vocabularies, 193
stored in arrays, 365
Drawing
animation systems for, 522–24
commands for, 138
paint systems for, 508–11
structured systems for, 511–12
Drawing editors, 477
commands in, 478
data input procedures in, 482–86
input devices for, 477
menu procedures in, 486–88
prompts and responses in, 480–82
screen organization in, 478–80
Drawings
program for viewing, 488–91
as sets of lines, 3
starting and finishing, 139
storage versus computation of, 440
stored as files, 384
stored in two-dimensional arrays, 364–68
transformation of, 416–19
Drum plotters, 11–12
device coordinates for, 16
Dynamic data structures, 391–97
Dynamic displays, 7
Dynamic windows, 479–80

Edges of figures, 326–28
EDVAC (computer), 76
Eight-bit microprocessor chips, 80

Electric light displays, 34
Electromagnetic arrays, 70
Electron guns, 40, 42
Electronic mail, 90
Electrostatic plotters, 58
Ellipses, 264–66
End conditions, 279–80
End statement, in Pascal, 118
for compound statements, 203
in nested loops, 243
in procedures, 164
Enfilades, 214–15
ENIAC (computer), 76
Eof (end-of-file) predicate, 384, 385
Erasing, 509
Error codes, 305
Error messages, 102, 104
Errors
conditional statements to detect, 304–5
in inputs to drawing editors, 481–82
in programs, 102–3
Ethernet, 85, 86
Executable statements, in Pascal, 114, 118–20
Execution registers, 73
Exponential progressions, 234–35
Exponents, 112
External procedures, 139

Fanlight windows, 464
Fibonacci sequence, 268
Fields, 374
File operators, 384
Files, 90, 95–97
read by graphics programs, 390–91
reading and writing, 384–89
File systems (of operating systems), 91
File transfer commands, 90
Filing, 440
Finish delimiting operator, 435
Finish_drawing command, 139
for procedures, 166
Finish_drawing viewing operator, 434
First-in-first-out (FIFO) structures, 395
Fixed windows, 478–79
Flat-bed plotters, 11, 12
device coordinates for, 16
Floppy disks, 67, 82
Flow of control, 203
Formal parameters, 148

For statement, in Pascal (in loops), 203
   arrays in, 360
   for nested loops, 241
   repetition parameters in, 247
Fortran (language), 101
Four-bit microprocessor chips, 80
Four-dimensional arrays, 374
Fractals, 404–7
Frame buffers, 10–11, 36
   color specified by, 39, 51
   image resolution of, 44
   look-up tables for, 39
   resolution of, 42
Framing, 427
   aesthetics of, 433–34
   clipping, 427–31
   viewing transformations and, 431–33
Fresnel subdivisions, 463–64
Frieze patterns, 238–39
Frieze symmetry, 446–49
Full-color pictures, 55
Functional parameters, 454
Function keys, 68
Functions
   arithmetic, 146–47
   Boolean, 277
   curves approximated by, 253–61
   to map between screen coordinate
      systems, 153–55
   with multiple parameters, 150–51
   procedures distinguished from, 177
   procedures similar to, 164
   rounding and truncating, 147
   scale conversion, 157
   trigonometric and analytic, 158–59
   user-written, 148–50

Generate-and-test procedures, 312–15
Geometric operators, 427
Geometric progressions, 230–31
Geometric transformations. *See*
   Transformations
Geometry. *See also* Coordinate
   systems
   of fractals, 404–7
   trigonometric and analytic functions
      for, 158–59
Gigabytes, 82
Global procedures, 335
Global variables, 155–57, 338
Goethe, Johann Wolfgang von, 41
Golden ratio, 268

Golden rectangle, 269
Gombrich, E. H. 46
Graphical Kernel System (GKS), 506
Graphic elements
   declaring procedures for, 192
   graphic vocabularies for, 193–96
   interfaces between, 329–35
   parameters for, 166–71
   parameters for shape and position of,
      177–86
   in subsystems, 324–25
   transformation of, 416–19
   variation in, 191
Graphics
   color in, 51–52
   compromising qualities for display
      of, 45–46
   coordinate calculations for, 145–59
   history of use of computers for, 77
   as Pascal output, 127–28
   programs to generate simple line
      drawings, 135–42
   on sixteen-bit personal computers,
      80
Graphics packages, 505–6
Graphics programs. *See also* Programs
   for exploring combinations, 497–502
   files read by, 390–91
   files written by, 386–89
   future of, 524–25
   for interactive parametric variation,
      491–97
   lists used by, 397–407
   for viewing drawings, 488–91
Graphic tablets, 69–70, 508
Graphic vocabularies, 193–96
   in loops, parameters for, 212–13
   with repetition parameters, 246–47
   in subsystems, 325
   in world coordinate systems, 439
Graphs, business graphics systems for,
   507

Halftones, 34, 49–51
Hardware. *See also* Central processing
   units; Processors
   cathode ray tubes, 3–11
   CPUs, 73–74
   memory, 72–73
   output devices, 83–84
   pen plotters, 11–15
   raster printers and plotters, 56–58

Hatchings, filling areas with, 22–24
    using arrays, 370–74
    using records, 378–83
Headings, in Pascal, 114–15, 338
HELP command, 95
Help facilities, 95
Hierarchical data structures, 408–9
High-level languages, 100–101
High-persistence phosphors, 4
High-resolution raster displays, 55
High-rise office buildings, 215
Hypostyle hall, 289

IBM 360 series (computers), 77
IBM 7090 (computer), 77
IBM PCs, 80
    color palettes for, 52
    graphics compromises in, 46
    screen resolution of, 135
Icons, 93
Identifiers, in Pascal, 110–11
If…then conditional statements, 285
If…then…else conditional statements,
    274–75
    Boolean expressions in, 275–77
    for error checking, 304–5
    for mathematical functions, 305–15
    for multiple design alternatives,
        290–304
    for pairs of design alternatives,
        278–90
IGES standard, 514
Images. *See also* Displays; Screens
    classes of, 46–55
    photographing, 58–60
    on raster displays, 9–11
    resolution of, 44–45
    on storage tube displays, 4–7
Impact printers, 57
Impressionists, 31–32
Independent variables, 145–46
Indexes, for arrays, 358
Indexes of raster grids, 33–34
Ingres, Jean-Auguste-Dominique, 51
Inkjet printers, 57
Input devices, 64
    direct, 68
    for drawing editors, 477, 486
    media for, 65–68
    pointing, 69–71
    positioning, 71
Inputs, 63

to computers, 64
direct devices for, 68
to drawing editors, 482–86
to drawing editors, errors in, 481–82
instructions for, 98
media for, 65–68
of parameters, read by repeat until
    loop, 212
pointing devices for, 69–71
positioning devices for, 71
Instruction cycles, 75
Instructions
    in high-level languages, 100–101
    in programs, 98–99
Instruction sets, 74
Integer arrays, 365
Integers, 112, 118, 122
    control variables limited to, 206
    odd function for, 278–79
    for parameters, 171–72
    rounding truncating, 147–48
    subrange types for, 189–91
Integrated circuits (ICs), 77
    very large scale (VLSI) chips, 78
Integrated graphics systems, 524
Intel Corporation, 78
    8088 microprocessor by, 80
Intensity
    of lines, 21
    of pixels, 37–39
Interactive graphics systems, 506–7
    animation, 522–24
    business graphics systems, 507
    curved surface–modeling systems,
        519
    drafting systems, 512–15
    images from data structures in, 522
    paint systems, 508–11
    polygon-modeling systems, 517–19
    solid-modeling systems, 519–20
    structured drawing systems, 511–12
    three-dimensional systems, 515
    two-dimensional systems, 507
    wire-frame systems, 515–17
Interactive operating systems, 91
Interactive parametric variation
        program, 491–97
Interfaces (in design), 329–35
Interlacing, 35
Interpretation (of programs), 90, 101
Interpreters, 100–102
    for Pascal, 104

Invoking procedures, 175–77
Irregular compositions, 273

Jacquard looms, 34
Jaggies (aliasing; pixel resolution), 44
    antialiasing techniques for, 45
    scan conversion methods for, 47
Joysticks, 71, 523
Jumbotron (Sony), 35

Kahn, Louis, 325
Kandinsky, Wassily, 18
    on aesthetics of frame, 433–34
    on graphic primitives, 63
    on lines, 3
    on picture plane, 15
    on points, 42
    on texture, 48
Kernels (of operating systems), 91
Keyboards, 68
Kilobytes, 81
Klee, Paul, 3, 6, 185, 407, 456

Languages (programming), compilers
        and interpreters for, 100–102. *See
        also* Pascal
Laser printers, 58
Last-in-first-out (LIFO) structures, 395
Le Corbusier, 329
Letarouilly, Paul, 261
Lettering, 24–26
    graphic vocabularies for, 196
Light pens, 69
Line drawings, 3
    color of, 21–22, 51–53
    CORE standard for, 506
    intensity of, 21
    lettering in, 24–26
    monochrome, 46–48
    on pen plotters, 11, 14
    programs for, 135–42
    raster displays of, 10–11
    thickness and quality of, 18–21
    tone and texture in, 22–24
    vectors for, 17
Line editors, 98
Line noise, 86
Lines. *See also* Arcs; Curved lines;
        Straight lines
    construction, 407
    parallel, 237–38
    scan conversion methods for, 47–48

Linking (of programs), 90
Liquid crystal displays (LCDs), 35
Lists, 397–99
    arbitrary curves represented by,
        402–3
    combining, 400–401
    construction lines and, 407
    curve smoothing and, 403–4
    fractals and, 404–7
    records inserted in and deleted
        from, 399–400
Local area networks (LANs), 84
Local procedures, 335
Local variables, 151–53
LOGOFF command, 105
Look-up tables, 39, 42
Loops, 99
    for animation, 523
    arrays handled in, 360
    for compositional repetition, 212
    counted, 205–7
    counted, within procedures, 207–8
    curves approximated by, 253–61
    downto, 235
    to draw arcs, 264
    to draw circles, 262–63
    to draw ellipses, 264–66
    to draw spirals, 267–68
    to input parameters, 212
    mathematical progressions in,
        229–36
    multiple shape parameters for,
        224–26
    nested, 240–46
    position and shape parameters for,
        226–29
    for recursion, 344
    repeat until statements in, 211–12
    repetition parameters in, 246–47
    sequences of, 237–39
    single position parameters for,
        213–21
    single shape parameters for, 223–24
    transformations and symmetries in,
        441–54
    two position parameters for, 221–23
    while statements in, 209–11
Low-persistence phosphors, 4, 8

Macdraw system, 512
Machine language, 100
Macintosh, Charles Rennie, 495

Macintosh Pascal (language), 104, 530
  Advanced_graphics library for,
    531–39, 541–42
Magnetic core memory, 78
Magnetic disks, 82
Magnetic ink character recognition
    (MICR) devices, 68
Magnetic tape, 67, 82, 384
Mainframes (computers), 82
Malevich, Kasimir, 31, 37
Mapping between screen coordinate
    systems, functions for, 153–55
Mathematical progressions, 213,
    229–36
Meaning of compositions, 337–38
Mechanical tablets, 70
Media, input, 65–68
Megabytes, 82
Megaliths of Carnac (Brittany), 213
Memory, 72–73
  auxiliary, 82–83
  development of, 76–79
  display buffers in, 8
  frame buffers in, 10–11
  look-up tables stored in, 39
  storage capacity, 81
  used by graphic characteristics, 46
Memory chips, 78–79
Menus, 93, 478
  in drawing editors, 486–88
Mice, 71, 508
Microcomputers, 82
Microphones, 68
Microprocessors, 78
Microprograms, 74
Middle conditions, 280–83
Minicomputers, 82
MIPS (millions of instructions per
    second), 80–81
Mixed mode arithmetic, 122
Mixed symmetries, 466–67
Modems, 84
Mod (modular) function, 122, 235–36,
    298–300
Modular arithmetic, 298–300
Mondrian, Piet, 258
Monitors. See Video monitors
Monochrome displays
  halftones on, 49–51
  of line drawings, 46–48
Monochrome video monitors, 35
  look-up tables for tones on, 42

Moore, Charles, 266
Mosaic art, 32, 34
Motifs, 49
  bilateral symmetry of, 442–43
  clipping of, 136
  constructed from arcs, 457–66
  dihedral symmetry of, 443–45
  frieze symmetry of, 446–49
  parameters for, 171
  rotational symmetry of, 441–42
  wallpaper symmetry of, 450–54
Motion choreography, 523
Motorola 68000 microprocessor chip,
    80
Move command, 128, 136–38
  under Advanced_graphics, 435
  in graphic vocabularies, 193
  stored in arrays, 365
MS-DOS operating system, 94
Multitasking operating systems, 91
Multi-user operating systems, 91
  sign-on procedures in, 95
Music, 68, 83

Names
  identifiers, in Pascal, 110–11
  local, 338
  for static variables, 394
  for variables, 100
Nested blocks, 338
Nested loops, 240–46
Networks, 64, 84–86
  operating systems for, 92
NOT Boolean operator, 276
Numbers. See also Integers
  odd function for, 278–79
  in Pascal, 112, 118
  random, 300–301
  rounding and truncating, 147–48
Numeric keypads, 68

Object programs, 101, 102
Odd function, 278–79
Ogees, 461
Oil painting, 31
One-dimensional arrays, 357–58
Operating systems, 90–92
  commands in, 95
  directories and, 97–98
  files in, 95–97
  sign-on procedures in, 93–95
  in start-up procedures, 89

text editors in, 98
windows, menus, and icons in, 92–93
Operators, in Pascal, 110, 121–23
  Boolean, 209
  file, 384
  geometric, 427
  viewing, 434
Optical character recognition (OCR), 68
OR Boolean operator, 276
Output devices, 64, 83–84
  cathode ray tubes, 3–4
  pen plotters, 11–15
  raster displays, 9–11
  raster printers and plotters, 56–58
  refreshed vector displays, 8–9
  storage tube displays, 4–7
Outputs, 63
  from computers, 64
  files as, 386–89
  instructions for, 99
  in Pascal, alphanumeric, 125–27
  in Pascal, graphic, 127–28
  photographic, 58–60
Ovals, 461
Ovolo, 310–12

Painting, tone and color in, 31–32
Paint systems, 508–11
Palladio, Andrea, 168, 325, 326
Parabolic curves, 253–55
Parallel lines, 237–38
Parallelograms, 183–84
Parameterized graphic elements, 169–71
Parameterized procedures, 193
Parameter lists, 338
Parameters
  functions with multiple, 150–51
  for graphic elements, 166–71
  for graphic vocabulary elements in loops, 212–13
  interactive parametric variation, program of, 491–97
  as interfaces between elements, 331–34
  multiple shape, in loops, 224–26
  position and shape, in loops, 226–29
  procedural and functonal, for transformations, 454–55
  for procedures, 171–77

read by repeat until loop, 212
for repetition, 246–47
restricting ranges of, 189–91
for shape and position, 177–86
single position, in loops, 213–21
single shape, in loops, 223–24
transformation, 419
two position, in loops, 221–23
for user-written functions, 148
variable, 331
viewing, 431
for viewing transformations, 432
under world coordinate systems, 439
Parametric elements, 171
Parentheses, in Pascal, 122–24
  in Boolean expressions, 276–77
Pascal, Blaise, 109–10
Pascal (language), 102, 109–14
  Advanced_graphics library for, 531–50
  alphanumeric output in, 125–27
  arithmetic functions in, 146–47
  arithmetic statements in, 121–25
  arrays in, 357–74
  assignment statements in, 120–21
  block structure in, 338–42
  Boolean operators in, 209
  case statement in, 296–98
  clarity and verifiability of, 131–32
  comment lines in programs in, 130–31
  control structures in, 203–4
  counted loops in, 205–8
  debugging in, 104
  designed for von Neumann machines, 75
  dynamic data structures in, 391–97
  external procedures used in, 139
  global variables in, 155–57
  trigonometric and analytic functions in, 158
  Turbo Pascal, 528–29
  user-written functions in, 148–50
  windows in, 480
Passwords, 95
Patterns, color in, 52–53
PDP-11 series (computers), 77
Pen plotters, 11–15
  device coordinates for, 16
  line colors on, 22
  line thickness on, 18
Pens

for plotters, 12–14
thickness controlled by, 18
Performance of processors, 79–82
Periodic functions, 235–36
Personal computers
business graphics systems on, 507
color capabilities of, 51
colored patterns on, 53
CPU speed of, 81
development of, 80
display generators for, 46–47
future of, 524
graphics compromises in, 46
graphic output in, 127–28
graphics programs using lists in,
397–407
graphic vocabularies in, 193–94
hierarchical data structures in,
408–9
hierarchies of subsystems in, 335–42
if…then…else conditional
statement in, 274–75
inputs in, 128–30
Macintosh Pascal, 530
nested loops in, 240–46
organization of programs in, 114–20
procedural and functional
parameters in, 454–55
procedures in, 163–77
punctuation in, 130
reading and writing files in, 384–91
records in, 374–83
recursion in, 342–48
rounding and truncating numbers
in, 147–48
scalar, structured and pointer data
types in, 357
subsystems in, 323–29
top-down programming in, 350–51
transformation procedures in,
419–27
mice used with, 71
operating systems for, 92
paint systems on, 511
screen resolution of, 135
start-up procedures for, 89
structured drawing systems on, 512
Phosphors, 4
on color video monitors, 35
in refreshed vector displays, 8
in storage tube displays, 5
Photographic output, 58–60

Picture plane, 15
Pictures
broken down into compound
statements, 203
with colored patterns, 52–53
full-color, 55
as programs, 161–63
Pigments, 31–32
Pixels (picture elements), 33
characters displayed with, 56
color of, 39–42
for halftones, 49–51
intensity of, 37–39
in paint systems, 510, 511
resolution of, 44–45
screen coordinate systems for, 135
shapes of, 42
Plasma panels, 35
Plotters, 11–15
device coordinates for, 16
line colors on, 22
line thickness on, 18
raster, 56–58
Pointed arches, 460–61
Pointed data type, 357, 391–92
dynamic allocation of variables by,
394–96
for tree structures, 408
values passed by, 399
variables, 393–94
Pointing devices, 69–71
Points
addressable, 6
lines composed of, 3
in mosaic art, 32–33
on raster displays, 10
transformations of, 415–16
Polygon-modeling systems, 517–19
Polygons
filled using arrays, 370–74
filled using records, 378–83
regular, 261–63, 325
solid-colored, 52
stored as arrays, 368–70
stored as files, 384
Polynomial curves, 254–58
Position
parameters for, 177–86
and shape parameters for, in loops,
226–29
single parameter for, in loops,
213–21

two parameters for, in loops, 221–23
Positioning devices, 71
Pound, Ezra, 251
Pressure-sensitive touchpads, 69
Primitive graphic commands, 136–38
Primitives, 17
Printers, 83
    raster, 56–58
Printing
    halftone, 34
    of transformed graphics, 440
Procedural parameters, 454
Procedures, in Pascal, 163–71
    called by other procedures, 334
    counted loops in, 207–8
    external, 139
    in graphic vocabularies, 193
    invoking, 175–77
    parameterized, 171–175
    passing values out of, 331
    recursive, 342–44
    top-down structure of, 350–51
    for transformations, 419–27
    for viewing transformations, 431–33
Processes, 63
    in computers, 64
Processors, 72–73
    CPUs, 73–74
    CPUs, development of, 76–79
    instruction set for, 74
    measurements of performance of,
        79–82
Programming
    debugging and, 102–4
    graphics packages for, 505–6
    top-down, 350–51
    variable parameters in, 331
Programs. *See also* Software
    applications, 90
    block structure of, 338–42
    compilation and interpretation of,
        101
    error checking in, 304–5
    for exploring combinations, 497–502
    files read by, 390–91
    files written by, 386–89
    to generate line drawings, 135–42
    graphic vocabularies as, 193–94
    for interactive parametric variation,
        491–97
    parts of, 163
    in Pascal, comments in, 130–31

in Pascal, organization of, 114–20
    pictures as, 161–63
    procedures as, 163–64
    running and debugging, 102–4
    storage in memory of, 73
    top-down structure of, 350–51
    for viewing drawings, 488–91
    writing, 98–100
Progressions, mathematical, 213,
    229–36
Prompts, 93, 480–81
Proportion, rules of, 186–88
Punch cards, 65–66, 91
Punched paper tape, 66
Punctuation, in Pascal, 130

Quadrangles, 184–85
Quality of lines, 18–21

Radians, 158
Radioconcentric subdivisions, 465
Rainbow (personal computer), 92
Random-access data structures, 384
Random access memory (RAM), 78, 82
Random choices, 300–304
Random number generators, 300–301
Raster displays, 9–11, 35
    bitplanes for, 37–38
    characters on, 56
    classes of images on, 46–55
    compromising graphic qualities in,
        45–46
    display generators for, 36
    high-resolution, 55
    line colors on, 22
    line quality on, 21
    resolution of, 44–45
    touch screens and light pens used
        with, 69
    on video monitors, 35
Raster grids, 33–34, 42
Raster printers and plotters, 56–58
Rasters, 33
Raster units, 15–16
Ratios, 168
    in geometric progressions, 230–31
Reading files, 384–89
    by graphics programs, 390–91
Readln statement, 128–29
Read only memory (ROM), 78–79, 89
Read operator, 385
Real numbers, 112, 118, 122

rounding and truncating, 147–48
Real-time animation, 523–24
Reciprocals, 305–6
Recording cameras, 60
Records, 374–76
    filling polygons using, 378–83
    inserted in and deleted from lists,
        399–400
    with statement for, 376–78
Rectangles, 182–83
Rectangular column girds, 242–46
Recursion, 342-47
    recursive subdivision, 347–48
Reflect_Y transformation operator, 434
Refresh cycles, 8, 9
Refreshed vector displays, 8–9, 46
    line colors on, 22
    raster units on, 15–16
Regular compositions, 273
Regular polygons, 261–63, 325
Relational operators, 209, 275, 276
Repeatability, of pen plotters, 14
Repeat until statement, 211-12
    repetition parameters in, 247
Repetition, 202, 204–5
    compositional use of, 212–29
    in mathematical progressions,
        229–36
    parameters for, 246–47
    of sine curves, 259–60
Reset statement, 386
Resolution
    of displays, 44–45
    of hatching or dot screens, 24
    logical and physical, 42
    of pen plotters, 14
    of personal computer screens, 135
    of recording cameras, 60
    of storage tube displays, 5
    of styluses and crosshair devices, 70
Resource management commands, 90
Reverse-video mode, 46
Rewrite statement, 385–86
Rhythms, 299–300
Risers, in stairs, 222–23
Rotate transformation operator, 434,
    455–56
Rotational symmetry, 441–42
Rotations, 180–81, 416, 422–23,
    425–26. See also Transformations
ROUND function, 147
Rounding numbers, 147–48

Rules of proportion, 186–88
Running programs, 102

Sampling techniques, 45
Scalar data types, 357
Scalar variables, 357
Scale conversion functions, 157
Scale transformation operator, 434,
    455–57
Scaling, 416, 423–25
    repetition of, 455–57
Scan conversion methods, 47
Scanning devices, 68
Scotia, 310
Screen editors, 98
Screens. See also Displays; Images
    aesthetics of frame of, 433–34
    cathode ray, 3–4
    clipping of boundaries of, 136
    coordinate systems for, 135
    in drawing editors, 478–80
    framing for, 427–34
    photographing, 58–60
    raster displays, 9–11
    refreshed vector displays, 8–9
    storage tube displays, 4–7
    touch-sensitive, 69
    viewing transformations on, 431–33
    windows, menus, and icons used on,
        92–93
Separators, in Pascal, 112
Sequential files, 384
Sequential memory, 82, 384
Serlio, Sebastiano, 517
Sets, 391
Seurat, Georges, 32
Shadow masks, 35
Shapes
    display of edges of, 45
    edges of, 326–28
    ellipses, 264–66
    multiple parameters for, in loops,
        224–26
    parameters for, 177–86
    of pixels, 42
    and position parameters for, in loops,
        226–29
    regular polygons and circles, 261–63
    single parameters for, in loops,
        223–24
    symmetries in, 325
Shell (for operating systems), 90–91

Sign-off procedures, 105
Sign-on procedures, 93–95
Sine curves, 234–35, 258–60
SIN (sine) function, 147, 258–59
Single-task operating systems, 91
Single-user operating systems, 91
Sixteen-bit microprocessor chips, 80
Size, conditional statements for,
   283–85
Smoothing of curves, 403–4
Snapping grids, 155
Software. *See also* Programs
   future of, 524–25
   graphics packages, 505–6
   interactive graphics systems, 506–22
   language compilers and interpreters,
     100–102
   operating systems, 90–98
   text editors, 98
Solid-modeling systems, 519–20
Solids, color in, 52
Sony (company), 35
Source programs, 101
Spacing, conditional statements for,
   283–85
Speakers, 83
Speech recognition, 68
Speech synthesis, 83
Speed
   of CPUs, 80–81
   of interpreted and compiled
     programs, 101
Spirals, 267–69
SQR (square) function, 146
   to generate parabolic curves, 253
SQRT (square root) function, 146
Square brackets, 358
Stairs, 221–23
Standard identifiers, in Pascal, 111
Standards, for graphics, 506, 514
Start delimiting operator, 435
Start_drawing command, 139
   for procedures, 166
Start_drawing viewing operator, 434
Statements, in Pascal, 110, 114
   arithmetic, 121–25
   assignment, 120–21
   compound, 203
   executable, 118–20
   input, 128–30
   output, 125–28
Static variables, 394

Stonehenge (England), 213
Storage, 81. *See also* Memory
   of drawings, 440
Storage tube displays, 4–7, 46
   raster units on, 15
   refreshed vector displays
     distinguished from, 8
Straight lines
   curves approximated by, 251–53
   scan conversion methods for, 47–48
   transformation of, 416
Structured data types, 357
Structured drawing systems, 511–12
Stylus, 70
Subdirectories, 98
Subdivisions
   of circles, 462–66
   recursive, 347–48
Subrange type, 189–91
Subsystems, 323–29
   alternative divisions of, 349–50
   hierarchies of, 335–42
   top-down structure of, 350–51
Sullivan, Louis, 407
Supercomputers, 82
Super-minicomputers, 82
Surface properties, 522
Sutherland, Ivan E., 77
Symmetries, 325–28
   bilateral, 442–43
   dihedral, 443–45
   frieze, 446–49
   mixed, 466–67
   procedural and functional
     parameters for, 454–55
   rotational, 441–42
   transformations and, 441
   wallpaper, 450–54
Syntax, in Pascal, 113–14
   for Boolean operators, 209
   of nested loops, 246
   for parts of compositions, 331–35
   for records, 375

Tablets, 70–71, 508
Taj Mahal (Agra, India), 347
Tangent function (user-written), 158
Tektronix, 505–6
Télématique, 84
Television sets, 9
   broadcast standards for, 35
Temples, program for, 339–42

Terminals, 84, 89, 91
Texas Instruments, TM 1000
  (computer), 79, 80
Text editors, 98, 477
Text outputs, 83
Textual sequence, 203
Texture, 48–49
  in line drawings, 22–24
Thermal transfer printing, 58
Thickness of lines, 18–21
Thirty-two-bit microprocessor chips,
  80
Three-dimensional arrays, 374
Three-dimensional graphics systems,
  515
  curved surface-modeling systems,
    519
  polygon-modeling systems, 517–19
  solid-modeling systems, 519–20
  ultrasonic styluses for, 70–71
  wire-frame systems, 515–17
Thumbwheels, 71
Tilting, 431
Tone
  bits per pixel for, 38
  continuous, 31
  in line drawings, 22–24
Top-down programming, 350–51
Torus, 310
Touchpads, 69
Touch screens, 69
Trackballs, 71
Transformation parameters, 419
Transformation procedures, 419–27
Transformations, 415
  for animation, 523
  framing, 427–34
  of graphic data structures, 416–19
  loops and symmetries in, 441–54
  with mixed symmetries, 466–67
  motifs constructed from arcs, 457–66
  of points, 415–16
  procedural and functional
    parameters for, 454–55
  procedures for, 419–27
  repetitions of scale, 455–57
  storage versus computation of, 440
  viewing system and, 434–39
Transistors, 76–77
Translate transformation operator, 434
Trees, program for, 344–47
Tree structures, 408–9

Trigonometric functions, 158–59
Truncating numbers, 147–48
TRUNC (truncate) function, 147
Turbo Pascal (language), 528–29
  Advanced-graphics library for,
    531–41
Turner, J. M. W., 31
Turnkey systems, 512
Two-dimensional arrays, 361–64
  drawings stored as, 364–68
Two-dimensional graphics systems, 507
  business graphics systems, 507
  drafting systems, 512–15
  paint systems, 508–11
  structured drawing systems, 511–12
TX-2 (computer), 77

Ultrasonic tablets, 70–71
Unit conversions, 483–84
UNIVAC (computer), 76
Unix (operating system), 90–92
Unstructured data types, 357
User-written functions, 148–50
  trigonometric and analytic, 158–59
Uses advanced-graphics command,
  434–35

Vacuum tubes, 76
Value parameters, 338
Values
  in arrays, 358
  passed by pointer variables, 399
  passed out of procedures, 331
  for variables, 100
Variables, 100
  in arrays, 357
  Boolean, 275, 277
  control, 205–6
  in design of stairs, 221–22
  dynamic generation of, 394–96
  for error codes, 305
  global, 155–57
  independent and dependent,
    145–46
  local, 151–53
  parameters as, 331, 338
  in Pascal, 117, 120
  pointer, 392–94, 399
  in repetition parameters, 247
  scalar, 357
  subrange types for, 189–91
  in while loops, 209–10

Var keyword, for variable parameters, 331
Vectors, 17–22
    connecting, 188–89
    curves approximated by, 251–53
    drawing, in programs, 138
    for hatching or dot screens, 24
    inputting into drawing editors, 484–86
for lettering, 24–26
    motifs expressed in, 171
    parameters for, 168
    in solid-modeling systems, 519–20
    in wire-frame systems, 515–17
Very large scale integrated circuits (VLSIs), 78, 79, 524
Video cameras, 68
Video monitors, 35
    color on, 39–42
    raster displays on, 9
Viewing drawings program, 488–491
Viewing operators, 434
Viewing parameters, 431
Viewing systems, 434–38
Viewing transformation procedures, 431–33
Viewing transformations, 431
Viewports, 431
Voice recognition, 68

Von Neumann, John, 75
Von Neumann machine, 75

Wallpaper symmetry, 450–54
Watercolor painting, 31
Weaving, 43
While statement, 209–11
    to read files, 391
    for recursion, 344
    repetition parameters in, 247
Whirlwind (computer), 76
Winchester disks, 82
Windows, 92–93
    in drawing editors, 478–80
    in Macintosh Pascal, 104
Windows (for files), 385
Wire-frame systems, 515–17
Wirth, Niklaus, 102
With statement, 376–78
Words, 73
World coordinate systems, 431
    graphic vocabularies under, 439
Wren, Sir Christopher, 467
Writeln statement, 125–26
Write operator, 385
Writing files, 384–89

Zero, testing for, 306
Zilog Z80 microprocessor chip, 80
Zooming, 431